C. Wragg

CW01649458

LAW M

The Made Simple series
has been created
especially for self-education
but can equally well
be used as
an aid to group study.
However complex the subject,
the reader is taken
step by step,
clearly and methodically
through the course. Each volume
has been prepared by
experts,
taking account of
modern educational requirements,
to ensure the most effective
way of acquiring knowledge.

In the same series

Accounting
Advertising
Auditing
Biology
Book-keeping
British Constitution
Business Calculations
Business and Enterprise Studies
Business Law
Calculus
Chemistry
Child Development
Commerce
Computer Electronics
Computer Programming
Computer Typing
Cost and Management Accounting
Economic and Social Geography
Economics
Education
Electricity
Electronics
Elements of Banking
English
Financial Management
First Aid
French
German
Graphic Communication
Italian
Latin
Law
Management
Marketing
Mathematics
Modern European History
Modern World History
MSX
Music
Office Practice
Personnel Management
Philosophy
Photography
Physical Geography
Physics
Politics
Psychiatry
Psychology
Russian
Salesmanship
Secretarial Practice
Social Services
Sociology
Spanish
Statistics
Statistics for Business
Teeline Shorthand
Typing

Law

Made Simple

C. F. Padfield, LLB, DPA
of Gray's Inn, Barrister

Revised by
D. L. A. Barker, LLB, MPhil, LLM, DipLG,
FCIS, ACIARB, FBIM, FAIM

Seventh edition

MADE SIMPLE
BOOKS

Made Simple
An imprint of Butterworth–Heinemann Ltd
Linacre House, Jordan Hill, Oxford OX2 8DP

PART OF REED INTERNATIONAL BOOKS

OXFORD LONDON BOSTON
MUNICH NEW DELHI SINGAPORE SYDNEY
TOKYO TORONTO WELLINGTON

First published 1970
Second edition 1972
Third edition 1973
Fourth edition 1975
Reprinted 1976
Fifth edition 1978
Reprinted 1979, 1980
Sixth edition 1981
Reprinted 1983, 1985, 1986, 1987, 1988
Seventh edition 1989
Reprinted 1990, 1991

© Mrs G. Padfield and D. L. A. Barker 1985, 1987, 1989

All rights reserved. No part of this publication may be reproduced in any material form (including photocopying or storing in any medium by electronic means and whether or not transiently or incidentally to some other use of this publication) without the written permission of the copyright holder except in accordance with the provisions of the Copyright, Designs and Patents Act 1988 or under the terms of a licence issued by the Copyright Licensing Agency Ltd, 90 Tottenham Court Road, London W1P 9HE. Applications for the copyright holder's written permission to reproduce any part of this publication should be addressed to the publishers

British Library Cataloguing in Publication Data

Padfield, Colin F.
Law made simple – 7th ed. – (Made simple books)
1. Law – England
I. Title II. Barker, D. L. A. III. Series
344.2 [LAW]

ISBN 0 7506 0255 4

Printed in England by Clays Ltd, St Ives plc

To G. T. P.

Preface to the First Edition

This book covers the elements of English Law, the law which is the basis of all legal systems throughout the English-speaking world. Today one-third of all mankind is ruled by laws that originally came from England, however much they may have become adapted to the needs and conditions of different countries.

The text is primarily designed for students of further education preparing for the examinations in (1) the law content of relevant BEC courses and for (2) the General Certificate of Education at 'A' level of the Associated Examining Board. In addition the book covers the syllabuses in law at intermediate stage set by many examining authorities for professional students such as Secretaries, Accountants, Bankers, Hospital Administrators, Surveyors, Estate Agents, and similar persons either attending colleges of further education or working alone.

For the general reader the book provides an excellent background to English legal practices and institutions. It is especially valuable as a guide to the Law of Contract, Law of Property, and Law of Tort. Throughout the text constant reference is made to cases and statutes available in major reference works.

I should like to offer my sincere thanks to Geoffrey Whitehead and Leslie Basford, both of whom gave most valuable and generous help during the preparation of the text. I should also like to thank Rigby Hart, Clive Hamblin, Robert Coram, and Frieda Morley for most helpful criticism at various stages.

C.P.
1970

Preface to the Seventh Edition

In writing this new edition I have endeavoured to retain the character of previous editions, while ensuring that the book continues to meet the changing needs of its readers.

Since the last revision a number of important statutes have been passed and many cases reported. The aim of this edition has been to take these into account as far as possible. Also, several changes have been made to the text particularly with regard to tort, contract and criminal law.

D. L. A. Barker
1989

Contents

PREFACE TO THE FIRST EDITION vii
PREFACE TO THE SEVENTH EDITION viii
1 INTRODUCTION 1
1. The Nature of Law 1
2. Custom, Morality and Law 1
3. Classification of Law 3
4. Characteristics of English Law 5
5. Exercises 7
2 HISTORICAL SOURCES OF ENGLISH LAW 8
1. The Common Law 8
The Norman Conquest 9
The Common Law Courts 11
2. Equity 13
Later History 15
3. Legislation 16
European Economic Community Law 18
4. Canon Law 18
5. The Law Merchant 19
6. Local Custom 21
7. The Nineteenth Century 21
Reorganization of the Courts 22
The House of Lords 22
Reforming the Rules 23
8. Exercises 23
3 LEGAL SOURCES 24
1. Judicial Precedent 24
The House of Lords and Precedent 25
Case Law: Advantages and Disadvantages 25
Law Reports 27
Citation of Cases 29
Declaratory Theory of the Common Law 29
2. Legislation 30
Statutes 30
Stages in Legislation 31
Obsolescence 32
Consolidation and Codification 33
Delegated Legislation 34
Forms of Delegated Legislation 34
Growth of Delegated Legislation 35
Criticism of Delegated Legislation 35

Control of Delegated Legislation 36
Publication 38
Interpretation of Statutes 38
Presumptions 40
Reference to Statutes 41
Reference to Statutory Instruments 41
European Economic Community Law 42
Law Revision and Reform 42
3. Textbooks 44
4. Local Custom 44
5. Exercises 46
4 THE COURTS TODAY 47
1. The Civil Courts 47
The House of Lords 47
Judicial Committee of the Privy Council 47
Court of Appeal (Civil Division) 48
The High Court of Justice 49
County Courts 51
2. Criminal Courts 52
The House of Lords 54
Court of Appeal (Criminal Division) 54
The Crown Court 54
Magistrates' Courts 58
3. Other Courts 62
Courts-Martial Appeal Court 62
Restrictive Practices Court 62
Employment Appeal Tribunal 62
Coroners' Courts 63
4. Court of Justice of the European Communities 64
5. Administrative Tribunals 64
Examples of Tribunals 66
6. Judicial Control of Administrative Tribunals 68
Supervision by the Queen's Bench Division 70
Tribunals and Inquiries Act, 1971 71
7. Arbitration 72
8. Juries 74
9. Legal Aid and Advice 75
Legal Advice and Assistance 76
Legal Aid in Civil Proceedings 76
Legal Aid in Criminal Proceedings 77
10. Laymen in the Courts 78
11. Exercises 79
5 THE JUDICIARY, LAW OFFICERS AND THE LEGAL PROFESSION 81
1. The Lord Chancellor 81
2. Judges 81

3. Attorney-General and Solicitor-General 83
4. Masters 83
5. Director of Public Prosecutions 84
6. Solicitors 84
7. Barristers 85
8. Queen's Counsel 86
9. Licensed Conveyancers 86
10. Exercises 86

6 OUTLINE OF THE LAW OF PERSONS 88
1. Legal Persons 88
2. Nationality and Domicile 88
British Nationality 89
Loss of Nationality 90
British Protected Persons 90
Aliens 90
Domicile 91
3. Marriage 92
4. Divorce 94
5. Domestic Proceedings in Magistrates' Courts 95
6. Legitimation 96
7. Adoption 96
8. Guardianship 97
9. Illegitimacy 98
10. Infants or Minors 99
11. Corporations 100
Classes of Corporations 101
Share Structure of a Company 104
The 'Ultra Vires' Rule 104
Termination of a Company 105
12. Unincorporated Associations 105
Legal Liability of Unincorporated Associations 105
13. Partnerships 106
14. Trade Unions and Employers' Associations 108
15. Crown Proceedings 108
The Crown as Employer 109
The Crown Proceedings Act, 1947 109
16. Exercises 111

7 THE LAW OF CONTRACT 112
1. Essentials of a Valid Contract 112
2. Classification of Contracts 113
3. Offer and Acceptance 115
Rules Regarding Acceptance 119
4. Intention to Create Legal Relations 121
5. Consideration 122
Rules of Consideration 123

6. Form 129
7. The Doctrine of Part Performance 132
8. Contractual Capacity 133
Infants or Minors 133
Corporations 138
Insane and Drunken Persons 139
Married Women 139
Aliens 140
9. Terms of a Contract 140
Exemption Clauses 143
The Unfair Contract Terms Act, 1977 145
Conditions and Warranties 146
10. Void, Voidable, and Illegal Contracts 147
Mistake 147
Misrepresentation 153
Contracts 'uberrimae fidei' 158
Duress and Undue Influence 159
11. Illegality 161
Contracts Declared Illegal by Statute 161
Contracts Illegal at Common Law 162
Effects of Illegality 166
12. Discharge of Contract 167
13. Remedies for Breach of Contract 176
14. Privity of Contract 183
15. Assignment 185
16. Interpretation of a Contract 188
17. Quasi-Contract 189
18. Exercises 190

8 THE LAW OF TORTS 191
1. The Nature of a Tort 192
Definition of a Tort 192
Damage and Liability 193
Malice 194
2. General Defences in Tort 195
3. Capacity of Parties 199
4. Remoteness of Damage 203
5. Vicarious Liability in Tort 204
Joint Tortfeasors 208
6. Trespass 209
7. Interference with Goods 215
8. Nuisance 217
9. Negligence 222
Contributory Negligence 227
10. Breach of Statutory Duty 229

11. Death: Survival of Actions 229
12. Occupiers' Liability 230
Dangerous Premises 231
Trespassers 232
Children 232
13. The Rule in 'Rylands v. Fletcher' 233
14. Defamation 236
15. Deceit 244
16. Malicious Falsehood 245
17. Limitation of Actions 246
18. Exercises 247
9 TRUSTS 248
1. Definition of a Trust 249
2. Private Trusts 249
3. Public (or Charitable) Trusts 252
4. Differences between Private and Charitable Trusts 253
5. The Rules against Perpetuities 254
6. Trustees 255
7. Trust Corporations 255
8. Appointment of Trustees 255
9. Termination of Trusteeship 256
10. Duties and Powers of Trustees 256
11. Liability for Breaches of Trust 257
12. Following the Trust Property (Tracing) 258
13. Relief from Liability for Breach 258
14. Exercises 259
10 THE LAW OF PROPERTY 260
1. Ownership 260
2. Possession 261
3. Property 262
4. Freehold and Leasehold Land 265
5. Reform of the Land Law 269
6. An Estate in Fee Simple Absolute in Possession 270
7. Future Estates 273
8. Settlements and Trusts for Sale 273
The Settled Land Act, 1925 275
9. Co-ownership 277
10. Leaseholds 279
Tenancies 279
Creation of Leases 281
Duties of Landlord and Tenant 281
Express Covenants 282
11. Servitudes 282
12. Restrictive Covenants 285
13. Mortgages 287

14. The Sale of Land 292
15. Registered Land 294
16. Exercises 295

11 THE LAW OF SUCCESSION 297
1. Wills 297
2. Legacies and Devises 302
3. Specimen Will 303
4. Family Provision 304
5. Personal Representatives 306
Probate and Letters of Administration 307
6. Intestacy 309
7. Gifts 'Inter Vivos' 311
8. 'Donatio Mortis Causa' 312
9. Exercises 312

12 CRIMINAL LAW 313
1. Definition of a Crime 313
2. Sources 313
3. Classifications 314
4. Criminal Liability 315
Actus reus 315
Mens rea 315
Negligence 316
Strict Liability 317
Vicarious Liability 317
Corporate Liability 318
5. Exemptions from Liability 319
6. Parties to a Crime 319
7. General Defences 320
Automatism 320
Mistake 321
Insanity 321
Intoxication by Drink or Drugs 322
Prevention of Crime: Arrest 323
Private Defence 323
Necessity 324
Duress 324
Coercion 324
Superior Orders 324
8. Inchoate Offences 325
9. Burden of Proof 326
10. Offences against the Person 327
Murder 327
Manslaughter 328
Involuntary Manslaughter 330
Infanticide 331

Causing Death by Reckless Driving 332
Child Destruction and Abortion 332
Assault and Battery 333
Assault occasioning Actual Bodily Harm 333
Malicious Wounding 334
Wounding with Intent 334
Administering Poison 334
Assault on, Resistance to, or Obstruction of a Police Constable in the Execution of his Duty 334
Firearms and Offensive Weapons 334
Sexual Offences 335
11. Offences against Property 336
Offences under Theft Act, 1968
Theft 336
Robbery 338
Burglary 338
Removal of Articles from Places open to the Public 339
Taking a Motor Vehicle or other Conveyance without Authority 339
Abstracting of Electricity 340
Obtaining Property by Deception 340
Obtaining a Pecuniary Advantage by Deception 341
False Accounting 341
Liability of Company Officers for Offences by the Company 342
False Statements by Company Directors, etc. 342
Suppression of Documents 342
Blackmail 342
Handling Stolen Goods 343
Offences under the Theft Act, 1978
Obtaining Services by Deception 344
Evasion of Liability by Deception 344
Making off Without Payment 344
Criminal Damage 345
Forgery 347
Trespass 347
Unlawful Eviction and Harassment of a Residential Occupier 348
12. Other Offences 348
Bigamy 348
Road Traffic Offences 349
Assisting Arrestable Offenders 350
Concealing an Arrestable Offence 351
Causing Wasteful Employment of the Police 351
13. Criminal Injuries Compensation Board 351

14. Exercises 352
13 PROCEDURE 353
1. Civil Procedure 353
2. County Court Procedure 353
Steps in an Ordinary Action 354
Steps in a Default Action 356
The Enforcement of County Court Judgments 357
Costs 358
3. Civil Proceedings in the Queen's Bench Division 358
Enforcement of Judgments in the High Court 361
4. Criminal Procedure 362
5. Proceedings in Magistrates' Courts 363
Process by Summons 363
Process by Warrant 364
6. Proceedings in the Crown Court 366
Indictment 366
Arraignment 366
Proceedings against Children and Young Persons 368
Arrest and Habeas Corpus 368
7. Standard Works 368
8. Exercises 369
APPENDIX 1—Glossary of Terms 370
APPENDIX 2—Examination Technique 374
APPENDIX 3—Test Papers 378
APPENDIX 4—List of Abbreviations: Law Reports 387
APPENDIX 5—Specimen Legislative Documents 390
Parliamentary Bill 390
Parliamentary Bill 391
Act of Parliament 392
Statutory Instrument 393
APPENDIX 6—Specimen Forms 394
Information 394
Summons 394
Recognizance 394
Warrant of Arrest 395
Indictment 395
APPENDIX 7—Financial Provision on Divorce, etc. 396
TABLE OF CASES 397
TABLE OF STATUTES 409
INDEX 414

1

INTRODUCTION

1. The Nature of Law

The term 'law' is used in many senses: we may speak of the laws of physics, mathematics, science, or the laws of football or health. When we speak of the law of a state we use the term 'law' in a special and strict sense, and in that sense law may be defined as *a rule of human conduct, imposed upon and enforced among, the members of a given state.*

Man is by nature a social animal desiring the companionship of his fellows, and in primitive times he tended to form tribes, groups, or societies, either for self-preservation or by reason of social instinct.

If a group or society is to continue, some form of social order is necessary. Rules or laws are, therefore, drawn up to ensure that members of the society may live and work together in an orderly and peaceable manner. The larger the community (or group or state), the more complex and numerous will be the rules.

If the rules or laws are broken, compulsion is used to enforce obedience. We may say, then, that two ideas underlie the concept of law: (*a*) **order**, in the sense of method or system; and (*b*) **compulsion**—i.e. the enforcement of obedience to the rules or laws laid down.

2. Custom, Morality and Law

When we examine the definition of law given above we notice certain important points.

(*a*) **Law is a body of rules.** When we speak of 'the law' we usually imply the whole of the law, however it may have been formed. As we shall see later, much of English law was formed out of the customs of the people. But a great part of the law has been created by statute. Common law and statutory law together comprise what we refer to as the 'Law of England'.

(*b*) **Law is for the guidance of human conduct.** Men resort to various kinds of rules to guide their lives. Thus moral rules and ethics remind us that it is immoral or wrong to covet, to tell lies, or to engage in drunkenness in private. If we transgress these moral or ethical precepts we may lose our friends or their respect. The law, however, is not concerned with these matters and leaves them to the individual's conscience or moral choice and the pressure of public opinion: no legal action results (unless a person tells lies under oath in a court, when he may be prosecuted under the Perjury Act, 1911).

(*c*) **Law is imposed.** We sometimes think of laws as being laid down by some authority such as a king, dictator, or group of people in whom special power is vested. In Britain we can point to statute law for examples of law laid down by a sovereign body, namely Parliament. The jurist John Austin (1790–1859) asserted that law was a command of a sovereign and that citizens were under a duty to obey that command. Other writers say that men and women in primitive societies formed rules themselves, i.e. that the rules or laws sprang from within the group itself. Only later were such rules laid down by a sovereign authority and imposed on the group or people subject to them.

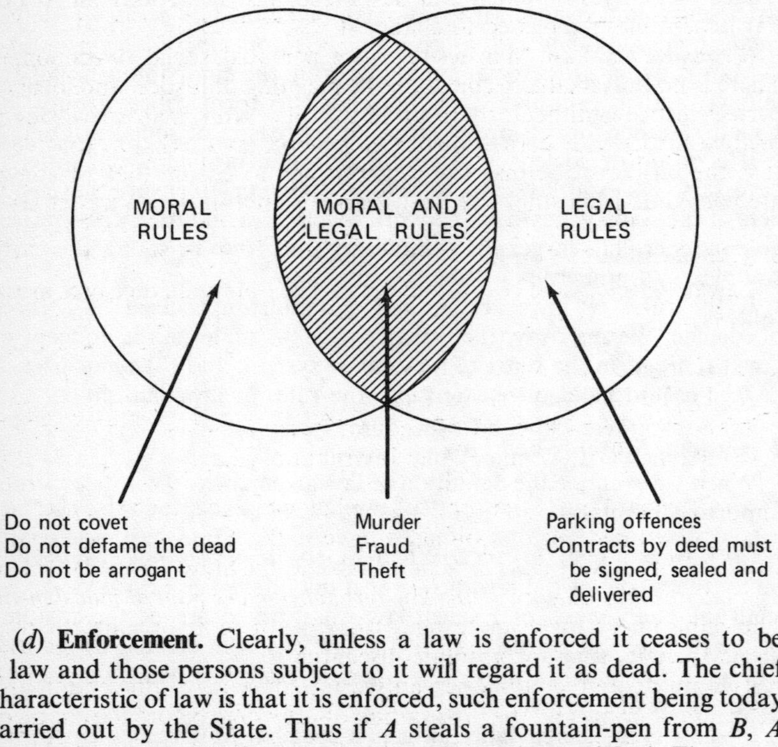

(*d*) **Enforcement.** Clearly, unless a law is enforced it ceases to be a law and those persons subject to it will regard it as dead. The chief characteristic of law is that it is enforced, such enforcement being today carried out by the State. Thus if *A* steals a fountain-pen from *B*, *A* may be prosecuted before the court and may be punished. The court may then order the restitution of the pen to its rightful owner, *B*. The 'force' used is known as a *sanction* and it is this sanction which the State administers to secure obedience to its rules.

(*e*) **The State.** A State is a territorial division in which a community or people lives subject to a uniform system of law administered by a sovereign authority, e.g. a parliament.

The United Kingdom, which comprises a parliamentary union of

England, Wales, Scotland, and Northern Ireland, is for our purposes the State. Parliament at Westminster legislates for England, Scotland, and Wales, and also in respect of some matters (such as defence and coinage) for Northern Ireland. Scotland has its own legal system, different in many ways from that of England and Wales, and has been influenced by Roman and Continental law to a far greater extent.

(*f*) **Content of Law.** The law is a living thing and it changes through the course of history. Changes are brought about by various factors such as invasion, contact with other races, material prosperity, education, the advent of new machines or new ideas or new religions. Law responds to public opinion and changes accordingly. Formerly the judges themselves moulded and developed the law. Today an Act of Parliament may be passed to change it.

(*g*) **Justice and Law.** Men desire justice, personal, social, or economic. There is no universal agreement on the meaning of justice, and ideal or perfect justice is difficult to attain in this life. What man strives for is relative justice, not perfect justice; and good laws assist to that end. It is the business of citizens in a democracy to ensure that wise laws are passed and that they are fairly administered in the courts of law.

3. Classification of Law

Law may be classified in various ways. The four main divisions are as follows:

(*a*) Criminal Law and Civil Law
(*b*) Public Law and Private Law
(*c*) Substantive Law and Procedural Law
(*d*) Municipal Law and Public International Law

(*a*) **Criminal Law** is that part of the law which characterizes certain kinds of wrongdoings as offences *against* the State, not necessarily violating any private right, and punishable *by* the State. Crime is defined as *an act of disobedience of the law forbidden under pain of punishment*. The punishment for crime ranges from death or imprisonment to a money penalty (fine) or absolute discharge.

The police are the public servants whose duty is the prevention and detection of crime and the prosecution of offenders before the courts of law. Private citizens may legally enforce the criminal law by beginning proceedings themselves, but, except in minor cases of common assault, rarely do so in practice.

Civil Law is concerned with the rights and duties of individuals towards each other. It includes the following:

(i) *Law of Contract*, dealing with that branch of the law which determines whether a promise is legally enforceable and what are its legal consequences.

(ii) *Law of Tort*. A tort is defined as *a civil wrong for which the remedy is a common law action for unliquidated (i.e. unspecified or unascertained) damages and which is not exclusively the breach of a contract or breach of trust or other merely equitable obligation.* (Salmond: *Law of Torts.*) Examples of torts are: nuisance, negligence, defamation, and trespass.

(iii) *Law of Property* is that part of the law which determines the nature and extent of the rights which people may enjoy over land and other property—for example, rights of 'ownership' of land, or rights under a lease.

(iv) *Law of Succession* is that part of the law which determines the devolution of property on the death of the former owner.

(v) *Family Law* is that branch of the law which defines the rights, duties, and status of husband and wife, parent and child, and other members of a household.

The above are the major branches of civil law. Its main distinction from criminal law is that in civil law the legal action is begun by the private citizen to establish rights (in which the State is not primarily concerned) against another citizen or group of citizens, whereas criminal law is enforced on behalf of or in the name of the State. Civil law is sometimes referred to as **Private Law** as distinct from Public Law.

(*b*) **Public Law** comprises (i) Constitutional Law, (ii) Administrative Law, and (iii) Criminal Law.

(i) *Constitutional Law* has been defined as *the rules which regulate the structure of the principal organs of government and their relationship to each other, and determine their principal functions.* This subject includes: choice of monarch, his powers and prerogative; the constitution of the legislature; powers and privileges of Members of Parliament; the relationship between the separate chambers of Parliament; the status of Ministers; the civil service; the armed forces; the police; the relations between the central government and local authorities; the making of treaties; admission and rights of aliens; the courts of justice; liberties of speech, of meeting, of association; and voting rights.

(ii) *Administrative Law* is defined as *that body of legal principles which concerns the rights and duties arising from the impact upon the individual of the actual functioning of the executive instruments of government.* (C. K. Allen: *Law and Orders.*) For example, administrative law determines the legal rights of a private citizen whose house a local authority intends to acquire compulsorily.

(iii) *Criminal Law* has already been described, with its distinction from civil law.

(*c*) **Substantive Law** is the body of rules of law in the above branches. Thus, murder is a common law offence. Bigamy is a statutory offence, contrary to section 57 of the Offences Against the Person Act, 1861. Negligence is a tort at common law.

Procedural Law lays down the rules governing the manner in which a right is enforced under civil law, or a crime prosecuted under the criminal law. Thus a legal action is started by taking out a writ in civil cases, by a summons or an arrest in criminal cases, and ends by the trial and judgment in the court itself, followed by the execution of the judgment. Procedural law governs the steps in the progress of the civil legal action or criminal prosecution.

The distinction between substantive law and procedural law is not always clear. It is an important rule of law that the prosecution may not (except in special circumstances) refer to the accused's bad character during the course of the trial, for this could clearly prejudice his case. (English law presumes that an accused person is innocent until proved guilty.) This rule may be regarded as either substantive or procedural, depending on the view taken of its nature. Some claims involving a conflict of laws are governed by the Civil Jurisdiction and Judgments Act, 1982.

(*d*) **Municipal or National Law** is the law operative within a State. One branch of that law is the law relating to conflict of laws, otherwise known as **Private International Law**, which determines which national law governs a case in which there is a foreign element.

Thus Jenkins, a British subject, makes a contract in Rome with Boussac, a Frenchman, for the supply of footballs to a team in Madrid. If Jenkins now takes action against Boussac in an English court of law for alleged breach of contract, the court will have to determine by the rules of private international law which law is to be applied: English, Italian, French, or Spanish.

(*e*) **Public International Law** is the body of rules of law which govern the relations of states *inter se*, particularly rules of war. Certain writers hold that there is no world authority with power to enforce the rules or laws and that, as public international law is incompatible with national sovereignty, the essential characteristics of law are absent.

4. Characteristics of English Law

The United Kingdom is a unitary State, not a federation of States. Nevertheless, it does not have a single system of law within that State. There are separate systems operating in (i) England and Wales, (ii) Northern Ireland, and (iii) Scotland. Due to the closeness of the association since the twelfth century between England and Wales on the one hand and Northern Ireland on the other, these countries have similar legal systems. There are, however, differences between the law of Scotland, influenced by Roman law, and that of the remainder of the United Kingdom, although since the Union with Scotland Act, 1707, these differences are now less marked on broad issues.

Two important links uniting the system are: (*a*) Parliament at Westminster is the supreme authority throughout the United Kingdom; (*b*) The House of Lords is the final court of appeal from the courts of (i) England and Wales, (ii) Northern Ireland, and (iii) Scotland.

English law is one of the great legal systems of the world, and one-third of all mankind is today ruled by laws that came originally from this small island. What, then, are the characteristics of English law which give it this pre-eminence? The most important are these:

(*a*) **Continuous Growth.** English law is traceable to Anglo-Saxon times. The common law, which forms the basis of English law, has endured for 900 years and has continuously adapted itself to changing social and economic needs.

Old rules of law remain law despite their age, unless expressly repealed. Thus in the case of *Ashford* v. *Thornton* (1818), an appeal against alleged murder, the appellor claimed and was granted the ancient Norman right of trial by battle. In point of fact the appellor's opponent refused to fight, and the right was abolished by statute in 1819.

The Treason Act, 1351, is still good law and may be invoked today despite its age.

Whereas Continental countries have been subject to continual invasions, revolutions, declarations of independence and the like, the geographical separation of England from the Continent, coupled with the Englishman's traditional respect for law, have tended to preserve the independent and uninterrupted growth of English law.

(*b*) **Absence of Codification**. A legal code is a systematic collection of laws so arranged as to avoid inconsistency and overlapping. Codification was a feature of Roman law and was adopted by certain Continental countries, notably France, Germany, Austria, and Switzerland. The English common law was formed from the customs of the people. Under the Norman kings these unwritten laws achieved a fairly uniform legal system. Certain parts only of English law have today been codified, e.g. the Bills of Exchange Act, 1882, and the Sale of Goods Act, 1979, though the Law Commission is working towards a codification of criminal law and contract (Law Commissions Act, 1965, see p. 43).

(*c*) **Judicial Character of the Law.** The early Norman judges were important figures appointed by the Crown whose justice they administered. The common law was largely 'judge-made' from the existing customary laws. It is from the records and reports of cases tried by the judges that we derive our knowledge of early case law. Judges formed or moulded the common law, and its growth and character can often be traced to outstanding men like Bracton, Coke, and Littleton. Although judges today may develop the common law within fairly narrow limits, they are mainly concerned with interpreting and applying statute law which is now the main source of legal development.

(*d*) **Independence of Judiciary.** Justice requires that a judge be impartial and independent of either party to a particular legal dispute. The Act of Settlement, 1701, provided that judges of superior courts 'hold office during good behaviour, that their salaries be ascertained and established, and that they be removed only on the address of both Houses of Parliament'.

(*e*) **Independence of Lawyers.** The two branches of the legal profession comprise barristers and solicitors. Each branch is controlled by independent bodies which maintain high professional standards of education, training, and conduct. Lawyers are not appointed by the State and are not civil servants. They are not subject to direct political control, and, like the judges, are traditionally independent. Their relations with clients are based on confidence and protected by privilege; they cannot be compelled to disclose what passes between them during their professional dealings.

(*f*) **Influence of Procedure.** Procedure has influenced substantive law. We shall see later that at one time the existence of a legal right depended on whether there was a suitable writ with which to begin the action. The writ system governed early law. Such procedural rules affected the law itself and they have left their imprint.

(*g*) **No Reception of Roman Law.** English common law was of native growth and little influenced by Roman Law, unlike the law of Continental countries and Scotland which was shaped by it.

(*h*) **The Doctrine of Precedent.** To achieve some consistency in decisions, the courts developed the practice of decisions in higher courts binding the lower courts.

(*i*) **Practical Nature of the Law**. It was emphasized by the House of Lords in *Ainsbury* v. *Millington* (1987) that it has always been a fundamental feature of the English judicial system that the courts decide disputes between the parties before them. They will not pronounce on abstract questions of law where there is no dispute to be resolved.

5. Exercises

1. Distinguish between (i) a legal rule and (ii) a principle of morality.
2. Distinguish between criminal law and civil law, and between public law and private law.
3. What are the main characteristics of English law?

2

HISTORICAL SOURCES OF ENGLISH LAW

English law has developed from a number of sources: custom, the rules worked out by the common law courts and the courts of equity, canon law, the law merchant, legislation, etc. Moreover, the growth of substantive civil law has at common law been bound up with procedure, since a right existed only if it could be enforced.

The following is an outline of the sources and of the courts and other institutions involved.

1. The Common Law

In Anglo-Saxon times there existed three fairly distinct legal systems: *The Dane Law*, which had been adopted after the invasions and settlement of Danish and Scandinavian warriors in the coastal areas of northern and north-eastern England; *Mercian Law*, which bore traces of Germanic origin, following the Saxon invasions, and extended around the Midlands; *Wessex Law*, which applied in south and west England.

In each of the three systems the law was based on customs, and the customs varied from place to place and shire to shire. There was little distinction between criminal wrongs and civil wrongs at this time; the laws were generally primitive but nevertheless served to produce such good order as could be expected. But there were courts of law where cases were heard. The Anglo-Saxon courts before 1066 were:

(i) **The Shire Court** (or **Moot**), presided over by the Sheriff, the Bishop, and the Ealdorman, and attended by the lords and freemen of the county, with the priest. This court sat twice a year.

(ii) **The Hundred Court** ('hundred' means a division of a shire), presided over by the Hundredman, assisted by twelve senior thanes.

(iii) **The Franchise Courts**, granted to certain persons by the monarch. The grantees were entitled to the profits, for the suitors or litigants who brought their cases to court for trial were required to pay fees. In Norman times the franchise courts were sometimes taken over by the lords of the manor who, in deciding disputes between tenants of land, continued the practice of charging fees.

Of these three courts the shire court was the most important, but all enforced the local laws and all had jurisdiction to deal with obvious criminal offences, such as murder, theft, violence to person and property, and also the civil claims concerning ownership or possession of land or cattle—both very important sources of wealth.

The Anglo-Saxon system of keeping the peace was based on *frank-pledge*, a police organization which required every male over the age of 12 to belong to a 'tithing', a group of ten or more persons under a headman. All in the tithing were mutually responsible for the offences of the others and were bound to produce the offender in court if called upon. Those who did not submit to justice in the courts were declared outlaws and could be killed with impunity.

In most parts of England the succession to land on the death of an owner was determined by the rule of *primogeniture*, i.e. the first-born son inherited his father's land. But in some places it was different, e.g. in Kent the system of landholding was known as *gavelkind* and under it all sons inherited equally. In Bristol and Nottingham a system of *borough-English* applied, which provided that the youngest son inherited.

The procedure and the proof of guilt in Anglo-Saxon courts were primitive. Trial might be by **ordeal**, which was in effect an appeal to God or the supernatural. It might consist of ducking someone in a pool, and he was guilty if the water 'rejected' him and innocent if he sank; or in an ordeal by fire a red-hot iron would be carried a distance of nine feet, whereby if the hands had not festered within a certain period after carrying the iron the offender had established his innocence.

Another form of proof in civil cases was **compurgation**. This consisted in the litigant repeating an oath word-perfect without stumbling. Sometimes the claimant was assisted by kinsmen who were oath helpers (or compurgators) and similarly swore. If they too repeated the oath sucessfully the claimant had 'waged his law' and won his claim. Juries (see p. 11) later superseded ordeal and compurgation.

Before the Norman Conquest there was no strong central government. The king with his council (or witan) had little control over his kingdom. Royal justice was difficult to obtain.

The Norman Conquest

English legal development stems from 1066 when William of Normandy gained the Crown of England by right of battle. William and his Norman successors distinguished themselves in many ways. They possessed orderly minds and were efficient administrators. They crushed the rebellious English into submission and established a strong central government.

William owned all England: all other persons possessed land either as tenants (not owners) or sub-tenants of the King himself. Feudalism, based on land tenure, was introduced into England. No immediate change was attempted in regard to the customary laws of the English, for this would have been an insuperable task. Primitive people do not take kindly to radical alterations in their way of living.

The changes made by William I include the following:

(*a*) The King's Council (*Magnum Concilium*) was set up. Here foregathered the barons, lords, bishops, and other important figures of the kingdom on whose advice and wisdom the monarch relied. Here was the stong central government.

(*b*) A new feudalism was introduced. The King owned (in theory) all the land, and the barons, lords, bishops, and freemen held of him as tenants or sub-tenants. All tenants, whether barons or freemen, were compelled to swear an oath of allegiance to the King himself. Freemen owed allegiance as sub-tenants not only to a lord of the manor but also to the King, an important fact making for closer royal control.

(*c*) Separation of lay courts and church (or clerical) courts, each with a definite jurisdiction. Bishops and clergy were henceforward to be tried in their own courts and Church (or canon) law was to be applied therein.

William and his successors achieved the uniformity of the law, making it the common law, by introducing the **general eyre**. This was a form of central control whereby representatives of the King were sent out from Westminster to all parts of the country to check the local administration in the shires. These representatives made records of the land and wealth of the country, they collected taxes and they adjudicated in disputes brought before them. In the course of time the general eyre became judicial rather than administrative. In the reign of Richard II the eyre was abolished, but the important practice of sending members of the Royal Council continued. These representatives of the King were the original *royal judges* and derived their authority from the King's command by Royal Commissions, namely:

(*a*) **The Commission of Gaol Delivery**, empowering the judges to clear the gaols of untried prisoners.

(*b*) **The Commission of Oyer and Terminer**, empowering the judges to hear (*oyer*) and determine (*terminer*) cases of serious crimes such as treason or felonies brought before them.

(*c*) **The Commission of Assize**, which granted the judges jurisdiction over civil matters normally triable in the royal courts at Westminster.

To appreciate the significance of the Commission of Assize we should remember that whenever a plaintiff wished to bring an action in a civil matter against another person he had to obtain a writ from the Lord Chancellor's writ office and serve it on his opponent. The writ commanded the defendant and the plaintiff to attend the royal courts at Westminster on a certain date, unless before that date (*nisi prius*) the King's justices could hear the case locally, i.e. where the action arose.

Attendance at Westminster was itself no easy matter in those days; journeys were long, delay in London was likely and witnesses could not always be found to attend. So a local hearing by the royal judges was a useful and attractive expedient readily grasped by those who could not obtain justice in the manorial court or other local courts—which were frequently corrupt, partial, and unfair.

Here, then, were the royal judges, known as **itinerant justices**, granting better justice which naturally proved popular with the people. Henry II (1154–89) reorganized the system by dividing the country into **circuits** and putting the excursions from Westminster on a regular basis.

We have seen that the judges were originally men appointed from the King's Council: they might be bishops, barons, or knights. Behind them stood the royal power as evidenced by the King's Commissions.

The original justices were for the most part untrained in law. When they visited a county court (the shires became counties after the Normans) they had to ascertain the customs applicable to the local court. The royal judges then applied the law thus discovered from the inhabitants. The twelfth and thirteenth centuries saw the introduction of **juries**. Juries were made up of local people who knew the facts of the local cases and the local customs relevant thereto, so that the justices could then enforce these customs in the name of the King.

On completing their circuits, the justices returned to the royal courts at Westminster. There they discussed together the customs ascertained in various parts of the country and their findings. By a process of sifting these customs, rejecting those which were unreasonable and accepting those which were not, and by the use of good sense and right reason, they formed a uniform pattern of customary law throughout England.

At the same time another important practice grew up: the judges began to apply the principle of *stare decisis* ('let the decision stand'). Whenever a new problem of law came to be decided a rule was formed and this rule was followed subsequently by all other judges. By this means the law became more certain and predictable, and acquired the character of a legal system. So, out of the varied and different customs, there was formed what is now known as the common law of England, so called because it is the law common to all parts of England and Wales.

It is estimated that the formation of the common law was complete by about 1250 when Bracton wrote his famous *Treatise on the Laws and Customs of England*, which was the first exposition of a part of the law that was destined to reach all parts of the world.

The Common Law Courts

The King's Council, sometimes called the *Curia Regis*, was the central government of the kingdom, performing legislative, executive, and judicial functions without distinction. From the King's Council special courts were instituted to deal with particular kinds of cases in which royal justice was sought. The various courts staffed by royal judges developed in the following order:

(*a*) **The Court of Exchequer**. This was formed during the reign of Henry I, and was primarily a Government department concerned with national revenue. It was named the 'Exchequer' because the method of accounting involved the use of counters which were moved about on a chequered board. The department split into two branches: one administrative, collecting taxes and dues; the other judicial, dealing with disputes over taxation. The court extended its jurisdiction to hear common-law actions only remotely connected with the royal revenue. The judges of the court were known as Barons of the Exchequer.

(*b*) **The Court of Common Pleas**. The itinerant or circuit judges were sent out by royal authority to dispense justice in the counties. These judges sat in the communal and feudal courts (e.g. manorial courts) and they claimed jurisdiction over disputes between persons, e.g. in relation to land. Their justice became popular and a special court called the *Court of Common Pleas* (so called because it dealt with pleas of the commoners as distinct from royal pleas, i.e. criminal cases) was set up to decide disputes of a civil nature between subject and subject. In 1273 the first Chief Justice was appointed. This court administered the common law and survived until the Judicature Acts, 1873–5.

(*c*) **The Court of King's Bench**. This was the youngest and the most durable of the courts to emerge from the *Curia Regis*. It owes its name to the close connexion with the monarch, for the King himself used to sit at a bench with the judges to decide disputes. This close connexion with the *Curia Regis* and the King also gave it a unique importance. Its jurisdiction included criminal cases (in addition to those tried by the itinerant justices in the local courts), and also civil cases, concurrent with the jurisdiction of the Court of Common Pleas. But the King's Bench had a supervisory jurisdiction over the activities of all inferior courts, which it enforced by means of prerogative writs.

This court survives today with its civil, criminal and supervisory jurisdiction, and is under the control of the Lord Chief Justice who is assisted (as were former courts) by *puisne* judges.

Some mention should be made here of legal procedure. In medieval times criminals were arrested and placed in the gaols until they could be tried, either by the local manorial courts or by the royal judges when they came to the district. In civil cases, however, procedure was more technical. The proceedings in the common-law courts started with the issue of an 'original' writ (so named because it originated the proceedings), which was purchased from the main royal office, the Chancery.

The writ was a formal document addressed to the sheriff of the county where the defendant resided, commanding him to secure the presence of the defendant at the trial and setting out the cause of action or ground of claim of the plaintiff. For every civil wrong or cause of action there was a separate writ. Important examples were the writ of trespass, the writ of debt, and the writ of detinue (detinue alleged that the defendant detained an article or chattel from the plaintiff and would not return it). The plaintiff had to select the particular writ which he considered fitted the facts of his case.

The plaintiff attended the Writ Office of the Chancery, where a register of the various writs was kept, and applied for the writ most suitable to his claim. If there was no writ suitable to the civil claim made or the relief required of the law, the plaintiff was at a severe disadvantage. We may say, therefore, that the writ system dominated the civil law: for only where there was a remedy was there a right (which is expressed in the Latin phrase *ubi remedium ibi jus*). Moreover, if the wrong kind of writ were selected by the plaintiff, the common law judges would throw out the case and refrain from inquiring into its merits. Under the rigid procedure of the writ system the remedy available to litigants became more important than the justice of the claim.

Some attempt to alleviate this system was made by the clerks in the Chancery. Where a writ was thrown out by the court, or where none existed to found the claim, the clerks endeavoured to accommodate litigants by issuing new writs, thus effectively expanding the rights available. At first the common law judges tolerated this procedure and accepted some new writs; but later their attitude stiffened and they refused to accept the new writs, since these amounted to new law.

The Provisions of Oxford, 1258, forbade the practice of creating new writs. As a result certain wrongs went unremedied merely because they did not fall within the limits of an existing writ. However, some alleviation was attempted by the Statute of Westminster II, 1285, which empowered the clerks in the Chancery to issue writs *in consimili casu* ('in like case to'), i.e. existing writs could be adapted to fit new circumstances. However, full use was not made of this provision, and litigants' claims still went unsatisfied by the ineffectual writ system: the common law did not expand to meet the urgent and growing needs of the community. Complaints to the King and his Council regarding the inelasticity of the common law led to the emergence of the Court of Chancery and its special field known as **equity**.

2. Equity

In a general sense equity means fairness. In English law, equity means that body of rules originally enforced only by the Court of Chancery. Equity has been described as 'a gloss [meaning a supplement] on the common law', filling in the gaps and making the English legal system more complete.

We have seen that petitions from persons unable to obtain justice in the common law courts were sent to the King as 'fountain of justice'. These petitions were sometimes examined by the King and his Council and the relief was granted or refused. Later, due to pressure of business in the Council, the petitions were sent to the Lord Chancellor who, as Chief Secretary of State and 'Keeper of the King's Conscience', dealt with them alone.

The petitions were usually in the form of allegations that:

(*a*) The common law was defective, e.g. the law of contract was undeveloped and inadequate to serve the growing needs of suitors.

(*b*) The remedy of the common law courts, namely damages, was not always a satisfactory relief.

(*c*) The defendant was too powerful; men of wealth and power in a county could overawe a court and intimidate jurors.

(*d*) The court lacked jurisdiction to decide certain cases, e.g. where foreign merchants were suitors.

By the end of the fifteenth century the Chancellor had set up his own court and dealt with petitions for relief. The Chancellor was not bound by the writ system or the technical and formal rules of the common law, and considered petitions on the basis of conscience and right.

At first the Chancellor used to consult the Council and sometimes the common law judges, but eventually it became his custom to summon the parties to the dispute to appear before him alone to answer 'interrogatories' (specific questions relevant to the issue) and to unburden their consciences so that the truth could be ascertained and justice done.

The Court of Chancery proved popular with litigants and this caused friction with the common law courts. Jurisdiction was lost to the Chancery Court. Sometimes the courts of common law and the Chancery Court issued contradictory verdicts, and relations between the courts became difficult. The dispute came to a head under James I (1603–25) in the *Earl of Oxford*'s case (1616). The common law courts, headed by Chief Justice Coke, gave a judgment which was alleged to have been obtained by fraud. The Chancellor, Lord Ellesmere, issued an injunction preventing the successful party from proceeding to enforce the judgment, whereupon the dispute was referred to the King for decision. The King sought the views of Sir Francis Bacon (Attorney-General) who advised that *where common law and equity conflicted, equity should prevail.* Although competition between the courts of common law and equity continued, the right of the Chancellor to grant injunctions thereafter was not seriously challenged. Matters were finally resolved by the passing of the Judicature Acts, 1873–5 (see p. 22).

Despite its early popularity, equity as administered in the Chancery was subject to criticism. Its initial flexibility led to uncertainty in the seventeenth century, and the jurist John Selden observed that 'Equity varies with the length of the Chancellor's foot'. Whatever the demerits of the common law, it was possible to estimate a probable verdict by considering similar cases already decided and the statutes enforced. Equity, which was dispensed as a matter of conscience, was unpredictable and the relief granted by one Chancellor might be refused by his successor. Between flexibility and certainty there is much tension. Flexibility was advantageous because it gave relief from the rigidity of law, but could be disadvantageous if it led to uncertainty and hardship.

Eventually equity emerged from vagueness and conscience and became formalized. Lord Nottingham (Lord Chancellor in 1673–82) held that equity should be administered where possible in accordance with known principles and not by arbitrary discretion. Only where there was no precedent or where there was conflict in the rules or principles should conscience determine the matter.

Nottingham's work was carried on by others, in particular Lord Hardwicke (Lord Chancellor in 1736–56) who held that a judge exercising equity jurisdiction should follow existing principles. With the adoption of the system of precedent, equity became predictable and intelligible.

Lord Eldon (Lord Chancellor in 1801–6 and 1807–27) further developed equity, establishing a system of case law, so that by the beginning of the nineteenth century equity became nearly as rigid as the common law.

Later History

The history of equity in the nineteenth century was notable for the delays which occurred in settling disputes, and the confusion over jurisdiction. Lord Eldon's rule as Lord Chancellor has been described as 'ponderous' (one case is reported to have lasted ten years). The delays may have been caused by the numerous duties which the Lord Chancel- lor was called upon to perform. Today the Lord Chancellor is similarl burdened, but he has a large staff at his disposal to assist him. In t nineteenth century complaint was also made of the cost of proceedin and we should remember that the clerks and assistants in the Chanc Court received emoluments from the litigants themselves, a sy which evoked much criticism.

The latter half of the nineteenth century was also a period of ju reform, which culminated in the Judicature Acts, 1873–5. Thes set up a new structure of courts known as the Supreme C Judicature (see p. 22). In addition the Acts laid down four in principles:

(*a*) Equity and common law should in future be admini by side in all courts.

(*b*) Where there is a conflict between a rule of equity and a rule of common law with reference to the same matter, the rule of equity should prevail.

(*c*) Evidence could be given in court orally.

(*d*) Rules of the Supreme Court of Judicature were to be formulated with regard to procedural matters.

The final result of the Acts was the fusion of administration of both common law and equity. Certain matters, e.g. trusts, originally dealt with by the Court of Chancery were assigned with other matters to the Chancery Division of the High Court. All courts could henceforward award common-law remedies, e.g. damages, and grant the special equitable remedies of which the following are the most important:

(*a*) **Injunction**, an order of the court in the form of a decree compelling the defendant in a case to cease from doing certain acts.

(*b*) **Specific Performance** of contracts where the common law remedy of damages is inadequate to compensate the plaintiff.

(*c*) **Rescission of Contracts** (see p. 157).

(*d*) **Rectification** (see p. 152).

(*e*) **Relief against Penalties** (see p. 179), **Fraud, and Undue Influence** (see p. 160).

These remedies are at the discretion of the court unlike the common law remedy of damages which is 'of right'. The discretion is exercised on equitable principles, e.g. 'He who comes to equity must come with lean hands'.

gislation

ave seen that the basis of English law is the common law, whose are to be found today in the case law built up by the judges the Norman Conquest.

al role of the King and his Council was merely to maintain e within the realm and to defend the state against external keep order and peace the King amended or altered suing ordinances, provisions, assizes and charters, vice of his Council. These ordinances, some temp- manent, were in effect statutes, but their number ll.

Frequently the King required to raise military rewith to carry out his duties and maintain This meant the taxation of those feudal the King's protection and from whom gly the Norman kings sometimes sum- s, bishops, and lords) to attend a 'parliament' (*parler*; to speak), a name first used in the thirteenth century.

In 1265 Simon de Montford summoned his famous parliament which for the first time contained representatives from the cities and boroughs as well as the shires. The practice of summoning representatives of the important groups in the land continued, and by 1300 the three estates of the realm, namely (i) the Lords Spiritual (the archbishops and bishops), (ii) the Lords Temporal (barons and lords) and (iii) the Commons (knights and freemen from the cities, boroughs, and the shires), met at Westminster. Sometimes the Lords and Commons met together, but more often in private and separate assemblies, to discuss what answers should be given 'in Parliament' to the King's demands for military supplies and money.

The grant of money to the King placed the Commons in a strong bargaining position, and eventually they began to present petitions or 'Bills' to the King requesting a change in the law in return for the grant of money. These petitions were originally requests; some were granted, and some were refused. Refusal meant a conflict between the Commons (expressing the will of the people), and the King with his advisers. But kings do not lightly relinquish their vast powers; many were despotic and claimed to rule by Divine Right.

In the time of the Tudors, Parliament was subjected to the wills of strong monarchs, including Henry VIII and Elizabeth I, who, while not overruling Parliament, ruled as they pleased *through* Parliament.

This uneasy balance of powers came to a head in the seventeenth century. James II (1685–8) reverted to unwise and arbitrary methods of government, and civil war broke out between the Royalists, supporting the King, and the Parliamentarians, supporting the Commons. James II fled to France, and, after the so-called 'Glorious Revolution' of 1688, William and Mary were invited to come to the throne of England. The Bill of Rights, 1689, meant that the King could not in future override Acts of Parliament or exercise the great powers of government without check from the representatives of Parliament. Because the Commons would grant money to the King for one year only, it became necessary for the King to call Parliament together at least once a year.

During the remainder of the seventeenth century and in the eighteenth and nineteenth centuries, great constitutional developments took place. First, the growth of political parties; secondly the rise of Cabinet government led by a Prime Minister; and, following the Reform Act, 1832, the grant of universal franchise. Today Britain has what is described as a **constitutional monarchy**, the chief characteristic of which is that the monarch is nominally head of the state, but has lost practically all actual power. By convention the monarch acts in accordance with the will of the Government of the day (headed by a Prime Minister and a Cabinet), which is itself responsible to Parliament composed of representatives of the people elected by popular vote.

Successive governments have interfered more and more positively with the social, economic, and industrial aspects of national affairs. The Welfare State was brought about by legislation, and many areas of the common law (civil and criminal) have been revoked or reformed. It follows, therefore, that the main source of law today is legislation.

Legislation may take the form of:

(*a*) **Statutes** or Acts of Parliament (see p. 30), and

(*b*) Delegated legislation, mainly in the form of what are called **Statutory Instruments** (see p. 34).

European Economic Community Law

Some of the legislation made by the Community institutions is directly applicable and immediately binding on the English Courts. Other legislation is not so, but Parliament of the United Kingdom is required to legislate on the matter.

4. Canon Law

After the Norman Conquest, William I separated the courts of law into *lay courts* administering the common law, and *ecclesiastical* (or *church*) *courts*. In the early days the church courts were very important locally and nationally and assumed a wide jurisdiction. The law enforced in the church courts was canon law which was influenced by Roman law. The matters dealt with included:

(*a*) clergy discipline;

(*b*) offences by clergy and laity against church doctrine, faith, and morality;

(*c*) marriage, e.g. declaring whether a lawful marriage had in fact taken place (if there was no valid marriage it was declared null); judicial separation (ordering that the parties be no longer bound to cohabit as man and wife, though not dissolving the marriage tie); and divorce (dissolving the marriage);

(*d*) legitimacy, e.g. declaring whether a child of a marriage was legitimate or the heir;

(*e*) wills of *personal* property, e.g. declaring whether a document was a lawful will, and the administration of the estates of deceased persons so far as *personal* property was concerned where the deceased left no will (i.e. was intestate). Realty (land) descended to the heir or other person in accordance with strict common law rules, and disputes as to ownership and possession of realty fell exclusively within the jurisdiction of the common law courts.

For church purposes England was divided into the Province of Canterbury and the Province of York, each in the charge of an archbishop. The two provinces were each divided into dioceses, each in the charge of a bishop. Each bishop had his Consistory Court for the diocese which he administered and which was in his spiritual charge. The presiding officer of this diocesan court was called a Chancellor and was appointed by the bishop as his representative in the court. Appeal from the bishops' diocesan courts went to the respective provincial courts of Canterbury (called the Court of Arches) and York (known as the York Chancery).

From the provincial courts appeal lay to the Pope, until this right was abolished after the Reformation by the Statute of Appeals Act, 1532. The Statute of Appeals Act brought the church courts in England more and more under the control of the State, but their separate jurisdiction continued on into the nineteenth century.

However, in 1857, the jurisdiction in divorce, judicial separation, nullity and legitimacy was transferred to the Divorce Court which was set up in that year by the Matrimonial Causes Act. Testamentary matters relating to wills were also transferred in 1857 from the church courts to a new Court of Probate.

The new civil courts of Probate and Divorce were staffed by civil lawyers who replaced the ecclesiastical lawyers, and the legal principles which had hitherto been enforced in the church courts and which had been based on canon law were incorporated in the law of England.

In 1875 the Probate Court and the Divorce Court were incorporated into the Supreme Court of Judicature set up by the Judicature Act, 1873. Probate is now dealt with in the Family Division and Chancery Division of the High Court. Divorce falls within the Family Division (see p. 51).

5. The Law Merchant

Mercantile law, or 'law merchant', has been described as

> 'Neither more nor less than the usages of merchants and traders . . . ratified by the decisions of the Courts of law which, upon such usages being proved before them, have adopted them as settled law' (*Goodwin* v. *Robarts*, 1875).

The law merchant in medieval times was applied in (*a*) maritime courts found in coastal towns, and (*b*) local courts found in certain market towns.

(*a*) **The Maritime Courts** applied the customary maritime law which operated generally in western Europe and which was derived from the Laws of Oleron, the Consolato del Mare, the Laws of Wisby, and other Mediterranean maritime laws.

Jurisdiction included such matters as the hiring of ships, charter-parties, carriage of goods by sea, marine insurance, piracy and crimes on the high seas.

As England became a trading and seafaring nation the jurisdiction of the maritime courts increased. In 1482 the Lord High Admiral of England appointed on behalf of the Crown a special judge to take over the jurisdiction of the local maritime courts and extended their jurisdiction to include prize matters. Prize jurisdiction determines whether a ship, with its cargo, captured during time by war by a belligerent is 'prize', and, if so, how it is to be disposed of.

(*b*) **Local Courts** administering mercantile or commercial law were of two kinds. In towns holding fairs at fixed times and places, courts were constituted on the spot and usually included the mayor assisted by one local trader and one foreign merchant. Justice was speedy and the unwritten law applied was based on the customs of merchants in buying, selling and delivering goods, bills of exchange, negotiable instruments and the like. The courts were sometimes called 'Piepowder' courts, because the merchants attending them often came into court with dusty feet (*pieds poudrés*).

The second group were known as the Courts of the Staple and were set up in certain 'staple' towns which had a monopoly in trading in such staple goods as wool and leather. These courts also applied the law merchant.

In both the local courts and the staple courts the law contained an international flavour. This was because the Crown, wishing to encourage Continental trade, gave the foreign merchants and traders the protection of the law which applied to men of their kind generally throughout Europe. Accordingly justice was administered on the spot by the special courts constituted by the mayor with one local and one foreign merchant. Merchants and traders moving from one fair to the next could not wait for the justice of either the ordinary English local courts or the royal courts. In any case the common law of England was inadequate to deal with the contractual disputes of the traders.

Gradually, however, the courts merchant declined in importance as the common law courts became more efficient and reliable and became centralized in London. Moreover, limitations were imposed by statute in 1477 on the jurisdiction of the local courts merchant.

By the middle of the eighteenth century the common law courts had absorbed nearly all the jurisdiction of the courts merchant, except for the maritime law and prize law applied in the maritime courts.

Lord Mansfield, Chief Justice in 1756, was notable for his work in regard to the law merchant. He established the principle that once a judgment had been given on a mercantile custom, that custom became judicially recognized and no further proof of it needed to be given in a similar case in the future. Specially selected juries of merchants ensured continuity in the administration of mercantile law. Mansfield's work was carried on by other judges and resulted in the absorption of this branch of the law into the common law of England.

6. Local Custom

We have described the common law as the unwritten part of English law or the common or universal custom of the realm. We have also mentioned that the principles of law formulated by the judges, which in fact make up the body of the common law, have been enforced by the courts of law for some 900 years.

It is well known that in some parts of England certain local customs are observed which, while different in character from the general custom of the realm, are nevertheless regarded as conferring rights or imposing duties. Moreover, many such customs have existed from time immemorial. English law takes account of these local customary rights, and even though they are apparent exceptions to the general law, they may nevertheless be enforced.

7. The Nineteenth Century

The law and the procedure by which justice is administered are always open to public criticism. In the nineteenth century there were ample grounds for general dissatisfaction. We have noted that the principles of common law and those of equity were separate and were administered in different courts. Where a litigant in a common law case (e.g. trespass) wished to obtain a equitable remedy or relief (e.g. an injunction) he had to commence a separate action in the Chancery Court, thus adding to expense and often causing great delay. The rules of common law sometimes conflicted with the principles of equity, so that confusion resulted. There was, moreover, a variety of courts, and some (e.g. the ecclesiastical courts and the Admiralty courts) had developed special rules and practices of their own. The system of appeals from the common law courts (civil and criminal) and the equity courts was irrational and confusing. The legal procedure for enforcing rights and obtaining remedies was inefficient, technical, antiquated, and slow.

The deficiencies in the law itself and in its administration were obvious to ordinary citizens (as well as litigants). They were noted by Charles Dickens and other writers, and were critically examined by outstanding political thinkers such as Jeremy Bentham (1748–1832).

Changes were, however, slow and piecemeal. We have mentioned (p. 19) the Court of Probate Act, 1857, which took away the probate jurisdiction of the ecclesiastical courts and set up a new Probate Court. By the Matrimonial Causes Act, 1857, a new Divorce Court was set up which took over the matrimonial jurisdiction of the old ecclesiastical courts.

The Common Law Procedure Act, 1854, empowered common law courts to grant injunctions and to take account of certain equitable defences. The Chancery Procedure Act, 1852, enabled the Chancery Court to decide points of common law arising in equity proceedings e.g. actions for breach of trust. The Chancery Amendment Act, 1858, enabled the Chancery Court to award damages (a common law remedy) in place of or in addition to its own equitable remedies, notably injunction and specific performance of contracts.

But the main reform was effected by the Judicature Acts, 1873–5, from the recommendations of the Judicature Commission of 1867.

Immediately before this important Act came into effect the following courts existed: King's Bench; Common Pleas; Exchequer; Chancery; Court of Probate; Court of Divorce; Court of Admiralty. Appeal courts were the Court of Appeal in Chancery and the Court of Exchequer. Appeals in criminal cases were heard by the Court of Crown Cases Reserved, established in 1848. This court was not affected by the reorganization of 1875.

Reorganization of the Courts

The Judicature Acts, 1873–5, set up a Supreme Court of Judicature comprising (*a*) the Court of Appeal and (*b*) the High Court of Justice. The latter included:

(i) the Queen's Bench Division;
(ii) the Chancery Division;
(iii) the Common Pleas Division;
(iv) the Exchequer Division;
(v) the Probate, Divorce, and Admiralty Division.

By an Order in Council of 1881, made under the Judicature Acts, 1873–5, the Common Pleas Division and the Exchequer Division were merged with the Queen's Bench Division, thus forming three divisions which existed till 1970.

(i) the Queen's Bench Division;
(ii) the Chancery Division;
(iii) the Probate, Divorce, and Admiralty Division.

The House of Lords

The jurisdiction of the House of Lords as a final court of appeal was abolished by the Judicature Act, 1873, mainly on the ground that there were insufficient legally qualified peers (lay members of the House, by convention, had not attended judicial meetings). By the Appellate Jurisdiction Act, 1876, the appellate jurisdiction was restored, and provision was made for the appointment of two Lords of Appeal in Ordinary. These are salaried life peers, holding or having held high judicial office for at least two years, or eminent barristers who have practised for a minimum of fifteen years. The maximum number of Lords of Appeal in Ordinary has now been increased to eleven.

Reforming the Rules

The Judicature Acts not only reformed the structure of the courts, they also made fundamental changes in the administration of law and equity. All branches of the Supreme Court were empowered to administer law and equity and to grant legal remedies and equitable remedies. Moreover, all divisions of the High Court were competent to try *any* action. For administrative purposes and convenience certain matters were reserved or allocated to each division, roughly corresponding to the jurisdiction of the courts that had been replaced.

The Acts further provided that, where a rule of equity and rule of common law were at variance with reference to the same matter, the rule of equity should prevail. The Acts did not fuse law and equity into a single set of rules. The rules of common law and the principles of equity stem from different sources and are still distinct.* What the Acts did was to ensure that for the future the two systems should be *administered* in the same courts. The rules of procedure, particularly in respect of the issue of writs, were simplified.

The relevant statute is now the Supreme Court Act, 1981, which has replaced earlier legislation.

8. Exercises

1. What is meant by 'common law'?
2. Name the early common law courts and give the jurisdiction of each.
3. What does 'equity' mean? Describe the growth of equity jurisdiction.
4. Of what importance was the *Earl of Oxford*'s case (1616)?
5. What is meant by 'mercantile law'? Whence did it derive, and who was mainly responsible for its incorporation into the common law?
6. What is canon law? With what matters did the canon law deal?
7. What courts existed before the Judicature Acts? What changes did the Acts make?

*The modern opinion (Lord Denning and Viscount Simonds) is that law and equity are now fused.

3

LEGAL SOURCES

In English law substantive rules of law derive their authority from the following: judicial precedents, legislation, certain ancient textbooks and, to a very limited extent, local custom. These are called the legal sources.

1. Judicial Precedent

The essentials of good law are, on the one hand, certainty; and on the other, uniformity and consistency. Common law was judge-made, i.e. the judges moulded or created out of the original customary rules the common law of England whose principles are today found in case law.

Once a regular system of law reporting had developed and reports published, judges began to be guided by decisions in previous cases; and eventually it became the established practice that judges were bound to follow the decisions of higher courts in similar cases. The general rule established in the nineteenth century and consistently followed since was of binding precedent.

The hierarchy of courts in this matter is as follows:

House of Lords. Its decisions bind all other courts but not necessarily the House of Lords itself.

Court of Appeal (Civil Division). Its decisions bind the High Court, county courts and Divisional Courts, and itself.

Court of Appeal (Criminal Division). Its decisions bind the Crown Court and the magistrates' courts. They probably bind the Queen's Bench Divisional Court. The Court normally follows its own decisions but on occasion does not do so.

Queen's Bench Divisional Court. Its decisions bind the magistrates' courts but not the Crown Court (*Colyer*, 1974) and normally the Court follows its own decisions.

High Court. Decisions of its judges do not bind other High Court judges, but they bind county court judges. If, however, the court is faced with two conflicting decisions on virtually the same point, then subsequent judges are bound to follow the second decision (*Colchester Estates* v. *Carlton Industries*, 1984).

Court of Justice of the European Communities. Its decisions on interpretation of the Treaties, validity of acts of Community institutions and interpretation of the statutes of Council bodies are binding on all English courts, though apparently not binding on itself.

It has not been determined whether decisions of the Crown Court are binding on magistrates' courts, but in effect they are not since they are not reported in the series of law reports and because appeals on points of law are by case stated to the Divisional Court of the Queen's Bench.

The two divisions of the Court of Appeal are of equal status and are not strictly bound by each other's decisions, but in practice each does pay attention to the rulings of the other and each has a strong persuasive influence on the other to ensure certainty and uniformity of the law.

The House of Lords and Precedent

In 1966 the Lord Chancellor, on behalf of the Lords of Appeal in Ordinary, made the following pronouncement in the House of Lords:

> 'Their Lordships regard the use of precedent as an indispensable foundation upon which to decide what is the law and its application to individual cases. It provides at least some degree of certainty upon which individuals can rely in the conduct of their affairs, as well as a basis for orderly development of legal rules.
>
> 'Their Lordships nevertheless recognize that too rigid adherence to precedent may lead to injustice in a particular case and also unduly restrict the proper development of the law. They propose, therefore, to modify their present practice and, while treating former decisions of this House as normally binding, to depart from a previous decision when it appears right to do so.
>
> 'In this connexion they will bear in mind the danger of disturbing retrospectively the basis on which contracts, settlements of property and fiscal arrangements have been entered into and also the especial need for certainty as to the criminal law.
>
> 'This announcement is not intended to affect the use of precedent elsewhere than in this House.'

Case Law: Advantages and Disadvantages

Prof. William Geldart has enumerated the advantages of case law as:

(*a*) Certainty.
(*b*) Possibility of growth.
(*c*) The great wealth of detailed rules.
(*d*) The practical character of these rules.

The disadvantages, according to the same writer, are:

(*a*) Rigidity: 'the binding force of precedent is a fetter on the discretion of the judge'.

(*b*) The danger of illogical distinctions: 'a judge will often avoid following a rule which works hardship in a present case by laying hold of minute distinctions. Moreover, rules which are logically inconsistent with each other are sometimes developed along distinct lines of cases which ultimately meet and come into conflict.'

(*c*) Bulk and complexity. There are over 1,000 volumes of law reports containing some 400,000 cases. These may be regarded as cumbersome and the legal rules difficult to learn and apply.

The points made by Prof. Geldart emphasize the need to achieve certainty and the need to ensure flexibility. While the former tends to make the law rigid, the latter tends to render the law uncertain and vague but does allow for development to meet the new needs of society.

Judges of the superior courts may, on appeal, *overrule* a decision, *reverse* a decision, or *disapprove* of a previous decision. Sometimes alterations can only be made by a statute which revokes previous law and reshapes the law to meet the changing conditions of men and society.

Overruling occurs where a higher court (e.g. the House of Lords) decides a similar case on the basis of a different legal principle. The previous rule laid down (e.g. by the Court of Appeal) is then said to be overruled.

Reversal occurs where an appeal court reverses a decision given in a lower court from which the appeal emanated. Thus in the case of *A* v. *B* a High Court may give judgment for *A*, while on appeal the higher court gives judgment for *B*.

Disapproval occurs where a superior court in the course of its judgment expresses doubt as to the validity of some previous rule but does not expressly overrule it.

The doctrine of *stare decisis* ('to stand by past decisions') is the technical name given to the rule that judges must follow the precedents and principles of law declared by superior courts.

Ratio decidendi is a technical phrase meaning the principle or reason for the decision. This portion of a judgment of a court is binding in similar cases which may subsequently be tried by lower courts. It is a vital part of a judgment and must be distinguished from *obiter dicta* ('things said by the way') meaning those words delivered by a judge which are not essential to his decision. Thus, a judge in the course of his judgment might discuss a hypothetical situation: 'If, however, *A* had done this and *B* had done that . . . I should have been obliged to find that *A* and *B* would be jointly responsible . . .' These words are said *obiter*, by the way, and are not binding. They might, however, be 'persuasive'; if the situation envisaged by the judge arose in fact at some later time his words could have an influence on the judge trying that case.

Judges of the High Court, county court judges, and magistrates are absolutely bound by the decisions of the House of Lords and Court of Appeal where those decisions are clearly in point. Such precedents which a judge *must* follow are called **Binding Precedents**. All other precedents are called **Persuasive Precedents**: these include decisions or principles laid down by the Judicial Committee of the Privy Council, decisions of

Commonwealth courts or of the United States Supreme Court. A judge of one division of the High Court is not bound by the decision of another High Court judge, though each pays attention to the other's decisions to ensure certainty and uniformity of the law.

Frequently there will be no relevant decided case for a judge to turn to. Notwithstanding the many volumes of law reports and the thousands of cases reported, representing a 'wealth of detailed rules', there may be no certainty of the rule to be applied. The judge must declare what the rule should be by arguing from analogous cases. Since the common law is 'complete' and capable of providing a remedy for every wrong, where there is no apparent rule the judge is expected to act creatively in declaring from his study of the common law or equity or jurisprudence what that rule should be.

Obviously no two cases coming before the courts of law are identical. This fact enables a judge to point to some material difference which justifies him in refusing to apply a rule of law previously laid down. The judge is **distinguishing** the present case from the earlier one, so avoiding hardship or injustice which was not envisaged when the earlier judgment was announced.

After hearing the evidence from both sides in a case and the address of counsel, the stage is reached when the judgment is delivered. The form the judgment takes is generally as follows:

(*a*) A statement of the relevant facts.
(*b*) Review of relevant precedents.
(*c*) Reasoning of the judge from one or more of the cases cited.
(*e*) Judgment, decree, or order made.

The judicial precedents which we have been considering above are found in law reports.

Law Reports

The records of Anglo-Saxon laws (or dooms) and of actual cases are few. Similarly, we have scant records of cases in the Norman period, and we have to remind ourselves that the common law was not completely formed until around A.D. 1250.

The first treatise on the English common law was written by Henricus de Bracton, who lived in the first part of the thirteenth century in the reign of Henry III. His work, in part a collection of cases, became the forerunner of the later law reports and was entitled *De legibus et consuetudinibus Angliae*.

Year Books. These contained fragmentary reports of cases in the period between 1289 and 1535. They were written in Anglo-Norman, were technical and procedural in content (covering points of practice) and dealt with civil law rather than the criminal law.

Abridgments. These were shortened versions of the Year Books which appeared in the sixteenth and seventeenth centuries and contained reports of cases, some of which were written by judges and counsel.

Private Publications. Some notable sixteenth-century lawyers and judges prepared private publications of reports on contemporary and earlier cases. Some were copied from imperfect manuscripts and contained much trivial detail. However, by the sixteenth century, pleadings in civil cases were written down, so that it was possible thereafter to cite a case in support of a particular argument. The notable reports during this period are Plowden's Reports (1550–80), Coke's Reports (1572–1616), Bridgman's Reports (1614–21), and Lord Raymond's Reports (1694–1732).

The first *regular* reports were known as Term Reports and were published by Durnford and East (1785–1800). Once reporting of cases became systematic and regular, the reports became authorized, i.e. accepted by the courts as accurately representing the judgment made. Nevertheless the system of reporting was expensive, the standard of reporting deteriorated and there were often lengthy delays between a judgment and the appearance of its report.

Council of Law Reporting. Because of the multiplicity of law reports in the nineteenth century, the Council of Law Reporting was set up in 1865 and barrister reporters were appointed. A series of authorized reports was established under the control of the legal profession.

The Council of Law Reporting is a quasi-official body consisting of representatives of the Inns of Court and the Law Society. The Council employs an editor and a staff of reporters (who are barristers) and produces a uniform series of reports of cases in all the superior courts. Not all cases are reported; a selection is made by the editor. Where it is decided to report a case, a copy of the report made by the reporter is passed to the judge who has an opportunity of revising the wording of his judgment. The reports so produced are known as the *Law Reports*. They include counsel's argument.

In 1953 the Council of Law Reporting began a weekly series known as the *Weekly Law Reports*.

The Council has no monopoly in the field of law reporting. Certain commercial companies produce reports, and the *All England Reports* begun in 1936 is an important example in this field. Moreover *The Times* publishes summary reports of important cases the day after judgment, and weekly journals such as *The Solicitors' Journal* (established 1857) and the *Justice of the Peace* (established 1837) contain summary reports of cases.

Where various reports of the same case reveal differences in wording, the *Law Reports* are taken to be the most authoritative since they are semi-official.

Reference to reports. The plaintiff is cited first and the defendant second; thus '*Brown* v. *Smith* [1968] 1 Q.B. 334' indicates that the report will be found in the first volume of Queen's Bench Division Reports of 1968 at p. 334. 'Ch' indicates Chancery Division Reports, while 'P' indicates those of the Probate, Divorce, and Admiralty Division. 'F' denotes the Family Division.

Reports of decisions of the Court of Appeal appear with the reports of the Division from which the appeal is made. 'A.C.' indicates an appeal case heard in the House of Lords or the Privy Council.

Citation of Cases

Where cases are determined by a court at first instance (i.e. heard for the first time), the proceedings are cited thus:

Civil Case

(*a*) *Brown* v. *Jones* (1969)
Brown is the plaintiff; Jones is the defendant.

Criminal Case

(*b*) *Regina* (or *R.*) v. *Smith* (1969)
Regina (the Queen) is the prosecutor; Smith is the defendant.

Appeal

If Jones and Smith decide to appeal against the decisions at (*a*) and (*b*), the appeal cases will appear as above, but in the past the names were reversed:

(*a*) *Jones* v. *Brown* (1969)
(*b*) *Smith* v. *Regina* (1969)

Jones and Smith are known as appellants; Brown and Regina are known as respondents.

Admiralty Cases

Where claims are made involving one ship only, the proceedings are named after the ship: e.g. *The Moorcock* (1889); *The Tubantia* (1924). Where two ships are involved, the owners of one claiming against the owners of the other, both ships are named.

Declaratory Theory of the Common Law

The declaratory theory encouraged the development of precedent and enabled a large body of rules to develop from a few customary rules. The judge applying those rules to new cases merely **declared** or enunciated a pre-existing rule or principle of common law. In no sense was he creating new law.

The declaratory theory of law applied only to the common law. It did not apply to equity, which is traceable to conscience, and whose principles were decided in many cases by individual judges. Moreover, many areas of jurisdiction, e.g. trusts, were not part of the common law at all. The development of equitable principles into a systematic form is attributable to the creativeness of judges, such rules being improved and refined in the course of time.

2. Legislation

The Sovereignty of Parliament means that Parliament is legislatively supreme and can make and unmake (i.e. repeal) laws to any extent. Moreover, there is no body which can declare its legal enactments to be of no effect; the only limit on the legislative power of Parliament is that it cannot bind its successors in power. This statement is now qualified since Britain's entry to the E.E.C. (see p. 42). The E.E.C. rules take precedence in the event of conflict with statute or common law.

Any Act passed by Parliament which is of general application is absolutely binding on all persons within the sphere of Parliament's jurisdiction. However controversial a particular statute may be, a judge is **bound** to enforce its provisions.

Statutes

A statute may be defined as *an express and formal laying-down of a rule or rules of conduct to be observed in the future by persons to whom the statute is expressly, or by implication, made applicable*. A statute and a judgment may be contrasted thus:

Statute	*Judgment*
(*a*) Creates new law	Disclaims any attempt to create new law
(*b*) Lays down general rules for the guidance of future conduct	Applies an existing law to a particular set of circumstances
(*c*) Is imperative	Gives reasons

The Making of a Statute. Parliament comprises the Queen, the House of Lords, and the House of Commons. Although legislation may be introduced by both Houses, the effective chamber from which most legislation springs is the House of Commons. This lower House contains some 635 members representing geographical areas of the country called constituencies. Such Members of Parliament are elected at General Elections, held usually every five years, by the vote of all subjects over eighteen years of age, unless disqualified.

The Government is formed by that party gaining a majority of seats in the House of Commons. A Prime Minister is appointed to lead the Government. He then forms his Cabinet from the important members of his party, and appoints junior officials to various posts in the

Government. When, however, no one party has a sufficient majority, or when a national emergency occurs, a coalition government may be formed by two or more parties temporarily uniting.

The Cabinet forms its policies of government and turns to legislation as the means of carrying the policies into effect, e.g. The Local Government Act, 1972 (as amended).

Stages in Legislation

The first step in legislation is the *drafting* of the Bill. This is a skilful and sometimes long process requiring the services of lawyers known as Parliamentary Counsel, attached to the Treasury.

Once drafted, the Bill passes through the following stages to enable Parliament to consider and reconsider its provisions as thoroughly as possible:

(*a*) *First Reading*. This is a formality. The Bill may be read a first time as a result of the House agreeing to a motion for leave to introduce it. The Bill is then printed and published.

(*b*) *Second Reading*. Here the Minister or Member in charge of the Bill explains its purpose and the main issues of policy involved. The debate is limited to the purpose of the Bill and the means proposed for giving it effect. The House votes on the Bill. If the Bill survives the vote it passes to the next stage.

(*c*) *Committee Stage*. At this stage the Bill is dealt with by (i) a committee of the whole House, or (ii) a Select Committee, or (iii) a Standing Committee. A Select Committee is a committee constituted on a party basis, while a Standing Committee is composed of 20–50 Members appointed to examine Public Bills, which, after a second reading, are not passed to a committee of the whole House or to Select Committees. The purpose of the Committee Stage is to consider the *details* of the Bill clause by clause.

(*d*) *Report Stage*. Having passed the Committee Stage the Bill is formally reported to the House by the chairman of the committee. At the Report Stage the amendments made in the committee are considered by the House, which may make any additional amendments.

(*e*) *Third Reading*. At this stage the Bill is reviewed in its final form. The debate is confined to verbal amendments only, not the principles of the Bill.

The House of Lords is the second tier in the legislative process which allows for reflection on the merits or faults of the Bill and for criticism from different points of view.

After its Third Reading in the Commons, the Bill is sent to the Lords where it goes through a procedure similar to that in the Commons. If the Bill is amended in the Lords, it is returned to the Commons for consideration of the amendments. These may be accepted or rejected, though attempt is made to reconcile the two points of view. If agreement is impossible, the Commons can invoke its powers under the Parliament Acts, 1911 and 1949, whereby it may present the Bill for Royal Assent after one year without the agreement of the Lords. A Money Bill must originate in the Commons and may be delayed by the Lords for one month only.

Royal Assent. Having passed the House of Lords the Bill is ready for the Royal Assent which may be given by the Queen personally or by three Lords Commissioners. The Royal Assent Act, 1967, now provides that an Act is duly enacted if the Royal Assent is notified to each House of Parliament, sitting separately by either the Speaker of that House or the acting Speaker. The Royal Assent is now simply a formality. Once the Royal Assent is given, the Bill becomes an Act of Parliament and takes effect immediately (unless some future date is specified in the Act).

Private Members' Bills. At the beginning of a Parliamentary Session (a session lasts one year), the Cabinet lays down its legislative programme. It is still possible for a Private Member of the House (i.e. an M.P. who is not a member of the Government) to introduce a Bill on some matter of importance to him or her. If the Private Member's Bill is of general importance and receives the support of the House it may be adopted by the Government and so form part of its legislative programme. Otherwise the Member may have difficulty in securing the passage of his Bill through Parliament. The Matrimonial Causes Act, 1937, and the Murder (Abolition of Death Penalty) Act, 1965, were the Private Members' Bills of Sir Alan Herbert and Mr. Sidney Silverman, respectively.

Private Bills. These are of two kinds: (i) Local and (ii) Personal.

Local Bills deal with purely local matters. Where a local authority or other public body wishes to acquire additional powers not available under the general law, it may obtain them by the promotion of a private Bill. After receiving Parliament's approval the Bill becomes an Act of Parliament. Local Bills usually deal with the construction or alteration of bridges, canals, docks, ports, roads, railways, tramways, waterworks, etc., or with extending the powers of local authorities, gas, electricity or other public-utility undertakings.

Personal Bills relate to private estates, names, naturalization, divorce, peerage and other matters. Such Bills are rare and must be started in the House of Lords.

Conflict with Common Law. Because Parliament is omnipotent in the field of law, it follows that a statute may abolish any rule of common law or any criminal offence at common law.

Obsolescence

It is obvious that the social conditions of today are vastly different from those obtaining in medieval and Tudor times. Some case law laid down in earlier times and applicable to wholly different social situations may therefore have to be disregarded on account of obsolescence.

Statute law, on the other hand, does not become obsolete on account of age. We may instance the well-known case of *Ashford* v. *Thornton* (1818), where the plaintiff asserted that a right of trial by wager of battle was available to him under a statute of Henry II. This long-forgotten statute was repealed the year after its existence was revealed by the plaintiff's application. The Treason Act, 1351, is still law despite its age, and was invoked in 1946 to prosecute a British subject for broadcasting enemy propaganda during the Second World War (*Joyce* v. *Director of Public Prosecutions*, 1946).

Though statute law does not become obsolete by reason of age, nevertheless there are some Acts which are so inappropriate to the changed conditions of today that *in practice* they are not enforced. The Sunday Observance Act, 1677, forbids meetings or assemblies of people out of their own parishes on the Lord's day for any sports and pastimes whatsoever. Every offender is to forfeit 3*s*. 4*d*. The Profane Oaths Act, 1745, made it an offence for any persons to curse or swear (penalty 1*s*. for a day labourer, common soldier, sailor, or seaman; 2*s*. for any person under the degree of gentleman; 5*s*. over the degree of gentleman). The Act was not enforced for many years, and was finally abolished by the Criminal Law Act, 1967.

Consolidation and Codification

By **consolidation** we mean the combination of all the statutes relating to a given matter, such statutes being incorporated into one consolidating Act. The statute law in relation to the given matter is, therefore, readily accessible in one Act. For example, the road-traffic problem is a pressing one, and numbers of statutes and statutory instruments are passed over the years regulating the different kinds of vehicles, their construction and their use on public roads. Amendments of road-traffic law appear yearly, and in time there are so many alterations or revocations or improvements that it is difficult to ascertain the law. Hence there is need for systematizing the law, and a consolidating statute is passed accordingly: in this case, the Road Traffic Act, 1972.

The Consolidation of Enactments (Procedure) Act, 1949, was passed to enable consolidating statutes to receive Parliamentary approval speedily. The Juries Act, 1974, the Magistrates' Courts Act, 1952, the Solicitors Act, 1974, and the Factories Act, 1961, are examples of consolidating statutes made under this new provision.

Whereas consolidation means the combination of statute law only, **codification** is a term which means the enactment of a statute incorporating all previous statute law *and* case law on a particular subject.

The Sale of Goods Act, 1893, and the Partnership Act, 1890, are examples of codification in English law.

Codification can mean, of course, a complete statement of *all* the law of a given State, and not, as in England, certain parts only. The French Civil Code is one example, though we may note that Germany and Switzerland have similar codes. The Law Commission (see p. 43) is charged with the duty of the codification of English law, a task which will take some years to fulfil.

Delegated Legislation

Because Parliament is legislatively omnipotent, it can grant to some other person or body the power to make orders, regulations or rules which have the force of law. In strict legal theory, Parliament ought to retain in its own hands the power and duty to enact all the laws and the rules affecting the State. In practice, Parliament cannot discharge this duty mainly because it has so much to do and so little time in which to do it. It overcomes this difficulty by resorting to **delegated legislation**, sometimes called subordinate legislation.

Acts of Parliament nowadays tend to lay down general principles or policy and to leave the working out of the administrative details to subordinate authorities who are responsible for carrying the Acts into effect. For example, the Road Traffic Act, 1972, empowers the Minister of Transport to make regulations in respect of road-traffic matters by means of statutory instruments. So too, the Home Secretary may make orders and regulations under the Police Act, 1964, in relation to the government, administration and conditions of service of police, and the Secretary of State for Education and Science may make orders under the Education Act, 1944.

Forms of Delegated Legislation

Delegated legislation comprises:

(*a*) **Orders in Council**, i.e. Orders made by the Queen in Council, have been described as the most dignified form of subordinate legislation. In practice, the Minister of a Government department usually drafts and makes the Order in the name of the Queen, whose approval 'in Council' is a formality.

(*b*) **Statutory Instruments, Rules and Orders** are normally made by Ministers in charge of Government departments, but such rules must be submitted to Parliament for approval.

(*c*) **By-laws** are made by local authorities, railways, water boards and other such bodies, and, like statutory instruments, draw their authority from Acts of Parliament. By-laws require the approval of the appropriate Minister before they have legislative force.

Government of a country of some fifty million people is a highly complex matter. The most that Parliament can manage in the legislative field is between 60 and 70 Acts of Parliament per session (one year). On the other hand there are today more than 2,000 statutory instruments issued each year.

All the forms of subordinate legislation noted above are enforced equally with statutes, provided the order or by-law is not *ultra vires* the Minister or local authority.

Growth of Delegated Legislation

The following reasons are advanced for the growth of delegated legislation:

(*a*) **Lack of Parliamentary time.** The legislature has insufficient time to deal with and debate all necessary measures for efficient government.

(*b*) **Urgency.** Parliament is not always in session, and its legislative procedures are slow. Emergencies and urgent problems arise, and delegated legislation is the best means of meeting the situation.

(*c*) **Flexibility.** A statute requires elaborate and cumbersome procedures for its enactment. It can be revoked or amended only by another statute. A ministerial order or statutory instrument can be made speedily; if it proves unworkable or impracticable, it can be quickly revoked.

(*d*) **Technicality of subject-matter.** Modern legislation tends to be technical and detailed, e.g. road-traffic matters which may deal with 'special type' vehicles; building regulations; dangerous-drugs regulations. Such legislation is best dealt with by Ministers (who are advised by experts familiar with the technical or scientific problem) rather than M.P.s who may be inexpert and unfamiliar with the technicalities involved.

(*e*) **Future needs.** Parliament cannot foresee the difficulties which may arise, particularly when new major schemes like the National Health Service or National Insurance are launched. Future difficulties are better dealt with by delegated legislation rather than statutes.

Criticism of Delegated Legislation

The processes of government and, in particular, the making of statutes are continuously subject to critical examination and analysis. Among the criticisms frequently levelled against delegated or subordinate legislation are:

(*a*) **Matters of principle**. Because these are the primary concern of the legislature, Ministers ought not to be entitled to legislate by means of orders in respect of matters of principle.

(*b*) **Delegation of taxing power.** Parliament fought for years for the sole and exclusive right to tax. History shows that the right can be abused and should not be yielded to subordinate authorities or Ministers. The Import Duties Act, 1932, gave the Treasury the power to legislate on taxation by fixing import duties and altering the 'free list', thus usurping the right of Parliament alone.

(*c*) **Sub-delegation.** The Emergency Powers (Defence) Act, 1939, provides a clear example of five-tier legislation as it embraces: (i) the parent statute; (ii) regulations made under the statute; (iii) orders made under the regulations; (iv) directions made under the orders; and (v) licences issued under the directions.

In its Report of 1946, the Select Committee on Statutory Instruments condemned the practice of delegation at four removes from Parliament of the power to make subordinate legislation.

(*d*) **Exclusion of the jurisdiction of courts.** The power of the courts to declare the regulations void on the ground of *ultra vires* ought not to be excluded either in the parent Act or the delegated legislation.

(*e*) **Authority to modify an Act of Parliament.** This power, known as 'the Henry VIII clause', enables a Minister to modify the Act itself and thus usurp the essential function and duty of Parliament.

(*f*) **Inadequate publicity.** The Press usually reports the effect of new statutes, but there is frequently inadequate publicity given to the numerous statutory instruments (over 2,000 annually) made by Ministers. A person charged with an offence against a statutory instrument of whose existence he was unaware, has only a limited defence since ignorance of the law is normally no excuse (see S. 3(2) of the Statutory Instruments Act, 1946).

Control of Delegated Legislation

The main forms of control over the power of a Minister to make delegated legislation are:

(*a*) consultation of interests;
(*b*) control by the courts; and
(*c*) control by Parliament.

(*a*) **Consultation.** In practice Ministers consult experts both within their own departments and outside, and take the advice of various interests and bodies likely to be affected by proposed legislation. Thus road-traffic legislation would involve consultation with local authorities, surveyors, the police, the A.A., the R.A.C., motor manufacturers and others likely to be intimately affected. Sometimes a Minister must, by statute, consult an advisory body or submit a draft of the statutory instrument to it for approval. For example, under the National Insurance Act, 1946, regulations proposed by the Secretary of State for Social Services must be submitted in draft to the National Insurance Advisory Committee. Where a Minister proposes to make rules of procedure for tribunals set up within his department, he must consult the Council on Tribunals (Tribunals and Inquiries Act, 1971—see page 71).

(*b*) **Control by the Courts.** Rules and regulations made by Ministers and other administrative bodies under statutory authority are liable to be subject to challenge in the courts on two grounds: (i) *ultra vires* and (ii) unreasonableness. While a court cannot invalidate an Act of Parliament, it may declare that statutory instruments, rules or by-laws are void on the ground that they are *ultra vires*, i.e. beyond the powers conferred by the Act under which they were made. In practice, ministerial rules and orders are only rarely challenged on this ground because great care is usually taken by the legal advisers of the Minister on such matters.

By-laws may be challenged on the grounds of **unreasonableness**, by which is meant that they are partial and unequal in their operation as between different classes. If rules are manifestly unjust, if they disclose bad faith, or if they involve 'such oppressive or gratuitous interference with the rights of those subject to them as can find no justification in the minds of reasonable men, the court might well say Parliament never intended to give authority to make such rules; they are unreasonable and *ultra vires*' (Lord Russell in *Kruse* v. *Johnson*, 1898).

(*c*) **Control by Parliament.** (i) Parliament may revoke or vary the delegated power. (ii) Certain Acts require that regulations made under them shall be laid before Parliament. This enables M.P.s to know what has been done by the Minister, or what he proposes to do. (iii) A Select Committee on Statutory Instruments (S.I.s) was set up in 1944 to consider every S.I., rule or Order laid before the Commons. A Special Orders Committee exists in the Lords to do similar work in that House.

In 1974, to avoid duplication in the two Houses, a Statutory Instruments (Joint Committee) was created comprising members of a Select Committee from the Commons and members of the Special Orders Committee of the Lords. The Joint Committee (which replaces the two former committees in the consideration of S.I.s) reports to each House on any order or regulation deserving special attention on the following grounds:

(i) that it imposes a charge on the public revenue, or imposes or prescribes charges for any licence or consent or for any services from a public authority;

(ii) that it is made under an Act which precludes challenge in the courts;

(iii) that it appears to make some unusual or unexpected use of the powers conferred by the statute under which it is made or there appears to be doubt as to whether it is *intra vires*;

(iv) that there appears to have been unjustifiable delay in publication or laying before Parliament;

(v) that for any special reason its form or purport calls for elucidation;
(vi) that it purports to have retrospective effect;
(vii) that the drafting is defective.

The Joint Committee may require a department to submit a memorandum or explanatory note on any instrument, and may request a representative of the department to appear and explain a document personally. Before the committee reports that the special attention of the House should be drawn to an instrument, it gives the department concerned the opportunity to furnish an explanation.

Publication

H.M. Stationery Office publishes lists showing dates of issue of statutory instruments, and the Statutory Instruments Act, 1946, provides that 'it shall be a defence to prove that the instrument had not been issued by H.M.S.O. at the date of the alleged contravention, unless it is proved that at that date reasonable steps had been taken for the purpose of bringing the purport of the instrument to the notice of the public or of persons likely to be affected by it, or of the person charged'.

Interpretation of Statutes

Statutes are drafted by Parliamentary draftsmen, who are lawyers skilled in this highly important work. Despite the great care taken to ensure that all statutes are clear and exact, it is certain that in due time legal actions will arise on points of doubt and the courts will be called upon to interpret the meaning and to adjudicate.

The rules adopted by the judges to discover the meaning of an Act may be classified as (*a*) statutory definitions and (*b*) common law rules.

(*a*) **Statutory Definitions.** The Interpretation Act, 1978, is a general statute which consolidates enactments regarding the construction of statutes and provides definitions and rules of construction. Thus, unless the contrary appears,

(i) words importing the masculine gender include females,

(ii) words in the singular include the plural and words in the plural include the singular,

(iii) the expression 'person' includes a body corporate,

(iv) expressions referring to writing are construed as including references to printing, lithography, photography, and other modes of representing or reproducing words in a visible form.

Modern statutes and statutory instruments frequently include a section expressly incorporating the Interpretation Act, 1978.

A statute usually contains an *interpretation section* which explains the meaning of words in that statute. Thus, section 34 of the Theft Act,

1968, contains a definition of the words 'goods' as follows: 'For the purpose of this Act "goods", except in so far as the context otherwise requires, includes money and every other description of property except land, and includes things severed from the land by stealing.'

The *preamble* is an introductory statement appearing immediately below the official title of a statute, and sets out the purposes of the Act. Judges may refer to the preamble as an aid to interpretation.

(*b*) **Common Law Rules.** Where a statute is not clarified by reference to the above statutory guides, a judge may look to the following common law rules:

(i) *'The Literal Rule'* lays down that words must be given their literal, grammatical meaning. Words in old statutes are given the meaning they had when the statute was passed, e.g. The Statute of Treason, 1351. Words appearing more than once must usually be given the same meaning throughout the Act. The duty of the court is to interpret the words that the legislature has used. If a statute so interpreted is clear and produces hardship, the remedy is a new statute; it is not the duty of a judge to fill in the gaps.

(ii) *'The Mischief Rule'*, also known as the Rule in *Heydon*'s case (1584), lays down that the court must look at the Act to see what 'mischief' or defect in the common law the Act was passed to prevent.

Four questions should be considered:

1. What was the common law before the Act was passed?
2. What was the mischief and defect for which the common law did not provide?
3. What remedy had Parliament resolved to provide?
4. What was the true reason for the remedy?

Judges were enjoined to make such construction 'as shall suppress the mischief and advance the remedy'.

(iii) '*The Golden Rule*' lays down that a judge should construe the statute in its grammatical and ordinary sense:

> 'It is a very useful rule in the construction of a statute to adhere to the ordinary meaning of the words used, and to the grammatical construction, unless that is at variance with the intention of the legislature to be collected from the statute itself, or leads to any manifest absurdity or repugnance, in which case the language may be varied or modified so as to avoid such inconvenience, but no further' (Parke, B., in *Becke* v. *Smith*, 1836).

For example, section 57 of the Offences Against the Person Act, 1861, defines the offence of bigamy and provides: 'Whosoever being married shall *marry* any other person during the life of the former husband or wife ... shall be guilty of bigamy.' Under English law a married person cannot 'marry', and to avoid absurdity or repugnance the word 'marry' in this section means 'to go through the form of marriage' (*R.* v. *Allen*, 1872).

(iv) *The 'Ejusdem Generis' Rule*. Where general words follow specific words, the general words must be construed as applying to the persons or things of the same class (*ejusdem generis*) as those already mentioned. Thus 'other person', 'other cattle', 'other animals' are vague and a reference in an Act to 'dogs, cats, and other animals' was held not to include lions and tigers, for 'other animals' meant those *ejusdem generis* with dogs and cats, i.e. domestic animals (*Evans* v. *Cross*, 1938).

(v) *Expressio unius est exclusio alterius* (the express mention of one thing implies the exclusion of another). This means that where specific words are used in a statute and are not followed by general words, the statute applies only to those things mentioned.

(vi) *Noscitur a sociis* (the meaning of a word can be comprehended from its context). Ambiguous or doubtful words may be determined by reference to those words appearing in association with them.

Presumptions

Certain presumptions or rules of evidence must also be borne in mind. These presumptions apply to the construction of a statute, unless there are express words to the contrary. The following examples are some of the more important presumptions in law:

(*a*) The presumption against criminal liability, unless *mens rea* (guilty mind) is shown to exist. Proof of criminal intent is generally necessary to secure a conviction. A motorist involved in a road accident of which he was unaware, could not rightly be convicted of 'failing to report the accident to the police within 24 hours', since he did not know that he had been involved, and the law does not compel the impossible (*Harding* v. *Price*, 1948).

(*b*) The presumption against the ouster of jurisdiction of the courts. Thus, where a particular statute provides that tribunals be set up to determine questions arising in administration (as under the National Service Act, 1948, to consider appeals for postponement of military service) and excludes the jurisdiction of the courts of law *expressly*, then the terms of the statute will be applied. Where no such express terms exist the jurisdiction of the courts is not ousted.

(*c*) The presumption that the Crown is not bound by statute, unless expressly stated therein.

(*d*) The presumption that a statute does not alter the general principles of the common law, unless expressly so stated.

(*e*) The presumption against the infringement of international law.

(*f*) The presumption against the deprivation of property. Statutes empowering the acquisition of private property will be strictly construed. Where private property is taken away from an owner, the law infers that compensation will be paid unless there are clear words in the statute to the contrary.

(g) The presumption against arbitrary conduct and abuse of a power given by statute.

Reference to Statutes

There are three forms of referring to an Act of Parliament: by its short title, by its official reference, or by its full title.

(*a*) *Short Title*. When we refer to an Act such as the Theft Act, 1968, or the Race Relations Act, 1968, we are using its short title.

(*b*) *Official Reference*. This shows the calendar year in which the Act was passed and the number of the Chapter (or Act) passed in that year. For example,

1968 CHAPTER 60

is the official reference to the Theft Act, 1968, and

1968 CHAPTER 71

is the official reference to the Race Relations Act, 1968.

(*c*) *Full Title*. This gives the official reference and a short description of the object of the statute. For example, the full title of the Theft Act, 1968, is

ELIZABETH II
1968 CHAPTER 60

> An Act to revise the law of England and Wales as to theft and similar associated offences, and in connexion therewith to make provision as to criminal proceedings by one party to a marriage against the other, and to make certain amendments extending beyond England and Wales in the Post Office Act, 1953 and other enactments; and for other purposes connected therewith.

The full title of the Race Relations Act, 1968, is

ELIZABETH II
1968 CHAPTER 71

> An Act to make fresh provision with respect to discrimination on racial grounds, and to make provision with respect to relations between people of different racial origins.

Reference to Statutory Instruments

The most common form of delegated legislation is the statutory instrument. Each statutory instrument is allocated a number, and reference to the instrument is to the year of issue followed by the number so allocated. For example,

S.I. 1968 No. 1911

relates to the Town and Country Planning (Planning Inquiry Commissions) Regulations, 1968.

The printing of Bills, Acts of Parliament and statutory instruments is done by Her Majesty's Stationery Office. Such documents are on sale to members of the public at that office in London.

European Economic Community Law

Since 1st January, 1973, the date of Britain's entry into the European Economic Community (European Communities Act, 1972), a new source of law is added to the above, namely the law of the European treaties (e.g. the Treaty of Rome, 1958) and of the secondary legislation made by the community institutions (e.g. the EEC Council, the Commission and the Parliament). This law constitutes a new legal order standing alongside both the statute and common law and, in the event of conflict, takes **precedence** over them.

Law Revision and Reform

The law is open to the criticism that in general it is conservative. Many statutes are ancient, appertaining to a bygone age and feudal system; some common law offences are inappropriate today. For example, the offences of challenging to fight, eavesdropping, being a common barrator, a common scold or common night walker were abolished only in 1967 by the Criminal Law Act of that year. Furthermore, it is argued that legal procedures are unduly formal and slow, and that the system of courts needs overhaul and remodelling.

Some of these criticisms may seem fair and reasonable; but it is clear that reform of the law and the machinery of the courts are matters which require careful planning. Nevertheless, law is a living thing and reform is continual. The agencies through which revision or reform is effected include the following:

(*a*) Law Reform Committee
(*b*) Criminal Law Revision Committee
(*c*) Law Commission
(*d*) Royal Commissions
(*e*) Committees appointed by Ministers or by Parliament
(*f*) Private Members' Bills.

(*a*) **The Law Reform Committee** began in 1952 and took over the work of the Law Revision Committee set up in 1934. It is made up of judges and practising and academic lawyers, and deals with civil law matters referred to it by the Lord Chancellor. Members of the committee, and the general public also, may raise matters and suggest subjects for consideration. The following statutes reformed parts of the civil law and were passed as a result of the recommendations of the committee:

The Limitation Act, 1939 (replaced by the 1980 Act)
The Law Reform (Contributory Negligence) Act, 1945
The Occupiers' Liability Act, 1957
The Law Reform (Husband and Wife) Act, 1962.

(*b*) **The Criminal Law Revision Committee.** While the Lord Chancellor is concerned with the Law Reform Committee and the reform of the civil law, the Home Secretary is primarily concerned with the administration of the criminal law. The Criminal Law Revision Committee (a standing committee) was set up in 1959 to examine aspects of the criminal law, to consider whether the law requires revision, and to make recommendations.

The committee has issued several reports; the seventh (Felonies and Misdemeanours) and eighth (Theft and Related Offences) have resulted in the Criminal Law Act, 1967, and the Theft Act, 1968, respectively.

(*c*) **The Law Commission.** The Law Commissions Act, 1965, set up a full-time commission whose duty is to keep under review the English law as a whole with a view to its systematic development and reform, including, in particular, its codification, the elimination of anomalies, the repeal of obsolete and unnecessary enactments, the reduction of the number of separate enactments, and, generally, the simplification and modernization of the law. Pursuant to programmes approved by the Lord Chancellor, the commission undertakes the examination of particular branches of the law and the formulation, by means of draft Bills, of proposals for reform.

The five commissioners and a legal staff are appointed by the Lord Chancellor. The commission issues an annual report, which is laid before Parliament.

(*d*) **Royal Commissions** are appointed by the Crown on the advice of a Minister who names a chairman. The membership of each Royal Commission varies, but it usually reflects expert, professional, and lay opinions. The duty of a Royal Commission is to investigate some matter of public importance, to take evidence and to make recommendations. On receipt of its report, the Government may give legislative effect to the recommendations. For example the main recommendations of the Royal Commission on Tribunals and Inquiries appointed in 1955 found expression in the Tribunals and Inquiries Act, 1958.

(*e*) **Committees appointed by Ministers or Parliament.** Committees of experts may be appointed to consider particular aspects of the law for the purpose of revising it, e.g. those appointed by the Lord Chancellor to consider civil procedure and legal aid, and by the Secretary of State for Trade and Industry to consider revision of the law of copyright.

(*f*) **Private Members' Bills** (see p. 32) may reform existing law in important respects. Examples include the Inheritance (Family Provision) Act, 1938, the Matrimonial Causes Act, 1937, and the Defamation Act, 1952. Parliamentary time is, however, limited, and Government Bills must come first. Hence the Private Member's Bill is not the most important medium of reform.

3. Textbooks

The first important work on the English common law was Glanvil's *Tractatus de Legibus et Consuetudinibus Angliae*, produced in the twelfth century. This work was followed by Bracton's *De Legibus et Consuetudinibus Angliae*, written in the thirteenth century, and described by Maitland as 'the crown and flower of English medieval jurisprudence'. It contained references to decided cases.

Later works included Littleton's *New Tenures* (1481), Sir Matthew Hale's *History of the Common Law* and *Pleas of the Crown*, which appeared in 1730, Sir Edward Coke's *Institutes* (1628–41), Sir William Blackstone's *Commentaries* (1765), and Sir Michael Foster's *Crown Law* (eighteenth century).

The above works and a few other early works, written when law reporting had barely begun, are accepted as books of authority and therefore as an original source of common law.

The modern textbook is not a source of law, and not a book of authority. However, such works may have persuasive authority; counsel may adopt the view of a distinguished academic writer and the court may accept that view of the law. In this way the writer is influencing the law. Works by Cheshire, Dicey, Winfield, Salmond, Williams and Smith and Hogan have often been referred to in this way, particularly on points which are not covered by authority or where there is some doubt about the authority. As Mr. R. J. Walker has commented, 'On the whole the persuasive authority of a standard textbook is of considerable weight.'

Similarly, articles in legal journals such as the *Criminal Law Review*, the *Law Quarterly Review* and the *Cambridge Law Journal* have been referred to in the courts.

4. Local Custom

A **local custom** is a usage or rule which has gathered the force of law and is binding within a defined area upon the persons affected thereby. Common examples are local rights of way or rights of common. A useful case which exemplifies the operation of law is the following:

> *Mercer* v. *Denne* (1905). Defendant owned part of a beach and proposed to erect houses thereon. Local fishermen sought to stop him by claiming

that they had a local customary right to dry their nets on the land. Witnesses proved that the custom dated back for some seventy years and reputedly earlier. This raised the presumption of antiquity. *Held:* that the defendant must not build the houses on the land: the local customary right was upheld.

The onus of proof of a local custom rests on the person claiming that such a custom exists. Judicial recognition will be given and the custom will be enforced if it is:

(*a*) Reasonable.

(*b*) Certain as to the subject-matter of the right, the persons benefited by it and the locality.

(*c*) Local, in the sense that the custom must be applicable to a district known to law, e.g. a parish, manor, or shire.

(*d*) Of immemorial existence, i.e. must have existed from 'the commencement of legal memory': arbitrarily fixed at 1189, the first year of the reign of Richard I. Because of the difficulty of proving this, courts presume that the custom existed then unless there is clear evidence to the contrary.

(*e*) Peaceably used. The custom must have been exercised peaceably, openly and as of right (*nec per vim, nec clam, nec precario*). If a right is exercised by permission, then it cannot be claimed to be exercised 'of right' for the right can only be exercised in accordance with the permission.

(*f*) Continuously observed. This does not mean that the right must have been continuously *exercised* but that it could have been, the right to do so being observed without interruption.

(*g*) Compulsory. Once established the custom must be local common law and legally effective because it is right and enforceable.

(*h*) Not contrary to any statute.

(*i*) Consistent, in the sense of being consistent with other customs and not contradictory to them.

Local customs must be distinguished from **conventional usages**, which are found and observed in particular occupations, trades or business or among professional groups. Following the analogy of the local custom, the courts have laid down certain principles. Every usage must be certain and reasonable and must have acquired notoriety (in the sense that the usage is well known and observed) in the trade or business to which it relates. In contracts, for example, there will usually be express terms, but in addition to these the court may, in construing the contract, imply a term or terms where the parties are deemed to have contracted on that basis. Thus, if a usage is shown to exist in a class of workers entitling members to, say, three months' notice terminating their engagements, this usage or trade custom will apply unless expressly negatived by the contract itself.

Dashwood v. *Magniac* (1891). *A* had devised an estate to *B* with 'a power to cut timber for the repair of the estate'. Evidence was admitted to show what trees were included in the term 'timber' in the locality. *Held:* that 'timber' included beech in addition to the usual meaning of oak, ash, and elm.

Grant v. *Maddox* (1846). Evidence was admitted in this case of a theatrical usage to show that the word 'year' in a theatrical contract means those parts of the year during which the theatre is open.

Smith v. *Wilson* (1832). A usage was proved and admitted that in a lease of a rabbit warren the words 'thousand rabbits' meant in that particular locality twelve hundred.

5. Exercises

1. Describe the principal and the subsidiary sources of English Law.
2. Distinguish between (i) *ratio decidendi* and (ii) *obiter dicta.* What is meant by *stare decisis*?
3. What are the advantages and disadvantages of case law?
4. What courts are bound by their own decisions?
5. What is the hierarchy of courts as regards judicial precedent?
6. What must be proved to enforce a local custom?
7. How far do judges make law?
8. What is meant by the phrase 'Sovereignty of Parliament'?
9. Define a statute, and distinguish between (i) a statute and (ii) a judgment of a court of law.
10. What forms of control over delegated legislation are exercised (i) by the courts and (ii) by Parliament?
11 What are the main rules applied by a court of law in the interpretation of a statute?

4

THE COURTS TODAY

1. Civil Courts

The House of Lords

The House of Lords stands at the apex of the judicial system, and is the final court of appeal in civil and criminal matters.

As a court of appeal, it is composed of the Lord Chancellor, the Lords of Appeal in Ordinary and other peers who have held high judicial office. A quorum of three is necessary to constitute the court. Each judge may deliver a separate speech, the verdict being by majority. Five members often sit.

Jurisdiction. In civil matters the court hears appeals from the Court of Session in Scotland, the Court of Appeal in Northern Ireland, and the Court of Appeal (Civil Division) in England. There is no general right of appeal: leave of the Court of Appeal or the House of Lords must first be obtained.

The Administration of Justice Act, 1969, provides a new form of appeal in *civil* actions from the High Court (or Divisional Court) direct to the House of Lords, 'leap-frogging' the Court of Appeal. An appeal will lie only subject to the following conditions: (i) that, on application of any of the parties, the trial judge grants a certificate of appeal; (ii) that the certificate will only be granted if the judge's decision involves a point of law of *general public importance*; (iii) that this point of law either relates to the construction of an enactment or statutory instrument, *or* is one in respect of which the judge is bound by the Court of Appeal or the House of Lords.

Judicial Committee of the Privy Council

The Privy Council originated as the *Curia Regis* of the Norman kings, to which reference has been made earlier (see p. 11). The Council retains certain advisory and formal functions, but it also exercises judicial authority through a committee known as the Judicial Committee of the Privy Council.

Composition. The 'court' is made up of all Privy Councillors who hold, or have held, high judicial office in the United Kingdom (including Lords of Appeal in Ordinary), the Lord Chancellor, former Lord Chancellors, and Commonwealth judges who are Privy Councillors. The quorum of the Committee is three, but in important cases five members are usually present.

Jurisdiction. The Committee hears appeals from those Commonwealth countries which have retained the right of appeal (some such countries on acquiring independence abolished the right) and from colonial territories. It also hears appeals from:

(i) Prize courts. Jurisdiction extends over claims to captured ships during time of war.
(ii) Ecclesiastical courts.
(iii) Courts of the Isle of Man, the Channel Islands.
(iv) Tribunals of the medical, dental, and opticians' professions.

Procedure. The Committee sits as an advisory board and its procedure is informal. Judges, for example, are not robed. No judgment is given as in a court of law. The committee tenders advice to the monarch upon which an Order in Council is made to dispose of the issue in question. Dissentient opinions are not usually given (but see *Abbott*, 1977).

The decisions of the Judicial Committee are not binding on itself or on other courts of law of the United Kingdom, but a decision on appeal from a colony is binding on the colonial courts of that territory. In practice the judicial strength of the Committee is such that its decisions are treated with great respect by other courts (see, for example, the *Wagon Mound* case, p. 203).

Court of Appeal (Civil Division)

This court is composed of the Lord Chancellor, the Lord Chief Justice, the Master of the Rolls and the President of the Family Division, who are all *ex officio* judges, and 28 Lords Justice of Appeal. Normally in civil cases the Master of the Rolls and the Lords Justice of Appeal sit. However, any High Court judge may be requested by the Lord Chancellor to sit. The Law Lords may also sit. The quorum of the court is three, and the court may sit in five divisions at the same time.

The court may uphold, amend, or reverse the decision of a lower court, or order a new trial.

Jurisdiction. The court hears civil appeals from the High Court, county courts, the Restrictive Practices Court, the Employment Appeal Tribunal and other tribunals. It also hears appeals on interlocutory orders made by judges in chambers and, exceptionally, masters and registrars (e.g. directions on procedure, evidence and other preliminary matters before actual trial).

The High Court of Justice

The High Court consists of:

(*a*) the Queen's Bench Division
(*b*) the Chancery Division
(*c*) the Family Division

THE CIVIL COURTS

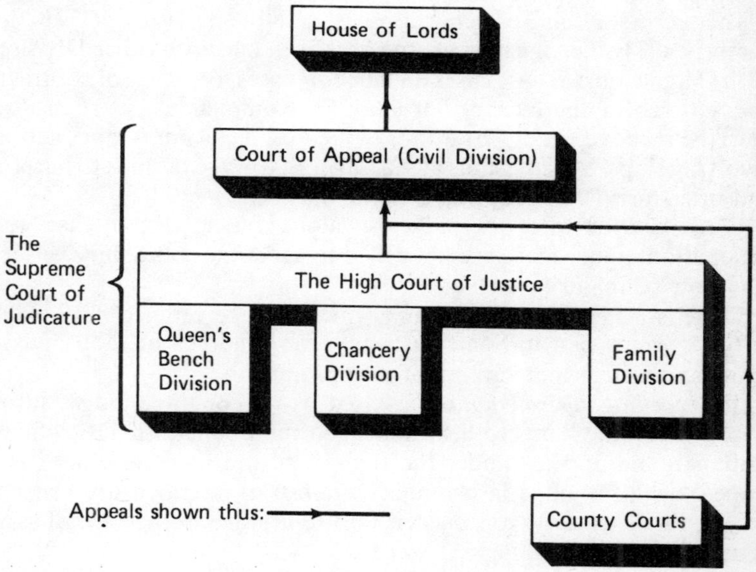

The three divisions are of equal competence, so each is empowered to try any action, but for administrative purposes and convenience specific matters are allocated to each division as described below.

The heads of the respective divisions are (*a*) Queen's Bench Division: The Lord Chief Justice; (*b*) Chancery Division: The Lord Chancellor (in practice the **Vice-Chancellor** presides); (*c*) Family Division: The President. These are assisted by approximately 85 puisne judges who are allocated to each division. The Lord Chancellor may require any judge to sit in any division.

(*a*) **The Queen's Bench Division.** This court is composed of the Lord Chief Justice and approximately 44 puisne judges. It exercises three kinds of jurisdiction: (i) original (i.e. at first instance); (ii) appellate; and (iii) supervisory.

(i) *Original Jurisdiction.* This is of three kinds. As a result of the Administration of Justice Act, 1970, the jurisdiction of the Admiralty Court (formerly a part of the Probate, Divorce and Admiralty Division) has now been added to the Queen's Bench Division. Further a new Commercial Court has been added to deal with commercial cases involving traders and merchants, e.g. insurance claims. The characteristics of this court are that procedure is more flexible than in other courts and disputes are dealt with more quickly.

The effect of this reorganization is that the Division jurisdiction comprises (1) all civil cases not specifically assigned to other Divisions of the High Court. These cases include tort cases, breaches of contracts, and actions for the recovery of land; (2) Commercial Court cases as described above, and (3) Admiralty cases, i.e. claims and actions involving ships, e.g. collisions at sea, salvage, towage of ships to harbour and prize jurisdiction (during time of war).

When hearing cases the judges sit alone, but in certain cases (e.g. defamation) a jury may be empanelled to assist the court. Jury verdicts may now be majority verdicts.

There is no limit to the amount which may be claimed in damages in the Queen's Bench. Some cases involve hundreds of thousands of pounds, e.g. negligent sinking of a ship.

(ii) *Appellate Jurisdiction* is exercised by two or three judges sitting as a 'Divisional Court' to hear appeals from a Solicitors' Disciplinary Tribunal, and appeals under the Rent Acts and in some other cases. Appeal lies to a judge in chambers against an interlocutory order of a Queen's Bench Division master; and to a judge in the case of some appeals from tribunals.

(iii) *Supervisory Jurisdiction* is exercised over inferior courts, tribunals, and administrative authorities 'acting judicially', by means of the writ of *habeas corpus* and the prerogative orders of *certiorari*, prohibition, and *mandamus* (see p. 70).

(*b*) **The Chancery Division** deals generally with matters which before 1873 fell within the jurisdiction of the old Court of Chancery. Certain other matters have, however, been added by statute, e.g. bankruptcy claims and company matters.

Composition. The court is composed of the Lord Chancellor who never sits, the Vice-Chancellor, and at least four other puisne judges. In 1971 a Vice-Chancellor was appointed to take charge under the official president, the Lord Chancellor.

Jurisdiction of the division includes (i) the administration of estates of deceased persons; (ii) the dissolution of partnerships and taking of partnership accounts; (iii) mortgages and charges on land; (iv) trusts, both private and public (or charitable); (v) the sale of property subject to a lien or charge; (vi) company matters, e.g. dissolution and winding up; (vii) revenue matters, e.g. taxation; (viii) partition and sale of real estates; (ix) rectification and setting aside or cancellation of deeds or other written instruments; (x) bankruptcy matters; (xi) specific performance of contracts; and (xii) probate (contentious matters only).

In addition, the Chancery Division hears appeals from certain lower courts, e.g. county courts, on such matters as bankruptcy or orders relating to trusts.

(*c*) **Family Division.** This Division was created by the Administration of Justice Act, 1970, and deals mainly with the following matters: divorce, granting decrees of judicial separation; decrees of nullity of marriage; orders as to the financial arrangements (maintenance) consequent upon decrees, e.g. for the wife, children or dependants; the marriage and wardship of minors; adoption; legitimacy; guardianship of minors; and non-contentious probate matters.

Probate jurisdiction (formerly exercised in the P.D.A. Division) has been divided thus: contentious probate matters (e.g. where a dispute arises between *A* and *B*, and *A* claims a will to be valid which *B* disputes), is allocated to the Chancery Division; non-contentious probate matters are dealt with in the Family Division.

The Family Division comprises a President and 16 puisne judges. Judges sit alone, except when adjudicating at a Divisional Court of the Family Division to hear appeals, e.g. from magistrates' and county courts.

County Courts

These courts were first established by the County Courts Act, 1846, to provide cheap, speedy, and local justice—so obviating the need for bringing actions at Westminster or before the courts at *nisi prius*. The county courts proved efficient, and their jurisdiction has been enlarged from time to time. The County Courts Act, 1984, which consolidated the County Courts Act, 1959, with certain later enactments, now governs the composition and the jurisdiction of these useful courts.

There are at present some 337 such courts in England and Wales; and there are about 125 Circuit judges (see p. 55). Some have charge of two or more courts. The number of cases dealt with annually amounts to over 1½ million. Most actions are, however, disposed of or settled out of court before hearing.

Composition. One judge sits alone. Circuit judges are appointed by the Lord Chancellor. They must be barristers of at least seven years' standing. In rare cases a jury of eight persons may assist the court.

The **registrar** of the court keeps the records of the court and performs the administrative work attached to it. He must be a solicitor of at least seven years' standing, and is appointed by the Lord Chancellor. A registrar may hear and deal with certain small claims in place of the judge.

Jurisdiction. As a general rule the plaintiff must bring his claim or action in the court of the district where the defendant (or one of several defendants) dwells or carries on business. Actions relating to land must be brought in the court of the district wherein the land is situated.

Matters falling within the jurisdiction of the county courts include: (i) actions founded on contract or tort (except defamation) up to £5,000; (ii) equity matters (trusts, mortgages, etc.) up to £15,000; (iii) actions for the recovery of land, and questions of title to land, where the net annual rateable value does not exceed £1,000; (iv) bankruptcies;* (v) probate proceedings where the value of the deceased's estate is less than £15,000; (vi) winding up of companies with a paid-up capital of less than £120,000;* (vii) supervision of the adoption of infants; (viii) Admiralty matters (in some courts only); and (ix) actions in relation to rent-restriction, hire-purchase, landlord-and-tenant and similar matters as laid down by statute.

To relieve the burden of work falling on the Family Division of the High Court in regard to divorce petitions, and with a view to reducing legal costs, the Matrimonial Causes Act, 1967, was passed giving county courts a limited divorce jurisdiction. Under this Act the Lord Chancellor may designate any county court as a 'divorce county court' with power to hear and determine any *undefended* matrimonial cause.

Appeal from a county court lies to the Court of Appeal.

Since 1974 **small claims**, e.g. for debts, whether for goods sold, work done or money lent, or for damages for negligence, where the amount in dispute does not exceed £500, may be dealt with informally before an arbitrator, who is usually the Registrar. The object is to enable persons to sue (and defend) actions without a solicitor, and without running up costs and long delays. A booklet is available at all county court offices showing the steps to be taken in simple actions of the kind described.

2. Criminal Courts

The courts which hear criminal cases are:

(*a*) The House of Lords
(*b*) The Court of Appeal (Criminal Division)
(*c*) Divisional Court of the Queen's Bench Division
(*d*) The Crown Court
(*e*) Magistrates' courts.

*Except in the Metropolitan area of London which has a special Bankruptcy Court and Commercial Court for company matters.

THE CRIMINAL COURTS

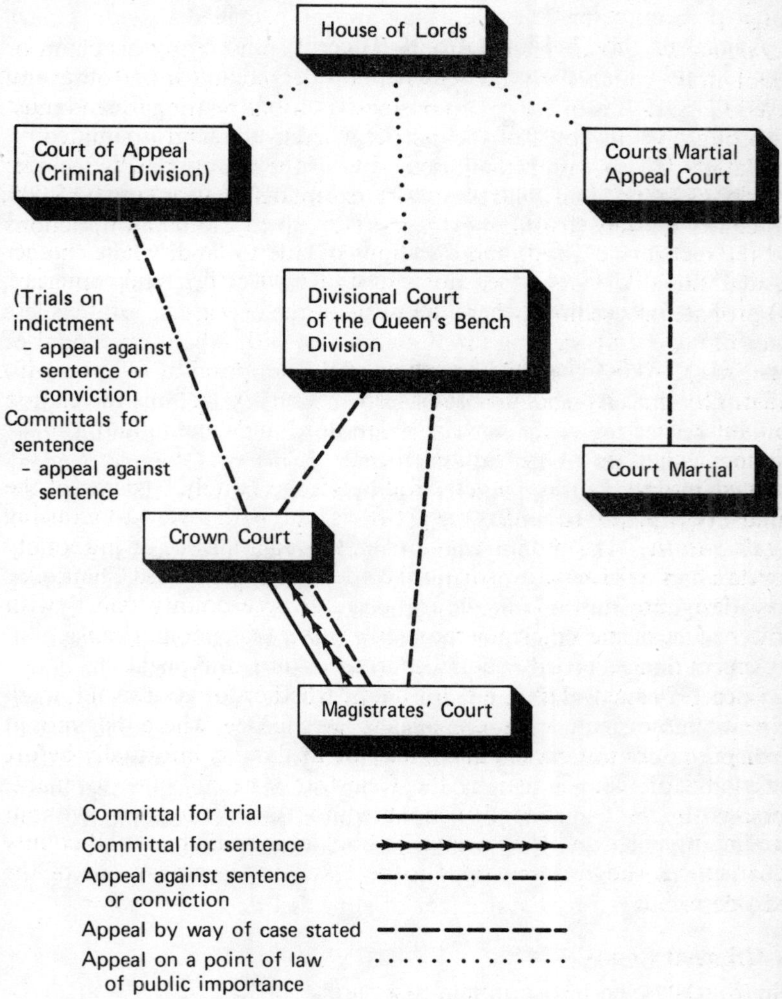

The House of Lords

This court hears appeals from the Court of Appeal (Criminal Division) and from the Divisional Court of Queen's Bench Division. Either prosecutor or defendant may appeal, provided that the Court of Appeal or the Divisional Court (i) certify that a point of law of general public importance is involved in its decision and (ii) either the Court of Appeal (or the Divisional Court) or the House of Lords gives leave to appeal on the ground that the point is one which ought to be considered by the House (Administration of Justice Act, 1960). This is to prevent frivolous or minor cases going to this final court.

Composition. This court is composed of the Lord Chancellor, the Lords of Appeal in Ordinary, and other peers who have held high judicial office. The quorum is three, and each judge delivers a separate speech, the verdict being by a majority.

Court of Appeal (Criminal Division)

The Criminal Appeal Act, 1968, provides that the Court of Appeal shall consist of two divisions: one exercising civil jurisdiction and one criminal. The Act abolished the former Court of Criminal Appeal (created in 1907); its jurisdiction is now exercised by the Court of Appeal (Criminal Division).

Composition. The judges who sit in this court are the Lord Chief Justice, the Lords Justice of Appeal, and judges of the Queen's Bench Division. A quorum of three is necessary.

The court may dismiss the appeal or allow it, and may order that any conviction recorded in a lower court shall be quashed. The court may order a new trial (Administration of Justice Act, 1964). The court may not increase the sentence against which appeal is being made. (Formerly a convicted person who wanted to appeal against what he considered too long a sentence ran the risk of having his sentence increased by the Court of Appeal, but this risk is now eliminated; the number of appeals on this ground has grown accordingly.)

To hear these appeals two courts sit full-time, while a third sits as and when required by the number of appeals listed.

The Crown Court

Before 1971 the more serious indictable offences were tried by a High Court judge at assizes; and the less serious by a recorder or a bench of magistrates at quarter sessions.

The Royal Commission on Assizes and Quarter Sessions recommended replacing the old circuit system and sweeping reorganization. It resulted in the Courts Act, 1971, which gave effect to most of the proposals. Only the main points can be noted here. The Act—

1. abolished Assize Courts and Quarter Sessions Courts; and
2. established the Crown Court.

Broadly, the Crown Court takes over all 'first instance' business above the magistrates' court level, and all appeal business of the Quarter Sessions mentioned above.

Jurisdiction. The Crown Court has jurisdiction over indictable offences and offences triable either way for which a defendant has been committed by the magistrates for trial by the Crown Court. The Court also sentences offenders committed for sentence by magistrates' courts, e.g. where the magistrates' court finds the accused guilty but has insufficient powers adequately to deal with the defendant. Finally, the Crown Court acts as an appeal court to hear appeals from magistrates' courts.

The judge in the Crown Court will be one of the following:

1. **A High Court Judge**, a puisne judge of the Queen's Bench Division. His position is similar to that of his predecessor sitting as an Assize Court Judge. The Judge is appointed to one of six circuits.

2. **A Circuit Judge** appointed by the Crown to serve in (1) the Crown Court and (2) a county court (see p. 51). He must be a barrister of 10 years' standing or a recorder who has held the office for 3 years. He retires at 72, but may be allowed to extend his period of office till 75 years.

3. **A Recorder**, who is a part-time judge of the Crown Court. Appointments are made from barristers and solicitors of ten years' standing who are prepared to commit themselves to not less than one month's work on the bench each year.

At the Lord Chancellor's request a Court of Appeal judge can sit in the Crown Court. All trials in the Crown Court take place before a jury.

The Crown Court has about 90 centres, chosen as far as practicable to be within travelling distance of the whole population. There are six circuits:

1. South-eastern (with London as its administrative centre);
2. Midland and Oxford (Birmingham);
3. North-eastern (Leeds);
4. Wales and Chester (Cardiff);
5. Western (Bristol);
6. Northern (Manchester).

On each of these circuits the towns where the judges sit are classified in three types:

1st tier centres, where High Court judges and Circuit judges deal with criminal cases, and High Court judges also take civil business.

CROWN COURT

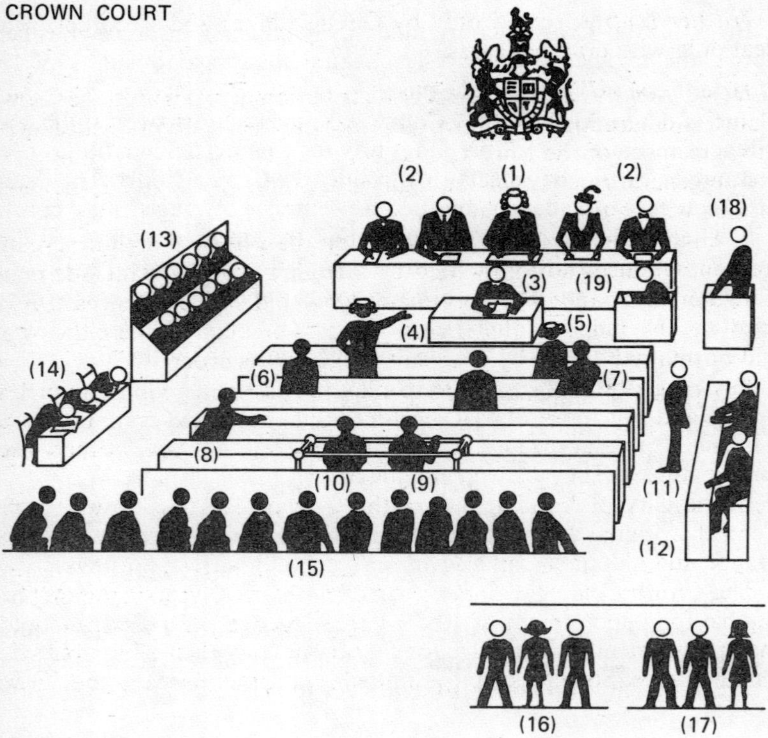

1. High Court Judge, Circuit Judge or Recorder
2. Justices of the Peace (not more than 4)
3. Clerk of the Crown Court
4. Defending Barrister (standing)
5. Prosecuting Barrister (seated)
6. Solicitor or solicitor's clerk in attendance (Defence)
7. Solicitor or solicitor's clerk in attendance (Prosecution)
8. Probation Officer
9. Accused
10. Warder from prison
11. Court Usher
12. Witnesses who have given evidence
13. Jury
14. Press reporters
15. Public
16. Witnesses for Prosecution outside court waiting to give evidence
17. Witnesses for Defence outside court waiting to give evidence
18. Witness
19. Shorthand writer

2nd tier centres, dealing only with criminal business, but served by both High Court and Circuit judges.

3rd tier centres, served only by Circuit judges and Recorders who deal only with criminal cases.

How Business is Distributed. The distribution of business in the Crown Court is determined by directions from the Lord Chief Justice, with the agreement of the Lord Chancellor.

The general rule is that the higher the status of the judge the more serious will be the cases he tries.

A High Court judge will always try the offences of murder and treason. Offences normally tried by a High Court judge include manslaughter and rape. The vast majority of indictable offences can be tried by any judge of the Crown Court. Offences triable either way will normally be tried by a Circuit judge or Recorder.

Lay magistrates have a role to play in the Crown Court. Not less than 2 and not more than 4 must sit for appeals and committals for sentence from magistrates' courts; and not more than 4 in other cases on indictment. They sit with the judge.

In the City of London, where the Crown Court is known as the Central Criminal Court, or more commonly the Old Bailey, the Lord Mayor and aldermen can sit with any judge in any type of case.

The *Crown Court and Solicitors.* Solicitors of 10 years' standing are eligible for appointment as Recorders. Moreover, if a solicitor holds the appointment of Recorder for 5 years he may then be appointed a Circuit Judge. Solicitors have a limited right of audience in the Crown Court.

Appeal by Way of Case Stated

This form of appeal may be used in magistrates' courts and in the Crown Court. The court to which appeal is made is the Divisional Court of Queen's Bench, which is constituted by not less than two judges of that Division (the usual number sitting is three).

Where either party (prosecutor or defendant) is dissatisfied on a point of law with the decision of the Crown Court, that party may require the Crown Court to 'state a case' for the opinion of the Divisional Court of Queen's Bench. The Crown Court then states the case in writing, giving the facts and the reasons for the decision. The Divisional Court then adjudicates on the written evidence submitted and gives its ruling.

There are two points to be noted: (i) the appeal must be on a point of law, not fact; (ii) both prosecutor and defendant may appeal. This is contrary to the general rule that where the defendant is acquitted, the prosecution has no general right of appeal to a higher court.

Magistrates' Courts

The first justices were appointed in 1327 as 'conservators of the peace'. For more than 600 years their successors, now known as justices of the peace or magistrates, have performed the duties of enforcing the common law and statute law and of preserving locally the public peace and good order.

In recent years Parliament has burdened the 900 magistrates' courts with enforcing increasing quantities of legislation, much of it highly complex. Magistrates' courts (or courts of petty sessions) today deal with more cases than any other court in the English legal system. For example, over 98 per cent of all criminal prosecutions in England and Wales are dealt with by magistrates. Magistrates also deal with some civil cases and perform certain administrative duties, particularly in licensing matters.

MAGISTRATES' COURT

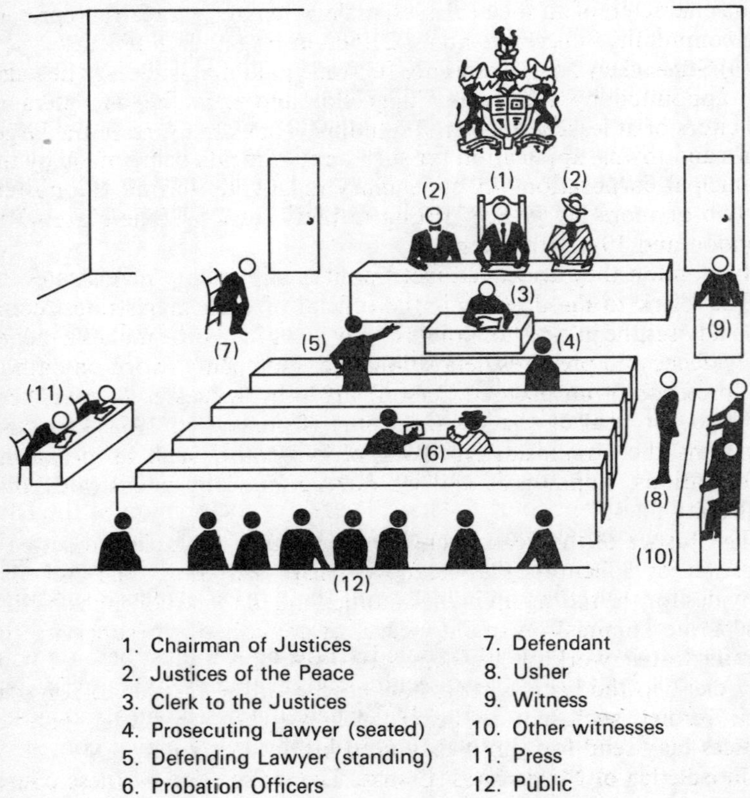

1. Chairman of Justices
2. Justices of the Peace
3. Clerk to the Justices
4. Prosecuting Lawyer (seated)
5. Defending Lawyer (standing)
6. Probation Officers
7. Defendant
8. Usher
9. Witness
10. Other witnesses
11. Press
12. Public

There are two kinds of magistrates:

(*a*) Justices of the Peace (lay magistrates) and
(*b*) Stipendiary Magistrates.

(*a*) **Justices of the Peace.** These are laymen appointed by the Lord Chancellor

(i) in respect of counties on the recommendation of the Lord Lieutenant of the county, assisted by an advisory committee;
(ii) in respect of large urban areas (e.g. Stoke on Trent) on the recommendation of its own advisory committee.

The important features of the county and urban magistrates are that they are local people, with some knowledge of the areas for which they are appointed, who are prepared to give up a certain amount of their time (say, one or more days a month) to the discharge of their judicial duties. They are unpaid (though they may receive out-of-pocket expenses when adjudicating).

The aim is to have on the bench a good cross-section of people of good character, of all social classes, male or female, who fairly represent the community. There are about 21,500 in England and Wales.

(*b*) **Stipendiary Magistrates** are full-time paid magistrates. They also are appointed by the Lord Chancellor and must be barristers or solicitors of at least seven years' standing. They are found in the larger cities and towns, application for such appointments being made by the municipal corporations. A stipendiary magistrate has all the powers of two or more lay justices sitting in petty sessions. There are 40 in London and 10 at other centres.

In London they are called metropolitan stipendiary magistrates.

The Clerk to the Justices is the official of each magistrates' court who advises the justices on points of law and procedure, makes a record of evidence and prepares depositions (i.e. statements sworn on oath in the presence of an accused person) made by witnesses in cases sent forward for trial at the Crown Court (Courts Act, 1971). He also performs the administrative work of the court, such as preparing informations, summonses and warrants granted by magistrates, and collecting fines.

The Justice of the Peace Act, 1949, provides that a clerk must be a barrister or solicitor of at least five years' standing. The Act also provides for the setting up in the counties and in those boroughs having a separate commission of the peace, of committees to supervise the administrative work of the magistrates' courts.

A clerk to the justices must not retire with the justices to consider their verdict, such matters being solely for the magistrates, but the justices may send for him if they need his advice.

Jurisdiction of Magistrates' Courts. The jurisdiction of these courts falls under three main headings: (*a*) as a court of trial; (*b*) as a court of preliminary investigation; (*c*) miscellaneous.

(*a*) *Court of Trial.* The jurisdiction is exercised by from two to seven justices, and the maximum punishment that may be imposed for any one offence is six months' imprisonment or a fine of £1,000. A single lay justice may try certain cases such as simple drunkenness.

Criminal offences can be divided into three classes:

(i) Offences triable only on indictment. Offences will be such if there is no express statutory provision otherwise. They are triable by judge and jury in the Crown Court. An indictment is the document used in jury trials which states the offences and gives particulars.

(ii) Offences triable only summarily, i.e. in a magistrates' court. Offences which can only be tried summarily include riding a pedal cycle at night without lights, begging in a public place, and being found drunk and incapable on the highway. A statute must expressly provide for such trial or prescribe a procedure for determining the matter (see s. 23 of the Criminal Law Act, 1977).

(iii) Offences triable either way. Schedule 3 of the Criminal Law Act, 1977, lists over 60 offences triable either way, i.e. summarily or on indictment. The Act also provides that offences made so triable by earlier statutes will now be in this class. The magistrates must offer the defendant the choice of trial either in the Crown Court or by the magistrates. If he chooses the latter, the magistrates will try the case there and then, i.e. summarily. If he chooses to be tried at the Crown Court, the magistrates will sit as a court of preliminary investigation.

The agenda of a typical magistrates' court reveals a wide variety of offences: petty theft, criminal damage, common assault, drunkenness, driving a motor-car without a driving licence, driving without insurance, failing to obey traffic signs, parking offences, driving without due care and attention, and similar road-traffic offences. Some offenders will be dealt with then and there (even though they qualify for trial by the Crown Court), while defendants who elect for trial by jury will be committed for trial if the prosecution makes out a *prima facie* case in respect of each. (A *prima facie* case is one which appears 'at first sight' or 'from the first impression' to be an offence.)

(*b*) *Court of Preliminary Investigation.* In this capacity the magistrates' court is called upon to determine whether an accused person, who is brought before it by means of a summons or by arrest, shall be committed to stand trial at the Crown Court.

The prosecution calls its witnesses and produces exhibits (e.g. a gun or knife). The evidence of the prosecution witnesses is taken down in writing in the presence of the accused, and the document (called a deposition) is signed by the witness (called a deponent) and by the justices present at the hearing. The accused may give evidence himself and call witnesses in his support, or he may reserve his defence until the actual trial. Usually an accused reserves his defence.

After hearing the evidence the magistrates decide whether the prosecution has made out a *prima facie* case. If it has, the accused and the witnesses are bound over to attend the trial at the Crown Court. These proceedings are known as **committal proceedings**, and although they may be taken before one justice, in practice two or more lay magistrates usually preside over this important step in the judicial process. A stipendiary magistrate acts alone.

If the prosecution has not made out a *prima facie* case against the accused, the magistrates must release him. When an accused is committed for trial he may be either remanded in custody (i.e. to a prison to await trial) or remanded on bail (i.e. released on condition that he appears at the trial court at a later date when his case will be heard).

The Criminal Justice Act, 1967, provides that, in certain circumstances, an accused person may be committed for trial on written statements alone.

The Act also restricts the publication of reports of committal proceedings to purely formal matters, i.e. the identity of the court and magistrates, the names of the parties, and the nature of the charges. The object is to avoid prejudicing the accused by pre-trial publicity. But the reporting restrictions can be lifted on application by the accused or one of the accused.

(*c*) *Miscellaneous Jurisdiction.* In addition to the foregoing duties, the magistrates perform administrative functions in regard to liquor licensing (approving applicants and premises), betting licensing, theatre and cinematograph licensing, and have a limited jurisdiction in regard to civil debts (e.g. unpaid income tax where the amount due is less than £30).

Other important duties include: (i) making matrimonial orders for separation and maintenance of spouses; (ii) affiliation orders; (iii) consent to marriage; (iv) guardianship of minors; (v) adoption of children; (vi) orders under the Mental Health Act, 1959; and (vii) orders in regard to children and young persons in need of care, protection, or control.

Juvenile Courts. Certain magistrates attached to a petty-sessional division form a special panel to deal with offences committed by children (i.e. persons under 14) and young persons (i.e. over 14 and under 17). The juvenile court is formed by three lay justices, under sixty-five years of age, one of whom must be a woman.

The juvenile court sits **separately** from the adult court: if it cannot sit in a different room it must sit on a different day. Proceedings in juvenile courts are shielded from publicity. The Press must not disclose the identity of the child or young person unless the court, in exceptional cases, permits.

Where a child or young person is charged jointly with an adult the case is dealt with in an adult court, i.e. the usual magistrates' court.

Appeals from Magistrates' Courts are organized as follows:

(*a*) Where the defendant wishes to appeal against (i) conviction and/or (ii) sentence, appeal lies to the Crown Court.

(*b*) Where the defendant or prosecutor wishes to appeal on a point of law, appeal lies to the Divisional Court of Queen's Bench by way of 'case stated'.

(*c*) Appeals concerning separation and maintenance orders, affiliation, adoption, and consent to marry lie to a Divisional Court of the Family Division.

(*d*) Further appeal may be made from the Divisional Court to the House of Lords.

3. Other Courts

Courts-Martial Appeal Court. This was established in 1951 to hear appeals from conviction by court-martial. It is composed of the judges of the Court of Appeal and the Queen's Bench Division nominated by the Lord Chief Justice, and the normal composition of the court is the same as that of the Court of Appeal (Criminal Division).

Restrictive Practices Court. This court was set up by the Restrictive Trade Practices Act, 1956, now replaced by the 1976 Act and it is a new superior court of record. Its purpose is to consider and adjudicate on agreements entered into between firms, suppliers or buyers, in which restrictions are imposed on the price, quantity, quality, or method of distribution of goods.

Under the Fair Trading Act, 1973, restrictive agreements must be registered with the Director General of Fair Trading, whose duties include protecting consumers against agreements offending the public interest (see p. 163). He also has powers of investigation under the Competition Act, 1980.

Composition. The court is equal in standing to the High Court, and consists of three judges of the High Court, a judge of the Court of Session of Scotland, and a judge of the Supreme Court of Northern Ireland. In addition there are ten lay members experienced in industry, commerce or public affairs, two of whom with one presiding judge form a quorum. The court may sit in two or more divisions. Appeal lies to the Court of Appeal (Restrictive Practices Court Act, 1976).

Employment Appeal Tribunal. This court was set up by the Employment Protection Act, 1975 (see now the consolidation Act of 1978), and replaced the National Industrial Relations Court which had ceased to exist. It is composed of Court of Appeal and High Court judges nominated by the Lord Chancellor, who appoints one as President, and other members with special knowledge or experience of industrial relations. A judge sits with two or four other members.

The court hears appeals on questions of law from industrial tribunals under the Equal Pay Act, 1970, the Sex Discrimination Acts, 1975 and 1986, the Race Relations Act, 1976, and the employment legislation, 1978 to 1982. Procedure is relatively informal.

Appeal lies on a point of law to the Court of Appeal.

Coroners' Courts. The office of coroner and the coroner's inquest (or inquiry) are of ancient origin. The first coroners were appointed in the reign of Richard I in 1194. Originally they had wide powers concerning local administration and the criminal law, but these have now been shed and the coroner of today carries out those duties laid down in the Coroners Acts, 1887 to 1980 (as amended by the Criminal Law Act, 1977) the Administration of Justice Act, 1982 and rules made thereunder.

The main duties of the coroner are to investigate the death of any person which has been (i) sudden, (ii) violent, or (iii) unnatural (i.e. against the course of nature), (iv) deaths of prisoners, (v) deaths of persons in mental institutions where there is no satisfactory medical evidence and (vi) deaths involving the police. The coroner may, however, hold an inquest into *any* case of death.

A coroner *must* summon a jury when there is reason to suspect that death is due to murder, manslaughter, infanticide, a road accident, poisoning, or notifiable disease. An inquest may be held in any place (e.g. a court or a private house). Proceedings are carried out in a formal manner. The public are admitted to the court except when this would be prejudicial to national security.

The purpose of the inquest is to enable the coroner, with the aid of a jury when so required, to ascertain the identity of the deceased person and the place and cause of death. If some person has already been arrested and charged with the murder, manslaughter, or infanticide of the subject of the inquest, the coroner must adjourn his inquiry until the criminal proceedings are ended.

Money, coin, gold, silver, plate, or bullion found hidden in the earth or a private place, the owner of which is unknown, is called **treasure trove** and belongs to the Crown. When such articles are uncovered, the coroner holds an inquest to establish whether they are in fact treasure trove. If so, the finder and the owner of the land on which they were found are customarily recompensed by the Treasury.

A coroner must be a barrister, solicitor, or medical practitioner of at least five years' standing. He is appointed by a county council or a borough council having a separate commission of the peace. The Lord Chancellor may remove a coroner for misbehaviour.

4. Court of Justice of the European Communities

The Court has jurisdiction to give preliminary rulings on the interpretation of the Treaties, the validity and interpretation of acts of the Community institutions and the interpretation of the statutes of bodies established by an act of the Council. Any national court or tribunal may request the European Court to give a ruling on these matters and courts or tribunals from which there is no appeal must make such referral.

The court consists of ten judges assisted by four Advocates-General.

5. Administrative Tribunals

In his book *Freedom Under the Law*, Lord Denning refers to administrative tribunals as

> 'a separate set of courts dealing with a set of rights and duties. Just as in the old days there were ecclesiastical courts dealing with matrimonial cases and the administration of estates, and just as there was the Chancellor dealing with the enforcement and administration of trusts, so in our day there are the new tribunals dealing with the rights and duties between man and the State.'

In the last fifty years successive governments have been concerned with regulating the social life of the community. Legislation for improving the general well-being has included the National Health Service Act, National Insurance Act, Education Act, Housing Acts, Town and Country Planning Acts, and Rent Restriction Acts. Although the collective good and welfare are admirable aims, the effect of much legislation is that, while promoting the public interest, it also circumscribes the rights of the private individual. There are now over 2,000 such tribunals which hear over 200,000 cases a year.

For example, Adams owns a field which the local Education Authority proposes to purchase compulsorily as a site for a technical college. Adams may wish to retain his field and to contest the right of the Education Authority to acquire it. If the field is compulsorily acquired, Adams may further dispute the amount payable to compensate him for his loss. Tribunals may decide (*a*) whether the field will be acquired, and (*b*) the amount of compensation.

Similarly, Black is injured at work which disables him from continuing his employment. He can claim a pension under the National Insurance Industrial Injuries Acts, but his claim may be repudiated by the National Insurance Officer on the ground that it is not within the Act.

Many such disputes occur between a private individual seeking to protect his own private rights and a Minister, Government department, local authority or other person to whom authority has been given by law to administer a particular Act.

It may be argued that disputes of this kind ought to be decided in the traditionally impartial and fair atmosphere of a court of law which follows a known procedure and applies a known system of law—common law or statute. But we find that such disputes are frequently decided by special tribunals, not on the basis of law, but on grounds of policy and discretion, and that as far as possible the tribunals endeavour to reconcile the rights of the individual with those of the public in whose general interest the particular legislation may have been passed.

The position occupied by administrative tribunals and the type of law applied therein, known as **administrative law**, is a matter of great importance. At this stage, therefore, we shall examine some of the reasons advanced for their creation, and the advantages and disadvantages which administrative tribunals display.

The **reasons** usually given for the establishment of administrative tribunals are:

(*a*) Ordinary courts are already overburdened with work, and additional jurisdiction would cause a breakdown.

(*b*) The costs of judicial proceedings in ordinary courts would be heavy.

(*c*) The courts of law are slow and the procedure elaborate.

(*d*) Matters involving a public service are best administered by specialists in that service, e.g. doctors at a medical appeal.

(*e*) Policy decisions are best settled by an administrative authority.

The **advantages** of administrative tribunals are said to be:

(i) Decisions are **quick** and delays are avoided.

(ii) The procedure is **cheap**; no fees are payable usually.

(iii) The **informal** atmosphere and straightforward procedure suit the litigant.

(iv) They have wide **discretionary** power. This avoids the rigidity which the doctrine of precedent imposes on the courts of law.

(v) Tribunals are often staffed by **experts**: e.g. doctors on Pensions Tribunals determine disability or extent of injury.

(vi) Tribunals ensure **efficient administration** of social or economic policies found in statutes; while courts of law sift facts and decide on the basis of established rules of law different in character from social policy.

The **disadvantages** are said to be:

(i) Administrative tribunals are sometimes held in **private** and lack publicity. Suspicion may be aroused as to 'administrative justice'.

(ii) The parties are sometimes prohibited from being represented by lawyers. The inarticulate person is therefore at a disadvantage in explaining his case. Legal aid is not generally available (see p. 76).

(iii) Reasons for decisions are not always published.

(iv) Technical experts and administrators are not always capable of acting impartially or of sifting the facts.

(v) Tribunals sometimes include a civil servant of the Ministry which is directly involved in the dispute. He is, therefore, not sufficiently independent or impartial to give a just decision.

(vi) Rights of appeal are limited in some cases.

(vii) Discretion of a tribunal is sometimes so wide as to make decisions inconsistent and unpredictable.

Examples of Tribunals

National Insurance. Claims for benefits under the National Insurance Act, 1965, are dealt with locally by an insurance officer. If disagreement arises the applicant for benefit has a right of appeal to a local tribunal made up of a chairman, who is a lawyer, and two lay members, one representing employers' organizations and one representing employees' organizations. From the tribunal's decision appeal lies to the National Insurance Commissioner, a barrister appointed by the Crown.

There is no right of appeal either on a point of law or fact from the Commissioner's finding. Some technical questions are reserved for decision by the Minister, who may refer the matter to a judge of the High Court. From the Minister's decision on such questions there is a right of appeal to the High Court (whose decision is final).

Industrial Injuries. There is a similar system of adjudication in respect of industrial injuries claims under the National Insurance (Industrial Injuries) Act, 1965. The insured person must establish that his injury arose during the course of his employment. If the insurance officer disallows the claim the applicant may appeal to the tribunal applicable to National Insurance (see above).

If the applicant establishes that his injury did arise in the course of his employment, the next question to consider is the extent of the disablement. This claim is decided first by a medical board of two doctors. Further appeal lies to a medical appeal tribunal made up of two doctors with a lawyer as chairman. From the medical appeal tribunal appeal lies to the National Insurance Commissioner.

Decisions of the Commissioner in national insurance and industrial injuries cases are published officially, and such decisions bind insurance officers and local tribunals.

Industrial Tribunals. The Industrial Training Act, 1964, provided for the establishment of these tribunals. Later legislation has considerably increased their jurisdiction, particularly the Redundancy Payments Act, 1965, the Trade Union and Labour Relations Act, 1974, and the Employment Protection Act, 1975. Most of the cases brought to the tribunals concern unfair dismissal or redundancy. The Employment Protection (Consolidation) Act, 1978, replaces earlier legislation. In addition to these areas the tribunals have jurisdiction over many aspects of industrial law. Thousands of cases are referred to the tribunals, which sit throughout the country.

The tribunal consists of a legally qualified chairman and two lay members.

The appellant may be legally represented or may be represented by a trade-union official; he may send written representations setting out the facts and arguments; he may require the production of documents, and may request the tribunal to order the attendance of any person to give evidence and to produce documents.

The decision of the tribunal, which is by majority, is given in writing with reasons therefor. The decision is subject to a right of appeal to the Employment Appeal Tribunal on a point of law.

Rent Tribunals. Under the Rent Acts the tenant of furnished accommodation may apply to a rent tribunal for the rent to be reduced. Similarly, the tenant of unfurnished accommodation below a certain rateable value may apply to a rent officer to fix a fair rent; and appeal from that decision lies to a rent assessment committee, which normally consists of a legally qualified chairman, a valuer or surveyor and a lay person.

Legal representation is allowed, hearings are open to the public and the Press, and evidence is never taken on oath. If requested, reasons for the decisions of the rent assessment committee may be given in writing or orally. Appeal, on a point of law only, lies to the High Court.

Domestic Tribunals. Domestic tribunals exist to determine questions, decide disputes and maintain discipline among members of a particular trade or profession. Thus a trade union or a professional body may lay down its set of rules governing membership. If the rules are infringed a tribunal may be set up to deal with the incident and it may punish or expel the offender.

Three important examples of domestic tribunals are:

(*a*) *Trade Unions*. The disciplinary tribunals of trade unions are created by members themselves. A governing committee frames the rules of membership, rules constituting a tribunal, rules of procedure and the forms of punishment. Members who violate the rules may be expelled or fined; expulsion could mean that the individual is prevented from following his former trade. The Trade Union and Labour Relations Act, 1974, alters the law in regard to Trade Unions. Registered Trade Unions maintain certain disciplinary powers in regard to members, but where a wrong is alleged to be done to a member he has a right of appeal to an industrial tribunal, e.g. where he has been wrongfully expelled or refused the right to take part in the activities of a registered trade union.

The right to belong to a registered union is repealed but employees will continue to be protected from dismissal for belonging to a union or taking part in its activities. This protection now extends to members of an independent union.

(*b*) *Solicitors.* The Solicitors Act, 1974, as amended by the Administration of Justice Act, 1982, provides for the setting up of a committee to exercise disciplinary powers over solicitors. The disciplinary committee sits as a board with a minimum of three members, and follows the usual legal procedure of a court of law. The board may strike a solicitor off the roll, suspend him from practice, impose a fine of up to £3,000, or order the payment of costs. Appeal from the committee lies to the High Court.

(*c*) *Doctors.* The General Medical Council has power under the Medical Act, 1956, to strike a doctor off the Medical Register for infamous conduct in his profession, and he can be barred from further practice. Appeal against the decision of the General Medical Council lies to the Judicial Committee of the Privy Council.

The General Dental Council has similar powers under the Dentists Act, 1957, concerning dentists; and the Central Midwives Board has similar authority over midwives. There are many more such tribunals, but lack of space precludes their description.

6. Judicial Control of Administrative Tribunals

A tribunal is another name for a court, but to avoid confusion the term is applied to those bodies possessing judicial powers which operate outside the traditional courts of law. The essential purpose of a tribunal is to adjudicate in a dispute, to follow proper procedures, to act fairly and impartially, and finally to reach a decision. We have seen that many of the tribunals have very wide powers indeed; therefore their judgments must be subject to the supervisory control of the courts of law. Such control is exercised mainly by the Queen's Bench Division which continues the ancient jurisdiction of the original royal court of King's Bench.

As a rule Parliament leaves the professional organizations to form their own rules and procedures to maintain control of their membership. Only in exceptional cases will the courts of law interfere with these. But where the administration of a statute, the exercise of powers under it, and the setting up of tribunals to decide disputes are entrusted to a Minister, Parliament generally requires that certain rules be framed to ensure fairness in the administration of the statute and of tribunals set up thereunder. Nevertheless injustices do occur, and the purpose of this section is to examine the grounds on which the courts of law exercise their supervisory jurisdiction, and the procedures that are followed.

Where a tribunal acts judicially it must follow certain unwritten rules of common law known as 'natural justice'. Natural justice embraces two sub-rules:

(*a*) The rule against bias ('no man may be a judge in his own cause'); and

(*b*) *Audi alteram partem* ('hear the other side').

(*a*) **The Rule against Bias.** A true judicial decision can be reached only if the judge himself is impartial. This is an obvious requirement in a court of law or a tribunal. In *R.* v. *Rand* (1866) it was held that a judge is disqualified where (i) he has a direct pecuniary interest, however small, in the subject-matter in dispute; or (ii) there is real likelihood that the judge would have a bias in favour of one of the parties.

For example, if a judge is related to, or is a friend of, one of the parties to a dispute there would be real likelihood of bias. It is immaterial whether a judicial decision was *in fact* biased, for as was said by Lord Chief Justice Hewart in *R.* v. *Sussex Justices, ex parte McCarthy* (1924): 'Justice should not only be done, but should manifestly and undoubtedly be seen to be done.'

As an example of pecuniary bias we may quote:

> *Dimes* v. *Grand Junction Canal* (1852). Lord Chancellor Cottenham made decrees in a Chancery suit in favour of a canal company. Lord Cottenham held several shares in the company. *Held* (by the House of Lords): that the decrees be set aside on the ground of pecuniary interest. No bias was proved in fact, nor could it be shown that Lord Cottenham was in any way influenced by his shareholding.

As an example of likelihood of bias we may quote:

> *R.* v. *Sussex Justices, ex parte McCarthy* (1924). *A* was summoned before magistrates for a motoring offence. The acting clerk to the justices was a member of a firm of solicitors representing *A* in civil proceedings arising out of the same accident. The acting clerk did not advise the magistrates, but he retired with them to consider their decision. *Held:* that as the acting clerk was connected with the case in the civil action he ought not to advise the magistrates in the criminal prosecution. Conviction accordingly quashed, despite the fact that the acting clerk took no part in the decision to convict and had not been asked by the justices to give his opinion or advice.

(*b*) **'Audi Alteram Partem.'** The second rule of natural justice is that a man has the right to be heard in his own defence. 'It is contrary to the spirit of our laws that anyone should be convicted without having an opportunity of being heard in his own defence' (*R.* v. *Benn and Church*, 1795).

The rule embraces the propositions that the party sued or prosecuted should have the opportunity to:

(i) know the case against him;
(ii) state his case (orally or in writing);

Ridge v. *Baldwin* (1964). The Chief Constable of Brighton was dismissed from the force by the watch committee. The Chief Constable was not present at the meeting of the Committee nor was he given an opportunity of stating his case. The Court of Appeal held in favour of the defendants. Ridge appealed to the House of Lords which overruled the Court of Appeal. *Held:* that, first, there were disciplinary regulations (Police Regs.) which laid down the procedure to be followed in dismissals; and, further, natural justice required that a hearing should have been given before the watch committee exercised its power. The failure to give a hearing as required by natural justice invalidated the dismissal.

A further rule is no doubt that parties have a right to be informed of the reason for the decision. The courts of law follow strict procedural rules which have been hammered out over the centuries to ensure fairness. Administrative tribunals, however, are not bound to follow these rules meticulously but must apply the general principles of justice as shown above.

Supervision by the Queen's Bench Division

We have mentioned earlier that the monarch is 'the fountain of justice' and that one part of the jurisdiction of the Queen's Bench Division is supervisory. Thus the Queen's Bench Division, acting for the Crown, supervises the administration of justice by inferior courts, administrative tribunals and other tribunals throughout the kingdom. Moreover the Queen's Bench Division exercises supervisory control over Ministers of the Crown, civil servants, local authorities or other authorities purporting to exercise statutory powers. If such authorities act *ultra vires* (i.e. beyond the powers conferred on them by statute), the Queen's Bench Division may declare such excess of power to be void.

The control exercised by the Queen's Bench Division is by means of prerogative orders of (*a*) *mandamus*, (*b*) prohibition, and (*c*) *certiorari*. Before the Administration of Justice (Miscellaneous Provisions) Act, 1938, these were known as prerogative writs.

In 1977 major changes were made to R.S.C. Order 53, to provide a new form of procedure known as 'application for judicial review' which enables an applicant to seek any one or more of the remedies: *certiorari*, prohibition *mandamus*, injunction, declaration or damages. This means that more than one remedy can be sought and remedies can be claimed in the alternative.

(*a*) **Mandamus** is an order issuing out of the Queen's Bench Division commanding (*mandamus*; we command) a person or body to perform a duty imposed by common law or statute. The order is available to enforce administrative duties, e.g. to compel a local authority to produce its accounts for inspection by a ratepayer; or judicial duties, e.g. to compel a housing tribunal to hear and determine an appeal, or magistrates to decide a case in petty sessions.

(*b*) **Prohibition** is an order issuing out of the Queen's Bench Division to prohibit an inferior court or tribunal from continuing to exceed, or threatening to exceed, its jurisdiction. Thus the order may be directed to recorders, magistrates, coroners, and all statutory tribunals.

(*c*) **Certiorari** is an order removing the decision of an inferior judicial body into the Queen's Bench Division to have its legality inquired into. The word *certiorari* means 'to be informed'. The order may be used (i) to secure an impartial trial; (ii) to review an excess of jurisdiction; (iii) to challenge an *ultra vires* act; (iv) to quash a judicial decision made contrary to natural justice; and (v) to correct errors of law on the face of the record.

An order of *certiorari* will lie 'wherever any body of persons having legal authority to determine questions affecting the rights of subjects, and having the duty to act judicially, act in excess of their legal authority' (Lord Atkin in *R.* v. *Electricity Commissioners*, 1924). Thus it can be issued to magistrates' courts, administrative tribunals, disciplinary tribunals of the police and fire service, and to arbitrators.

Tribunals and Inquiries Act, 1971

We have already mentioned some of the disadvantages of administrative tribunals (see p. 65). The wide powers granted to, and the procedures followed by, tribunals in disputes involving private rights of individuals caused considerable disquiet in the period following the Second World War. This came to a head in the *Crichel Down* case in 1954 (concerning the acquisition by a Government department of land owned by a private individual), which revealed inefficient administrative procedures and apparent injustices. As a result, a committee was set up in 1955 by the Government under Sir Oliver Franks (now Lord Franks). Its terms of reference were to examine and make recommendations on (i) the constitution and working of tribunals set up by statute, and (ii) the working of administrative procedures, e.g. the holding of an official inquiry or the hearing of appeals by a Minister as the result of objections, particularly in relation to the compulsory purchase of land.

This important committee reported in 1957, and some of its main recommendations passed into law in the Tribunals and Inquiries Act, 1958. The Tribunals and Inquiries Act, 1971 (a consolidating Act) operates today.

The provisions of the Act include:

(*a*) *A Council on Tribunals* shall be formed of 10–15 members appointed by the Lord Chancellor and Secretary of State for Scotland. (A Scottish committee is appointed to deal with Scottish matters.)

(*b*) *Duties* of the Council are to keep under review the constitution and working of the tribunals listed in Schedule 1 of the 1971 Act and other tribunals and inquiries. The Council acts in advisory capacity and does not itself hear appeals.

(*c*) *Reports* of the Council are to be made annually and laid before Parliament.

(*d*) *Chairmen* of the various tribunals to which the Act applies are selected by the appropriate Ministers from a panel of names suggested by the Lord Chancellor. This ensures that nominees have the qualifications, legal or otherwise, for the appointment.

(*e*) *Membership* of tribunals can be terminated only with the Lord Chancellor's consent. The Parliamentary Commissioner is an *ex officio* member of the Council and the Scottish Committee.

(*f*) *Reasons for decisions* made by tribunals must be given, if requested before or when the decision is given.

(*g*) *Appeal* on a point of law to the High Court is given in the case of a number of tribunals (e.g. rent, schools', and employment tribunals) where the right had not existed before the Act.

(*h*) *Prerogative Orders*; judicial control by resort to *certiorari, mandamus*, and prohibition is safeguarded.

7. Arbitration

Arbitration is the reference of a matter in dispute to one or more persons called arbitrators. We commonly find arbitrators, usually three, appointed to consider wage disputes between employers' and employees' organizations if both sides so agree. But arbitration may be used as an alternative proceeding to litigation. So instead of bringing an action in a court of law the parties may agree to submit a dispute to arbitration.

Contracts often include a clause for arbitration in the event of disagreement between the parties, and a clause is often incorporated in partnership agreements should disputes occur among partners. A clause may provide for the appointment of (*a*) a sole arbitrator, or (*b*) two arbitrators (one may be appointed by each party to a dispute). Where the appointment of two arbitrators is expressly provided for, it is implied that on appointment they should appoint an umpire to take up the reference in the event of failure of the arbitrators to agree. High Court judges may now be appointed as arbitrators in certain cases. Members of the Bar are often appointed.

The **advantages** of arbitration are said to be:

(*a*) Privacy: the dispute which may involve private and personal matters or confidential commercial matters is not debated in open court.

(*b*) Convenience: the arbitration is held at a place and time convenient to the parties and the arbitrator(s).

(*c*) Speedy settlement: delays often met in litigation are overcome. Time is money to commercial men.

(*d*) Informality: technical procedural rules of a court of law are not rigidly applied.

(*e*) Expert knowledge: the arbitrator may be appointed because he is an expert in the matter under dispute. Frequently the matter is purely a factual one not involving law at all.

(*f*) Where contracts involve a foreign element (see Conflict of Laws, p. 5) foreign courts may be more likely to enforce the arbitration award (as opposed to a court order) when the parties have clearly so agreed to arbitration.

(*g*) Expenses are generally less than litigation fees.

The **disadvantages** are said to be:

(*a*) The dispute may hinge on difficult points of law. An arbitrator may not have the requisite expertise.

(*b*) The doctrine of precedent does not apply. Each case is decided on its merits; and is therefore no guide to future similar cases.

Arbitration procedure is governed by the Arbitration Acts of 1950, 1975 and 1979 and the statutes which provide for statutory references. Unless the parties have agreed otherwise, the case must be decided according to the normal rules of English law and procedure. The parties often agree to dispense with strict rules of evidence. The arbitrator has power to order discovery and inspection of documents and to examine witnesses, etc.

After hearing the evidence it is usual for the arbitrator to notify each party when he has come to his decision, and he may require payment of his fees before publishing his award. The losing party may be required to pay the costs of the arbitration proceedings, including the arbitrator's fees.

If a losing party refuses to carry out the terms of an award, an order may be obtained from the High Court to compel its enforcement in the same way as a judgment of that court.

The High Court has jurisdiction on application with consent of the arbitrator or the other parties to determine a question of law arising in the case.

There is now a right of appeal to the High Court on a question of law arising out of the award with the consent of the parties or by leave of the court, unless validly excluded by agreement.

There is a limited right of appeal with leave from the High Court to the Court of Appeal. In *Pioneer Shipping Ltd.* v. *B. T. P. Tioxide Ltd.* (1980) the Court of Appeal held that decisions of arbitrators in arbitrations begun after 1st August, 1979 to which the 1979 Act applies, are only to be questioned on points of law if the judge gives leave, usually with no appeal from him to the Court of Appeal; and leave should not be given where the sole question is the proper interpretation of a commercial contract in a commercial sense, as an arbitrator is better placed to do that than a judge.

The court may remove an arbitrator for misconduct and set aside the award.

8. Juries

(*a*) **The Criminal Jury** consisting of twelve persons of either sex is found in the Crown Court (see p. 54). Juries are not used in magistrates' courts. The sworn duty of the jury is 'to faithfully try the defendant and give a true verdict according to the evidence'.

The defendant has a right of challenge to the array of jurors or to individual jurors. The Crown has a right to a provisional challenge to 'stand by' jurors. Those jurors objected to will be asked to stand down and others will be empanelled to take their places.

Formerly the verdict of a jury had to be unanimous. Now, the Criminal Justice Act, 1967, provides that a majority verdict may be allowed. The court cannot, however, accept a majority verdict unless the jury has been deliberating for not less than two hours, when the verdict need not then be unanimous if (i) in a case where there are not less than eleven jurors, ten of them agree; or (ii) in a case where there are ten jurors, nine of them agree. It must be stated in open court as to the number of jurors who respectively agreed to and dissented from the verdict (*R.* v. *Reynolds*, 1981).

Where a juror dies or is ill, provided that both sides agree and the number of jurors is not reduced below ten, the case may continue and a verdict may be given.

(*b*) **The Civil Jury** is now a rarity. The general rule following the Administration of Justice (Miscellaneous Provisions) Act, 1933, is that the civil court has a discretion in its use of a jury. A jury may, however, be ordered on the application of either party in cases of defamation, malicious prosecution, false imprisonment, and cases of fraud (called Deceit—see p. 244), unless the court considers that the trial will involve prolonged examination of documents or accounts, or a scientific or local investigation.

In actions in the Chancery Division juries are not used. In defended divorce cases or contested probate actions a jury may be applied for.

In High Court cases the jury comprises 12 persons; and a majority verdict may be accepted. In county court actions the jury numbers eight. In coroners' courts the jury comprises from seven to 11 persons; the coroner may accept a majority verdict, provided that the number of dissentients does not exceed two.

When a judge sits without a jury, he determines questions of law and fact.

Qualifications of Jurymen. The Criminal Justice Act, 1972, abolished the former property qualification for jury service in England and Wales.

The basic qualification is that of citizenship as evidenced by inclusion in the Electoral Register. Anyone between the ages of 18 and 65 registered as an elector who has lived here for five years or more since the age of 13 becomes liable for jury service.

Payments in respect of jury service for travelling, subsistence and financial loss are made to jurors.

Ex-prisoners are disqualified from serving on a jury as is anyone who has been on probation during the previous five years.

Peers, judges, M.P.s, clergymen, barristers, solicitors, medical practitioners, members of H.M. Forces and police officers are among the persons exempt from jury service. Mentally ill persons are ineligible.

The Juries Act, 1974 (as amended), consolidates the law on this subject.

The **advantages** of trial by jury may be said to be:

(*a*) A finding of fact is better left to several persons than to one person.
(*b*) Juries represent the verdict of ordinary people.
(*c*) There is public confidence in jury trials.

The **disadvantages** of trial by jury are:

(*a*) Jurors of 18 may be too inexperienced for jury service.
(*b*) Jurors have no physical or educational test for their task.
(*c*) Jurors may be too easily impressed and swayed by advocacy of experienced counsel.
(*d*) Juries are prone to leniency to an accused in certain cases e.g. manslaughter by motor car.
(*e*) Local prejudice may exist in certain trials, and this may be reflected in local jurors.
(*f*) Corrupt influences, threats and intimidation from outside parties.
(*g*) Some trials are long and may cause inconvenience to jurors, who may suffer financially. The cost to the State will also be high.

9. Legal Aid and Advice

The Legal Aid Act, 1949, replaced previous provision for people of limited means to obtain some legal help. The Act created a scheme for providing legal aid to people within certain means limits, the expense to be paid out of the Legal Aid Fund financed by the State. A later Act made provision also for legal advice. The scheme is now governed by the Acts of 1974, 1979 and 1982 and the regulations made under them.

The administration of legal aid in civil litigation and in legal advice is carried out by the Law Society acting in consultation with the Bar Council and under the general guidance of the Lord Chancellor. Fourteen Area Committees supervise lawyers' remuneration under the scheme and the preparation of the lists of lawyers willing to act, and complaints against lawyers on these lists. Local Committees consider applications for legal aid certificates. Both Committees consist of practising barristers and solicitors. Legal aid in criminal matters is granted by the courts.

The Government has announced its intention to transfer the administration of legal aid to an independent Legal Aid Board.

Legal Advice and Assistance

Known as 'the £25 scheme' or 'the green form scheme', this scheme is governed by sections 1 to 5 of the 1974 Act, as amended by the 1979 Act, and by the regulations. The scheme provides for general advice to be given by a solicitor and if necessary a barrister on any question of English law and the steps which might be taken by an applicant with regard to his problem, other than any matter for which a legal aid certificate or order already exists. Apart from negotiating a settlement the scheme does not cover taking steps in proceedings, except that representation is covered in magistrates' and county courts where the court requests a solicitor present in the court, e.g. a duty solicitor, to undertake it (now regulated by Schedule 1 of the 1982 Act).

The 1979 Act added 'assistance by way of representation' before a court or tribunal, but regulations are necessary to bring this into operation. At present Legal Aid does not extend to tribunals other than Mental Health Tribunals.

Legal advice and assistance is available to applicants within specified means limits, at present if his disposable income does not exceed £108 a week, or he receives supplementary benefit or family income supplement and his disposable capital does not exceed £800 (£3,000 if represented).

On receiving the green form from the applicant, the solicitor will decide whether the applicant is eligible, and will assess any contribution to be paid by the applicant. If the latter receives supplementary benefit or family income supplement or has no more than £58 a week disposable income, no contribution is payable. If his income is above that figure a contribution is payable, calculated on the basis of income.

If the solicitor considers that the cost of giving advice or assistance will not exceed £25, or £90 in divorce proceedings, the advice can be given immediately, otherwise approval of the Area Committee must be obtained.

Legal Aid in Civil Proceedings

Courts in which legal aid is authorized. Legal Aid is available in the House of Lords, Judicial Committee of the Privy Council, Court of Appeal, High Court, Restrictive Practices Court, county courts, coroners' courts and in magistrates' courts in respect of civil proceedings; and for proceedings in the Lands Tribunal and the Employment Appeal Tribunal.

Legal aid is not available for proceedings wholly or partly in respect of defamation, undefended matrimonial proceedings, proceedings before administrative tribunals or arbitration proceedings.

Eligibility. The applicant must be within the prescribed financial limits, at present (1986) a disposable income not exceeding £5,415 a year and a disposable capital not exceeding £4,710. Disposable income is much less than gross income, since deductions from the latter are allowed. The applicant must also show that he has reasonable grounds for taking the proceedings. The Local Committee will not grant a certificate if it considers the matter too trivial or simple to require legal assistance.

A contribution will be payable by the applicant where his disposable capital is above £3,000 and disposable income above £2,255 to the extent of all the capital above that figure and a quarter of the excess of income above the figure. The contribution will be marked on the certificate.

Application for a certificate is to be made to the Area Committee in respect of proceedings in an appellate court, and to a Local Committee in respect of proceedings in other courts. The Committee will state the conditions on which a certificate will be issued and the applicant if he accepts these must choose a solicitor from the panel.

Costs. Apart from his liability to a contribution, if any, to the Legal Aid Fund an assisted person has no further liability to his lawyer for costs. But if he is unsuccessful in his action, he may have to pay the other side's costs, limited to what is a reasonable amount for him to pay, bearing in mind the means of the parties and their conduct in the proceedings.

If the assisted person is awarded costs, these are paid into the Legal Aid Fund. The Fund also has a first charge on property recovered or preserved in the proceedings if these costs and the assisted person's contribution exceed the amount paid to his lawyer.

If the unassisted party loses his case he will have to pay full costs. If he wins, s. 13 of the 1974 Act provides that he may be awarded a part or the whole of his costs out of the Fund provided that (1) the proceedings are decided in his favour, (2) they were begun at first instance by the assisted party and (3) the court is satisfied that the unassisted party will suffer serious financial hardship unless the order is made.

In cases where both parties are legally aided the court may make such order as it thinks fit in the circumstances of the case.

Legal Aid in Criminal Proceedings

Application is usually made to the trial court, which before making an order must have a written statement of means from the applicant. Assessment of means and contribution may be made after the order has been made.

Legal aid must be granted where desirable in the interests of justice, particularly in the case of serious crimes.

Curiously, in appeals to or from a Queen's Bench Divisional Court application is to the Area Committee.

As regards appearances before the Crown Court, an order may be made either by that court or the magistrates' court.

Legal aid in criminal cases will cover advice and representation by a solicitor or a barrister, except in magistrates' courts where normally only representation by a solicitor is covered.

After the trial the Court may order an assisted person to pay such contribution as seems reasonable in the circumstances.

Law Centres. Law Centres are local centres, with solicitors employed on a full-time basis, who will handle free of charge a person's case from start to finish, including representation in court or at a tribunal, if necessary. There are 14 in London, distributed in the Boroughs, and there are 3 outside London in Birmingham, Cardiff and Manchester. Finance for the centres is provided by local authorities and through the Government's Urban Aid Programme for areas in special need. Some are staffed with community social workers to deal with special social problems best settled through social or community means rather than by legal action.

Legal Advice Centres. These centres are for the giving of advice. If the applicant needs further help he will be advised where to go, e.g. to a solicitor operating under the Legal Aid Scheme who will be able to devote adequate time to the applicant's case. There are about 40 legal advice centres in London, and about 50 outside London. Some operate in conjunction with the Citizens' Advice Bureau.

10. Laymen in the Courts

As to administration of the law today, we may note particularly the part played by laymen (*a*) as justices of the peace, (*b*) as jurors, and (*c*) as lay assessors who assist a professional judge or lawyer acting judicially in the special courts and administrative tribunals already described.

(*a*) **Justices of the Peace.** A description of the composition of the magistrates' courts and Crown Courts has already been given. All we need to note here is that there are some 21,500 lay justices regularly adjudicating on a wide variety of matters and performing numerous administrative duties. These justices deal with more than 98 per cent of the criminal cases in Britain.

Lay justices appointed after 1 January 1966, are required to undergo training in the basic duties of their office. This does not render them lawyers, but assists them in understanding the meaning of 'acting judicially' so that they may more efficiently administer justice to the local people, from whose numbers they are drawn and whose public interests they serve.

(*b*) **Juries.** A detailed description of the different kinds of juries is given on p. 74. We should bear in mind that juries are composed of laymen on whose shoulders rests the final determination of verdicts in criminal cases.

(*c*) **Lay Assessors in Special Courts.** Examples of this form of participation are found in:

(i) *The Admiralty Court of the Queen's Bench Division.* This is presided over by a High Court judge with jurisdiction to decide shipping disputes, collisions at sea, etc. There is no jury, but in suitable cases (e.g. negligent navigation) the judge may call on the assistance of two nautical assessors (Elder Brethren of Trinity House) who are competent to advise on technical maritime matters.

(ii) *The Restrictive Practices Court.* The jurisdiction of this court has been dealt with on p. 62. It is a superior Court of Record and is composed of professional judges and men experienced in commerce and business. Each court sits with a High Court judge and two laymen.

(iii) *Administrative Tribunals.* These have an increasingly important part to play in the lives of all people, and mention may be made of Rent Tribunals, National Insurance Tribunals, National Insurance Industrial Injuries Tribunals, Pensions Tribunals, National Health Service Tribunals, Transport Tribunals, and those of the Area Traffic Commissioners.

Although the constitution of each may vary in detail, the common factor is the presence of laymen, usually drawn from bodies such as local authorities, employers' organizations and employees' organizations. Usually the chairmen are legally qualified (Tribunals and Inquiries Act, 1971), but the presence of the laymen ensures that tribunals have the benefit of industrial or other experience.

11. Exercises

1. Outline the jurisdiction of the civil courts.
2. Describe the system of appeal in criminal cases.
3. Describe the composition and jurisdiction of: (*a*) county courts and (*b*) magistrates' courts.
4. What are the main duties of a coroner? What qualifications must he possess, and by whom is he appointed?
5. What is the importance of the Tribunals and Inquiries Act, 1971, and what are its main provisions?

6. What part does a jury play in a court of law? What are (i) the advantages and (ii) the disadvantages of jury trial?
7. Give an account of legal aid and advice. Deal with its history and describe its operation today in the English legal system.
8. A party to arbitration proceedings considers the arbitrator has wrongly applied the law. Advise the party how an appeal may be made and to whom.

5

THE JUDICIARY, LAW OFFICERS AND THE LEGAL PROFESSION

1. The Lord Chancellor

The Lord High Chancellor of Great Britain, more usually known as the Lord Chancellor, ranks eighth in order of precedence in England after the Queen: a status which reflects his importance as a Minister of the Crown chiefly responsible for the administration of justice.

The Lord Chancellor is appointed by the Queen on the advice of the Prime Minister. His position combines duties which are legislative, executive, and judicial: it is therefore an exception to the constitutional doctrine of the 'Separation of Powers'.

In his legislative capacity the Lord Chancellor presides over the House of Lords. He may take part in its debates and can vote in all of its divisions.

In his executive capacity he is a member of the Cabinet, its chief legal and constitutional adviser and one of its representatives in the House of Lords. He is responsible for the custody and use of the Great Seal, which authenticates important legal documents such as Letters Patent.

In his judicial capacity the Lord Chancellor is head of the Judiciary, and presides over the House of Lords sitting as a court of appeal. He is a member of the Judicial Committee of the Privy Council, is head of the Chancery Division of the High Court and a member of the Court of Appeal. However, he never sits as a judge other than in the House of Lords and the Judicial Committee of the Privy Council. He advises the Queen on the appointment of puisne judges of the High Court, circuit judges and recorders; and appoints magistrates and the chairmen of certain administrative tribunals.

2. Judges

(*a*) **The Lord Chief Justice** (L.C.J.) is appointed by the Queen on the advice of the Prime Minister. He is head of the Court of Appeal (Criminal Division) and of the Queen's Bench Division. He is a member of the House of Lords.

(*b*) **The Master of the Rolls** (M.R.) is appointed by the Queen on the advice of the Prime Minister. He is head of the Court of Appeal (Civil Division). He supervises the admission of solicitors to the Rolls of the Supreme Court.

(*c*) **The President of the Family Division** is appointed by the Queen on the advice of the Prime Minister, and is responsible for the work of this Division of the High Court.

(*d*) **The Lords of Appeal in Ordinary** are known as Law Lords and are appointed by the Queen on the advice of the Prime Minister from among existing judges or barristers of at least fifteen years' standing. They are life peers and adjudicate in appeal cases heard in the House of Lords. They are also members of the Judicial Committee of the Privy Council. There are nine Law Lords.

(*e*) **Lords Justice of Appeal** are appointed by the Queen on the advice of the Prime Minister from among existing judges or barristers of at least fifteen years' standing. They are judges of the Court of Appeal. They are twenty-three in number.

(*f*) **Judges of the High Court** are known as puisne judges and are appointed by the Queen on the recommendation of the Lord Chancellor from among barristers of at least ten years' standing. Twelve judges are assigned to the Chancery Division, forty-five to the Queen's Bench Division and sixteen to the Family Division of the High Court.

All the judges referred to in (*a*) to (*f*) above hold office 'during good behaviour' and may be removed by the Crown on an address presented by both Houses of Parliament. Their salaries are fixed by statute and form a charge on the Consolidated Fund. The effect of these two important provisions is to ensure judicial independence: a vital feature in the administration of law and justice within the State.

Judges of the High Court retire at the age of 75, and are eligible for pensions granted by statute.

(*g*) **Circuit Judges.** These are judges appointed by the Queen on the advice of the Lord Chancellor to serve in (1) the Crown Court (see p. 54, and (2) county courts (see p. 51). A circuit judge must be a barrister of 10 years' standing or a person who has held the office of a recorder (see below) for 5 years. The retiring age is 72, with the possibility of extension to 75. All county court judges who existed in 1971 became circuit judges, as did the recorders of Liverpool and Manchester, a number of whole-time chairmen and deputy chairmen of Quarter Sessions and certain other holders of judicial offices. (Courts Act, 1971.)

(*h*) **Recorders.** Under the Courts Act, 1971 these are designated *part-time* judges of the Crown Court. Appointments are made by the Queen on the recommendation of the Lord Chancellor to men of standing who are prepared to commit themselves to not less than one month's work on the bench each year. Barristers and solicitors of 10 years' standing are eligible for appointment to this office. If a solicitor holds the appointment for 5 years he may then be appointed a circuit judge (see above).

3. Attorney-General and Solicitor-General

Together these are known as Law Officers. Both are appointed by the Prime Minister. They are political appointments, and the holders are precluded from private practice while holding office.

(*a*) **The Attorney-General** is a member of the House of Commons (not cabinet rank). His duties comprise the following:

(i) He represents the Crown in the courts in civil matters where the public interest is concerned, and may prosecute in important and difficult cases in the criminal courts.

(ii) He advises the Cabinet and Government departments on important legal matters and may take part in many judicial and quasi-judicial proceedings affecting the public interest, e.g. the administration of charities and patent law.

(iii) Certain criminal offences must be reported to the Attorney-General, and his consent is necessary before criminal proceedings may be taken in certain cases, e.g. bribery, incest, corrupt practices, and offences against the Official Secrets Act, 1911 and 1939, the Dangerous Drugs Acts, the Public Order Act, 1936, and various other Acts. He is head of the English Bar.

(*b*) **The Solicitor-General** is deputy to the Attorney-General and his duties are similar. He is a barrister and is a member of the House of Commons. By the Law Officers Act, 1944, any functions authorized or required to be discharged by the Attorney-General may, unless expressly excluded, be discharged by the Solicitor-General if the Office of Attorney-General is vacant, if the Attorney-General is absent or ill, or if the Attorney-General authorizes his deputy to act in any particular case.

4. Masters

Masters of the Supreme Court are salaried officials, lawyers of at least ten years' standing, attached either to the Queen's Bench Division or to the Chancery Division of the High Court.

Masters of the Queen's Bench Division adjudicate on all matters preliminary to a trial. These preliminaries are known as 'interlocutory matters'. Thus one party may wish to inspect documents in the possession of his opponent, or one party may wish to put questions to his opponent to clarify certain points in issue. In these circumstances application may be made to a master for an order for discovery or an order for interrogatories commanding the opponent to produce the required documents or to answer on oath written questions. Disputes may arise as to the most convenient time or place of trial, or whether the trial should be with or without a jury. Such disputes may be decided by a master, from whose decision appeal lies to a judge in chambers. They are appointed from barristers.

Chancery Division Masters perform similar work in their Division of the High Court. They are appointed from among solicitors.

Taxing Masters are officers of the Supreme Court whose function is the checking, determining, and levying of costs to be paid by parties to the trial when the court so directs.

5. Director of Public Prosecutions

The office of the Director of Public Prosecutions is governed by the Prosecution of Offences Act, 1985. The Director must be a barrister or solicitor of at least ten years' standing. He is an official appointed by the Attorney General and is responsible for the Crown Prosecution Service. This service, set up under the 1985 Act, is staffed by barristers and solicitors, certain of whom are designated Crown Prosecutors and Chief Crown Prosecutors (who are responsible for the service in each area in England and Wales).

The Director, in his capacity as head of the Service, is responsible for all criminal proceedings on behalf of the police (other than minor criminal offences). He must also conduct all binding-over proceedings instigated on behalf of the police force and any other proceedings where, because of the importance, difficulty or otherwise of the case, he considers it necessary.

The Legal Profession

There are two branches of the legal profession in Britain: (i) barristers and (ii) solicitors of the Supreme Court. In most other countries, including some parts of the Commonwealth, there is no such division.

6. Solicitors

The modern solicitor is the successor of three former ancient professions known as attorney (or representative), solicitor, and proctor. These assisted judges in the King's Bench in the early stages of litigation or carried out the less skilled work in the ecclesiastical and Admiralty courts. By a succession of Solicitors Acts, 1939 to 1974, the profession has been unified and regulated (the 1974 Act consolidates the law).

The regulations of the Law Society provide for:

(i) the scales of remuneration and fees of solicitors;
(ii) the terms and conditions of articles of clerkship for new entrants;
(iii) courses for the education and training of students;
(iv) the conduct of examinations;
(v) the discipline of all solicitors.

A person who has served articles (from 2–4 years) to a solicitor, and who passes the examinations of the Law Society, may be admitted a solicitor by having his name enrolled. He thereby becomes an officer of the Supreme Court, and receives his Certificate to Practise which is renewable annually. As from 1 October 1984 solicitors are permitted to advertise on certain terms and also advertise properties for sale.

Duties of a Solicitor. Most solicitors are employed in private practice, either alone or in a partnership firm, with the right to incorporate with limited or unlimited liability. Others are employed in the public service, industry, and commerce.

Practising solicitors are consulted by, and receive instructions from, lay clients on a wide variety of matters both civil and criminal, e.g. the making of wills, administration of estates, family matters, the formation of companies, drawing up of documents, conveyancing, and criminal offences of all kinds. In cases of unusual difficulty or where a trial is to take place in the superior courts, the solicitor takes his instructions from the client, prepares a brief and approaches a barrister (counsel) to give an 'opinion' or represent the client at the trial.

Solicitors have a right of audience only in the magistrates' courts, county courts with limited rights of audience in the Crown Court and the Supreme Court.

The relationship between solicitor and client is based on professional confidence, and a solicitor cannot be compelled to disclose in court communications made in a professional relationship. Nor is a solicitor liable for defamation in respect of statements made in court during the course of a trial. A solicitor is, however, liable to be sued for damages for negligence in the conduct of his profession: e.g. where he has carelessly lost documents entrusted to him. In certain situations it has also been held that a solicitor might owe a duty of care in tort to a third party (*Ross* v. *Caunters*, 1980 and *Al-Kandari* v. *J. R. Brown & Co.*, 1987).

7. Barristers

Anyone wishing to become a barrister must join one of the four Inns of Court: Gray's Inn, Lincoln's Inn, Inner Temple, or Middle Temple. These four Inns of Court are unincorporated bodies of medieval origin, owned and controlled by their senior members called the Masters of the Bench.

The Senate of the Inns of Court and the Bar, formed in 1974, can be regarded as the governing body of the Bar today, since the Inns follow the general policy laid down by the Senate and the judges have agreed that disciplinary powers shall be exercised in accordance with the Senate's regulations.

Each intending barrister must make a certain number of attendances (known as 'keeping terms') at his Inn, and to qualify for Call to the Bar he must pass the examinations conducted by the Council of Legal

Education. After passing the examinations a barrister intending to practise must undertake one year's pupillage in chambers. After six months he has the right of audience in any court of law in England and Wales. As noted above, he may take instructions only from a solicitor, not from a lay client direct. Unlike the solicitor, he may not sue for his fees and is not liable in negligence in the conduct of a case. (See p. 226.)

Duties of a Barrister. A barrister intending to practise must choose in which part of the law he intends to specialize. A barrister is essentially an advocate whose task is to present his client's case effectively in court. His work includes the drafting of opinions on difficult points of law, the settling of pleadings and advice on evidence and procedural matters.

The difference between the two branches of the profession may be summarized as follows:

(*a*) Barristers are advocates; solicitors are not necessarily so.

(*b*) Barristers have the right of audience in all courts; solicitors have only a limited right.

(*c*) Barristers specialize in certain branches of the law; solicitors tend not to do so but to be general practitioners.

(*d*) Barristers deal with legal matters; solicitors may be consulted about many non-legal matters, e.g. family, business or financial matters.

(*e*) Barristers are instructed by solicitors, who are instructed by the lay client.

(*f*) Barristers cannot sue for their fees; solicitors can.

(*g*) Barristers may not be liable for negligence in the conduct of a case; solicitors may.

(*h*) Solicitors are controlled under the Solicitors Acts, 1839–1974; barristers are controlled by their Inns of Court and the recently established Senate, non-statutory bodies.

8. Queen's Counsel

When a barrister has acquired a substantial practice, he may apply to the Lord Chancellor to 'take silk', i.e. become a Queen's Counsel. If the applicant's request is granted, letters patent are issued and he will then be called 'within the bar' thus relinquishing his former status of 'outer' or 'utter' barrister. Henceforth he wears a silk gown.

By his new status the successful applicant will expect to attract more important cases and to command higher fees. He will no longer draft pleadings, conveyances, or similar documents. Thenceforward he will have the assistance of junior counsel who will be briefed with him. A Queen's Counsel is distinguished by the letters Q.C. after his name, and is referred to as a 'Leader'.

9. Licensed Conveyancers

A licensed conveyancer is authorized to carry out the legal formalities relating to the transfer of land (Administration of Justice Act, 1985).

The governing body of licensed conveyancers is the Council for Licensed Conveyancers who are responsible for making and enforcing rules on conduct and discipline, including accounts rules. The Council is also responsible for the licensing of conveyancers, the first licence being granted on 1 May 1987

Licensed conveyancers are permitted to practise in partnership with each other, or in partnership or association with non-licensed conveyancers (but not with solicitors). In addition to this, licensed conveyancers may practise through the medium of a 'recognized body', which means a body corporate recognized by the Council for Licensed Conveyancers.

10. Exercises

1. Describe (*a*) the appointment of, and (*b*) the duties performed by, each of the following:

(i) The Lord Chancellor
(ii) The Lord Chief Justice
(iii) The Master of the Rolls
(iv) Circuit Judges.

2. Discuss the appointment and functions of the Law Officers of the Crown.
3. What are the functions of (i) Masters of the Supreme Court and (ii) the Director of Public Prosecutions?
4. Describe the duties of (i) solicitors and (ii) barristers. Is the division of the legal profession justifiable and necessary today?

6

OUTLINE OF THE LAW OF PERSONS

All human beings are 'persons' under English law. One of the most important concepts of English law is that all persons within the realm, including aliens, have rights and are subject to certain duties.

1. Legal Persons

This state of affairs is not universal. A slave in early Roman and Anglo-Saxon times, for example, had no rights. He was regarded as a chattel: a thing to be owned and used or even killed at the will of his master or owner. A slave had, in law, no 'legal personality'. Similarly in early Norman times a criminal could be declared an outlaw: someone outside the law's protection whom any man could kill with impunity. In early times also, animals which had 'misbehaved' by attacking humans or cattle were sometimes hanged. In the East gods and idols were offered gifts or appeased in some way as if they were persons. Whether a human being or some other creation is a 'legal person' depends, therefore, on the law of the state where that being or creature is.

In English law legal personality generally attaches to a human being at birth and ends at death. Although certain parts of the criminal law recognize and protect the existence of a child not yet 'in being', e.g. it is an offence to commit abortion or child destruction (which means unlawfully causing the death of a child before it has an existence independent of the mother), this does not necessarily attribute legal personality to the unborn infant.

Death puts an end to both the physical and legal personality. For example, the defamation of a deceased person is not actionable in English law by his personal representatives or near relations.

So far we have been dealing with human beings. We shall later discuss a different kind of legal person, the corporation, which is an artificial or juristic person, created by law, with a legal personality distinct from the individual persons who control the corporation.

2. Nationality and Domicile

By a person's nationality we mean his status as a citizen or member of a particular state to which he owes allegiance. Apart from stateless persons everyone is the subject of some state to which he owes political allegiance and loyalty, for which he may be called upon to fight, pay taxes and support, and from which he may expect protection. These are broad general statements only. For instance, although we say that all persons must be national subjects of some state or other, we know that due to upheavals of war there are some unfortunate 'stateless' persons who have been disowned by, or expelled from, their country of birth and origin.

Nationality is of great importance in the field of public law. Thus, British subjects enjoy universal franchise, i.e. the right to vote at local and Parliamentary elections. Aliens in Great Britain have no such right. They are subject to certain restrictions concerning entry into the United Kingdom and employment after entry; furthermore they must register certain particulars with the police.

Apart from these requirements, English law treats aliens in much the same way as ordinary British subjects: for example, they are subject to the same rules of criminal law and the same laws of tort and contract. Special disabilities or restrictions will be mentioned later. Here we may note that an alien may not own, or become part-owner of, a British ship registered at a British port and sailing under the British flag.

In the following pages we shall deal with the acquisition of British nationality and the allied question of domicile, which is becoming increasingly important as travel makes it easier for people to move from one country to another.

British Nationality

The British Nationality Act, 1981, which replaces the 1948 Act, divides citizenship into three classes:

(i) British citizenship.

(ii) British Dependent Territories citizenship, conferred upon citizens of a number of specified countries, e.g. Bermuda, Hong Kong.

(iii) British Overseas citizenship—a residual category.

British citizenship may be acquired in the following ways:

(i) *By Birth* in the United Kingdom to a parent who is a British citizen or who is settled in the United Kingdom, or who becomes a British citizen or becomes settled in the United Kingdom.

(ii) *By Adoption* under an order made by any court in the United Kingdom authorizing the adoption of a minor who is not a British citizen.

(iii) *By Descent:* i.e. birth outside the United Kingdom to a parent who is a British citizen by birth, adoption, registration or naturalization (not by descent).

(iv) *By Registration.* Any minor may apply for British citizenship, which is granted at the Home Secretary's discretion. Persons who are British Dependent Territories citizens, or British Overseas citizens or British subjects or British protected persons may apply after satisfying periods of residence in the United Kingdom. There is a special entitlement for British Dependent citizens who are nationals of the United Kingdom for the purposes of the EEC (in practice, Gibraltarians).

(v) *By Naturalization.* Any person may apply to the Secretary of State for a certificate of naturalization. The conditions of grant (which is at the discretion of the Home Secretary) are that the applicant must be of full age and capacity, of good character, have sufficient knowledge of the English, Welsh or Scottish Gaelic language, and have satisfied residence requirements and intend that the United Kingdom will be their home or their principal home.

(vi) *By Marriage.* An alien woman who immediately before commencement of the Act was the wife of a citizen of the United Kingdom and Colonies may acquire British citizenship if she chooses to do so by registration as in (iii) above within five years provided the marriage subsists.

Loss of Nationality

British citizenship may be lost by

(i) *Renunciation.* This is effected by a person of full age and capacity making a declaration of renunciation, which must be registered with the Home Secretary. Any person who has married is deemed to be of full age. A person who has renounced British citizenship in order to retain or acquire some other citizenship or nationality may resume it but this right can only be exercised once.

(ii) *Deprivation.* This applies *only* to citizens who acquired citizenship by naturalization or by registration, and may be ordered by the Home Secretary for serious misconduct, e.g. criminal acts.

British Protected Persons

So far we have been dealing with British citizens and aliens. A third group of persons, known as British Protected Persons, must be mentioned. These are members of those territories described as Protectorates, Protected States or Mandated or Trust Territories and declared as such by an Order in Council.

Aliens

All persons other than Commonwealth citizens, British protected persons and citizens of the Republic of Ireland are aliens. The following general restrictions apply to an alien:

(i) He may not vote at local or Parliamentary elections.

(ii) He may not become a Member of Parliament.

(iii) He may not work in the United Kingdom unless specially permitted.

(iv) He must register with the police and notify changes of address to them.

(v) He is liable to deportation if he engages in crime.

Domicile

Domicile is a concept distinct from nationality. Thus a person may be a British subject and yet be domiciled, for example, in France.

The concept of domicile, under English law, involves two elements: (i) actual residence; and (ii) *animus manendi*, i.e. the intention to remain in that place or country. Where these two elements co-exist a person is said to have a domicile in that country.

Whereas nationality implies a political relation existing between a person and the state to which he owes allegiance, domicile determines important civil rights and obligations which will be discussed later.

First we must note that under English law it is an inflexible rule that (i) every person must possess a domicile, and (ii) no person can have more than one domicile.

There are three classes of domicile:

(*a*) *Domicile of origin.* This domicile attaches at birth. A legitimate child takes the domicile of the father; an illegitimate child that of its mother. A foundling (deserted infant without known parents) acquires the domicile of the place where found.

A domicile of origin cannot be entirely lost or extinguished. If a person with a 'domicile of choice' (see later) abandons his present domicile, the domicile of origin revives and attaches to him until he acquires a new domicile.

(*b*) *Domicile of choice.* Where a person of full age and capacity establishes his home in a country with the intention of remaining there permanently (such country being different from his last domicile), he is regarded as acquiring a domicile of choice.

(*c*) *Domicile of Dependent Persons.* (i) A minor takes the domicile of his parent, as at (*a*) above. A child may take his mother's domicile instead of his father's where the spouses are separated and the child makes his home with his mother. (ii) A woman who marries normally acquires her husband's domicile immediately on marriage. However, under the Domicile and Matrimonial Proceedings Act, 1973, a married woman is now capable of acquiring a domicile independent of her husband. This statute also states that a person is capable of acquiring an independent domicile when he attains the age of sixteen.

The above represent the main rules regarding the concept of domicile in English law. The law of domicile is important in regard to the following matters:

(*a*) *Jurisdiction in Divorce.* For example, Atkins, a British subject domiciled in Nevada, U.S.A., is granted a divorce by the Divorce

Court in Nevada on the grounds of 'incompatibility of temperament'. The divorce is recognized in English law even though the grounds are much less than those required to sustain a divorce in England.

(*b*) *Validity of Wills of Movable Property and the distribution of such property on an intestacy.* For example, Brown, a British subject domiciled in Ruritania, makes a will attested by one witness. English law requires two witnesses to a will, whereas the law of Ruritania requires one witness only. Brown's will is regarded as valid in English law because it complies with the law of the domicile.

(*c*) *Legitimation.* This is discussed on p. 96.

(*d*) *The Essential Validity of Marriage.* The 'essential validity' includes the form of celebration, age of parties, etc. It is possible for an English court to decide that a marriage contracted without the form required in England is valid because it complies with the law of the domicile.

Proof of Domicile. The English court decides the question of domicile by applying English law, taking account of the *intention* of the party. Evidence of intention may include correspondence, oral or written declarations, the purchase of a house, or even a grave. Inquiry by the English court may range over the whole of a person's life to enable the court to establish where a domicile has been acquired.

3. Marriage

The legal view of marriage is that it is a contract between two persons. Because it fundamentally affects the status of each of the contracting parties and imposes rights and obligations of a special kind, marriage is accorded a particular importance legally as well as socially.

Lord Penzance defined marriage as *the voluntary union for life of one man and one woman to the exclusion of all others* (*Hyde* v. *Hyde*, 1866).

It follows from the above definition that forcible marriage and marriage by deceit or by mistake must be void. Deceit means misrepresentation of the essential nature of the transaction; mistake means an essential mistake, e.g. the identity of the other party, or the ceremony itself. The free and voluntary consent of the parties is essential.

Capacity to Marry. A person domiciled in England or Wales must comply with English law as to capacity to marry. The requirements are that at the time of the marriage neither party must be (i) under 16 years of age, (ii) already married, (iii) certified of unsound mind, or (iv) within the 'prohibited degrees'.

The 'prohibited degrees' means close members of the family, e.g. brother and sister, set out in the first schedule to the Marriage Act, 1949 as amended. Under the Marriage (Enabling) Act, 1960, it is now lawful to contract a marriage with a sister, aunt or niece of a former wife (living or dead).

A marriage under English law may be contracted either (*a*) according to the rites of the Church of England, or (*b*) under a certificate of a Superintendent Registrar.

(*a*) **Marriage by the Church of England** may be solemnized provided that the following requirements have been complied with:

(i) *Banns* have been published, or

(ii) a *Special Licence* has been issued by the Archbishop of Canterbury under special circumstances, or

(iii) a *Common Licence* has been issued by a bishop (or his surrogate, i.e. deputy) for the marriage of persons residing within his diocese within three months of the issue of such licence, or

(iv) a *Certificate* has been issued by a Superintendent Registrar.

The publication of banns means an announcement made by a priest on three Sundays preceding the solemnization of the marriage. Where the parties to the marriage reside in different parishes the banns must be published in the parish churches of both. Otherwise they may be published in the parish church within the parish where both reside.

The marriage must be solemnized by a clergyman of the Church of England in the presence of two witnesses.

(*b*) **Marriage under a Certificate of a Superintendent Registrar.** The following marriages may be solemnized on the authority of a Superintendent Registrar's certificate:

(i) A marriage in a registered building (e.g. a non-conformist church registered for the solemnization of marriages therein).

(ii) A marriage in a register office (i.e. the office of a Superintendent Registrar).

(iii) A marriage according to the usages of the Society of Friends (commonly called Quakers).

(iv) A marriage between two persons professing the Jewish religion according to the usages of the Jews.

(v) A marriage according to the rites of the Church of England.

In all these cases the marriage must take place in the register office or in 'a building which is registered for the purpose' (except that the Marriage Act, 1983, provides for marriages of house-bound and detained persons to be solemnized at the place where they reside). Such buildings inside a Roman Catholic church, a church of one of the non-established denominations (e.g. the Congregational Church), a meeting house of the Society of Friends, a synagogue of the Jewish community. A further requirement is that only 'an authorized person' may solemnize the marriage. Such a person is usually the minister or other official of the building wherein the marriage is solemnized, or the Superintendent Registrar.

Two witnesses must be present at the ceremony, and the building must remain open throughout the proceedings to allow public access. The permitted times of marriage in a 'registered building' or in a register office are between 8 a.m. and 6 p.m.

As well as valid marriages, we need to consider marriages that are either void or voidable.

Void Marriages are those destitute of legal effect. By the Matrimonial Causes Act, 1973, a marriage after July 31, 1971, is void if:

(i) The parties are within the prohibited degrees (see p. 92).
(ii) Either party is under 16.
(iii) Certain formal requirements are not complied with (e.g. marriage took place elsewhere than in a registered building).
(iv) Either party is already legally married.
(v) Parties are not respectively male and female.
(vi) In the case of polygamous marriages entered into outside England and Wales, either party was at the time of the marriage domiciled in England and Wales.

A declaration of nullity by the High Court will have effect *ab initio*, i.e. from the date of 'celebration'.

Voidable Marriages are valid until they are declared void by a competent court. The Matrimonial Causes Act, 1973, provides that a marriage taking place after July 31, 1971, is voidable if:

(i) It has not been consummated owing to incapacity of either party.
(ii) There is wilful refusal to consummate the marriage by the respondent.
(iii) Either party did not validly consent, whether by duress, mistake, unsoundness of mind or otherwise.
(iv) Either party was suffering from mental disorder within the meaning of the Mental Health Act, 1959, of such a kind or to such extent as to be unfit for marriage.
(v) The respondent was at the time of the marriage suffering from venereal disease in a communicable form.
(vi) The respondent was at the time of the marriage pregnant by another man.

Proceedings in respect of (iii), (iv), (v) and (vi) must be taken within 3 years of the date of the marriage. The court has a discretion to refuse a petition brought under (i) to (vi) if it would be unjust to the respondent spouse.

Any child born of a voidable marriage is legitimate irrespective of the fact that the marriage is subsequently annulled.

4. Divorce

Under the Matrimonial Causes Act, 1973 (as amended), a consolidating Act, it is provided that the sole ground on which a petition for divorce may be presented to the court shall be that the marriage has **broken down irretrievably**. To establish this the petitioner must satisfy the court on one or more of the following grounds:

(i) The respondent has committed adultery and the petitioner finds it intolerable to live with the respondent.

(ii) The respondent has behaved in such a way that the petitioner cannot reasonably be expected to live with the respondent.

(iii) The respondent has deserted the petitioner for a continuous period of at least two years immediately preceding the presentation of the petition.

(iv) The parties to the marriage have lived apart for a continuous period of at least two years immediately preceding the presentation of the petition and the respondent consents to a decree being granted.

(v) The parties to the marriage have lived apart for a continuous period of at least five years immediately preceding the presentation of the petition.

A divorce petition cannot normally be presented within three years of the marriage. (There is an absolute bar during the first year of marriage.)

The Act contains provisions designed to encourage reconciliation of the parties, but where this is impossible and divorce is granted the court has wide powers to order financial relief for either party (see Appendix Seven).

Presumption of Death. A person who can show good grounds for believing his or her spouse to be dead may apply to the Family Division of the High Court for an order to presume death, and to dissolve the marriage. Continuous absence for a period of seven years, provided that the petitioner has no reason to believe the absent spouse to have been alive within that time, is accepted as *prima facie* evidence that the absent spouse is dead.

Judicial Separation. This is an order of the courts which absolves the parties from their duty of cohabitation, i.e. living together as man and wife. Whereas divorce dissolves the marriage tie, judicial separation does not. The court may still order financial relief.

5. Domestic Proceedings in Magistrates' Courts

Magistrates' courts exercise certain jurisdiction in regard to married persons, and may make orders for (i) the protection of the spouses, (ii) the maintenance of spouses and children of the family, and (iii) the custody of such children. Formerly orders to provide maintenance could only be made against the husband, since he was traditionally regarded as the breadwinner. Since 1960, an order may be made against the wife to provide maintenance in certain circumstances for the husband and children of the family. The Domestic Proceedings and

Magistrates' Courts Act, 1978, has replaced the 1960 Act.

Domestic proceedings are, as far as possible, separated from the other business of the court. The proceedings are not open to the public, and Press reports are limited to minimum details (Magistrates' Courts Acts, 1952). The court must contain not more than three justices, including one man and one woman.

6. Legitimation

A child born illegitimate becomes legitimate if his parents subsequently marry. By the Legitimacy Act, 1926, an illegitimate person is legitimated by the marriage of his parents provided that at the date of the marriage (i) the illegitimate person is alive and (ii) the father is domiciled in England and Wales.

The Legitimacy Act, 1959, further provides that it shall be no bar to legitimation that either of the parents was married to a third party at the time of the birth of the child. For example, *A* and *B* are married. *B* conceives a child (*L*) by *Z*. *A* then divorces *B*, who thereupon marries *Z*. The child *L* will be legitimated from the date of the subsequent marriage of *B* and *Z*.

The legal effect is that the legitimated child is treated in nearly all respects as though he were legitimate or a lawful child. Should the parents die intestate, the legitimated child will succeed to their property. Moreover, he will have the same rights of maintenance by parents as a lawful child.

7. Adoption

The present law is contained in the Adoption Act, 1958, the Children Act, 1975, and the Adoption Act, 1976.

The Effect of Adoption. An adoption order made by a court extinguishes the rights, duties and obligations of the natural parents or guardian and vests them in adopters. On adoption the child is deemed to be the legitimate child of its adoptive parents to the exclusion, with minor exceptions, of all its former ties. The adopted child has the same rights of inheritance under wills, deeds and intestacies (unless the adopted child is expressly excluded) as natural children born in wedlock to the adopters. Titles of honour are, however, excepted.

A person is eligible for adoption at any age under 18, provided he or she is unmarried. In practice about 90 per cent of all adoptions are of children under 10.

Who may Adopt? A married couple, domiciled in the U.K., may adopt jointly. Otherwise adoption by more than one person is not allowed. The applicant or one of the joint applicants for an adoption must (*a*) have attained the age of 25, or (*b*) have attained the age of 21 and be a relative, e.g. grandparent, brother, sister, uncle or aunt, or (*c*) be the mother or father of the infant, e.g. with an illegitimate child. Under the Adoption Act, 1958, a man cannot be the sole adopter of a girl, except in special circumstances.

Procedure. The following are the competent courts, each having jurisdiction: the High Court, the county court, and the magistrates' court. The court has to be satisfied that

(*a*) the adoptive parents are suitable;

(*b*) the consent of the natural parent(s) has been obtained;

(*c*) the consent of the other of two spouses, one of whom makes the application to adopt, has been obtained.

The court may dispense with the natural parent's consent if, for example, the parent has abandoned the child, or has persistently ill-treated the child or has seriously ill-treated the child and it is unlikely that the child will be able to live with such parent, or is unreasonably withholding consent. Such consent of the natural parents may also be dispensed with where they have already indicated that they would consent to a custodianship order being made.

The court's first consideration is to safeguard and promote the welfare of the child, whose wishes and feelings (having regard to his age and understanding) must also be taken into account. So far as practicable, the court must consider the natural parents' religious preferences before placing a child for adoption.

8. Guardianship

Guardianship is the relationship existing between an infant (known as a ward) and some person who has the right of control over him and of ensuring his maintenance, education, and welfare.

Such powers are, of course, normally exercised by parents who have a duty to provide care, protection, and control. Where, however, either or both parents are deceased, or unable or unwilling to exercise these powers and duties, the question of appointing a successor in the form of a guardian will arise. Every infant must have some adult to safeguard his interests.

By the Guardianship of Minors Acts, 1971 and 1973, the father and mother are equally entitled to care and custody of their infant children; if either parent dies, the duties devolve on the survivor. Where a dispute arises, or divorce proceedings occur, an application may be made to the court. The court will examine the circumstances and determine the matter of guardianship, bearing in mind that the *paramount consideration is the welfare of the infant.*

Appointment of Guardians. Guardians may be appointed by:

(*a*) A deed or will of a parent (Guardianship of Minors Act, 1971).

(*b*) The High Court, county courts, and magistrates' courts, where no guardian has been appointed by deed or will and the infant has no parent, guardian or other person exercising control over him.

Where an infant or minor has been made a *ward of court* (which may result where both parents are dead or divorced) all important decisions affecting the child, such as his upbringing, property, investments, etc. may only be made by authority of the court, usually the Family Division. Other incidents of wardship are:

(i) The court may appoint any person to be guardian. Thus a parent can be appointed 'guardian' but would act under the control of the court.

(ii) Interference with a ward or a guardian amounts to contempt of court, punishable by imprisonment.

(iii) A ward may not marry or leave the country without the consent of the court.

(iv) A ward who refuses to carry out a direction of the court may be punished for contempt of court.

9. Illegitimacy

A child born during wedlock is *prima facie* legitimate. Similarly a child born within the normal time after the termination of a marriage by the death of the husband or by divorce is presumed legitimate.

A child will only be illegitimate when the mother does not marry the father. If the mother does, however, marry the father following the birth of the child, the child may be *legitimated* (see p. 96).

If the mother marries some other person, the mother and the husband may in such a case jointly adopt the mother's illegitimate child, although her husband will be bound to maintain the child and can claim custody as a 'child of the family'.

Custody and Maintenance. An illegitimate child is in the custody of its mother, and the mother is bound to maintain him until the age of 16. The putative father, as he is generally called, is under no legal obligation to provide for the child except when an *affiliation order* has been made against him by a magistrates' court. If so ordered, the putative father is liable to maintain the child until the age of 16, although it may be extended beyond 16 if the child needs further education or training.

Property Rights. Where either parent of an illegitimate child dies intestate in respect of either real or personal property, the illegitimate child enjoys the same rights of succession as if he had been born legitimate. Moreover, where an illegitimate child dies intestate, each of his parents can 'take any interest in the child's property to which that parent would have been entitled if the child had been born legitimate' (Family Law Reform Act, 1969, s. 14).

Section 15 of the above Act provides that in any dispositions of property (e.g. sales, gifts, and trusts) after 31 December 1969, references to children and other relatives include references to, and to persons related through, illegitimate children, unless the contrary intention appears.

Similarly, section 16 provides that, from January 1970, where a testator makes a gift to his children or other 'issue', the reference will include any illegitimate child of the testator.

The modern law has gone a long way to assimilate the position of the legitimate and illegitimate child. The following points should be noted:

(i) Domicile and nationality. A legitimate child usually takes the father's domicile and nationality. An illegitimate child takes the mother's domicile and nationality.

(ii) Surname. A legitimate child takes his father's surname whilst an illegitimate child takes his mother's.

(iii) Rights of succession. Certain of these rights are different by reason of illegitimacy.

(iv) No reference on a child's birth certificate need be made as to his illegitimacy.

10. Infants or Minors

Section 1(1) of the Family Law Reform Act, 1969, provides that as from 1 January 1970, a person 'shall attain full age on attaining the age of eighteen instead of on attaining the age of twenty-one; and a person shall attain full age on that date if he has then already attained the age of eighteen but not the age of twenty-one'.

Section 9(1) provides that 'the time at which a person attains a particular age expressed in years shall be the commencement of the relevant anniversary of the date of his birth'. For example, a child born on 31 December 1970, will reach his majority at the first moment of 31 December 1988.

The following is a summary of the rights and liabilities of minors under the law:

(*a*) **Under the Criminal Law.** A child under the age of 10 is not criminally liable for any offence, and cannot, therefore, be convicted. Between the ages of 10 and 14 a child is liable for any crime he may commit if the court finds that such a child knew his conduct to be wrongful. Children over the age of 14 years are liable for criminal acts.

Children (i.e. persons under 14) and young persons (i.e. persons over the age of 14 and under 17 years) are as a general rule tried in a Juvenile Court by magistrates. If the case is a serious indictable offence, e.g. homicide, the child or young person will usually be committed for trial at the Crown Court. No person under 17 may be sent to prison, however. Other institutions, e.g. Borstal, Community Homes and Detention Centres, are used for custodial treatment or punishment. A child or young person may be fined for any offence committed.

(*b*) **Under the Civil Law.** A minor is liable for all *torts* he commits.

(Torts are civil wrongs, which are not breaches of contracts or trust.) Usually the minor is without means and, unless a parent or guardian is directly and personally involved in the commission of the tort, an injured party is left without remedy since a parent or guardian as such is not liable. Where the tort complained of is also a breach of contract, a plaintiff will not be able to sue in contract in respect of damage so caused. The position and liability of minors in respect of torts will be considered on p. 201.

The law as to infants' **contracts** is discussed on p. 133.

Voting Rights. Under the Representation of the People Act, 1969, the voting age for Parliamentary and local elections is 18 years and over.

Property Rights. A minor may own all kinds of personal or movable property, but he cannot, however, legally own land (Law of Property Act, 1925, s. 19).

Litigation Rights. Where a minor wishes to enforce or protect rights in a civil court, a responsible person (e.g. father) must be appointed to act as 'next friend'. Where a minor is sued, a responsible person is similarly appointed to act as his 'guardian *ad litem*', i.e. a guardian with respect to a suit at law. In criminal proceedings a minor may act in his own name by taking out a summons against another person: for example, *A* aged 16, may prosecute *B* aged 25, for common assault if the police do not prosecute on behalf of the public.

Wills. A minor has no legal capacity to make a valid will. Where, however, he is a serving member of H.M. Forces on military service, or is a mariner or seaman at sea he may make an informal will (see page 299).

Miscellaneous. Persons under 16 may not hold a driving licence to ride a motor-cycle on a public road. Persons under 17 may not hold a driving licence to drive a motor-car on a road. Persons under 16 may not contract a valid marriage. Restrictions are placed on the possession and use of firearms. Generally persons under 18 may not consume liquor on licensed premises.

11. Corporations

We have mentioned that as well as natural persons recognized as such by law, there are artificial or juristic persons called corporations. *A corporation is a legal entity, or artificial person, with a distinctive name, perpetual succession and a common seal.*

The essential feature of a corporation is that it has a legal personality distinct from that of its members or those who control it. It is clear, of course that a corporation once created by law will only be able to act if there are human servants or agents who for example order goods and make contracts for it, or perform other functions which the corporation itself may lawfully be empowered to do.

The next point to note is that the corporation continues in existence irrespective of the death or expulsion of any or all its members. Its independent existence and survival is known as 'perpetual succession'. This technical expression means that once the corporation is created by law it will continue until it is destroyed, annulled or dissolved by law. For example a monarch may, in the past, have granted a charter to create a corporation. The corporation will continue until such time as Her Majesty or Parliament (by statute) revokes the charter. Unless the dissolution or revocation is effected by law, the corporation continues in existence for ever. A corporation does not die: it must be 'killed'.

Limited-liability companies constitute what may appear to be an exception to this observation. The Companies Act, 1985, provides that where there is a reduction of membership below the statutory minimum of two members, the company may be wound up by the courts. Nevertheless, until the winding up is completed, the company continues in existence.

Classes of Corporations

Sir Edward Coke, L.C.J. (1552–1634) wrote: 'Persons are natural, created by God, and incorporate created by the policy of man, and these latter are either sole or aggregate of many.' In accordance with Coke's definition we may classify corporations thus:

(*a*) Corporations Sole; and
(*b*) Corporations Aggregate.

Alternatively we may classify them according to their mode of creation:

(*c*) Corporations created by Charter (common law)
(*d*) Corporations created by Statute
(*e*) Corporations created by Registration under the Companies Acts.

(*a*) **Corporations Sole.** This class of corporation consists of one person only at any time. Examples include the Queen, a bishop, the Public Trustee. In all the above examples there is a natural person and a 'corporation', each separate and distinct from the other. When the bishop dies a new incumbent assumes office, and there is no break in the powers vested in the corporation sole, whether of ownership of land or any other rights attaching to his office in his corporate capacity.

(*b*) **Corporations Aggregate.** Whereas a corporation sole consists of one member only, corporations aggregate comprise many members or groups of people. Common examples include the mayor, aldermen, and burgesses of a borough; the National Coal Board; the British Broadcasting Corporation; and all companies registered under the Companies Acts (see paragraph (*e*) below).

Corporations may be classified according to their manner or mode of creation.

(*c*) **By Charter.** Under the common law the Crown still has the power to create corporations at the royal pleasure. The Monarch may grant a charter to groups of subjects who petition for the purpose. A large district council may wish to become a borough to give itself added dignity and status: its council will then petition Her Majesty for the grant of a charter. The method is used today, usually to give corporate status to educational, charitable or scientific bodies, e.g. the new universities, the B.B.C.

(*d*) **By Statute.** These corporations are created by Acts of Parliament. Thus, the National Coal Board was created by the Coal Industry Nationalization Act, 1946. The County Councils were created by the Local Government Act, 1888 (and re-created by the Local Government Act, 1972), the British Railways Board by the Transport Act, 1962, and the Independent Broadcasting Authority by the Television Act, 1954 (renewed until 1996 in 1980). Parliament has generally adopted this form of incorporation in creating all the nationalized boards.

(*e*) **Corporations Registered under the Companies Acts.** From the mid-nineteenth century Companies Acts were passed which conferred the benefits of incorporation and limited liability of members on previously unincorporated associations of people if they wished to achieve this by registering under the Acts. The present law is to be found in the Companies Act, 1985, which replaced earlier Acts. The organization of companies is as follows:

Registration of a company is effected by depositing the following documents with the Registrar of Companies:

(i) *Memorandum of Association.* This document is in effect the charter of the company defining its *constitution* and the scope of its *powers.* The Memorandum of a public limited company must state:

1. The name of the company, ending with 'public limited company' (plc) or their equivalent in Welsh (ccc) in the case of a company whose registered office is situate in Wales.
2. Whether the registered office of the company is situate in England, Wales or Scotland.
3. The objects of the company.
4. That the liability of the members is limited.
5. The amount of share capital, and the division of it.

A private company limited by shares must have 'Limited' as the last word in its name (or its Welsh equivalent, 'cyfyngedig'), the remaining features of its memorandum being items 2 to 5 above.

(ii) *Articles of Association.* These are regulations governing the *internal* management of the company. They define the duties of the directors and the mode or form in which the business will be carried on.

These two documents (i) and (ii) may be distinguished by noting that the Memorandum of Association governs the *external* working of a company, and the Articles of Association govern the *internal* workings.

If no Articles are deposited with the Registrar of Companies, model sets of Articles (described in the Companies Act) will apply, depending on the type of company to be registered.

In addition to the above documents, various written declarations must be made by the persons responsible for the promotion or direction of the intended company stating that the statutory requirements of the Companies Act, 1985, have been complied with.

The three kinds of registered companies are (i) those limited by *shares*, (ii) those limited by *guarantee*, and (iii) *unlimited* companies.

(i) **Companies Limited by Shares.** This is the usual form of company, whether public or private. Where a company is limited by shares each member is liable to the amount (if any) unpaid on his shares. For example, Robinson buys 100 £1 shares in the Xanadu plc, for which he pays £50 on application to the company. Robinson's liability in the event of Xanadu plc being wound up is to pay the outstanding £50.

(ii) **Companies Limited by Guarantee.** In this type of company each member undertakes to contribute a certain sum in the event of its winding-up. Thus a member who has guaranteed £10,000 will be liable for that amount if the company becomes insolvent and unable to pay its debts. The member cannot be compelled to contribute more. Under the 1985 Act those having a share capital are classed as public companies and may continue in existence, but no such companies may be created in future. Those limited by guarantee without a share capital are classed as private companies.

(iii) **Unlimited Companies.** An unlimited company is one in which the liability of the members to pay the debts of the company is unlimited. The unlimited company is not common in the business world. Its main use is to hold property or provide services where outside indebtedness will not be large and secrecy of financial affairs is desired. Under the 1985 Act unlimited companies are classed as private companies.

In addition to the above classes of companies distinguished by financial liability of members, we should note also the distinction between public and private companies.

Public Limited Companies must have a minimum of two members (no maximum) and must at all times maintain a minimum issued share capital of £50,000. The shares of such members are freely transferable by sale on the Stock Exchange or elsewhere. The largest industrial and trading companies are public limited companies whose shares are quoted on the Stock Exchange lists.

Private Companies must have a minimum of two members (no maximum). They are guilty of an offence if they offer their shares or debentures to the public.

Share Structure of a Company

The capital of a company may be divided into the following classes:

(*a*) **Preference Shares.** Holders of these shares are entitled to a dividend at a fixed rate out of profits in priority to holders of any of the company's other shares.

(*b*) **Ordinary Shares.** The dividend paid is not fixed but fluctuates with the profits of the company.

(*c*) **Deferred Shares.** These are shares which may receive a higher dividend after the payment of preference and ordinary share dividends.

If the capital is insufficient to run the company, additional money may be raised by means of **debentures.** These are loans to the company, such loans being usually secured by means of a charge on the company's assets.

The 'Ultra Vires' Rule

The doctrine of *ultra vires* ('beyond the powers') applies particularly to corporations. Where a corporation has been created by law, it *must* act within the powers which have been granted to it. As we have seen, these powers are defined in the Charter in respect of common law corporations, in the Statute in respect of statutory corporations, and in the Memorandum of Association in respect of registered companies.

There is, however, a distinction between chartered corporations and the remainder. The chartered corporations have the same rights and powers as ordinary individuals and are subject to the same liabilities. Where a chartered corporation acts beyond the powers defined in its charter, such acts are not in law void. Thus a contract between such a corporation and a private person may be enforced in the same way as a contract between two adults. The only effect of acting beyond the powers defined in the charter is that the Crown (which granted the charter) may revoke it at its pleasure, or a statute may be passed with similar effect.

Where a statutory or registered company exceeds the powers granted to it by the statute of incorporation or the Memorandum of Association, any contract made beyond the powers laid down is void.

> *Ashbury Carriage & Iron Co.* v. *Riche* (1875). The company was formed with the following objects (defined in the Memorandum of Association): to make, sell, or lend on hire railway carriages and wagons. The company, however, contracted to build a railway in Belgium. *Held:* that the contract was *ultra vires* and void; the contract could not, therefore, be ratified by a meeting of shareholders.

The doctrine of *ultra vires* has been weakened by the European Communities Act, 1972 s. 9(1), which states:

'In favour of a person dealing with a company in good faith, any transaction decided on by the directors shall be deemed to be one which it is within the capacity of the company to enter into, and the power of the directors to bind the company shall be deemed to be free of any limitation under the memorandum or articles of association; and a party to a transaction so decided on shall not be bound to inquire as to the capacity of the company to enter into it or as to any such limitation on the powers of the directors, and shall be presumed to have acted in good faith unless the contrary is proved.'

The company cannot rely on the *ultra vires* rule against someone dealing in good faith with the company.

Termination of a Company

The existence of a company may be ended either (i) by the Registrar of Companies striking the name of the company off the register (after satisfying himself that it is defunct) or (ii) by winding up.

The winding up of a company is either voluntary or compulsory. A **voluntary** winding up is begun when the members of a company resolve so to do. A **compulsory** winding up is undertaken following an order of a court on a petition presented by a member of the company, or a creditor or the Department of Trade. The petition may allege one or a number of grounds: for example, inability to pay its debts; failure to commence business within a year; or maintain the minimum numbers; that it is just and equitable to wind up.

12. Unincorporated Associations

As the name implies, these associations of people differ from corporations in that they (the associations) do not have a distinct legal personality separate from the members themselves. Common examples include societies and clubs such as a local tennis club, a college literary society, or arts group. Trades unions and partnerships are also unincorporated associations.

Legal Liability of Unincorporated Associations

The law regards these groups as a collection of persons bearing individual responsibility for the association's actions. So, where an official of an association (e.g. a secretary) makes a contract for the purchase of goods for the common use of the group, the official is personally liable on such contract either alone or jointly with the committee which authorized it.

Where a tort is committed by an individual member, that person will be responsible in law. Where a committee is appointed to act on behalf of a number of people, the committee may, however, be held liable for any action which they authorized.

> *Brown* v. *Lewis* (1896). The committee of a football club authorized the repair of a football stand for use by the public. The repair was faultily performed and a member of the public was injured when the stand collapsed. *Held:* that the committee authorizing the repair was liable.

There are certain important points of law which affect unincorporated associations with regard to:

(*a*) **Ownership of Land.** The Law of Property Act, 1925, places certain restrictions on the number of people who may own land together. Consequently the association may nominate four of their members to hold land as trustees. These trustees may sue and be sued in respect of the property vested in them.

(*b*) **Representative Action.** One representative or more may bring or defend actions on the part of the other members of the group. 'Where numerous persons have the same interest in any proceedings ... the proceedings may be begun and, unless the Court otherwise orders, continued by or against any one or more of them as representing all ...' (Rules of the Supreme Court, Order 15, rule 12).

(*c*) **Committee.** An unincorporated association may confer powers on a committee to control membership and where necessary to expel members. It may therefore act as a disciplinary tribunal, but while so acting it is subject to the rules of natural justice which may be enforced by the courts. An example of such a group is the Jockey Club, the Stewards of which are empowered to control members.

(*d*) **Trade Unions and Friendly Societies.** Some statutory recognition has been given to both these forms of unincorporated associations, and they may, in certain circumstances, sue and be sued (see page 108).

(*e*) **Partnerships.** These may sue and be sued in the partnership's name (Rules of the Supreme Court, Order 80, rule 1).

(*f*) **Credit Unions.** These thrift and loan societies have received statutory recognition in the Credit Unions Act, 1979.

13. Partnerships

A partnership is defined by the Partnership Act, 1890, as *the relation which subsists between persons carrying on business in common with a view of profit.*

The relationship between the partners may be created orally, in writing or by conduct. Frequently, of course, a deed of partnership is drawn up legally to define the rights and duties of the partners.

The carrying on of business does not necessarily imply the buying and selling of goods; the partnership may well consist in the provision of services. Where persons engage in business and they share profits, the law will presume that a partnership has been formed even though the persons have never mentioned their intention orally or in writing.

The following is a summary of the main distinctions between a partnership and a registered corporation:

(*a*) **Personality.** A partnership has no legal personality apart from the personalities of its members. A registered company is a legal person distinct from its members.

(*b*) **Management.** In the absence of contrary agreement, all partners are entitled to share in managing the firm. The members of a company have no such right: they have vested the management of the company in its directors.

(*c*) **Contractual Authority.** A partner is presumed in law to have authority to enter into contracts on behalf of the firm in the ordinary course of its business. Members of a company, as such, have no such right.

(*d*) **Liability.** A partner, other than a *limited partner*, is liable for the debts of the partnership to the full extent of his private estate. A shareholder member of an ordinary limited company bears liability limited to the amount, if any, unpaid on his shares. If the company is limited by guarantee, he is limited to the amount of his guarantee.

(*e*) **Numbers.** A partnership cannot generally have more than twenty members (exceptions are: bankers, accountants, stock exchange brokers, solicitors, estate agents and building designers such as architects, surveyors and the like). Any type of company can be formed by at least two persons, and there is no maximum.

(*f*) **Dissolution.** A partnership firm is dissolved by (i) the expiration of the agreed period of its duration; (ii) the completion of the particular undertaking for which the firm was formed; (iii) death or bankruptcy of any partner; (iv) mutual agreement; or (v) by order of a competent court. Companies are wound up compulsorily or voluntarily. The death of a member of a company does not affect the existence of the corporation itself.

Where a partner commits a tort while 'in actual or apparent furtherance of the business', the partnership firm will be liable for that tort.

The law requires that partners observe the utmost good faith in their mutual dealings. This means that a partner must disclose all profits made in relation to the business so that such profits may be shared in common.

There are two types of partner, general and limited. A **general partner** is a partner in the fullest sense, while a **limited partner** is one who takes no part in the management of the firm and whose liability is limited to the amount of his capital investment. Limited partnerships must be registered under the Limited Partnerships Act, 1907. In any such firms, however, one general partner at least must be fully liable for the partnership debts.

14. Trade Unions and Employers' Associations

A trade union may be defined as a combination of workmen whose principal object is collective bargaining for wages or conditions of work.

As everyone knows, the legal control of trade unions is the subject of political debate. The Trade Union and Labour Relations Act, 1974, as amended in 1976, 1980, 1982 and 1984, is the main statute operating today.

So far as the status and regulation of trade union and employers' associations are concerned, no union can be a corporate body (s. 2). An exception is made in the case of organizations on the Special Register maintained under the Industrial Relations Act, 1971 (now repealed), which fall within the definition of trade union. The 1974 Act provides that all unions, except Special Register organizations, are to have certain of the attributes of corporate bodies, e.g. the power to sue and be sued in their own names.

The Acts require the Certification Officer to maintain lists of trade unions and employers' associations, and lay down administrative and accounting requirements with which trade unions and employers' organizations have to comply.

Employers' associations are permitted to be either (*a*) bodies corporate or (*b*) unincorporated associations (s. 3(1)).

Legal immunities currently include:

(*a*) protection against action for civil conspiracy;
(*b*) protection for peaceful picketing;
(*c*) provision prohibiting any court from ordering someone to work;
(*d*) protection for persons inducing breaches of contracts of employment in contemplation or furtherance of a trade dispute:

but these immunities have been to some extent reduced by the Employment Acts 1980 and 1982, and the Trade Union Act, 1984.

Under the 1974 Act collective agreements are presumed to be legally unenforceable unless the parties specifically provided otherwise.

15. Crown Proceedings

The expression 'the Crown' may be used to describe (i) the Sovereign in her personal capacity, and (ii) the Sovereign as Head of State, in her corporate capacity. The Crown, in its corporate capacity, includes Her Majesty's Ministers, the Government departments and the Civil Service.

Two ancient maxims of the common law determined the relationship of the Crown to a subject: 'No action can be brought against the King (or Queen) personally, for he cannot be sued in his Courts'; and 'The King can do no wrong'. The Sovereign could not and still cannot be sued personally for any alleged wrongs he may have committed in person. As a corporate body, the Crown was similarly immune from legal liability. The doctrine of vicarious liability (whereby at common law a master is liable for the wrongs of a servant committed in the course of his employment) did not apply to the Crown.

The Crown as Employer

The Crown is now one of the largest employers of labour in the State. Until 1971 a civil servant held office 'at the pleasure of the Crown'. Thus, he was dismissible at the Royal pleasure.

The Trade Union and Labour Relations Act, 1974, applies to Crown employment in the same way that it does to other employment. The effect now is that a civil servant can no longer be dismissed at the Crown's pleasure; his dismissal will have to be a **fair** dismissal, the onus of proving fairness lies on the Crown. The Act does not affect members of the Armed Forces who can be discharged 'at the pleasure of the Crown'.

The Crown Proceedings Act, 1947

This Act was passed as a result of the unsatisfactory state of the law regarding legal proceedings against the Crown. The main object was to place the Crown in the same position, as far as possible, as a private person or employer, i.e. able to sue and be sued for breaches of contracts or for torts committed by servants. The Act does not affect the Queen's personal immunity from legal proceedings.

Liability in Contract. The Act provides that actions for breach of contract may now be brought as of right against the Crown, without the need to obtain the *fiat* of the Attorney-General.

Liability in Tort. Section 2(1) of the Act provides that 'the Crown shall be subject to all those liabilities in tort to which, if it were a person of full age and capacity, it would be subject:

(*a*) in respect of torts committed by its servants or agents;

(*b*) in respect of any breach of those duties which a person owes to his servants or agents at common law by reason of being their employer; and

(*c*) in respect of any breach of the duties attaching at common law to the ownership, occupation, possession or control of property'.

As an example of (*b*): A master is under a common law duty to provide reasonably safe plant and machinery for his employees. If, therefore, the Crown provides a faulty vehicle for use by its servant *B*, as a result of which *C* is injured, an action will lie against the Crown under s. 2(1).

As an example of (*c*): A private person visits the local office of the Inspector of Taxes to discuss his income-tax assessment. A defective electric light fitting falls from the ceiling and cuts the caller's head. An action will lie for the tort at the instance of the injured person.

Procedure. Action is brought against the appropriate Government department. The Treasury publishes a list of the departments and names the solicitor to accept service of process on behalf of each department. Where the department is not named, or uncertainty exists as to the department's identity, the Attorney-General may be made defendant.

The legal action then follows the usual procedure of a High Court or county court action. The Act provides, however, that

(*a*) Judgment against the department cannot be enforced by the ordinary methods of levying execution or attachment. The department is required to pay the amount certified due as damages.

(*b*) An injunction and a decree of specific performance are inappropriate to the Crown. Instead, the court makes an order declaratory of the rights of the parties.

(*c*) No order for restitution of property will be made against the Crown. Instead, the court may declare the plaintiff entitled as against the Crown.

Special provision is made in the Act with regard to (i) the Post Office, and (ii) the Armed Forces of the Crown.

The Post Office. This was formerly a Government Department. The Post Office Act, 1969, constituted the Post Office as a public corporation and the staff ceased to be Crown servants. The corporation is headed by a chairman and board of control who are responsible for the day-to-day administration. The telecommunications business of the Post Office has been separated off under another public corporation, British Telecom plc.

The corporation may sue and be sued in its corporate name. Special regulations as to compensation obtainable against the Post Office for damage or loss or misdelivery of letters or parcels apply, and reference should be made to the Post Office Guide.

Postmen and other officials may be prosecuted for theft of postal packets, etc. in the same way as other individuals; but punishment is usually more severe by reason of their special position.

The Armed Forces. Nothing done or omitted by a member of the Armed Forces of the Crown while on duty shall subject him or the Crown to liability for inflicting death or personal injury on another member of the Armed Forces if (i) the latter is on duty or is on any land, premises, ship, aircraft, or vehicle used for the purposes of the Armed Forces, and if (ii) the Minister of Social Security certifies that the victim will receive an award.

Adams v. *War Office* (1955). *A* was killed on duty by a shell fired by other members of the Armed Forces on duty. The Minister certified that *A*'s death was attributable to service for the purpose of entitlement to an award, but it was also held that *A*'s father did not satisfy the conditions of the Royal Warrant under which parents might claim a pension in respect of the loss of a son.

Section 10 of the Crown Proceedings Act, 1947, has now been repealed by the Crown Proceedings (Armed Forces) Act, 1987. This allows members of the Armed Forces to sue the Crown in personal injury cases. However, the Government has reserved the right to reactivate the provisions of Section 10 in the event of impending, or actual, hostilities or grave national emergency.

Crown Servant. Section 2(6) of the Act defines the term 'officer' (in respect of whose actions the Crown now assumes liability in tort) as follows: the 'officer' shall (i) be appointed directly or indirectly by the Crown; and (ii) be paid in respect of his duties as an officer of the Crown at the material time *wholly* out of the Consolidated Fund, moneys provided by Parliament, the Road Fund, or any fund certified by the Treasury.

The police are not *wholly* paid out of such funds, hence the Crown is not subject to liability for torts committed by them.

16. Exercises

1. By what means may British nationality be acquired?
2. What are the three classes of domicile? Why is it important to establish the domicile of a person for the purposes of English law?
3. Distinguish between (i) void marriage and (ii) voidable marriage.
4. What 'domestic proceedings' may be taken in a magistrates' court?
5. What special rules apply to mentally disordered persons?
6. Define a 'corporation' in law. What are the distinguishing features of a corporation?
7. Distinguish between (i) a company limited by shares, (ii) a company limited by guarantee, and (iii) an unlimited company.
8. Describe the operation of the *ultra vires* rule in regard to companies.
9. 'The King can do no wrong.' How far is this maxim true today?
10. Outline the main provisions of the Crown Proceedings Act, 1947.

7

THE LAW OF CONTRACT

In his book *Principles of the Law of Contracts*, Sir William Anson defined a contract as *a legally binding agreement made between two or more parties, by which rights are acquired by one or more to acts or forebearances on the part of the other or others*. Shortly it may be defined as an agreement between two or more parties which is intended to have legal consequences.

The agreement referred to in the definition means a meeting of minds, called in law *consensus ad idem*, signifying that the parties are agreed together about the same thing. The definition also emphasizes that the parties to the contract must intend that their agreement shall be legally enforceable. Unless the law regognizes this and enforces the agreements of parties, it would be impossible to carry on commercial or business life. For this reason the law of contract plays a leading role in courses on business studies.

These contractual agreements give rise to rights and obligations which the law recognizes and enforces. But certain agreements, such as domestic and social arrangements, are not intended by the parties to be legally binding. The law allows for this. Thus, if Cumming and Gowing agree to meet for dinner and Gowing fails to turn up, the law will do nothing in the matter. The agreement was not intended to create legal rights and duties, and, as such, it is not a contract in law. Every contract is an agreement, but not every agreement is a contract.

The object of the law of contract is to identify those agreements which it will enforce and those which it will not. This is of prime importance and will be referred to later in more detail.

1. Essentials of a Valid Contract

An agreement will be enforced when the following essential elements exist:

(*a*) *Offer and Acceptance*. There must be an offer by one party and an acceptance of it by the other.

(*b*) *Intention* to create legal relations.

(*c*) *Capacity* of the parties. Each party must have the legal capacity to make the contract.

(*d*) *Consent* must be genuine. The consent must not be obtained by fraud, or duress, for example.

(*e*) *Consideration* must be present (except in contracts under seal, i.e. by deed).

(*f*) *Legality* of object. The object of the contract must not be one of which the law disapproves.

(*g*) *Possibility* of performance.

All the above elements must be present. If one or more is absent the contract will be (i) void, (ii) voidable, or (iii) unenforceable.

Void Contracts are destitute of legal effect; that is, they are not contracts, and agreements of this kind do not confer legal rights on the parties thereto. For example, a contract by an infant to buy goods other than 'necessaries'. Similarly, if *A* agrees with *B* to break into *C*'s house and steal if *B* pays *A* £10, the contract is void for it is illegal. Neither party can recover from the other on a void contract, but goods delivered may be recovered by an action in tort because no property (ownership) passes. Money paid under the agreement may be recovered in quasi-contract (see p. 189).

Voidable Contracts are those which may be made void at the instance of one of the parties. For example, a contract which is induced by fraud can be avoided by the party deceived.

Unenforceable Contracts are those which are valid but are unenforceable at law because of the absence of (i) evidence of the contract or (ii) the form required by law. For example, some contracts which are not 'evidenced in writing' are unenforceable at law. So, too, are contracts barred by the Limitation Act, 1980.

2. Classification of Contracts

Contracts may be classified under the following headings: (*a*) Contracts of Record, (*b*) Specialty Contracts, and (*c*) Simple Contracts.

(*a*) **Contracts of Record** include (i) Judgments of a Court and (ii) Recognizances.

(i) *Judgments of a Court*. The previous rights under a contract are merged in the judgment. Thus, *A* owes *B* £10 on a contract. *B* sues *A* and obtains judgment. The previous rights become merged in the judgment of the court, and execution may be levied upon *A* to enforce payment, if need be.

(ii) *Recognizances*. In the criminal courts an offender may on conviction be 'bound over to be of good behaviour and to keep the peace'. The person so bound acknowledges that he owes the Crown a certain sum of money (say, £10 or £20) if he fails to observe the terms of the recognizance. (See example on p. 394.)

(*b*) **Specialty Contracts** (or **Contracts by Deed**). This type of contract is the only formal contract in the law. Specialty contracts are used for various transactions such as conveyances of land, a lease of property for more than three years, and articles of partnership.

The characteristics of a contract by deed are that it is (i) signed, (ii) sealed, and (iii) delivered. Signing needs no explanation. An *X* will suffice if the signatory is unable to write. Sealing is today the affixing of a paper wafer which is touched by the person making the deed. Delivery is made by handing over the deed physically to the other party (or his agent, e.g. solicitor) or, constructively, by touching the seal and uttering the words 'I deliver this as my act and deed'.

When delivery is made subject to a condition, it is termed an *escrow*; this means that although the deed has been 'delivered' it will not become effective until the specified condition has been fulfilled.

The Law Commission have recommended that the requirement for sealing should be abolished but that of delivery retained.

Where there are two or more parties, the deed is sometimes called an *indenture*.

(*c*) **Simple Contracts.** These are contracts not under seal. They may be made (i) orally, (ii) in writing, or (iii) implied by conduct.

We have considered the essential elements in a valid simple contract and we have noted that it must be supported by valuable consideration (see p. 113). In the absence of such consideration, the contract will be void.

In addition to the above, we may note the following types of contract:

An **express contract** is one where the terms are stated in words (orally or in writing) by the parties.

An **implied contract** is one in which the terms are not expressed but are implied from the conduct or position of the parties. For example, if someone goes into a restaurant, takes a seat and is supplied with a meal, the law will imply a contract from the very nature of the circumstances, and the customer will be obliged to pay for what he has had. Similarly, where money which is not due is paid by mistake, the law implies a contract by the person paid to refund the money (see quasi-contract, p. 189).

An **executed contract** is one wholly performed on one or both sides. For example, on 1 June Arnold agrees to dig Basset's garden in August if Basset will pay Arnold £10 on 1 July. When Basset pays the £10 and Arnold digs the garden the contract will be executed so far as Arnold and Basset are concerned.

An **executory contract** is one which is wholly unperformed, or in which there remains something further to be done on both sides. For instance, the contract in the above example is executory between 1 June and 1 July, for the contract is wholly unperformed until Basset pays Arnold £10. Many examples occur in relation to goods, as when a customer agrees to buy a car for £1,000 in the following year, payment to be made on delivery.

3. Offer and Acceptance

As already mentioned, to constitute a contract there must be an offer and an acceptance. The party making the offer is known as the *offeror;* the party to whom the offer is made is known as the *offeree.* The contract comes into existence when an offer has been *unconditionally* accepted.

How made. An offer may be made orally, in writing or by conduct. An example of an offer made by conduct is where a customer in a supermarket chooses goods and hands them to the cashier, who then accepts the customer's offer to buy.

To Whom Made. An offer may be made to a definite person (or group of persons) or to the whole world, i.e. generally. Where an offer is made to one person only, or a group of persons, only that person or that group may accept. Where an offer is made to the whole world, anyone may accept by complying with the terms of the offer.

> *Boulton* v. *Jones* (1857). *B* bought a hose-pipe business from one Brocklehurst. *J*, the defendant, to whom Brocklehurst owed a debt, addressed an order to Brocklehurst for some piping. *B* supplied the order even though it was not addressed to him. *J* refused to pay *B* for the piping, and contended that he meant to deal with Brocklehurst only because he had a set-off (contra) account against Brocklehurst. *Held:* that the offer was made to Brocklehurst and that *J* was not liable to *B* for the goods as there was no contract. 'Now the rule of law is clear, that if you propose to make a contract with *A*, then *B* cannot substitute himself for *A* without your consent and to your disadvantage, securing to himself all the benefits of the contract' (Pollock, C.B.).

Where a reward is offered to any person who does a certain thing, e.g. finding lost property, it follows that any person may accept. Providing the finder knows of the offer he may claim any reward for returning the property.

> *Carlill* v. *Carbolic Smoke Ball Co.* (1893). A patent-medicine company advertised that it would give £100 to anyone who contracted influenza after using their smoke ball for a certain period. Plaintiff (Mrs. Carlill) bought the article, used it as directed and contracted influenza nevertheless. She claimed the reward of £100. *Held:* that plaintiff accepted by complying with the conditions of the offer. There was an offer capable of acceptance by all who used the smoke ball and it mattered not that the plaintiff did not communicate her acceptance to the offeror.

The Offer must be Communicated to the Offeree. An offer must be communicated to the offeree before it can be accepted. A person cannot be said to accept an offer of which he is ignorant. If *A* by public notice advertises a £10 reward to the finder of a lost brooch, and *B*, who is unaware of the notice and the offer, finds the brooch and returns it to the loser, *B* is not entitled to claim the reward.

Taylor v. *Laird* (1856). A ship's captain, *T*, threw up his command of a vessel in the course of a voyage, but nevertheless helped to work the ship home. He then claimed compensation for his services. *Held:* that as *T* had not communicated his offer to work the ship home, the defendant owners had no opportunity of accepting or rejecting the services, *T* could not recover compensation.

An Offer must be Distinguished from an Invitation to Treat. An 'invitation to treat' means an invitation to make offers. Thus when an auctioneer requests bids he invites the assembly to make offers to him. An offer is accepted by the auctioneer by the fall of the hammer.

Where goods are displayed in a shop window or on shelves in a self-service store, the display is construed as an invitation to treat, not an offer to sell. Where a customer picks up an article in a self-service store and takes it to the cashier's desk to pay, the taker's action is an offer to buy. It is for the cashier (or shopkeeper) to accept the offer and take the purchase money in payment (*Pharmaceutical Society of Gt. Britain* v. *Boots Cash Chemists* (*Southern*) *Ltd.*, 1953).

Fisher v. *Bell* (1960). A shopkeeper displayed in his shop window a flick-knife behind which was a ticket reading 'Ejector knife—4*s*.'. He was charged with offering for sale a flick-knife, contrary to the Restriction of Offensive Weapons Act, 1959. *Held:* that the display of goods in a shop window is not in itself an offer for sale. 'According to the law of contract, the display of an article with a price on it in a shop window is merely an invitation to treat. It is in no sense an offer for sale the acceptance of which constitutes a contract' (Lord Chief Justice Parker).

As a consequence of this decision a further Act was passed in 1961 to include the words 'exposes or has in his possession for the purpose of sale', thus giving effect to the intention of Parliament.

Harris v. *Nickerson* (1873). An auctioneer, *N*, advertised that a sale of office furniture would take place at Bury St. Edmunds. *H* travelled down from London to attend the sale, but found the furniture was withdrawn from the sale. *H* thereupon sued the auctioneer for his loss of time and expenses. *Held:* that the advertisement was a mere declaration of intention and did not create a binding contract with *H* when he acted on it.

A statement of price is not necessarily an offer.

Harvey v. *Facey* (1893). The following telegraph messages were exchanged between the parties. *H:* 'Will you sell us Bumper Hall Pen? Telegraph lowest price.' *F:* 'Lowest price for Bumper Hall Pen £900.' *H:* 'We agree to buy Bumper Hall Pen for £900 asked by you.' To this last telegram *F* made no reply. *H* claimed that there was a contract between himself and *F. Held* (by the Judicial Committee of the Privy Council): that there was no contract. The second telegram was not an offer but in the nature of an invitation to treat (i.e. the lowest price if it were decided to sell). The final message could not be looked upon as an acceptance.

Termination of an Offer. An offer terminates

(*a*) On the death of either offeror or offeree *before* acceptance.
(*b*) By non-acceptance within the time stipulated for acceptance, or within a reasonable time.
(*c*) When revoked *before* acceptance.
(*d*) When rejected by the offeree.

Termination by methods (*a*) and (*b*) above is sometimes referred to as **Lapse of Offer.** Students should note that although death of offeror or offeree before acceptance terminates the offer, death after acceptance has no effect on the majority of contracts. Where an offeree dies after acceptance the contract will be valid. Thus, Potts offers to sell building land to Kettle. Kettle accepts the offer but dies before conveyance. Kettle's personal representatives may compel Potts to convey the land to themselves.

As to (*b*) above, what constitutes 'a reasonable time' is a matter for the court and varies with the type of contract. Some offers must be accepted almost immediately. Where an offer is made by telegram, the mode of offer indicates *prima facie* that the acceptance should be quick also, and in this case a reply by letter may be too late. Other offers may be accepted within a month or even longer.

Ramsgate Victoria Hotel Co. Ltd. v. *Montefiore* (1866). *M* by letter on 8 June offered to purchase shares in a company. The shares were allotted on 23 November; *M* refused the shares. *Held:* that the offer to take shares lapsed through unreasonable delay in accepting.

Revocation of Offer. Withdrawal or revocation of an offer must be communicated to the offeree before acceptance. The revocation may be made directly by the offeror himself, or indirectly. The important point to note is that revocation is of no effect until it is actually brought to the notice of the offeree.

Byrne v. *Van Tienhoven* (1880). On 1 October, defendant *V* offered by letter goods for sale to *B*. On 11 October *B* received the letter, and accepted by telegraph immediately. On 8 October, *V* wrote to *B* revoking the offer. On 20 October *B* received the letter of revocation. *Held:* that *B* had accepted the offer on 11 October. Revocation to be effective must be communicated to the offeree before he has accepted. The fact that a letter of revocation had been posted or was on its way was immaterial.

Where notice of revocation of an offer does not come directly from the offeror or his agent, but from a *reliable source*, this is deemed indirect revocation.

Dickinson v. *Dodds* (1876). *X* offered to sell a house to *Y*, the letter stating: 'This offer to be left over until Friday, 9 a.m.' On Thursday, *Y* heard from *A* that *X* had sold the house to *Z*. On Friday at 7 a.m. *Y* handed to *X* his acceptance of the offer. *Held:* that there was no contract between *X* and *Y*, since *X* had revoked his offer and the revocation had been communicated to *Y* by *A* before the purported 'acceptance' by *Y*.

Rejection of offer may take two forms: (i) where the offeree communicates his rejection to the offeror, and (ii) where the offeree makes a counter-offer.

An example of (ii) occurred in the following case:

Hyde v. *Wrench* (1840). *W* offered to sell a farm to *H* for £1,000. *H* said he would give £950. *W* refused, and *H* then said he would give £1,000. When *W* refused, *H* sought to obtain an order of specific performance. *Held:* that there was no contract. *H*'s offer of £950 was a counter-offer which evidently rejected the original offer.

Where the offeree accepts subject to a condition, this also amounts to a rejection.

Jordan v. *Norton* (1838). *N* offered to buy *J*'s horse if warranted quiet in harness. *J* agreed to the price and said he would warrant the horse quiet in *double* harness. *Held:* that *N*'s offer was rejected.

But note that a mere request for further information of the offer does not amount to a counter-offer so as to bring about a rejection.

The methods of communicating acceptance are varied, and it is advisable to note the following decisions.

Mental Acceptance. This means assenting to an offer in one's mind, but not actually communicating acceptance.

Felthouse v. *Bindley* (1862). *F* offered by letter to buy his nephew's horse for £30. *F* wrote: 'If I hear no more about him, I shall consider the horse is mine at £30.' The nephew did not reply, but he asked the auctioneer who was engaged to sell the horse to keep the horse out of the sale because he had sold it to his uncle. By error the auctioneer, Bindley, included the horse in the sale, and *F* sued *B* for conversion. *Held:* that *F* had no claim since his offer to buy had only been mentally accepted by the nephew. It had not been communicated to the offeror.

Particular method of acceptance. Where the offeror prescribes a particular method of acceptance, it follows that the method prescribed should normally be followed. Thus where acceptance of an offer is to be by telegram, acceptance by air mail would be insufficient because it does not comply with the terms of the offer.

Where acceptance consists in the performance of an act, as in *Carlill* v. *Carbolic Smoke Ball Co. Ltd.* (1893) summarized on p. 115, this may be sufficient acceptance since the offer does not contemplate that the offeree should notify the offeror orally or by letter. The finder of a lost dog or other article, provided that he returns it, will be able to claim any reward offered, assuming in this case the finder knew of the reward beforehand.

Options. An option is an offer to keep a contract 'open' for a specified time. An option is not binding unless made by deed or is supported by valuable consideration. Thus Potts, the owner of a building site, may give Kettle an option to buy the land, in consideration of Kettle paying £50, such offer to remain open for one month. This is not an offer to sell the land but is a contract to allow Kettle to buy it within the time (one month) on the terms of the contract. Potts is lawfully binding himself to sell to Kettle, and if Potts revokes the option, Kettle can on the terms of the option compel Potts to sell the land to him.

Rules Regarding Acceptance

How Made. Acceptance of an offer may be made orally, in writing or by conduct. The first two modes of acceptance are self-evident. Acceptance by conduct is exemplified in the case of *Carlill* v. *Carbolic Smoke Ball Co. Ltd.* (1893) summarized on p. 115.

Acceptance must be Unqualified. This means that the acceptance must be absolute and must conform exactly with the terms of the offer. Thus if the offeree is required to perform an act or to pay a sum of money, the act must be performed or the sum mentioned paid exactly.

> *Neale* v. *Merrett* (1930). *M* offered to sell land to *N* for £280. *N* replied purporting to accept and enclosed £80, promising to pay the balance of £200 by monthly instalments of £50 each. *Held:* that *N* could not enforce acceptance because his acceptance was not an unqualified one.

Acceptance Subject to Contract. Acceptance 'subject to contract' means that the parties do not intend to be bound, and are not bound, until a formal contract is prepared and signed by them. The object of the phrase, which often appears in sales of land and property, is to give the parties an opportunity to reflect on the matter, to obtain legal advice, and to change their minds if need be.

> *Chillingworth* v. *Esche* (1924). *C* agreed to purchase *E*'s nursery for £4,800 'subject to a proper contract to be prepared by the vendor's solicitors'. A contract was prepared by *C*'s solicitors and approved by *E*'s solicitors, but *E* refused to sign it. *Held:* that there was no contract as the agreement was only conditional.

> *Eccles* v. *Bryant* (1948). The plaintiff bought a house subject to contract. The terms of the formal contract were agreed, and each party signed his part. The plaintiff posted his part, but the vendor changed his mind before posting his part. *Held:* that there was no binding contract.

> *Branca* v. *Cobarro* (1947). The parties negotiated for the sale of a farm and signed a document containing the statement: 'This is a provisional agreement until a fully legalized agreement drawn up by a solicitor and embodying all the conditions herewith stated is signed.' *Held* (by the

Court of Appeal): that the use of the word 'provisional' indicated that the parties intended the document to be binding, although to be replaced subsequently by a more formal contract.

Acceptance by Post. Where the post is the proper means of communication between the parties to a contract the following rules apply:

(*a*) An offer has no effect until it reaches the offeree. Where an offer is made by post, it takes effect (i.e. it is communicated) when it reaches the offeree, not when the letter is posted.

Adams v. *Lindsell* (1818). On 2 September, *L* wrote offering to sell wool at a price, and requesting an answer in course of post. The letter was misdirected and reached *A* on 5 September. The reply of acceptance was sent at once and reached *L* on 9 September, but the wool had been sold on 8 September. *Held:* that there was a good contract between *A* and *L*, because the offer was accepted at once on being received.

(*b*) Where an offer is made and accepted by letters sent through the post, the contract is made the moment the letter accepting the offer is posted, even though it never reaches its destination.

Household Fire Insurance Co. v. *Grant* (1879). *G* applied for shares in a company. A letter of allotment of shares was posted to *G* but never reached him. *Held:* that the contract was complete on posting, and *G* became a shareholder of the company.

For the above rules to apply, the letter of acceptance must be prepaid, properly addressed and properly posted. The handing of a letter to a postman is not a proper posting.

(*c*) Revocation of an offer is communicated when the letter of revocation is received and read by the offeree. (See *Byrne* v. *Van Tienhoven* (1800), summarized on p. 117).

As to instantaneous communications, e.g. by telephone, the contract is complete only when the acceptance is received by the offeror at his end of the line. If the line 'goes dead' during the communication of the acceptance, there is no contract.

Entores Ltd. v. *Miles Far East Corporation* (1955). Plaintiffs in London made an offer by Telex (teleprinter) to defendants in Amsterdam. The defendants accepted by Telex message transmitted to London. Later, defendants were in breach of contract, and the plaintiffs wished to establish that the contract by Telex was made in London where the acceptance took place, in which case the legal action could be decided in English courts. *Held:* that the contract had been made in London, since the defendant's acceptance of plaintiff's offer was not complete until actually received by plaintiff. This Court of Appeal decision was upheld by the House of Lords in *Brinkibon Ltd.* v. *Stahag Stahl* (1982).

If *A* telephones his acceptance of an offer made by *B*, and *B* does not hear *A*'s voice at the moment of acceptance *B* should request *A* to repeat the message. Otherwise *B* may be estopped from denying that there has been a communication of acceptance.

Tenders. A tender is an offer. Tenders commonly arise where, for example, a corporation invites offers to supply goods or services. Two kinds of tender must, however, be distinguished: (*a*) where the tender is an offer to supply a *specified* or definite quantity of goods or services; and (*b*) where the tender is a *standing* offer, i.e. an offer to supply goods or services periodically or as required.

The rules may be summarized as follows:

(*a*) Where tenders are invited for the supply of goods or services, each tender submitted is a separate offer any one of which may be accepted. On acceptance of a tender a contract is formed. For example, *A* invites tenders for the supply of 100 tons of coal: *B* submits a tender which is accepted; the contract is formed immediately the tender is accepted.

(*b*) Where the tender is a standing offer to supply goods or services as required by the buyer (or offeree), a separate acceptance is made each time an order is placed.

> *G.N. Rly. Co.* v. *Witham* (1873). A railway company advertised for tenders for the supply of stores. *W* made a tender and undertook 'to supply the company for 12 months with such quantities of specified articles as the company may order from time to time'. The tender was accepted. Orders were placed and goods supplied for some time, but later *W* refused to execute an order given. *Held:* *W* was bound to supply goods which had been specifically ordered but was free to refuse to supply any further goods which might be ordered in the future.

If the buyer gives no order or fails to order the full quantity of goods set out in a tender, there is no breach of contract; but where a buyer binds himself 'to buy all the goods he needs' from the person submitting a tender, the contract is broken if the buyer does need some of the goods and does not obtain them from the tenderer (*Kier* v. *Whitehead Iron Co*, 1918).

4. Intention to Create Legal Relations

A contract is an agreement that is intended to have legal consequences. Whether or not an agreement is intended to have such consequences is not always easily determined. We have mentioned that agreements of a purely social or domestic nature are not contracts. However, there are some 'domestic' agreements which do create legal obligations.

> *Simpkins* v. *Pays* (1955). *S* agreed with *P* and *P*'s grand-daughter to 'go shares' in a weekly coupon submitted in a fashion competition. A forecast by the grand-daughter proved correct, and defendant received a prize of £750. Plaintiff sued for his share of £250. *Held:* that there was an intention to create legal relations. Evidence showed there was a joint

enterprise, and the parties expected to share any prize won in the competition. It was not a mere domestic arrangement.

Parker v. *Clark* (1960). An aged couple made an arrangement by correspondence with their niece and her husband whereby the latter couple sold up their home in Sussex in order to live with the aged couple and to share the household and other expenses. The two couples subsequently quarrelled and the Parkers were ordered to leave the house. *Held:* that there was an intention to create legal relations, and damages were awarded to plaintiff.

Commercial and Business Agreements. In all cases coming before the courts, evidence (oral or written) will be required to substantiate the existence of a legal agreement. In commercial and business relations the law will presume that the parties entering into agreement intend those agreements to have legal consequences. Examples abound in this book.

However, this presumption may be negatived by express terms.

Rose & Frank Co. v. *J. R. Crompton & Bros. Ltd.* (1925). Plaintiffs were appointed selling agents in North America for the defendants, and the parties entered into an agreement which included the following: 'This arrangement is not, nor is this memorandum written as, a formal or legal agreement and shall not be subject to legal jurisdiction in the law courts.' *Held:* that this agreement was not a legally binding contract. The court stated it would respect the intention of the parties as shown in the agreement.

Appleson v. *Littlewood Ltd.* (1939). *A* sent in a football-pools coupon, bearing a written condition that 'it shall not be attended by or give rise to any legal relationship, rights, duties, consequences'. *Held:* that in view of this condition the agreement was not actionable.

Similarly, where a coupon contains the words that the entry 'shall not give rise to any legal relationships, or be legally enforceable, but binding in honour only', the clause manifests that the agreement is not a contract creating legal relations (*Jones* v. *Vernon's Pools Ltd.*, 1938).

Although the terms used in the agreements noted above considerably limit the effect of the rights of the parties, we must observe that it is not possible to make an agreement which ousts the jurisdiction of the courts of law. Such a term is void. Access to the courts of law is open to all persons to test their rights, and it is for the courts to decide whether rights do or do not exist or whether a remedy will or will not be granted. Moreover, parties may agree to arbitration (see p. 72) which is a common method of settling disputes in commercial contracts.

5. Consideration

One of the fundamental rules of this branch of the law is that 'consideration' is a necessary element in the formation of a valid simple contract. In *Rann* v. *Hughes* (1778), the principle was stated clearly that 'if contracts be merely written and not specialties (i.e. by deed), they are parol (i.e. oral) and a consideration must be proved'.

A bare promise (*nudum pactum*) is not legally binding, so that if *A* promises £10 to *B*, it follows that *B* cannot enforce the payment of the sum at law if *A* subsequently changes his mind. 'A promise without consideration is a gift; one made for consideration is a bargain.'

In *Currie* v. *Misa* (1875) the term **Valuable Consideration** was defined as *some right, interest, profit or benefit accruing to one party, or some forbearance, detriment, loss or responsibility given, suffered or undertaken by the other*. Valuable consideration means, therefore, any benefit to the promisor, or detriment to the promisee, which is sufficient in law to support the promise. In other words, it is the price for which the promise of the other is bought.

'Good consideration' is another form altogether and consists in some moral obligation such as natural love and affection. It is not sufficient to support a valid simple contract.

Executed Consideration means that consideration which is wholly performed on one side immediately the contract is entered into. For example, Aston sells his bicycle to Bray for £20, which Bray agrees to pay next week. If Aston delivers the machine straight away, the consideration is 'executed' by Aston.

Executory Consideration is a promise to confer a benefit or to suffer some detriment at some future time. For example, so far as Bray is concerned (in the example above) his consideration is 'executory' since the £20 is payable in the future. Similarly, if *M* and *N* agree to form a partnership on January 1 of next year, both parties give mutual promises, and the consideration will be executory.

Rules of Consideration

The general rules relating to consideration are that (*a*) it must be real or genuine, (*b*) it need not be adequate, (*c*) it must be legal, (*d*) it must move from the promisee, (*e*) it must be possible, and (*f*) it must not be past.

(*a*) **Consideration must be real or genuine.** The courts will not enforce vague or sham promises, or promises in which there is no benefit at all, or where no detriment is imposed on the parties. The 'reality' of the consideration will be understood by reference to the following cases.

> *White* v. *Bluett* (1853). An undertaking by a son 'to cease complaining that he was not as well treated as his brother' was held insufficient consideration and was nothing more than a promise 'not to bore' his father.

Similarly a promise 'to do the right thing' is too indefinite and vague to support a contract.

Glasbrook Bros. v. *Glamorgan C.C.* (1925). The managers of a colliery requested police protection during a strike, and asked that police be billeted on the premises. The police arranged for this to be done, and thus gave more secure police protection than applied generally throughout the area. When sued for the cost by the police authority, the colliery owners refused to pay on the ground that the police were under a public duty to give police-protection. *Held:* that police had done more than they were bound to do and that the special protection was sufficient consideration in support of the contract.

Collins v. *Godefroy* (1813). *G* obtained from the Court a *subpoena* requiring *C*'s attendance as a witness for *G*. *G* promised to pay *C* six guineas as compensation for loss of time by *C*. *G* refused to pay and *C* sued *G*. *Held:* the issue of a *subpoena* imposed on *C* a duty to attend court by law, and the performance by *C* could not be consideration for *G*'s promise to pay the sum stated.

Ward v. *Byham* (1956). The father of an illegitimate child promised £1 a week to the mother provided that 'the child will be well looked after and happy'. *Held:* that the promise was binding since the mother's undertaking amounted to something more than her mere legal obligation to the child.

Shadwell v. *Shadwell* (1860). An uncle promised his nephew an annuity of £150 if he should marry Ellen Nicholl, to whom the nephew had already become engaged. The nephew married the lady. Certain payments were made by the uncle, and on his death the nephew sued the uncle's executors for the balance outstanding. *Held:* that by marrying, the nephew had incurred responsibilities and changed his position and status, and the uncle had derived some benefit in seeing his nephew settled.

(*b*) **Consideration need not be adequate.** The general rule of the law of contract is that the parties are free to make what contracts they desire, e.g. by naming the price for which they are prepared to sell their goods. A person cannot seek the assistance of a court of law merely because he has made a bad bargain. *Caveat emptor* ('let the buyer beware') is a basic rule. If I buy for £1 a picture which turns out to be a Rembrandt, I am lucky; the seller is not. The contract is good.

Bainbridge v. *Firmstone* (1838). *B* allowed *F* to weigh two boilers owned by *B*, on condition that they were returned as they were lent. *F*. took them to pieces to weigh them and returned them in this condition. *B* sued for damages. *Held:* that there was a contract for the returning of the boilers in a complete state. The consideration given by the plaintiff, *B*, was the parting with the possession of the boilers for however short a period. Damages for plaintiff, *B*.

Haigh v. *Brooks* (1839). *B* promised to pay certain bills if *H* would hand over a guarantee to him. *H* handed over the guarantee, which turned out to be unenforceable. *Held:* that the consideration was valid as the plaintiff was induced to part with something which he might have kept and the defendant obtained what he desired.

Where an intending litigant genuinely forbears from taking legal action, such forbearance is valuable consideration provided that the action itself is not vexatious, frivolous or one which the person forbearing knows must fail (*Callisher* v. *Bischoffsheim*, 1870; and *Wade* v. *Simeon*, 1846).

The adequacy of the consideration is not irrelevant where fraud is alleged. Thus if *A* states fraudulently that a picture is a genuine Van Gogh, and *B* pays £50,000 for the picture, which is in fact valueless, the adequacy of the consideration is highly relevant to the intention of the seller to deceive the purchaser.

Sufficiency of Consideration. Can a promise to pay less than the amount due be consideration? The general rule laid down in *Pinnel*'s case (1602) is that payment of a lesser sum than the amount due cannot be treated as satisfaction for an existing debt.

> *Pinnel*'s case (1602). *P* sued *C* for £8 10*s*. due on 11 November 1600. *C* alleged that, at *P*'s request, he had paid to *P* £5 2*s*. 6*d*. on 1 October, and that *P* had agreed to accept this payment in full satisfaction of the original debt of £8 10*s*.

Although the court gave judgment for Pinnel on a technical point, it was also laid down that *payment of a lesser sum on the day cannot be any satisfaction for the whole*. But to this general rule there are the following exceptions:

(i) Where the debtor, at the creditor's request, makes an *earlier* payment. The earlier payment gives the creditor something to which he is not strictly entitled, and this is consideration. A later payment of a lesser sum than the amount due, however, will not be sufficient.

(ii) Where the *mode of payment* is altered. The payment of a debt must be by legal tender. In *Goddard* v. *O'Brien* (1882) it was held that the giving of a cheque for a smaller sum in satisfaction of a debt of a greater amount was the giving of 'something collateral' and the debt was thereby extinguished. The modern view is that the giving of a cheque in payment of an existing debt is not an alteration of the mode of payment: per Lord Denning in *D & C Builders Ltd.* v. *Rees*, summarized on p. 129. Similarly, where *A* is bound to pay for example £20 to *B* at London, and *B* requests *A* to pay £15 on the day at York, there will be a good discharge if *A* accedes to the request and pays £15 at York.

(iii) Where something is *added*. For example, if *A* owes £20 to *B* on a certain date, and *B* agrees to accept £10 plus an article, such as a tom-tit or canary (as in Pinnel's case) or a transistor radio, however small in value, there will be a good discharge.

In these cases the change of time or mode of payment or the addition of something of value must be with the agreement of and to the benefit of the creditor to amount to a good discharge.

(iv) *'Composition'* agreements. To avoid bankruptcy a debtor may reach an agreement with his creditors to pay them, say, 50p in the £ in full settlement of their debts; the payment of the lesser sum discharges the greater amount. The consideration is the agreement by the creditors with each other and with the debtor not to insist on their full claims. If any creditor were to do so he would be defrauding the others.

(v) Payment of a lesser sum by a third party.

(*c*) **Consideration must be legal.** This is obvious. A promise to break into a house for £100 must inevitably be regarded as unlawful and therefore void. No criminal would have the nerve to sue on such a contract and would receive prompt attention from the police if he did, for his agreement would amount to criminal conspiracy at least.

Pearce v. *Brooks* (1866). The owner of a cab let it out on hire to a known prostitute for use by her. *Held:* that the owner, *P*, could not sue for the cost of the hire since he knew of the nature of the use to which the cab would be put.

Foster v. *Driscoll* (1929). A contract was entered into for the shipment of whisky from England to the United States during the time when prohibition was in force. *Held:* that the consideration (whisky), the import of which was illegal (according to the law of the United States, a friendly country), rendered the contract void.

(*d*) **Consideration must move from the promisee** (i.e. the person to whom the promise was made). The relationship which exists between promisor and promisee is known as *privity of contract*. Since the parties to the contract must provide consideration, it follows that as a general rule a person who receives a benefit under a contract may not, unless he has supplied consideration, enforce rights under the contract. In other words, no stranger to the consideration may sue on a contract.

Tweddle v. *Atkinson* (1861). *T* was married to the daughter of *X*. To assist the married couple, *X* promised to pay *T* £200 in consideration of *T*'s father paying *T* £100. *X*, however, died before he had paid the £200, and in consequence *T* sued Atkinson, *X*'s executor. *Held:* that *T* could not sue as no consideration had been given by *T*. Only *T*'s father was entitled to sue.

(*e*) **Consideration must be possible.** The law will not enforce a contract to do that which is quite outside human capability. Thus a promise to go to the centre of the Earth in consideration of the payment of £100, would be absurd and impossible, and brings into question whether the parties could genuinely have contemplated legal relations on that basis. However, a promise to do the impossible must be distinguished from a promise which, although possible of performance when the contract was entered into, becomes impossible subsequently. This is discussed under the doctrine of Frustration (see p. 171).

(*f*) **Consideration must not be past.** This means that a benefit conferred in the past is not consideration for a present promise. In everyday life this may seem harsh, since most of us have received great benefits from others, e.g. parents, teachers, friends who have given a helping hand in moments of crisis. Apart from these moral obligations of indebtedness, the rule of law concerning past consideration is practical and sound.

> *Roscorla* v. *Thomas* (1842). *T* sold a horse to *R* for £30. After the actual sale, *T* stated that the horse was sound and free from vice. The horse proved, in fact, to be vicious, and *R* sued *T*. *Held:* that *R* could not recover on the warranty that the horse was not vicious. The sale had already taken place when the warranty as to the soundness and quiet temperament was given. The warranty did not, therefore, form part of the consideration.

> *Re McArdle* (1951). The occupants carried out certain improvements and decorations to a house at a cost of £488. After the work was done, those beneficially interested in the house executed a document by which they promised, in consideration of the execution of the work, to pay £488. *Held:* that the consideration for the promise was past, as the work had been completed when the promise was made; the claim to recover £488 therefore failed.

There are two exceptions to this rule, as follows:

(i) *Bills of Exchange Act, 1882*. Section 27 of this Act lays down that, in addition to any consideration sufficient to support a simple contract, the consideration for a bill of exchange may be any *antecedent debt or liability*, provided that such debt or liability is not that of a stranger to the instrument.

(ii) *Services Rendered*. Where it is proved that services have been rendered at the express or implied request of the promisor, it has been held that this is sufficient consideration to support a *subsequent* promise to pay.

> *Lampleigh* v. *Braithwait* (1615). *B* had unlawfully killed a man, and he requested *L* to obtain the King's pardon for him. *L* did as requested and went to considerable trouble to do so. *B* then promised *L* £100 for his services. *Held:* that as *L*'s services were rendered at the defendant's request, there was consideration for defendant's promise.

Today's view of such services would probably be that the defendant's request to the plaintiff would imply a promise to pay a reasonable sum for those services.

(N.B. The further exception, that a statute-barred debt could be revived by a subsequent acknowledgment or payment, was abolished by the Limitation Act, 1980.)

Of the two foregoing exceptions, (i) is the only true exception; (ii) is looked upon merely as an *apparent* exception to the rule that consideration must not be past.

Equitable Estoppel. Although the basic rule of common law is that consideration is essential to support a valid simple contract, there are exceptions to the rule. These exceptions demonstrate how equitable principles operate to do justice in the particular case and to soften the rigid rules of common law.

Hughes v. *Metropolitan Railway Co.* (1877). *H*, landlord, gave *MR* (lessee) 6 months' notice to repair some houses in accordance with the lease. A month later *H* negotiated with *MR* to purchase the freehold. Relying on this *MR* did not repair the houses. Negotiations failed after 2 months. After 6 months *H* sued for ejectment of *MR* for failure to repair. *Held* (House of Lords): equity should override the common law. *MR* relied on the negotiations as being, in effect, a promise that *H* would not enforce his demands while negotiations continued. So no repairs were done. *H* failed in his action. 'It is the first principle upon which all courts of equity proceed that if parties who have entered into definite and distinct terms involving certain legal results ... afterwards by their own act ... enter upon a course of negotiations which has the effect of leading one of the parties to suppose that the strict rights arising under the contract will not be enforced, or will be kept in suspense ... the person who otherwise might have enforced those rights will not be allowed to enforce them where it would be inequitable having regard to the dealings which have thus taken place between the parties (per Lord Cairns, L.C.).

Central London Property Trust Ltd. v. *High Trees House Ltd.* (1947). In 1937 the plaintiffs let to the defendants a block of flats on a 99-year lease (by deed) at a rental of £2,500 a year. Only a few flats were let owing to the outbreak of war, and the consequent departure of people from London. Plaintiffs then entered into an agreement with the defendants to reduce the rent to £1,250 a year. The defendants, who were contemplating terminating the lease, continued it in these circumstances. The agreement was in writing, not under seal, and operated from 1941 to 1945. Then, when the flats were fully let, plaintiffs claimed for the full rent of £2,500 from 1941. The basis of the claim was that there was no consideration for the reduction agreed in 1941. *Held* (Denning, J.): that plaintiffs were entitled to the full rent from 1945, since implied in the 1940 agreement there was a term that the rent should revert to the original rent when the war-time situation ended. It would be inequitable to allow the plaintiffs to go back on their promise as to 1941/45 because, on the strength of it the defendants had reduced the rents to their tenants, relying on the fact that the agreement prevented the strict legal effects of the first contract from being enforced. It was a case of *equitable estoppel.*

The principle in this case is that a promise intended to create legal relations which, to the knowledge of the promisor, will be acted upon by the promisee, and which is in fact acted upon (e.g. by retaining the lease as above), must be honoured. The law does not, however, give cause for action in damages if such a promise is broken; and it will not allow the promisor to act inconsistently with the promise, even though the promise is not supported by consideration in the strict sense.

D & C Builders Ltd. v. *Rees* (1966). D & C Builders claimed £482 for work done for *R*, debtor. Mrs. R, knowing D & C Builders were in financial difficulties, offered £300 by cheque in full settlement and stated that if the builders would not accept that sum they would get nothing. D & C Builders reluctantly accepted, but later sued for the balance of £182. *Held:* that D & C Builders could recover. There was no consideration for the builders' agreement to take less, nor were they estopped from claiming the balance, because Mr. and Mrs. Rees had acted inequitably by making threats to the builders. Therefore the remedy of promissory estoppel was not available to them. The payment by cheque was not sufficient alteration of mode to amount to consideration, for it was not done at the request of the builders.

The principle operates as a shield to the party sued, and is not a weapon of attack enabling the other party to sue on a gratuitous promise.

Combe v. *Combe* (1951). A husband and wife were divorced in 1943. The husband agreed to make an annual allowance to the wife. Accordingly, and because of this agreement, the wife failed to apply for a court order for maintenance against the husband. He, however, did not make any payments. In 1950 the wife sued the husband on his promise to pay the annual allowance. *Held* (by Lord Justice Birkett): that as the husband had not requested the wife to refrain from making an application to the court, there was no consideration for his promise moving from the wife. Therefore the action by the wife failed. 'The principle in the High Trees House case must be used as a shield and not a sword.'

'It is not thought right that a man who has indicated that he is not going to insist on his strict legal rights, as a result of which the other party has altered his position, should be able at a minute's notice to insist upon his rights however inconvenient it may be to the other party' (Lord Cohen in *Tool Metal Manufacturing Co. Ltd.* v. *Tungsten Electric Co. Ltd.*, (1955).

6. Form

We have already seen (p. 113) that unless contracts are valid, they may be classified as void, voidable, or unenforceable. A void contract is entirely without legal effect, does not give rise to any legal rights and duties, and is, in fact, no contract at all. A voidable contract is one which may be repudiated at the will of one of the parties, but until it is so repudiated it remains valid and binding. It is affected by a flaw (e.g. fraud, innocent misrepresentation, undue influence or duress), and the presence of any one of these defects enables the person adversely affected to take steps to set the contract aside.

Unenforceable contracts are neither void nor voidable, but they cannot be enforced in the courts because they lack some item of evidence essential to a valid contract. Some contracts must be made by deed, some must be in writing, and some must be evidenced by writing. Unless the writing (in the form laid down by law) is available, the courts will not lend their aid to the enforcement of the agreements. So they are stated to be unenforceable, but it does not mean that they are invalid. The purpose of these formal requirements is to achieve certainty and thus avoid disputes arising in the transfer of ownership or possession or rights in various kinds of property.

Contracts which must be by deed. The following *must* be by deed, otherwise the transaction is invalid:

(*a*) Contracts not supported by valuable consideration, e.g. promise of gifts.
(*b*) Leases of land for more than three years (Law of Property Act, 1925).
(*c*) Transfers of British ships or shares in British ships.
(*d*) Transfers of title to land (Law of Property Act, 1925).

Contracts which must be in writing. The following *must* be in writing, a requirement laid down by statute in each case:

(*a*) Bills of exchange, cheques and promissory notes (Bills of Exchange Act, 1882).
(*b*) A contract of marine insurance (Stamps Act, 1891).
(*c*) A contract under the Moneylenders Act, 1927.
(*d*) A hire-purchase contract (Hire Purchase Act, 1965).
(*e*) An assignment of copyright (Copyright Act, 1956).
(*f*) Transfer of shares in a registered company (Companies Act, 1985).

Contracts which must be evidenced in writing. The following will not be enforced in the courts unless a sufficient *note or memorandum* (the nature of which will be examined later) signed by the defendant or his agent is available as proof of the agreement entered into:

(*a*) contracts of guarantee;

(*b*) contracts for the sale or other disposition of land (Law of Property Act, 1925, s. 40);

(*c*) contracts of employment (Contracts of Employment Act, 1972).

Contracts of Guarantee. Under section 4 of the Statute of Frauds, 1677, as amended by the Law Reform (Enforcement of Contracts) Act, 1954, 'any special promise to answer for the debt, default or miscarriage of another person' is required to be evidenced by writing. Section 4 applies to contracts of guarantee, by which we mean the undertaking by one person to hold himself responsible to another (e.g. a creditor) for the debt or wrongful action (tort) of a third party. For example, let us suppose that you and I enter a shop in which you want to make a purchase. The shopkeeper may not wish to sell the goods to you unless you have a guarantor, i.e. a person who will undertake to pay for the goods if you default in payment. I inform the shopkeeper that I will pay for the goods if you do not (or are unable to) pay. This is a **guarantee**. You are *primarily* liable on the contract, while I am *secondarily* liable in the event of your default. The shopkeeper should ensure that some document (the 'note or memorandum') is completed, and signed by me as guarantor signifying the agreement.

A contract of guarantee must be distinguished from an indemnity. Thus, if you and I go into a shop and I say to the shopkeeper: 'Let him have the goods, I will ensure you are paid' (or 'I will pay for them'), I am indemnifying the shopkeeper against loss on the contract. I am primarily liable on the contract, and may be sued by the creditor. Such is not a guarantee; it is an **indemnity**, and no writing is required to evidence the agreement.

Contracts subject to s. 40 of the Law of Property Act, 1925. Section 40 provides that

> No action may be brought upon any contract for the sale or other disposition of land or any other interest in land, unless the agreement upon which such action is brought, or some memorandum or note thereof, is in writing, and signed by the party to be charged or by some other person thereunto by him lawfully authorized.

Contracts for the sale of land* are obviously highly important, first because land itself has always been of great value, and secondly because the law insists that particularly strong evidence should be necessary to prove the dispositions of land by way of sale or transfer. The phrase 'or other disposition' of land refers to leases, mortgages, etc., and these too require to be evidenced in writing.

'Note or Memorandum.' Ideally, contracts of the above kind (guarantees or sales or transfers of land) should be wholly in writing in one clearly written or printed form. Unfortunately mankind is not always tidy and efficient, and the written evidence may consist in a number

* This refers to the preliminary agreement, and not to the conveyance which must be by deed.

of documents, e.g. letters. Provided that there is some indication, oral or written, connecting them, the various documents taken together may evidence the contract and thus constitute the 'memorandum' to satisfy the evidential requirements of the law.

The memorandum must contain the following:

(*a*) The names of the parties (or sufficient description to identify them).

(*b*) The subject-matter of the contract (i.e. the goods, land, etc.).

(*c*) The consideration agreed upon. This is not necessary in contracts of guarantee.

(*d*) The signature of the person to be charged (i.e. the guarantor, or the person against whom the document will be used in evidence and who has accepted responsibility).

> *Pearce* v. *Gardner* (1887). *G* agreed to sell *P* gravel situated on *G*'s land. *P* sued for breach of contract and sought to put in evidence a letter signed by *G* and starting 'Dear Sir'. The letter did not contain *P*'s name, but *P* produced the envelope which was addressed to him and in which the letter was contained. *Held:* that the letter and the envelope together constituted a sufficient memorandum.

7. The Doctrine of Part Performance

We have noted in the contracts just described that, in the absence of the required evidence in writing, the courts would do nothing. Such was the attitude of the common law: in effect a refusal to act because the parties failed to comply with the requirements laid down as to evidence. Equity, however, took a different view, and the doctrine of Part Performance shows how it dispensed its fairness and justice in cases where there was no note or memorandum. If, in the circumstances, the enforcement of the rigid rule of law would assist fraud rather than prevent it, equity would intervene as a matter of conscience.

In consequence of a number of judicial decisions it is now established that the equitable remedy will be granted where:

(*a*) The contract is of such a nature that the court can effectively compel performance. The doctrine does not, therefore, apply to contracts of personal service.

(*b*) The plaintiff has committed some act of part performance which is unequivocally referable to the contract.

(*c*) The circumstances are such that it would be fraudulent on the defendant's part to take advantage of the lack of written evidence.

(*d*) There is adequate and admissible oral evidence of the terms of the contract.

> *Wakeham* v. *Mackenzie* (1968). A widow, aged 67, gave up her council

house to look after a widower of 72 in poor health. He promised orally that he would leave her his house when he died. The widow contributed to household expenses but had no remuneration from her friend. *Held:* the widow's acts were consistent with the oral contract, clearly referred to it and she was entitled to specific performance to convey the house to her, despite the absence of a written memorandum.

Rawlinson v. *Ames* (1925). Mrs. *A* agreed orally to take a lease of Mrs. *R*'s flat. Mrs. *A* requested Mrs. *R* to carry out certain alterations which Mrs. *A* supervised. Mrs. *A* refused to complete, and when sued upon the contract pleaded the Statute of Frauds and the absence of a memorandum. *Held:* that the alterations made by Mrs. *R* at Mrs. *A*'s request clearly constituted acts of part performance and were 'unequivocally referable to the contract'. Accordingly Mrs. *A* must complete the contract by signing a proper lease.

Maddison v. *Alderson* (1883). Mrs. *M* was employed as housekeeper to Mr. *A*, a farmer, for a number of years. *A* made an oral promise that if *M* would carry on working for the rest of *A*'s life without wages he would by his will leave her a life interest in the farm. *A* made a will in those terms, but it was declared void. *M* sued, alleging part performance. *Held:* that there were many reasons why *M* might have worked without wages. The work was equivocal; for example, she might have wanted a home. It did not follow that she was entitled to a life interest.

8. Contractual Capacity

The general rule is that any person, of whatever nationality or sex, may enter into a binding contract. To this rule there are certain exceptions. First, we remember that the word 'person' includes both natural and artificial (or juristic) persons such as corporations. By the very nature of things certain special rules apply to these. Secondly, there are special rules of common law and statute law formed for the protection of certain classes of person who by reason of want of age or deficiency in mental ability and understanding might be taken advantage of by experienced and mature adults.

The special rules affecting each class of person are detailed below.

Infants or Minors

As we have noted, a person attains his majority 'at the commencement of the relevant anniversary of the date of his birth' (Family Law Reform Act, 1969). From the moment he reaches 18 he assumes the full responsibilities of an adult.

Certain contracts made by a minor are classified as (*a*) void, (*b*) valid or (*c*) voidable.

(*a*) **Void Contracts.** As a result of the recommendations of the Law Commission published in their Report on Minors Contracts (Law Com. No. 134) the Minors' Contracts Act 1987 was passed with the aim of removing certain restrictions on the enforceability of contracts entered into by minors.

Previously, parts of the law of contract relating to minors, particularly those classified as 'void' contracts were governed by the Infants Relief Act, 1874; Section 1 of which rendered 'absolutely void' all contracts with minors for the payment of money lent, or for goods supplied or to be supplied (other than contracts for 'necessaries'—the legal meaning of which is explained below) and all accounts stated with minors.

The effect of the Minors' Contracts Act 1987 is to disapply (i.e. repeal) the Infants Relief Act, 1874. As a consequence, Section 1 of the 1874 Act will cease to govern these contracts which will become subject to the rules of common law.

Section 1 of the Minors' Contracts Act, 1987 also repeals Section 5 of the Betting and Loans (Infants) Act, 1892, which rendered void any new agreement by a minor, after attaining full age, to repay a loan obtained during his minority; it also invalidated any negotiable instrument given in connection with such agreement. By disapplying this provision the 1987 Act makes any future such agreement and any negotiable agreement effective.

Section 2 of the Minors' Contracts Act 1987 provides that where:

(i) a guarantee is given in respect of an obligation of a party; and

(ii) the obligation is unenforceable against him (or he repudiates the contract) because he was a minor when the contract was made, the guarantee shall not, for that reason alone, be unenforceable against the guarantor.

The effect of this section is to make a guarantee of a minor's contractual obligation enforceable against the guarantor even though the main contractual obligation is not enforceable against the minor. It ensures that the guarantee of an unenforceable minor's contract is as effective as if the minor had been an adult. Prior to this section coming into force Section 1 of the Infants Relief Act, 1874 had the effect of invalidating guarantees on the basis that the main contract itself was 'absolutely void'. This means that the rule in *Coutts & Co.* v. *Browne-Lecky* (1947) is now repealed.

It is no longer necessary for a creditor to ensure that a separate indemnity is taken instead of a guarantee, although the distinction between them for all other purposes is apparently unaffected.

It is important to note that these changes in no way alter the circumstances in which a guarantor who has honoured the guarantee is entitled to recover against the minor. He is in the same position as any of the minor's creditors.

Section 3 of the 1987 Act alters the common law as to recovery of property from defaulting minors under unenforceable contracts. The disappointed creditor is now allowed even in the absence of fraud and where it is 'just and equitable' to obtain a court order for the return of property acquired by a minor 'or any property representing it'. It will be necessary to wait and see how this part of the new Act will affect the decision in *Leslie* v. *Shiell* (1914).

However, in case it should be thought that minors are free to do as they wish in regard to loans it must not be forgotten that if a minor misrepresents his age fraudulently and obtains money or goods, he renders himself liable to prosecution for 'dishonestly obtaining the property of another by deception'—an arrestable offence under the Theft Act, 1968, and punishable with imprisonment.

The decision in *Ballett* v. *Mingay* (1943) relating to wrongful interference to goods by a minor would appear to be unaffected by the new Act.

(*b*) **Valid Contracts.** These are of two types: (i) contracts for 'necessaries' and (ii) contracts for the minor's benefit.

(i) *Contracts for 'necessaries'* are contracts for 'goods suitable to the condition in life of the minor *and* to his actual requirements at the time of sale *and* delivery' (Sale of Goods Act, 1979, s. 3). In any legal action, therefore, the courts will have to decide whether the goods in dispute are, as a matter of fact, necessaries for that particular minor having regard to his 'condition in life' (or status or standard of living).

The next question to be considered is whether, even though the goods may be 'necessaries' in themselves, the minor is in fact already plentifully supplied with the goods; for one must connect the word 'necessaries' with the minor's 'actual requirements' at the time of sale *and* at the time of delivery, where these times are different.

Examples of necessaries include such obvious things as food, clothing, medical attention, and educational books. Even services such as legal advice or hire of a car have been held to fall into this class. But in all cases it is for the court to decide as a matter of fact whether the goods supplied or services given are necessaries to that minor. Where a minor is married, the term will include necessaries for his wife and any children he may have.

Nash v. *Inman* (1908). Plaintiff was a Savile Row tailor and the defendant an undergraduate of Trinity College, Cambridge, who was under

21. Defendant ordered clothes (including 11 fancy waistcoats) which together amounted to £145. The plaintiff sued the defendant for the sum. Defendant's father, an architect, proved that his son was already supplied with adequate clothes suitabe to his condition in life when the clothes made by plaintiff were delivered. *Held:* that in view of these facts, the plaintiff's clothes were not 'necessaries' and accordingly the action failed.

(ii) *Contracts for the Minor's Benefit.* The question of what is 'for the minor's benefit' is one for the court to decide from the particular facts of each case. Decided cases show that contracts of apprenticeship, training or education fall within this class. The court will look at the contract as a whole; isolated terms that are not for the minor's benefit will not necessarily invalidate the contract, and it may be enforced against the minor.

Doyle v. *White City Stadium Ltd.* (1953). *D*, an infant professional boxer, made a contract with the British Boxing Board of Control. A term in the contract provided that if *D* were disqualified for certain reasons the prize money would be withheld. *D* fought a contest and was disqualified. He sued the Board to recover the money, contending that due to his infancy he was not bound. *Held:* that *D*'s action must fail. The agreement was closely analogous to a contract of employment and the contract was on the whole for his benefit.

Roberts v. *Gray* (1913). *G* a young professional billiards player agreed with *R* (a leading professional player) to go on a world tour, competing against each other in matches. *R* accordingly made arrangements, but a dispute arose and *G* declined to go and repudiated the contract. *R* sued the infant and claimed damages for breach of their contract. *Held:* that the contract was for the infant's benefit in that he would in effect be receiving instruction. Damages were awarded to *R*.

If a minor is a trader and agrees to sell goods and receives payment for them he cannot, if he has committed no fraud, be compelled to refund the money or deliver the goods.

Cowern v. *Nield* (1912). *N*, an infant hay and straw dealer, failed to deliver a consignment of hay to *C*, to whom he had contracted to sell the goods. *C* paid for the goods. *Held:* that the contract was a trading contract which was not binding on the infant. Moreover, the infant, *N*, was not compelled to repay the price paid by *C*.

Mercantile Union Guarantee Corpn. v. *Ball* (1937). *B*, an infant haulage contractor aged 20, contracted to buy a lorry on hire-purchase terms for use in his business. *Held:* that the infant was not liable for the instalments due under the agreement.

(*c*) **Voidable Contracts.** In this class we include (i) contracts of a continuing nature and (ii) contracts under which a minor acquires an interest in property of a permanent kind, e.g. leases of property, partnership agreements, or the taking of shares in a company.

These contracts are described as voidable because they will be binding upon a minor unless he repudiates them before he reaches his majority, or within a reasonable time thereafter.

> *Steinberg* v. *Scala* (*Leeds*) *Ltd.* (1923). The plaintiff, an infant, applied for and was allotted shares in the defendant company. She paid sums on allotment and on the first call on the shares. She was unable to pay further calls and repudiated the contract. She requested, while still an infant, that her name be removed from the register of shareholders and also requested the return of all money she had paid. *Held:* that the infant was entitled to the removal of her name from the register, so avoiding future calls on her shares, but she could not recover the moneys paid because there had not been a *total* failure of consideration; although no dividends had been paid on the shares, nevertheless the shares had some value.

> *Valentini* v. *Canali* (1889). An infant took a lease of a house and agreed to buy the furniture in it for £102. The infant paid £68 on account. After some months, however, he repudiated the contract and then claimed to recover the sum of £68 paid. *Held:* that the infant was entitled to have the contract set aside, but having used the furniture he could not recover the £68 already paid under the contract, for there was no *total* failure of consideration.

Similarly, when a minor becomes a partner in a firm he is not liable for the firm's debts contracted during his minority. He may, however, on or before reaching majority repudiate the contract of partnership. If he omits so to do and continues as a partner he will be responsible for all the firm's debts contracted after he reaches 18.

We have mentioned that a minor may repudiate this class of contract before or within a 'reasonable time after' he reaches 18. What is a 'reasonable time' is a matter for decision by the court and varies with each type of contract.

Section 2 of the Infants' Relief Act, 1874, provided that 'no action shall be brought whereby to charge upon any promise made after full age to pay any debt contracted during minority, or upon any ratification made after full age of any promise or contract made during minority, whether there shall or shall not be any new consideration for such promise or ratification after full age'.

A creditor will no longer be concerned with this distinction between ratification and a fresh agreement as Section 2 has been repealed by the Minors' Contracts Act, 1987.

Corporations

We have already discussed the position and status of corporations in English law (see p. 100). The contractual capacity of a corporation depends on whether it is (*a*) a chartered corporation, (*b*) a statutory corporation or (*c*) a corporation by registration under the Companies Act, 1985.

By the nature of things corporations are incapable of making certain contracts of a personal nature, e.g. a contract to marry.

(*a*) **Chartered Corporations.** These are formed by royal charter, and the powers of the corporation are found in the charter granting it corporate status. There are no legal limits to the contractual capacity of these corporations. If, therefore, contracts are made outside the powers defined in the particular charter, such contracts are not void. However, the activities of the corporation may be controlled by law to some extent. Thus, an application may be made to the court for an injunction to prevent or restrain a corporation from making contracts outside the terms of its charter. Further, the Crown which grants the charter may revoke it if the corporation wilfully persists in operating outside the limits of its powers (*Baroness Wenlock* v. *River Dee Co.*, 1888).

(*b*) **Statutory Corporations.** These corporations derive their powers from the statutes which create them. Sometimes the powers are increased by subsequent statutes or statutory instruments, but in all cases any acts or contracts formed beyond the powers contained in the statutes or statutory instruments are *ultra vires* and void.

(*c*) **Registered Companies.** These corporations have the powers detailed in the 'Objects' clause of the Memorandum of Association. An act in excess of the powers defined in the memorandum is *ultra vires* and void (but see page 104). Sometimes it is difficult to determine whether an act or a contract is within the meaning of the memorandum or 'fairly incidental' thereto. Because of this, it is customary to draft the terms defining the powers very widely to prevent legal actions against the company on the ground of *ultra vires*.

> *Re Jon Beauforte Ltd.* (1953). A company was empowered to carry on business as clothing manufacturers. It then began making veneered wall panels and no alteration was made to the 'Objects' clause of the Memorandum of Association. The company then made contracts for the construction of a company building and for the supply of veneers and coke. The company later went into liquidation. *Held:* that these contracts were *ultra vires* and therefore void.

Any act or contract which is *ultra vires* the memorandum cannot be ratified subsequently, even if all the shareholders of the company assent thereto (*Ashbury Railway and Carriage Co. Ltd.* v. *Riche*, 1875).

In law the Memorandum of Association, Articles of Association and the Certificate of Incorporation of a company are public documents. Any member of the public proposing to make an important contract with a registered company may, therefore, inspect those documents at the office of the Registrar of Companies on payment of a small fee. In practical business life this precaution is not always taken.

The Form of Contracts Made by Corporations. The common law laid down the general rule that contracts made by corporations must be made under seal. The seal of the corporation is its signature to authenticate its action and to show that the corporation is bound in the same way that an individual is bound by his signature to legal documents or contracts. This requirement of sealing became highly inconvenient, particularly for the making of contracts of a trivial or repetitive nature.

The above rule has now been modified, and section 36 of the Companies Act, 1985, provides that a registered company need not contract under seal except in those cases where an ordinary person is required to do so. Similarly, under the Corporate Bodies' Contracts Act, 1960, other corporations (including local authorities) are permitted to contract in the same way as, or in the manner required of, a private person.

Insane and Drunken Persons

Contracts entered into by an **insane person** are voidable, but liability exists to pay a reasonable price for 'necessaries' (Sale of Goods Act, 1979, s. 2).

Two points must be proved by the person who pleads insanity:

(i) That he was insane at the time of making the contract and that he was incapable of understanding the importance of the transaction; and

(ii) That the other party knew of his condition.

The contracts being voidable, they may be repudiated at the will of the insane party. Unless so repudiated within a reasonable time after his disability has ceased, he will be liable. Any such contract, however, binds the other party to the contract.

Drunken or intoxicated persons are treated in the same way as those suffering from insanity.

Married Women

By virtue of the Law Reform (Married Women and Tortfeasors) Act, 1935, a married woman now has full legal capacity. Accordingly a married woman has the same contractual capacity as a man or an unmarried woman.

A husband will incur liability for his wife's contracts if he expressly authorizes his wife to act as his agent, or impliedly authorizes her to pledge his credit. Thus where a wife purports to contract on his behalf and the husband pays the bills without question or demur, the law will infer that the wife has implied authority to pledge the husband's credit.

Where a wife is, for example, deserted by a husband she may be an 'agent of necessity'. This means that for any 'necessaries' (e.g. food, shelter, and clothing for herself and her family) purchased, the law infers that the husband will be liable. Where, however, the wife has means of her own or is earning her own living the presumption of law may be rebutted.

Aliens

Except that he cannot acquire property in a British ship (Mercantile Shipping Act, 1894, s. 1), an alien has the same contractual capacity in peacetime as a British subject.

In wartime an enemy alien cannot enter into a contract with a British subject, and where an alien made such a contract before the outbreak of war he cannot enforce his rights under the contract in an English court. Where on the other hand the alien is sued in England on such a pre-war contract, he may defend the action.

The contracts of an enemy alien present in England by licence of the Crown are valid and enforceable even during wartime.

The test of whether a person is an 'enemy alien' is not his nationality but the place where he resides or carries on business. So a British subject resident in hostile or enemy-occupied territory may be classed as an enemy alien.

Foreign sovereigns or governments cannot be sued in the English courts unless they voluntarily submit to the jurisdiction (*Mighell* v. *Sultan of Johore*, 1894). Immunity from the jurisdiction of the English courts is extended to foreign ambassadors, High Commissioners of Commonwealth countries, and certain representatives of international organizations including the United Nations. Members of the suites of such persons enjoy similar immunity under the Diplomatic Privileges Act, 1964.

Any such person who is sued (or even prosecuted) may claim immunity from the jurisdiction of the court by arranging for the production in court of a certificate from the Secretary of State for Foreign Affairs. Furthermore, persons enjoying this immunity may not be subpoenaed as witnesses.

9. Terms of a Contract

We have noted that the contents of a contract may be expressed orally or in writing, or by conduct. The terms of a contract define the rights and duties arising under the contract. These terms are of two kinds: (*a*) express and (*b*) implied.

(*a*) **Express Terms.** Where a contract has been put into writing the parties are precluded from adducing evidence to add to, vary or contradict its terms. Therefore, oral evidence will not be admitted to prove that some other term (even though agreed to orally) has been omitted from the written instrument. However, this does not prevent the rectification of a mistake in the written contract, provided that the conditions for rectification are present (see p. 152). Further, if the written contract is not complete and does not, in fact, represent the whole transaction, oral evidence will be admitted by the court to prove a collateral agreement, i.e. one which is subsidiary to the main purpose of the contract.

> *Couchman* v. *Hill* (1947). Plaintiff bought a heifer at an auction, and the catalogue described the animal as 'unserved'. The printed conditions of sale provided that the auctioneer 'gave no warranty whatever' in respect of the condition or description of any animal. Before he bid for the heifer, plaintiff asked the auctioneer and the owner of the heifer to confirm that it was 'unserved'. Both replied in the affirmative. The heifer died within eight weeks of the sale as a result of carrying a calf at too young an age for breeding. *Held* (by the Court of Appeal): that the verbal statements that the heifer was 'unserved' overrode the conditions of sale; plaintiff was able to recover damages for breach of warranty.

Certainty of Terms. Unless the parties make their contract in terms which are certain, their contract will fail.

> *Scammell and Nephew Ltd.* v. *Ouston* (1941). The respondents (*O*) agreed to purchase a motor-van from the appellants. *O* sent an order to appellants thus: 'This order is given on the understanding that the balance of the purchase price can be had on hire-purchase terms over a period of two years.' A dispute arose and the appellants' defence was that there was no contract until 'hire-purchase terms' had been ascertained. *Held:* that no precise meaning could be given to the clause as to 'hire-purchase terms'. They were too vague, and as there was no previous trade practice between the parties to guide the court on what was meant, the contract failed.

Moreover, there cannot be a contract to make a contract. The parties cannot, in other words, make an agreement to agree in the future. The parties must agree on terms which are definite or 'capable of being made definite without further agreement of the parties'.

> *Loftus* v. *Roberts* (1902). *L*, an actress, was engaged for a provincial tour. The contractual agreement provided that if the play came to London *L* would be engaged at a salary 'to be mutually arranged between us'. *Held:* that there was no contract.

This case may be distinguished from the following, where although the parties themselves had not agreed the terms, they nevertheless agreed on a form of proceeding whereby the terms could be determined, as by conferring on a court of law or an arbitrator the power to fill in a term or gap in their agreement.

> *Foley* v. *Classique Coaches Ltd.* (1934). *F* sold part of his land to a motor company on condition that the company would buy all their petrol from him. The agreement between *F* and the company laid down that petrol would be bought from *F* 'at a price to be agreed by the parties in writing and from time to time'. The agreement also provided that in any dispute the agreement should be submitted to arbitration. The price was never agreed and the company refused to purchase the petrol. *Held:* that there was a binding contract, and a method was provided by which the price could be ascertained, namely by arbitration. An injunction was granted against the company restraining them from breach.

Meaningless terms are disregarded in law. If the whole contract is meaningless the contract is void. Where the meaningless term is subsidiary, the contract may be held valid although the meaningless term is ignored.

(*b*) **Implied Terms.** We have noted that one of the basic rules of contract is that the parties are free to make their own terms. It is not the function of the courts to make the parties' contract for them. However, in the following exceptional cases the law may imply terms into the contract.

(i) *To give the contract business efficacy.* What is meant by 'business efficacy' can be seen from the remarks of Lord Justice Bowen in the following case.

> *The Moorcock* (1889). Appellants agreed with the respondent to use the appellants' jetty and wharf to load and store cargo from the *Moorcock*. The river bed was owned by a third party. It was beyond the appellants' control and they had taken no steps to ascertain whether it was safe for the ship to lie, as was inevitable at low water on each tide. The ship grounded and suffered damage because of the uneven river bed. *Held:* that appellants were liable as the jetty could not have been used without the *Moorcock* grounding. In these circumstances the appellants were deemed to have impliedly represented that they had taken reasonable care to ascertain that the river bed adjoining the jetty was in such a condition as not to cause damage to the vessel. 'What the law desires to effect by the implication is to give such business efficacy to the transaction as must have been intended at all events by both parties who are businessmen.'

(ii) *Custom.* Terms may be implied by custom of a locality or a particular trade. The custom, or usage as it is sometimes called to distinguish it from the general custom of the realm, must be certain, reasonable, and well-known (notorious) to all affected by it, and must not offend any statute.

(iii) *Sale of Goods Act, 1979.* Sections 12–15 of this Act imply certain terms into contracts for the sale of goods which are for the protection of the buyer. For example, s. 13 makes it an implied condition that goods shall correspond with the description of them; and s. 15 lays down that in a sale by sample, the bulk shall correspond with the sample.

Exemption Clauses

The basic rule regarding conditions contained in an offer is that the offeror can attach any conditions he pleases and any terms of acceptance he chooses. Conditions may be made orally or in writing. In the latter event the writing is generally stated on the face of the document itself (e.g. hire-purchase agreements). But, in some instances (e.g. railway tickets) an authority may impose conditions too numerous to be included on these small documents. Usually railway tickets bear on the face the words 'For conditions, see over'. On the reverse side of the ticket may be printed: 'Issued subject to the conditions and regulations contained in the Board's publications and notices.' It follows that offerees should read such publications and notices, but only very few ever do. Such conditions are binding.

In recent years commercial companies and public authorities have imposed similar conditions in their contracts exempting or excluding themselves from liability for breaches of contract or from liability for torts, particularly negligence, arising during the contract. The rules applicable in this situation may be summarized thus:

(*a*) The offeror must do all that is reasonably necessary to bring the conditions to the notice of the offeree. This is a question of fact in each case (*Thornton* v. *Shoe Lane Parking Ltd*., 1971)

(*b*) The conditions must be brought to the notice of the offeree either before or contemporaneously with the making of the contract (*Olley* v. *Marlborough Court, Ltd.*, 1949).

(*c*) An exemption clause printed on a receipt after the contract is not valid (*Chapelton* v. *Barry U.D.C.*, 1940).

(*d*) Where the party seeking to rely on an exemption clause misrepresents the extent of the clause, it will not be binding (*Curtis* v. *Chemical Cleaning & Dyeing Co.*, 1951).

(*e*) Where the terms are signed, the parties are bound as a general rule (*L'Estrange* v. *Graucob*, 1934).

(*f*) Where there has been a fundamental breach of contract it is a question of construction whether the terms of the contract give exemption from the consequences of the breach.

> *Olley* v. *Marlborough Court, Ltd.* (1949). *O* booked into a hotel, having paid in advance. *O* went to the room allotted, and on one of the walls was a notice: 'The proprietors will not hold themselves responsible for articles lost or stolen unless handed to the manageress for safe custody.' *O* closed the self-locking door of the bedroom and handed the key to the reception clerk downstairs. A third person took the key and stole certain

of *O*'s furs from her room. *O* sued for the loss. *Held:* that the contract was completed at the reception desk, and no *subsequent* notice (e.g. in a bedroom) could affect *O*'s rights.

Note: Had *O* previously visited the hotel and seen the notice she would have been bound by its conditions (*Spurling* v. *Bradshaw*, 1956).

But by the 1977 Act (see below) the terms must also be reasonable for *O* to be bound.

L'Estrange v. *Graucob* (1934). *L*, a shopkeeper, bought from *G* a slot machine. *L* signed a sales agreement containing the following clause: 'Any express or implied condition, statement or warranty, statutory or otherwise, is hereby excluded.' *L* did not read the relevant clause, which was in small print. The machine did not work and *L* sued for damages. *Held:* that the clause was binding on *L* because she had signed the document and there had been no misrepresentation.

Chapelton v. *Barry U.D.C.* (1940). *C* wished to hire deckchairs on a beach. He went to a stack near which was a notice: 'Hire of chairs 2*d.* per session of three hours.' He took two chairs, later he paid 4*d.* to the attendant and received two tickets which he put into his pocket without reading what was on them. Printed on the back of the tickets were the words: 'The Council will not be liable for any accident or damage arising from hire of chair.' When *C* sat on the chair it collapsed and he was injured. *C* sued the local council who had provided the chair. *Held:* that the ticket was a mere voucher or receipt, so that the condition printed on it could not form part of the contract. The only conditions of the contract were those contained in the notice displayed near the pile of chairs. *C* was entitled to succeed in damages.

Curtis v. *Chemical Cleaning and Dyeing Co.* (1951). *C* took a dress with beads and sequins to defendants (cleaners and dyers) for cleaning. *C* was asked to sign a paper headed 'Receipt'. When *C* asked about the terms of the document the defendant's assistant informed her that it exempted the company from liability for certain types of damage such as damage to beads and sequins. *C* signed. In fact the paper contained a clause excluding *all* liability for damage to the garment. The dress was returned stained, and *C* sued. *Held:* that defendants could not rely upon the signed document because the assistant had misrepresented its terms so that *C* ran the risk of damage merely to beads and sequins.

Alexander v. *Railway Executive* (1951). *A* deposited luggage at a left-luggage department at a railway station and was handed a ticket, a condition of which exempted the Railway Executive from liability for misdelivery. The luggage was later delivered to *X* who fraudulently claimed authority from the depositor, *A*; *X* was not asked to furnish evidence as to such authority. *A* sued accordingly. *Held:* that there was a fundamental breach of the bailment contract, and the Railway Executive could not rely on the exemption clause.

Karsales (*Harrow*) *Ltd.* v. *Wallis* (1956). *W* inspected a second-hand

Buick car, found it in running order and arranged to purchase it for £600 through a finance company. The contract contained the clause: 'No condition or warranty that the vehicle is roadworthy or as to its age, condition or fitness for any purpose is given by the owner or implied herein.' On delivery it was found that the new tyres had been replaced by old ones, many parts were missing and other parts originally on the car when inspected had been replaced by old parts. The car would not go at all. *Held:* that the exclusion clause did not apply. The sale was for a car. What was delivered was incapable of propulsion and therefore not really a car at all. There had been a fundamental breach and plaintiffs were unable to rely on the clause.

The Unfair Contract Terms Act, 1977

Judges had tried over the years to prevent the operation of exemption clauses, which often deprived a consumer of virtually all his rights, by strict interpretation of terms and by propounding the doctrine of 'fundamental breach'. The Law Commission produced a Report on the dilemma, and, as a result, the Unfair Contract Terms Act, 1977, came into force on 1st February, 1978, and applies to all contracts entered into after that date. Basically the Act limits the extent to which civil liability for breach, *or for negligence or other breach of duty*, can be avoided by means of contract terms or by warning notices.

The Act covers the supply of goods and services, contracts of employment and the liability of occupiers of premises and of land to persons entering upon or using those premises or the land. The Act will do a number of things which can be listed thus:

Negligence liability (both in contract and tort). 1. Liability for negligence resulting in death or personal injury can no longer be excluded or restricted by contract or by notice in the course of a business (S. 2(1)).

2. Liability for other loss or damage resulting from negligence can no longer be excluded or restricted in a 'guarantee' given with consumer goods (s. 2(2)) as in *Phillips Products Ltd.* v. *Hyland and Another*, 1987.

3. Except as provided for in 1 above, liability for negligence not resulting in death or personal injury can be excluded or restricted, but only in so far as the contract term or notice satisfies the test of reasonableness (see below). 'Attempts to exclude liability for negligence must be clearly and unambiguously expressed' (*Ailsa Craig Fishing Co. Ltd.* v. *Malvern Fishing Co. Ltd.*, 1983).

Contractual obligations. When (1) dealing with consumers or (2) on its own written standard terms, a business cannot by means of a contract term, unless the term satisfies the test of reasonableness, (*a*) exclude or restrict its liability for breach of contract, (*b*) claim to be entitled to render no performance or a performance substantially different from that which was reasonably expected of it (s. 3).

Contracts where both parties are businesses and which are not on standard terms are not subject to this control.

Supply of Goods. The rules in the Supply of Goods (Implied Terms) Act, 1973, now replaced by the Sale of Goods Act, 1979, in general deal with the exclusion or restriction of liability for breach of the obligations implied by law into contracts for the sale of goods and hire purchase agreements. Work and materials and services contracts are now governed by the provisions of the Supply of Goods and Services Act, 1982. These rules are now extended to all other contracts for the supply of goods (not just sale). In short, the right of the consumer to goods which (*a*) correspond with description or sample, (*b*) are of merchantable quality, and (*c*) are fit for the purpose cannot be excluded or restricted by contract whether he (the consumer) buys the goods or obtains them by way of hire, hire purchase, exchange or under a contract for work and materials. Attempts to deny any of the corresponding rights to a business customer are now subject to the reasonableness tests. Terms excluding or restricting liability for breach of the implied obligations as to title (i.e. ownership) or quiet possession are also subject to control, both in consumer contracts and in contracts where both parties are businesses.

Auctions are exempted under s. 12(2).

Indemnity Clauses. The reasonableness test is applied to contract terms requiring a consumer to indemnify another person (whether a party to the contract or not) in respect of the other's liability for negligence or breach of contract.

Reasonableness Test. For a contract term, the test is whether 'the term is a fair and reasonable one to be included having regard to the circumstances which were, or ought reasonably to have been, known to or in the contemplation of the parties when the contract was made' (s. 11(1)). The party alleging 'reasonableness' must prove it.

For *notices* not having contractual effect, the requirement of reasonableness under the Act is 'that it should be fair and reasonable to allow reliance on it, having regard to all the circumstances obtaining when the liability arose or (but for the notice) would have arisen.' (s. 11(3)).

Moreover, where a contract term or notice purports to exclude or restrict liability for negligence a person's agreement to or awareness of it is not of itself to be taken as indicating his voluntary acceptance of any risk (s. 2(3)) as in *G. Mitchell (Chesterhall) Ltd.* v. *Finney Lock Seeds Ltd.* (1983).

Fundamental Breach. S. 9 of the Unfair Contract Terms Act, 1977, provides that an exemption clause may apply where there has been a fundamental breach of contract, provided that it satisfies the requirement of reasonableness. A case where an exemption clause was upheld by the House of Lords in such circumstances is *Photo Production Ltd.* v. *Securicor Transport Ltd.* (1980).

Conditions and Warranties

At this point it is advisable to distinguish between the terms 'condition' and 'warranty' which appear in the law of contract.

A **condition** is a term (oral or written) which goes directly 'to the root of the contract', or is so essential to its very nature that if it is broken the innocent party can treat the contract as discharged. He will not therefore be bound to do anything further under that contract.

A **warranty** is a term of the contract which is collateral or subsidiary to the main purpose of the contract. It is therefore not so vital as to effect a discharge of the contract. A breach of warranty only entitles the innocent party to an action for damages, he cannot treat the contract as discharged.

Both conditions and warranties are terms in a contract and it is for the court to decide in each contract whether, having regard to the intentions of the parties, a term is a condition or a warranty. The importance lies in the remedy in the event of breach.

10. Void, Voidable, and Illegal Contracts

We have already mentioned (p. 112) that one of the essential elements in a valid contract is that there must be genuineness of consent of the parties. That consent may be vitiated (i.e. harmed) by the following factors: (i) mistake, (ii) misrepresentation, (iii) duress, (iv) undue influence, and (v) illegality. Where one of these factors exists in relation to a contract, there is no true consent and the contract may be rendered void or voidable. For example, an illegal contract is void, and a contract affected by misrepresentation, duress or undue influence is voidable, i.e. able to be repudiated at the instance of the party prejudiced.

Mistake

The general rule of common law is that mistake does not affect the validity of a contract. If I sell you a painting for £10 and, after the sale, you discover that the painting is a Rembrandt worth £100,000, you are fortunate: I am not. I merely sold a painting, not knowing that it was a very valuable old master. I mistook its real value, and the law will do nothing to assist me.

There are, however, some kinds of mistake which operate on the agreement and really undermine it so that there is no true consent. Such a mistake is known as an 'operative' mistake, the effect of which is to render the contract void.

First we must observe that the mistake has to be one of fact and not of law. If I make a mistake about some general rule of law, I cannot plead in court that I did not know the legal rule existed. The maxim *ignorantia juris haud excusat* ('ignorance of the law is no excuse') applies. A mistake of private rights or of foreign law is, however, treated as a mistake of fact and not of law. Thus, where *A* agrees to lease to *B* some land which in fact already belongs to *B*, such a mistake (relating to private property) is treated as a mistake of fact. The lease would in the circumstances be void (*Cooper* v. *Phibbs*, 1867).

(*a*) **Mistake as to the Identity of the Subject-matter.** Where two parties intend to contract, and the first party intends to contract with regard to one thing while the second intends another thing, there is no true agreement and hence no contract.

> *Raffles* v. *Wichelhaus* (1864). *W* agreed to buy cotton 'to arrive on the *Peerless* sailing from Bombay'. *W* intended the ship *Peerless* sailing from Bombay in October. *R* offered the cotton from another ship *Peerless* sailing in December. *Held:* that there was no binding contract between the parties as the defendant meant one ship and the plaintiff another.

> *Scriven* v. *Hindley* (1913). An auctioneer put up for sale some lots of hemp and tow. Owing to ambiguity in the auction particulars the defendant bid an excessive price for an item of tow, thinking it was hemp. From the price bid the auctioneer must have realized there was a mistake. *Held:* that there was no contract.

Where each party makes a different kind of mistake it is known as 'mutual' mistake; where both parties make the same mistake it is known as 'common' mistake. Unilateral mistake means a mistake by one party, e.g. *Cundy* v. *Lindsay* (1878), see p. 150.

(*b*) **Mistake as to the Existence of the Subject-matter.** Where both parties contract in the mistaken belief that a particular thing is in existence when, in fact, it has ceased to exist, there is a fundamental mistake which renders the contract void. For example, if I agree to sell to you my motor-car which both of us believe to be at my home, but unfortunately was destroyed by fire a day before the contract, we have both made a mistake (a 'common' mistake) and the contract is void. The law presumes in this type of situation a condition that the thing about which we agreed was in existence.

> *Couturier* v. *Hastie* (1852). A contract was made between two parties for the sale of Indian corn, which, at the time, was believed to be on the high seas. Unknown to both parties the corn had become overheated during the voyage and had been landed at the nearest port and sold. *Held:* that there was no contract. The agreement contemplated that there was in existence something to be sold and bought, but as at the time of the contract the goods had already been sold, defendants were not liable.

(*c*) **Mistake as to the Quality of the Subject-matter.** The general rule in this type of agreement is that mistake as to the quality of the thing contracted for does not invalidate the contract. If, for example, I sell you a painting which we both think to be an old master, but turns out to be a cheap imitation, the contract is good. No representation is made as to the painting. All that is bought and sold is a painting. There is no mistake as to its identity, but both parties are mistaken as to its quality. You get what you bargained for: a particular painting. In such a case the law is not concerned with the quality or the value paid, for the general rule is *caveat emptor* ('let the buyer beware').

Equity, however, may grant relief in certain circumstances, and the contract may be set aside on terms which are fair and just.

Bell v. *Lever Bros.* (1932). *B* was under a contract of service with Lever Bros. Amalgamations of the company took place and *B* became redundant. Lever Bros. contracted to pay *B* £30,000 as compensation for his loss of office. After the contract had been made it was discovered that *B*, in breach of his employment contract, had engaged in secret trading during his service, for which he could have been summarily dismissed from office without payment of compensation. Lever Bros. sought to recover the sum of £30,000 which it had paid (it was alleged) on the ground of mistake. *Held:* that the contract was not void. Lever Bros. had got what it had bargained for, i.e. the termination of the agreement of service which was in existence at the time of payment. The mistake was one of quality, and this did not avoid the contract. (But see the decision in *Sybron* v. *Rochem* (1983).)

Solle v. *Butcher* (1950). *B* agreed to lease a flat to *S* at a rental of £250 per annum. Both parties assumed that the rent was not restricted under the Rent Acts. In fact, the statutory rent was £140 unless the landlord carried out certain formalities. When the tenant found out that the flat was still controlled he sought to recover the difference between the two rents. *Held:* that both parties made a 'common' mistake which was fundamental to the lease. At common law the contract was valid since the mistake was one of quality. However, the contract could be set aside (rescinded) by the court provided a new lease was granted at a rent of £250 after proper statutory notice of increase.

Grist v. *Bailey* (1966). *G* bought a house from *B* for £850. Both parties believed that the house was occupied by a statutory tenant who therefore could not be compelled to quit. In fact the occupier was not a statutory tenant. The value of the house with vacant possession was £2,250. *Held:* that *G* and *B* made a 'common' mistake of a fundamental kind. The contract was not void at common law, but in exercise of its equitable jurisdiction the court set the contract aside on terms that the vendor should offer the house to the purchaser at its 'open-market' price.

(*d*) **Mistake as to the Identity of the Other Party.** This type of mistake arises where, for example, *A* intends to contract with *B*, but by mistake contracts with *C*. Is the contract with *C* valid? The answer here depends on whether the identity of the party (in the above case, *B*) is material to the contract in the sense that *A* intended to contract with *B* and no other person. *Boulton* v. *Jones*, 1857, summarized on p. 115, indicates that in these circumstances there is no contract.

Mistake of identity, therefore, will nullify the contract if it is proved

(i) that the identity of the party contracted with is *material* to the contract; and

(ii) that the party contracted with knows that he is not the person that the other party intended to enter into contractual relations with.

In ordinary contracts for the sale of goods in a shop, for example, the identity of the customer is immaterial. He is a mere customer, and as long as he is willing to pay the price for the goods, the shopkeeper is usually unconcerned with personal identity. Whoever the customer, it matters not as long as a bargain is made. But in some contracts personal identity is material, and in such cases the contracts with the mistaken person are void.

A study of the following cases shows the application of the rules. In each case the test of mistake of identity is: Did the party intend to contract with one particular person only, and none other than him?

Cundy v. *Lindsay & Co.* (1878). A fraudulent person named Blenkarn ordered goods from Lindsay & Co. and imitated the signature of an old customer of Lindsay's named Blenkiron. Lindsay's sent the goods. Blenkarn then sold the goods to Cundy who paid for them. Lindsay claimed the goods from Cundy who refused to part with them. Cundy claimed that the contract between the fraud (Blenkarn) and Lindsay was voidable. Lindsay claimed that their contract with Blenkarn was void by reason of the mistake of identity of the person they were contracting with. *Held:* that Cundy must return the goods. The contract was void by reason of the mistake of identity. Lindsay had only one person in mind and that was their genuine customer Blenkiron. There was no contract; no title passed to Blenkarn, and he could not give a good title to Cundy.

Phillips v. *Brooks* (1919). A rogue, *X*, entered a jeweller's shop to purchase jewellery. The rogue offered to pay by cheque. The cheque was accepted by the jeweller who said delivery would be delayed until the cheque was cleared by the bank. The rogue said 'I am Sir George Bullough', and gave an address at St. James' Square. He asked to take some of the jewels with him. The jeweller agreed, and the rogue then went to Brooks, Ltd. and pawned them for a sum of money. The cheque later proved worthless. The jeweller then sued the pawnbroker for the jewels. *Held:* that Brooks obtained a good title. The contract was not void for mistake, but voidable for fraud. At the time of the contract the jeweller intended to deal with the person physically in his shop and his identity was immaterial.

Note: the fraud by the rogue was that by drawing a cheque he impliedly represented that he had an account at a bank with sufficient funds. He had no such account.

Lewis v. *Averay* (1971). *L* advertised his car for sale. *X*, a fraud, replied to the advertisement, met *L* and said he was 'Richard Green' a well known film star. *L* and *X* agreed a price (£450). *X* drew a cheque for £450 and signed it 'R. A. Green', producing a pass to Pinewood Studios as proof of his identity. *X* obtained the car and sold it to *A* (a *bona fide* purchaser) for a sum of money. *X*'s cheque was worthless. *L* thereupon sued *A* in conversion. *Held* (Court of Appeal): *L* intended to contract with the person (*X*) actually before him despite the fraudulent impersonation as Richard Green. Judgment given for *A* who could retain the car.

(*e*) **Mistake as to the Nature of the Document.** The general rule of law is that a person is bound by the terms of any instrument which he signs. This is so even though the signer did not read the document or did not understand its contents (*L'Estrange* v. *Graucob*, 1934), see p. 144.

Where, however, a person signs a contract in the mistaken belief that it is a totally different document he can escape liability. In such a case he may plead *non est factum*, i.e. 'not my deed'.

Foster v. *Mackinnon* (1869). *M*, an old man of feeble sight, was induced to endorse a bill of exchange for £3,000, on the assurance that it was a guarantee. The bill was endorsed for value to Foster who sued *M* on the bill. *Held:* that *M*'s plea of *non est factum* was good, and he was not liable on the bill.

If the document is a negotiable instrument the plea of *non est factum* can only be used if the signer has not been negligent. Mackinnon in the above case, being senile and poor-sighted, was held not to have been negligent.

Saunders v. *Anglia Building Society* (1970) (also known as *Gallie* v. *Lee*). Mrs. *G*, an aged woman, handed over to *P*, her nephew, the deeds of her house. *P* needed money and consulted his business associate, *Lee*. The latter caused a deed to be prepared and presented it to Mrs. *G* to sign, saying it was a deed of gift to *P*. Mrs. *G* had broken her spectacles and had difficulty in reading without them. She knew the document was to raise money and that *Lee* was involved. The deed in fact transferred the property to *Lee* (a fraud), who mortgaged it to a building society for £3,000, and absconded. Mrs. *G* sued for a declaration that the deed was void and that the building society should deliver up the mortgage. Judgment was given for Mrs. *G*. *Held* (on appeal to House of Lords): The plea of *non est factum* failed. 'The essence of the plea of *non est factum* is that the person signing believed the document he signed had one character and one effect whereas in fact its character or effect was quite different' (per Lord Reid). Mrs. *G* signed a document of the same character as she intended to sign and was bound by it.

Where a person knows the nature of the document he signs but is mistaken as to the contents, the contract is not avoided.

Howatson v. *Webb* (1908). A solicitor, *W* was asked to execute a deed and did so on being told (fraudulently) it was a conveyance of property of which he was a trustee. The deed was in fact a mortgage of the property. *W* was subsequently sued on the mortgage. *Held:* that *W* was bound by the terms of the mortgage; the misrepresentation related to the contents, not the character of the deed.

Mistake in Equity. The general rule of common law was that mistake, by one or both parties, showed that there was no true agreement (*consensus ad idem*) and that accordingly the contract was void, as in *Raffles* v. *Wichelhaus* (p. 148) for instance. If the mistake was, however, not fundamental, as in *Bell* v. *Lever Bros.* (p. 149), the contract was held valid or good.

Where the simple division of contracts as either void or valid is inappropriate and unfairness results, equitable principles may be applied to effect a compromise and to do justice in the particular case where a strict application of common law rules leads to hardship.

The forms of equitable relief are these:

(*a*) The court may set aside an agreement on terms which are fair and just (*Solle* v. *Butcher*, 1950), see p. 149.

(*b*) It may rectify a written instrument which does not truly express the agreed intention of the parties.

> *Craddock Bros.* v. *Hunt* (1923). *A* orally agreed to sell a house, exclusive of an adjoining yard, to *B*. Owing to a mistake the later formal and written conveyance included the house and the yard. The mistake was common to *A* and *B*. *Held:* that the court could rectify the conveyance to accord with the intention of the parties.

(*c*) It may grant an order of specific performance of a contract where appropriate.

> *Webster* v. *Cecil* (1861). *C* wrote to *W* to offer to sell some property to *W* for £1,250. *C* had already refused to sell the same land to *W* for £2,000. *W*, knowing a mistake must have occurred, wrote to *C* accepting the offer contained in *C*'s letter. *C* had intended the price to be £2,250, and immediately gave notice of the error to *W*. *Held:* that the decree of specific performance would not be granted.

We remember that all forms of equitable relief or remedy are discretionary. The plaintiff cannot claim equitable remedies as of right, as he can with the common law remedy of damages once he has proved his claim.

Rectification. The above case of *Craddock Bros.* v. *Hunt* is a good example of the decree of rectification in action. Where the parties make an agreement, but the written instrument to which they have reduced their agreement does not accurately express the agreement, the court may rectify the instrument so as to make it express the agreement of the parties, and enforce it as rectified. To obtain the equitable remedy of rectification the following conditions must be satisfied:

(*a*) The mistake must be one of expression only.

(*b*) There must be an actually concluded contract before the written instrument is drawn up. (The court will not make a new agreement for the parties.)

(*c*) There must be clear evidence of intention.

(*d*) The mistake must be *common* to both parties.

(*e*) The mistake must have existed at the time of the execution of the instrument.

(*f*) The mistake must be exactly proved. The plaintiff must show the precise form in which the instrument should be drawn up.

Misrepresentation

> 'A representation is a statement made by one party to the other, before or at the time of the contract, with regard to some existing fact or to some past event, which is material to the contract.' (Cheshire and Fifoot: *Law of Contract*.)

Misrepresentations are of two kinds: innocent and fraudulent. **Innocent misrepresentations** are those statements of fact which the maker believes to be true but are, in fact, false. **Fraudulent misrepresentations** are those statements of fact which the maker knows to be false, so fraud means *dishonest belief*. Fraudulent misrepresentation is a distinct tort, known as **deceit**. Its relevance and importance to the law of contract are obvious, and for these reasons it is treated fully in this portion of the book. The next important point to consider is the distinction between (i) representations, (ii) conditions, and (iii) warranties.

Representations are those statements which are made for the purpose of *inducing* persons to make contracts. They may be made before or at the time of the contract, but are not part of the contract themselves as is the case with conditions and warranties. **Conditions** are terms of the contract which are vital, i.e. 'go to the root of the contract'. A **warranty**, on the other hand, is a term in an agreement which is subsidiary or collateral to the main purpose of the contract. In other words a warranty is not so vital to the performance of the contract as to enable the contract to be set aside for breach. It is not always easy, in some contracts, to distinguish the three categories or descriptions mentioned above, and careful study of cases is usually necessary to achieve a fair understanding. But, in every case, it is for the court to determine whether a particular statement is a representation, a condition or a warranty. This can only be done by examining closely the circumstances of each case and the intention of the parties as disclosed by the evidence.

Misrepresentation is defined as *an untrue statement of fact made by one party to the other party to a contract, either before or at the time of making the contract, with the intention that the person to whom the statement is made shall act upon such misrepresentation, and he does so act.*

The features common to innocent and fraudulent misrepresentation are:

(*a*) The misrepresentation must be one of fact, not law.
(*b*) The misrepresentation must be made by a party to the contract (or his agent).
(*c*) The party seeking legal redress must have relied upon and acted upon the misrepresentation when entering into the contract.
(*d*) The plaintiff must have suffered damage as a result of the misrepresentation.

(*a*) *A misrepresentation must be a statement of fact*. 'I am a bank manager', 'The watch is solid gold': these are obviously statements of fact. Statements of general law are immaterial, and are not grounds for relief or remedy to the party suffering loss. 'Ignorance of the law is no excuse', and since this implies that everyone is presumed to know the law, a party cannot aver that he has been led into a contract by a misstatement of general law.

Statements of opinion and 'trade puffs' as they are sometimes called are not statements of fact. 'This powder washes whitest', 'This is some of the best land in England', 'This medicine will put you on top of the world': such statements are the stock-in-trade of advertisers, and are not actionable unless they are statements of fact.

A statement of intention is not, as a rule, a representation. The statement must be of a present or past fact. However, a statement of intention *may* contain within itself a representation of an existing fact.

> *Edgington* v. *Fitzmaurice* (1885). A company issued a prospectus inviting the public to subscribe for its debentures. The company stated that the money raised was to complete alterations to the company's premises, to purchase horses and vans and to develop trade. Plaintiff advanced money, but it turned out that the real object of the loan was to enable the directors to pay off pressing liabilities. *Held:* that the misstatement of the purpose for which the debentures were issued was a material misstatement of fact which rendered the directors liable in deceit.

In this case Lord Justice Bowen said: 'The state of a man's mind is as much a fact as the state of his digestion.'

(*b*) *The misrepresentation must be made by a party to the contract or by his agent*. A representation made by a third party or a bystander is immaterial.

(*c*) *The representee must have relied on the misrepresentation*. If therefore, the representee (i) never knew of the existence of the misrepresentation, or (ii) did not allow the misrepresentation to affect his own judgment, or (iii) was aware of the untruth, he cannot state that he relied on the misrepresentation. Moreover, the misrepresentation must relate to a material element in the contract. Thus a misrepresentation as to a trivial matter cannot avail to enable the plaintiff to claim relief. What is material is a question for the court to decide.

Smith v. *Chadwick* (1884). A prospectus contained a false statement that a certain man was on the board of directors of a company. Plaintiff admitted that on purchasing his shares this statement had not influenced him. *Held:* that he could not obtain relief.

Where a party makes a statement which was true when made but which subsequently becomes untrue before the other party enters into the contract, the party making the misrepresentation owes a duty to the representee to tell him the true position before he acts.

With v. *O'Flanagan* (1936). A doctor, *X*, represented in January that the takings of his medical practice were £2,000. Five months later when the contract was signed the takings had fallen considerably due to the doctor's own illness. *X* failed to disclose the reduction. *Held:* that the contract could be rescinded owing to *X*'s failure to disclose the fall in the takings.

Fraudulent Misrepresentation. A fraudulent misrepresentation is an untrue statement made (i) knowingly, or (ii) without belief in its truth, or (iii) recklessly, careless whether it be true or false (Lord Herschell in *Derry* v. *Peek*, 1889).

Derry v. *Peek* (1889). The Plymouth Tramways Co. had power under a special Act of Parliament to run trams by animal power and, with the Board of Trade's consent, by mechanical or steam power. The directors of the company issued a prospectus inviting subscriptions from the public for shares. The prospectus stated that the company had authority to run trams by steam power. They assumed the Board of Trade would grant permission as a matter of course. But the Board refused permission, and in consequence the company was wound up. A subscriber sued the directors for fraud. *Held:* that the directors were not fraudulent; they honestly believed the statement in the prospectus to be true.

As a consequence of this case the law in relation to statements in the prospectuses of companies was altered, and now, by section 67 of the Companies Act, 1985, directors are liable to pay compensation for innocent misrepresentations appearing in prospectuses.

Remedies for Fraudulent Misrepresentation. A party who has been deceived by a fraudulent misrepresentation has the following remedies open to him. He may:

(*a*) Bring an action in tort for damages for deceit.

(*b*) Bring an action for rescission (with or without a claim for damages).

(*c*) Repudiate the contract and refuse further performance.

(*d*) Prosecute, or notify police (obtaining property or pecuniary advantage by deception: Theft Act, 1968, see p. 340).

The party deceived may treat the contract as voidable. He may affirm the contract or not as he chooses. In effect it is up to him to take any of the above courses or to do nothing in regard to (*a*) to (*c*) and treat the contract as binding. If he is sued he may plead fraud as a defence and counterclaim for damages.

Remedies for Innocent Misrepresentation. At common law, before 1967, when a person claimed he entered into a contract as a result of an innocent misrepresentation the party misled could not claim damages. He could, however, take action in court for rescission (see p. 157), or he could repudiate the contract by his own act, e.g. by notifying the other party personally that he ceased to regard the contract as binding. The contract affected by innocent misrepresentation is voidable at the option of the party misled.

The Misrepresentation Act, 1967, now governs the remedies available for innocent misrepresentation. The contracting party may:

(*a*) Claim for damages (see s. 2(1) and (2) below).
(*b*) Apply for rescission (see s. 2(2) below).
(*c*) Repudiate the contract and refuse to perform further obligations under the contract.
(*d*) Affirm the contract.

As to (*a*) the judge (or arbitrator) may award damages 'if of the opinion that it would be equitable to do so, having regard to the nature of the misrepresentation and the loss that would be caused by it if the contract were upheld, as well as to the loss that rescission would cause to the other party' (s. 2(1)).

As to (*b*), the judge (or arbitrator) 'may, if it is equitable to do so, award damages in *lieu* of rescission and may declare the contract subsisting'. The court must have regard to the nature of the misrepresentation, the loss that would be caused if the contract were upheld and the loss that rescission would cause to the other party (s. 2(2)).

As to (*d*) the party misled may choose to ignore the misrepresentation and treat the contract as binding. The contract is voidable, and it is a matter for him.

Negligent Misrepresentation. So far we have considered two kinds of misrepresentation: (i) fraudulent and (ii) innocent. Recently a further development has arisen in this complicated portion of the law. We have now 'negligent misrepresentation'. Note that in fraudulent misrepresentation, there must be dishonesty; in negligent misrepresentation there is a careless (or negligent) statement, though not dishonest. We look at two factors:

(*a*) The *Hedley Byrne* case (1964) (see p. 226) rules that where *A* makes a negligent mis-statement to *B*, as a result of which *B* suffers damage in reliance on it, *B* may sue *A* in tort for negligence providing a 'special relationship' exists between *A* and *B*, such as banker and customer, solicitor and client, surveyor and house-purchaser, etc. Hitherto the tort of negligence had been confined to acts, not words.

(*b*) The Misrepresentation Act, 1967, s. 2(1), distinguished between (i) negligent and (ii) entirely innocent misrepresentation. Thus:

> 'Where a person (*A*) has entered into a contract after a misrepresentation has been made to him by another party (*B*) and as a result thereof he (*A*) has suffered loss, then, if the person making the misrepresentation (i.e. (*B*)) would be liable to damages in respect thereof had the misrepresentation been made fraudulently, that person (*B*) shall be so liable notwithstanding that the misrepresentation was not made fraudulently, unless he (*B*) proves that he (*B*) had reasonable ground to believe and did believe up to the time the contract was made that the facts represented were true' (s. 2(1)).
>
> (Note: the writer has inserted the *A*'s and *B*'s to assist in grasping the meaning of this complicated section.)

Neither 'negligence' nor 'duty of care' are mentioned in this section. What the section does is to place on the defendant the burden of proving that he had reasonable ground for believing the facts represented were true; in short, that he had not been careless or negligent in his statement. In the tort of negligence the burden of proof of duty of care and breach of duty is placed on the plaintiff. So there is a procedural advantage to the plaintiff if he sues under s. 2(1). Damages are, however, obtainable only if they would have been obtained 'had the misrepresentation been made fraudulently'.

The remedies for negligent misrepresentation in the sense we have been discussing are:

(*a*) Damages, either under the *Hedley Byrne* type of action, or under the Misrepresentation Act, 1967, s. 2(1).

(*b*) Rescission, either by the party misled cancelling the contract himself, or by the court. But, in the latter case, the judge (or arbitrator) has a discretion to declare the contract as subsisting and may award damages in *lieu* of rescission (s. 2(2)).

Rescission (i.e. cancellation or annulment) is a discretionary remedy, and in any legal action on the contract it is granted subject to certain important principles. In particular the party misled will lose his right to rescission if:

(i) The parties cannot be restored to their original positions. This is known as *restitutio in integrum*.

(ii) The party, knowing of the misrepresentation, takes a benefit under the contract, or in some other way affirms the contract.

(iii) Third parties have acquired rights under the contract.

(iv) There has been long delay in taking legal action to rescind the contract. Delay indicates to the court that the party misled affirms the contract.

> *Leaf* v. *International Galleries* (1950). *L* bought a painting of Salisbury Cathedral described innocently by the seller as a genuine Constable. After five years *L* discovered that the painting was not a genuine Constable, and he claimed rescission on the ground of innocent misrepresentation. *Held:* that *L*'s claim must fail. His action was too long delayed.

Exemption Clauses. Section 3 of the Act provides that if an agreement contains an exemption clause purporting to give immunity or to protect a party from liability for misrepresenting or excluding or restricting any remedy available to the representee, the exemption clause shall be void unless the court allows reliance on it as being fair and reasonable in the circumstances.

Damages for Misrepresentation. The general rule of law that damages cannot be claimed for innocent misrepresentation is subject to certain exceptions as follows:

(*a*) Under the Misrepresentation Act, 1967, just noted.

(*b*) Under the Companies Act, 1985, s. 67, where an innocent misrepresentation is included in a prospectus inviting the public to subscribe for shares in a company. In this case *compensation* is payable by the directors to a subscriber for the shares.

(*c*) In an action for breach of warranty of authority by an agent. In this case damages may be claimed from the agent who has represented that he has authority to act as agent for another when in fact he has no such authority, or where an agent exceeds his authority. It is immaterial that the agent acted innocently. The agent is liable in damages.

Trade Descriptions Act, 1968. This Act (see p. 317) includes new provisions designed to give greater protection to consumers, particularly against their being deceived by false or misleading trade descriptions. Where, therefore, a misrepresentation is made in a contract the misrepresentor may be liable criminally under the Act, as in *Wings Ltd.* v. *Ellis* (1984). Section 11 of the Act (Misleading Price Indications) has now been replaced by Part III of the Consumer Protection Act, 1987.

Contracts 'uberrimae fidei'

In the law of contract silence by a party does not in general amount to misrepresentation. But there is one class of contracts in which disclosure of material facts must be made. Agreements falling within this class are known as contracts *uberrimae fidei* ('of the utmost good faith'). Failure to disclose material facts, whether they are asked for or not, renders the contract voidable at the option of the party prejudiced, i.e. the party to whom disclosure ought to have been made.

Examples of contracts to which this rule applies are as follows:

(*a*) **Contracts of Insurance.** In contracts of marine, fire, and life insurance the insured party must disclose all facts which might influence the judgment of the other party, i.e. the insurer, whether or not to take the risk of insuring or to increase the premium. If, therefore, the insured omits the information required, the insurer may repudiate the contract. It may also be owed by the insurer to the insured (*Banque Keyser Ullmann SA* v. *Skandia* (*UK*) *Ins. Co. Ltd. and Others*, 1987).

(*b*) **Company Prospectuses.** These documents invite persons to subscribe for shares in a company. Under section 56 of the Companies Act, 1985, full disclosure of material facts must be contained in all prospectuses. Failure to include these facts renders the contract voidable, and the directors or promoters liable for damages (see p. 158).

(*c*) **Contracts for the Sale of Land.** A vendor of land must disclose all defects in his title to the land, e.g. restrictive covenants, easements, etc. A vendor is under no duty to disclose obvious defects in the land itself which could be discovered on reasonable inspection.

(*d*) **Suretyship and Partnership Contracts.** These contracts are not, in their inception, of the utmost good faith; once the relationship is entered into, however, a duty is imposed on the surety and his principal and between partners to disclose to each other all material facts affecting their fiduciary relationship.

(*e*) **Family Arrangements.** Under this heading are included settlements of family property or agreements relating to family property and similar matters. Each member of the family is bound to disclose to the others any sums of money and details of property received without the knowledge of the remaining members.

> *Gordon* v. *Gordon* (1821). An advantage was gained under a family settlement by one brother who withheld valid information. *Held:* that the agreement should be rescinded, notwithstanding that nineteen years had elapsed after its making.

But in addition to all the above classes of contracts, the relationship of the parties to each other may give rise to a duty in law to disclose. Thus, for example, in contracts or agreements between trustee and beneficiary, solicitor and client, and principal and agent, the utmost good faith must be observed. Failure to observe this standard renders the agreement voidable at the instance of the person prejudiced.

Duress and Undue Influence

The general rule of law is that a valid agreement may be made only where the parties exercise their own free will unconstrained by force or the fear of force or other pressure. The two forms of pressure of which the law takes account are: (*a*) duress and (*b*) undue influence.

(*a*) **Duress** at common law means violence or threatened violence to a party to a contract or to a member of his family, or threatened unlawful imprisonment. The effect on the agreement is that it is probably voidable at the instance of the party threatened; but arguably it is void.

> *Cumming* v. *Ince* (1847). An agreement to give up deeds made under threat of confinement in an asylum was held not to be binding on the plaintiff.

> *Welch* v. *Cheeseman* (1973). In fear of violence from the man with whom she lived, *W* transferred her home to him. *Held:* the transfer would be set aside for duress.

> *Barton* v. *Armstrong* (1975). A deed executed under threats to kill was held to be void for duress.

(*b*) **Undue Influence**, an equitable doctrine, is a more subtle form of pressure exerted upon a party to a contract. According to Ashburner the doctrine is that 'If *A* obtains any benefit from *B*, whether under a contract or as a gift, by exerting an influence over *B* which, in the opinion of the court, prevents *B* from exercising an independent judgment in the matter in question, *B* can set aside the contract or recover the gift'.

Where no special relationship exists between the parties, the party alleging undue influence has the burden of proving it.

> *Williams* v. *Bayley* (1866). *W*'s son had forged *W*'s signature on some promissory notes and given them to his bank. His bank manager called upon *W* and persuaded him to make a mortgage to the bank in return for the notes, under threat of prosecuting the son. *Held:* the agreement was invalid on the grounds of undue influence in that an unfair advantage was taken of *W*.

But where a confidential relationship exists between the parties, undue influence may be presumed by the court, in which case the party in whom confidence is reposed has the burden of rebutting the presumption; for example, a solicitor who buys property from his client may need to show that the client has acted upon independent advice.

The special relationships which have been held by the courts to raise the presumption are solicitor and client, doctor and patient, trustee and beneficiary, guardian and ward, parent and child, religious adviser and disciple; but not husband and wife. However, the presumption may be raised in the case of other persons; the list is not closed.

A contract induced by undue influence is voidable, and confers a right to rescission. But the party seeking to avoid will be deprived of this remedy if a third party has obtained rights under the contract, or if there has been delay in asserting his claim. Delay implies that the party affirms the contract, and as 'delay defeats the equities' the court may, in its discretion, refuse aid to the applicant.

Allcard v. *Skinner* (1887). Plaintiff, in middle age, joined a Protestant sisterhood, taking vows of poverty and obedience. She gave property to the value of £7,000 to the sisterhood in accordance with her vows. Some nine years later she left the order to become a Roman Catholic. Only £1,671 of her property remained with the sisterhood, the balance having been spent. Plaintiff claimed the return of the £1,671 from the Mother Superior (Miss Skinner) and alleged undue influence. *Held:* that undue influence existed in this case since the plaintiff was bound not to seek independent advice while in the Order. However, the plaintiff's claim was barred by her delay of five years after leaving the sisterhood in claiming the money.

Lancashire Loans Ltd. v. *Black* (1934). *B*, a young married woman, acting under the influence of her mother, made unwise moneylending contracts which were for the benefit of the mother. The moneylenders knew of the facts, and subsequently sued mother and daughter on a promissory note. *Held:* that although of full age and a married woman, *B* was unduly influenced by her mother. The contract was therefore voidable by *B*.

Whilst inequality of bargaining power may also be regarded as undue influence, the House of Lords in *National Westminster Bank PLC.* v. *Morgan* (1985) stated that there was no general principle for the granting of such relief. The decision in this case was further explained in *Goldsworthy* v. *Brickell and Another* (1987).

11. Illegality

A contract is illegal if it contravenes a statute or the common law. Illegality may exist in regard to the *making* of a contract, e.g. making a contract to break into a house to steal amounts to a criminal conspiracy; or in regard to the *performance* as in a contract to perform an illegal operation.

Contracts containing criminal elements such as those mentioned above are illegal. So, too, are contracts which involve the commission of a tort. But a contract may be illegal for reasons quite unconnected with crime or tort. Thus a contract 'in restraint of trade' is illegal, as we shall see. These and similar contracts are declared illegal because they offend against certain fundamental rules of common law laid down by the judges and collectively described as 'public policy'. The broad limits of this doctrine in its application to illegal contracts will be examined later.

The general rule is that an illegal contract is void. The maxim applied by the courts is *ex turpi causa non oritur actio* ('no action arises from a base or wrongful cause').

Contracts Declared Illegal by Statute

Certain statutes declare that some kinds of contracts are illegal and void. Thus, the Gaming Act, 1845, declares certain gaming and wagering contracts to be of this kind. The Moneylenders Act, 1927, renders certain moneylending contracts void, e.g. those of an extortionate or unconscionable kind. *Note:* The Truck Acts, 1831 to 1940, which prohibited the payment or part-payment of wages in kind, have been repealed by the Wages Act, 1986.

Contracts Illegal at Common Law

(*a*) **Contracts to commit a crime or a tort.** Contracts to make counterfeit coin, commit theft or maim another are examples of this kind. It is illegal in some cases to agree for a consideration not to prosecute an offender. To contract with a police officer, for a consideration, not to prosecute an offender amounts to corruption and is of course illegal.

Beresford v. *Royal Insurance Co. Ltd.* (1937). *B* insured his life for £50,000. This amount was to be paid on his death (even if by suicide). Some years after taking out his policy, *B* shot himself in a taxi-cab, intending that the insurance money should be used to pay off his heavy debts. *Held:* that *B*'s personal representatives could not recover from the insurance company the £50,000, for it is contrary to public policy to permit *B*'s estate to benefit by reason of the commission of a crime (suicide was at that time a crime).

An agreement to perform in a foreign and friendly country an action which is unlawful in that country is illegal and void as contrary to public policy.

Foster v. *Driscoll* (1929). A partnership agreement was entered into in England for the purpose of smuggling whisky into the United States at a time when the American prohibition laws were in force. An action on the agreement was begun in England. *Held:* that the agreement was illegal and void.

(*b*) **Contracts tending to sexual immorality.** A contract involving prostitution is contrary to good morals and is illegal.

Pearce v. *Brooks* (1866). A prostitute bought a brougham (carriage) on hire-purchase terms from a firm of coachbuilders. It was known that she intended to use the carriage for the purpose of attracting men customers. The woman failed to keep up her contractual payments for the carriage and the coachbuilders sued for arrears. *Held:* that as the plaintiff knew the purpose for which the carriage was to be used the contract was void.

(*c*) **Contracts affecting the freedom of marriage.** A contract in absolute restraint of marriage, i.e. to restrain a person from marrying at all, is void. Partial restraints, e.g. not to marry a person of a particular religious faith or of a particular nationality, may, if reasonable, be upheld.

Marriage-brokage contracts, i.e contracts for reward to introduce men and women with a view to subsequent marriage, are void.

(*d*) **Contracts of champerty and maintenance.** *Maintenance* occurs where one person having no interest in the subject-matter of litigation encourages another to take civil action against a third party as, for example, by giving financial assistance. It is a good defence to show that the person assisted has a common interest with the maintaining party, or that the maintenance is actuated by motives of charity.

Champerty is similar to maintenance, except that the assistance is given on the understanding that the person giving the assistance will share in the recovered damages.

Both were abolished by the Criminal Law Act, 1967, but by s. 14(2) this does not affect contracts contrary to public policy.

(*e*) **Agreements tending to injure the public service.** A contract involving bribery and corruption and contracts to buy honours are illegal.

> *Parkinson* v. *College of Ambulance* (1925). *P* was induced to give a large sum of money (£3,000) to a charitable institution, the secretary of which undertook to secure a knighthood for *P* in return. The knighthood was not bestowed, and *P* sued for the return of his money. *Held:* that the agreement was illegal and void and *P* was, therefore, unable to recover the sum.

(*f*) **Contracts of trading with the enemy.** These contracts are illegal at common law, and also by statute (Trading with the Enemy Act, 1939). All such contracts made with a person voluntarily residing in enemy territory during war are illegal unless permitted by licence of the Crown.

(*g*) **Contracts in restraint of trade.** Every agreement in restraint of trade is *prima facie* illegal and void. An agreement in restraint of trade will, however, be valid if it is reasonable between the parties, and if it is reasonable having regard to the interests of the public. In such agreements the doctrine of public policy applies with particular emphasis. There are three classes:

(i) Contracts between the buyer and seller of the goodwill of a business, restraining the seller from competing with the buyer.

(ii) Contracts between an employer and an employee.

(iii) Contracts between traders regulating conditions of trade, price-maintenance agreements and similar agreements. These may contravene the Restrictive Trade Practices Act, 1976, the provisions of which are noted on p. 62.

(i) *Restrictions on the Sale of a Business.* There is said to be greater freedom of contract between the seller and purchaser of the goodwill of a business than there is between an employer and an employee. Consequently, the rule as to the 'reasonableness' of an agreement will be less strictly applied in the case of sellers and purchasers in a position of equality and competent to make their own terms and conditions.

The reasonableness of an agreement which is in restraint of trade is a matter for the court and not the jury. This applies to all types of contracts, whether between employer and employee or between seller and purchaser of a business. Frequently contracts of this kind contain several clauses, some of which may be controversial. Accordingly where the reasonable part of a contract can be safely severed from the unreasonable, a court may, in its discretion, enforce the former part only. If the whole contract is indivisible and severance cannot effectively be made, the contract is void.

Nordenfeldt v. *Maxim-Nordenfeldt Gun Co.* (1894). *N*, an inventor and manufacturer of guns and ammunition, sold his business to a company, and promised that for twenty-five years he would not manufacture guns and ammunition henceforward in any part of the world. *Held:* that the agreement was reasonable and binding.

In this case a world-wide restraint was imposed. The fact that Nordenfeldt was liberally compensated, however, rendered the contract reasonable in itself.

British Reinforced Concrete Co. Ltd. v. *Schelff* (1921). *S*, the owner of a local business, sold it to the plaintiff company which had branches all over England. *S* covenanted not to carry on a business similar to that sold within ten miles of any of the branches of the plaintiff company. *Held:* that the covenant was void. The restraint was more than was necessary to protect the plaintiff company and the goodwill of the business purchased from *S*.

(ii) *Restraints on Employees.* The question arises whether an employee's contractual undertaking not to compete with his employer when he leaves is enforceable when he does so. In determining whether an agreement is reasonable, the courts pay regard to the class of business of the employer; the status and class of work of the employee; the area covered by the restriction; and the duration of the restraint clause in the agreement (*John Michael Design Plc* v. *Cooke and Another*, 1987).

As to the employer's protection from competition with his former employee, we may note that a restraint has 'never been upheld if directed only to the prevention of competition or against the use of the personal skill and knowledge acquired by the employee in his employer's business' (*Morris* v. *Saxelby*, 1916).

An employer may protect himself against the misuse of knowledge gained by an employee of the following kinds: lists of trade connexions; trade secrets; confidential information; and lists of names and addresses of an employer's customers. An injunction may be obtained from the court to restrain the misuse of such information in suitable cases. Further, a skilled employee having access to an employer's trade secrets may be prevented by injunction from working in his spare time for a rival business (*Hivac Ltd.* v. *Park Royal Scientific Instruments Ltd.*, 1946). There is an implied term in employment contracts that an employee must render faithful service during his employment.

A servant who is wrongfully dismissed by his employer is thereby released from liability under a restrictive agreement of the kind we are discussing here. It is, of course, otherwise where the dismissal is lawful.

In determining the reasonableness of an agreement in restraint of trade, the court has regard to the nature of the employer's business and also the capacity in which the employee serves. A wider restriction may be permissible in relation to an employee occupying a managerial position than would be upheld in the case of a subordinate employee. Moreover, some confidential relationship must subsist between employer and employee, e.g. the confidential relationship which exists between a solicitor and his managing clerk. But not all such relationships are held to be confidential in this sense, and restrictive agreements between the following classes of person have been held unreasonable and void: a newspaper proprietor and a reporter; a clothing company and a canvasser; a firm of motor-car dealers and a motor-salesman; an estate agent and a clerk.

Attwood v. *Lamont* (1920). *A*, a tailor and draper at Kidderminster, employed *L* under a contract containing a restriction that *L* would not, on leaving his employment, carry on a business as a tailor within ten miles of Kidderminster. *Held:* that the restriction was merely to prevent *L* from using his skill in competition with *A* and the agreement was void.

Fitch v. *Dewes* (1921). *D*, a solicitor at Tamworth, employed *F* as managing clerk. A covenant in a service agreement contained a clause restraining *F*, on leaving *D*'s employment, from practising as a solicitor within seven miles of Tamworth. *Held:* that the covenant was good. *F* had become acquainted with the solicitor's clients and their business, and therefore could be restrained from using that knowledge to the detriment of *D*. Accordingly a lifelong restriction was not too wide.

M & S Drapers v. *Reynolds* (1956). A collector-salesman, *R*, working for a firm of credit drapers, covenanted that he would not for five years after leaving his employment canvass orders from any person on the firm's list of customers during the three years immediately preceding the determination of his employment. *R* sold goods in breach of the covenant and was sued by plaintiffs. *Held:* that the restraint for five years in *R*'s position was too long and was an unreasonable restraint of trade.

(iii) *The Restrictive Trade Practices Acts, 1956, 1968, 1976 and 1977.* The Acts require restrictive trade agreements to be registered with the Director General of Fair Trading (Fair Trading Act, 1973).

The registrable agreements are set out in Part I of the Act and include any agreement between two or more persons carrying on business in the United Kingdom restricting: (i) the prices to be charged for goods; (ii) the conditions subject to which goods are supplied or processed; (iii) the quantities or descriptions of goods to be produced, supplied or acquired; and (iv) the persons or class of persons to or for whom, the areas or places in or from which, goods are to be supplied or acquired.

The general rule is that a restrictive agreement is presumed to be contrary to the public interest and, therefore, void. Thus, if *A* and *B* are two independent companies producing the same commodity, and they agree to fix the price at which certain goods may be bought, the agreement must be registered.

The Director General may then summon *A* and *B* before the court to justify the restrictive agreement. The grounds upon which *A* and *B* may validate the agreement are set out in the Act, and include the following: that the agreement (i) protects the public from danger or injury; (ii) counteracts similar practices abroad; (iii) maintains employment in a concentrated area; (iv) maintains the export trade; and (v) maintains another restrictive agreement already approved by the court.

The Restrictive Practices Court is of equal standing with the High Court, and consists of a full-time judge assisted by laymen with experience in business or commerce (Restrictive Practices Court Act, 1976). The court has power to enforce its rulings by injunction, but in practice resort to this form of control is not found necessary. Most agreements upon which the court has adjudicated have been found to be against the public interest, and the parties to the agreements have accepted the court's ruling and acted upon the findings accordingly. Recourse to injunction is thus unnecessary.

Effects of Illegality

An illegal contract is void, and consequently the court will not assist a party to such an agreement either directly or indirectly: *ex turpi causa non oritur actio* ('no action arises on a base cause'). Accordingly, no money or goods delivered under such a contract can be recovered by action.

Where money or goods have passed under an illegal contract the defendant is in a stronger position than the plaintiff who seeks the aid of the court to recover his property. Because the court usually refuses its aid once it discovers the illegality, the defendant to whom goods have been delivered or money has been paid may sometimes keep the goods or money. The maxim applied is *in pari delicto potior est conditio defendentis* ('where there is equal wrongdoing the position of the defendant is stronger').

There are certain exceptions to the above rule. Thus (i) where the parties are not *in pari delicto* (equal in wrongdoing), e.g. where one is subservient or has entered into the contract due to the oppression, duress or fraud of the other, the innocent party may recover money paid or property transferred; (ii) where the illegal purpose of the contract has not been carried out, one party may repent and recover back any money or property transferred. There must be true repentance, and the non-performance must result from the repentance, not that the contract was frustrated for other cause (see *Bigos* v. *Bousted* below).

Bigos v. *Bousted* (1951). *P* wanted to send his wife to Italy for health reasons. P agreed with *D* that *D* should make available £150 in Italian money for the purpose, contrary to the Exchange Control Act, 1947. *P* deposited a share certificate with *D* as security, but *D* failed to make available the Italian currency. *P* claimed the return of the share certificate. *Held:* that the contract was illegal and the fact that the contract had not been carried out was not due to repentance of *P*.

Berg v. *Sadler & Moore* (1937). *B*, a tobacconist, was placed on a stop-list by a tobacco association for breach of its rules. *B* concealed his identity, and to obtain supplies induced another member of the association to obtain tobacco for him from the defendants. *B* paid £72 19*s*. for cigarettes to the defendants. The latter became suspicious and refused to supply the goods or refund the money. *Held:* that *B*'s claim failed as he had attempted to obtain cigarettes by false pretence (an illegal act).

Severance. Sometimes a contract is illegal as to a part only. In these circumstances the court may divide the contract, enforcing the valid portion and refusing assistance in regard to the illegal part.

Where the whole purpose of the contract is illegal, severance of the good from the illegal is impossible, and the court will do nothing to assist and will not make a new contract for the parties.

Napier v. *National Business Agency Ltd.* (1951). *P* was employed by a company as secretary and accountant at a salary of £13 per week, plus £6 per week expenses. Both parties knew that *P*'s expenses were never more than £1 per week. The company dismissed *P* who then claimed his salary for the period in lieu of notice. *Held:* that the contract was to evade tax and was, therefore, illegal. It was impossible to sever the salary from the expenses, and the whole agreement was therefore unenforceable as tainted with illegality.

As a general rule the court will more readily sever covenants in restraint of trade affecting vendor and purchaser than similar contracts between master and servant.

12. Discharge of Contract

A contract may be discharged by (*a*) agreement, (*b*) performance, (*c*) breach, (*d*) a subsequent impossibility or frustration, and (*e*) operation of law.

(*a*) **Discharge by Agreement.** Since the parties to a contract enter into their relationship by agreement, it follows that they may also by agreement release each other from their obligations. The mutual release of each party from his obligations under the agreement provides the consideration for the agreement to discharge the contract. This form of release is known as **waiver**, each party waiving his rights under the contract, and is available where the consideration is still executory.

Where one of the parties has performed his obligations under the contract, an agreement to discharge the contract must (i) be supported by fresh consideration, or (ii) the release must be by deed. The form of release in (i) above is known as 'accord and satisfaction', and arises where the party to whom the obligation is owed agrees to accept from the other party something different in place of the original obligation. For example, Arnold agrees to dig Basset's garden for £10. Arnold digs the garden as promised. The parties may agree to rescind the former contract and to substitute one where Basset agrees to provide Arnold with a bicycle instead of the £10. If Arnold accepts there will be accord and satisfaction: 'accord' indicating the agreement, and 'satisfaction' indicating the new consideration (the bicycle).

Substituted Agreement. Where parties to a contract enter into a new agreement the question to be determined is whether the new agreement is a variation of an existing contract or whether a new contract is substituted for the original. This is sometimes difficult to decide.

(*b*) **Discharge by Performance.** A contract may be discharged by performance, each party fulfilling completely his obligations under the contract so that nothing remains to be done. Where, however, one party has done all that is required and the other has not, the contract is not discharged, for only one party has fulfilled his obligations.

Time. The time for performance may be agreed by the parties. Where time is 'of the essence of the contract', failure to perform within the stated time amounts to a breach. Time is 'of the essence of the contract' when the parties have expressly agreed or where it is implied from the circumstances. A contract for the supply of buns for a garden fête must be performed on the day of the event, not one day after, for obvious reasons. The general rule in mercantile contracts is that where time for performance is stated, the contract must be performed in that time: if not so performed there is breach.

Where time is not 'of the essence of the contract', performance must be within a reasonable time.

Though time may not be 'of the essence' at the inception of the contract, it may become so on giving reasonable notice to the other party on whom performance depends.

> *Chas. Rickards Ltd.* v. *Oppenheim* (1950). *O* ordered from *R* a Rolls-Royce chassis and car body, delivery to take place within six or seven months expiring March 1948. No delivery was made. *O* still pressed for delivery, and in June 1948, *O* wrote to *R* instructing that the car must be delivered within four weeks, otherwise the order would be cancelled. The car was not, in fact, delivered until October 1948, and *O* refused to

accept. *Held* (in an action by *R* for the price): that defendant *O* had waived the original time for delivery, but he was entitled on giving reasonable notice to make time 'of the essence of the contract', and did so.

Tender. Tender may mean 'attempted performance' of a contract. Where, therefore, performance of a contract is prevented or frustrated by the other party, it is a good defence in any subsequent action that performance was attempted (tender) but was prevented by the opponent. Accordingly, if tender of performance is made but prevented by the other party, the party tendering is freed from liability under the contract, which is thereby discharged. So, if goods are offered, as specified in the contract, but are rejected by the purchaser, the seller is freed from liability.

The second use of the word 'tender' relates to the payment of money. Where a person is obliged to pay a sum of money and attempts to do so, but payment is refused, the party tendering may, when sued, protect himself by paying into court the sum offered. If no greater sum is awarded to the plaintiff, the defendant will be awarded his costs incurred in the action.

A valid legal tender of money must comply with the terms of the contract as to place, mode, and time of payment. Moreover, payment must be unconditional. The following points should be noted:

(i) The exact amount must be tendered.

(ii) The tender must be made to the creditor or to his duly constituted agent (e.g. solicitor).

(iii) The tender must be a continuing one, i.e. the party paying must be always ready and willing to pay the sum due.

(iv) The money must be **legal tender**, i.e. Bank of England notes to any amount; 50p. pieces for payments not exceeding £10; 10p. and 5p. pieces for payments not exceeding £5; 2p. 1p. and ½p. pieces for payments not exceeding 20p.

A cheque is a good tender only if the creditor agrees to this method of payment. If the cheque is dishonoured the creditor may sue either under the original contract or on the dishonoured cheque, a separate action.

A receipt is evidence of payment, though not conclusive evidence. Where a receipt is lost, the payment may be proved by oral evidence of the payer or some other witness who knows the facts, or by other written evidence.

Appropriation of payments. Where a debtor owes several debts to a creditor and makes a payment which is insufficient to satisfy all the debts outstanding, the question arises as to which of the several debts the one payment will be appropriated.

Certain rules have been laid down to regulate this matter as follows:

(i) The debtor can appropriate any payment he makes to any debt. The appropriation can be made expressly or impliedly. If *A* owes a £100 debt and a £50·27 debt to *B*, payment by *A* of a £50·27 cheque implies payment of the lesser amount, irrespective of when the smaller debt was created.

(ii) If the debtor fails to appropriate expressly or impliedly the creditor may do so. Appropriation by the creditor may be to any legal or equitable claim and to debts which are statute-barred. Such debts are not extinguished; the right of action only is lost (Limitation Act, 1939).

(iii) In current accounts between creditor and debtor, e.g. ordinary bank current accounts, the rule laid down in *Clayton*'s case (1816) applies. This states that if neither party appropriates expressly or impliedly, the money first paid in discharges the earliest outstanding debt.

(*c*) **Discharge by Breach.** A breach of contract may take one of the following three forms: where one party

(i) repudiates his liability under the contract before performance is due;

(ii) disables himself from performing his promise or part under the contract; or

(iii) fails to perform his obligations under the contract.

A breach of contract entitles the injured party to an action in damages. But it may also entitle him to treat the contract as discharged, provided that the injured party is able to show that the breach is of the whole contract or of some term which is vital to, or 'goes to the root of' the contract. Breach of warranty, as distinct from a condition, gives a right to damages only but does not entitle the party injured to treat the contract as discharged.

Before the time for performance of the contract arrives, a party may expressly declare that he no longer intends to fulfil his obligations. He thus repudiates liability while the contract is still executory. This form of repudiation is sometimes called **anticipatory breach**, and its effect is to entitle the other party to sue immediately for breach even though time for performance has not yet arrived.

> *Hochster* v. *De La Tour* (1853). In April 1853, *D* agreed to engage *H* as a courier for a European tour to commence on 1 June. On 11 May *D* informed *H* that he no longer required his services. *H* began legal action. *Held:* that *D* had broken his contract by repudiation, and *H* could bring an action at once.

Repudiation may be of the whole contract or of part only. Repudiation which is sufficient to enable the contract to be discharged must be of a vital term in the contract.

Repudiation by one party entitles the innocent party (i) to sue at once (as in *Hochster* v. *De La Tour*), or (ii) to treat the contract as still continuing and to wait until the time for performance arrives. In the latter case, the contract continuing in existence, the party in default may take advantage of any circumstances or events which may subsequently release him from liability under the contract.

Avery v. *Bowden* (1855). *B* chartered *A*'s ship at Odessa, and *B* agreed to load her with a cargo of wheat within forty-five days. Before this period elapsed *B* informed *A* that he had no cargo for the ship and told *A* to leave the port. But *A* refused and stayed on at Odessa hoping *B* would change his mind. Before the forty-five days expired the Crimean War broke out, and performance of the contract would have been illegal. *Held:* that *A* might have treated *B*'s refusal to load the cargo as a breach of contract. By staying on at the port he had waived his right against *B*. The contract was discharged, not by repudiation, but by the outbreak of war. *B* was accordingly under no liability.

(*d*) **Discharge by Subsequent Impossibility** (or **Frustration**). An agreement may be held to be void at the outset owing to operative mistake, e.g. common mistake as to existence of subject matter. But a perfectly valid contract may be frustrated by subsequent impossibility. The common law rule for the latter was that if the parties failed to provide for it in their contract, the party liable to perform could be sued for damages for breach. The courts have modified this rule to the extent that though they will not regard a contract as frustrated merely because performance has become more difficult or more costly or less likely to yield the anticipated profit, they are prepared to find that a contract is discharged by frustration in the following circumstances:

(i) *Supervening illegality*. A contract, legal when made, may subsequently become illegal by outbreak of war or by a change in the law. (*Avery* v. *Bowden* (1855)—see above).

Baily v. *De Crespigny* (1869). *D* leased land to *B* and covenanted that he (*D*) would not build on adjoining land which he retained. A railway company compulsorily acquired *D*'s land under a *subsequent* statute, and the company built upon it. *Held:* that *D* was excused from his covenant with *B*, because the company's statutory powers made performance of the covenant impossible.

This case should be contrasted with the following:

Walton Harvey Ltd. v. *Walker & Homfrays* (1931). A contract by *X*, the lessees of an hotel, permitted *Y* to exhibit advertisements on the hotel roof for a period of seven years. During this time the hotel was acquired by a local authority under powers *existing at the time* of the formation of the contract. *Y* sued *X* for breach. *Held:* that the contract was not discharged, as *X* was aware of the possibility of compulsory acquisition, and must be taken to have accepted the risk. *X* was liable in damages for breach.

(ii) *Where there is destruction of a specific thing necessary for the performance of the contract.* If the contract depends on the existence of a certain thing and that thing is destroyed, the contract cannot be performed and is discharged.

Taylor v. *Caldwell* (1865). *C* let a music-hall to *T* for a series of concerts on certain days. The hall was accidentally burnt down before the concerts opened. *Held:* that the contract was discharged.

(iii) *Where the contract depends on the happening of a certain event.* If the event does not occur, the contract is regarded as discharged.

Krell v. *Henry* (1903). Defendant agreed to hire plaintiff's flat to watch the coronation procession of Edward VII. The King was taken ill and the procession was cancelled. *Held:* that the contract was discharged and no rent was payable by defendant.

This case should be contrasted with the following:

Herne Bay Steamboat Co. v. *Hutton* (1903). *D* agreed to hire *P*'s steamboat on a certain day to take passengers from Herne Bay for the purpose of viewing the Royal Naval review and for a cruise round the fleet. The review was cancelled, but the fleet remained, and the steamboat might have been used for the intended cruise. *D* did not use the boat, however, and *P* claimed the hiring fee. *Held:* that the contract was not discharged as the review was not the sole foundation of the contract. Judgment for the plaintiff, *P*.

(iv) *Where there is death or personal incapacity.* In contracts for personal services, the death or illness of the party who is to render the personal services discharges the contract. Thus a pianist who contracts to give a concert performance but falls ill on the date of the concert will be excused if too ill to perform. The contract is frustrated. The illness must be sufficiently serious to go to the root of the contract (*Robinson* v. *Davison*, 1871).

Condor v. *The Barron Knights, Ltd.* (1966). *C*, aged 16, was drummer employed by the Barron Knights band under a contract for 5 years. His duties were to play on 7 nights a week when the band had engagements. *C* fell ill and his doctor ordered that he was fit to play only on 4 nights a week. The band thereupon terminated his contract. *Held:* that, being ill, it was impossible for *C* to continue the contract in a business sense and the contract was properly terminated.

(v) *Where there is a vital change in the circumstances*, i.e. where events occur of such gravity that they result in a greatly different situation from that contemplated by the parties when the contract was made.

Metropolitan Water Board v. *Dick, Kerr & Co.* (1918). *D* contracted with *M* to construct a reservoir within six years. After two years, a Government department, acting under statutory powers, ordered *D* to cease work on the reservoir. *Held:* that the contract was frustrated. The character and duration of the interruption ordered by the Ministry would make the contract a really different contract based on changed conditions.

J. Constantine Steamship Line Ltd. v. *Imperial Smelting Corporation, Ltd.* (1942). Respondents chartered a ship to go to Port Pirie, Australia, to load a cargo. The day before the ship was due to load her cargo, an explosion in her boilers occurred, the cause of which was unknown. The ship was unable to perform the charter. Respondents sued in damages for breach of contract. *Held:* that the explosion frustrated the contract, and appellants were not liable in damages. Negligence against the appellants was not proved.

There must be a fundamental change in the circumstances which, in effect, goes to the root of the contract so that to hold the parties to their agreement would be to hold them to 'a new adventure or a new agreement'. Increased costs or delay are not by themselves enough.

Davis Contractors Ltd. v. *Fareham U.D.C.* (1956). *D* contracted with Fareham U.D.C. to build 78 houses for a certain sum within eight months. Because of inadequate supplies of labour and bad weather it took 22 months to complete. Building costs rose meanwhile, and *D* claimed the contract was frustrated and that he was entitled to a higher sum than agreed on the basis of *quantum meruit* (see p. 180). *Held* (by the House of Lords): that the shortage of labour and the increased costs made the contract more burdensome, but these factors did not operate to make the contract radically different from the original contract and did not frustrate it.

Tsakiroglou & Co. Ltd. v. *Noblee Thorl G.m.b.H.* (1961). *A* sold a quantity of groundnuts to *B*, shipment being from the Sudan to Germany, c.i.f. Hamburg, November/December 1956. The usual route was via the Suez Canal, but this was suddenly closed on 2 November 1956, after the contract was made. Shipment via the Cape of Good Hope was still possible. *A* did not ship the groundnuts and *B* sued. *Held:* that *A* was liable for breach. The change in circumstances did not make the contract fundamentally different from that agreed upon, and shipment through the Suez Canal was not an implied term.

A contract automatically comes to an end when frustration occurs. It is not necessary for either party to give notice to the other that the contract is discharged.

The Effects of Frustration. The old common law rule was that the loss resulting from the event causing the frustration lay where it fell. Money paid under the contract could not be recovered, and any sums due and payable before that time could be claimed, even though performance became impossible. These rules were formulated in the well-known case of *Chandler* v. *Webster* (1904), but as a result of the *Fibrosa* case (1943) the law was changed and is now embodied in the Law Reform (Frustrated Contracts) Act, 1943, the new rules of which are summarized below.

Where a contract is discharged by frustration:

(i) All sums paid before frustration are recoverable.

(ii) Money payable before frustration ceases to be payable.

(iii) Where *expenses* have been incurred before frustration, the court may allow a party to retain a reasonable sum out of money already received from the other or to recover from the other reasonable expenses.

(iv) Where a *benefit*, other than money payment, has been conferred before frustration by one party on another, the court may permit that party to recover a reasonable sum as compensation for such benefit.

The Act does not apply (i) where a contract contains special provisions in the event of frustration; (ii) where an **absolute** agreement exists, e.g. where the parties intend the agreement to be binding irrespective of frustrating circumstances; (iii) to charter parties; (iv) to carriage of goods by sea; (v) to contracts of insurance; (vi) to any contract for the sale of specific goods under section 7 of the Sale of Goods Act, 1979. (This section states that where goods have perished, the loss lies with the seller if ownership in the goods has not passed, or with the buyer if it has.)

(*e*) **Discharge by Operation of Law.** (i) *Lapse of Time*. Where a contract is entered into for a particular period of time the contract is discharged at the expiration of that period. Apart from provisions in the contract itself, therefore, the general rule is that lapse of time does not discharge a contract.

However, lapse of time may render the contract unenforceable in a court of law, and the important statute here is the Limitation Act, 1980, which sets out periods of time within which action must be taken by an aggrieved party. What the Act does is to extinguish the remedy by action at law. The provisions of this Act may be summarized as follows:

Actions on simple contracts are barred after six years from the date on which the plaintiff could have first brought an action.

Actions on specialty contracts (i.e. by deed) are barred after twelve years.

Special time limits are set for actions in respect of certain loans.

Actions to recover money due on a judgment by a court are barred after twelve years.

The Limitation Act, 1980, thus ensures that where a party has a cause of action he should not be able to keep alive the cause for a lengthy period of time, for this would be unfair to the other party and is against the public interest. By s. 29(6) a payment of part of the interest does not extend the period for claiming the remainder of interest then due, but the payment is treated as a repayment of principal (and so restarts the limitation period running against the principal debt). Subject to the above, s. 29(7) provides that a current period of limitation may be repeatedly extended by further acknowledgments or payment, but once a debt has become statute-barred, it cannot be revived subsequently.

Time runs not from the date of the contract but from the date when the plaintiff can first bring his action. Where a contracting party is under disability (such as minority or insanity) when the cause of action accrues, the period of limitation does not run against him until the contractual disability ends, or from the death of the plaintiff, whichever first occurs. Once, however, time has started to run under the Limitation Act, any subsequent disabilities do not affect the operation of the Act.

Where the action is based on fraud, or where, for example, the fraud of the defendant has prevented the plaintiff knowing of his right of action or where the action by the plaintiff is one for relief from the consequences of mistake, the period under the Limitation Act will begin to run when the fraud or the mistake could, by the use of reasonable diligence, have been discovered.

Finally, where an action for personal injuries arises out of breach of a contractual duty, the right of action is barred after three years under the Limitation Act, 1980, which has replaced an Act in 1954.

(ii) *Merger* arises where a simple contract is made and subsequently the parties make a specialty contract (by deed) embodying all the former terms. The contract is said to be merged, and the rights under the simple contract are discharged by this process. Similarly, where action is brought in a court of law on a simple contract and the court makes its judgment, the contract debt on which action is brought is merged in the judgment itself. Future action is brought on the judgment, e.g. by execution of the judgment, and not on the original contract.

(iii) *Material Alteration.* Where parties enter into a written contract or one by deed, the written form is in a sense sacrosanct. Any alteration which varies the legal significance of the contract, e.g. by incorporating false dates, names or money prices, will discharge the contract. However, the insertion of a correction in a document, as by inserting 'John S. Smith' in place of 'John Smith', is immaterial and does not operate to discharge the contract.

(iv) *Bankruptcy.* Where a person becomes bankrupt, a trustee in bankruptcy may be appointed and given statutory power to sue for debts due to the bankrupt party. Certain rights of action will not pass to the trustee, however. Thus he may not sue in respect of personal services to be rendered by the bankrupt, nor may the trustee sue in respect of rights of action which the bankrupt may have in defamation. The trustee may also disclaim onerous contracts which the bankrupt may have made, thus discharging the debtor from his obligations.

(v) *Death.* The death of either party to a contract discharges the contract where personal services are concerned. Thus, if a painter agrees for £100 to paint a portrait of *B*, the contract will be discharged if the painter dies one week after being commissioned.

Contracts other than these are not discharged, and the contractual rights and duties survive for the benefit of, or against, the estate of the deceased (see p. 311).

13. Remedies for Breach of Contract

On breach of contract the following remedies are available to the injured party: (*a*) refusal of further performance; (*b*) action for damages; (*c*) action on a *quantum meruit*; (*d*) action for specific performance; (*e*) action for an injunction; (*f*) rescission (see p. 157).

(*a*) **Refusal of Further Performance.** On breach of a condition of a contract, the injured party may of his own accord treat the contract as at an end (or rescinded) and refuse to perform or fulfil his part of the contract. In effect the injured party does nothing and the initiative passes to the contract-breaker who may sue for any sums due to him. The injured party may in any subsequent action set up the breach as a defence and may then counterclaim for any loss he sustains. Where an injured party treats the contract as rescinded, he must return any benefits he has received under the contract (*restitutio in integrum*).

(*b*) **An Action for Damages.** The object of this common law remedy is to compensate the injured party for loss caused by breach of contract, i.e. to put the injured party in the same financial position as he would have occupied had the contract been performed in its entirety. The measure of damages is the value of performance to the plaintiff, not the cost of it to the defendant. In sales of goods the measure of damages when there is an available market for the goods is the difference between the market price at the date of breach and the contract price. Where the market price is equal to, or less than, the contract price the injured party will be entitled only to nominal damages for the breach.

Not all damage resulting from or arising out of a breach of contract is recoverable. Some damage is regarded in law as too remote. No compensation will be awarded for such loss. For example, *A* takes a train journey on a certain day for an appointment for a new job. The train arrives half an hour late. *A* in consequence hurries through the streets and slips on the road, injuring himself. He also arrives too late for the interview. It may be said that the injuries and the loss of the job arise from the lateness of the train. But *A* may not recover damages from the railway authority for these losses which might be held to be too remote in law. A line has to be drawn somewhere, and the law does this by applying the following principles established in certain well-known cases, of which *Hadley* v. *Baxendale* (1854) is the most important.

The plaintiff will be entitled to:

(i) such damages as may fairly and reasonably be considered as *arising naturally*, i.e. according to the usual course of things, from the breach of contract; or

(ii) such damages as may reasonably be supposed to have been *in the contemplation of both parties*, at the time when they made the contract, as the probable result of the breach.

> *Hadley* v. *Baxendale* (1854). A miller sent a broken crankshaft by a carrier to deliver to an engineer for copying and to make a new one. The miller informed the carrier that the matter was urgent and that there should be no delay. The carrier accepted the consignment on those terms. The miller did not inform the carrier that the mill would be idle and unable to work. The carrier had no reason to believe that the crankshaft was an essential mechanism of the mill. The carrier delayed delivery of the crankshaft to the engineer, and, as a consequence, the mill was idle for longer than it need have been. *Held:* that the carrier was not liable for the loss of profits during the period of the delay.

The court in its judgment laid down the principles as at (i) and (ii) above.

The above case should be compared with the following. In this second type of case loss of profits for non-delivery or delayed delivery may be recoverable if the parties concerned could reasonably have foreseen such a loss.

> *Victoria Laundry* (*Windsor*) *Ltd.* v. *Newman Industries Ltd.* (1949). *V*, launderers and dyers, required another boiler to expand their lucrative dyeing contracts. *N* agreed to sell to *V* a second-hand boiler and to deliver on 5 June. The boiler was damaged on being dismantled, and was not delivered till 8 November. *V* claimed for (i) loss of profits on laundry business which would have been earned had the boiler been delivered on time, and (ii) loss of profits on a certain remunerative dyeing contract from the Ministry of Supply. *Held:* (i) that laundry profits were recoverable as *N* must have foreseen their loss if there was delay; (ii) that the loss of the dyeing contracts, which could not have been contemplated, was not recoverable.

Mitigation of damages. The party suffering damage as a result of breach must do all in his power to minimize his losses. If an employee is dismissed from his job he should try to secure other suitable work, not merely sit down and do nothing. Similarly, if rooms at a hotel are cancelled by a guest the hotelier should re-let the rooms if possible to another guest.

Brace v. *Calder* (1895). *B* was employed by a partnership for two years. After six months two partners died, leaving two surviving partners. A change in the partnership having taken place, this, by law, operated to dismiss all employees. The two remaining partners offered *B* re-employment on his previous terms, but *B* declined re-employment and sued for wrongful dismissal. *Held:* that *B* was entitled to nominal damages only since he should as a reasonable man have accepted the offer.

Damages may be classified in various ways according to the opinion of text writers. The following types are commonly found in practice:

General damages. This is pecuniary (money) compensation a judge (or jury in cases where a jury is summoned) is entitled to award on proof that a breach of contract has been committed. It is that kind of damage which the law presumes to follow from the breach of contract, and the amount is in the court's discretion having regard to all the circumstances.

Special damages. These are damages which do not arise naturally from the breach, but must be specially proved if they are to be claimed. Thus, loss of earnings during the period of incapacity of the plaintiff, damages for medical expenses, hire of car, etc., may be claimed under this head if such damages do not follow naturally from a breach. Special damages must be brought to the court's notice and be pleaded.

Nominal damages. Where only a technical breach has occurred and the plaintiff has suffered no real loss, the court may find for the plaintiff and award a nominal sum only, e.g. £1. These damages merely acknowledge that the plaintiff has proved his case and won.

Contemptuous damages. Here the court expresses its contempt of the plaintiff in bringing his action by awarding him a minimal sum, e.g. one penny. The award registers the fact that the plaintiff has technically won, but that the action ought not to have been brought at all.

Exemplary damages. These are partly punitive and serve to make an example of the defendant. They are more than would normally be awarded and may be given in tort but not contract, e.g. where the defendant's conduct is calculated to make a profit by his tort greater than normal compensation (*Cassell & Co. Ltd.* v. *Broome*, 1972).

Liquidated damages. These are damages which are ascertained and agreed beforehand by the parties to the contract. Having laid down the amount to be paid by either party on breach, it follows that the only dispute will be as to the breach itself, not the damages.

Unliquidated damages. These are unascertained damages. When breach of contract occurs and a legal action is undertaken, it is for the court to determine the amount of such damages to be paid by the defendant, having regard to all the circumstances of the case. It is up to the plaintiff to prove the circumstances from which the court can deduce the loss.

Penalties. We have seen that liquidated damages are predetermined by the parties themselves, and the court normally awards the amount of liquidated damages so agreed. Sometimes, however, the amount of damages payable on breach is not merely an agreed and reasonable compensation but is more in the nature of a **penalty**. Where a minor breach occurs and a heavy payment has to be paid by way of compensation, there is obviously injustice. Accordingly the party in breach complains against his fate. The common law attitude was that the parties agreed to the amount payable and no relief was available. Equity took a different view, however, and has laid down certain principles in the giving of relief where the sum specified has been inserted in the contract *in terrorem*, i.e. as a **frightener** to ensure performance of the contracts.

The court will base its decision on the following principles:

(i) The sum agreed must be treated as a penalty if it is extravagant and unreasonable in amount by comparison with the greatest loss that can ensue from breach of the contract.

(ii) Where the payment of a smaller sum is secured by a larger sum, the latter is a penalty.

(iii) When 'a single lump sum is made payable by way of compensation on the occurrence of one or more or all of several events, some of which may occasion serious damage, and others but trifling damage', there is a *presumption* that the sum so inserted is a penalty.

The relief afforded by the court where a penalty is found to exist is to excuse payment of that amount. The court has power to substitute its own award of damages computed on the basis of compensation for loss sustained. On the other hand, where an agreed sum is in the nature of liquidated damages, no greater sum will be awarded by the court even if it is proved that the consequences of breach have been more serious than the parties had foreseen.

Dunlop v. *New Garage Co*. (1915). Dunlops sold tyres at reduced rates to wholesale traders on the terms that no private customer should be supplied with tyres at a lower rate than the retail prices laid down. New Garage Co. agreed to this clause and to pay the sum of £5 as 'liquidated damages' for each tyre sold in breach of the term. New Garage Co. sold a tyre at less than the agreed current list price and was sued by Dunlops. New Garage pleaded that the £5 per tyre was a penalty. *Held* (by the House of Lords): that it was liquidated damages. The sum of £5 was really and genuinely a pre-estimate of the interest of Dunlops in the due performance of the contract.

Cellulose Acetate Silk Co. Ltd. v. *Widnes Foundry (1925) Ltd.* (1933). Manufacturers agreed to erect certain machinery within 18 weeks from the date of the final approval of drawings. They also agreed that if they took longer the machinery manufacturers would pay £20 per week for every week exceeding 18. There was serious delay in making the machine, and the buyers claimed £5,850, which greatly exceeded the agreed sum. *Held:* that the sum of £20 per week was agreed damages and that no more could be recovered.

Recovery of Interest. The rules are that interest is payable in the following circumstances:

(i) Where the parties have so agreed in the contract.
(ii) Where there is an implied agreement, e.g. from the course of dealing between the parties themselves, or from a trade usage.
(iii) On overdue bills of exchange and promissory notes.

Under the Law Reform (Miscellaneous Provisions) Act, 1934, the court may allow interest at such rate as it thinks fit on all claims for debt or damages from the date when the claim arose to the judgment date.

(*c*) **An action on a 'Quantum Meruit'.** In the event of a breach of contract, the injured party may have a claim other than that for damages, in particular he may claim payment for what he has done under the contract. His right to sue on a *quantum meruit* ('as much as he has earned') arises not out of the original contract but on an implied promise by the other party who has accepted an executed consideration to pay a reasonable sum for it.

The claim arises in cases of two kinds:

(i) Where one party abandons or refuses to perform the contract.

Planché v. *Colburn* (1831). *P* agreed with *C* to write a volume on ancient armour for a periodical called *The Juvenile Library* for a fee of £100. After *P* had written part of his work the defendant *C* abandoned the periodical. The contract could not, therefore, be completely performed, and *P* sued. *Held:* that the defendant had repudiated the contract and *P* was entitled to treat it as discharged and recover on a *quantum meruit* for the work he had already done.

(ii) Where work has been performed and accepted under a void contract.

Craven-Ellis v. *Canons Ltd.* (1939). Plaintiff was employed as managing director of Canons Ltd. under a deed which provided for salary. The directors who made the contract were unqualified (they had never obtained the required number of shares) so the deed was invalid. Plaintiff had rendered his services and now sued on a *quantum meruit* for a reasonable sum. *Held:* that he could recover on a *quantum meruit*, there being no valid contract.

A claim under *quantum meruit* does not apply, however, where the contract requires *complete* performance as a condition of payment, e.g. a contract to do one piece of work in its entirety in consideration for a lump-sum payment.

Sumpter v. *Hedges* (1898). *S* agreed to build a house for a certain sum on *H*'s land. When the house was half finished *S* ran out of money and could not complete. *H* refused payment, and *S* brought an action on a *quantum meruit* for the value of materials used and the labour he had expended. *Held:* that the claim must fail. The contract was to do certain work for a lump sum which was not payable until completion. *H* had no choice but to accept the work.

Cutter v. *Powell* (1795). *P* agreed to pay *C* 30 guineas 'provided he proceeds, continues and does his duty as second mate' on a voyage from Jamaica to Liverpool. *C* died shortly before the end of the voyage, and his widow (*C*'s personal representative) claimed a proportion of the agreed payment in respect of that part of the work he had completed. *Held:* that the widow's claim must fail. *C*'s obligation remained undischarged, the contract imposed one indivisible obligation which had not been performed.

Such cases are exceptional; but if *A* agrees, for example, to make an article for *B* on *B*'s promising to pay for the article when it is completed, nothing less than complete performance will bind *B*. But if *B* has the choice of rejecting or accepting partial performance, he must pay a reasonable price if he accepts the work.

However, not every breach of contractual term to complete a piece of work will absolve an employer from his promise to pay. Only a breach which goes to the root of the contract (c.f. *Sumpter* v. *Hedges* above) will enable the employer to refuse payment. It follows, therefore, that where the work is *substantially completed*, but certain small defects are manifest or differences exist from what was contractually agreed, the full amount due may be claimed, less allowances for the defects and differences.

Hoenig v. *Isaacs* (1952). An interior decorator, *A*, agreed to furnish *B*'s flat with a wardrobe and bookcase for £750. The work was performed, but *B* complained that it was faulty workmanship and paid £400 only, claiming that he (*B*) was not liable in law to pay anything, as some of the work was defective. *A* sued for the full £750. *Held:* that the contract was a lump-sum contract; it had been substantially performed, and *A* was entitled to the contract price of £750 less a deduction in respect of the defective work amounting to £294.

(*d*) **An Action for Specific Performance.** This is an equitable remedy and was available only in the courts of equity before the Judicature

Acts, 1873–5. It is now available in all civil courts. The remedy is supplementary to the common law remedies and is in all cases issued at the discretion of the court so that in *Patel* v. *Ali* (1984) the court refused specific performance on the grounds of hardship.

The order essentially instructs that the parties to a contract carry out, or perform, the terms of their agreement, hence its name.

The principles on which the order is granted are as follows:

(i) Where damages are an adequate remedy, specific performance will not be granted. *Beswick* v. *Beswick* (1967), see p. 185.

(ii) Where the court cannot supervise the performance or execution of the contract, the remedy is not available. Thus, it cannot be granted in a building contract of a continuing nature where the 'performance' is usually by stages, or in contracts of personal services.

(iii) Where one of the parties is a minor the remedy is not granted. Equity states that there must be 'mutuality', i.e. the contract must be specifically enforceable by both parties. A contract between a minor and an adult lacks mutuality and the remedy will therefore be refused.

(iv) The remedy is not granted in contracts to lend money.

(v) The contract itself must be certain, fair and just, and the conduct of the party seeking performance must be irreproachable.

The most common types of contract in which specific performance is granted are those connected with land, and contracts to take debentures in a company.

It is not ordinarily granted in the case of sales of goods, but it is a suitable remedy where the contract is for the purchase of a rare or unique article.

(*e*) **An Injunction.** This too is an equitable remedy, and is commonly used in torts such as where the owner of property wishes to restrain another from continual trespass to his property or goods. An injunction is an order of the court restraining a person from the doing of an act. It will be granted to enforce a **negative** stipulation in a contract where damages would not be an adequate remedy. Thus, in a contract for personal services where *A* binds himself not to work for any person other than *B* (the other contracting party), this negative stipulation may be enforced by injunction.

Lumley v. *Wagner* (1852). *W* agreed to sing at *L*'s theatre for a certain period, and during that time not to sing elsewhere. Later *W* contracted to sing at another theatre and refused to perform her contract with *L*. *Held:* that an injunction should be granted to prevent *W* from singing elsewhere. The court would not, however, grant an order of specific performance to compel *W* to sing for *L*.

Warner Bros v. *Nelson* (1937). *N* agreed to give her services exclusively for a certain period to *W*, and also during the period of the agreement not to give her services to any other person. During the time *N* contracted to act for *X*. *Held:* that an injunction be granted restraining her from entering into the more favourable employment with *X*.

The court will not intervene if the granting of an injunction would compel a defendant either to work for the plaintiff alone or remain workless, as this would amount to an indirect enforcement of a contract for personal services. This rule is confirmed in the Trade Union and Labour Relations Act, 1974.

Whitwood Chemical Co. v. *Hardman* (1891). *H* was employed by *W* as manager and agreed to devote all his time to the business of the company for a term of 10 years. Later he gave some of his time to a rival company and wished to relinquish his post with *W*. *W* sued. *Held:* that the grant of an injunction would have been in effect to compel specific performance of a contract for personal services. Other remedies were available.

An injunction is granted only where it is just and equitable to do so, having regard to all the circumstances of the case. It is a discretionary remedy.

(*f*) **Rescission.** This remedy has been described on p. 157.

14. Privity of Contract

By its very nature a contractual agreement is private to the contracting parties, each of whom is given rights which are enforceable at law. The general rule, therefore, is that *only a person who is a party to a contract can sue on it* (Lord Haldane in *Dunlop* v. *Selfridge*, 1915). To permit a person who had no part in the original agreement whatsoever to obtain benefits, or to impose upon such a person an obligation to which he was not a party or had never agreed, would be clearly contrary to the basic rules of justice.

Dunlop v. *Selfridge* (1915). *D* sold tyres to Dew & Co. on condition that the latter would not re-sell Dunlop's tyres below a certain price and that they (Dew & Co.) would obtain a similar agreement from any of their customers. Selfridges bought tyres from Dew & Co. and agreed not to sell tyres below list price. Selfridges sold some tyres below the list price in breach of the agreement between Selfridges and Dews. The manufacturers (*D*) sued Selfridges on the breach of the agreement. *Held:* that Dunlops could not enforce the agreement between Selfridges and Dews, because they (Dunlops) were not party to the agreement and could not therefore obtain rights under it.

This rule is distinct from the rule that consideration must move from the promisee. Here, the basis of the decision is that Dunlops were not party to the agreement made between Dew & Co. and Selfridges.

The Resale Prices Act, 1976, allows individual enforcement of restrictions as to minimum resale prices, so *Dunlop* v. *Selfridge* (1915) would be decided differently today.

Once a contract is formed there is a general duty on third persons not to interfere with the contractual relationship. If a third person, *C*, knowingly and without lawful justification induces *A* to break his contract with *B*, so causing damage to *B*, *B* may sue *C* in tort.

Similarly where *X* threatens to do some unlawful act to *Y* unless *Y* does something which will cause loss to *Z*; *X* commits the tort of intimidation actionable at the suit of *Z*. Where a trade union threatened to strike if the employers did not dismiss a non-union employee it was held that the strike, involving breach of contract of employment, would be an unlawful act and that the threat was an actionable wrong to the non-union employee (*Rookes* v. *Barnard*, 1964). The Trade Disputes Act, 1965, now provides that such a threat shall not be actionable in tort if made in contemplation or furtherance of a trade dispute.

The doctrine of privity of contract as stated has existed for more than a century and has been reaffirmed in decisions ranging from *Tweddle* v. *Atkinson* (1861) to *Scruttons Ltd.* v. *Midland Silicones Ltd.* (1962).

> *Scruttons Ltd.* v. *Midland Silicones Ltd.* (1962). *A* and *B* contracted for the carriage of a cargo owned by *B*. A further contract existed between *A* and *C* regarding the unloading of the goods from *B*'s ship. The goods were damaged through *C*'s negligence during the unloading, and *B* claimed damages from *C*. An exemption clause existed in the contract between *A* and *B*, and on that clause *C* relied. *Held* (by the House of Lords): that *C* was a stranger to the contract between *A* and *B*, and as a result could not rely on the exemption clause. His defence therefore failed.

Exceptions to the general rule as to privity of contract are listed below:

(*a*) *Action by a beneficiary under a trust*. If the facts show that the person entitled is a beneficiary (or *cestui que trust*) he may sue under the trust itself though not on the contract.

(*b*) *Certain contracts of insurance*. Section 207 of the Road Traffic Act, 1972, compels insurance against third-party risks in respect of vehicles driven on roads. If *A*, a third party, is injured he will have rights against the negligent driver *B* personally, and against the insurance company. The following Acts of Parliament are also relevant: The Marine Insurance Act, 1906 (s. 14); the Married Women's Property Act, 1882 (s. 11); and the Law of Property Act, 1925 (s. 47).

(*c*) *Negotiable instruments* (e.g. cheques).

(*d*) *Restrictive covenants* (see p. 285).

(*e*) *Law of agency*.

(*f*) *Price-maintenance agreements* under the Restrictive Trade Practices Acts, 1956 and 1976 (see p. 165).

The following case offers an important illustration of the general rule as to privity and the effect of the Law of Property Act, 1925, s. 56(1), which states that 'a person may take an immediate or other interest in land *or other property* or the benefit of any condition, right of entry, covenant or agreement over or respecting land or other property although he may not be named as party to the conveyance or other instrument'.

Beswick v. *Beswick* (1967). *A* owned a small coal round, and his nephew, *B*, helped him to run it. *A*, being in poor health and wishing to retire from the business, drew up an agreement under which *A*, the uncle, transferred his business to the nephew, *B*. *A* would be retained as adviser and consultant at £6 10*s*. per week, and on his death his widow, *C*, would receive an annuity of £5 per week. *A* retired and was paid the £6 10*s*. per week. *A* died later but *B* made no payment to the widow, *C*. Accordingly *C* sued the nephew: (i) as administratrix of her husband's estate, and (ii) in her personal capacity for the arrears of the annuity and for specific performance of the agreement. *Held:* that as administratrix, the widow could obtain an order of specific performance which would enforce the provision in the contract for the benefit of herself; but that in her personal capacity she could derive no action from the statute.

The case history of *Beswick* v. *Beswick* is interesting in that at the first hearing the court applied the general principle of *Tweddle* v. *Atkinson* and disallowed the widow's claim; it was the Court of Appeal's verdict given above that the widow could succeed at common law, in equity and by statute (Law of Property Act, 1925, s. 56). The House of Lords affirmed the decision of the Court of Appeal on the ground that the widow could succeed as personal representative of the deceased and was entitled to enforce the agreement by an order of specific performance. The House of Lords expressed the view that the Law of Property Act, 1925, was a consolidating Act, and Section 56 could not be construed as changing the law so as to enable the widow to sue in her personal capacity. The House of Lords reaffirmed the general principle that a person not a party to a contract cannot sue upon it, and that although the Law Revision Committee of 1937 had long ago suggested changing the rule, this change must be left to the legislature.

15. Assignment

Assignment means transfer, and we consider here the law affecting the transference of rights and liabilities to a third person who is not a party to the original contract. The general rule is that the only persons who possess rights and liabilities under a contract are the parties to it. But in certain circumstances the contracting parties may drop out and others may take their places, thereby succeeding to the rights and liabilities. If one of the contracting parties dies, his rights and liabilities may pass to his personal representatives: this is described as an 'assignment by operation of law' (see below).

Liabilities under a contract cannot be assigned without the consent of the other party to the contract. The only means by which a liability can be effectively assigned is by 'novation' (see below), which requires the consent of the other party.

Rights under a contract can usually be assigned, but where the contract is for personal services, and personal performance by the promisor is of the essence of the contract, rights may only be assigned with the consent of the other party.

> *Robson and Sharpe* v. *Drummond* (1831). *D* hired a carriage from one Sharpe who undertook to paint it every year and keep it in repair. After three years Sharpe retired from his business and informed *D* that thereafter *R* would be responsible for the repairs. *D* refused to deal with *R*, and *R* sued on the agreement. *Held:* that *D* was entitled at law to refuse to deal with *R*, and further that Sharpe could not assign his liabilities under the contract without *D*'s consent.

The assignment of rights under a contract may be carried out by: (*a*) novation, (*b*) legal assignment, (*c*) equitable assignment, or (*d*) operation of law.

(*a*) **Novation.** This is the making of a new contract between the parties whereby *A*, the person possessing rights under a contract (e.g. a creditor), at the request of *B*, the person under liability (e.g. a debtor), agrees to *X* assuming or taking over *B*'s liability.

The two original contracting parties, *A* and *B*, and the third party, *X*, must all agree together to form a new contract under which *X* undertakes *B*'s liability to *A* in consideration of *A* releasing *B*.

There must be consideration for the transaction which is constituted by the release of an existing debt or other contractual obligation. Thus a new party is introduced and a *new* contract is formed, hence the term 'novation'.

Novation arises most frequently in a partnership when, on a change in the membership of the firm, the creditors agree, expressly or impliedly, to accept the liability of the new firm and to discharge the old firm from liability.

(*b*) **Legal Assignment.** The old rule of common law was that contracting parties could not assign rights to a third party. Equity, however, allowed assignment subject to certain conditions. The law was altered by the Judicature Act, 1873, and was re-enacted in the Law of Property Act, 1925, s. 136, which states that all debts and other legal choses in action (see below) may be assigned, provided that:

(i) The assignment is in writing, signed by the assignor.
(ii) It is absolute and not by way of charge.
(iii) Express notice in writing is given to the debtor, trustee or other

person from whom the assignor would have been entitled to claim such a debt or chose in action.

A legal 'chose in action' means a right which may only be enforced by taking legal action and not by taking physical possession. Examples include a debt, a patent right, a right under a copyright, and a right under a contract. These cannot be physically touched. A 'chose in possession', on the other hand, is a tangible object, e.g. a chair, a table, a ring, a painting, coins, etc.

As a simple example of the operation of section 136 of the Law of Property Act, 1925, let us assume that *A* owes £100 to *B*, and *B* owes £100 to *C*. *B* wishes to assign to *C* his right in *A*'s debt. *B* does so by written letter assigning the £100 to *C*. *B* (the assignor) then notifies *A* (the debtor) in writing that *C* (the assignee) is entitled to the debt. If *A* pays the £100 to *C*, the debt is discharged at law.

The assignment must be 'absolute', i.e. it must be of the whole debt (£100 in our example) and not a portion of it. This is to ensure that *A* will not be inconvenienced by having to seek out and pay numerous assignees to whom *B* may have attempted to transfer parts of the £100. Conditional assignments or part assignments of a debt are not, therefore, absolute.

The assignment is subject to any claims or defences open to the debtor (*A*) against the assignor (*B*) existing at the time of the receipt of notice of assignment. Suppose that *B* owes *A* the sum of £10. If the debt arises out of the same contract as that under which the £100 is due, *A* will be entitled to deduct the sum of £10; then a payment of only £90 to *C* will be a good discharge of *A*'s obligations. This is an example of what is meant by 'subject to equities'.

The effect of the assignment is to transfer to the assignee:

(i) the legal right to the debt or chose in action;
(ii) the legal and other remedies for the debt or other legal chose in action; and
(iii) the power to give a good discharge, e.g. a valid receipt.

Consideration is not necessary to support the assignment of a legal chose in action.

(*c*) **Equitable Assignment.** An assignment which does not comply with the requirements of a legal assignment (under section 136 of the Law of Property Act) may nevertheless take effect as an equitable assignment. But to do so the intention to assign must be clear from the circumstances. If it is clear, no particular formalities need be complied with, e.g. the assignment need not be in writing. Notice of the assignment *need* not be given to the debtor, but it should be given for two reasons:

(i) The debtor can set up any defences against the assignee which he (the debtor) had against the assignor up to the date of his receipt of notice of the assignment. If, therefore, the debtor makes a payment to the assignor before he receives notice of the assignment, this payment is good as against the assignee.

(ii) To gain priority over any subsequent assignee without notice of his assignment.

> *Brandt* v. *Dunlop Rubber Co. Ltd.* (1905). *K* & Co. agreed with *B* (plaintiff) who financed *K* & Co. that the purchase price of all goods sold by *K* & Co. should be paid direct to *B*. *K* & Co. sold goods to Dunlops, and *B* gave notice to Dunlops to pay the price to *B*. Dunlops disregarded the notice and paid *K* & Co. *Held:* there was evidence of an equitable assignment of the price and Dunlops were liable to pay *B* notwithstanding that they (Dunlops) had already paid *K* & Co.

Certain assignments must be carried out in the manner laid down in the statutes appropriate to those assignments, and not in accordance with section 136 of the Law of Property Act. For example:

(i) Shares in companies are transferred in accordance with the Companies Act, 1985.

(ii) Policies of life assurance are transferred in accordance with the Policies of Assurance Act, 1867.

(iii) Bills of exchange and promissory notes are transferred in accordance with the Bills of Exchange Act, 1882.

(*d*) **Assignments by Operation of Law.** The foregoing assignments take effect by an act of the party (or parties). The following assignments take effect by operation of law, i.e. without any voluntary act by the parties.

(i) *On Death.* The personal representative (i.e. executor or administrator) of a deceased person acquires the rights and liabilities of the deceased, and pays the debts of the deceased to the extent of the latter's estate. Rights and obligations arising out of contracts for personal services are extinguished by the death of either party to such a contract.

(ii) *On Bankruptcy.* A trustee in bankruptcy has vested in him all the rights of the bankrupt. Rights of action for slander and assault, and other rights of a purely personal nature do not pass to the trustee.

The rules relating to bankruptcy are too detailed to be examined here, but we should mention that contracts for personal services to be performed by the bankrupt are not usually affected by the bankruptcy proceedings. The trustee is primarily liable to pay the debts of the bankrupt to the extent of the estate, though the trustee can disclaim onerous contracts of the bankrupt. Any party prejudiced by such disclaimer may petition in the bankruptcy proceedings for any loss suffered thereby.

16. Interpretation of a Contract

The general rule is that a written contract cannot be varied by parol (i.e. oral) evidence, either by the parties thereto or by others. But there are exceptions to this main rule.

The duty of the court is to interpret the contract itself and to give effect to the intentions of the parties. It does so by giving to the words used in the writing their ordinary and literal sense.

Parol evidence will, however, be admitted in the following cases:

(i) To show that a commercial custom or a trade usage may be read into the contract (unless such custom or usage is expressly excluded).

(ii) To explain a latent, as opposed to a patent, ambiguity. A latent ambiguity is one which is not apparent from the face of the document. For example, *A* leaves his car by will to his nephew, John: but *A* has two nephews named John, and evidence may be admitted to explain which nephew *A* intended to benefit.

(iii) To prove collateral terms or warranties not expressly provided for in the contract.

(iv) To prove rescission of a written contract. Thus where *A* and *B* make a contract in writing but later rescind it orally, evidence may be given of the oral rescission.

(v) The court may receive oral evidence to imply a term to give 'business efficacy' to the contract, in accordance with the intention of the parties thereto (see *The Moorcock* (1889) at p. 142).

17. Quasi-Contract

We have noted that the essence of a legal contract is that it is based on agreement of the parties. Sometimes, however, the law imposes an obligation on a party and allows an action to be brought on that obligation despite the fact that no agreement was present. These types of obligation are known as 'quasi-contracts' (quasi means 'as if it were' or 'seemingly').

The following are examples:

(*a*) A contract of record, e.g. a recognizance (see p. 113).

(*b*) An account stated (see p. 134).

(*c*) Actions for money had and received, e.g. where Smith pays money by mistake to Black instead of White; or where under a valid contract John pays money to William who fails entirely to keep his side of the bargain. Here John has a quasi-contractual remedy to recover his money as an alternative to a legal remedy in damages.

(*d*) Actions for money paid to the use of another, e.g. where a surety (Harry) pays the debt owed by the principal debtor (Thomas), an action will lie against Thomas.

(*e*) Claims on a *quantum meruit*. This type of action arises where a contract which has been partly performed by one party has become discharged by breach by the other party. Here the law implies an agreement by the person who has benefited to pay for what has been done for him. The right is founded not on the original contract (which is discharged or void), but on an implied agreement to pay for what has been done. See *Planché* v. *Colburn* (1831), p. 180.

18. Exercises

1. Define a contract, and state the essential elements of a valid contract.
2. Distinguish between (i) an offer, and (ii) an invitation to treat.
3. What is the effect of an acceptance 'subject to contract'?
4. Describe the main rules regarding consideration.
5. Distinguish between (i) a guarantee, and (ii) an indemnity.
6. What is the 'doctrine of part performance'? What are the four points which must be proved before the equitable remedy will be applied?
7. What does s. 1 of the Infants' Relief Act, 1874, provide?
8. What special rules apply to contracts by corporations?
9. When will an 'implied term' be imported into a contract?
10. Distinguish between (i) a condition, and (ii) a warranty, in a contract.
11. What are the rules as to mistake of the identity of the person with whom a contract is made? Discuss with reference to decided cases.
12. Define a 'representation', and distinguish between fraudulent and innocent misrepresentation.
13. Distinguish, with examples, between contracts made as a result of duress and those effected by undue influence.
14. Enumerate contracts which are illegal (i) by statute, and (ii) at common law.
15. In what ways may a contract be said to be discharged? What is meant by the statement that 'a contract may be discharged by frustration'?
16. What remedies are available at law to a person who claims there has been a breach of contract?
17. Distinguish between general and special damages.
18. What is meant by 'an equitable assignment' of a debt or other chose in action? Give an example.

8

THE LAW OF TORTS

The word 'tort' derives from the Latin *tortus*, meaning crooked or twisted, and the Norman-French *tort*, meaning wrong. In English law we use the word tort to denote certain civil wrongs as distinct from criminal wrongs.

The early Anglo-Saxon did not distinguish between civil wrongs and criminal wrongs. In the Middle Ages, however, the idea sprang up that certain wrongs of an anti-social kind, e.g. treason, murder, theft, arson, and the like, were offences against the King or the State. The King's peace, as it was called, extended to every corner of the land, and all crimes were at the same time breaches of the peace. Certain other wrongs, done by one person to another, were disregarded by the King and the State. These were left to be enforced by the person claiming to be injured or wronged. The injured plaintiff decided for himself whether to take action or not. His claim, if any, was for damages, i.e. money compensation or reparation for the injury inflicted upon him by the defendant.

Whether or not a plaintiff had a right of action against another for an alleged wrong depended on the existence of a writ wherewith to begin the action. The rights available depended in practice on the writs available. The Forms of Action, as these were called, enshrined the rights. If there was no writ there was no remedy available in the courts of law.

The most important all-purpose writ which covered the common civil wrongs in medieval society was **trespass**. This was available for all *direct* injuries to the person, goods, or lands. Thus a personal injury to another, e.g. assault and battery, damage to personal goods, to gates, hedges, lands, or mere entry on lands or cattle trespass, fell within the ambit of trespass.

The writ of trespass was aptly called 'the fertile mother of actions'. After the Statute of Westminster II, 1285, there grew up offshoots of trespass, named **trespass on the case**. Whereas the writ of trespass was available for all direct and forcible injuries, the writs of trespass on the case were used for all injuries which were *indirect*.

For example, where *A* walks across *B*'s land, or lifts *B*'s gate off its hinges, or punches *B* on the nose, there is a direct and forcible injury to the property or person of another: the writ of trespass lay.

But where *A* lights a fire on his own property which spreads to his neighbour's house and burns it, or where *A* digs a hole into which *B* falls, or *A* leaves a log in the road and *B* trips over it injuring himself, *A*'s action is not direct and forcible: the writ of trespass did not lie. The plaintiff proceeded by trespass on the case.

1. The Nature of a Tort

First, we must examine the distinctions between (*a*) a tort and a crime, (*b*) a tort and a breach of contract, and (*c*) a tort and a breach of trust.

(*a*) **A Crime.** The object of criminal proceedings is primarily punishment. The police are the principal agents to enforce the criminal law, though a private person may also prosecute a criminal offence. If the defendant is found guilty the court may award the proper punishment. The object of proceedings in tort is not punishment, but compensation or reparation to the plaintiff for the loss or injury caused by the defendant, i.e. damages.

The same facts may disclose a crime and a tort. Thus, if *A* steals *B*'s coat, there is (i) a crime of theft, and (ii) trespass to goods (a tort) and conversion (also a tort). If *X* assaults *Y*, there is both a crime and a tort.

(*b*) **A Breach of Contract.** In contract the duties are fixed by the parties themselves. They impose terms and conditions themselves by their agreement. In tort, on the other hand, the duties are fixed by law (common law or statute) and arise by the operation of the law itself.

Here, too, the same circumstances may give rise to a breach of contract and a tort. Thus, if *A* hires a taxi-cab driven by *B*, and *B* by dangerous driving injures his fare, (*A*), the latter will have a cause of action for (i) breach of the contractual duty of care, and (ii) the tort of negligence.

So, too, where *A* employs privately a surgeon, *B*, to operate on *A*'s son, *B* owes *A* a contractual duty of care. If he fails in that duty he is also liable to *A*'s son in tort.

(*c*) **A Breach of Trust.** As we have seen (p. 16) a breach of trust fell within the jurisdiction of the Chancery Courts, and although compensation may be awarded for damage suffered by reason of the breach of trust, the real distinction is due to the history of equity and common law rather than to logical reasons and development.

Definition of a Tort

'The province of tort is to allocate responsibility for injurious conduct' (Lord Denning). Such is the area of the law with which we are concerned.

A tort has been defined as '*a civil wrong for which the remedy is a common law action for unliquidated damages, and which is not exclusively the breach of a contract or the breach of trust or other merely equitable obligation*' (Salmond: *Law of Torts*).

Prof. P. H. Winfield, another important authority in this field, asserts that '*tortious liability arises from the breach of a duty primarily fixed by law; such duty is towards persons generally, and its breach is redressible by an action for unliquidated damages*'. (*Law of Tort*)

What is the essential difference between these two writers? One school maintains there is a general principle of liability in tort, and that all harm is actionable in the absence of just cause or excuse: i.e. there is a law of tort (not torts). The other school maintains that there are a number of specific torts, and that unless the damage or injury suffered can be brought within the scope of one or more of these torts there is no remedy.

Damage and Liability

As a general rule, where one person suffers unlawful harm or damage at the hands of another, an action in tort for that damage or injury arises. An action in tort lies, for example, in the situation where *A* negligently collides with *B*'s stationary car on a road and causes damage to it.

Sometimes we find instances where harm is done by one person to another yet the law does not provide a remedy: this is described as *damnum sine injuria* ('damage without legal wrong'). Ordinary trade competition is the most common example. Let us suppose that a giant supermarket sets up adjacent to, and in competition with, a small family grocer, selling all goods cheaper and thereby commanding the custom of the housewives. The result could well be that the family grocer, unable to compete, is forced out of business. Harm is done to him in that he loses his livelihood, yet the law offers no remedy to him.

> *Mogul Steamship Co.* v. *McGregor, Gow & Co.* (1892). The *X* company and the *Y* company were rival traders in China tea. The *Y* company persuaded merchants in China not to act as the *X* company's agents, otherwise the *Y* company would withdraw their agency. *Held:* that the *Y* company acted with the lawful object of protecting and extending their trade and the means used were not unlawful.

In contrast to the above, we can imagine a situation where there is a legal wrong but no loss or damage. This is described as *injuria sine damno*, and is an exception to the general rule that there must be damage or injury before action may be brought. Certain torts are actionable *per se* (i.e. actionable in themselves). Examples are trespass and libel: in either of these cases no loss need be alleged or proved.

If *A* trespasses on *B*'s land, or if *A* removes *B*'s goods without lawful authority, *A* may be sued in trespass; the mere entry on the land or the mere removal of the article constitutes in each case a trespass.

Similarly in libel, as we shall see, the mere publication of the libel constitutes the wrong even though the party defamed may have suffered no loss whatsoever.

In torts not actionable *per se*, the plaintiff will succeed only if he can prove that the defendant has infringed his legal right and that thereby the plaintiff has suffered damage.

Malice

Malice in its popular and narrow sense means spite and ill-will. In law the term has two distinct meanings which should be understood. Malice in its legal sense means:

(i) The doing of a wrongful act intentionally, without just cause or excuse. In other words 'wilful and conscious wrongdoing'.

(ii) The doing of an act from some *improper motive*, i.e. a motive of which the law disapproves for the act in question.

To act maliciously means, therefore, to do the act from some wrong and improper motive, or merely to do the act intentionally.

In tort, the intention or motive for an action *is generally irrelevant*.

> *Bradford Corporation* v. *Pickles* (1895). *P*, with a view to inducing Bradford Corporation to buy his land at a high price, sank a shaft on his land which interfered with the water flowing in undefined channels into the corporation reservoir. The corporation applied for an injunction to restrain *P* from collecting the underground water. *Held:* that an injunction would not lie. *P* was entitled as owner to draw from his land the underground water. His 'malice', if any, in trying to force the purchase of the land, was irrelevant. No use of property which would be legal if done with a proper motive can be illegal if done with an improper motive.

A good or innocent motive will not be a lawful excuse for the commission of a tort; and a bad (malicious) motive will not make a lawful act unlawful. In general the law of tort is more concerned with the effect of injurious conduct than with the motive or intent which inspired it. It is the act, not the motive for it, that must be regarded.

> *Wilkinson* v. *Downton* (1897). *A*, as a practical joke, told Mrs. *B* that her husband had met with an accident. Mrs. *B* suffered a nervous shock and was ill as a result. Mrs. *B* brought an action against *A* for false and malicious representation. The fact that *A* passed the information as a joke was irrelevant, and Mrs. *B* was entitled to damages.

Malice in the sense of improper motive is, however, relevant to the following cases:

(*a*) *Malicious Prosecution*. For example, *A* prosecutes *B* without just cause; *B* is acquitted. If it can be proved that *A* brought his prosecution out of private spite, *B* may sue *A* for the offence of malicious prosecution.

(*b*) *Malicious Falsehood.* For example, *A* makes an allegation that a ship is unseaworthy; as a result the crew refuses to sail, thereby causing loss. If the allegation is proved to be untrue, *A* may be sued for the offence of malicious falsehood.

(*c*) *Defamation.* The presence of malice will destroy the defence of 'qualified privilege' in a case of defamation, and is relevant also to the defence of 'fair comment' in libel (see p. 240).

(*d*) *Conspiracy*, i.e. a combination of persons to cause illegal harm to another. Malice is relevant here in the sense of improper motive.

(*e*) *Nuisance*, see *Christie* v. *Davey* (1893) p. 221.

2. General Defences in Tort

A frequent form of defence in an action in tort is a *denial* of the facts alleged in a claim. Thus, in a claim in negligence arising out of a road accident, the defendant may deny driving at 60 m.p.h. or that he was on the wrong side of the road. Sometimes the defence is on a point of law, e.g. that no duty of care was owed by the defendant to the plaintiff.

Certain special defences are available for particular torts, e.g. in defamation there is a special defence of qualified privilege in libel (see p. 241).

The following general defences are available to a defendant in every action for tort *where they are appropriate*.

(*a*) **'Volenti non fit injuria'** ('no injury can be done to a willing person'). This means that a person who has voluntarily consented to the commission of a tort may not sue on it. Obvious examples occur in sport. A boxer voluntarily runs the risk of being punched on the nose by his opponent, and cannot complain if he is. If *X*, a soccer player, kicks the ball towards goal and the ball strikes *Y*'s head, *Y* has no cause of action against *X*. Participants in sport voluntarily undertake to run the lawful risks and hazards inherent in the game. On the same principle, spectators voluntarily undertake the lawful risks in attending sports meetings, and may have no cause of action if injured during the performance.

> *Hall* v. *Brooklands Auto-Racing Club* (1933). *H* paid for admission to Brooklands to watch the car races. During one race a car shot over the railings after a collision and killed two spectators. It was the first time that a car had gone through the railings. The court found the precautions taken by the defendants were adequate. *Held:* that the type of danger to spectators was inherent in the sport, and the plaintiff, *H*, must be taken to have assented to the risk of such an accident.

The consent of the plaintiff must be a true consent to both the physical and legal risks. The consent may be *expressed* (orally or in writing), or may be *implied* from the circumstances of the case. Mere knowledge (*sciens*) of a risk is not usually sufficient: there must be consent (*volens*) to the risk, for the maxim is *volenti non fit injuria*, not *scienti non fit injuria*. The distinction is important, but is not always easy to determine.

Difficulties arise in two types of case: (i) those involving the relationship of master and servant, and (ii) those where a person acting under the compulsion of a legal or moral duty undertakes risks to save others or even the person rescued if he has failed to take reasonable care for his own safety ('rescue' cases).

Bowater v. *Rowley Regis Corporation* (1944). *B*, a carter, was injured by a bolting horse and sued his employers, the corporation. The horse was known by *B* to be vicious and to have bolted on other occasions; *B* had protested previously to his employers about the animal. *Held:* that the corporation was liable, and the defence of *volenti non fit injuria* did not apply. 'To rely on this doctrine the master must show that the workman undertook that the risk should be on him. It is not enough that, whether under protest or not, he obeyed an order or complied with a request which he might have declined as one which he was not bound either to obey or comply with. *It must be shown that he agreed that what risk there was should lie on him.*' (Lord Chief Justice Goddard.)

The defence does not apply where a dangerous situation has been created by a defendant's negligent action and a person is placed in an emergency to decide to act to save or protect the lives of others or the defendant. A person of reasonable courage who acts and is injured in these circumstances cannot be described as 'acting willingly'.

Haynes v. *Harwood* (1935). Plaintiff, a constable, was injured stopping defendant's horses which had bolted due to the defendant's negligence. *Held:* that the defendant was liable in negligence while the plaintiff, who was doing his duty, was not contributorily negligent.

Owgo v. *Taylor* (1987). *O*, a fireman, was injured by scalding caused by hose water and flames, while fighting a fire in loft of *T*'s house. *Held: T* was liable, as his negligence had created a foreseeable risk and there had been no break in the chain of causation.

Baker v. *T. E. Hopkins & Son, Ltd.* (1959). Two men descended a well where a petrol pump was not working properly and were overcome by fumes causing their collapse. A doctor went to their assistance and was himself overcome and died from the poisonous fumes. *Held:* defendants were liable since they created the dangerous situation. The doctor acted under the compulsion of a moral duty and *volenti non fit injuria* did not apply.

The tests applied in such cases are: (i) Did the rescuer intervene to rescue someone who was put in peril by the negligence of another or of himself and (ii) Was the act such as could be expected of a man of ordinary courage and ability situated in similar circumstances?

The case of *Haynes* v. *Harwood* must be distinguished from the following where the facts were different in an important respect.

Cutler v. *United Dairies* (*London*) *Ltd.* (1933). Defendant's milk roundsman left a horse and van, two wheels of which were chained, while he delivered milk. The horse was frightened by noise from a river steamer and bolted down the road into a meadow. The roundsman followed it, became excited and shouted for help. Plaintiff, a spectator of the incident, went to the roundsman's help and tried to hold the horse's head. The horse lunged and the plaintiff was injured. He then sued defendants for negligence. *Held:* that in the circumstances plaintiff freely and voluntarily assumed the risk. It was not an attempt to stop a runaway horse; there was no sense of urgency to impel the plaintiff. He knew the risk, had time to consider it and impliedly agreed to incur it.

Accidents on the highway show one important application of the doctrine of *volenti.* Road-users may expect to run the risk of pure accident, but not injury due to carelessness. 'For the convenience of mankind in carrying on the affairs of life, people as they go along roads must expect, or put up with, such mischief as reasonable care on the part of others cannot avoid' (*Holmes* v. *Mather*, 1875). In this claim the plaintiff was knocked down by the defendant's horse which was being driven with proper care: the court found that the defendant was not liable.

The following cases are of interest in regard to accepting lifts in cars when the driver is under the influence of drink and an accident occurs:

Dann v. *Hamilton* (1939). *Held: Volenti non fit injuria* did not apply. *D* had knowledge of a potential danger and was aware of *H*'s state when accepting the lift, but she did not assent to his negligent driving. (Nowadays, the plaintiff's knowledge of the driver's state is treated as contributory negligence, e.g. in *Owens* v. *Brimmell* (1976) 20 per cent was deducted from the damages.)

(*b*) **Mistake.** The general rule is that mistake, either of law or of fact, is no defence in tort.

As to mistake of law, the maxim *ignorantia legis non excusat* ('ignorance of the law is no excuse') applies. To allow a defendant to say that he mistook, or did not know there was a particular law, would bring the whole of the administration of justice to a standstill. Many defendants would avail themselves of such a loophole.

As to mistake of fact, there are exceptions to the rule that it is no defence. For example, in actions such as malicious prosecution or false imprisonment, a *reasonable* mistake may afford a defence. Thus where a police constable arrests *X* on reasonable suspicion of crime, and it subsequently turns out that *X* is innocent and that the real culprit is *Y*, the constable is not liable. The test is: had the constable who made the mistake reasonable grounds for his belief?

A trespass is actionable even if the trespasser acted under a mistaken but honest belief that the land belonged to him or that he had a right of entry (*Basely* v. *Clarkson*, 1682). An auctioneer who in good faith and without negligence sells goods as the agent of a customer who has, in fact, no title thereto is guilty of conversion and is liable to the true owner for the value thereof (*Consolidated Co.* v. *Curtis*, 1892).

(*c*) **Necessity.** In some cases damage done intentionally may be excused if done from necessity. The defence is a rare one and is available only when the defendant was compelled by the circumstance to prevent a greater evil. This is illustrated in the following cases.

Cope v. *Sharpe* (1912). Defendant (a gamekeeper) went on to adjoining land of the plaintiff and made a firebreak in order to prevent the spread of fire to his own land where he had sitting pheasants. Plaintiff sued for trespass. *Held:* that the defendant had acted reasonably, and the threat of fire was a real one.

Leigh v. *Gladstone* (1909). A suffragette in prison went on hunger strike. She was forcibly fed by warders. The suffragette later sued the prison staff for assault and battery. *Held:* that the defence of necessity was good. Had the prison staff not fed the plaintiff she would have died.

(*d*) **Inevitable Accident.** This means some happening which cannot be avoided by the taking of ordinary precautions.

Stanley v. *Powell* (1891). *P*, a member of a shooting party, fired a shotgun and a pellet hit a tree and ricocheted into the eye of a beater, *S*, who was working with the shooting party. *Held:* that *P* was not liable to *S* for trespass; *S* had failed to establish that *P* had been negligent.

N.C.B. v. *Evans & Co. and another* (1951). Evans & Co. were employed by the Glamorgan County Council to do work on land owned by the council. A trench had to be cut across the land, and Evans & Co. employed a sub-contractor to do this. An electric cable passed under the land, but neither the council nor Evans & Co. nor the sub-contractors knew this, and the cable was not marked on any available map. During the excavation of the trench a mechanical digger damaged the cable; water seeped in causing an explosion. The electricity supply to the plaintiff's colliery was cut off. Plaintiff sued in trespass and negligence. *Held* (by the Court of Appeal): that defendants were entirely free from fault and there was no trespass by them.

At the hearing of the case at first instance the court held that the defendants were not liable in negligence, but were liable in trespass.

(*e*) **Statutory Authority.** It is a defence to an action in tort to show that a statute (or subordinate legislation) authorizes the alleged wrong. The authority given by statute may be either (i) absolute or (ii) conditional. Absolute authority allows the act even though it may cause harm to other persons; conditional authority, on the other hand, merely allows the act provided that it causes no harm to others. Where the authority is imperative it is absolute; where the authority is permissive, it is conditional only.

Vaughan v. *Taff Vale Railway Co.* (1860). A railway company was authorized by statute to run a railway which traversed the plaintiff's land. Sparks from the engine set fire to the plaintiff's woods. *Held:* that the railway company was not liable. It had taken all known care to prevent emission of sparks. The running of locomotives was statutorily authorized.

Metropolitan District Asylum Board v. *Hill* (1881). A hospital authority (appellants) were empowered by statute to erect a smallpox hospital. The hospital was erected in a residential district where it caused danger of infection to residents near by. *Held:* that the erection of the hospital was a nuisance. The statute gave the hospital authority general power to erect such hospitals but did not sanction the erection in places where this would constitute danger. An injunction was granted. The statutory authority was conditional.

(*f*) **Self-Defence.** A person may use reasonable force to defend himself (or any other person) against unlawful force. A defendant will not be liable provided that the amount of force used is reasonable and proportionate to the harm threatened.

It appears that a person may also use reasonable force in the defence of his goods.

Cresswell v. *Sirl* (1948). A dog owned by plaintiff, *C*, attacked during the night some in-lamb ewes owned by *S*. The dog had just stopped worrying the sheep and started towards *S*, who shot it when it was 40 yards away. *C* sued for trespass to goods (dog). *Held: S* was justified in shooting the dog if (i) it was actually attacking the sheep; or (ii) if left the dog would renew the attack on them, *and* shooting was the only practicable and reasonable means of preventing renewal. The onus on justifying the trespass lay on the defendant. (Protecting livestock against dogs is now on a statutory basis: s. 9 of the Animals Act, 1971.)

An occupier of property may protect that property by using reasonable means, e.g. barbed-wire fencing. He may not set spring guns to injure trespassers who come on to his property, nor may he shoot at them, for such an amount of force is not proportionate to the harm or threat.

3. Capacity of Parties

The general rule is that anyone of full age may sue and be sued in tort. Mention has already been made in Chapter 6 of certain categories of persons. Nevertheless the following list is appropriately dealt with here since special rules apply in torts.

(*a*) **The Crown.** At common law the maxim 'The King can do no wrong' applied until 1947. We have seen (p. 109) that it was not possible to sue the Crown or its servants for tort. The Crown Proceedings Act,

1947, altered the common law, and section 2(1) now provides that 'the Crown shall be subject to all those liabilities in tort to which, if it were a person of full age and capacity, it would be subject:

(i) in respect of torts committed by its servants and agents;

(ii) in respect of any breach of those duties which a person owes to his servants or agents at common law by reason of being their employer; and

(iii) in respect of any breach of the duties attaching at common law to the ownership, occupation, possession, or control of property'.

The only respect in which the former common law maxim applies is that no proceedings in tort may be brought against the Monarch in his or her private capacity.

The Crown is not liable for torts committed by the police (Police Act, 1946, s. 48), by other public officers who are appointed and paid by *local* authorities, or by members of public corporations such as the Coal Board, Gas Board, and Electricity Board.

(*b*) **Judicial Immunity.** A judge has absolute immunity for acts within his judicial capacity. This immunity probably also applies to justices of the peace acting within their jurisdiction. Thus, in *Law* v. *Llewellyn* (1906), a magistrate at Bridgend court uttered words which implied that the prosecutor (Law) was a blackmailer and had brought unfounded criminal charges, whereupon Law sued. It was held that judicial immunity extended to the magistrate, Llewellyn, and he was not liable for slander.

Counsel and witnesses have similar immunity in respect of all matters relating to the case with which they are concerned.

(*c*) **Foreign Sovereigns and Diplomats.** A foreign sovereign is not liable in tort in the English courts of law unless he submits to the jurisdiction, thereby waiving his immunity from legal process. He may however, sue in an English court. Ambassadors, High Commissioners and certain other diplomats cannot be sued in tort during their terms of office. Once the period of office is ended such persons become amenable to the jurisdiction of the English courts and they may be sued at any time between recall and their departure from the jurisdiction.

The privilege enjoyed by ambassadors and other diplomats extends to members of their families and to some employees. A full list of such persons is maintained by the Foreign and Commonwealth Office.

(*d*) **Corporations.** A corporation can sue and be sued in its corporate name. It is liable vicariously (i.e. on their behalf) for torts committed by its servants or agents acting within the scope of their authority.

(*e*) **Trades Unions.** These unincorporated bodies enjoy special protection in tort; in certain cases in accordance with the Trade Union Act, 1984, to ensure immunity a ballot must be held prior to a strike.

Trades unions may, however, sue in tort in their registered names.

(*f*) **Infants or Minors.** As a general rule minority is no defence in tort. Where however, a tort is founded on malice or where negligence is a necessary ingredient of the tort, the age of the minor is relevant; through want of age a minor may be incapable of forming the specific intent, and what may be negligent in an adult may not be so in respect of a child. If an unborn child is injured by a tort it may sue provided it is born alive and disabled (Congenital Disabilities (Civil Liability) Act, 1976).

Where the act complained of is also a breach of contract the plaintiff cannot avoid the defence of minority by framing his action in tort.

> *Jennings* v. *Randall* (1799). An infant hired a mare for riding (not a 'necessary'). He injured the animal by over-riding her and was sued in tort for damage. *Held:* that the infant was not liable in tort for negligence since his act was substantially a breach of contract.

This means that where a minor because of his minority is not liable on a contract (e.g. a contract for the supply of an article which is not a 'necessary') he will not be liable for a tort which arises *directly out of the contract.* Where the tort is independent of the contract the minor will be liable.

> *Burnard* v. *Haggis* (1863). A minor hired a horse for riding, but, against the express instructions of the owner, he jumped the horse and injured it. *Held:* that the minor was liable since his wrong was independent of the contract, though the injury occurred because there had been a contract.

Where a minor was in law a bailee of property and lent the property to another person contrary to the terms of the bailment, the minor was held liable in tort for detinue (*Ballet* v. *Mingay*, 1943, summarized on p. 135). Further, where a minor fraudulently misrepresented his age and thereby obtained a loan of money from a moneylender, contrary to section 1 of the Infants' Relief Act, 1874, it was held that the minor could not be sued in deceit. To allow the plaintiff so to frame his action would be to enforce a void contract (*Leslie* v. *Shiell*, 1914, summarized on p. 135).

A parent is not liable, merely because he is a parent, for the torts of his children. But, a parent will be liable where he has authorized or commissioned or ordered a tort, in which case the parent incurs vicarious liability. Secondly a parent may also be held liable for his own personal negligence where he gives the child opportunity for doing harm.

A parent permitted his son aged 15 to remain in possession of a shotgun, with which the son had already caused harm and in respect of which complaints had been made. The father was then held liable for injury to another boy's eye (*Bebee* v. *Sales*, 1916). If, however, the parent took reasonable precautions and could not reasonably foresee that the child would disobey his instructions the parent would not be liable (*Donaldson* v. *McNiven*, 1952).

(*g*) **Persons of Unsound Mind.** A person of unsound mind is, in general, liable for his torts. However, a person of unsound mind who is incapable of forming the intention or malice as required in torts of malicious prosecution or deceit, will not be held liable. Similarly, a person who is so insane that his actions are involuntary, will escape liability.

> *Morriss* v. *Marsden* (1952). Defendant took a room at a Brighton hotel. While there he attacked the manager of the hotel (plaintiff). It was established that defendant was suffering from disease of the mind at the time of the attack; that he knew the nature and quality of his act, but he did not know that what he was doing was wrong. *Held:* that as defendant knew the nature and quality of his act he was liable in tort for the assault and battery. It was immaterial that he did not know that what he was doing was wrong.

(*h*) **Married Women.** At common law a husband could not sue his wife in tort, and a wife could not sue her husband in tort except for the protection and security of her own property. This rule has been altered by the Law Reform (Husband and Wife) Act, 1962, so that now 'each of the parties to a marriage shall have the like right of action in tort against the other as if they were not married'. Thus, if Mrs. *A* is being driven by Mr. *A* in his car and he negligently collides with a wall, whereby Mrs. *A* is injured, she may claim damages against her husband in negligence.

The proceedings between husband and wife may, however, be stayed by the court if it appears that (i) no substantial benefit will accrue to either party from the continuation of the proceedings; or (ii) that the case can more conveniently be disposed of under section 17 of the Married Women's Property Act, 1882, which provides for the summary determination of questions between husband and wife as to the title to, or possession of, property.

The above relates to actions between the spouses. The wife may now sue and be sued in tort as a *feme sole* (i.e. as a single woman), and the husband is no longer liable for his wife's torts by reason only of being her husband. Where, however, the wife is agent or servant of her husband he may render himself vicariously liable (Law Reform (Married Women and Tortfeasors) Act, 1935).

(*i*) **Aliens.** These fall into two classes: enemy aliens and other aliens. Enemy aliens are members of a state with which England is at war, or persons (including British subjects) who 'voluntarily reside or carry on business' in that state. Such persons cannot bring an action in tort, but they may if sued defend one, and they may appeal. Other aliens have neither disability nor immunity.

4. Remoteness of Damage

A plaintiff is only entitled to compensation if the damage suffered is, in the eyes of the law, not too remote from the original wrong. If the damage is too remote, it follows that the defendant will not be liable for such damage.

> 'The law cannot take account of everything that follows from a wrongful act; it regards some subsequent matters as outside the scope of its selection, because "it were infinite for the law to judge the cause of causes or consequence of consequences".' (Lord Wright in *Liesbosch Dredger* v. *Edison*, 1933.)

A line must be drawn somewhere. To determine where that line is two tests have been propounded: (*a*) the test of directness, and (*b*) the test of reasonable foresight.

(*a*) **The Test of Directness.** Under this test a defendant is liable for all damage which is the *direct* consequence of his act, whether such damage is or is not foreseeable by a reasonable man.

> *Re Polemis and Furness Withy & Co.* (1921). Stevedores, employed by the charterers of a ship, were unloading the hold of a ship which contained drums of petrol. Due to leakage the hold contained inflammable vapours. A stevedore negligently knocked a plank into the hold which caused a spark to ignite the petrol vapour. The ensuing fire destroyed the ship. *Held:* that even though the stevedore could not reasonably have foreseen that his negligent act would destroy the ship, the loss of the ship was a direct consequence of the negligent act. The charterers were liable for loss of the ship.

(*b*) **The Test of Reasonable Foresight.** The second view is that the defendant is only liable for that damage which he, as a reasonable man, should have foreseen. Foreseeability is the test for (i) liability and (ii) remoteness of damage.

> *The Wagon Mound* case (1961). Owing to negligence, fuel oil spilt into Sydney harbour from the appellants' ship. The oil was carried by the tide to the respondents' wharf where their employees were welding. A piece of cotton waste on the oil was ignited by sparks from oxy-acetylene equipment. The oil burnt and set fire to the wharf, damaging the ship which the respondents were refitting. *Held* (by the Judicial Committee of the Privy Council): that the appellants were not liable. The test was that the appellants could not reasonably have foreseen that the floating oil would catch fire; they were not liable even though the damage caused was the direct result of their servants' negligence.

Under the doctrine of precedent, the decisions of the Judicial Committee of the Privy Council are of only persuasive authority on English courts. Notwithstanding this, the new rule propounded in the *Wagon*

Mound case has been followed in important cases: by the House of Lords in *Hughes* v. *Lord Advocate* (1963), and by the Court of Appeal in the following case.

Doughty v. *Turner Manufacturing Co. Ltd.* (1964). *D* was employed by the T. M. Co. A fellow employee of *D* let slip into a cauldron of molten metal an asbestos cement cover. At that time it was unknown that asbestos cement coming into contact with the molten metal would cause an explosion. An explosion resulted and *D* was injured. No similar accident had been known to occur previously. *Held:* that the accident (though a direct result of the action of the defendant's servant) was not reasonably foreseeable, and therefore the defendants were not liable.

There is a further important rule, namely, that damage which is intended is never too remote. Moreover, although the type of damage must (to come within the rule) be foreseen, the amount of damage done need not be foreseen. For example, let us suppose that *A* negligently knocks down *B* with his car, or strikes *C* an intentional blow with his fist. The injuries inflicted are very great because, as it is later found, *B* has a thin skull and *C* has a weak heart. It is no defence for *A* to claim that if *B* and *C* had been normal persons the injuries or damage would not have occurred: the tortfeasor 'takes his victim as he finds him'.

Smith v. *Leech Braine & Co. Ltd.* (1962). Plaintiff's husband was a workman employed by defendants. Through the defendant's negligence a piece of molten zinc flew out of a galvanizing tank and hit the husband's lip, causing a burn. Cancer developed on the site of the burn, and three years later the man died. *Held:* that defendants were liable, although the man's death was clearly not a foreseeable result of the accident.

In this case Lord Chief Justice Parker said: 'I am satisfied that the Judicial Committee of the Privy Council did not have what are called "thin-skull" cases in mind. It has always been the common law that a tortfeasor must take his victim as he finds him.' Lord Parker also approved of the decision in the *Wagon Mound* case, but argued that it had overruled *Re Polemis* only where the actual damage differed from the foreseeable one not only in extent but also in type. In *Smith* v. *Leech Braine* the fatal injury to the employee differed from the foreseeable one (a burn) in extent only but not in type.

As a result of the decision in the *Wagon Mound* case the law as to remoteness in contract and in tort appears to be the same.

5. Vicarious Liability in Tort

We have now to consider the circumstances in which one person will be liable for the torts of another, even though he (the person liable) is not a party to the tort or did not himself commit the tort in question. Thus, where *A* instructs *B* to commit a tort against *C*, it is common-sense and justice that *A* should be liable, whatever the liability may be which attaches to *B*. *A* is said to be **vicariously** liable, and, therefore, may be sued for the act which he himself ordered, even though he did not commit the tort. This subject will be dealt with under two headings: (*a*) the liability of a master for the torts of a servant, and (*b*) the liability of a principal for the torts of an independent contractor.

(*a*) **Master and Servant.** The general rule regarding the master-and-servant relationship is that the master is vicariously liable for the torts of his servant committed during the course of his employment, whether the master authorized them or not. The liability lies in respect of:

(i) a wrongful act or omission expressly or impliedly authorized by the master; or
(ii) a wrongful act or omission which is an unauthorized manner of doing something authorized by the master; or
(iii) a wrongful and unauthorized act or omission which is ratified by the master.

In the case of an independent contractor, the principal is in general liable only for those torts which he has expressly or impliedly authorized the contractor to commit. This liability will be dealt with specifically later.

Who is a servant? The relationship of master and servant exists when one person employs another to do work for him on the terms that the servant is subject to the control of his employer as to the manner in which that work is to be done. The test is one of control. Does the master control (i) the work to be done, and (ii) the way in which the work is done? Common examples of servants include chauffeurs, domestic servants, clerks, and labourers. These persons are employed under a 'contract *of service*'.

An independent contractor, on the other hand, is under the control of his employer as to what he must do, but the employer cannot control the actual manner in which he does the work. He is free to select his own method. Independent contractors are said to work under a 'contract *for services*'. Examples of independent contractors are a builder who contracts to build a house for a client, electricians, plumbers, carpenters, and the like who may be called in by a householder to effect a repair in the house. Such persons are not the servants of the householder. Similarly, a taxi-cab driver is an independent contractor, while a chauffeur is a servant. The term 'master' or 'employer' can be applied to a body corporate, e.g. a company or local authority.

It is for the courts to decide on the evidence in each case whether a person is a servant or independent contractor: a task which is sometimes difficult, particularly in view of the expanding categories of skilled employment in modern society.

The 'Course of Employment'. An employer will not be liable for a tort committed in the course of employment if the servant was performing that act solely for his own purposes. For example, let us suppose that a servant (Smith) is instructed to drive his master's car from Oxbridge to Camford; but instead of proceeding directly to the destination, Smith goes off to London on a 'frolic' of his own. The master will not be liable for any tort which Smith may commit while so deviating from the route (*Storey* v. *Ashton*, 1869). If the deviation from the authorized route is slight or is unavoidable, the master remains liable.

An act is done in the course of a servant's employment if it is of a class of act which he is expressly or impliedly authorized to do. The master does not escape liability merely by forbidding the act which constitutes the tort: otherwise employers would evade liability by simply prohibiting all kinds of things connected with the work (cf. *Limpus* v. *London General Omnibus Co.*, below). It is immaterial, too, that the particular act was done for the servant's own fraudulent purpose. Moreover, the master will be liable if the act complained of was merely a mode of doing what the servant was employed to do.

Century Insurance Co. v. *Northern Ireland Road Transport Board* (1942). The driver of a petrol lorry was engaged in transferring petrol into an underground storage tank. The driver struck a match to light a cigarette and this caused an explosion resulting in great damage. *Held:* that the driver was negligent in carrying out his authorized work, and his employers were therefore liable.

Limpus v. *London General Omnibus Co.* (1862). A bus driver racing to a stop to collect passengers deliberately obstructed the driver of a bus of a rival company, overturning the latter's vehicle. The bus driver had been given strict instructions against obstructing other buses. *Held:* that defendants were liable. The driver was acting within the course of his employment at the time. It was immaterial whether his act was forbidden.

Beard v. *London General Omnibus Co.* (1900). A bus conductor drove a bus in London and negligently collided with plaintiff. The conductor was not authorized to drive the bus. *Held:* that the servant was not acting within the scope of his employment. Accordingly the claim against the employer failed.

Lloyd v. *Grace, Smith & Co.* (1912). A firm of solicitors employed a managing clerk to deal with conveyancing matters. Plaintiff, a widow, wished to sell some cottages and went to the solicitors. The managing clerk induced plaintiff to transfer the cottages to him and misappropriated certain mortgage moneys. Plaintiff sued the employers. *Held:* that the solicitors were liable to the client for the fraud of the managing clerk though it was committed solely for his benefit.

Harrison v. *Michelin Tyre Co. Ltd.* (1985). The plaintiff was injured by a 'practical joke' of a fellow-employee. His employers argued that the employee's action constituted a 'frolic of his own'. *Held:* that two mutually exclusive questions should be asked. (1) Although unauthorised or prohibited, was the employee's action incidental to his employment? If 'Yes', *D* was liable. (2) Was it so divergent from the employment as to be plainly alien to and wholly distinguishable from the employment? If 'Yes', *D* was not liable. On the basis of the facts the answer to question (1) was 'Yes', so that the employers were vicariously liable.

It should be observed that the master *and* the servant are liable and may be sued jointly and severally. Usually the master only is sued, he being the more likely to be able to pay the damages. If the master is sued, he may recover contribution from the employee for the loss, and in some cases an indemnity.

Lister v. *Romford Ice and Cold Storage Co. Ltd.* (1957). *L*, a lorry driver employed by the company, reversed his lorry negligently and knocked down his father who was also employed by the company. The father recovered damages from the company which was held vicariously liable for the tort of its servant, *L*. The insurers of the company paid the amount and thereupon sued *L*, in the name of the company, for an indemnity. *Held, inter alia:* that *L* had broken his obligation to the company to take reasonable care in the performance of his duties and the company could recover on an indemnity.

Where a servant is lent by one master to another, the identity of the employer is sometimes difficult to establish. Thus, Smith, the servant of *A*, is sent by *A* to work for *B*. If Smith commits a tort during 'the course of employment', is *A* or *B* liable? This question is resolved by adopting the 'control' test already mentioned; and the onus of proving that control has passed to the new employer (*B*) rests on the first employer (*A*).

(*b*) **Liability for Independent Contractors.** The general rule is that an employer is *not* liable for the torts of an independent contractor or of the servant employed by the latter. There are, however, the following exceptions to the rule:

(i) Where the contract is to do something which is itself a tort, e.g. a nuisance.

Ellis v. *Sheffield Gas Consumers Co.* (1853). A company which had no authority to dig up streets in Sheffield employed a contractor to open trenches in a street. The contractor's servants left a heap of stones in the road over which the plaintiff fell and injured himself. *Held:* that the defendant company was liable for the consequences of their unlawful act.

(ii) In operations on or adjoining a highway, other than normal use for the purpose of passage.

> *Tarry* v. *Ashton* (1876). *A* was occupier of a house from the front of which a heavy lamp protruded over the highway. The lamp fell into disrepair and *A* instructed a contractor to inspect and renew it. The contractor negligently repaired the lamp which later collapsed and injured *T*. *Held: A* was liable in public nuisance. It was his duty to repair the lamp, and the duty was not discharged. It was no excuse that the injury was caused by the negligence of the contractor.

(iii) Under the rule in *Rylands* v. *Fletcher* (see p. 233). In this case the employer was liable notwithstanding the fact that no negligence was imputed to the independent contractor who built the reservoir.

(iv) Where an independent contractor is employed to do 'extra hazardous' acts.

> *Honeywill & Stein* v. *Larkin Bros.* (1934). Plaintiffs instructed defendants (independent contractors) to take flashlight photographs of the interior of a cinema. A flash with magnesium powder caused a fire which damaged the cinema. *Held:* that the cinema owners were entitled to claim damages from the plaintiffs, who, in turn, were granted an indemnity from defendants (the photographers).

Joint Tortfeasors

A tort may be committed by two persons acting together, i.e. jointly. Thus if *A* holds one end of a log while *B* holds the other, and together they heave it through a window, the law holds that *both* are liable.

The liability of joint tortfeasors is said to be 'joint and several', which means that a plaintiff may sue both (or all, if more than two) defendants, or he may recover the full amount of his claim from one only of the tortfeasors.

Until 1935 there was no right of contribution between joint tortfeasors, but under the Civil Liability (Contribution) Act, 1978 (replacing a statutory provision in 1935), it is enacted that where one tortfeasor is sued and pays the damages, he may claim contribution from his fellow-tortfeasors. The amount recoverable is such 'as may be found by the court to be just and equitable having regard to the extent of that person's responsibility for the damage'. Thus if *A* is sued in damages for £1,000, he may recover from *B* (a joint tortfeasor) by legal action against *B*, such sum as the court determines, e.g. £250 if *B* is quarter responsible only.

If, in the last example, *A* were a servant of *B* and damages were awarded against *A* (say for £1,000) and if *A* were merely carrying out the instructions of his employer, he (*A*) would be entitled to be indemnified by action against *B* for the amount of £1,000 which *A* has been compelled to pay. An indemnity may arise out of a contractual agreement as well as in the relationship of master and servant as noted above.

6. Trespass

There are three types of trespass: (*a*) trespass to the person, (*b*) trespass to goods, and (*c*) trespass to land.

(*a*) **Trespass to the Person.** This action takes three forms: (i) assault, (ii) battery, and (iii) false imprisonment.

(i) **Assault** is an act which causes another person to apprehend immediate and unlawful personal violence. Thus, striking at another with a stick or fist (even though the party misses his aim), drawing a sword, and throwing a bottle are common examples. Where *A* points a firearm at *B*, which *A* knows to be unloaded though *B* does not, and is so near that it might produce injury if it were loaded and went off, this constitutes an assault (*R.* v. *St. George*, 1840).

Mere words do not constitute an assault, however. The intent must be shown in acts not just in speech (*Wilson* v. *Pringle*, 1986). Words are nevertheless relevant in certain circumstances and may prevent what, in other circumstances, would amount to an assault. Thus in *Tuberville* v. *Savage* (1669) a man laid his hand on his sword (a menace) and said: 'If it were not assize time I would not take such language from you.' This was held not to be an assault.

(ii) **Battery** consists in applying force, however slight, to the person of another hostilely or against his will. The charge of battery is usually combined with assault, namely 'assault and battery'. Common examples include giving a man a black eye, or throwing water at him, or holding him by the arm, or spitting in his face, or removing a chair from under him, or throwing a squib at him (*Scott* v. *Shepherd*, 1773).

Volenti non fit injuria (consent) is a notable defence in this type of action, e.g. where a doctor makes a medical examination of a patient with his consent. Merely touching a person (without undue force) to engage his attention is not a battery. In an action for trespass to the person it is essential to prove that the defendant acted intentionally or negligently. In *Fowler* v. *Lanning* (1959) it was held that where the defendant shot the plaintiff accidentally no cause of action arose in the absence of intent or negligence.

(iii) **False Imprisonment** consists in the infliction of bodily restraint of another without lawful justification. As with assault and battery, false imprisonment is actionable *per se* (i.e. in itself) without proof of damage. There need be no imprisonment such as incarceration in police cells. The mere holding of the arm of another, as when a constable makes an arrest, is sufficient.

It is not, however, necessary that actual force be used: the threat of force is sufficient. 'Stay there or I'll shoot you' may be evidence of imprisonment. Neither is it necessary for the person to know that he is being detained, for he may be imprisoned while he is asleep (applied in *Murray* v. *Ministry of Defence*, 1988).

The restraint of another must be total or complete. Thus, to restrain a person from going in three ways but leaving him free to go in a fourth is not false imprisonment (*Bird* v. *Jones*, 1845).

Bird v. *Jones* (1845). A bridge company lawfully stopped a public footpath on Hammersmith Bridge. A spectator insisted on using the footpath, but was stopped by two policemen who barred his entry. Plaintiff was told he might proceed to another point around the obstruction but that he could not go forward. He declined and remained for about half an hour, and then sued in false imprisonment. *Held:* that there was no false imprisonment since plaintiff was free to go another way.

Herd v. *Weardale Steel Coke & Coal Co*. (1915). A dispute arose between a miner and his employers while the miner was at work in the mine. The miner demanded his return to the surface, but the employers refused to grant the use of the cage for him to come to the surface, and he was stranded in the pit for some 20 minutes. The miner sued the employers for false imprisonment. *Held:* that the claim must fail. The miner entered the pit of his own free will and the employers were under no duty to bring him to the surface until the end of his shift.

Meering v. *Grahame White Aviation Co. Ltd*. (1919). Plaintiff was suspected of stealing paint from his employers (defendants) and was asked to accompany two works' policemen to defendants' office to be interrogated. Plaintiff did not know he was suspected and agreed to the request. He remained in the office while the two policemen remained outside the room without plaintiff's knowledge. *Held:* that plaintiff was imprisoned and his knowledge was irrelevant.

The following **defences** may be offered to an action for trespass to the person.

(i) *Self-defence*. It is lawful for a person to defend himself against an assault or battery. The defence must be proportionate to the attack, no more force being used in defence of oneself than is reasonably necessary. What is reasonable or commensurate with the necessity is a matter for decision by the court on the particular facts of each case. If, for example, *A* throws a jug of water at *B* which splashes *B* (an assault and battery), it follows that *B* cannot lawfully resist or defend himself by shooting *A*.

(ii) *Defence of Property*. Similar rules apply to the defence of one's property, including a house. An occupier may use reasonable force to eject a trespasser. Where the trespass is not forcible, the occupier should first request the trespasser to leave; secondly allow him sufficient time to do so peaceably; and finally, if he still refuses to leave, the occupier may use reasonable force to eject him.

(iii) *Consent of Plaintiff*. The normal rules of *volenti non fit injuria* apply (see p. 195).

(iv) *Parental or other Authority*. A parent may administer reasonable punishment to a child or young person. This punishment includes locking him in a room, if need be, though one must stress that in all cases the test is reasonableness. Long imprisonment might amount to the criminal offence of cruelty to a child.

This parental authority may be delegated to another, e.g. a schoolmaster who may (providing the regulations of the Education Authority permit) also administer reasonable punishment. Thus, the detention of a child after school hours is not false imprisonment, and reasonable chastisement with, say, a cane is not a battery.

(v) *Inevitable Accident*. The rules of *Stanley* v. *Powell* (1891) and *N.C.B.* v. *Evans* (1951) demonstrate the defence of inevitable accident, and the case of *Fowler* v. *Lanning* (1959) is of special note as demonstrating the necessity of intent or negligence.

(vi) *Judicial Authority*. A judge who acts within his judicial authority may grant a warrant of arrest, in which case the person executing the arrest may use reasonable force to detain the person named. Prisoners under terms of imprisonment in H.M. Prisons, for example, are there pursuant to the judicial authority of a magistrate or a judge who sentences them and signs the requisite committal warrants.

(vii) *Preservation of the Peace*. All persons owe a duty not to disturb the public peace either by committing crime or causing public disorders and the like. The police have wide common law and statutory powers to make arrests to enforce the law and to preserve the peace. If the individual constable acts lawfully, no action lies against him in trespass, provided that he uses no more force than is reasonably necessary to effect the arrest.

(*b*) **Trespass to Land.** Trespass to land may take three forms:

(i) entry on the land of another;
(ii) remaining on the land of another; and
(iii) placing or throwing any material object upon the land of another.

Again we may note it is not necessary to prove actual damage to the land, the tort being actionable *per se*.

'Land' includes not only the soil itself but things under the soil, and buildings or houses affixed to the surface. The general rule is that the owner of the land owns all the land below the surface and all the space above the land (*cujus est solum ejus est usque ad caelum et ad inferos*). Trespass may, therefore, occur by delving into the subsoil, e.g. to lay a cable or to take coal from another's mine.

Common examples of trespass to land include putting a hand on a fence or through an open window of a house, entering another's forecourt and removing a dustbin, and throwing bricks on to another's land. (Merely to allow bricks from a chimney which is ruinous and in disrepair to fall on a neighbour's land constitutes a nuisance, but is not trespass.)

As to the flight of aircraft over land, it is provided by the Civil Aviation Act, 1949, that 'no action shall lie in respect of trespass or nuisance by reason only of the flight of aircraft over any property at a height above the ground which, having regard to wind, weather and all the circumstances of the case is reasonable or the ordinary incidents of such flight'. But the Act makes the owner of the civil aircraft (not R.N., Army, or R.A.F. aircraft) strictly liable for any damage caused.

The sign 'Trespassers will be prosecuted' is not true. Mere trespass on land is not a *crime* and no *prosecution* for it may be brought, though a civil action may be. If, however, the trespass is accompanied by damage, e.g. by breaking fences or treading down growing corn, an offence of wilful damage is committed contrary to the Criminal Damage Act, 1971. In civil trespass no damage need be proved. Moreover, a person may be sued even though he did not know he was trespassing, for mistake is no defence.

Personal entry on land of another may be lawful, as for example, where the occupier grants permission on payment (by licence) or gratuitously. Where permission to enter and remain on land is revoked or where the time limit for entry has expired a person may become, from that moment, a trespasser. Subject to the foregoing rules the trespasser may be requested to leave, given time to do so, and if he still refuses to go, ejected.

Trespass 'ab initio'. Where a person enters on the land of another by authority of law (as distinct from authority conferred by the plaintiff occupier) he may become a trespasser if, by his subsequent conduct, he abuses his right of entry. This doctrine is known as trespass *ab initio* and is exemplified by the ancient case given below. The subsequent conduct which abuses the right of entry may be stealing an article from the occupier. The abuse relates back to the *original* entry and he becomes a trespasser. The abuse must consist of a *misfeasance* (i.e. some positive act of wrong-doing, such as stealing) not a *non-feasance* (i.e. an omission to do something, such as failing to pay for food or drink).

> *The Six Carpenters* case (1610). Carpenters entered an inn (entry being the exercise of a public and lawful right). They ordered bread and wine for which they paid. They then ordered more wine, but refused to pay. *Held:* that they were not trespassers *ab initio* because they had authority by law to enter the inn and their offence was one of *non-feasance* not *misfeasance*.

Who may sue and be sued. Trespass is essentially a wrong against possession, not against ownership. Thus an owner out of possession cannot sue, but if he later recovers possession the right relates back to the time when his right of entry accrued, and he may sue for any trespass committed in the meantime. A landlord may sue in trespass only if some permanent injury to his property has been done or its value has been seriously impaired. The person who may sue is he who is in possession. For example a landlord cannot sue in respect of a trespass to land in the occupation and possession of a tenant. Though he (the landlord) may sue where the trespass has done some actual harm to the property and that harm has adversely affected his reversionary interest. A mere licensee, e.g. a person attending a theatre as a member of an audience, a lodger, or a guest at a hotel, is not deemed to be 'in possession' of land (theatre, hotel, etc.) so as to enable him to sue in trespass to that land.

Justification for Entry. We have noted that to constitute actionable trespass an entry on land must be unlawful. Nevertheless there are several instances where the supposed trespasser may claim that his entry is justifiable either by common law or by statute. The justification may, therefore, be a defence, as follows:

(i) Entry by lawful authority: e.g. by police to make an arrest or to search premises (Criminal Law Act, 1967); or by bailiffs to distrain for rent or to eject a tenant.

(ii) Entry to abate a nuisance in emergency (see p. 220).

(iii) Entry made to retake a chattel owned by defendant provided the chattel is placed there by the plaintiff (occupier of the land) or, possibly, by a third person, and the plaintiff acts reasonably.

(iv) Entry by licence or permission of the occupier, express or implied. A licence is 'that consent which, without passing any interest in the property to which it relates, merely prevents the acts for which consent is given from being wrongful' (Pollock).

(v) Peaceable entry on the land by a person entitled to possession of it.

Remedies for Trespass to Land. The following remedies are available to a plaintiff.

(i) *Damages*. This is in general the amount by which the value of the property is diminished as a result of the trespass; not the cost of reinstatement.

(ii) *Injunction*. This may be used to prevent the continuance or repetition of the act of trespass. The plaintiff may apply to the court for both damages and an injunction.

(iii) *Ejection*. The occupier of the land may eject a trespasser after first requesting him to leave and allowing him peaceably so to do. No more force may be used than is reasonable in the circumstances, otherwise the occupier himself may be sued for assault.

(iv) *An action of ejectment* may be brought for recovery of land.

Where trespass consists in entry by cattle or sheep on the land of another, the occupier's rights are now governed by the Animals Act, 1971, which replaces the common law rules.

S. 4(1) provides that where the defendant's livestock strays on the plaintiff's land, the defendant is, generally, liable for the damage done to the land or to the property on it and for any expenses reasonably incurred by the plaintiff in keeping the livestock, while it cannot be restored to the defendant, or while it is being detained for certain other purposes.

S. 7 gives the occupier of land on to which livestock strays limited rights of detention and sale in certain cases.

Dispossession means wrongfully depriving another of possession of land. This may occur where, for example, *A* enters a field or a house and assumes possession of it, or where *A* retains possession of land after the expiration of any lease granted to him. If now *B* claims possession of the land or house in the above example, his (*B*'s) proper course should *A* prevent possession is to take action in the courts for recovery of possession of the property. The court will then examine the respective claims of *A* and *B* and make an order as to the right of possession to the one who has the stronger claim. Where *B* is successful in regaining possession he may claim damages, which includes the right of *mesne* (i.e. intermediate) profits. These are profits of the land during the period when it was wrongfully possessed by *A*.

The general rule is that a claimant to possession must prove his claim by the strength of his own title; he may not support his claim by alleging that a third party has a better title than that claimed by the party in possession. This right outstanding in a third party is known as the *jus tertii*.

Re-entry on Land. Where a person is lawfully entitled to take possession of land he should exercise those rights peaceably otherwise he renders himself liable. Where a person is *wrongfully* in possession, it is no tort for a person claiming under a legal title to eject the wrongful possessor forcibly, provided that no more force is used on the wrongful possessor or his goods than is reasonably necessary (*Hemming* v. *Stoke Poges Golf Club*, 1920). The Statute of Forcible Entry, 1381, which made forcible entry, even by the person entitled to possession, a criminal offence, was repealed by the Criminal Law Act, 1977.

When *B* (the person lawfully entitled to possession) has re-entered, the possession re-vests in him, and the former occupant *A* (i.e. the person against whom the incoming tenant re-entered) becomes a trespasser. Action may, therefore be taken against *A* for trespass.

(*c*) **Trespass to Goods.** The wrong of trespass to goods is the intentional or negligent interference with the possession of goods of another. The interference must be direct and forcible (though a mere touching may be trespass). Trespass is actionable *per se*.

An omission does not give rise to an action in trespass unless it was done intentionally or negligently (*N.C.B.* v. *Evans*, 1951; and *Fowler* v. *Lanning*, 1959). Accidental touching of goods is not actionable.

As examples we may note that it is a trespass to throw another's book out of the window, to remove a bicycle from a shed, or to remove the wheels of another's motor-car.

Trespass is essentially a wrong to possession, as distinct from ownership. To maintain trespass, the plaintiff must show he had possession of the goods at the time of the trespass. Thus, a borrower, hirer or a bailee of goods (e.g. a shoemaker to whom shoes are sent for repair) possesses the goods lent, hired or bailed, and he may maintain action against any person who wrongfully interferes with the goods in his possession. It follows, therefore, that a bailor cannot sue in trespass during the term of bailment.

7. Interference with Goods

Detinue means 'the wrongful detention of the goods of another to the immediate possession of which that other is entitled', e.g. *A* lends a book to *B* for one week and *B* refuses to return it at the proper time; *X* hands his watch to *Y*, a watchmaker, and *Y* declines to return it after demand by *X*. The essence of the claim was for the return of the plaintiff's property of which he was owner.

Conversion is defined as 'an act or complex series of acts of wilful interference, without lawful justification, with any chattel in a manner inconsistent with the right of another, whereby that other is deprived of the use and possession of it' (*Salmond on Torts*).

In practice the torts of (*a*) trespass to goods, (*b*) detinue (detention), and (*c*) conversion of goods overlapped and archaic procedures applied to each. The Torts (Interference with Goods) Act, 1977, abolished the tort of detinue and simplified the law and procedure. Each of the various torts is now treated in the same way.

Wrongful interference with goods is defined as:

(*a*) conversion of goods (also called trover);

(*b*) trespass to goods;

(*c*) negligence so far as it results in damage to goods or to an interest in goods;

(*d*) any other tort so far as it results in damage to goods or to an interest in goods (s. 1).

Detention of goods now becomes conversion, including such cases as loss or destruction of goods by a bailee in breach of his duty to the bailor, e.g. where *B* (see above) loses the book, or *Y* (above) destroys the watch, now becomes conversion.

Court's powers. The court may order: (*a*) specific delivery of goods; or (*b*) damages; or (*c*) specific delivery, with the alternative to defendant of paying damages. Specific delivery is a *discretionary* remedy, and may be ordered subject to conditions.

Damages. Payment of damages or settlement extinguishes the title to the goods of the plaintiff, including where damages are reduced by reason of contributory negligence of plaintiff.

If defendant improved goods, e.g. *A* has a car which *B* steals and sells to *C*, a *bona fide* purchaser, who fits a new engine, then the defendant (*C*) is entitled to an allowance to the value of the goods attributable to the improvement (s. 6).

Jus Tertii. This rule is abolished and a defendant is now entitled to prove that a third party has a better right to the goods than the plaintiff. The plaintiff must now give particulars of his title and identify any person who, to his knowledge, has or claims to have any interest in the goods, and the defendant may apply to join any person in the action (s. 8(2)). The court determines the respective claims to the goods at one time.

Co-ownership is not a defence to an action (*a*) in conversion or (*b*) trespass to goods where the defendant without the authority of the co-owner:

(*a*) destroys the goods, or disposes of the goods in a way giving a good title to the entire property in the goods, or otherwise does anything equivalent to the destruction of the other's interest in the goods, or

(*b*) purports to dispose of the goods in a way which would give a good title to the entire property in the goods if he was acting with the authority of all co-owners of the goods (s. 10(1)).

Conversion may be committed in the following ways:

(i) *By Taking.* Where *A* takes chattels out of the possession of *B* (the true owner) without lawful justification with the intention of exercising dominion over the goods permanently or even temporarily. Every simple theft, as where *X* steals *Y*'s mackintosh, is a conversion. Mere shifting the goods of another, as where a station-porter puts suitcases at the side of a railway platform, may be trespass but not conversion.

(ii) *By Detention.* Where *A* detains goods of *B* in defiance of *B*'s right to the chattels, *B* may sue in conversion.

(iii) *By Wrongful Delivery.* If *A* without lawful justification delivers *B*'s goods to *C* (a stranger), *A* is liable in conversion. Similarly, if a bailee of goods sells them before the period of the bailment has expired, the bailee renders himself liable in conversion.

(iv) *By Destruction.* The wilful and unlawful destruction of another's goods amount to conversion. There must be a complete destruction, mere damage of goods being insufficient.

Fouldes v. *Willoughby* (1841). *W* was manager of a ferry boat. *F* embarked his horses on the ferry. *W* and *F* had a dispute, and in order to induce *F* to leave the boat, *W* turned the horses off into the highway. *F* remained on the boat and crossed to the other side of the river. *F* then sued *W*. *Held:* that there was trespass to the horses, but no conversion.

Hollins v. *Fowler* (1875). A cotton broker, acting on behalf of a customer for whom he had often made purchases, bought cotton from a person who had obtained it by fraud. The broker sold it to the customer and received only his commission. *Held:* that the broker was liable in conversion for the entire value of the goods.

Armory v. *Delamirie* (1722). A chimney sweep's boy found a jewel and handed it to a jeweller for valuation. The latter took the jewel from the setting, and refused to return it to the boy, who thereupon sued the jeweller in trover (the original form of conversion). *Held:* that the jeweller was liable; the finder had a good title except as against the true owner. (This case was applied by the Court of Appeal in *Parker* v. *British Airways Board* (1982), where the plaintiff passenger at London Airport found a gold bracelet in the executive lounge, and it was held that his claim prevailed.)

8. Nuisance

Nuisances are of two kinds: (i) public, and (ii) private.

A public nuisance is some unlawful act or omission which endangers or interferes with the lives, safety or comfort of the public generally or of some section of the public, or by which the public, or some section of it, is obstructed in the exercise of a common right.

It is a public nuisance to keep a brothel; to obstruct the public highway; and to erect a factory which emits excessive smoke, fumes or dirt so as to cause discomfort to persons in the locality.

A public nuisance is a *crime*, punishable at common law on indictment before a jury. Usually the criminal proceedings are undertaken by the police. Action may also be taken by the Attorney-General on behalf of the public, who may *sue* also for an injunction to restrain further offences. In addition, a private person may also *sue* (not prosecute) the person committing the public nuisance if he can show that he has suffered peculiar damage over and above that suffered by the public generally. Thus, to dig a trench in a public highway without lawful authority is a public nuisance and a crime. If *A* falls into the trench, or if the trench interferes with *A*'s right of way into his own premises, he may show peculiar damage to himself and sue the person who excavated the trench.

Benjamin v. *Storr* (1874). *B* kept a coffee-house in Covent Garden. *S continually kept his horses and vans outside the coffee-house, so obstructing the highway. B* alleged he suffered damage because the vans obstructed light to the shop windows (he having to provide gas lights all day long) and that the smell from the horses made the premises objectionable and deterred customers. *Held:* that *B* could lawfully sue inasmuch as he had suffered special damage.

Lyons, Sons & Co. v. *Gulliver* (1914). Defendants were occupiers of a theatre. Popular performances at 2.30 p.m. and 6.30 p.m. caused queues to form which obstructed customers to an adjacent shop. *Held:* that the plaintiff suffered particular damage and the nuisance was actionable at the suit of the adjacent shop owner.

Attorney-General v. *P.Y.A. Quarries, Ltd.* (1957). Defendants owned and used a quarry at which blasting of rocks took place. Some stones and splinters were hurled out of the quarry, and dust and vibration caused discomfort to near-by dwellers. *Held:* that this was a public nuisance.

Miller v. *Jackson* (1977). Balls were often struck out of a cricket ground (long used for the game) on to *M*'s house recently built nearby. The Court of Appeal awarded damages for negligence and nuisance, but discharged an injunction against playing cricket because in modern conditions the interest of the public should prevail over that of the individual.

A private nuisance is an unlawful interference with a man's use of his property, or with his health, comfort or convenience. It is, in fact, a wrongful act or omission causing (i) material injury to property, or (ii) sensible personal discomfort.

There are two main classes of private nuisance: (i) interference with the enjoyment of land generally; and (ii) injuries to servitudes. Of these two classes the first is the more important; the second deals with servitudes or easements (e.g. rights of way, rights of light, and rights of support to land) and is more appropriate to a specialized study of English land law rather than the present book.

There are, of course, many varied acts which may constitute nuisance. Noise, vibrations, fumes, smell, smoke, dirt, and damp are fairly obvious ones, and are part of man's existence in some degree or other.

Nuisance is not (in contrast to trespass) actionable *per se*. Some damage must have occurred to the plaintiff to enable him to sue.

The basic rule is that you should so use your property that you cause no harm to another (expressed by the Latin maxim: *sic utere tuo ut alienum non laedas*). More simply, one should 'live and let live' and be reasonable as to one's acts or omissions in regard to neighbours.

> 'A balance has to be maintained between the right of the occupier to do what he likes with his own, and the right of a neighbour not to be interfered with. It is impossible to give any precise formula, but it may broadly be said that a useful test is perhaps what is reasonable according to the ordinary uses of mankind living in society.' (Lord Wright in *Sedleigh-Denfield* v. *O'Callaghan*, 1940.)

The following points are relevant to private nuisance and are helpful in understanding the field of law affecting this tort.

(i) *Health and Comfort*. There need be no direct injury to health. It is sufficient that a person has, to an appreciable extent, been prevented from enjoying the ordinary comforts of life.

(ii) *Standard of Comfort*. The standard of the 'ordinary comfort of life' varies with the locality affected. Thus, for example, in London there is a difference between Mayfair and Stepney. One area may be relatively quiet and peaceful, another bustling and noisy. The only exception, under this head, seems to be that an interference with light to a building will be dealt with equally whether it occurs in one area or another, for 'one requires as much light to sew in Belgravia as in Whitechapel'.

(iii) *Variety*. The modes of annoyance are infinitely diverse: stenches, filth, the use of radio, church bell-ringing, circus performing may all be nuisances.

(iv) *Several Wrongdoers*. A nuisance may be caused by the combined operation of several wrongdoers. Their joint action or cumulative action (if operating separately) may result in nuisance. Thus let us suppose *A*, *B*, *C*, and *D* are the persons involved. In this case a plaintiff may sue all jointly or he may sue one only, *A* for example, for the total damage. If this is done *A* will have a right of contribution from *B*, *C*, and *D*, the joint tortfeasors, for their portion of the damage caused.

(v) *Extra Sensitivity*. Reasonableness is, as we have observed, the test. A person cannot take advantage of his personal sensitivity or that of his property. Moreover one cannot expect the same standards to obtain in a crowded industrial city as those which hold in a country market town. There must be 'give and take'.

(vi) *Utility of the Nuisance*. Pig sties, tanneries, lime-kilns, quarries and fried-fish shops are perhaps useful for the general well-being, but if their operation causes serious or appreciable discomfort they are a nuisance. The allegation that the trade or industry is 'for the public benefit' is no defence in law.

(vii) *Malice or Evil Motive*. This may in some cases be the essence of the tort, inasmuch as the wrongdoer's improper motive may show that he is not acting reasonably and lawfully. The wantonness of an act to annoy a neighbour may therefore be a nuisance (*Hollywood Silver Fox Farm* v. *Emmett* (1936), (see p. 221).

(viii) *Prescription*. A person may acquire a right to commit a nuisance by long usage, e.g. twenty years' continuous operation since the act complained of first became a nuisance. Prescription is a defence in private nuisance, but *not* in public nuisance (which is a crime).

Who may Sue and be Sued. The occupier of the property (e.g. a tenant) affected by the nuisance is the person who brings the action (*Malone* v. *Laskey*, 1907). A landlord may, however, sue in some cases, e.g. where a permanent injury is caused, or will be caused, to his property.

The person to be sued is he who creates the nuisance. Where premises are leased, a landlord may, however, be liable if (i) he creates the nuisance and then leases the property; or if (ii) he authorized, expressly or impliedly, a tenant to commit or continue the nuisance (*Harris* v. *James*, 1876).

Defences. The following defences may be raised in nuisance.

(i) *Statutory Authority*. It is a defence to show that a statute authorizes the act or omission in question. (See p. 198 for further discussion on this defence.)

(ii) *Triviality*. A defendant may prove that the act or omission is small and trivial, e.g. smoke from an ordinary garden fire on one morning only. The maxim is *de minimus non curat lex* ('the law does not concern itself with trifles'). Minimum discomfort must be expected on the basis of 'give and take'.

(iii) *Lawful Use of Land*. The defendant may prove that his use of his land is lawful (*Mayor of Bradford* v. *Pickles*, 1895).

(iv) *Reasonableness*. The act or omission is reasonable having regard to the locality concerned.

The following defences are **ineffectual**:

(i) That the plaintiff came to the nuisance. If a man goes to the place where a nuisance exists he is not barred from his claim. The question is whether the act is reasonable in that locality (*Sturges* v. *Bridgman*, 1879; and *Bliss* v. *Hall*, 1838).

(ii) That the particular act is for the public benefit.

(iii) That all care and skill have been used to prevent a nuisance.

Remedies. The following legal remedies exist:

(i) *Abatement*. This means 'self help'. The injured party may stop the nuisance by removing the cause. But the abater must not, in the process, infringe another's rights, e.g. by trespass on a neighbour's property or land, or injure an innocent person's rights, such as a tenant's. Abatement is not favoured as a remedy by the law, and where entry on another's land is contemplated, notice to the alleged tortfeasor should first be given to remedy the alleged nuisance before entry is effected, unless there is an emergency (*Lemmon* v. *Webb*, 1895).

A common example of abatement is the cutting of roots and branches projecting from a neighbour's trees: such roots and branches may be sawn off, but they remain the property of the person owning the tree (*Mills* v. *Brooker*, 1919).

(ii) *Damages*. This is the ordinary common-law remedy.

(iii) *Injunction*. Application may be made to the court for an order to restrain further acts constituting the nuisance, if it can be proved that the nuisance will recur and do irreparable damage to the plaintiff.

Distinction between Trespass and Nuisance. The torts of nuisance and trespass to land are similar in that both affect land. Nevertheless there are important distinctions as indicated below.

Trespass	*Nuisance*
1. Actionable *per se*.	Must prove *damage*.
2. *Direct* physical interference to land (e.g. placing rubbish on a neighbour's land).	Need not be direct (e.g. allowing bricks from a ruinous chimney to fall on a neighbour's land).
3. Wrongful *entry* of an object or person on another's land.	No entry necessary. Can be created on defendant's own land.
4. May consist of *one act* only.	Usually more than one act is necessary.
5. Trespass to land is *not a crime*.	*Public* nuisance is a crime.

Robinson v. *Kilvert* (1889). Defendant manufactured paper boxes in a cellar of a house, and leased the floor above to the plaintiff. Defendant heated the cellar with hot dry air. This raised the temperature of plaintiff's premises above which were used for storing brown paper which (because of its special quality) lost its value. Plaintiff sued in nuisance. *Held:* that defendant was not liable. His heating of the premises would not have damaged ordinary brown paper, though it did damage plaintiff's particularly sensitive paper.

Christie v. *Davey* (1893). *C*, a music teacher, used her house for frequent practice and musical evenings. *D*'s premises were separated by a party-wall. *D* became exasperated with the playing and retaliated by knocking on the wall, beating trays, whistling and shrieking. *Held:* that defendant acted maliciously and unreasonably and was liable. He purposely annoyed the plaintiff.

Mint v. *Good* (1951). Plaintiff, an infant, was walking on the highway when a wall collapsed. Plaintiff was injured by the collapse and sued the landlords (defendants) responsible for the wall. *Held:* that there was nuisance and the defendants were liable. (The Court of Appeal held that there was a duty to repair which lay on the landlords in this case.)

St. Helen's Smelting Co. v. *Tipping* (1865). Fumes from factory injured plaintiff's trees and shrubs. *Held:* that this was an actionable nuisance.

Hollywood Silver Fox Farm v. *Emmett* (1936). Plaintiff bred silver foxes on land where they erected a sign. Defendant owned an adjacent field. A dispute arose over the sign, and defendant sent his son to discharge a 12-bore shot gun near the plaintiff's land, which frightened the vixen, affected their breeding habits and caused them to miscarry their young. Plaintiff sued in nuisance. *Held:* that this was an actionable nuisance. Defendant's malicious motive rendered his actions a nuisance, and an injunction was granted to restrain him in future.

Adams v. *Ursell* (1913). A fried-fish shop was alleged to be a nuisance which caused plaintiff's house to be permeated with the odour and vapour from the stoves. *Held:* that an injunction be granted. It was immaterial that the shop served a working-class area and supplied a public need.

Castle v. *St. Augustine's Links* (1922). A taxi-cab driver, plaintiff, lost an eye when he was hit by a sliced golf ball. The golf-links adjoined a road, and the golf hole was near it. *Held:* that there was a public nuisance.

Bolton v. *Stone* (1951). A cricket field was near a highway and it was proved that only six or ten cricket balls during thirty-five years had been known to be hit into the road. No one had been previously injured until the plaintiff was struck by a ball. *Held:* that there was no nuisance.

Sturges v. *Bridgman* (1879). Defendant, a confectioner and baker in Wigmore Street, London, used a pestle and mortar for some twenty years on his premises. Plaintiff, a doctor, built consulting rooms in his garden next to the confectioner's premises. Noises and vibration interfered with plaintiff's practice, and accordingly he sued defendant in nuisance. *Held:* that although defendant could acquire a prescriptive right to create a nuisance, the nuisance in this case arose only when the doctor's consulting room was built.

Bliss v. *Hall* (1838). The defendant used his tallow factory for making candles. The factory emitted 'divers noisome smells' for some three years. Then the plaintiff took up residence nearby. *Held:* that there was nuisance. It was no defence that the plaintiff came to the nuisance.

9. Negligence

Negligence is one of the most important and common torts in the law. Although its origins are to be found in trespass and trespass on the case, the action was developed and formulated only in the nineteenth century; it now exists in its own right as a separate and independent tort.

In the law of tort, negligence may mean

(i) a state of mind in which a particular tort may be committed, e.g. where *A* commits a trespass through inadvertence or carelessness; and

(ii) an independent tort. It is this aspect alone that will be dealt with in the following pages.

The plaintiff suing in negligence must prove three points to maintain a successful claim:

(*a*) That the defendant was under a *duty of care* to the plaintiff.
(*b*) That there had been a *breach* of that duty.
(*c*) That as a result the plaintiff has suffered damage.

The Duty of Care. It has been said that a man may be as negligent as he pleases towards the whole world, if he owes no duty to them (*Le Lievre* v. *Gould*, 1893). This is of course true, and it is good law. If, having given no one permission to be in my field and having no knowledge of any other person's presence, I enter my property I can do what I like there. I can drive my tractor, shoot a rabbit, and hit a golf ball anywhere I please. I owe no duty to anyone, and I can be as negligent as I please.

Negligence is not a ground of liability unless the person whose conduct is impeached is under a duty of taking care (*Butler* v. *Fife Coal Co. Ltd.*, 1912). The important question we may ask is when does such a duty of care arise in real life? There are, of course, many situations where one person owes a duty of care to another; the most common arise on the highways. All persons, whether driving motor-cars, riding pedal cycles or merely walking as ordinary pedestrians, owe a duty of care to all other road users. Doctors owe a duty of care to patients; employers to work-people; and teachers to students. The list is endless, and the forms of negligence and the situations in which the duty of care arises are varied. 'The categories of negligence are never closed' (Lord Macmillan in *Donoghue* v. *Stevenson*, 1932).

> *Donoghue* v. *Stevenson* (1932). A man bought from a retailer a bottle of ginger-beer manufactured by the defendant. The man gave the bottle to his lady friend who became ill from drinking the contents. The bottle contained the decomposed remains of a snail. The bottle was opaque so that the noxious substance could not have been seen and was not discovered until the lady was refilling her glass. The consumer sued the manufacturer in negligence. *Held* (by the House of Lords): that the manufacturer was liable to the consumer in negligence.

The consumer had no cause of action in contract against either the retailer or the manufacturer, because it was not she but her friend who bought the bottle. In this most important case Lord Atkin laid down a broad definition of the duty of care:

(i) 'You must take reasonable care to avoid acts or omissions which you can reasonably foresee would be likely to injure your neighbour.'

(ii) 'Who then is my neighbour? The answer seems to be persons who are so closely and directly affected by my act that I ought reasonably to have them in contemplation as being so affected when I am directing my mind to the acts or omissions which are called in question.'

The rule enunciated has been applied to manufacturers of foodstuffs, clothing, hair-dyes and similar matters.

Recognized Duties in Law. The list is not exhaustive.

(i) *Highway*. This duty of care for other users has already been mentioned. The duty of care applies to railways, shipping at sea, and canal navigation.

(ii) *Employers' liability*. An employer owes a duty of care to employees. He is expected to provide a reasonably safe system of work, reasonably safe machinery and competent fellow employees. Under the Employers' Liability (Compulsory Insurance) Act, 1969, an employer must insure against liability for bodily injury or disease sustained by his employees in the course of their employment. This applies even where the injury is caused by defective equipment supplied by a third party (Employers' Liability (Defective Equipment) Act, 1969).

(iii) *Professional persons.* Doctors, surgeons, dentists, solicitors, and similar professional persons owe a duty of care in the discharge of their duties to their patients, clients, or other persons with whom they are in professional relationship. In *Anns* v. *L. B. of Merton* (1977), where a building inspector had passed defective foundations of a house, the House of Lords held that a local authority owes a duty of care in the application of its bye-laws to owners and occupiers who might suffer injury as a result of its negligence. However, in *Investors in Industry Commercial Properties Ltd.* v. *South Beds. D.C.* (1986), the Court of Appeal held the local authority to be not liable for the approval of plans for warehouses and design for their foundations which proved to be faulty.

(iv) *Carriers.* These owe a duty of care for the passengers and goods, whether fee-paying or not, independently of the contractual terms of their agreement to transport.

(v) *Schools.* A duty of care is owed to the children, and this duty is also owed to third parties injured by the children: *Carmarthenshire C.C.* v. *Lewis* (1955).

(vi) *Police.* A duty of care owed to the general public, but not to an individual in respect of losses caused by their failure to apprehend a criminal: *Hill* v. *Chief Constable of West Yorkshire* (1988).

The Standard of Care. Granted a person in a given situation must use care to another; the question is what standard of care is he required in law to use? The answer here is that the standard of care is that of an ordinary prudent man. In other words, that care which a reasonable man would use or show in the circumstances of the particular case under consideration. The degree or amount of care (to be distinguished from the standard) is variable. For example, one is expected to take more care in handling a loaded gun than in handling a walking stick. Where serious consequences may follow from carelessness in a particular situation, the greater the degree of care which must be exercised. One expects a manufacturer of, or dealer in, explosives to manifest a high degree of care; similarly a manufacturer of poisons and drugs and such like matters.

Where a person sets himself up as possessing a particular skill, e.g. a surgeon, industrial chemist or accountant, he must exhibit in following his calling that skill which is usually found in such a person. A plumber, carpenter or labourer may not display the same amount of skill as a highly qualified heart specialist, but the same legal standard applies to both. The test to be applied is: What is reasonable in the circumstances of the case, having regard to his particular profession or occupation?

Dorset Yacht Co. Ltd. v. *Home Office* (1969). Some boys escaped from a borstal institution and set adrift and damaged a motor-yacht in Poole harbour. The Yacht Co. (owners) sued the Home Office as the Government department responsible for prisons and borstals. *Held:* that the Home Office was liable for damage done by persons who escaped from custody or while on parole if the escape was due to the negligence of prison or borstal officers.

Smith & Others v. *Littlewoods Organisation Ltd.* (1987). Vandals started fire in the defendant's empty building which damaged adjoining property. *Held:* occupier's duty did not extend to preventing deliberate acts of third party vandals in these circumstances.

Yachuk v. *Oliver Blais Co.* (1949). A boy of nine persuaded a garage attendant to let him have a tin of petrol by a false tale that his mother's car had run out of petrol some distance from the garage. The boy poured the petrol over some timber and then set it alight. The fire caused an explosion and the boy was seriously injured. *Held* (by the Judicial Committee of the Privy Council): that it was negligence on the part of the garage attendant to entrust the child with such a dangerous commodity as petrol.

Condon v. *Basi* (1985). During a football match the defendant recklessly tackled the plaintiff, breaking his leg. The defendant was sent off by the referee. *Held:* defendant was liable in negligence, the foul tackle falling below the standard of care reasonably expected in any match.

McLoughlin v. *O'Brian* (1983). One of the plaintiff's children was killed and her husband and two other children badly injured in a road accident caused by defendant's negligence. Plaintiff was at home two miles away, when she was informed of the accident and taken to the hospital where she saw the injured members of her family, and heard her daughter had been killed. She suffered severe nervous shock. The House of Lords extended the doctrine of nervous shock, holding that her injury was foreseeable by the defendant, who owed her a duty of care, and was liable. *Note:* Decision extended to shock of seeing damage caused to own property (*Attia* v. *British Gas Plc*, 1987).

Brice v. *Brown* (1984). Mother alarmed by injuries to her daughter when both were passengers in a taxi involved in a collision caused by the negligence of the defendant. *Held:* defendant liable in negligence for the mother's resulting mental illness.

Negligent Misstatement. Formerly the general rule was that a person was liable for negligent acts but not for negligent words. Where, therefore a negligent statement was made even though it was intended to be acted on by the plaintiff and was, in fact, acted on by him to his loss, no liability fell on the defendant.

We must distinguish *fraudulent misrepresentations* which give rise to an action of deceit (cf. *Derry* v. *Peek*, 1889), from *negligent misstatements*.

In *Candler* v. *Crane, Christmas & Co.* (1951), it was held that an accountant who negligently prepared certain accounts for a particular transaction was under no liability in tort in respect of those accounts, even though a plaintiff in reliance on the accounts invested money in a company and suffered financial injury as a consequence.

This case was overruled by the following:

> *Hedley Byrne & Co. Ltd.* v. *Heller & Partners Ltd.* (1964). H.B. contacted *A*'s bankers, H. & P. (defendants) for references. H. & P. gave a favourable report of *A*'s credit-worthiness. H. & P. headed the document 'Without Responsibility'. H.B. acted on the misleading report, gave substantial credit, and suffered heavy loss when *A* went into liquidation shortly after. H.B. sued H. & P. in negligence. *Held* (House of Lords): the defendant bankers (H. & P.) would have been liable in negligence had they not expressly disclaimed liability. 'Where in a sphere in which a person is so placed that others could reasonably rely on his judgment or his skill or on his ability to make careful inquiry, a person takes it on himself to give information or advice to, or allows his information or advice to be passed on to, another, who, as he knows or should know, will place reliance on it, then a duty of care will arise' (per Lord Morris).

This rule was applied in *Cornish* v. *Midland Bank PLC.* (1985).

Since the Unfair Contract Terms Act, 1977 (which despite its name also affects the law of torts), the 'without responsibility' clause will only be effective if it is 'reasonable' having regard to all the circumstances.

In *Clay* v. *A. J. Crump & Sons* (1963), an architect inspected a site in course of demolition and negligently stated that a particular wall was safe and could be left. However, the wall collapsed injuring a labourer. It was held that the architect was liable for his negligent statement.

A barrister is partially excepted from the rule; he is not liable for careless advocacy, *Rondel* v. *Worsley* (1967), but he may be liable for careless advice not intimately connected with the conduct of a case in court (*Saif Ali* v. *Sydney Mitchell & Co.*, 1978).

'Res Ipsa Loquitur.' Where the duty is so plain as to admit of no denial, the presumption that failure in performance indicates fault is expressed by the maxim *res ipsa loquitur* ('the thing speaks for itself').

As a general rule the plaintiff must prove that the defendant has by his act or omission been negligent in the discharge of a legal duty owed to the plaintiff.

There must be reasonable evidence of negligence, but where the thing is shown to be under the management of the defendant or his servants, and the accident is one which in the ordinary course of things does not happen if those who have the management use proper care, it affords reasonable evidence, in the absence of explanation by the defendant, that the accident arose from want of care (*Scott* v. *London and St. Katherine's Docks Co.*, 1865). If the defendant produces a reasonable explanation, equally consistent with negligence or no negligence, the burden of proof of negligence remains with the plaintiff. The presumption is one of fact not law.

> *Byrne* v. *Boadle* (1863). A barrel of flour fell from an open door on an upper floor of defendant's warehouse, injuring a passer-by in the street. *Held:* that this was evidence to go to the jury without further explanation. Barrels which are properly handled do not generally so fall, and a jury might reasonably infer negligence on the part of defendant.

Similar examples of *res ipsa loquitur* are found in the following cases. A pedestrian was knocked down by a car which mounted the pavement and struck him from behind (*McGowan* v. *Scott*, 1923). Two trains collided on the same railway line (*Skinner* v. *L.B. & S.C. Rly.*, 1850). Excess sulphites were present in underwear, causing plaintiff dermatitis (*Grant* v. *Australian Knitting Mills*, 1936). Collapse of scaffolding (*Kealey* v. *Heard*, 1983). Although in *Mahon* v. *Osborne* (1939) it was said the doctrine could not apply to surgical cases, the modern trend is to allow it (*Cassidy* v. *Ministry of Health*, 1951).

Contributory Negligence

Before 1945 a defendant could escape liability by showing that the accident would not have happened had not the plaintiff contributed to it by his own negligence. This common law rule was altered, and the present law is contained in the Law Reform (Contributory Negligence) Act, 1945, which adopts the principle applied in regard to collisions of ships at sea. Section 1(1) of the Act provides that

> 'Where any person suffers damage as a result partly of his own fault and partly of the fault of any other person or persons, a claim in respect of that damage shall not be defeated by reason of the fault of the person suffering the damage, but the damages recoverable in respect thereof shall be reduced to such extent as the court thinks just and equitable having regard to the claimant's share in the responsibility for the damage.'

To take a simple illustration, let us suppose that *X* is a pedestrian who negligently walks into the path of a car driven carelessly along the road by *Y*. *X* claims damages for injuries sustained to the extent of £6,000 from *Y*. The court may find that *X* was one-third to blame for the accident. Accordingly damages may be awarded of £4,000 (i.e. £6,000 less one-third).

Doctrine of Novus Actus Interveniens. A *novus actus interveniens* (a new act intervening) occurs when some act of a third person intervenes between the wrongful act or omission of the defendant and the subsequent damage to the plaintiff.

In this type of case it is for the court to decide whether the new act ought reasonably to have been foreseen by the defendant. If it ought to have been foreseen the defendant remains liable. Thus in *Scott* v. *Shepherd* (1773) *A* lit a squib at a market fair and threw it on to *B*'s stall. *B* threw it away to *C*'s stall, and *C* threw the squib to *D*'s stall where the squib exploded injuring *D*. *Held: A* was liable to *D*. The chain of causation was not broken by the actions of *B* and *C*.

If the defendant could not foresee the intervening actions, the originator(s) of the *novus actus may* be liable, and the defendant's act or omission will not be treated as the cause of the damage.

Where a person is placed in imminent personal danger by the negligence of another, any unwise act he does in 'the agony of the moment' (as it is put) is not treated as contributory negligence. There is a qualification that the person so acting imprudently should show as much judgment and control as can reasonably be expected in the unusual and dangerous circumstances. This is sometimes referred to as the doctrine of alternative danger.

For example, a motor-coach being driven negligently gets out of control going down a hill. A passenger, realizing the situation, decides to jump from the coach as it moves on, and injures himself in the fall. The coach subsequently comes to rest safely. The passenger is not debarred from his claim against the driver of the coach merely because, had he (the passenger) remained seated, no harm would have come to him. In such circumstances the passenger is not contributorily negligent, for he acted on the spur of the moment in a difficult situation.

> *Sayers* v. *Harlow U.D.C.* (1958). Plaintiff, a woman, entered a public lavatory owned and operated by defendants. Owing to a defective lock without a handle, she could not get out of the cubicle. Her bus was due to leave, and she tried to climb over the door. She placed her foot on a revolving toilet roll, fell to the ground and injured herself. She sued the local authority. *Held:* (i) that the defendants were negligent; (ii) that plaintiff herself was guilty of contributory negligence in trying to balance on a revolving object. Her claim would be reduced by one-quarter.

> *Froom and others* v. *Butcher* (1976). *B* drove a car negligently on a road and collided with *F*'s car injuring the driver, *F*, who was not wearing a seat-belt. The accident was *solely* caused by *B*. *Held:* (CA): *F*'s claim for damages was reduced by 25 per cent, because *F* was contributorily negligent in not wearing the seat-belt.

> *Jones* v. *Boyce* (1816). A horse-drawn coach got out of control going down a hill due to defendant's negligence. A passenger (plaintiff) feared the coach would overturn, jumped and was injured. *Held:* that plaintiff was not guilty of contributory negligence.

> *O'Connell* v. *Jackson* (1971). *A* rode a moped and had no crash helmet. *B* negligently collided with *A* who received severe head injuries. *Held:* although accident caused by *B*, the absence of a crash helmet was a contributory causative factor in the damages. *A*'s claim was reduced.

10. Breach of Statutory Duty

A plaintiff may have a right of action in tort as the result of a breach of duty imposed by a statute: in fact most breach of statutory duty claims arise out of industrial injuries (e.g. under the Mines and Quarries Act, 1954, and the Factories Act, 1961) which will gradually be covered by new provisions under the Health and Safety at Work Act, 1974.

11. Death: Survival of Actions

At common law the general rule known as *actio personalis moritur cum persona* ('a personal action dies with the person') applied. Thus, if an injury were done either to the person or property of another for which damages was the only remedy, the action died with the person to whom (the would-be plaintiff), or by whom (the would-be defendant), the wrong was done. If *A* negligently drove his car and knocked down a pedestrian (*B*) walking along a footpath, and either *A* or *B* died before action was brought, the claim died too.

The common law rule was mitigated to some extent by the Fatal Accidents Act, 1846, under which certain dependants of the deceased may recover damages from a tortfeasor responsible for the death, if the dependants can show that they have suffered financial loss. The Fatal Accidents Act, 1976 (as amended by the Administration of Justice Act, 1982), consolidates the law. The following points should be noted:

(*a*) The specified class of relatives who may sue are: (i) wife, husband, former spouse or any person who at the deceased's death and for at least two years before had lived with the deceased as his or her husband or wife, (ii) children including posthumous, illegitimate, step-children or those treated by the deceased as a child of his family, (iii) grandchildren, (iv) parents, step-parents or treated by the deceased as his parent, (v) grandparents, (vi) brothers and sisters and their issue, and (vii) uncles and aunts and their issue.

(*b*) The plaintiff must show that the death was caused by the wrongful act, neglect or default of the defendant. Non-tortious acts will not qualify.

(*c*) The plaintiff must have suffered some 'actual pecuniary loss' (this term includes reasonable probability of financial benefit) and the loss must arise out of the death of 'the breadwinner'.

(*d*) Action must be brought by the deceased's personal representatives on behalf of the claimant relative(s).

(*e*) Action must be begun within three years of the death.

The old common law rule referred to above was fundamentally altered by the Law Reform (Miscellaneous Provisions) Act, 1934, as amended by section 4 of the Law Reform (Limitation of Actions) Act, 1954. The 1934 Act provided that on the death of any person 'all causes of action subsisting against or vested in him shall survive against, or, as the case may be, for the benefit of, his estate'.

The following points are relevant here:

(*a*) Actions in defamation do not survive.

(*b*) The cause of action must exist at the time of death.

(*c*) Damages may be recovered for (i) pain and suffering, (ii) loss of earnings (during the period between the injury and the death), and (iii) medical and hospital expenses. The Administration of Justice Act, 1982 abolished loss of 'expectation of life' as a separate head of general damages but the knowledge of such reduction is to be taken into account in assessing damages in respect of pain and suffering.

(*d*) Exemplary damages cannot be awarded in favour of the deceased plaintiff's estate.

(*e*) Funeral expenses may be recovered if not already recovered under the Fatal Accidents Act.

(*f*) The following special periods of limitation apply:

(i) If the tortfeasor dies, no action may be brought against his estate unless *either* the proceedings were pending against him at the date of his death, *or* proceedings are begun not later than six months after his personal representatives have taken out representation. (Unless this rule were made the personal representatives would never be able to wind up the estate.)

(ii) If the injured (i.e. aggrieved) person dies, there is no special period of limitation; the ordinary rules apply in such a case.

Common examples occur in road-accident cases where legal action is taken under the Fatal Accidents Act on behalf of dependants for the loss of the breadwinner, and under the 1934 Act in respect of any cause of action arising before death. In these circumstances the court will ensure that no award has the effect of giving a dependant a benefit twice over. Damages recoverable on behalf of the deceased's estate under the 1934 Act are subject to estate duty (claims under the Fatal Accidents Act are not so subject), and such damages are to be calculated without reference to any loss or gain to the estate consequent upon the death, e.g. under a policy of insurance.

12. Occupiers' Liability

Before 1957 at common law the liability of an occupier to a person coming on to his premises depended on the category in which the entrant fell, i.e. whether as an *invitee* or a *licensee*, and the Occupiers' Liability Act, 1957, was passed to simplify the position.

The Act abolished the distinctions between the categories and the varied duties of care applicable to each. The Act now establishes one category of persons, namely that of *visitor*. A visitor is anyone who has express or implied permission to be on the property, e.g. a guest at dinner, a postman, a shopper, and so on. S. 1 of the Occupiers' Liability Act, 1984, has introduced statutory rules for the safety of persons outside the scope of the 1957 Act.

Dangerous Premises

Section 2 of the Occupiers' Liability Act, 1957, provides as follows:

(*a*) An occupier of premises owes the same duty, the 'common duty of care', to all his visitors, except, in so far as he is free to and does extend, restrict, modify or exclude his duty to any visitor or visitors by agreement or otherwise. (This section allows, therefore, an occupier to contract with a visitor to absolve himself from liability.)

(*b*) The 'common duty of care' is a duty to take such care as in all the circumstances of the case is reasonable to see that the visitor will be reasonably safe in using the premises for the purpose for which he is invited or permitted by the occupier to be there.

(*c*) The circumstances relevant for the present purpose include the degree of care, and want of care, which would ordinarily be looked for in such a visitor. For example.

(i) an occupier must be prepared for children to be less careful than adults; and

(ii) an occupier may expect that a person, in the exercise of his calling, will appreciate and guard against any special risks ordinarily incident to it, so far as the occupier leaves him free to do so.

(*d*) In determining whether the occupier of premises has discharged the common duty of care to a visitor, regard is to be had to all the circumstances. For example

(i) where damage is caused to a visitor by a danger of which he had been warned by the occupier, the warning is not to be treated as absolving the occupier from liability, unless in all circumstances it was enough to enable the visitor to be reasonably safe; and

(ii) where damage is caused to a visitor by a danger due to the faulty execution of any work of construction, maintenance or repair by an independent contractor employed by the occupier, the occupier is not to be treated as answerable for the danger if in all the circumstances he has acted reasonably in entrusting the work to an independent contractor and has taken such steps (if any) as he reasonably ought in order to satisfy himself that the contractor was competent and that the work had been properly done.

(*e*) The 'common duty of care' does not impose on an occupier any obligation to a visitor in respect of risks willingly accepted by the visitor.

(*f*) Persons who enter premises for any purpose in the exercise of a right conferred by law are to be treated by the occupier to be there for that purpose, whether they in fact have his permission or not.

For example, a police officer may enter premises under authority of a search warrant; the 'common duty of care' is owed to him while he is so exercising the right conferred by law.

Defences. The following defences deserve note:

(i) That the occupier warned the visitor (see paragraph *d* (i) above).

(ii) That the plaintiff consented, *volenti non fit injuria* (see paragraph (*e*) above).

(iii) That the occupier employed a competent independent contractor (see paragraph *d* (ii) above).

> *O'Connor* v. *Swan & Edgar and Carmichael Contractors* (1963). Plaintiff was working as a demonstrator in a store when part of the ceiling fell and injured her. Plaintiff sued the store owners (as first defendants) and the plasterers (independent contractors employed by first defendants). *Held:* that first defendants (store owners) were not liable; second defendants (plasterers) were liable since they had been guilty of faulty workmanship in plastering the ceiling.

Under the Defective Premises Act, 1972, the builder, the specialist subcontractor, the developer and the professional people involved come under a non-excludable statutory duty of care in respect of new houses towards the purchaser and his successors in title, unless the National House Builders Registration Council scheme, or a similar scheme of protection, applies.

Trespassers

A trespasser has been defined as 'one who goes on to the land without any invitation of any sort and whose presence is either unknown to the proprietor, or, if known, is practically objected to' (*Addie and Sons* v. *Dumbreck*, 1929).

A burglar or a poacher is clearly a trespasser; but difficulties can arise in borderline cases, e.g. hawkers or canvassers, unless there is a notice specifically excluding them.

The general rule is that an occupier of premises owes no active duty to trespassers. A trespasser enters property of another at his own risk. Where, however, a trespasser is known to be present, an occupier may not inflict damage on him recklessly or intentionally. An occupier may not create dangers intentionally to injure a trespasser. Thus, he may not set spring guns (*Bird* v. *Holbrook*, 1828), though it is possible to take defensive measures, such as covering the tops of high walls with broken glass.

Children

The general rules as to trespass apply to children. There are, however, some special points which should be noted.

(*a*) An occupier must be prepared for the fact that children are less careful than adults.

(*b*) What may be a warning to an adult may not be so to a child.

(*c*) If with the knowledge of child trespassers on his land the occupier makes no attempt to prevent recurrence of the trespass, e.g. by repairing his fences, his inactivity might be evidence of implied permission, in which case the child may qualify as a 'visitor'.

(*d*) Where a child is lawfully on land and there is something on the land which acts as an 'allurement' to a child, e.g. machinery or attractive poisonous berries, the occupier may be liable even though the child is a trespasser so far as the allurement itself is concerned.

As to (*d*) above, an occupier of land is entitled to assume that young children will be in the charge of competent adults. In *Phipps* v. *Rochester Corporation* (1955), where a boy aged five, who was accompanied by his sister aged seven, fell into a hole and broke his leg, it was held that the responsibility for the safety of young children rests primarily with their parents.

B.R. Board v. *Herrington* (1972). *H*, aged 6, trespassed through a defective fence adjoining an electrified railway line and was badly injured. *H* sued the Board in negligence for permitting the fence to be in a dilapidated condition. The Board knew previous trespasses had occurred. *Held* (House of Lords): the Board was liable. An occupier's liability to a child trespasser depends on what a conscientious, humane man (with his knowledge, skill, and resources) could reasonably have been expected to have done or refrained from doing which would have avoided the accident. A poor person would often be excused where a large organization would not (per Lord Reid.)

Cook v. *Midland G.W.Rly. of Ireland* (1909). Defendants kept a turntable on their land near a public road. To the knowledge of defendant children habitually came on to the land and played with the turntable. Defendants took no effective steps to prevent them doing so. A child aged four, injured himself on the turntable. *Held:* that there was sufficient evidence to find the defendants liable. As they had acquiesced in the trespasses by the children, the particular child was in the position of a visitor, and to him the turntable was an allurement.

Glasgow Corporation v. *Taylor* (1922). A child, seven years of age, picked some attractive, but poisonous, berries growing on a shrub in a public park controlled by Glasgow Corporation. The child died after eating the berries. Defendants (the corporation) knew the berries were poisonous and that children went to the park, but they had done nothing to give effective warning, intelligible to children, of their danger. *Held:* that the corporation was liable in an action by the child's parent; the berries constituted an allurement.

13. The Rule in 'Rylands v. Fletcher' (1868)

'A person who for his own purposes brings on his lands and collects and keeps there anything likely to do mischief if it escapes, must keep it in at his peril, and, if he does not do so, is *prima facie* answerable for all the damage which is the natural consequence of its escape' (per Blackburn J in the Court of Exchequer Chamber).

The circumstances of the case were that the defendant employed independent contractors to construct a reservoir on his land and to use the water power for his mill. In the course of construction the contractors came across some disused mine-shafts and passages filled with earth and marl which, unknown to defendant and the independent contractors, communicated with the plaintiff's mines. When the reservoir was filled, the water escaped through the shafts and flooded the plaintiff's mine. It was found as a fact that the defendant had not been negligent. Nevertheless the defendant was held liable, first by the Court of Exchequer Chamber and secondly on appeal to the House of Lords where the judgment was confirmed but the rule was restricted to damage due to a non-natural user of the land.

Rylands v. *Fletcher*

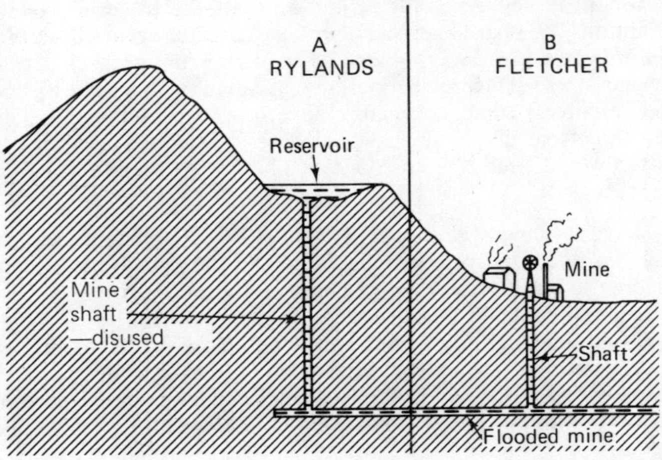

Note: That the original action was brought by *Fletcher* (the mine owner) against *Rylands* (the mill owner), the names being reversed on appeal.

The rule is one of *strict* liability, i.e. the defendant is liable independently of wrongful intent or negligence.

The celebrated case described here related to an escape of water, but the rule has been applied to various kinds of 'escape', for example: electricity (*National Telephone Co.* v. *Baker* (1893)), yew trees (*Crowhurst* v. *Amersham Burial Board* (1878)), wire fencing (*Firth* v. *Bowling Iron Co.* (1878)), sewage (*Jones* v. *Llanrwst U.D.C.* (1911)), and explosives (*Rainham Chemical Works* v. *Belvedere Fish Guano Co.* (1921)).

The tort is not actionable *per se*; some damage must be proved to sustain a successful claim.

There are several important points to observe in the rule. One is that the defendant is liable notwithstanding his employment of a competent independent contractor, and whether or not there is any default by the contractor. Moreover, there must be an actual 'escape' or leakage from the defendant's land of the dangerous or harmful thing, and the dangerous thing must move from the defendant's land to the plaintiff's.

Things 'naturally on land' include thistles, insects, rats (unless their numbers increased as a result of defendant's acts or omissions), rocks (when these crumble and fall naturally there is no liability on the defendant, though it would be otherwise if the fall were due to negligent quarrying or if increased falls resulted from quarrying). Liability for such things may, however, be actionable in nuisance or trespass. Many things are brought on to land by landowners, and the question arises as to whether their introduction and use amounts to 'non-natural usage'. Natural usage includes the working of mines and the planting of trees, though if these are poisonous and they escape, the defendant will be liable. The storage of water in quantities and the storage of electricity have been held as non-natural.

Defences. The defences to this tort are:

(i) *Act of God.* The defendant may evade liability if he can prove that there was an escape due to what is described as an Act of God, e.g. extraordinary rainfall which could not reasonably have been anticipated (*Nichols* v. *Marsland*, 1876).

(ii) *Act of a Stranger.* The defendant can evade liability if he can prove that the escape was due to the unlawful act of a third party ('stranger') over whom the defendant had no control (*Rickards* v. *Lothian*, 1913).

(iii) *Default of Plaintiff.* If the escape of the dangerous thing was caused by the default of the plaintiff.

(iv) *Consent of Plaintiff.* Where the plaintiff voluntarily consented to the presence or existence on the defendant's land of the dangerous thing or source of the mischief. For example, fire-extinguishers, water-pipes or water cisterns in a block of flats. Common benefit is evidence of consent.

(v) *Statutory Authority.* A local authority or public-utility corporation may escape liability if the terms of the statute are clear (*Green* v. *Chelsea Waterworks Co.* 1894). This does not apply to escape of water from reservoirs (Reservoirs Act, 1975).

> *Rickards* v. *Lothian* (1913). *R*, the lessee of a building, sub-let the second floor to *L*. A third person unknown blocked the waste pipes of a wash-basin on the fourth floor (which was in *R*'s control) and turned the tap on. *L*'s stock on the second floor was damaged by the overflow of water. *Held:* that *R* was not liable since the damage was due to the act of a stranger which *R* could not reasonably have prevented.

Home Brewery Co. Ltd. v. *William Davis & Co.* (*Leicester*) *Ltd.* (1987). Defendants filled in clay pit which caused water to percolate on to plaintiff's land and also temporary flooding. *Held: Rylands* v. *Fletcher* not applicable as there was no escape. Defendants liable either in trespass or nuisance for temporary flooding.

Peters v. *Prince of Wales Theatres Ltd.* (1943). Defendants leased to *P* a shop in a building used as a theatre. The theatre, with knowledge of *P*, contained a water-sprinkler system against fire risk, the system extending to *P*'s shop. During a frost, water poured from the system, damaging *P*'s stock. *P* claimed damages under '*Rylands* v. *Fletcher*'. *Held:* that the water-sprinkler system had been installed for the common benefit of plaintiff and defendant; the rule in *Rylands* v. *Fletcher* did not apply; and, as there was no negligence on the part of defendant, there was no liability under that head.

Green v. *Chelsea Waterworks Co.* (1894). Defendants were authorized by statute to lay a water main. The main burst and flooded the plaintiff's premises. *Held:* that statutory authority precluded liability under *Rylands* v. *Fletcher*; and as there was no negligence on the part of the defendants, they were not liable.

Crowhurst v. *Amersham Burial Board* (1878). Yew trees were planted by defendants on the boundaries of their land. The yew-tree branches protruded over the land occupied by plaintiff. The plaintiff's horse ate some leaves and was poisoned and died. *Held:* that defendants were liable, for it was a non-natural use of land to plant such poisonous trees, and the branches had 'escaped' into plaintiff's field.

Read v. *Lyons* (1947). Plaintiff was an inspector of the Ministry of Supply and was injured by an explosion in defendant's munition factory while she was carrying out her duties. The plaintiff was unable to prove negligence by defendants, but she alleged that they were liable under the rule of *Rylands* v. *Fletcher*. *Held* (by the House of Lords): that there had been no escape sufficient to render the defendant liable under the rule. The House gave the opinion (not part of the decision) that the making of munitions in wartime was a natural usage of land.

Giles v. *Walker* (1890). The occupier of land ploughed it up, and shortly afterwards a large crop of thistles grew up. As a consequence, thistle seeds were blown on to the land of neighbours. *Held:* that the rule of *Rylands* v. *Fletcher* did not apply. The defendant had not brought the thistles on to his land, for they had accumulated there naturally. (The case has been overruled in *Leakey* v. *National Trust* (1980) on the ground that there would now be liability in nuisance.)

14. Defamation

Defamation is the publication of a *statement which exposes a man to hatred, ridicule or contempt or causes him to be shunned or avoided by right-thinking members of society generally*. In other words it is a 'false statement about a man to his discredit'.

There are two classes of defamation: (i) **libel**, which is a statement made in *permanent* form, and (ii) **slander**, which is a statement in *transitory* form.

The permanent form, as far as libel is concerned, may be in a written or printed statement, an effigy, a statue, a caricature, or a film. Section 1 of the Defamation Act, 1952, made defamation by broadcasting (radio and television) libel, not slander. A talking film was held to be libel in *Youssoupoff* v. *Metro Goldwyn Mayer Ltd.* (1934).

The transitory form, as far as slander is concerned, is usually by speech or gesture.

Two further distinctions may be drawn. Libel, if it tends to a breach of the peace, is a crime. Slander, as such, is not a crime.

Thirdly, libel is actionable *per se*, i.e. on mere publication, and the plaintiff need not show that he has suffered any pecuniary loss following the libel. In slander the plaintiff must prove actual damage (i.e., financial loss) except in the following cases:

(i) Imputation of any crime that is punishable by imprisonment.

(ii) Imputation that the plaintiff is suffering from a contagious disease rendering the person so infected liable to be excluded from society, e.g. venereal disease.

(iii) Imputation of unchastity in a woman (Slander of Women Act, 1891). This includes lesbianism (*Kerr* v. *Kennedy*, 1942).

(iv) Imputation of unfitness for any office, profession, calling, trade or business held or carried on by the plaintiff at the time of the publication (Defamation Act, 1952). Thus it is defamatory to say of a solicitor that he knows no law; or of a carpenter that he cannot make a simple joint.

In a trial the question whether the statement is defamatory is one of fact to be decided by the jury. As a matter of practice and law, however, the judge first decides whether the statement is *capable* of being defamatory, i.e. whether a reasonable person could take such a view; it is for the jury to say whether the statement is *in fact* defamatory.

Proof of Defamation. In a successful claim in defamation the plaintiff must prove four points:

(i) that the statement was defamatory;
(ii) that the statement referred to him;
(iii) that the statement was published;
(iv) that damage was suffered (in slander, outside the four exceptions).

As to (i) above, the variety of the forms of defamation can be gleaned from the definition appearing at the head of this section. Moreover, a study of the examples below will assist in grasping how the law is applied in the particular circumstances of each individual case.

One special form of defamation which needs particular mention is *innuendo*. Although words may not on the face of them appear defamatory, they may nevertheless be such by reason of peculiar surrounding circumstances or facts, or because a special meaning is attributable to them. There is, we may say, a hidden meaning or implication, possibly more telling and harmful in its effect than a bold and obvious statement. In such cases, the plaintiff who alleges he is defamed by innuendo must show that the facts were known to the person to whom the defamatory statement was made, and that reasonable persons would interpret the words used as defamatory. To say '*A* drinks a lot' is ambiguous: it may be a harmless statement, or it may insinuate that *A* is a heavy drinker of intoxicants and may, in certain circumstances, be defamatory.

Cassidy v. *Daily Mirror Newspapers Ltd.* (1929). A newspaper published a photograph of a man and a woman. Underneath appeared the words 'Mr. *C* and Miss *B* whose engagement has been announced'. Mr. *C* was already married to Mrs. *C*, and the latter sued the newspaper proprietors, alleging that the words imputed 'by innuendo' that she was immorally cohabiting with Mr. *C* and that several friends thought this to be the case. *Held:* that plaintiff should be awarded £500 damages, although the defendants acted quite innocently.

Tolley v. *Fry* (1931). Defendants, chocolate manufacturers, published without the plaintiff's consent an advertisement which showed the plaintiff, a golfer, with a packet of their chocolate in his pocket. Plaintiff alleged an innuendo that he had prostituted his amateur golf status. *Held:* that defamation was proved; damages were awarded to plaintiff.

Reference to Plaintiff. The plaintiff must prove that he was the person marked out by the words, i.e. identified. Nevertheless, he need not be the person to whom the defendant intended to refer. The question to be asked is: Would a reasonably-minded person who knew the plaintiff connect the defamatory statement with him?

It follows from the above that a *class* of persons cannot as such be defamed. To say 'All lawyers are rogues who fleece the public', or 'All priests are immoral and dishonest' is not defamatory.

Hulton v. *Jones* (1910). A newspaper article contained words which defamed one Artemus Jones who was intended to be a fictional character in a fanciful sketch of life in Dieppe. Artemus Jones was described as a churchwarden at Peckham. Unfortunately the name Artemus Jones was also that of an English barrister and journalist. Evidence was adduced that those who knew him thought the article referred to the barrister and journalist. *Held:* that the newspaper was responsible for the libel. Damages awarded to the respondent, Jones.

Newstead v. *London Express Newspaper, Ltd.* (1940). Defendants published in their newspaper a report of the trial and conviction of bigamy of one 'Harold Newstead, a thirty-year old Camberwell man'. The account was true of a barman of that name. But it so happened that there was also another man, Harold Newstead, thirty years old, and living in Camberwell. The latter sued the defendants. *Held:* that plaintiff was entitled to damages.

Publication consists in making known in writing, or orally, or in other form, to some person other than the plaintiff. If *A* orally tells *B* that he, *B*, is a thief or a rogue, this is not actionable. If *C* is present and overhears the remark, there is publication to *C*. Where *A* authorizes another, say *B*, to make a defamatory statement, *A* is liable. Moreover *A* will be liable if he could have reasonably foreseen the likelihood of a publication which he initiated.

Where a postcard is sent through the post, there is a 'publication'. The presumption is that a postcard is likely to be read by post-office staff. This rule does not apply to a letter, either sealed or unsealed, for it cannot reasonably be foreseen that someone will open it and read the contents.

Where the author of a letter reveals its contents to a secretary or to the writer's clerks or officials, there is a publication. In such cases, however, the occasion may be privileged.

Special rules apply to communications between husbands and wives. The communication of a statement which defames a third person made by a husband to his wife is not publication. The same rule applies where the communication is made by a wife to a husband. So if *H* (husband) writes a letter defaming *X* (a third party) and shows the letter to *W* (*H*'s wife), there is no publication of the letter sufficient to sustain an action in libel by *X*. Where *X*, a third party, writes a letter defaming *H* (husband), and *X* shows the letter to *W* (*H*'s wife), there is a publication. Where a servant wrongfully opened his master's letter it was held that there was no publication to the servant (*Huth* v. *Huth*, 1915).

Repetition and Dissemination. The repetition of a defamatory statement orally, or in writing, is a fresh 'publication'. It is no defence in such cases to plead that the person who repeats the statement did not originate it.

Repetition is highly relevant to the Press. Where a book or newspaper article is defamatory, the printer and the publisher are each liable as well as the author. Subsidiary distributors such as booksellers and newsvendors are not liable, however, if they can prove the following points. The distributor must show that:

(i) he did not know the statement was libellous;
(ii) there were no circumstances which ought to have led him to suspect the book or paper was libellous; and
(iii) his lack of knowledge was not due to negligence.

A circulating library is in the same position as a bookseller or newsvendor.

Vizetelly v. *Mudie's Select Library Ltd.* (1900). A book contained a libel. Defendants, librarians, had copies in stock, but were unaware of the libellous contents. They employed a reader of their books and took other precautions, but they did not observe in a trade publication that the publishers of the libellous book requested return of all copies for correction. The library continued to lend the book. *Held:* that the library was negligent and thus liable in damages as 'publishers' of the particular libel in the book.

Defences. The following defences may be raised in defamation:

(*a*) Justification.
(*b*) Fair Comment.
(*c*) Privilege.
(*d*) Apology.
(*e*) Offers of Amends.

(*a*) **Justification.** It is a good defence to plead that the alleged defamatory statement is *substantially true*, even though some details may be untrue. If an alleged defamatory statement is true, the plaintiff cannot, by the nature of things, have suffered damage to his reputation.

In an action for libel or slander in respect of words containing two or more charges against the plaintiff, the defence of justification will not fail merely because the truth of every charge is not proved, if the unproved charges do not materially injure the plaintiff's reputation having regard to the truth of the remaining charges (Defamation Act, 1952, s. 5).

In practice justification is only rarely pleaded. If the defence fails, the defendant will usually be required to pay substantial damages by reason of his having persisted in his assertion of the truth of the defamatory statement.

(*b*) **Fair Comment.** This defence is restricted to fair comment on *a matter of public interest*. What constitutes 'a matter of public interest' is for the judge to decide in each individual case. The following subjects fall within this category: central and local government; the conduct and speeches of persons in public offices and affairs generally; trade unions; the police; works of art; books; plays; television and other broadcasts. The private lives of authors, actors, playwrights are not matters of public interest in this context.

As to the meaning of 'fair comment', the defendant must be able to prove that his remark is honest, relevant and free from malice or improper motive. The defendant's statement must consist of opinion or comment and not a statement of fact. Proof of actual spite or of malice towards an author (and similar persons) negatives the defence. Moreover the statement must not be a comment on a person's moral character.

In each case the judge decides whether a reasonable person might consider the comment as fair. The jury decides in each case whether it is unfair.

(*c*) **Privilege.** This defence protects certain defamatory statements from action at law on the grounds of public policy. The free expression of opinion and facts in Parliament is so important to our democratic way of life that this freedom (protected by absolute privilege) overrides any private right or interest of the person who might be defamed. No action may be taken against the person, e.g. a Member of Parliament, giving utterance to his words. There are two classes of privilege: absolute and qualified.

Absolute Privilege exists in the following cases:

(i) *Statements made in Parliament.* Whatever is said in Parliament cannot be the subject of legal proceedings (Bill of Rights, 1689).

(ii) *Reports ordered to be published by either House of Parliament.* For example, 'Hansard' and Government White Papers (Parliamentary Papers Act, 1840).

(iii) *Judicial Proceedings.* Statements made in the course of judicial proceedings by a judge, jury, parties, witnesses and advocates. The proceedings *must* be judicial. Statements made in the course of licensing applications dealt with by magistrates enjoy qualified privilege only, the proceedings being administrative not judicial.

(iv) *Matters of State.* Communications between one Officer of State and another in the course of his duty. Secretaries of State and Ministers fall within the category of 'Officer of State', but it is uncertain how far this privilege extends to those in subordinate rank. Such persons would, however, be protected by qualified privilege (*Chatterton* v. *Secretary of State for India*, 1895).

(v) *Communications between Solicitor and Client*, i.e. statements made in the course of their professional relationship. (There is some doubt as to whether this privilege is absolute or qualified, but its importance in the administration of the law justifies inclusion here as absolute.)

Qualified Privilege means that the defence is qualified to the extent that the statement in question was made without malice and with an honest belief in its truth. If a statement is made maliciously the law withdraws the protection of privilege and the defendant will be liable for defamation.

Qualified privilege exists in respect of the following matters:

(i) *Legal or Moral Duty.* Statements where the maker has a duty to inform, or an interest in informing, some person who has a duty or interest to receive the information. For example where employer *A* writes to employer *B* concerning *X*, an applicant for a post with *B*.

(ii) *Private Interests.* Statements in protection of one's private interests.

(iii) *Statements to Authorities.* Letters of complaint or report to a proper authority, e.g. petitions to Parliament, complaints to local government officials and police.

(iv) *Reports of Parliamentary Proceedings.* Fair and accurate reports of Parliamentary Proceedings.

(v) *Reports of Judicial Proceedings.* Fair and accurate reports of public judicial proceedings.

(vi) *Reports of Public Proceedings.* Fair and accurate reports of various matters of public interest and importance such as proceedings of the U.N.O., International Court of Justice, British courts martial outside the U.K.; and proceedings of public meetings of local authorities, public authorities, public companies, or any tribunal or body exercising functions under an Act of Parliament.

Addis v. *Crocker* (1961). The plaintiff (not a solicitor) alleged he was libelled by the findings of the Disciplinary Committee of the Law Society. *Held:* that the Disciplinary Committee, a statutory committee, was exercising judicial functions, and the publication of its findings was absolutely privileged.

Chatterton v. *Secretary of State for India* (1895). Plaintiff alleged that a letter from the Secretary of State for India to his Parliamentary Under-Secretary giving material with which to answer a Parliamentary question, was libellous. *Held:* that the statement was absolutely privileged, since it concerned a matter of State.

Osborn v. *Thomas Boulter & Son* (1930). Plaintiff was a licensee of an inn. He wrote to the defendants (his brewers) complaining of the quality of the beer. Defendants sent one of their men to investigate and report. After receiving the report, defendant (Boulter) dictated a letter to his secretary suggesting that plaintiff had been adding water to the beer, and pointed out the penalties attaching to this practice. Plaintiff sued, alleging publication to the secretary and other clerks. *Held:* that the occasion was privileged; as the plaintiff could not prove malice, his claim failed.

Jackson v. *Hopperton* (1864). A prospective employer, *A*, wrote to a former employer, *B*, concerning the character of *C*, an employee of *B*. *B* replied. *Held:* that information about the character of the employee, *C*, was privileged.

(*d*) **Apology.** By the Libel Act, 1843 (as amended by the Libel Act, 1845), a defendant in an action for libel contained in a newspaper and other periodical may plead:

(i) that the publication was made without malice or gross negligence;
(ii) that a full apology was published at the earliest opportunity; and
(iii) that compensation has been paid into court.

This is a special plea, but it is seldom used since no other defence can be set up if the statutory apology under this Act is relied on.

(*e*) **Offer of Amends.** The defence of offer of amends under the Defamation Act, 1952, is available when words have been published *innocently*, i.e. if the publisher used reasonable care and either:

(i) did not intend to publish them of the plaintiff and did not know of circumstances by which they might be understood to refer to him (see *Newstead* v. *London Express Newspapers Ltd.*, p. 238); or

(ii) did not know of circumstances by which words innocent on the face of it might be understood to be defamatory of the plaintiff (see *Cassidy* v. *Daily Mirror Newspapers Ltd.*, p. 238).

An 'offer of amends' does not mean the payment of money. It does mean that at the same time the defendant offers:

(i) to publish a correction and an apology; and

(ii) to take reasonable steps to notify persons to whom copies of the defamatory matter have been distributed that the words used are alleged to be defamatory of the aggrieved party.

If the offer is accepted by the aggrieved party, no further proceedings can be taken against the person making the offer. The court may, however, order the defendant to pay costs and expenses.

If the offer of amends is rejected, the defendant must prove that the words were published innocently and that the offer of amends was made as soon as practicable after it came to his knowledge, and that the offer has not been withdrawn.

Remedies. The main legal remedies for defamation are (i) damages, and (ii) injunction. We have noted that in slander, as a general rule, some damage must be proved as grounds for the action. A loss of the voluntary hospitality of friends has been held in one case as sufficient. Damages may be compensatory (i.e. recompense for the actual loss sustained) or exemplary.

The following matters may, however, be taken into account in mitigation of damages:

(i) if the defendant made a full apology at the earliest practicable moment;

(ii) if the plaintiff had a bad reputation;

(iii) if there was provocation by certain counter-libels;

(iv) if the plaintiff had already recovered damages for the publication of words to the same effect as those in which the action is brought;

(v) whether the damage was too remote.

Injunctions may also be granted, but the court is reluctant to grant an interim injunction since this involves a decision that *prima facie* the case is one of libel before the jury has itself decided this important fact.

The plaintiff must act quickly in his petition for an injunction, and prove that the offending publication will be made or continued, and that any such intended or continued publication will entail immediate and irreparable injury.

15. Deceit

We have already discussed fraudulent misrepresentation (or deceit) in the law of contract (see p. 155). Deceit is a separate tort, and its essential features are considered below.

The tort of deceit consists in making a wilfully false statement with the intent that the plaintiff shall act in reliance on it, and with the result that he does so act and suffers harm in consequence (*Bradford B. S.* v. *Borders*, 1941).

The essentials of the tort are:

(*a*) A statement of *fact*.
(*b*) That the maker knew it to be *false* or had no genuine belief in its truth.
(*c*) That it was made with *intent* that it should be acted upon.
(*d*) That it was acted upon.
(*e*) Damage was suffered.

(*a*) **Statement of fact.** Mere expressions of opinion are insufficient. The statements are usually made orally or in writing, but a 'statement' or representation may be made by conduct, without words even. Thus, where a person at Oxford, who was not a member of the University, went into a shop, wearing a cap and gown, and obtained goods, by the fraud, this was held to be a sufficient 'false pretence' (*R.* v. *Barnard*, 1837).

(*b*) **The representation was false.** The classic definition of fraud is in *Derry* v. *Peek* (1889). It is 'a false representation of fact, made with knowledge of its falsity or without belief in its truth, or recklessly careless whether it be true or false'. The test is whether the defendant had an honest and genuine belief in the truth of the statement. Recklessness indicates the absence of such a belief; and if the defendant honestly believed the representation to be true in the sense in which he understood it, however erroneously, this will be a good defence.

(*c*) **The intent.** The statement must be made with the intent that the plaintiff should act upon it, and that he did so act. If the plaintiff was not deceived by the statement he will not be able to recover.

(*d*) **The statement must be acted upon.** The plaintiff must have relied on the fraudulent misrepresentation, and in consequence of the deceit must have acted upon it, e.g. by transferring goods or money to the defendant.

(*e*) **Damage.** Damage or loss must have been suffered by the plaintiff.

Peek v. *Gurney* (1873). Plaintiff, in reliance on a fraudulent prospectus issued by company promoters, bought shares which were already in the market and so suffered loss. *Held:* that plaintiff could not recover. The purpose of a prospectus is to induce persons to apply for shares from the company, not to induce them to purchase shares in the market and already issued. The plaintiff was not, therefore, one of the persons intended to act on the false representation in the prospectus.

Burrows v. *Rhodes* (1899). Defendant induced the plaintiff to take part in the Jameson Raid in South Africa, by the false statement that British women and children needed protection. Plaintiff lost certain property (his kit) and suffered personal injuries in the loss of a leg. *Held:* that he could recover.

Langridge v. *Levy* (1837). A gunmaker sold a gun to *A* for the use of *A* and his (*A*'s) sons, and fraudulently represented the gun to be sound. While *B*, one of *A*'s sons, was using it the gun burst and *B* was injured. *Held*: that *B* could bring an action in deceit by the gunmaker because the statement as to the soundness of the gun, though made to *A*, was intended to be communicated to and acted upon by *B*.

16. Malicious Falsehood

This tort is committed when a person causes damage to another by making false and injurious imputations. The damage here contemplated is damage to business interests, not to reputation.

The essentials of malicious falsehood are:

(i) that the statement *is* false;

(ii) that there is *malice*, i.e. a desire to injure, or some other improper motive.

(iii) that it tends to make *others* act on the statement to the plaintiff's detriment.

The distinction from deceit is that in deceit the plaintiff is induced by the false representation to act to his own detriment; and the distinction from defamation is that in defamation the person's reputation is primarily attacked.

There are three types of injurious or malicious falsehood:

(*a*) **Slander of title**, where a defendant falsely and maliciously disparages or denies another person's title to property in a manner calculated to cause him damage. An example occurs where *A* falsely and maliciously alleges that *B* is offering certain goods for sale, in infringement of a patent vested in *C* (*Wren* v. *Weild*, 1869).

(*b*) **Slander of goods**, e.g. where a person falsely and maliciously disparages goods manufactured or sold by another, though the motive may be to boost the first person's sales. But a false statement that one's own goods are the best is not actionable. The court will not allow litigation to be used as a method of advertising by using the forum of the court to give publicity to a litigant's products.

(*c*) **Other false words which damage a man's business.** Thus, where a defendant falsely and maliciously published in a newspaper that the plaintiff had ceased to carry on business, it was held that the plaintiff was entitled to recover damages for loss of trade attributable to the false statement (*Ratcliffe* v. *Evans*, 1892).

17. Limitation of Actions

The law governing this matter is found in the Limitation Act, 1980, which has replaced earlier Acts.

Actions in tort must be brought within six years of the cause of action accruing. This is the general rule, and the calculation of the period presents little difficulty where the tort consists of one independent and simple tort. Time begins to run from the date of that event. Where, however, the damage arising from a tort does not become immediately apparent, e.g. where a person by continual digging on his own land disturbs the supports of a neighbour's property (a nuisance), time begins to run from the date of the damage accruing.

> *Pirelli General Cable Works Ltd.* v. *Oscar Faber & Partners* (1983). Defendants designed a chimney which was constructed from unsuitable materials in June and July 1969. As a result cracks developed in the chimney in April 1970, although the plaintiffs did not discover the damage until November 1977. In October 1978 the plaintiffs brought an action for negligence. *Held:* Although it was agreed that the damage could not with reasonable diligence have been discovered before October 1972, the claim was statute barred as the action accrued when the damage came into existence and not when the damage was discovered or could have been discovered with reasonable diligence.

> *Dove* v. *Banhams Patent Locks Ltd.* (1983). Defendants fitted an insecure security gate to the plaintiff's premises. The house was burgled in 1979 when thieves forced the top of the security gate. The defendants pleaded that the cause of action arose in 1967 when the gate was installed. *Held:* That the plaintiff's cause of action was not statute barred. The damage and, therefore, the cause of action arose in 1979 on the forcing of the gate and the resulting burglary.

Where the tort consists of a continuing wrong, e.g. noise, vibration or stench (nuisances), a new cause of action arises daily. Where any such nuisance has been continuously committed for, say, nine years, the plaintiff will be able to recover only for the six years immediately preceding the date action commences. The first three years in this example are outside the limit, and damage occurring within that time is not actionable.

If the injured party was under disability (e.g. a minor or of unsound mind) when the cause of action accrued, the period runs from the time when the disability ceases or the injured party dies, whichever first occurs.

Special periods of limitation operate in the following cases.

(i) *Fatal Accidents Act, 1976.* Action must be commenced within three years after the death of the deceased person.

(ii) *Personal Injuries.* Actions for damages for negligence or nuisance where *personal injuries* are involved must be begun within three years from the date on which the cause of action accrued, or the date (if later) of the plaintiff's knowledge. The court has a discretionary power to override the time limit if it thinks it equitable to do so (*Conry* v. *Simpson*, 1983). In accordance with S.6 of the Administration of Justice Act, 1982, provisional damages can be awarded where there is a possibility of further serious disease or deterioration.

(iii) *Defamation.* The Administration of Justice 1985, S.57, has reduced the limitation period for libel and slander actions from six to three years.

(iv) *Latent Damage Act, 1986.* Provides that in actions relating to property, where the damage is latent, the time limit is either six years from the date on which the action accrued, or three years from when the knowledge was acquired, whichever is the later, and a right to bring the action.

(v) *Joint Tortfeasors.* A tortfeasor wishing to recover contribution from a joint tortfeasor must bring his action within two years from the date when judgment was entered against him.

18. Exercises

1. Define a tort, and distinguish a tort from (i) a crime, and (ii) a breach of contract.
2. How far is malice and intention relevant to an action for a tort?
3. How far is mistake a defence in tort?
4. Discuss the defence in tort of (i) necessity, and (ii) inevitable accident.
5. The liability of two or more persons who together commit a tort is said to be 'joint and several'. What is meant by this statement?
6. 'A person may be imprisoned without being conscious of the fact.' Explain.
7. Distinguish between (i) detinue, and (ii) conversion.
8. Explain, with examples, what is meant by 'a public nuisance'.
9. What do you understand by 'the duty of care' in relation to the tort of negligence?
10. How far is it true to say that negligent misstatement is now a tort?
11. Distinguish between (i) the liability of joint tortfeasors, and (ii) contributory negligence.
12. Summarize the provisions of the Occupiers' Liability Act, 1957, in relation to visitors on premises.
13. Define 'defamation'. List the points to be proved in a successful claim for libel.
14. What special rules govern 'publication' in the law of libel?
15. Distinguish, with examples, between (i) absolute privilege, and (ii) qualified privilege, in regard to the law of libel.

9

TRUSTS

The modern trust derived from the feudal 'use', which was invented by medieval lawyers in order to overcome the hardship of the common law rules preventing land from being devised (i.e. left by will), and the harshness of the feudal burdens imposed on freehold tenants.

Suppose that *A* was a feudal tenant who wanted to escape the heavy burdens and services attaching to his holding. *A* would 'enfeoff' three friends, *X*, *Y*, and *Z*, of his land to the 'use' of his son, *B*. (Enfeoff means to transfer the interests in land to another.) So far as the lord of the manor was concerned, *X*, *Y*, and *Z* were the legal owners. On *A*'s death no feudal dues were payable, because the legal ownership in the land was vested in *X*, *Y*, and *Z*. If one friend died there was no interruption of ownership since the property passed to the remaining two, and if one of these died the property passed to the survivor under the doctrine of survivorship which applied at common law to joint tenants (see p. 278).

If *X*, *Y*, and *Z* attempted to deal with the land in a way incompatible with their obligations towards *B* (e.g. by using the land themselves or selling it), the Court of Chancery would intervene on *B*'s behalf. *B* could not, however, obtain any redress in the courts of common law, for these were concerned only with the legal rights and the legal owner or owners.

B's right, at least originally, was a personal one against the legal owners *X*, *Y*, and *Z*. But it was soon realized that to permit the remedy to prevail against only the feoffees to 'uses' was to open the door to fraud. Consequently, a remedy for *B* was afterwards made available against a purchaser from the legal owners (i.e. the feoffees), provided that the purchaser took the land *with notice* of the 'use' attached to it. If, however, the purchaser bought the legal estate in the land without notice of the rights of the beneficiary, the latter had no right against him either at law or in equity. Herein lies the origin of the doctrine of 'the purchaser for value of the legal estate without notice' (see p. 294).

The adoption of the 'use' led to loss of income and valuable rights which were exacted from the tenants by the feudal lords and land-owners: particularly the Crown, the greatest landowner of all. The Statute of Uses, 1535, was passed to stop evasion of death duties and feudal dues or payments. The statute enacted that where land was granted 'To *A* to hold it for the use of *B*', *B* should be regarded as the legal owner and *A* should be excluded from the grant. *B* was intended to bear responsibility for the discharge of the feudal burdens. However, the statute was unpopular and lawyers invented technical ways of evading its operation. Uses persisted and came in due course of time to be called 'trusts'. Gradually they achieved popularity and came to be one of the most distinctive features of English law.

1. Definition of a Trust

> 'A trust is the relationship which arises wherever a person called the trustee is compelled in Equity to hold property, whether real or personal, . . . for the benefit of some persons (of whom he may be one) or for some object permitted by law, in such a way that the real benefit of the property accrues, not to the trustee, but to the beneficiaries or other objects of the trust.' (Professor Keeton, *The Law of Trusts*).

The trust device is used for many different purposes, notably:

(i) To enable property to be held for persons who cannot hold the legal title themselves, e.g. a minor cannot be the legal owner of land, but land can be held in *trust* for a minor.
(ii) To enable property to be used to benefit persons in succession, e.g. settlements.
(iii) To enable two or more persons to own land.
(iv) To further a charitable purpose.
(v) To avoid or minimize liability to various forms of taxation.

The distinctive feature of the trust is the duality of ownership. The **trustee** is the legal owner; the **beneficiary** is the equitable owner. This split in ownership is possible because, whilst admitting that the trustee has the legal title, equity acts on the trustee's conscience and will compel him to hold the property for the beneficiaries.

Trusts may be classified as (*a*) private trusts and (*b*) charitable trusts. These must be considered separately as there are important differences between them.

2. Private Trusts

Private trusts can be categorized as (*a*) express, (*b*) implied, or (*c*) constructive.

(*a*) **Express Trusts.** An express trust is one expressly created by the settlor *inter vivos* (i.e. during life), or by will, for the benefit of one or more specified persons or a group of persons. It may be created in writing, by deed, by will or merely orally in certain cases.

The essential elements of an express private trust were laid down in *Knight* v. *Knight* (1840) by Lord Langdale, who declared that three 'certainties' are necessary for the creation of a trust: (i) certainty of intention, (ii) certainty of subject-matter, and (iii) certainty of objects.

(i) *Certainty of intention.* The settlor must show by his words a clear intention to create a trust. The words must be imperative, not precatory (i.e. words merely beseeching or hoping); there must be a positive command that a thing shall be done and that a trust shall be created. If there is lack of certainty of intention the grantee can take the property absolutely. Thus in *Re Adams and the Kensington Vestry* (1884), the testator left property in his will to his widow 'in full confidence that she will do what is right as to the disposal thereof between my children'. This was held not to create a trust so the widow took the property for herself.

(ii) *Certainty of subject-matter*. This refers both to the property to which the trust is to apply and to the interests in the property that the beneficiaries are to take. Thus if a testator attempts in his will to create a trust of 'the bulk' of his property or a trust of 'a nice round sum', the trust will fail. Again, if a settlor conveys his houses to his trustees to hold some in trust for Mary and the rest for Ann, the trust will fail and the trustees will hold the houses on a resulting trust (see below) for the settlor.

(iii) *Certainty of objects*. This means that the persons whom the trust is intended to benefit must be ascertainable or at least capable of ascertainment. If a settlor has conveyed property to trustees and the objects of the trust are uncertain, the trustees will hold on a resulting trust for the settlor.

Completely and Incompletely Constituted Trusts. A settlor can create a trust either:

(i) by declaring himself to be a trustee, or
(ii) by conveying the property to trustees.

If the settlor chooses (ii), the trust will not be fully constituted (i.e. fully made) until he has done all he can to vest the legal title in the trustees. What the settlor must do depends on the type of property involved, e.g. if it is unregistered land there must be a conveyance; if it is a chattel (such as a painting) he must physically hand it over; if it is shares the share transfer must be registered in the company's books; if the trust is created by will then the will must comply with the formalities of the Wills Act, 1837 (see page 298).

Once a trust is fully constituted equity will assist any beneficiary under the trust to enforce his rights. Before the trust is fully constituted however, it does not exist—an incompletely constituted trust is no trust at all—and no person can have any rights as beneficiary under a trust that does not exist.

Equity will assist would-be beneficiaries under an incompletely constituted trust if they have provided consideration. Consideration in equity's eyes means either valuable consideration in the common law sense (money or money's worth) or marriage consideration, i.e. where the would-be beneficiaries are the spouse and children of the settlor and the settlement was made before and in consideration of marriage. Equity will assist them by compelling the settlor to convey the property to the trustees, thus completely constituting the trust.

If, however, the would-be beneficiaries have provided no such consideration, then they are known as 'volunteers' and equity will not help them to completely constitute the trust. This is summed up in the maxim 'Equity will not assist a volunteer'.

(*b*) **Implied Trusts.** An implied trust is based upon the presumed intention of the settlor. The most common type of implied trust is the **resulting trust**. For example, suppose a settlor conveys property to trustees to hold on trust for *B* for life. If the settlor does not state where the property is to go on *B*'s death, then when *B* dies the trustees will hold on a resulting trust for the settlor; thus the equitable interest returns to the settlor. Similarly, if a settlor conveys property to trustees but the trusts are void, e.g. because they offend one of the rules against perpetuities, then the trustees hold on a resulting trust for the settlor.

Another example of a resulting trust can be seen in the following situation: suppose *A*, a purchaser of property, has it conveyed into the name of *B*. In the absence of any evidence to show that *A* intended to make a gift of the property to *B*, equity will treat *B* as holding the property on a resulting trust for *A*, i.e. there is a presumption of a resulting trust. Sometimes there is a presumption the other way; this is known as the presumption of advancement. Thus if the person providing the purchase money has the property conveyed into the name of his wife or child, it is presumed that a gift was intended. In this case there is no resulting trust and the recipient can enjoy the property for himself. These presumptions can be rebutted by evidence of what was actually intended.

(*c*) **Constructive Trusts.** These are trusts imposed by equity regardless of the intention of the parties. An important example of this type is where a trustee, *X*, in breach of trust conveys the trust property to another person, *Y*, who knows of the breach of trust but nevertheless accepts the trust property. In these circumstances, *Y* will be treated as a 'constructive trustee' and will be compelled by equity to hold the property in trust for the beneficiaries. *Y* will be a constructive trustee whether he consents or not.

A person will also be treated as a constructive trustee where he acquires a benefit under the trust to which he is not entitled. He will be compelled by equity to hold the benefit for the beneficiaries, as in the following case:

> *Keech* v. *Sandford* (1726). A trustee held a lease of Romford Market on trust for an infant beneficiary. The trustee attempted to renew the lease for the benefit of the infant, but the lessor refused to grant a renewal to

the infant. The lessor agreed, however, to renew the lease in favour of the trustee personally. The lease was accordingly made out to the trustee. *Held:* that the trustee held the new lease on a constructive trust for the infant.

3. Public (or Charitable) Trusts

For a trust to be charitable it must satisfy three requirements:

(*a*) **It must be charitable in the legal sense.** 'Charity' in a legal context does not accord with the popular meaning of the word. For example, fee-paying public schools like Eton or Harrow are charitable in the legal sense and enjoy the same privileges, including tax exemptions, as say, Barnardo's or the Spastics Society.

There is no statutory definition of a charity. The preamble to the Statute of Charitable Uses, 1601, listed a number of charitable objects, but the classification most frequently quoted is that of Lord Macnaghten in *Income Tax Special Commissioners* v. *Pemsel* (1891), who classified charitable trusts under four heads:

(i) for the relief of poverty;
(ii) for the advancement of education;
(iii) for the advancement of religion; and
(iv) for other purposes beneficial to the community.

The last category includes such purposes as the welfare of animals, the provision of public works such as bridges and museums, the setting up of fire brigades and distress funds, and the promotion of efficiency in the armed forces. Trusts for political purposes are not charitable and will therefore fail (*re Koeppler's Will Trusts* v. *Slack*, 1985).

In re South Place Ethical Society (*1980*). This was an agnostic society; it held public meetings and gave high quality concerts. Its objects were held to be charitable under heads (ii) and (iv) above, but not under head (iii).

Inland Revenue Commissioners v. *McMullen* (1980). The Football Association Youth Trust was set up to promote football and other sports in schools and universities. The House of Lords held that this was a charitable trust within head (ii) above, as the physical development of the young is part of their education.

Under the Recreational Charities Act, 1958, it is charitable to provide facilities for recreation or leisure-time occupations if the facilities improve the conditions of life of the persons for whom they are primarily intended. The persons must have need of the facilities by reason of age, youth, infirmity, disablement, poverty or social or economic circumstances; or the facilities must be available to members or female members of the public at large. Trusts in favour of Women's Institutes would thus be held valid.

(*b*) **It must benefit the public as a whole or at least a section of it.**

If the main intention of the trust is to benefit certain specified individuals, no charitable trust arises. Thus a trust to provide for the education of the lawful descendants of three named persons is not charitable (*Re Compton*, 1945). Employees of a company do not form a section of the public for this purpose. Thus a trust to educate children of employees of a company has been held not charitable (*Oppenheim* v. *Tobacco Securities Trust Co. Ltd.*, 1951).

Trusts for the relief of poverty are, however, exempt from this public benefit requirement. Such trusts are charitable even if restricted to the relatives of the donor or to the employees or ex-employees of his firm.

(*c*) **It must be wholly and exclusively charitable.** This requirement is not satisfied if, under the terms of the trust, the property can be applied to non-charitable as well as to charitable purposes. Thus trusts for 'charitable or benevolent purposes' have been held void.

4. Differences between Private and Charitable Trusts

(*a*) **The persons to benefit.** Private trusts are created for the benefit of specified persons or classes of persons; charitable trusts are created to further a purpose that will benefit society at large or an appreciable part of it.

(*b*) **The application of the perpetuity rules** (see below).

(*c*) **Taxation.** Charities are wholly or partially exempt from many taxes that affect private trusts, and they also enjoy reduced rates. The income of a charity, if used for charitable purposes, is largely exempt from income tax.

(*d*) **Uncertainty of objects.** If the persons who are to be beneficiaries under a private trust are not defined with sufficient certainty the trust will fail. However, a trust whose objects are clearly charitable will not fail merely because those purposes are vague; the court can order a scheme for the application of the property.

(*e*) **The Cy-Pres Doctrine.** This applies only to charitable trusts. Where the literal execution of a charitable trust is or becomes inexpedient or impractical, the court will apply the property *cy-pres*, i.e. to some charitable purpose as near as possible to the original purpose named by the donor. This is done by means of a scheme established by the Charity Commissioners or the court.

The Charities Act, 1960 extended the doctrine of *cy-pres* to include cases where:

(i) The original purposes have as far as possible been fulfilled or cannot be carried out.

(ii) The original purposes provide a use for part only of the property.

(iii) The property given can be more effectively employed if used in conjunction with other property applicable for similar purposes.

(iv) The original purposes were laid down by reference to an area which has ceased to be a unit, or by reference to a class of persons which has ceased to be suitable.

(v) The original purposes since being laid down have been provided for by other means, or have ceased to be an effective method of using the property.

If the charitable gift fails from the start, then the property cannot be applied *cy-pres* unless the court can find a **general charitable intention**, i.e. an intention on the part of the donor to benefit charity in any event. Thus if there is a gift by will to a charity that ceases to exist before the testator's death, the gift cannot be applied *cy-pres* in the absence of a general charitable intention.

(*f*) **Enforcement.** Private trusts are enforced by the beneficiaries; charitable trusts are enforced by the Attorney-General on behalf of the Crown.

(*g*) **Registration.** Most charities must be registered with the Charity Commissioners, who have general supervision over charities. They may sanction new charitable schemes and authorize legal proceedings.

5. The Rules Against Perpetuities

As a matter of policy, the law has always discouraged the tying up of land or other property for excessive periods of time. Two rules have been developed to deal with this, both of which apply to private trusts:

(*a*) **The rule against remoteness of vesting.** This was laid down in *Cadell* v. *Palmer* (1833):

> 'Every attempted disposition of land or goods is void unless, at the time when the instrument creating it takes effect, one can say that it *must* take effect (if it takes effect at all) within a life or lives *then* in being and 21 years after the termination of such life or lives, with the possible addition of the period of gestation.'

This has now been amended by the Perpetuities and Accumulations Act, 1964. The effect now is that where property is held on trust, the beneficiaries must become absolutely entitled to the property either within a period no longer than that of a life in being at the time when the trust came into existence, plus 21 years after the end of that life, *or* within a period not exceeding 80 years specified in the trust instrument. Under the pre-1964 rule, *possible* events, and not actual or likely events, had to be considered. Where a gift might have failed under the pre-1964 rule because there was a *possibility* that it would vest outside the perpetuity period, the Act introduces a 'wait-and-see' rule. The effect is that such a disposition is to be treated as if it were not affected by the rule against remote vesting until such time as it is established that the disposition will *in fact* vest outside the perpetuity period.

Charitable trusts *are* basically subject to this rule.

(*b*) **The rule against perpetual trusts.** This renders void any disposition that attempts to tie up property for a period longer than a life in being plus 21 years. This rule does *not* apply to charitable trusts, which can therefore continue indefinitely.

6. Trustees

Most of the law relating to trusts has evolved from the decisions of the Court of Chancery, but there are also important statutory provisions, notably the Trustee Act, 1925.

Any person of full age, sound mind and legal capacity may be a trustee under an express trust. An infant cannot be an express trustee, though he may become a *constructive* trustee or hold on a *resulting* trust in certain circumstances.

If the trust property is land a maximum of four trustees is permitted. Where land is sold, at least two trustees (or a trust corporation) are needed to give a valid receipt for the purchase money.

7. Trust Corporations

A trust corporation is empowered to act as a trustee. Because this is not a human trustee there is never any problem of the trustee dying or retiring. Common examples include the trustee departments of banks and large insurance companies. The Public Trustee is a trust corporation and a government office: if the Public Trustee acts improperly the State makes good any loss.

8. Appointment of Trustees

The initial trustees are usually appointed by the settlor in the trust instrument. It is one of the maxims of equity that a trust shall never fail for want of a trustee. Thus, if a testator creates a trust by will but does not name trustees, or if those named refuse to act, then the testator's personal representatives must act as trustees until others are appointed.

Subsequent trustees are appointed by the person given power to appoint in the trust instrument; failing that, the existing trustees or the personal representatives of the last surviving trustee can appoint. As a last resort the court can appoint under section 41 of the Trustee Act.

Under section 36 of the Trustee Act a new trustee can be appointed by writing. This can be either an additional trustee or a replacement trustee for one who is (i) dead, or (ii) remains outside the U.K. for more than 12 months, or (iii) wishes to retire, or (iv) refuses to act, or (v) is unfit or incapable of acting, or is an infant, or (vi) is a corporation which is dissolved.

A person may decline to accept the office of trustee, but unless he does so promptly he may be presumed to have accepted.

9. Termination of Trusteeship

Apart from death, this may be effected either:

(*a*) **By removal.** A trustee can be removed under an express power in the trust instrument, under section 36 of the Trustee Act (where a replacement trustee is appointed), or, in extreme cases, by the court; or

(*b*) **By retirement.** This can be effected under section 36 of the Trustee Act if a replacement trustee is appointed. If no replacement trustee is appointed, a trustee can retire under section 39 provided (i) at least two trustees or a trust corporation will remain; and (ii) he obtains the consent of his co-trustees and any person empowered to appoint trustees; and (iii) the retirement is by deed. As a last resort a trustee can apply to the court to be discharged.

10. Duties and Powers of Trustees

(*a*) **Administration.** A trustee must take the same care of the trust property as an ordinary prudent man of business would take of his own property. Moreover, a professional trustee must exercise the special skill that he professes to have. (*Bartlett* v. *Barclay's Bank Trust Co.*, 1980.) If a trustee is careless or fails to comply strictly with the terms of the trust he may be personally liable for losses. He will not, however, be liable for mere accidental losses or errors of judgment. A trustee must actively consider exercising all his powers—Equity does not countenance a sleeping trustee. He must obtain control of the trust property and must collect all debts owing to the trust, taking legal action if this is necessary.

(*b*) **Investment.** The Trustee Investments Act, 1961, gives trustees statutory power to invest up to one half of the trust fund in the ordinary shares of companies. The remainder must be invested in safer items, such as National Savings Certificates, government stocks and local authority loans. These statutory powers are often extended by a clause in the trust instrument which may give unrestricted powers of investment. Trustees must select investments of a type suitable to the trust and must secure a balance between income-producing and capital-producing investments so that all beneficiaries are treated fairly.

(*c*) **Trustees must not profit from their trust.** This rule is strictly applied. If a trustee makes a profit to which he is not entitled he must account for it to the beneficiaries: *Keech* v. *Sandford* (see above).

(*d*) **Delegation of duties.** A trustee can employ and pay an agent provided the agent is employed in his proper field e.g. a solicitor to prepare a mortgage deed, a surveyor to carry out a valuation. However, a trustee cannot delegate his discretions; he must always consider these himself, e.g. he may employ a stockbroker to give advice on investments and to make the investments, but the decision as to the choice of investments must be made by the trustee himself.

(*e*) **Keeping accounts.** Trustees must keep proper accounts and must produce them for inspection by a beneficiary.

(*f*) **Variation of trusts.** If all the beneficiaries are of full age and capacity and are entitled to the whole beneficial interest in the trust, they may together authorize the trustees to deal with the trust in any manner desired. Apart from this the trustees have no power to vary the trust. However, under the Variation of Trusts Act, 1958, where the beneficiaries belong to certain specified classes (e.g. those under incapacity by age or unsoundness of mind), the court may approve an arrangement varying or revoking any of the trusts or enlarging the trustees' powers. The court must be satisfied that the variation is for the benefit of those persons on whose behalf it is giving its approval.

(*g*) **Remuneration of trustees.** A trustee is not permitted to charge for his services unless authorized (i) by the trust instrument, (ii) by all the beneficiaries if of full age and capacity, or (iii) by the court. A trustee is entitled to be reimbursed out of the trust funds for any expenses properly incurred by him in the performance of his duties.

11. Liability for Breaches of Trust

Where a loss occurs to the trust estate from some improper act, neglect, default or omission of the trustee, the following actions are available to the beneficiaries:

(i) An action against the trustees to compensate the trust for the loss sustained.

(ii) A criminal prosecution in certain cases (Theft Act, 1968).

(iii) 'Following' the trust property (see below).

A trustee is liable only for his own acts or defaults. He is not liable for losses occasioned by the acts or defaults of his co-trustees or of other persons with whom trust money is deposited, unless this happens through his own wilful default (section 30, Trustee Act, 1925). 'Wilful default' means deliberate intention to commit a breach of trust, or reckless carelessness as to whether there is a breach of trust or not.

Where more than one trustee is liable for a breach of trust, their liability is joint and several. Thus, the beneficiaries may sue any one or more of those trustees liable for the breach and may recover from them the whole amount of the loss. Where a single trustee is compelled to satisfy a claim, he may recover by way of contribution from his co-trustees such amount as the court thinks just (Civil Liability (Contribution) Act, 1978).

In three cases a trustee will be bound to indemnify his co-trustees:

(i) Where the trustee is a solicitor to the trust and the breach of trust was committed on his advice.

(ii) Where the trustee has obtained the benefit of the breach of trust.

(iii) Where one of the trustees is a beneficiary, and in particular where he (the beneficiary) instigated the breach, the breach will be made good out of his interest so far as possible.

12. Following the Trust Property (Tracing)

This remedy is best understood by example. Suppose that *X*, a trustee, holds a valuable painting in trust for *B*. If *X*, in breach of trust, sells the painting to *Q*, the question arises as to whether the beneficiary, *B*, can sue *Q* for the return of the painting. *B* has a right of action against *X* for the money realized on his sale. If *Q* had no notice, actual or constructive, that the painting bought by him was held in trust, he may keep the painting. *Q* in this case falls within the category of a person who *bona fide* (i.e. in good faith) purchased trust property without notice that it is such, and he will be protected. *B*'s only remedy is against *X*, the trustee. If instead of selling the painting to *Q*, *X* had *given* it to him, the beneficiary (*B*) may lawfully claim the painting from *Q*, for the latter is not a *bona fide* purchaser. Therefore the beneficiary can follow (i.e. trace) the trust property.

Another example of tracing is where the trustee, in breach of trust, uses trust money to purchase an asset, say land. The beneficiaries can trace into the land, i.e. they can claim the land because it is identifiable as their property, albeit in a different form.

If a trustee or a recipient of trust property (e.g. money) mixes it with his own, special tracing rules apply that are outside the scope of this book.

A tracing claim has two important advantages over a personal action for damages. First, if a person who has received trust property becomes bankrupt, a beneficiary who can trace will in effect gain priority over that bankrupt's creditors. Secondly, a beneficiary may reap the benefit of any increase in the value of property into which he can trace.

13. Relief from Liability for Breach

The standard of care required of a trustee is high. Some breaches occur even though there was no deliberate intent to defraud or harm the beneficiaries or diminish the trust fund. Accordingly, relief may be granted by the court to a trustee if he has acted honestly and reasonably and ought fairly to be excused (section 61, Trustee Act, 1925).

Under the Limitation Act, 1980, an action for breach of trust cannot usually be brought more than six years from the date of the breach. Exceptions to this rule may be made where there has been fraud by the trustee, or other circumstances obtained which prevented the time from running, e.g. where a breach was not discovered until some time after it was committed.

14. Exercises

1. Define a trust, and give a short history of its development.
2. What are 'the three certainties' of an express private trust?
3. When is a trust said to be completely constituted?
4. What is (i) a 'resulting trust' and (ii) a 'constructive trust'?
5. What are the four heads of charitable trusts laid down in *Income Tax Special Commissioners* v. *Pemsel* (1891)?
6. Certain special rules apply to charitable trusts. Describe them. What are the main provisions of the Charities Act, 1960?
7. What is a 'trust corporation'? What advantages have these over other types of trustee?
8. 'Equity never wants for a trustee.' Explain.
9. What are the main duties of a trustee? What standard of care must a trustee adopt in regard to trust property? May he delegate any of his duties? If so, to whom?
10. What types of action are available to a beneficiary who alleges breach of trust and loss of trust funds caused by a trustee?
11. Describe the advantages of a tracing claim over a personal action for damages.

10

THE LAW OF PROPERTY

1. Ownership

Ownership has been described as 'the entirety of the powers of use and disposal allowed by law' (Pollock: *First Book of Jurisprudence*). The owner of a thing has an aggregate of rights, namely (i) the right of enjoyment, (ii) the right of destruction, and (iii) the right of disposition, subject to the rights of others. Thus if *A* owns a hat he can wear it, alter it, burn it, or merely throw it away. There are, however, limits to these rights. If *A* throws his hat at *B*, this might be an assault on *B* (or a battery if the hat strikes him), for under the general law *B* has a right not to be interfered with. Similarly in regard to land, *A* may enjoy and use his land, he may sell it or give it away; but his use of his land is subject to the rights of others as allowed by law, e.g. in nuisance and tort. Today a landowner's rights are much circumscribed by legislation aimed at social control, e.g. the Town and Country Planning Act, 1971. Permission for any change in the use of the land owned has to be obtained from the local planning authorities. Moreover, Government departments and local authorities may compulsorily acquire privately-owned land and use it for public purposes, e.g. as a site for a school or college. A person may own land notwithstanding that another has an easement, such as a right of way, over it.

As already mentioned, the ownership of land grew out of possession. An early landowner's rights were possessory, and in medieval law his title to the land was based on the concept of *seisin* (a possessory right). The word 'ownership' was not found in use in England before 1583, and the word 'property' was uncommon before the nineteenth century. People spoke of 'possessions' and 'estates'.

In course of time the idea of ownership grew with an advancing industrial and capitalistic economy. The *right of possession* changed into the *right of ownership* which we know today.

Ownership may be acquired in the following ways.

(*a*) **Originally.** Ownership may be thus obtained by (i) *creating* something, e.g. a clay jar or a picture; (ii) *occupation*, where a person claims something not owned by anyone, e.g. a wild bird or animal, or by occupation of property abandoned by another; or (iii) *accession*, e.g. if *A* owns an animal which begets young, the young animals become the property of *A* by accession.

(*b*) **Derivatively**, through sale, gift or compulsory acquisition by law, e.g. where goods or land are compulsorily acquired by statute, or taken by distress in execution of judgment.

(*c*) **By Succession.** On the death of a previous owner another person may succeed to the property and thus acquire ownership, e.g. a beneficiary under a will.

2. Possession

Possession in law is based on possession in fact. It involves two concepts:

(*a*) the *corpus possessionis*, meaning the control over the thing itself which may be exercised by a person, his servant or his agent; and

(*b*) the *animus possidendi*, which is the intent to exercise exclusive possession of the thing itself and thus to prevent others from using it.

Possession is, therefore, largely a question of fact, as is borne out by common experience. Thus, if *A* lends a fountain-pen to *B* for his examinations, *B* is in temporary physical possession of the pen. If *A* sends his shoes to the shoe repairer, *B*, to be mended, the shoe repairer possesses them while the articles are under repair. In each case *B* is known as a **bailee** in law. The *ownership* of the pen and the shoes remains in both cases with *A*, while the *possession* resides with others who exercise temporary control.

Possession may be obtained lawfully and unlawfully. Lawful possession needs no explanation, as the above examples demonstrate. As to unlawful possession we may note that if *X*, a thief, steals *Y*'s watch, *X* acquires possession but *not* ownership. Clearly *X* acquires no rights to the watch as against the lawful owner. Moreover, if *X* sells the watch to another person, *Z*, the rights of ownership in *Y* are not destroyed. Nevertheless the thief has possession, and usually endeavours to maintain exclusive control over the thing stolen until such time as he decides to sell it, discard it or throw it away.

It is possible to possess things without being aware of them. I possess the books in my library, even though they may be individual books on my shelves whose existence or particular disposition I have forgotten. I nevertheless control them and, as I have the intent to exclude others, I possess them in law. Possession is not lost even though I may have temporarily mislaid an article.

In English law even wrongful possession may, if continued for a length of time, ripen into a claim which is indistinguishable from ownership itself. Thus, where a squatter occupies derelict land or land in respect of which the true owner is unknown or untraceable, and continues in uninterrupted possession for twelve years, using it in a way inconsistent with the true owner's right, the owner's title to the land is destroyed. The squatter thereupon acquires a lawful title of ownership with rights against the whole world.

Although possession is, as we have noted, largely a question of fact, it also has considerable legal significance. When we speak of 'possession being nine points of the law' we refer to the legal rights attaching to possession itself and to the protection given to it by law. First, actual possession is evidence (though not conclusive evidence) of ownership. Proof of ownership of a thing is sometimes difficult. Let us suppose that I purchase a dictionary from a bookshop. I may not keep the receipt, and there may be many similar dictionaries. Conclusive and incontrovertible proof that the dictionary is mine becomes difficult. I may only be able to prove that it is mine by my signature on the book and by my having had possession of it for some time so that I can identify it.

Similarly it is sometimes difficult to prove ownership of land. *A* may claim that he owns land by right of inheritance or purchase from some other person, *C*, who may be able to prove ownership or 'a good root of title', e.g. by a deed showing the devolution of the property on himself. If one can go back far into the past, the title may be traced ultimately to someone who took possession, so originating the ownership of the particular portion of land in dispute. All ownership of land finally derives from possession. *A*'s claim may, of course, be defeated by a rival claimant, *C*, who can prove that he or his predecessor in title was in possession or that *A* wrongfully dispossessed *C*. The law has always protected the rights of possession.

Secondly, the law protects possession by various procedural rules. Suppose *X* possesses something (e.g. a pen) to which *Y* lays claim. If the latter uses force in retaking (called in law *recaption*), the physical act of recovery may involve an assault or breach of the peace for which *Y* may be held responsible. As regards premises, the Criminal Law Act, 1977, provides that squatters may be charged with criminal offences in certain circumstances.

A finder of goods is entitled to them as against all persons other than the true owner (*Hannah* v. *Peel*, 1945). As a general rule the right to take action in respect of trespass to land inheres in the occupier (i.e. the person in possession), for it is the right of possession or the enjoyment of possession which is disturbed or infringed by trespass.

Finally, we may note the law's acknowledgment that wrongful possession of land for twelve years, and goods for six years, may mature into lawful ownership, thereby destroying the previous owner's title and even his legal right to recover the land or goods by action (Limitation Act, 1980).

3. Property

The word 'property' has several meanings, and in law we must be careful to distinguish between two of them.

(i) Property may mean the thing or things *capable* of ownership. In this sense the word includes not only physical (or corporeal) things such as a pen, desk, watch, and land, but also non-physical (incorporeal) things such as patent rights, copyrights, debts, etc. This is the popular sense of the term 'property'.

(ii) Property may mean *ownership*. Thus, we may say in law that '*A* has the property in a watch', or in other words, '*A* owns a watch'. Both statements mean the same. In a sale of goods where, for example, a

PROPERTY RIGHTS

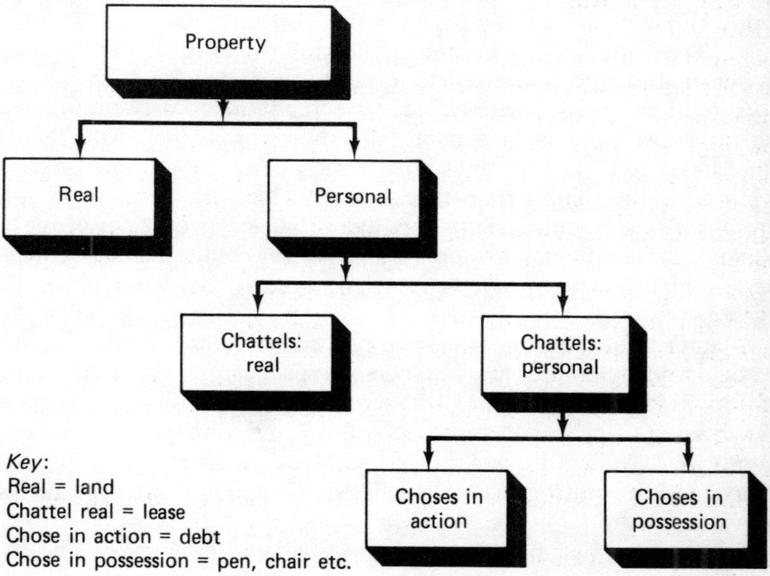

student buys a pen, the shopkeeper delivers the pen to the buyer, and, at the same time, the shopkeeper passes 'the property in the goods' (i.e. the ownership) to the buyer by delivery on the sale.

Classification of Property. English law has classified property in various ways. Land, the main source of wealth, is by the very nature of things treated differently from most other kinds of property, as we shall see later. Property may be divided into two classes:

(*a*) *Real Property* (i.e. freehold interests in land); and

(*b*) *Personal Property*, which may be subdivided into (i) *Chattels Real* and (ii) *Chattels Personal.*

'Chattels real' means leaseholds in land. 'Chattels personal' comprises *choses in action* and *choses in possession.*

The meaning of the terms mentioned above are explained in the following pages.

Real Property. In medieval law property was said to be 'real' if the courts of law would restore to a dispossessed owner the thing (*res*) itself. For example, if *A*, the owner of freehold land (the term freehold will be explained later) were dispossessed or evicted or turned out of his land by *B*, *A* could bring a 'real' action against *B* for the recovery of the land.

If *B* took away, let us say, a horse and harness owned by *A*, the remedy available to *A* was a personal action at civil law against *B* for the recovery of the specific property (i.e. the horse and harness) or its value. The horse and the harness in the present example are referred to as **personalty**; land is referred to as **realty**.

A right *in rem* (sometimes called a real right) corresponds to a right against persons in general. In other words, the owner of the right has a right against the whole world not to be interfered with in relation to the thing (the *res*), e.g. land, which he owns. A right *in personam* is a personal right only against one person or a group of persons; the commonest example is an ordinary contract made between, say, *A* and *B* where each has a right against the other under the agreement.

As a result of these historical and procedural rules, a distinction was made between real property and personal property, and the distinction continues to this day. On the Continent, and in most other legal systems, the division of property is into 'movables' and 'immovables'. Land is immovable, while all other things which can be taken up and carried away (and are not permanently affixed to the land) are regarded as movable.

The term 'real property' in general signifies all interests in land. An important exception exists in regard to **leaseholds**, or 'terms of years' as they are sometimes called. A leasehold arises, for example, where *A*, the owner of land, grants to *B* a lease for (say) two years. *A* is called a lessor, and *B* is a lessee.

A dispossessed leaseholder had no right at law to recover the land from anyone except the lessor who granted the lease. Until the thirteenth century the lessee could recover damages, but not possession. Later, in 1499, a lessee was permitted to recover the land itself by action. The law had by this time come to look upon leases as personalty, and has done so ever since. A lease has, therefore, acquired a different status in the eye of the law. Even today, if for example *X* dies leaving his realty to *A* and his personalty to *B*, any leaseholds held by *X* on his death will pass to *B*.

The relationship of landlord to tenant is mainly contractual; the tenant pays the rent to the landlord who for his part agrees to allow the tenant to occupy the land or house, as the case may be. The lease in law is classified as personalty, but it is also specially described as a **chattel real**. The word 'chattel' derives from the Latin *cattala* (cattle) and means in general terms 'goods'. The word 'real' signifies, as we have noted, connexion with land. A lease partakes of both goods and land, and to distinguish it from 'real property' and from 'personal chattels' it is called a chattel real.

Chattels Personal. There are, as we have noted, two types: (i) choses in possession, and (ii) choses in action. The word 'chose', derived from the French, means in law 'a thing'.

Choses in possession. The characteristic of a chose in possession is that it is a physical thing and can be touched. A pen, book, chair, and a horse are all choses in possession. As each has a physical existence, they are sometimes called corporeal (i.e. material) chattels to distinguish them from the so-called choses in action.

Choses in action. The main characteristic of a chose in action is that it can be owned but not touched. It has no physical existence. A common example is a debt, which is a 'thing' in law yet has no tangible existence. If *A* owes *B* £10, this is obviously of value to *B* who may sue on the debt to recover the amount of £10 from the debtor *A*. We have discussed (see p. 185) the transfer or assignment of the right which *B* has. Provided that certain formalities are complied with, *B* may assign to *C*, a third party, the right to the debt and the right to sue *A*.

The phrase 'chose in action' provides a clue to another characteristic. It is not possible to take *physical* possession of a debt, but it is possible to assert the right by taking *legal action* for the debt, hence it is called a chose *in action.*

Other examples of choses in action include patent rights, copyrights, rights in trade marks, stocks and shares, registered designs, goodwill of a business, insurance moneys, and cheques.

All rights existing in the items listed above can be protected or enforced or transferred at law by taking action, if need be, in the courts. But we must be careful to distinguish the thing itself from the rights which attach to it. A cheque, for example, is in common experience merely a piece of paper on which appear words and figures. That is its physical manifestation. However, *in law* it represents certain rights, the most important of which is the right (enforceable by action) to payment of a sum of money.

4. Freehold and Leasehold Land

The basic rule of English land law is, as we have noted elsewhere, that all land in England is owned by the Crown. When William I defeated the English, he made grants of land to his followers, to certain of the English barons and to those who submitted to his control. The grantees thereupon became holders or 'tenants' of the land. Since under feudal law there could not be two owners (the King was lord paramount and owned the land by right of conquest), it follows that the interest in the land possessed or held by a grantee was certainly less than that of the royal grantor.

Tenure. The grants of land were made in return for services to be rendered by the tenant. The terms on which the tenant held (called the tenure) were of various kinds. The chief division was between free and unfree tenure. **Free tenure** included the following:

FEUDAL TENURE

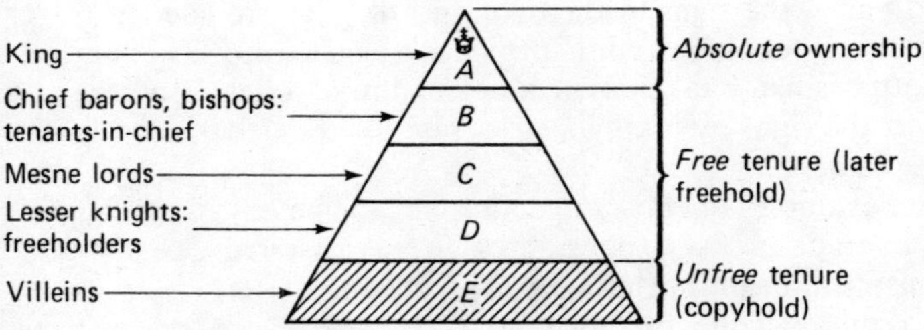

A grants land to *B* in return for services,
B grants land to *C* in return for services,
C to *D*, and *D* to *E* in return for services.

(i) *Military Tenure*. This consisted in the provision of armed horsemen and knights for a certain number of days in each year (Knight Service).

(ii) *Spiritual Tenure*. This consisted in praying for the lord and saying masses for him. Spiritual tenure was sometimes called Frankalmoign.

(iii) *Socage Tenure*. This consisted of services of a non-military kind, usually agricultural, e.g. provision of crops and beasts to a lord.

(iv) *Serjeanty*. This consisted of a personal service to the King or a lord.

These forms of tenure were for *fixed* services. Once the specified services were performed by the tenant, his time was his own and he was free to use the land as he desired. In course of time all four tenures became known as **freehold**, as distinct from copyhold (villeinage) tenure or **unfree tenure**.

Medieval serfs (or villeins) held their land by unfree tenure. The villeins were bound to their lord, and they were at his beck and call to do whatsoever he willed. Their services were not defined or limited as were those of free tenure. They were in a real sense bound to the soil and could not leave the holding. In the course of time the tenure of land became known as **copyhold**, because a tenant's right to land depended on the possession of a copy of the rolls of the manorial court kept by the steward of the court. Copyhold tenure was finally abolished in 1922, the land becoming freehold.

LAND GRANTS

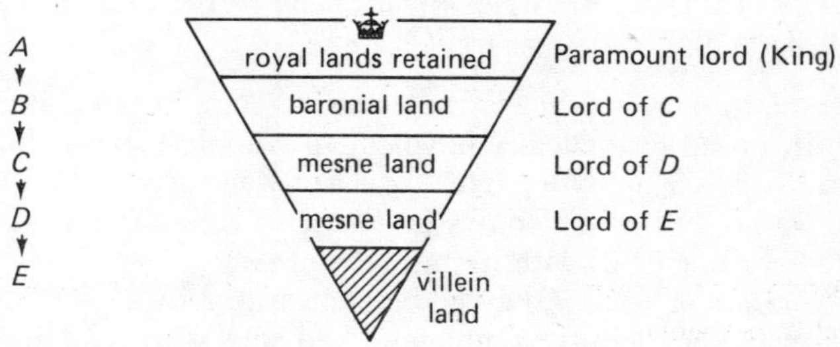

B held land of *A* (King) as tenant-in-chief.
C held of *B*, and *D* of *C*. Sub-infeudation (i.e. grant of land to another over whom the grantor became lord) was abolished by Statute of *Quia Emptores*, 1289.

In the limited space available it is impossible to give more than a very brief outline of the history of the land. The accompanying diagram shows the structure of the feudal grants of land, and the sub-grants made by one person to another. Where a person sub-granted a freehold estate to two or more other tenants to hold of him, he became a 'lord of the manor'. Subinfeudation, as this process was called, was stopped by the statute of *Quia Emptores*, 1289.

The feudal system broke down in the Middle Ages, and the various forms of tenure already described disappeared after 1660, with the exception of socage tenure which was retained as the only form of free tenure.

An important point to note in early land law is that a person *possessed* land. That possession which a freeholder of land had or enjoyed was of a special kind known as *seisin*. Seisin was, therefore, the interest of a freeholder in his land. His right of seisin was protected in the courts of common law and was enforced against all persons except those with a prior right to seisin acquired by lawful means.

The Meaning of Estate. A person who owned the seisin in land owned in truth a collection of rights in relation to the land. The tenant's interest in his land was known as his **estate**. Estates in land were of various kinds and they differed as to the length of time for which they might exist. The word 'estate' does not in law mean the vast rolling acres often implied in the everyday use of the word.

Classification of Estates. Estates are classified according to the duration of a tenant's rights to the land as either

(*a*) Estates of freehold (of uncertain length of duration), or

(*b*) Estates less than freehold (e.g. leaseholds), where the duration is either certain or may be ascertained from the terms of the grant.

Estates of freehold may be subdivided into: (i) estates in fee simple; (ii) estates in fee tail; (iii) estates for life; and (iv) estates *pur autre vie* ('for another's life').

(i) *The estate in fee simple* is the greatest estate in land which may be held. In broad terms it is equivalent to complete ownership; so if in common speech today we refer to *A* as owner of a certain portion of land, we imply that he enjoys an estate in fee simple in the land. This estate will be dealt with in more detail later.

(ii) *The estate in fee tail* may be best illustrated by example. Where a father owned lands in fee simple and had sons who were dependent on him, he might wish to make a grant of a portion of land to son *A*, but so limited that the land be kept within the family. He could, therefore, make a grant of an estate in fee tail, which meant that on *A*'s death the land would devolve on *A*'s lineal descendants only. If there were no lineal descendants the estate reverted to the grantor, or, if he were dead, to his (the grantor's) own successors, i.e. his next son.

(iii) *The estate for life*. Where an owner (*X*) in fee simple wished to grant an estate for the life of the grantee only, he could do so at common law. He merely made a formal grant indicating his intentions: 'To *A* for life.' *A* became the owner of a limited estate in that he could not, of course, dispose of the estate by his will. On *A*'s death the land reverted to the grantor, *X*. The interest of *X* was known as an interest in reversion. Sometimes he might wish to make a grant 'To *A* for life, remainder in fee simple to *B*'. In this case the estate would not revert to the grantor, but it would vest in *B*. The interest of *B* was known as an *interest in remainder*, so called because the estate remained away from the grantor, *X*.

(iv) *The estate 'pur autre vie'*, endured for the life of a person other than a tenant. Thus, let us assume *X* is owner in fee simple of land which he grants to *A* in the following terms: 'To *A* for the life of *B*.'

A becomes tenant of the land for the duration of the life of *B*. On *B*'s death the estate terminates, and will revert to the grantor or become vested in some other person to whom the 'remainder' has been granted.

5. Reform of the Land Law

In the course of some 900 years following the Norman invasion, the English land law became highly complex, highly technical, and artificial. The distinction between real property, chattels real, and personal property is one example. The rules of the devolution of property on death differed as to real property and personal property. A multitude of rights and interests in relation to land were created, making the transfer of land a most complicated task and sometimes impossible. Certain interests were legal interests, while others, known as equitable interests, took effect only in equity. Landowners tried to keep the land within their families, and constantly endeavoured to tie up the land so as to prevent alienation (i.e. transfer, by sale or otherwise) by a tenant for life. The public policy of the law was against tying the land up, and hence there arose a battle of wills and wits.

Some attempts at piecemeal reform had been undertaken, but it was left to one of the most famous of English Lord Chancellors, Lord Birkenhead, to undertake a thorough reform of the land law. Lord Birkenhead's reforms resulted in the following five Acts of Parliament.

(i) Law of Property Act, 1925.
(ii) Settled Land Act, 1925.
(iii) Administration of Estates Act, 1925.
(iv) Land Charges Act, 1925.
(v) Land Registration Act, 1925.

The main aims of the 1925 legislation were:

(*a*) To abolish the distinction between real property and chattels real, and to assimilate the law relating to land as far as possible into the law relating to chattels.

(*b*) To simplify land law, and thus to make it cheaper and easier to transfer land.

(*c*) To make the rules for intestate succession the same for all forms of property.

(*d*) To abolish the antiquated form of tenure of land known as copyhold tenure.

(*e*) To reduce the number of *legal* estates in land to two:

(i) a fee simple absolute in possession; and
(ii) a term of years absolute.

(*f*) To reduce the number of legal *interests* to five.

Reduction of the Number of Legal Estates. Under section 1 of the

Law of Property Act, 1925, the number of legal estates and interests which can exist in land has been reduced as follows:

(*a*) The only estates in land which are capable of subsisting or of being conveyed or created at law are:

(i) an estate in fee simple absolute in possession; and
(ii) a term of years absolute.

(*b*) The only interests or charges in or over land which are capable of subsisting or of being conveyed or created at law are:

(i) An easement, right or privilege for an interest equivalent to either of the above estates. (Thus 'an easement for life' would not be a *legal* interest.)

(ii) A rentcharge in possession issuing out of or charged on land being either perpetual or for a term of years absolute. (A rentcharge is a right which, independently of any lease or mortgage, entitles the owner of it to a periodical sum of money with the payment of which the land is charged. For example, where the owner in fee simple of Whiteacre charges the land with the payment of £500 per annum for John Smith.)

(iii) A charge by way of legal mortgage.

(iv) Land tax and other similar charge on land which is not created by an instrument. (This means a land tax, etc. created by a statute.)

(v) Rights of entry exercisable over or in respect of a legal term of years absolute, or annexed, for any purpose, to a legal rentcharge.

It should be noted that the section does not provide that all the estates and interests mentioned at (*a*) and (*b*) are necessarily *legal*, but no *other* estate or interest can be a *legal* estate or interest. All other estates in land can now only exist as *equitable* interests.

6. An Estate in Fee Simple Absolute in Possession

This is one of the two estates in land which since 1925 may exist as *legal* estates. The expression is admittedly a technical one, but the meaning may be ascertained by analysis of each of the terms used.

'Fee' denotes that the estate is an estate of inheritance, i.e. one that may be inherited under the laws of intestacy or given by will.

'Simple' denotes that the estate is not a fee tail (an estate limited to certain lineal descendants only of the grantee). 'Simple' means that the estate is capable of passing to the *general heirs* of the grantee.

'Absolute' signifies the grant is not subject to a condition but will continue for ever, and distinguishes it from a fee or an estate which may be determinable on the happening of an event.

'In Possession' signifies that the grantee must be entitled to immediate possession of the estate. This *may* be physical possession, though not necessarily, for the phrase 'in possession' includes 'the receipt of rents

and profits and the right to receive rents and profits'. A grantee need not, therefore, take physical possession to qualify as being 'in possession'.

A tenant in fee simple absolute in possession is, for all practical purposes, in the same position as owner. Those ownership rights extend down to the centre of the earth and up to the sky (*usque ad inferos et usque ad caelum*). An owner is not, of course, absolutely free to do what he likes with his own property, be it land or any other thing. As we have noted elsewhere, he is subject to the general law of torts, including nuisance, negligence, and particularly to modern statute law which circumscribes the rights of the individual owner in the interest of the community, e.g. Town and Country Planning Acts. Moreover, certain mineral rights (e.g. coal, iron ore, and petroleum) in an owner's land have been taken away and vested in the State.

Creation of an Estate in Fee Simple Absolute in Possession. It is clear that a legal owner of land wishing to transfer the ownership may do so in various ways, e.g. gift, sale or by will. Land is transferred by means of a **conveyance**, which is a legal document conveying the ownership of the property from one person to another. Words in the conveyance must be used with exactness to define or delimit the right to be transferred. The words marking out the interest in the land to be taken by another are known as 'words of limitation'.

The common law rules on words of limitation were exceedingly strict, but section 60 of the Law of Property Act, 1925, states that the 'grantee will take the whole interest which the grantor had power to convey in such land, unless a contrary intention appears in the conveyance'. Today, therefore, where *X* who, let us say, owns the fee simple in Blackacre, wishes to transfer the land to *Y* he may 'convey Blackacre to *Y*'. In such a case *Y* will 'take the fee simple in the land known as Blackacre'. The same rules regarding words of limitation apply to wills as to conveyances.

Words of limitation must be distinguished from 'words of purchase'. Words of limitation *define* or *delimit* an estate or interest; words of purchase *confer* one. To make this clearer, let us suppose that a grant of land is made thus:

(*a*) 'To *A* and his heirs.' The entire phrase is taken together to delimit *A*'s estate. *A* receives the fee simple estate which he can thereupon sell or give away or leave by will. There is no interest conveyed to the heirs.

(*b*) 'To *X* for life, remainder to *Y*.' The effect of this grant is that *X* takes a life interest, and on *X*'s death the estate will pass to *Y*. The effect of the words of purchase here is to confer an interest on the two persons, *X* and *Y*.

In example (*a*) the words are words of limitation. In example (*b*) the words are words of purchase, since they define or mark out and *confer* the estate or interest to be taken by *X* and *Y*. Words of purchase do not necessarily mean that the recipient bought the estate. They mean that the estate or interest was handed over by grant which may take the form of a sale or a gift, as distinct from entitlement arising by operation of law (as when an owner dies intestate).

To understand the meaning and legal effect of the phrase 'an estate in fee simple absolute in possession', it is useful to mention some forms of grant which may be made today and to consider what interest passes to the grantee. A grantor may today use such phrases as 'To *X* for life'; 'To *X* and the heirs of his body'; 'To *X* provided he adopts the name of Dickens'; 'To *X* in fee simple absolute from 1984'; 'To *X* in fee simple'; and 'To *X* and his heirs'.

The common law had formed rigid rules of interpretation before 1925, and these have been carried over into current use. They must now, however, be interpreted in the light of the Law of Property Act, 1925 and its provisions.

(i) *'To X for life.'* A grant in this form does not create a legal estate. It is of limited duration and can now take effect only as an equitable interest.

(ii) *'To X and the heirs of his body.'* This again does not create a legal estate. This form of words formerly created an entailed estate capable of being inherited only by the lineal descendants of *X*. It now creates an entailed interest which is equitable.

(iii) *'To X provided he adopts the name of Dickens.'* This does not create a legal estate, for it is not absolute, being subject to the condition of the adoption of the name Dickens.

(iv) *'To X in fee simple absolute from 1984.'* This does not create a legal estate. It does not take effect in possession, being postponed until 1984. It is not of certain duration since *X* may not be alive in 1984.

(v) *'To X in fee simple.'* This does create a legal estate in fee simple absolute in possession. The Conveyancing Act, 1881, enabled this phrase to be used to convey the whole interest of the grantor. Where the date for possession is not mentioned the estate is deemed to take effect in possession immediately, i.e. forthwith.

(vi) *'To X and his heirs.'* This phrase creates a legal estate in fee simple absolute in possession. The words here used are words of limitation and not words of purchase. The mention of the words 'his heirs' does not transfer to them any interest in the property.

The interests in (i), (ii), (iii), and (iv) which are passed will take effect, if they take effect at all, as equitable interests. Only in cases (v) and (vi) do the words create a legal estate, i.e. a fee simple absolute in possession.

7. Future Estates

Before 1925 there were three main varieties of future legal estates:

(*a*) Reversions and remainders
(*b*) Shifting and springing uses
(*c*) Executory devises.

(*a*) *Reversions and Remainders.* Where a grant of land is made by a tenant in fee simple to another for life or in fee tail, the grantor loses his right to present possession and enjoyment of his land. His estate becomes a future estate, and is called a **reversion**.

Suppose the tenant (*A*) owner in fee simple of Blackacre makes the following grant: 'To *B* for life.' When *B*'s life comes to an end, the 'particular estate' carved out of *A*'s fee simple estate also ends, and the estate reverts to *A* in possession. The same rule applied to the fee tail when the lineal descendants of the grantee became extinct.

Where a grant was made by *A* (fee simple owner of Blackacre): 'To *B* for life, then to *C* in fee simple', the future interest to be taken by *C* was known as a *remainder*. And even if *C* died before *B*, the effect would be that *C*'s heirs would take the fee simple in Blackacre.

The tenant for life and the tenant of the fee tail estate were known as 'limited owners', as distinct from the tenant in fee simple when in possession who was a full owner.

(*b*) *Shifting and Springing Uses.* These kinds of future interests were created by means of a trust (which evolved from the medieval 'use'), and were always equitable as they are today.

(*c*) *Executory Devises.* These future interests were created by means of wills. The details need not concern us.

8. Settlements and Trusts for Sale

In former times where a person owned considerable land he would not infrequently consider some ways in which he might provide for his family out of his resources. It was also a matter of family pride to keep the land within the family. These were the main reasons for the creation of family settlements.

A settlement is a legal instrument by which land or other property is limited in trust for a number of persons successively. Settlements fall into two classes: (*a*) strict settlements, and (*b*) settlements by way of trust for sale.

(*a*) **Strict Settlements.** The means adopted to keep the land within the family was the trust (see p. 248). The land was so limited that it descended as a whole from father to the eldest son. If the father had no son, it was so arranged that the land descended to daughters. The claims of the other members of the family, i.e. his wife (or widow), and other sons and daughters dependent upon the father, were satisfied by giving them an income or capital sum charged upon the land.

We remember that before 1 January 1926, the life estate and the estate tail existed as legal estates. These forms were used to effect the intention of the creator of the trust or settlement.

The operation of the strict settlement may best be explained by example. Let us go back in time to before 1926 and suppose that William Smith was the owner of property known as Blackacre and that he was about to marry Jane. He would execute a so-called 'marriage settlement', transferring his estate in Blackacre to trustees on the following trusts.

(i) To William Smith (himself) to hold for a life interest in Blackacre.

(ii) With remainder to his eldest son in tail, and successive remainders should the eldest son die without issue.

(iii) A provision for his wife (Jane), i.e. an annual payment (called a *jointure*) to her during her widowhood.

(iv) A provision for other children of the marriage who would be granted *portions*, i.e. capital sums of money raised out of the estate in Blackacre.

The jointure to the wife and the portions to the children were secured on the property by means of a *rentcharge*. Payment of these annual sums was a first charge on the proceeds and profits arising out of the land. These grants could be enforced at law (they were legal grants) and the person liable could be sued for them, if need be. The person liable was the life tenant or other person entitled to the estate.

Let us now suppose that William Smith had a son, Robert Smith, and that Robert Smith reached 21 years. It was the practice when the son reached maturity for the father and the son to join together to make a resettlement of the property. The land was then re-conveyed to the trustees in trust to hold on the following terms:

(i) To William Smith for the rest of his life.

(ii) An annual charge upon the land is secured to Robert Smith, with remainder to Robert Smith for life, with remainder to Robert Smith's son in tail.

On the death of William Smith, Robert Smith would, as life tenant, take the place of his father. In due time when he himself had a son, Robert Smith would make a similar resettlement with his eldest son to avoid the possibility of the son barring the entail. The process was continued generation by generation.

The exact details of these settlements varied from family to family, but the main principles outlined above to keep the land with the Smith family prevailed almost universally among those persons with sufficient land at their disposal. Consequently there was no person, not even the life tenant, having the power of sale. This led to unfortunate consequences, however laudable the family motives might be. The tenant for life had to pay for all repairs, maintenance, taxes, etc. out of his own pocket, and he was unable to pay for improvements or to secure capital for these. But his chief limitation was that he was unable to sell the estate. In later times increased taxation added to the burdens facing life tenants.

The policy of the law generally was that land ought to be freely alienable, i.e. transferable from person to person, and at long last the Settled Land Act, 1882, and the Settled Land Act, 1925, were passed.

The Settled Land Act, 1925

The Settled Land Act, 1925, applies to settled land and not to land held on trust for sale (to be described later). Since 1 January 1926, where land is settled, the *legal* estate in the land is vested in the tenant for life. He is now in a dual position: he is (i) absolute owner for the purpose of any disposition (e.g. sale) of the land; but as regards his interest under the settlement he is (ii) a trustee of the settled land on behalf of himself and the other beneficiaries under the settlement.

The Act further provides that settlements must now be made by two deeds: (*a*) the vesting deed, and (*b*) the trust instrument.

The **vesting deed** must contain:

(i) a description of the settled land;

(ii) a statement that the land is vested in the life tenant on the trusts of the settlement;

(iii) the names of the settlement trustees;

(iv) the names of the person(s) entitled to appoint additional trustees; and

(v) a statement of any additional powers of the tenant for life over and above those conferred by the Act.

There is no mention in the vesting deed of the trusts upon which the tenant for life holds the land.

The **trust deed**, which is made out at the same time, contains the description of the trusts on which the land is held, i.e. giving the details of the beneficiaries and the interests which each is to have (following the pattern of the settlement already described) which will necessarily be equitable interests.

Where a settlement arises under a will, the will itself is treated as the trust instrument, and the testator's personal representatives (the executors of the will) hold the land on trust to vest the legal estate in the first person entitled as life tenant. This is done by means of a vesting assent in writing.

The advantage of creating these two instruments (vesting deed and trust instrument) is that a purchaser of the land is normally only permitted to examine the vesting deed which deals with the legal estate he is purchasing. As far as the purchaser is concerned, the owner of the land is the tenant for life—not the trustees. The details of the trust on which the land has been settled, contained in the trust deed, are not disclosed to the buyer. They lie behind the curtain of the vesting deed, and they can be overreached by the purchaser of the land, provided the purchase money is paid to the trustees of the settlement, not to the tenant for life. It is the duty of the trustees on receipt of the purchase price to ensure that the trusts of the settlement are discharged, i.e. by paying to the beneficiaries their interests which attach to the money, and not to the land once sale has taken place. This is what is meant by 'overreaching'.

The Settled Land Act, 1925, also lays down the powers of the tenant for life concerning the settled land. These powers include the general management of the settled property, in regard to which he may use his own discretion. But, to protect the interests of the beneficiaries of the settlement, the tenant may exercise certain powers only after giving notice to the trustees, or, in some cases, obtaining their consent. Thus consent is required where the tenant for life proposes to sell the principal mansion house, to cut and sell timber, to use capital money for improvements, and to modify restrictive covenants attaching to the land.

(*b*) **Trusts for Sale.** The strict settlement just described must be distinguished from a settlement by way of trust for sale. In the latter case the purpose of creating a trust was not to keep the land in the family but to sell the land and to provide a regular income for the beneficiaries out of the money realized on the sale. Accordingly the trust for sale imposes on the trustees an absolute duty to sell the land, and to hold the proceeds of the sale and the rents and profits until the sale for the beneficiaries.

The trustees were usually given power to postpone the sale at their discretion and to manage the land until the sale. As long as it produced a satisfactory income, the land could be retained. Often the consent of the beneficiaries under the trust was made necessary before a sale could take place.

The effect of creating a trust for sale was that, even before sale, the rights of the beneficiaries were deemed to be rights in personalty, not in the land. Since there was a *binding obligation* to sell the land, the beneficiaries were treated as having immediate interests in the purchase money into which the land would ultimately be converted; but they had no interest in the land itself. This doctrine, known as **conversion**, is based on the principle that equity 'looks upon that as done which ought to be done'. Thus from the moment of the conveyance of the property to the trustees, whether there has been an actual sale or not, the land is regarded in equity as if it were *purchase money* already.

In a trust for sale there is no need for a 'tenant for life'. The trustees exercise the power of sale, since they are the legal owners. Moreover, under section 28(1) of the Law of Property Act, the trustees for sale are given all the powers of a tenant for life under a settlement, e.g. they have power to exchange the land for other land, to grant leases, to obtain mortgages, to manage the property and to make improvements to the land. The trustees may delegate their powers of leasing, accepting surrenders of leases, and management, at any time before sale to 'any person of full age for the time being beneficially entitled in possession to the rents and profits' under the terms of the trust.

Since the rights which encumber the land are (in theory) rights only in respect of a share of the purchase money, notice of them will have no effect upon a purchaser. Once the latter pays the trustees on the sale, the distribution of the money among those beneficially entitled is the responsibility and business of the trustees; the purchaser takes the land free from those interests, which again are said to be over-reached. There is, therefore, no need for special machinery (e.g. the making of two deeds) to conceal these rights. Although only one deed is strictly necessary in a trust for sale, in practice and for the sake of simplicity two are generally used.

Trusts for sale may arise (*a*) expressly, as where land is deliberately limited by a settlor on trust for sale, or (*b*) by operation of law. The most common circumstances under which a trust for sale arises by operation of law are:

(i) where there is co-ownership of land by two or more persons (Law of Property Act, 1925, s. 36); and

(ii) where a person dies intestate (Administration of Estates Act, 1925, s. 33).

9. Co-ownership

Although property rights in relation to land are often held by one person only at a time, it is, of course, possible for two or more persons to own land together, e.g. a husband and wife may both own the matrimonial home. This form of ownership is known as co-ownership, and is of two kinds: (*a*) joint ownership, and (*b*) ownership in common.

(*a*) **Joint Ownership.** The owners are known as *joint tenants* and each is the owner of the whole land, though, of course, the rights of ownership of each is subject to the right of the other party or parties.

(*b*) **Ownership in Common.** In this case each owner is regarded as owning an individual share in the property though not a specific part, e.g. if there are three owners in common each is entitled to a third.

There are important distinctions between these two forms of ownership. In the first place, a joint tenancy arises where land is conveyed to two or more persons and no words of severance, such as 'in equal shares', are used in the grant. Thus a grant: 'To *A* and *B*', or To *A* and *B* jointly' creates a joint tenancy, while a conveyance 'To *A* and *B* equally', or 'To *A* and *B* in common' creates a tenancy in common. Wherever land is granted in such a way as to suggest that the grantor intends the tenants to have *distinct* shares, even though the land remains physically undivided, a tenancy in common arises. Words which show this intention of distinct shares are known as *words of severance*.

The difference between the two forms of ownership is best observed by looking at the position when one owner (joint or in common) dies. Where a joint owner dies his share in the property passes to the survivor(s). Let us suppose that *A*, *B*, and *C* are joint tenants. When *C* dies his share in the property passes automatically to *A* and *B* equally. When *B* dies his share in the property passes to *A*, who thereupon becomes the sole owner of the land. This is known as the *jus accrescendi* or right of survivorship. If, however, the land is held in common, the deceased owner's share will pass to his heir and does not accrue to the surviving co-tenant. Thus, where *A*, *B*, and *C* are tenants in common, on the death of *C* his share will form part of *C*'s estate and will be disposed of accordingly.

The advantage of the joint tenancy was that it avoided splitting the estate into many different parts, and thus prevents the creation of too many interests in one portion of land. A joint tenant cannot leave any part of the jointly owned property by will. With a joint tenancy there would be only a few persons whose consents and signature are necessary for a sale and conveyance of the land to a purchaser. With land held in common, however, the transfer of ownership raised difficulties as each co-owner had to sign the necessary deeds of transfer or conveyance. Moreover each co-owner may leave his interest by will, thus creating further complications. A joint tenancy as described above is of course unjust in that the right to the sole ownership depends on the length of one's days; and longevity is uncertain.

The Law of Property Act, 1925, amended the law in respect of co-ownership. After 1925 a tenancy in common cannot exist at law and all co-owners (or the first four named in the grant if there are more than four) are joint tenants of the legal estate, which is subject to a trust for sale. The right of survivorship applies to the joint tenancy, so that on the death of one trustee, the legal estate automatically vests equally in the remaining trustees. In equity, however, they and any other co-owners will be either joint tenants or tenants in common according to the terms of the grant or the presumptions of equity. For example, equity will presume a tenancy in common of the equitable estate where two or more purchasers contribute the purchase moneys in unequal shares, or where partners purchase land.

The effect is that anyone buying property from co-owners (joint or in common) is concerned with, at the most, only four persons as legal owners from whom he takes a conveyance of the legal estate. The rights of the co-owners attach to the sum resulting from the sale in proportion to the shares held by each. If, therefore, a co-owner who is a tenant in common in equity dies his heirs will succeed not to his interest in the land, but to his interest in the money realized on the sale and held in trust for them. If a co-owner who is a joint tenant in equity dies, however, the right of survivorship applies to his equitable joint tenancy and his share accrues equally to the other equitable joint tenants. This is the form of co-ownership used very frequently where a husband and wife purchase the matrimonial home as co-owners.

10. Leaseholds

We have already mentioned that before 1925 a freeholder could grant leases of his land to others. Much of the property (land and houses) in the United Kingdom is occupied by tenants under leases. As a result of the 1925 legislation the only legal estate in land other than the fee simple absolute in possession is the **term of years absolute**, which is the interest created by a lease.

The essential nature of a lease is that it is a grant by a landlord to a tenant of exclusive possession of the property leased, together with an intention to create the relationship of landlord and tenant. In doubtful cases it is for the courts to decide whether the agreement (oral, in writing or by conduct) into which the parties have entered is a tenancy agreement in law. The further essential feature of a leasehold interest is that it will start and end at some definite time in the future and will not continue indefinitely, i.e. it is of a determinate nature.

The expression 'a term of years' is misleading in that it includes weekly, monthly, quarterly or yearly tenancies (called **periodic tenancies**), as well as long leases for 99 years or 999 years which are common in practice. Other types of tenancies are known as **tenancies at will**, and **tenancies at sufferance**.

A leasehold interest may subsist as a legal estate even though the tenant is not to take possession at once. Thus a *term of years* can be made to take effect in, say, five years' time. Under section 149(3) of the Law of Property Act, 1925, a term granted at a rent must be limited to take effect within twenty-one years. Any grant purporting to postpone the taking of effect of the term for a longer period than twenty-one years is invalid.

Tenancies

(*a*) **Lease for a Fixed Period.** The characteristics of this tenancy are (i) that it is created by express agreement, and (ii) that the commencement and the termination of the lease must be certain or ascertainable before the lease comes into effect.

(*b*) **Yearly Tenancies.** A yearly tenancy continues from year to year or until determined by proper notice. It may be created (i) expressly, or (ii) by implication, e.g. where a person occupies land with the owner's consent and pays rent which is calculated on an annual basis. The period of notice necessary to determine the tenancy is agreed upon between the parties. If no such agreed notice has been arrived at, a yearly tenancy must be determined by at least half a year's notice to expire at the end of the year of the tenancy; where the tenancy began on one of the official quarter days, this means two-quarters' notice. Quarterly, monthly or weekly tenancies (which are included under this classification) are determined by notice for the full period, i.e. quarter, month or week.

(*c*) **Tenancy at Will.** This arises where a person takes possession of property with the owner's consent (i.e. not as servant or agent) on the understanding that the term can be brought to an end at any time by either party giving notice. The tenancy may be rent-free, but unless this has been expressly agreed between the parties the tenant must pay rent. In addition to notice, the tenancy may come to an end if either landlord or tenant does some act inconsistent with the tenancy and automatically terminates after twelve months. Where there is no agreement as to rent, the tenancy can become a periodic tenancy if the tenant pays and the owner accepts rent paid at given periods of time.

(*d*) **Tenancy at Sufferance.** This can only arise by implication of law. It comes into existence where, on the expiration of his tenancy, a tenant holds over without the landlord's permission. The distinction between this and the tenancy at will is that in the one case the landlord does not consent and in the other he does. No rent is payable, but the tenant must compensate the owner by a payment (called *mesne profits*) for the use and occupation of the land. The tenancy may be brought to an end at any time, or it may be converted into a periodic tenancy if rent is paid and accepted periodically.

Statutory Protection. Because of the shortage of houses and accommodation the Government has more and more interfered in the landlord and tenant relationship which was originally purely contractual. This involves detailed legislation which cannot be described here. The main purpose is to give some degree of security to tenants and to restrict rents. The most important statutes are:

(*a*) The Agricultural Holdings Act, 1948, as amended.

(*b*) The Landlord and Tenant Act, 1954.

(*c*) The Leasehold Reform Act, 1967, under which a tenant holding a long lease may, in certain cases, acquire the freehold or the extended long lease of the house where he resides.

(*d*) The Rent Act, 1977, which imposes certain rent control and gives some security of tenure in respect of unfurnished lettings; and imposes rent control and, again, a limited security in respect of furnished lettings.

Creation of Leases

(*a*) **Leases for more than three years.** This type must be created by deed in order to become a legal estate. A mere written lease (not a deed) creates only an equitable interest which is capable of being converted into a legal estate by order for specific performance. If the lease is merely oral it may be enforced by equity as above, provided that the equitable doctrine of part performance applies (see p. 132).

(*b*) **Leases for not more than three years.** These need not be by deed to be legal; a written or oral lease will suffice, so long as the lease takes effect in possession at once at the best rent obtainable and without payment of a capital sum.

Duties of Landlord and Tenant

In any lease the lessor may require the tenant to sign certain express covenants, e.g. to insure against fire. Apart from these expressed covenants there are certain implied covenants.

Landlord's duties. The following are the main duties owed by the landlord to the tenant:

(*a*) The landlord has to ensure that the tenant gets 'quiet enjoyment' of the land. This does not mean there will be no noise, but that the lessor guarantees to the tenant that no third party will be lawfully able to question the title of the tenant to the land.

(*b*) The landlord must not derogate from his grant, i.e. he must not interfere with the tenant's enjoyment of the premises. He must not, therefore, do anything which would render the land unfit for the purpose for which it was let, e.g. by using the adjoining premises in a manner inconsistent with the lease.

(*c*) The landlord has no obligation to ensure that the premises should be fit for habitation. There is an implied covenant that a furnished house which is let must be fit for human habitation at the time of the letting. Houses let at an annual rental of less than £26 (£40 in London) must be fit for human habitation at the time of letting and maintained in that state during the tenancy (Housing Act, 1957).

(*d*) Certain statutes and cases now impose limited obligations on the landlord to repair.

Tenant's duties. The main duties of the tenant are:

(*a*) To pay the rent.

(*b*) To pay rates and taxes, except those which are legally the landlord's personal obligation.

(*c*) Not to commit waste. This means that he must not do deliberate damage to the property leased or permit it to depreciate unreasonably by neglect.

Express Covenants

The most important express covenants usually contained in a lease are: (i) to pay rent; (ii) to pay rates and taxes; (iii) to repair; (iv) to permit the lessor to enter and inspect the state of repair; (v) to obtain insurance; (vi) not to carry on any trade or business; and (vii) not to assign or underlet without consent.

Two of the above call for mention:

(*a*) **Covenant not to assign or underlet.** Where such a covenant exists, the tenant may neither assign or underlet; in the absence of such a covenant a tenant may do so. In an assignment the lessee parts with his whole interest to the purchaser who becomes in his place the tenant of the freeholder. Such an assignee is bound, as long as he owns the leasehold interest, to observe and perform all the covenants binding on the vendor (the assignor) which touch and concern the land. In an underletting, the original lessee himself grants an underlease to the purchaser for the residue of the lease, less the last few days. For example, *A* is fee simple owner and leases Blackacre to *B* for twenty years. *B*, the lessee, may then sublet Blackacre to *C* (who becomes sub-lessee) for the residue of the term held by *B* less the last ten days thereof. *B* will, therefore, retain the reversion of ten days on the expiration of *C*'s underlease. Generally the sub-lessee is not bound by the covenants in the lease granted by the freeholder, but he will be bound by those in the underlease of which he is himself sub-lessee.

Where a landlord imposes a covenant binding on the lessee not to assign or underlet without consent, there is a statutory duty on the landlord not to withhold his consent unreasonably (section 19(1) (*a*) of the Landlord and Tenant Act, 1927). To justify a refusal to consent, the landlord must have a good reason, e.g. the unsuitability of the use to which the sub-tenant proposes to put the land.

The Court of Appeal in *International Drilling Fluids Ltd.* v. *Louisville Investments* (*Uxbridge*) *Ltd.* (1986) set out seven propositions which can be deduced from the authorities on the reasonableness of withholding consent.

(*b*) **Covenant to repair.** In long leases the tenant usually covenants to repair. In short leases the landlord frequently assumes the liability for external repairs and structural repairs, and the tenant assumes responsibility for internal repairs only. The standard of repair is the standard which a reasonable landowner would adopt in relation to his own premises.

If the lease makes no mention of the liability to repair, neither party is liable. The tenant is liable for committing waste, and must generally keep the property in a reasonable state of repair (an implied duty).

11. Servitudes

In addition to the ordinary rights of property which a landowner may exercise over his own land, the law recognizes certain rights which extend over the land of a neighbour. These are known as *servitudes* and may be either (*a*) easements, or (*b*) profits à prendre.

(*a*) **Easements.** An easement may be defined as the right to use, or to restrict the use of, the land of another person in some way. The most important easements are rights of way, rights of light, rights to abstract water and rights to the support of buildings.

The main features of an easement are as follows:

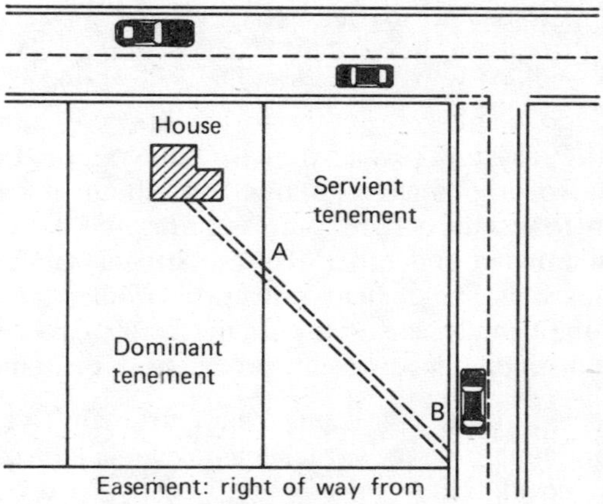

Easement: right of way from A to B

Right of support: easement

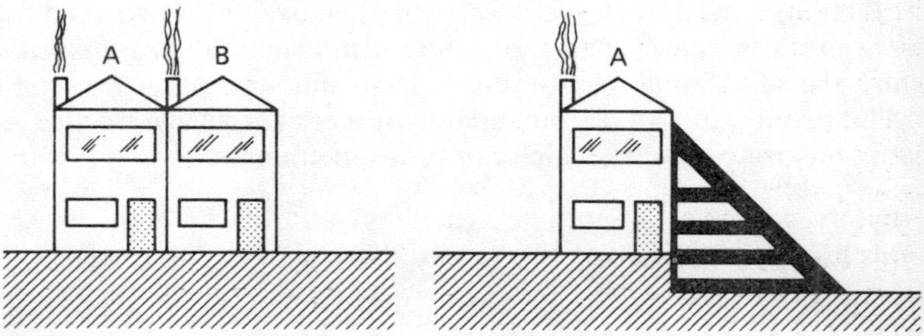

(i) There must be a **dominant** and a **servient** tenement. The land in favour of which the easement exists is known as the dominant tenement; that in respect of which the right is exercised is called the servient tenement. Thus, if *X* gives *Y* permission to cross his land, *Y* will have no easement. It is a personal grant only and, at most, may be a licence so that *Y* does not become a trespasser. If, however, *X*, the owner of Blackacre, grants a similar right to *Z* the owner of neighbouring Whiteacre, this is an easement. In this example, Whiteacre is the dominant tenement and Blackacre is the servient tenement. The easement must contribute in some way to the better enjoyment of the dominant tenement, e.g. by facilitating access to house or land, and not merely benefit the owner personally in a way unconnected with the enjoyment of the dominant tenement.

(ii) The easement must be capable of forming the subject-matter of a grant by deed. Thus there must be a capable grantor and a capable grantee, and the grant must relate to something which is capable of reasonable definition, and have the characteristics of an easement.

(iii) There must be separate ownership of the dominant and servient tenements. If the two pieces of land are under the same ownership, or at some future date come under the same ownership, the easement will cease to exist.

(*b*) **Profits à Prendre.** A profit à prendre is the right to take something from the land of another, e.g. a right of fishing in another's river, grazing rights for cattle, a right to collect firewood or to cut turf. The right to draw water from another's river or stream is an exception since it is treated in law as an easement, not a profit. (This apparent anomaly is based on the proposition that running water cannot be privately owned.) The distinctions between a profit and an easement are:

(i) An easement must, as it is put, be appurtenant to land (i.e. there must be a dominant and servient tenement), while a profit may exist *in gross*, which means that it may be enjoyed by its owner or owners independently of any dominant tenement and unconnected with the enjoyment of land.

(ii) A profit may be a 'several profit', i.e. enjoyed by one person only to the exclusion of all others, or a 'profit in common', i.e. enjoyed by many people. Thus *A* may have a right to shoot game on *B*'s land (a several profit), and all the inhabitants of a certain village may have a right to graze cattle on *B*'s land (a profit in common).

Easements and profits may be created by (i) statute, (ii) grant (express, implied or presumed), and (iii) prescription.

(i) **By Statute.** Where these exist, the statute is usually a local one.

(ii) **By Grant.** This is the most usual method of acquisition of a servitude. **Express** grants exist where the owner of the servient tenement creates the servitude by deed. An **implied** grant is one implied by law. Let us suppose that *A* owns a field and a bungalow in the middle of it. If *A* sells the field, without reserving a right of way from the bungalow to the road, he will have no means of access. A reservation of way is, therefore, implied in favour of the bungalow retained by *A*. This is called an easement or 'way of necessity'.

(iii) **By Prescription.** At common law, proof of use of a servitude from 'time immemorial', i.e. since 1189, is regarded as giving a prescriptive right to the servitude. In practice the courts regard any long usage as sufficient to raise the presumption that the right has existed since 1189, but the presumption may be rebutted by proof that the right did not exist, or by its nature could not have existed, at some time since 1189.

Because of the obvious difficulty of proof of continuous use since 1189, the courts evolved the doctrine of the **Lost Modern Grant.** Under this doctrine a court will sometimes presume, provided that long use (usually twenty years) can be proved, that a grant was made at some time since 1189 but that it has subsequently been lost (*Bridle* v. *Ruby and Another*, 1988).

Under the Prescription Act, 1832, which was passed to remedy some of the defects in the common law prescriptive rights, the grant of a servitude may be presumed from long usage of the right involved. In the case of an easement, the usage must be for twenty years; and in the case of a profit, thirty years. Where the servitude has been held or enjoyed by right of *oral* permission from the owner of the servient tenement, the periods of prescription are (under the Prescription Act, 1832) forty years for an easement, and sixty years for a profit. Written permission defeats prescription.

The Rights of Light Act, 1959, provides for a permanent change in the methods of preventing the acquisition of a right of light by enjoyment of the right for one period of twenty years. Under the Prescription Act, 1832, a servient owner could avoid the creation of a right of light by statutory prescription only if he (i) gave his written permission, or (ii) interrupted the enjoyment of the right for a continuous period of one year. This interruption could be effected by, for example, putting up a screen to prevent access of light to the dominant premises. The latter method may not always be practical because the permission of the planning authority is necessary for the erection of such a physical structure, and that permission is discretionary. Now, under the Rights of Light Act, 1959, a servient owner may substitute for the actual screen a 'notional' screen. He does this by registering in the register of local land charges a statutory notice indicating the exact site of the screen which he would have liked to erect. The effect of such registration is the same as if the access to light of the dominant tenement had been obstructed for one year.

12. Restrictive Covenants

Restrictive covenants are agreements restricting the use of freehold land which are enforceable not only between the original contracting parties, but also between assignees of the respective lands. In spite of the doctrine of privity of contract such a contract may be enforced by applying the principles of equity, namely that a person who acquires property with knowledge that some other person has rights in relation thereto will, in conscience, be bound to observe those rights provided that certain conditions are satisfied. An example will help to make this clear:

> *Tulk* v. *Moxhay* (1848). Tulk sold the central part of Leicester Square to Elms, who covenanted on behalf of himself, his heirs and assigns not to build on the land. The land was later sold to Moxhay who knew of this covenant, but nevertheless proceeded to build on the land. *Held:* that Moxhay was bound by the covenant. It would be inequitable that Elms, who gave a small price for the land because of the restrictions, should be able to sell it for a larger price free from those restrictions.

It was laid down in the above case that the purchaser was bound, even if he had only 'constructive' notice of the covenants, i.e. those covenants which he would have discovered if he had made a proper investigation of title. We may note here also that, under the doctrine of constructive notice, any sub-lessees are deemed to have notice of the contents of the head lease and are, therefore, bound in equity by any negative covenants contained therein.

Restrictive covenants may be enforced today subject to the following conditions:

(i) The covenant must be *negative* in nature, i.e. one which does not require the expenditure of money. For example, a covenant not to use dwellings as shops is negative, but a covenant to build or maintain a house or a wall is positive.

(ii) The covenant must 'touch and concern' the land, i.e. it must in some way be beneficial in protecting the value of the land or the amenities of some other piece of land or a house in respect of which the covenant was created.

(iii) The land in respect of which the covenant is claimed must be owned by the person who seeks to enforce it.

(iv) Where the claimant of the benefit of the covenant is not the original covenantee, he must show that the benefit of the covenant has been expressly assigned to him or that it was originally annexed to the land, or relates to land subject to a building scheme or a scheme of development.

By s. 78 of the Law of Property Act, 1925, the benefit of a covenant entered into after 1925 is deemed to be annexed to the covenantee's land, and by s. 79 the burden is deemed to be annexed to the covenantor's land.

Under the Land Charges Act, 1925, all restrictive covenants entered into since 1 January 1926, are registrable as 'land charges'. Thus the doctrine of notice no longer applies to them, although they remain equitable interests. It is, therefore, no longer necessary to prove that the buyer of land bought it with knowledge of the existence of the covenant, registration of the covenant being treated as notice to any subsequent purchaser. The doctrine of notice still applies, however, to covenants entered into before 1 January 1926.

13. Mortgages

A loan of money may be obtained in various ways. The borrower may approach a friend who may agree to the loan quite freely, making no charge; or the borrower may obtain a loan from a stranger who may insist on some form of security against repayment. This security may be personal, e.g. where a third person (a guarantor) undertakes to repay the loan should the borrower default. Alternatively, the lender may agree to advance the required loan provided that the borrower offers some form of property against which the lender may lawfully make a claim should the borrower default in repayment of the debt.

Personal property (e.g. a gold watch) is a simple form of security; it is easily deliverable and is the kind sometimes transferred to a pawnbroker as security for a loan which the latter is prepared to advance to the borrower (the pawner). When the loan is repaid with interest on the date agreed the property is returned to the borrower.

Real property, such as valuable lands and houses, provides a good form of security, but by the very nature of things this form of property cannot be 'delivered' in the straightforward way applicable to personal property; the lands or houses must be *conveyed*, which means the preparation of a formal deed.

The *mortgage* (Norman-French, meaning 'dead pledge') is the name given to the transaction by which a borrower (a mortgagor) obtains a loan from another person (a mortgagee) on the security of property.

Before the Law of Property Act, 1925, the usual method of creating a mortgage of freehold land was for the borrower (the mortgagor) to convey the fee simple, i.e. his freehold estate, to the lender (the mortgagee) with the condition that if the mortgagor repaid the loan plus interest on a specified date (usually six months later) the mortgagee would reconvey the land to him. In the early days the common law courts held the parties to their agreement (into which they had freely entered), strictly construed the contract, and enforced its terms. If the loan was not repaid on the date named in the mortgage deed the borrower would be deprived permanently of his land, the land then becoming a 'dead pledge'.

This caused some hardship; the lender obtained the land itself (more valuable than the loan advanced), and in addition he could sue the mortgagor on the agreement to repay the sum advanced, plus interest thereon. Mortgagors could obtain no relief from this situation from the common law courts, and eventually approached the Court of Chancery. As a result, equity intervened in the mortgage transaction and gave borrowers certain rights, the most notable being the right to get back their lands (taken as security) if the loans were able to be repaid at some time later than the date of redemption named in the contract. This right became known as the 'Equity of Redemption'. As was said by Lord Nottingham in 1675, 'The principal right of the mortgagee is to the money, and his right to the land is only as a security for the money.' From the earliest days equity gave valuable rights to mortgagors on the ground of conscience, such rights being termed equitable rights.

Since the Law of Property Act, 1925, it is no longer possible to create a mortgage in the way just described, i.e. by transferring the whole of the interest of the mortgagor in the land to the mortgagee, but the principle of the 'equity of redemption' remains, with other equitable principles, today. The forms of mortgages of land today are (*a*) Legal Mortgages, and (*b*) Equitable Mortgages.

(*a*) **Legal Mortgages.** These take two forms: (i) mortgage by demise (i.e. lease), and (ii) a charge by deed expressed to be by way of legal mortgage.

(i) *Mortgage by Demise.* This is effected by the creation of a lease. Suppose *A* is owner of Blackacre in fee simple. *A* (mortgagor) wishes to borrow money from *B* (mortgagee). *A* may grant to *B* a legal term of years, usually for 3,000 years, with a proviso in the deed that if the principal loan plus interest is repaid on a date named (usually six months later), the term of years shall cease. *A* further agrees that he will repay the sum due plus interest on the date named.

(ii) *Charge by way of Legal Mortgage.* This is created by a short deed which confers on the mortgagee a legal *interest*, not a legal estate. The legal interest entitles the mortgagee to the same remedies as if the mortgage were by lease for a long term of years as in (i) above.

Where the mortgagor owns leasehold property (this is sometimes as valuable as freehold, e.g. where the lease is for 999 years), the mortgagor may adopt one of two methods:

(i) A grant of a sub-lease to the mortgagee for a term of years subject to the proviso that the sub-lease will cease or determine on repayment of the principal sum secured plus interest. The sub-lease will be at least one day shorter than the lease vested in the mortgagor. In practice the term of the first sub-lease is usually for ten days less than that held by the mortgagor.

(ii) A charge by way of legal mortgage. The advantage of the charge by way of legal mortgage over the mortgage by demise is that where the mortgagor owns both freeholds and leaseholds he may on one document charge both types of property with the mortgage debt. Moreover, where a holder of a lease wishes to create a mortgage on the lease he may be obliged to obtain the lessor's consent to sub-let. No consent is required if the charge by way of legal mortgage is adopted.

(*b*) **Equitable Mortgages.** An equitable mortgage is one in which the mortgagee receives merely an equitable interest in the land. There are two distinct types:

(i) A mortgage of an equitable interest owned by the mortgagor, e.g. a life interest or other interest under a trust. In these cases the mortgagor may assign his equitable interest to the mortgagee with a proviso for reassignment of the equitable interest on repayment of the debt, plus interest.

(ii) An informal mortgage of a legal estate or legal interest. Sometimes a borrower requires a loan urgently, and he wishes to avoid the trouble and expense of drawing up a formal legal mortgage. In cases of this type an agreement in writing to create a mortgage or the deposit of title deeds as an act of part performance of an oral agreement operates to create an *equitable* mortgage. This will be treated in equity as a mortgage since 'equity looks upon that as done which ought to be done'.

The three usual methods of creating such equitable mortgages are:

(i) A written agreement (signed as required by section 40 of the Law of Property Act) which is not accompanied by a deposit of title deeds.

(ii) A deposit of deeds alone, without written agreement, if the deposit of the deeds amounts to part performance of an agreement to give security.

(iii) A combination of (i) and (ii) above, i.e. a written agreement *plus* a deposit of deeds.

The agreement is usually by deed as this gives the mortgagee certain valuable remedies under the Law of Property Act, 1925.

Remedies of the Mortgagee. The mortgagee of a legal mortgage has the following rights:

(*a*) *To sue for the debt.* The amount due on the mortgagor's covenant to repay is the principal sum plus interest. Where the date fixed for redemption has passed, the mortgagee may sue for that amount.

(*b*) *To take possession.* This remedy is available to the mortgagee since he is legal tenant of the land. He may take possession at once or 'before the ink is dry on the mortgage' (per Harman J. in *Four Maids Ltd.* v. *Dudley Marshall* (*Properties*) *Ltd.*, 1957). The remedy of taking possession is not, in practice, desirable since the mortgagee is strictly accountable to the mortgagor for any loss occasioned by his own default. He is accountable not only for such rents and other income from the property which he in fact receives, but also for those rents, incomes, etc. which he *might* have received had he exercised due diligence and proper management. A mortgagee's right to obtain possession of a dwelling house is restricted by the Administration of Justice Acts of 1970 and 1973.

(*c*) *To foreclose*. If the mortgagor fails to pay the sum due for an unreasonable time, the mortgagee may obtain a court order extinguishing the mortgagor's equitable right to redeem the property and vesting the full legal estate in the mortgagee. The first order is a *foreclosure order nisi*, which directs that the money due must be repaid within a given time, e.g. six months. If not so paid, the court order is made *absolute*, the property then vesting in the mortgagee free from the equity of redemption. Foreclosure is a rare remedy in practice since the court may reopen the foreclosure, thus giving the mortgagor a further opportunity to redeem his mortgage. Also, the mortgagor may apply to the court for an order for sale instead.

(*d*) *To sell the land*. This is the most frequently used right and is implied in all mortgages made by deed. Subject to the exceptions below, the mortgagee has a power to sell the property as soon as the legal date for redemption has passed. The power of sale cannot be exercised until

(i) three months' notice has been served on the mortgagor requiring repayment of the debt, and the notice has expired; or

(ii) interest on the loan is in arrears for two months; or

(iii) there has been a breach of some covenant in the mortgage other than the covenant to repay.

A mortgagee cannot purchase the land for himself. The sale of the property is usually by public auction. Out of the proceeds of sale the mortgagee may recover (i) any expenses incurred in the sale of the property, and (ii) the principal sum due, plus interest. Any surplus money belongs to the mortgagor. A sale with vacant possession is preferable but where a husband mortgaged the matrimonial home, of which his wife was in actual occupation and to which she had contributed, the mortgagee was refused an order for possession: *Williams and Glyn's Bank Ltd.* v. *Boland* (1981).

(*e*) *To appoint a receiver*. The power to appoint a receiver is also implied in all mortgages by deed, unless a contrary intention is expressed. The receiver's duties are to receive the rents and profits on the mortgagee's behalf in order to discharge the sum due to him. The receiver is deemed in law to be the agent of the mortgagor, and the latter is liable for the receiver's acts or defaults, unless the mortgage otherwise provides. For this reason it is usually more advantageous to appoint a receiver than for the mortgagee himself to take possession.

Where the mortgage is equitable and is created by deed, the mortgagee has practically the same remedies as those stated above. Unless, however, the power to do so is expressly reserved to him, the equitable mortgagee has no right to take possession. If the mortgage is created by a deposit of title deeds, the mortgagee must apply to the court for an order to sell the property and for an order appointing a receiver.

Remedies of the Mortgagor. The main weapon of the mortgagor is his right to redeem the mortgaged property on payment of the principal sum borrowed, plus interest. This amount falls due on the contractual date specified (usually six months later). We have already discussed the equity of redemption evolved by the Court of Chancery which applied two equitable principles in its jurisdiction: 'Once a mortgage, always a mortgage', and 'Equity looks at the intent rather than the form.' Accordingly, even after the date for redemption had passed, the mortgagor could get back the land when he was in a position to repay the debt plus interest.

As long as an order of foreclosure has not been issued by a court, that right of redemption exists. But there are conditions. The mortgagor must conduct himself properly, and he must, for example, give to the mortgagee six months' notice of his desire to redeem (or give six months' interest in lieu), unless the legal charge states some shorter period. This period gives the mortgagee, who regards the mortgage transaction as an investment, time to reinvest his money in a suitable security elsewhere.

Equity treated the right of redemption with special care. Any provision in the mortgage deed which tended to make the mortgage irredeemable, or which encumbered the property or land, or which encumbered the mortgagor's enjoyment of it in the future, after paying off the sum due, was regarded as inequitable. The mortgagor had the right, in essence, to get his property back in exactly the same condition as it was before the mortgage deed. Any term in a mortgage deed which greatly benefits the mortgagee at the expense of the mortgagor has always been viewed with suspicion.

> *Carritt* v. *Bradley* (1903). *B* held most of the shares in a tea company. He mortgaged them to *C*. The mortgage contained a term that *B*, as a shareholder, would induce the company to employ *C* as the company's agent to sell tea. The company paid off the mortgage, and ceased to employ *C*, whereupon *C* claimed damages for breach of the agreement to employ him. *Held:* that the proviso in the mortgage as to employment of *C* ceased to exist after the mortgage was paid off.

> *Noakes* v. *Rice* (1902). The tenant of a 'free' public house, under a twenty-six-year lease, mortgaged the premises to a brewery company as security for a loan, and covenanted that during the remainder of the twenty-six years he would not sell any beers except those provided by the brewery company (the mortgagees). The tenant paid off the mortgage three years later, and sued for a declaration that he was free from the covenant. *Held:* that the covenant was inconsistent with the express proviso for redemption (which entitled the tenant to demand a reconveyance of the premises upon repayment of the loan with interest) and was a clog upon the equity. Tenant became entitled to trade as a 'free' public house.

Nevertheless, not every collateral advantage to the mortgagee is void, as will be seen from the following case.

> *Kreglinger* v. *New Patagonia Meat and Cold Storage Co.* (1914). A firm of woolbrokers (mortgagees) lent £10,000 to a meat company on mortgage. The woolbrokers agreed not to demand repayment for five years, but the mortgagors (the meat company) could repay the debt earlier on giving notice. The parties covenanted also that the meat company would not sell sheepskins to anyone except the woolbrokers for five years from the date of the agreement, as long as the woolbrokers were willing to purchase the skins at the agreed price. The loan was paid off before the five years. *Held:* that the option of purchasing the sheepskins did not end on repayment, but continued for five years. It was a collateral contract and did not affect the right to redeem.

Where the parties to a mortgage agree to postpone redemption for a long period, it is a matter for decision by the court in each case whether it is unreasonable. In *Knightsbridge Estates Ltd.* v. *Byrne* (1939), where the mortgagee required a long-term investment, it was held that the postponement of the period of repayment for forty years was not oppressive or unconscionable in the circumstances, although such a period would be unreasonable between *private* persons who mortgage property of small value in return for a small loan.

14. The Sale of Land

The sale of land involves two elements: (*a*) the contract of sale, and (*b*) the delivery of the land and transfer of title in it.

As to the contract of sale, the general rules of the law of contract already considered apply. The parties to the sale must have contractual capacity, the contract must not be illegal, there must be an 'agreement', and the acceptance of the offer must be unconditional. Where the offer of the sale is made 'subject to contract', no agreement comes into effect until a formal contract is approved by both parties. The decision in *Alpenstow Ltd.* v. *Regalian Properties PLC.* (1985) illustrates an exception to this rule.

Under section 40 of the Law of Property Act, 1925, contracts for the sale of land must be evidenced in writing. In the absence of a 'note or memorandum' the contract is unenforceable by legal action, although valid. The above are the general rules, and are subject to the proviso that where the doctrine of 'part performance' applies, the contract may be enforced notwithstanding that the agreement does not comply with section 40 of the Law of Property Act. The memorandum must contain: (i) an agreement for sale, (ii) a description of the parties, (iii) a description of the property, (iv) a statement of the price, and (v) it must also be signed by the person to be charged or his agent (see p. 132).

Under an *open* contract for sale (i.e. a contract which does not set out the terms of the sale, but merely specifies the names of the parties, the description of the property and the price), there is a most important condition implied by law that the vendor must show title for at least fifteen years, starting with 'a good root of title'.

A good root of title may be defined as a disposition of the land dealing with the whole of the legal and equitable estate in the property to be sold, containing an adequate description of the property and revealing no defect in title thereto. The vendor must, at his own expense, abstract and, if under his control, produce the document which forms the root of his title and all subsequent documents which affect the legal estate. He must also prove all facts which have affected the legal estate in the last 15 years. This is called 'deducing title'. The purchaser on his part 'investigates the title'.

Upon the satisfactory investigation of title the transaction proceeds to the **conveyance** of the property to the purchasers.

The stages in this process are as follows:

(i) The preparation of the contract.

(ii) The exchange of contracts between the vendor's solicitor and the purchaser's solicitor, when the purchaser pays a deposit (usually 10 per cent of the purchase money). The transaction has now become binding on both parties.

(iii) Delivery by the vendor's solicitors of an 'abstract of title'.

(iv) Examination of this title by the purchaser's solicitor and comparison of the abstract with the title deeds to check accuracy. The time allowed for this is usually fourteen days.

(v) The purchaser's solicitor may deliver requisitions (i.e. written questions) on title to the vendor to give the purchaser full details of the property concerned, and to clear up doubts.

(vi) Search by purchaser's solicitor in the Land Charges Register and in the register maintained by the local authority to ascertain what encumbrances exist in relation to the property.

(vii) Once the conveyance has been drawn up it has to be completed. Completion is usually carried out at the office of the vendor's solicitor. The purchaser hands over the money, and the vendor hands over the conveyance which he has himself signed, together with the title deeds of the property. The deed must be stamped as required by the Stamp Act, 1891, as amended.

Registration of Land Charges. It is of great importance to a prospective purchaser of land to discover what charges exist in favour of third parties. Certain rights and charges are legal and will bind the purchaser in all cases, e.g. a purchaser would be bound by a legal lease of the property.

The 1925 legislation has greatly affected the 'doctrine of notice' to which reference has been made previously. By the very nature of land, there may be many rights of others in relation to a property. *A* may be a fee simple owner of Blackacre, but the property may be in the occupation of *B*, under a lease, and may be subject to an easement (e.g. a right of way) in favour of *C*, and *D* may have an equitable mortgage on the property. Before 1926 the rule was that a purchaser from *A* was bound by the *legal* rights of *B*, *C*, and *D*, irrespective of notice. However, a purchaser from *A* would be free from any *equitable* interests only if he acquired the legal estate for value *without notice* of equitable rights.

To simplify the investigation as to these rights, the Land Charges Act, 1925, introduced the principle of registration of certain equitable interests and charges affecting land. Registration of such interests constitutes notice to a purchaser, whether he knows of them or not. Conversely, an interest requiring registration and which is not in fact registered, is not binding on a purchaser even though he knows that such an interest exists.

The most important charges which should be registered are:

(*a*) *Puisne mortgages*, i.e. legal mortgages not protected by a deposit of title deeds.

(*b*) *Limited owners' charges*, i.e. an equitable charge on settled property arising by statute in favour of the tenant for life of such property, e.g. where he pays estate duty out of his own pocket.

(*c*) *General equitable charges*, i.e. an equitable charge not secured by a deposit of documents relating to the legal estate. For example, an equitable mortgage not protected by deposit of the title deeds; or the right of an unpaid vendor who has parted with the deeds.

(*d*) *Estate contracts*, i.e. contracts by estate owners to convey or create a legal estate. The object of registration is to protect the purchaser's rights under the contract against other purchasers who may acquire a legal estate from the vendor before the completion of the purchase.

(*e*) *Restrictive covenants* (see p. 285).

In addition to the above, section 15 of the Land Charges Act, 1972, which contains the modern law on the subject, requires local authorities to keep registers of local land charges. These charges are constituted under various statutes: for example the Private Street Works Act enables local authorities to recover the cost of road construction, etc. from local property owners; and certain plans and orders made under the Town and Country Planning Acts have to be registered. If the charges are not registered they are void against a purchaser of the legal estate, and he takes the estate free from them.

15. Registered Land

The investigation of title to land is sometimes very difficult and complicated. The parties to the conveyance are responsible for ensuring accuracy.

In many countries a system of compulsory land registration is in force, the purpose of which is to provide an official guarantee certifying who is the owner of a particular piece of land and disclosing certain of the encumbrances to which the land is or may be subjected. A purchaser need only consult a single publicly operated register to find out whether the vendor has a good title to the property and the nature of the rights and encumbrances affecting the land he proposes to buy.

The Land Registration Act, 1925, introduced the system of land registration into Britain. In areas to which an Order in Council has made the system applicable, registration of title is compulsory upon sale of freeholds or of leaseholds having more than forty years to run.

The mechanism of registration is as follows. The Government lawyers of the Land Registry or a district registry investigate the title of every freehold or leasehold sold after the appropriate date once and for all. If they are satisfied that it is in order, they record the owner as registered proprietor of the land with absolute (freehold) title or good leasehold title, as the case may be. The title is, in effect, guaranteed by the State.

Where the title does not come up to the above standard, or where there is doubt, the person in possession of the land may be granted a possessory title only, which can be subsequently upgraded in accordance with Section 1 of the Land Registration Act, 1986.

The Land Registry issues to the registered proprietor a **land certificate,** certifying that a registered title of the appropriate kind has been granted. This corresponds to the title deeds of property. In any further transactions affecting that particular land the purchaser's solicitor need not concern himself (except in rare cases) with the original deeds: the land certificate and the certified statements made therein can generally be relied upon. The name of the new registered proprietor is entered by the Land Registry officials when a transfer is made in his favour, or a grant of a lease is made to him.

Registration of title is compulsory in the counties of London, Middlesex, Kent, Surrey and Berkshire, and in most of the built-up areas.

In addition to the Property Register, giving details of land, and the Proprietorship Register, giving details of title (absolute, good leasehold, qualified or possessory) and the name and address and description of the proprietor, there is a Charges Register which contains charges and encumbrances affecting the land, all dealings with registered charges and encumbrances and notices relating to covenants, conditions, and other rights *adversely* affecting the land. It contains all the matters which would be registered under the Land Charges Act if the title to the land were unregistered.

16. Exercises

1. 'Possession' and 'ownership' are common terms in ordinary life, yet in law each has a special significance. Discuss the two concepts and explain what 'possession is nine points of the law' means.
2. Distinguish between (i) real property and (ii) personal property, and between (iii) choses in possession and (iv) choses in action.
3. Describe the main aims of the 1925 legislation.
4. Explain in detail what is meant by the phrase 'an estate in fee simple absolute in possession'.
5. What are the main duties of (i) a landlord and (ii) a tenant?
6. How may an equitable mortgage be created?
7. Outline the remedies available to a mortgagee of a legal mortgage.
8. The sale of land involves two major steps: (i) the contract for sale, and (ii) the delivery. Enumerate the stages leading to 'completion'.
9. What do you understand by 'registered land'? Explain 'registration of land charges'. Estimate the importance of registration to the rational development of land law.

11

THE LAW OF SUCCESSION

When *A* transfers property to *B* we may say that *B* 'succeeds' to that property, i.e. he takes over the rights owned by the transferor. In law the word 'succession' has a special meaning. Thus when we speak of 'universal succession' we refer to two classes: (*a*) succession on death, and (*b*) succession on bankruptcy. This chapter deals with succession on death.

Obviously a person cannot own property or exercise rights over property when dead. The law bows to inevitable facts: other persons will succeed to the property owned or possessed by the deceased. All systems of law have certain rules of succession which lay down how, and to whom, the property of a deceased person is to be distributed.

Where a person makes a valid will stating how his property is to be distributed he is said to die 'testate' (from the Latin word *testari*, to make a will). Where he leaves no will, or an invalid will, he is said to die 'intestate'.

1. Wills

From an early date the law recognized the right of a man to make a will showing to whom his *personal* property should descend. In medieval times he had no right to dispose of freehold land as the strict feudal law laid down that the land had to devolve on the heir at law. Later, the Statute of Military Tenures, 1660, permitted a freeholder to devise (i.e. leave by will) his lands, and the introduction of the 'use' provided a further means of making dispositions of freehold property on death.

Birth, marriage, and death have always been of immediate concern to the Church. In Norman and medieval times the Church courts (separate from the lay courts) adjudicated on wills of personal property, including leaseholds. The Court of Probate Act, 1857, transferred the jurisdiction relating to wills to the ordinary civil courts, where it has been exercised ever since. However, many of the rules applied today are derived from the early Church courts which applied canon law (i.e. Church law), not the common law.

Nature of a Will. A will is a declaration of a person's intentions concerning the descent of his property after his death. A will is said to be *ambulatory* (i.e. not permanent: subject to revocation or alteration) until the death of the testator. The will speaks from death. If *A* makes a disposition of 'All my property to *Z*', the successor (*Z*) will receive all the property which *A* owns at the moment of death. The gift will include property which *A* acquires between the time of making the will and his death. It will not, however, include property which *A* has disposed of between these times.

Testamentary Capacity. The general rule is that any person of full age and sound mind may make a valid will. The testator is presumed sane at the time when he made his will; but if the will is contested on the ground that the testator was of unsound mind when he made it, the person propounding the will has the burden of proving that the testator was of sound mind.

Married women were formerly incapable of making valid wills, but legislation in the past century has remedied this, so that now they have full testamentary capacity (Married Women's Property Acts, 1882–93, and the Law Reform (Married Women and Tortfeasors) Act, 1935).

An infant cannot make a valid will, but there is an exception in regard to infant soldiers, sailors, and airmen (see p. 299).

Formalities. The Wills Act, 1837, is the main Act governing this important matter. Its main provisions are:

(*a*) *Writing*. A will must be in the form of a written document. Any document, e.g. a letter, can suffice and may include other documents existing at the time the will was made and referred to in the will. Oral evidence may be given to identify these documents if they are so referred to. 'In writing' includes handwriting, print, and typescript.

(*b*) *Signature*. The will must be signed by the testator or by someone in his presence and by his directions. Initials, a partial signature, a mark (e.g. a cross) or a thumb print in ink may be used, as long as the mark is clearly ascribable to the testator. A seal stamped with the testator's initials has been held to be a signature.

The Administration of Justice Act, 1982, s. 17 substituted a new section for s. 9 of the Wills Act, 1837 and the Wills Act Amendment Act, 1852 dealing with the signing and attestation of wills and relaxes the law governing the position of the testator's signature and the acknowledgement of signature by an attesting witness. The result of this new s. 9 is that the signature by or on behalf of the testator can be anywhere on the will provided that the testator intended by his signature to give effect to the will.

Attestation. The signature of the testator 'shall be made or acknowledged by the testator in the presence of two or more witnesses present at the same time', and 'each witness either attests and signs the will or acknowledges his signature in the presence of the testator (but not necessarily in the presence of any other witness)'.

The purpose of attestation is to authenticate the testator's signature. The witnesses need not be present at the time of the actual signing of the will by the testator. They must, however, both be *present to-*

gether at this time *or* at some later time when the testator acknowledges the signature as his. Although in practice a witness signs or acknowledges his signature in the presence of the other witness, this is not a legal requirement. Addresses and occupations are added to assist in identification and subsequent tracing. If a dispute should arise over the validity of the will, the evidence of the witnesses will be vital. Witnesses need not read the will or know its contents.

A blind person may not 'witness' a will or a codicil, because he cannot 'see' the signature (*Re Gibson*, 1949). A person under the age of majority is a competent witness for the purpose of attestation, provided that he is a credible person.

Section 9 of the Wills Act, 1837, expressly provides that no particular form of attestation shall be necessary. It is enough if the witnesses merely subscribe their names, their initials (*In the Goods of Christian*, 1849), or their marks (*In the Goods of Ashmore*, 1843).

All amendments made to the Wills Act, 1837 introduced by the Administration of Justice Act, 1982 came into operation on January 1, 1983 but did not affect the wills of testators who died before that date.

Additions and Alterations. A will having been made is alterable. Any changes may be made in the body of an existing will, *provided that* they are initialled by the testator and the witnesses. Moreover, additions may be made even below the testator's signature if they are signed and attested in the same manner as the will itself. Further, a will may be supplemented or added to by properly signed and attested codicils.

Anyone to whom, or to whose husband or wife, the testator had left property, and who acted as a witness was not entitled to benefit under the will (Wills Act, 1837, s. 15). The Wills Act, 1968, restricts the operation of this section and provides that if a will is attested by a person who is, or whose spouse is, a beneficiary, the gift will not be avoided if the will is duly executed without his attestation.

Provided there are two qualified witnesses, the attestation of any other witnesses can be disregarded and they become entitled to any dispositions made to them under the will.

Rectification and Extrinsic Evidence. The Administration of Justice Act, 1982, introduced some further measures to assist the court in carrying out the testator's intentions. S. 20 provides for rectification of a clerical error or failure to understand the testator intentions; s. 21 for admission in certain circumstances of all available extrinsic evidence (*Re Williams* (dec.) v. *Madgin*, 1985).

As a matter of public policy no one convicted of murder or manslaughter may benefit under the will of his victim (Forfeiture Acts 1970 and 1982).

Wills of Soldiers, Sailors, and Airmen. Roman law allowed a soldier 'in the field' to make an informal will. During hostilities death in battle is likely; a soldier may have no legal advice near by, and pen and paper are not readily available. The law, by the very nature of things, cannot apply stringent rules in the abnormal situations mentioned. It has, therefore, allowed oral declarations and other informal dispositions to take effect notwithstanding their non-compliance with the technical rules of regular law applicable to civilians.

These practical rules found their way into English common law and they are now incorporated in section 7 of the Wills Act, 1837, as extended by the Wills (Soldiers and Sailors) Act, 1918. The effect of these provisions is to grant special privileges to soldiers, sailors, and airmen who are *on actual military service* and to seamen who are *at sea* (under any conditions). Such persons may make wills even though infants, and such wills may be made informally.

Where a soldier about to embark overseas declared orally: 'If anything happens to me, this is for *R*', the disposition was held to be a valid will. Where a soldier, sailor, etc., writes his will there is no need for witnesses. Whether the declaration is oral or written, the court will give effect to its terms, provided that the person wanted it to be a binding will.

The phrase 'actual military service' means that the serviceman is called up for service, is engaged in hostilities, is about to proceed to a hostile engagement, or is on embarkation leave for a foreign station in connexion with operations of war, imminent or taking place. In *Re Wingham* (1949) it was held that a trainee pilot on an R.A.F. instructional course in Canada was on 'actual military service'. A soldier in England in *peace-time* is not. Seamen (including those serving in the Merchant Navy) may make informal wills when at sea or about to embark for a voyage, not if they are on leave and do not have orders to join a ship (*Re Rapley's Estate, Rapley* v. *Rapley* (1983)).

Women serving as army nurses, typists, etc., under military or naval orders, enjoy the same privilege as soldiers on 'actual military service'.

An informal will made by any of the above persons remains valid even after the testator ceases to be a seaman or completes his service in the Armed Forces.

Revocation. It is of the very nature of a will, according to English law, that it shall be revocable until the testator dies. Revocation may be express, or it may be implied from the conduct of the testator.

Revocation may be effected by (*a*) subsequent will or codicil; (*b*) a writing executed like a will; (*c*) subsequent marriage (*per subsequens matrimonium*); or (*d*) destruction of the will with *animus revocandi.*

(*a*) *Revocation by a subsequent will or codicil.* A will usually begins with a clause revoking all former wills. If such a clause is not inserted, the later will (or codicil) does not revoke the former will except in so far as it is inconsistent therewith. Thus, if a testator, *T*, in his first will leaves a specified named house to *A*, and in a later will leaves the same house to *B*, the house will go to *B*. If, however, *T* in his first will leaves £500 to *X*, and in a later will (which does not contain a revocation clause) leaves £500 to *Y*, both *X* and *Y* will receive legacies of £500.

(*b*) *Revocation by writing executed as a will.* A will may be revoked by a writing which, though not itself a will, is signed and attested. It is sufficient that it should declare the testator's intention to revoke his will without containing any dispositions in lieu of those contained in the instrument revoked. Thus a letter signed by a testator and attested by two witnesses directing his will to be destroyed has been held sufficient to revoke the will (*In the Goods of Durance*, 1872).

(*c*) *Revocation 'per subsequens matrimonium'*. A will is revoked by the subsequent marriage of the testator, whether the testator be male or female (Wills Act, 1837, s. 18). The Administration of Justice Act, 1982 has substituted a new section for s. 18 and has added a new s. 18A to the Act whilst repealing s. 177 of the Law of Property Act, 1925. It has re-enacted the general rule that a testator's will is revoked by marriage, but provides that where it appears from a will that at the time it was made the testator was expecting to be married to a particular person and that he intended that the will should not be revoked by the marriage, the will is not revoked by his marriage to that person. In addition, where it appears from a will that at the time it was made the testator was expecting to be married to a particular person and that he intended that a disposition in the will should not be revoked by his marriage to that person then that particular disposition shall take effect. Any other disposition will also take effect unless it appears from the will that the testator intended the disposition to be revoked by the marriage. S. 18A provides that, except where there is a contrary intention in the will, where a marriage of a testator has ended by divorce, annulment or by being declared void, any appointment of a former spouse as an executor or executor and trustee will be ineffective, as will any gift to such a former spouse.

(*d*) *Revocation by destruction of the will with 'animus revocandi'*. This is effected by the testator (or someone in his presence and by his direction) destroying the will, provided that the act of destruction, e.g. burning, tearing, is done with the intention to revoke the will. The following points must be proved: a physical destruction; an intention (*animus revocandi*) to revoke by such destruction; and the destruction must be effected by the testator or someone *in his presence and by his direction*.

As to destruction, a partial destruction is sufficient if there is clear evidence that cancellation of the will was intended, e.g. tearing off the signature and attestation clause. 'All the destroying in the world without the intention will not revoke a will, nor intention without destroying. There must be the two.' (Lord Justice James in *Cheese* v. *Lovejoy*, 1877.)

The destruction cannot be delegated to a solicitor or other agent unless the will is destroyed in the presence of the testator and by his authority. 'If it was not done with his (the testator's) authority at the time . . . no amount of authority afterwards can be brought into play so as to ratify an act done without authority at the time' (*Gill* v. *Gill*, 1909).

Where a will is lost or is destroyed without being revoked, its contents may be proved by other evidence, e.g. a copy, a draft or oral evidence (*Sugden* v. *Lord St. Leonards*, 1876).

Revival of Revoked Wills. Where a will has been revoked in any of the above ways it may nevertheless be revived either by re-execution as a will or by a properly executed codicil which expresses a clear intention that the earlier will shall stand. We may note here that it is not possible to revive a will which has been revoked by a later will merely by destroying the later will. For example, let us suppose a testator makes will No. 1; later he makes will No. 2 revoking will No. 1. The testator now desires to revive will No. 1. It is not possible to do this merely by destroying will No. 2. The only effect of this is that the testator would have left no will at all, and he would die intestate.

Doctrine of Dependent Relative Revocation. Where a testator revokes his will with the intention of making a new one, and for some reason (e.g. he dies before executing it) fails to make a new one, the original (i.e. the revoked will) remains valid and is treated as the will of the testator. This applies only where the court is satisfied that the testator did not intend to revoke the will *absolutely*, but merely revoked it as a first step towards making a new will. For example, a man destroyed his will, made out in favour of his wife, under the mistaken belief that all his property would pass automatically to her if he died intestate. It was held in these circumstances that a copy of the will could be admitted to probate (*In the estate of Greenstreet*, 1930).

2. Legacies and Devises

A *devise* is a disposition of freehold land contained in a will. A *legacy* or a *bequest* is a disposition of any other form of property, including leaseholds. The terms used for recipients of the gift by will are 'devisees' and 'legatees', respectively.

Classes of Dispositions. A legacy (or bequest) may be (*a*) a general legacy, (*b*) a specific legacy or (*c*) a demonstrative legacy.

(*a*) *A general legacy*. Where a gift is made which does not refer to a specific or particular object, it is described as a general legacy. For example, a gift of 'a horse', or 'a motor-car', or '£1,000'.

(*b*) *A specific legacy*. This is a gift which is specifically described. For example: 'my Daimler car' or 'my Chippendale chairs'.

(*c*) *A demonstrative legacy*. A gift of a sum of money to be paid out of a particular fund is referred to as demonstrative. For example: 'a sum of £500 from my Post Office deposit account'.

In the specimen will on p. 303, mention is made of a 'residuary gift'. The residue of an estate is that which remains after all the debts have been paid, and the devises and legacies have been distributed. Unless the residue is disposed of, e.g. by gift to some person, the testator will be presumed in law to be intestate as to that part.

The importance of distinguishing these different classes of legacies will be seen when we come to discuss the effect of abatement and ademption.

Lapsing of Gifts. Where a legatee or devisee dies before the testator, and is not issue of the testator, the gift to him or her lapses. The property allocated to the deceased beneficiary falls into the residue of the estate. Where however the deceased beneficiary is issue, the Wills Act, 1837, raises the fiction that the child (grandchild, etc.) who had died before the testator had in fact died immediately after the testator. It is, of course, open to a testator to make provision against the contingency of death of a legatee or devisee, but in the absence of such a provision the property will fall into residue for the benefit of the residuary legatee or devisee.

Abatement. The first duty of the personal representative responsible for winding up the testator's estate is to pay the testator's debts before his estate is distributed among the beneficiaries. Where there is insufficient property remaining after the debts have been paid to satisfy all the beneficiaries, it follows that some of the legacies will have to be reduced or even repudiated altogether. The legacies are said to 'abate', and they will do so in a certain order. Residuary gifts abate first, then general legacies, then specific legacies. Demonstrative gifts will not abate unless the fund out of which they are to be paid is itself exhausted. If that happens the demonstrative legacies will be treated as general legacies and will abate with them.

Ademption. If a specific thing to be given by will to a legatee is not in existence or no longer belongs to the testator at the time of the testator's death, the gift is 'adeemed', and the legatee gets nothing. Thus, if *X* bequeaths a specific painting to *Y*, and the painting is destroyed by a fire before *X* dies, *Y* will get nothing. The rule as to ademption does not apply to general legacies or to demonstrative gifts.

3. Specimen Will

I, EDWARD COKE, of 14 Acacia Avenue, Oxbridge, in the County of Somerset, company director, HEREBY REVOKE all Wills and testamentary documents heretofore made by me AND DECLARE this to be my LAST WILL

1. I APPOINT my wife *Gladys Coke*, and my solicitor, *Thomas B. Macaulay*, to be jointly the executors of this my will.
2. I DEVISE my freehold cottage known as THE LILACS, at Tone Dale, Oxbridge, unto my son, *Hugh Coke*, in fee simple.
3. I BEQUEATH the following specific legacies:

   (i) To my son, *John Coke*, any motor-car I may own at the date of my death.

   (ii) To my daughter, *Carolyn Coke*, all my ordinary shares in the company known as Imperial Chemical Industries plc.

   (iii) To my said wife all my personal chattels not hereby bequeathed for her absolute use and benefit.

4. I BEQUEATH the following pecuniary legacies:

(i) to my daughter *Rosalyn Coke* the sum of Three Thousand Pounds.

(ii) to my daughter *Elizabeth Coke* the sum of Three Thousand Pounds.

5. I DEVISE AND BEQUEATH all the residue of my real and personal estate whatsoever and wheresoever not hereby or by any codicil hereto otherwise expressly disposed of as to my freeholds in fee simple and as to my personal estate absolutely unto my said wife *Gladys Coke* for her own absolute use and benefit.

6. I DIRECT that any executor of this my Will being a solicitor or a person engaged in any profession or business may be so employed and act and shall be entitled to make all proper professional charges for any work done by him or his firm in connexion with my Estate including work which an executor not being a solicitor or a person engaged as aforesaid could have done personally.

IN WITNESS whereof I the said *Edward Coke* the Testator have to this my LAST WILL set my hand this thirty-first day of March One Thousand Nine Hundred and Eight-Three.

SIGNED AND ACKNOWLEDGED by the above-named *Edward Coke* the Testator as and for his LAST WILL in the presence of us both present at the same time who at his request in his presence and in the presence of each other have hereunto subscribed our names as witnesses:	*Edward Coke* (signed)

Thomas More, (signed)
6, High St.,
Oxbridge,
Somerset.
Clerk.

Jeremy Bentham, (signed)
3 North St.,
Oxbridge,
Somerset.
Chartered Accountant.

4. Family Provision

Until 1938 a testator had complete freedom to dispose of his property, real or personal, in any manner he thought fit. He was not obliged to make any will. Moreover, if he made a will he was not obliged by law to include any provision for his wife and children, and he could leave to any other person the whole of his property if he so decided. Such was his testamentary freedom.

By the Inheritance (Family Provision) Act, 1938, as amended by the Intestates' Estates Act, 1952, the court was given power to vary a will on the application of certain persons. Where the court considered that either the dispositions of the will or the law relating to intestacy did not make reasonable provision for certain **dependants** of a deceased person, payment of reasonable provision out of the net estate might be ordered for his or her maintenance.

The Inheritance (Provision for Family and Dependants) Act, 1975, replaced the 1938 Act (as amended) and applies to the death on or after 1st April 1976, of a person domiciled in England and Wales.

The 1975 Act expands the list of claimants surviving the deceased to include:

(*a*) the wife or husband;

(*b*) a former spouse who has not remarried;

(*c*) a child;

(*d*) any person who was treated by the deceased as a child of the family (in relation to any marriage of his);

(*e*) any person who immediately before the death of the deceased was being maintained by the deceased without reciprocal consideration.

A mistress or other person with whom the deceased was cohabiting may claim under (*e*) above.

Any such person (*a*) to (*e*) may apply to the court for an order on the ground that the disposition of the deceased's estate effected by his will or the law relating to intestacy is not such as to make *reasonable financial provision* for such person.

'Reasonable financial provision' means in the case of a surviving spouse, other than one under a continuing separation following a decree of judicial separation, 'such financial provision as it would be reasonable in all the circumstances of the case for a husband or wife to receive, whether or not the provision is required for his or her maintenance'. In other cases the financial provision should be such as 'would be reasonable in all the circumstances of the case for the applicant to receive for his or her maintenance'.

Application under the Act must be made within 6 months from the date on which representation in respect of the estate is first taken out.

The court may make an order for periodical or lump sum payments from the estate. In making the order the Court must have regard to a number of matters including, e.g. the applicant's resources, the size of the estate, and the applicant's conduct towards the testator (or the person dying intestate). There are wide powers under the Act to upset dispositions intended to defeat or frustrate applications under the Act.

An objective test of 'reasonable financial provision' is made. As to the nature of the conduct of an applicant spouse living with the deceased at the time of his or her death, this is of marginal effect only in the majority of cases. In *Wachtel* v. *Wachtel* (1973), Lord Denning, M.R., stated (in regard to financial provision in divorce proceedings) that the conduct of a party was relevant only where it was ' "both obvious and gross", so much so that to order one party to support another whose conduct falls into this category is repugnant to anyone's sense of justice. . . .' An unmarried daughter who devoted considerable time to looking after the deceased at considerable sacrifice will have a strong moral claim for provision—*Re Cook* (1956). A child who lost contact with deceased for a long time, and was not dependent on him in any way, has little, if any, claim on the deceased for provision—*Re Andrews* (1955). In *Re Callaghan* (dec.) (1984), it was held that 'child' was not limited to a minor or dependent child but could include a stepson if treated as one of the family or as in *Re Leach* (dec.) (1985), an adult stepdaughter.

5. Personal Representatives

It is a feature of the English legal system that a deceased's estate does not vest in the persons to whom he has left it by will, or among whom it has by law to be distributed on an intestacy. The estate vests, in the first instance, in the deceased's personal representatives. These are interposed, as it were, between the estate and the beneficiaries.

The personal representatives are recognized by law as representing the deceased person for all purposes under the law of property, and for most purposes under the law of contract and tort. In general terms the deceased's rights and liabilities are transferred or transmitted to his lawfully appointed personal representatives, and can be enforced by or against them as soon as they are officially able so to act.

There are two **classes** of personal representative:

(*a*) **Executors,** who are appointed usually by a testator in his will. Sometimes an appointment may be implied, as where a testator nominates a certain person to pay off his debts. In this event, the executor is technically called 'an executor according to the tenor'.

(*b*) **Administrators,** i.e. personal representatives of someone who has died intestate.

We must beware of oversimplifying the division between these two classes, because although a testator may appoint an executor in his will there is no certainty that the appointee will act when the time comes. Where no executor is appointed, or where an executor dies, becomes incapacitated through illness, or refuses to act, the court itself will appoint a person to administer the estate 'with the will annexed'. This means that the appointee will administer the estate in accordance with the terms of the will as though he were an executor. This special type of administrator is called an *administrator cum testamento annexo*.

If an infant is appointed an administrator, an adult will be required to act for him during his minority. Such an appointee is called an *administrator durante minore aetate* ('during infancy').

An executor appointed under a will of which the validity is in dispute cannot take office, for if the will should be declared invalid he would be acting under a void authority. In this type of case an *administrator pendente lite* ('during the litigation') has to be appointed; he may proceed with the administration but must not distribute the property among the beneficiaries.

Probate and Letters of Administration

An executor can begin his duties immediately following the death of the testator. His *right to dispose of the estate* is not complete, however, until he has obtained a **grant of probate** of the will.

Probate (from the Latin *probatum*, 'proved') is nothing more than an official acceptance that the will is a genuine one, and that the executor's right to administer the estate is officially sanctioned. Probate may be obtained in two ways: (*a*) Probate in Common Form (the usual one); and (*b*) Probate in Solemn Form.

Application for probate may be made by the executors in person at the Principal Probate Registry (Somerset House, London) or at a district registry. Applicants should present the following documents: (i) the will, if any; (ii) a certificate of death, (iii) particulars of property liable to capital transfer tax; and (iv) a list of debts and funeral expenses.

Where the deceased has many complicated business interests the collection of information as at (iv) above may take some time. If the documents are in order, and payment of estate duty is made, probate can then be granted and a *copy* of the will handed to the executor. The original will is retained at the Probate Registry.

Probate in common form is usually a matter of course. Where a dispute arises as to the validity of the will, **probate in solemn form** will have to be obtained. This involves an action taken usually before a judge of the Chancery Division of the High Court in London.

Letters of Administration are granted at the registries mentioned above, and in broadly the same way as probate of a will. Whereas an executor is selected because, at least in the opinion of the deceased, he is an honest and prudent person, an administrator enjoys no such confidence. Therefore the court will not usually appoint an administrator unless he produces what is called an 'administration bond'. This is a solemn undertaking by the administrator to pay to the Principal Registrar double the value of the estate if he does not administer it in accordance with the law. Two sureties who guarantee to be liable if the administrator defaults in this obligation are also obtained.

Who may be appointed. The naming of an executor is within the discretion of the testator. Usually more than one executor is nominated, because it is always open to a sole executor to refuse to act, but only the first four named can act. Probate will not be granted to more than four executors. Nor will it be granted to (*a*) a person of unsound mind, or (*b*) an infant during his minority.

As to administrators, the appointment is within the discretion of the court. The order of priority of appointment follows that of the persons entitled to take on intestacy: surviving spouse, children, father and mother of deceased, etc. Sometimes a creditor may be appointed, e.g. where the estate is insolvent.

Not more than four administrators may be appointed. Where an infant is beneficiary there must normally be at least two, although a trust corporation may act as sole trustee. Trust corporations include the Public Trustee and any corporation such as a bank which is either appointed by the court to act as custodian trustee, or is qualified as such under the Public Trustee (Custodian Trustee) Rules, 1926.

Powers and Liabilities of Personal Representatives. The personal representatives have absolute power to dispose of the property for the purpose of administration of the estate. On a total intestacy a trust for sale automatically arises, and the powers of trustees for sale are conferred upon the executors (Administration of Estates Act, 1925, s. 39).

Personal representatives have one year in which to wind up the estate, such time being extended if need be. Where a beneficiary or creditor is prejudiced by delay, he may complain to the court but will have to prove that neglect on the part of the personal representatives was the cause of the delay.

Personal representatives hold a fiduciary position in respect to the administration, and are therefore in the position of trustees. If they distribute the estate imprudently, e.g. by paying the beneficiaries before the creditors, they render themselves personally liable. However, the court has power to relieve a personal representative where he has acted honestly and reasonably and ought fairly to be excused.

Revocation. A grant of probate or letters of administration may be revoked if good reason can be shown. For example, if the grant was obtained by fraud, or if a later will has been discovered, or if it can be shown that the testator is alive, or if probate was granted to the wrong persons or was irregular, there would be good reason for revocation.

Duties of Personal Representatives. The four main duties of personal representatives are:

(*a*) To collect all debts due to the estate.

(*b*) To pay all the debts and satisfy all the liabilities of the estate.

(*c*) To convert unauthorized investments into authorized ones (if need be). There is usually power to postpone this duty for as long as the personal representatives think fit.

(*d*) To distribute the remainder of the estate according to (i) the will, or (ii) the rules of intestacy.

Where the estate is sufficient to pay off all debts and the beneficiaries in full, there is no difficulty. Where, on the other hand, the estate is insolvent there will necessarily be conflicting claims. Accordingly rules must be laid down as to the order or priority of payment.

Insolvent Estates. The following rules apply where the estate is insufficient to meet the claims of creditors in full:

(*a*) Funeral expenses, testamentary expenses, and the costs of administration have first priority. They must be paid in full, if possible.

(*b*) Debts have next priority. These are paid in the order set out in the Insolvency Act, 1986, thus:

(i) Preferred debts, e.g. arrears of rates and taxes for one year, and wages of clerks and workmen (up to £200) due for a period of four months prior to the death.

(ii) Ordinary debts. These are debts not falling into the categories of Preferred or Deferred.

(iii) Deferred debts, e.g. claims by a husband or wife for money lent to the deceased for the purpose of business, and claims for money lent to the deceased on terms that it is to bear interest at a rate varying with the profits of the deceased's business.

Secured creditors, e.g. persons holding a mortgage, charge or lien on property, are also entitled to special rights in regard to payment.

6. Intestacy

Before 1926, the freehold land owned by a person dying intestate passed to his heir at law, while his personalty (including leaseholds) passed to his next of kin.

Descent upon an intestacy is now governed by the Administration of Estates Act, 1925, and the Intestates' Estates Act, 1952. After paying funeral expenses, testamentary expenses and debts, the administrators hold the estate on trust for sale (with power to postpone the sale), and distribute the proceeds of sale according to rules laid down below.

Five main groups of people must be considered: (i) a surviving husband or wife; (ii) surviving children; (iii) surviving parents; (iv) surviving brothers and sisters of the whole blood; and (v) surviving relations of remoter degree.

The right of the intestate's widow or widower depends largely on whether there are any children of the marriage.

(*a*) *Where the intestate leaves a surviving spouse.* If there is no issue and no surviving parent or brothers and sisters of the whole blood, the estate passes to the surviving husband or wife. If there is issue, the surviving husband or wife takes

(i) personal chattels, e.g. furniture, motor-cars, and jewellery, but not chattels used for business purposes; and

(ii) £75,000 free of death duty and costs, with (if possible) interest at 4 per cent; and

(iii) a life interest in half of the residue (this involves the investment of capital from which the surviving spouse will derive income for life). The remaining property then goes to the issue on 'the statutory trusts' (see below).

If there is a surviving parent, brother or sister of the whole blood, but *no issue*, the surviving spouse takes

(i) personal chattels (as above); and
(ii) £125,000 free of duty and costs with interest (payable out of income) at 4 per cent from the date of death; and
(iii) half the residue absolutely.

The remaining property goes to the parents of the intestate absolutely; if there are no parents, it goes to the brother or sisters of the whole blood (or the issue thereof) on 'the statutory trusts'.

Section 14 of the Family Law Reform Act, 1969, provides that where either parent of an illegitimate child dies intestate in respect of all or any of his real or personal property, the illegitimate child (or, if he is dead, his issue) shall be entitled to take any interest therein to which he would have been entitled if he had been born legitimate.

Where an illegitimate child dies intestate, each of his parents (if surviving) shall be entitled to take any interest therein to which that parent would have been entitled if the child had been born legitimate.

(*b*) *Where the intestate leaves no surviving spouse.* The residue is held on 'the statutory trusts' for the issue, if any.

If there is no issue but one or both parents survive, the residue passes to the parents absolutely.

If there is neither issue nor parents, but other relatives survive, the property is distributed in the following order:

(i) brothers and sisters (or their issue) of the *whole* blood;
(ii) brothers and sisters (or their issue) of the *half* blood;
(iii) grandparents absolutely, if there is no one in class (i) and (ii) above;
(iv) uncles and aunts (or issue) of the *whole* blood;
(v) uncles and aunts (or issue) of the *half* blood.

In cases (i), (ii), (iv), and (v) above the property is held on 'the statutory trusts'.

Where the deceased leaves no relatives whatsoever, the property goes to the Crown as *bona vacantia* ('ownerless property').

The Statutory Trusts. This means that the administrators are to divide the property equally among the beneficiaries within the class, each share vesting at the age of majority or on a prior marriage of the beneficiary. Where a beneficiary predeceases the intestate, his share goes to his issue (if any). If he has no issue, the property falls into the common fund.

We should note in passing that on an intestacy the surviving spouse has, in normal circumstances, the right to require the personal representatives to appropriate to him or her the matrimonial home. The market value of the home on such an appropriation has to be deducted from the other benefits accruing to the surviving spouse under the intestacy.

Where a testator fails to dispose of all his property he is described as dying 'partially intestate'. The property not disposed of specifically is taken by the residuary legatee, if any. In the absence of such a person, the property not disposed of by will is distributed by the testator's executors in accordance with the rules of intestacy as set out above.

Hotchpot. In a total intestacy, s. 47(1) (iii) of the Administration of Estates Act, 1925, requires money or property transferred to his child by the intestate during his lifetime to be brought into account on the division of his residuary estate under the statutory trusts, and treated as having been paid on account of the child's share under the intestacy, unless a contrary intention is shown. This is called the hotchpot rule.

Similarly, in a partial intestacy, under s. 49 a surviving spouse must bring into hotchpot any beneficial interest received under the operative part of the will; and so must children bring into account any substantial benefit received from the deceased during his lifetime; and issue, any beneficial interests under the operative part of the will.

7. Gifts 'Inter Vivos'

So far in this section we have considered the disposition of a person's estate in the event of his death. A person may make dispositions of his property with the intention that they be effective or become operative during his lifetime.

A gift may be defined as *a transfer of property whereby the transferor* (the donor) *receives no valuable consideration from the transferee* (the donee). Gifts may be made by deed or, more usually, by a transfer of the property by the donor to the donee with the intention that the *ownership* in the goods (as distinct from mere possession) shall be transferred. A gift is not complete therefore until *possession* of the thing has actually been transferred to the donee: the mere intention alone is insufficient; there must be an actual transfer of possession. Where the gift is by deed, the physical transfer of possession or delivery is not necessary. A donee can, of course, refuse a gift. The law presumes that a donee has accepted the gift unless he has shown clearly that he does not wish to do so.

Once a gift is made it is irrevocable. On the Continent, however, some legal systems permit a donor to revoke a gift on the grounds of ingratitude by the donee. A gift may be conditional. Thus a gift of an engagement ring may be conditional on the fiancée being prepared to marry the donor of the ring.

8. 'Donatio Mortis Causa'

A *donatio* (gift) *mortis causa* (in anticipation of death) is the delivery of property to another in contemplation of the donor's imminent death on condition that the gift is not to be absolute until the donor dies.

A *donatio mortis causa* resembles a gift by will in that: that donor has the right to revoke the gift; the gift lapses if the donee happens to die before the donor; the gift is subject to death duties, and is also liable for the donor's debts.

A *donatio* resembles a gift *inter vivos* ('between the living') in that it takes effect when the delivery occurs, subject to the condition (as stated above) that the gift will only become absolute if the donor dies. The donor must be in imminent peril of death, i.e. *in extremis*, either by illness or otherwise.

Revocation of the gift is automatic on recovery of the donor from his illness. Revocation may be express, as where the donor informs the donee that the gift is revoked; or implied, as where the donor resumes possession of the property.

Delivery of the gift may be actual or constructive. Actual delivery occurs where, for example, *A* who is about to die hands a ring to *B*. Constructive delivery occurs where, for example, *A* hands the keys of his safe where the property is kept to *B*, the donee, coupled with the intention to transfer ownership.

Anything capable of passing by mere delivery can be the subject of a *donatio*. Examples include a Post Office Savings Book, National Savings Certificates, and a Bank Deposit Book. Freehold land and leasehold land cannot pass by means of a *donatio*.

9. Exercises

1. Outline the main provisions of the Wills Act, 1837.
2. What is the purpose of 'attestation' in regard to a will?
3. How may a will be revoked?
4. What is meant by the doctrine of dependent-relative revocation?
5. What are the three kinds of legacies? Give an example from your own experience of each.
6. Draw up a specimen will for yourself, disposing of all your property.
7. Name the powers, duties and liabilities of personal representatives.
8. Outline the legal provisions in regard to intestacy. State the Acts which apply particularly to this part of the law and show how an estate devolves (i) where an intestate leaves a surviving spouse, and (ii) where an intestate leaves no surviving spouse.
9. In relation to the law of intestacy what is meant by the phrase 'the statutory trusts'?
10. Explain the law in regard to *donatio mortis causa*.
11. Consider the importance of the changes made to the Law of Wills by the Administration of Justice Act, 1982.

12

CRIMINAL LAW

1. Definition of Crime

Criminal law is concerned with conduct which the State considers should be punished, whereas civil law is concerned with private rights. A crime may be regarded as a public wrong; but conduct which is harmful to the public is not necessarily criminal. 'Crimes, then, are wrongs which the judges have held, or Parliament has from time to time laid down, are sufficiently injurious to the public to warrant the application of criminal procedure to deal with them.' (Smith and Hogan.) Nor is immoral conduct necessarily criminal; but conduct which would not be regarded as immoral may be criminal on grounds of social expediency. 'The domain of criminal jurisprudence can only be ascertained by examining what acts at any particular period are declared by the State to be crimes ...' (Lord Atkin.)

This means that crime can only usefully be defined by reference to procedure: 'A crime (or offence) is a legal wrong that can be followed by criminal proceedings which may result in punishment.' (Glanville Williams).

2. Sources

(*a*) **Common Law.** Many criminal offences were created by the common law courts and the definitions of some of these offences are to be found even today only in case law, e.g. murder, involuntary manslaughter, common assault.

An offence remains a common law offence even when statute provides defences or penalties, e.g. Homicide Act, 1957.

Today the courts have no power to create new offences; and this was acknowledged by the House of Lords in *Knuller* v. *D.P.P.* (1973). In an earlier case before the House of Lords, *Shaw* v. *D.P.P.* (1962), Lord Simonds L.C. seemed to be claiming otherwise when he stated that 'there remains in the courts of law a residual power to enforce the supreme and fundamental purpose of the law to conserve not only the safety and order but also the moral welfare of the state'.

(*b*) **Textbooks.** These are not sources, but certain early works—e.g. Coke, Foster, Hawkins, Hale—are accepted by the courts as authoritative of the law as it stood at the time when the book was written.

Note: In this chapter, *D* denotes the defendant and *P* the prosecutor or the person affected by *D*'s act.

Modern books are not authoritative but may be used persuasively by counsel and thus influence the courts, e.g. Kenny, Williams, Smith and Hogan.

(*c*) **Statute.** This is the main source of law today. Some statutes may merely amend common law offences, e.g. Homicide Act, 1957. Others may abolish earlier law and start afresh, e.g. Theft Act, 1968, Criminal Damage Act, 1971. But a great number of modern statutes which have no apparent connexion with criminal law contain criminal offences, e.g. Income Tax Acts, National Insurance Act, Health and Safety at Work Act. Ministers appear to accept that the best way of ensuring compliance with the statute is to have a criminal law sanction; and as most of the charges are heard by unpaid magistrates this is no doubt an economic method. But it may be doubted whether the criminal law should be so vastly widened since even the minor offences involve prosecution before the criminal courts (see, for example, 'Breaking the Rules'—a report by Justice 1980).

(*d*) **Subordinate Legislation.** Statute may empower a minister or some other body, e.g. a local authority, to make rules, orders, or byelaws which may contain offences. If the minister exceeds the authority given by the statute he is said to have acted *ultra vires* and the rule will be invalid.

3. Classifications

Crimes may be classified as follows:

(*a*) *According to source* (see above).

(*b*) *According to method of trial.* The Criminal Law Act, 1977, provides as follows:

(i) Indictable offences—triable in the Crown Court by judge and jury; e.g. murder, robbery.

(ii) Summary offences—triable by lay or stipendiary magistrates; e.g. most traffic offences.

(iii) Offences triable either way; e.g. theft.

(*c*) *Treason, arrestable offences, other offences.*

Treason is an offence against the State. Arrestable offences are the more serious offences for which arrest may be made without a warrant. By s. 2 of the Criminal Law Act, 1967 they are ones which have a fixed penalty, e.g. murder, or for which a person, not previously convicted, may under any enactment be sentenced for a term of five years, or attempts to commit such offences. Also, a statute may declare an offence which has a lesser sentence than five years to be arrestable, e.g. s. 12 of the Theft Act, 1968.

Other offences are the less serious ones.

4. Criminal Liability

Almost all common law offences and serious statutory offences require two elements, **actus reus** and **mens rea**; in the words of the Latin maxim: *actus non facit reum nisi mens sit rea*. Some offences are satisfied with negligence instead of *mens rea*. Many minor statutory offences require proof only of the *actus reus*: these are called strict liability offences. In addition, a person may sometimes be criminally liable for the act and even *mens rea* of another; this is known as **vicarious liability**. Lastly a corporation, a non-human, may be held personally liable for acts of its directors or servants.

Actus reus

This is the prohibited act which is necessary for all crimes and is to be found in the definition of the crime. Professor Glanville Williams defines *actus reus* as 'the conduct that is forbidden by the rule of the criminal law on the assumption that any necessary *mens rea* is found to exist ... the external elements of the offence, including the negative of defences'. The *actus reus* may consist of three elements: (i) the willed movement or omission, (ii) the surrounding circumstances and (in some cases) (iii) the prohibited consequences.

The following may amount to conduct:

(i) A physical act, e.g. a blow.

(ii) Words, in such offences as incitement, conspiracy, blackmail; and where the words induce an act by an innocent agent.

(iii) An omission, where there is a legal duty to act either at common law, or by statute or by undertaking, e.g. a parent has a duty to provide food and medical attention for his child.

> *Instan* (1893). A niece who had undertaken to look after her elderly aunt at her aunt's expense and failed to provide food and to call medical assistance when the aunt was seriously ill, was convicted of manslaughter.

(iv) Possession, e.g. drug offences.

(v) A state of affairs, e.g. 'being found in a dwelling-house for an unlawful purpose'.

(vi) Conduct of others in vicarious liability.

If the conduct is not willed by a person it will not count as his act, e.g. where *A* is pushed by *B* into *C*, it is not *A*'s act. Similarly, the conduct of a sleepwalker in his sleep is not willed conduct (see **automatism**, p. 320).

The word 'unlawfully' in the definition of a crime indicates merely that there are defences.

Mens rea

This consists of intention or recklessness. It is necessary to distinguish them since some crimes require nothing less than intention, e.g. attempt and wounding with intent under s. 18 of the Offences Against the Person Act, 1861 (Belfon, 1976).

(*a*) **Intention.** The hallmark of intention is desire or purpose. Professor Williams defines it as 'a volitional movement (or omission), knowledge of the relevant circumstances and a desire that any relevant consequences shall follow'. Foresight of certainty without desire must also be counted as intention. The Law Commission has proposed the following definition: 'A person intends an event not only (*a*) when his purpose is to cause that event but also (*b*) when he has no substantial doubt that the event will result from his conduct.'

The words 'has no substantial doubt' seem less clear than 'is certain'.

(*b*) **Recklessness.** Here there is foresight of the consequences but not desire. The Law Commission has proposed the following definition: 'A person is reckless if (*a*) knowing that there is a risk that an event may result from his conduct or that a circumstance may exist, he takes that risk, and (*b*) it is unreasonable for him to take it having regard to the degree and nature of the risk which he knows to be present.'

However, in *Caldwell* (1981), where *D*, while drunk, had set fire to a hotel and was indicted for arson, the House of Lords stated that recklessness had a wider meaning than that which had previously been ascribed to it. It was used as an ordinary English word and as such included not only deciding to ignore a risk which one has recognized as existing but also failing to give any thought to whether or not there is a risk in circumstances where, if any thought were given to the matter, the existence of risk would be obvious. The decision in this case and in *Lawrence* (1981) has been to bring a marked change in the approach to recklessness, very different from that recommended by the Law Commission. This test of recklessness was followed in Miller (1983) where *D* was convicted of reckless arson

Negligence

Mens rea involves foresight or awareness. Negligence does not; it is conduct which fails to measure up to the conduct of a reasonable person, i.e. the test is objective. Negligence has been long established in the law of tort, e.g. the negligent motorist will have to compensate anyone injured by his act. In criminal law there is less scope for this since the sanction is punishment. Some writers doubt therefore whether negligence ought to feature at all in criminal law (e.g. Hart). There are, however, some statutory offences based on negligence, e.g. careless driving, neglect of children and some offences under the Health and Safety at Work Act, 1974; and some offences may be regarded as offences of negligence where there is a defence of due diligence, e.g. Trade Descriptions Act, 1968. There is also one serious offence, manslaughter, which can be committed by grossly negligent conduct.

Strict Liability

Common law offences require *mens rea*; and until the middle of the nineteenth century the courts always presumed that a statutory offence also required *mens rea* even where the statute did not expressly say so. However, when the courts came to construe the social legislation which Parliament had begun to pass they felt that the statutes would be rendered more or less ineffective if the prosecution had to prove *mens rea* before the lay magistrates, who heard these minor cases. The courts therefore began to hold in this class of offence, called 'public welfare offences' in America, that where the statute neither expressly nor by necessary implication required *mens rea*, then Parliament had intended that it was not necessary, and thus the prosecution could succeed by proving merely the *actus reus*. The following are two examples of this:

> *Parker* v. *Alder* (1899). *D* was convicted under the Food and Drugs Act of selling impure milk. He had sent pure milk by train to London but when it was delivered it was found to have been adulterated by water and the culprit was unknown.

> *Quelch* v. *Collett* (1948). Provisions as to third party insurance in the Road Traffic Act were held to be strict and *D* was liable even though he was without fault.

Offences which the courts have construed in this way are to be found in such statutes as Sale of Food and Drugs Act, Road Traffic Acts, Trade Descriptions Act, Consumer Protection Act, Pollution Act, Factories Acts and similar statutes whose object is protection of the public against such activities. In *Westminster City Council* v. *Croyalgrange Ltd.* (1986) it was stated that caution should be exercised in reaching a guilty verdict where the word 'knowingly' is incorporated into the offence. Occasionally the courts have extended the notion of strict liability to offences outside the field of social legislation. For example:

> *Prince* (1875). A conviction under s. 55 of the Offences against the Person Act, 1861, of unlawfully taking an unmarried girl under sixteen out of the possession and against the will of her father was upheld even though *D* believed on reasonable grounds that the girl was over 16, the court holding that it was an offence of strict liability so far as the age of the girl was concerned.

Vicarious Liability

In tort a master may be liable for the tort of his servant committed in the course of his employment. At common law there was no vicarious liability in criminal law (*Huggins*, 1730). But from the late nineteenth century the courts began to hold that it could arise in statutory offences in the following circumstances:

(i) Where the statute expressly says so (Pharmacy and Poisons Act, 1933, s. 24).

(ii) In licensing cases, (*a*) where the licensee knows that his servant is contravening the statute and fails to stop him, or (*b*) where the licensee has delegated control of the business.

Allen v. *Whitehead* (1930). The licensee of a refreshment house employed a manager for it and instructed him not to allow prostitutes to frequent the house. The manager knew that they were resorting to it. The licensee did not but was convicted because he had delegated control to the manager.

(iii) Where the offence is one of strict liability and the master can legitimately be regarded as coming within the *actus reus*. A master can be held guilty of a 'selling' or 'using' offence even though the act is that of his servant. But he will not be held liable for a 'driving' offence by his servant.

Coppen v. *Moore* (1898). The owner of a shop was convicted under the Merchandise Marks Act of selling goods to which a false trade description was applied, when without his knowledge an assistant sold an American ham as a 'Scotch ham'.

Green v. *Burnett* (1955). A company was convicted under the Motor Vehicles (Construction and Use) Regulations of using a vehicle on the road with defective brakes, even though the defect leading to the failure could only have been discovered by dismantling the cylinder.

There are one or two other cases which cannot be brought under the above headings, e.g. *Newton* v. *Smith* (1962).

Corporate liability

A corporation may be liable (i) vicariously where an ordinary master can be liable (see above), and (ii) under the '*alter ego*' doctrine.

Under (ii) a corporation can be held personally liable for most offences provided:

(*a*) it is a fineable offence;
(*b*) it is committed by a 'controlling mind', i.e. a director,
(*c*) it is committed in the course of his corporate duties.

I.C.R. Haulage (1944). A company, its managing director and persons outside the company were indicted for conspiracy to defraud. The Court of Criminal Appeal held that the company could be liable through its director.

Henshall v. *Harvey* (1965). A weighbridge operator employed by a company by oversight allowed an overladen lorry to be driven away. The company was held not guilty of aiding and abetting the driver's offence, since the knowledge of an inferior servant is not knowledge of the company.

5. Exemptions from Liability

(*a*) **The Sovereign.** The Crown cannot be prosecuted, nor can government departments.

(*b*) **Foreign Sovereigns, Ambassadors.** Visiting foreign sovereigns and diplomats are exempt from criminal liability; so are members of armed forces unless a statute provides otherwise.

(*c*) **Children.** There is an irrebuttable presumption that a child under ten cannot commit a crime. If a child is between ten and fourteen there is a rebuttable presumption that he cannot do so; but the prosecution can rebut this by evidence of 'a mischievous discretion', i.e. that he knows that what he is doing is gravely wrong (*Gorrie*, 1919).

The criminal liability of children over fourteen is the same as for adults.

6. Parties to a Crime

By s. 1 of the Criminal Law Act, 1967, which abolished the distinction between felonies and misdemeanours, parties may now all be charged as principals. But there are reasons for distinguishing the parts actually played: (i) for the purpose of punishment; (ii) an accessory cannot be guilty of an offence unless he has *mens rea*, whereas a principal may in strict liability offences; (iii) duress is available to an accessory as a defence in murder but not to a principal.

The courts therefore distinguish between a principal or perpetrator who does the act and the accessory who counsels, procures, aids or abets him. However, the parties may be charged as joint principals. A person who commits an act through an innocent agent will be charged as a principal. So will the master in vicarious liability.

To constitute counselling or procuring there must be instigation, not mere knowledge; or facilitating the commission of the offence by providing the instrument knowing that it is to be used for a crime of the type committed. In *Bainbridge* (1960) *D*'s oxygen cutting equipment was used for burglary.

Prior to 1967 aiding and abetting was assisting at the scene of the crime: there had to be help or encouragement, not mere presence; common purpose; power to prevent the offence. Since the Act, presence would not seem to be necessary.

If the principal exceeds the agreed purpose the accessory will not be held liable for the excess if he did not agree.

> *Davies* v. *D.P.P.* (1954). The agreed purpose was common assault but *D* had a knife and killed. *D*'s confederates were held not to be parties to the homicide.

Both the principal and the accessory may be liable for unforeseen consequences:

Buck (1960). *D* carried out an illegal abortion on *P* at the request of her friend *E*. The girl died. The Court of Criminal Appeal held that *D* was rightly convicted as principal and *E* as accessory to manslaughter.

Normally a person cannot be convicted as an accessory if there is no principal—*Thornton* v. *Mitchell* (1940). But there are a number of exceptions to this rule.

The *mens rea* may consist of knowledge of the circumstances, or knowledge of the type of crime planned, or in some cases 'wilful blindness' (*Carter* v. *Mace*, 1949). Negligence is not sufficient.

7. General Defences

It is convenient to group these together, although mistake is no more than a negating of *mens rea*.

Automatism

If the act is involuntary, there is no act in law. This means that it would be a defence even to an offence of strict liability.

According to Lord Denning in *Bratty* (1963) automatism is confined to acts done while *D* is unconscious and to spasms, reflex actions and convulsions. The usual instances are: sleepwalking or other behaviour during sleep (*Boshears*, 1961), concussion, epilepsy, hypoglycaemia (*Quick*, 1973) and dissociative states or hysterical neurosis. An act which does not arise from automatism may nevertheless be involuntary, e.g. where a driver's brakes fail without his fault (*Burns* v. *Bidder*, 1967) or where a driver is attacked by a swarm of bees and cannot control his vehicle (*Hill* v. *Baxter*, 1958).

A successful defence of automatism entitles the defendant to an absolute acquittal. But the courts have qualified the defence in three ways: (i) *D* will not be entitled to the defence if there was prior fault on his part, e.g. if he does not stop driving when he realizes that he is likely to fall asleep; (ii) self-induced intoxication will never amount to automatism; (iii) if the automatism arises from disease of the mind the M'Naghten rules will be applied. Devlin J. in *Kemp* (1957) held that the issue of insanity was a question of law for the judge; and this was approved by Lord Denning in *Bratty*.

In *Quick* (1973), *D*, a diabetic, had taken insulin which had produced a hypoglycaemic episode during which he assaulted a patient. Following *Kemp* and *Bratty* the trial judge did not allow the jury to consider the defence of automatism. The Court of Appeal in quashing the conviction distinguished *Kemp* on the ground that there the blackout resulted from inherent disease whereas in Quick it resulted from an external event, i.e. the insulin injection, and therefore *D* was entitled to the defence of non-insane automatism.

In putting forward the defence *D* must put it on a proper foundation;

and according to Lord Denning *D*'s own word must be supported by medical evidence.

Mistake

According to the maxim, ignorance of the law is no defence. But ignorance or mistake may be a defence where:

(i) The definition of the crime involves a concept of civil law, e.g. bigamy—being married.
(ii) There is a claim of right—this is a defence to theft and criminal damage (*Smith*, 1974).

Mistake of fact may be a defence if it negatives the *mens rea* of the offence, e.g. if *A*, believing it to be his, takes *B*'s umbrella he does not have the *mens rea* for theft. The House of Lords in *Morgan* (1976) held that mistake will be a defence if it is an honest mistake; except in bigamy where the mistake must be based on reasonable grounds, i.e. an objective test (*Tolson*, 1889). In other than bigamy cases courts have sometimes held that the mistake must be reasonable. But the ruling in *Morgan* presumably now applies to such cases; though not apparently to mistake as to a defence (*Rose*, 1884).

Insanity

According to the **M'Naghten rules**, which a committee of judges stated in 1843, an accused is presumed sane until he proves otherwise. In order to succeed in the defence of insanity he must show that at the time of committing the act he was labouring under such a defect of reason, from diseases of the mind, as not to know:

(i) The nature and quality of the act he was doing or if he did know it.
(ii) That he did not know he was doing what was wrong.

The judges added:

(iii) That if the accused 'labours under a partial delusion only, and is not in other respects insane, we think he must be considered in the same situation as to responsibility as if the facts with respect to which the delusion exists were real'.

The accused who puts forward this defence must prove on balance of probabilities that (i) medically he is insane and (ii) that he comes within the M'Naghten rules. If the defence is successful the verdict is not guilty by reason of insanity; but the accused will be detained in a hospital such as Broadmoor.

Since the abolition of the death penalty this defence is rarely used, diminished responsibility being preferred. But if the accused raises the defence of diminished responsibility or automatism the prosecution will be allowed to rebut with evidence of insanity—*Kemp* (1957).

The courts have also given a wide meaning to disease of the mind:

> *Kemp* (1957). *D* injured his wife in a blackout caused by arteriosclerosis. His defence was automatism. Devlin J. ruled that physical disease of the brain could amount to disease of the mind and could therefore come within the rules.

This decision was approved by Lord Denning in the House of Lords case of *Bratty* (1963), where he said, 'It seems to me that any mental disorder which has manifested itself in violence and is prone to recur is a disease of the mind. At any rate it is the sort of disease for which a person should be detained in hospital rather than be given an unqualified acquittal.'

Intoxication by Drink or Drugs

In the House of Lords case of *D.P.P.* v. *Beard* (1920), Lord Birkenhead stated the law with regard to this defence as follows:

(i) If the intoxication causes actual insanity, e.g. delirium tremens, then the M'Naghten rules will be applied.
(ii) Intoxication is a defence if it rendered *D* incapable of forming the specific intent essential to constitute the crime.
(iii) Intoxication not negativing *mens rea* but merely leading *D* more readily to behave as he did is no defence.

The charge in Beard was murder, and in (ii) Lord Birkenhead was no doubt drawing a distinction between murder and negligent manslaughter which needs no intent; just as Lord Denning was doing in *A.-G. for Northern Ireland* (1963) when he referred to the case of the nurse at a christening party who was so drunk that she put the baby on the fire in mistake for a log of wood; Lord Denning said there would be a defence to murder but not to manslaughter. However, later courts held that intoxication was a defence only to crimes of 'specific intent'; and over the years held that murder, wounding with intent, theft, robbery, burglary with intent to steal, handling stolen goods, criminal damage under s. 1(2) of the Act, and attempt, were such offences; whereas manslaughter, malicious wounding, assault occasioning actual bodily harm, common assault, indecent assault, assault on a constable, rape, criminal damage under s. 1(1) of the Act, and taking a conveyance without consent have been held to be offences of basic intent, not requiring a specific intent, and therefore intoxication is no defence. Only the decisions will show which are which. The leading case today is *Majewski* (1976) in which the House of Lords considered the history of the defence and approved the classification adopted by the courts after Beard. The actual decision was that intoxication was not a defence to assault occasioning actual bodily harm.

In *Pordage* (1978) the Court of Appeal held that the question to be asked is not whether *D* had the capacity to form the intent but whether he in fact formed it.

In *O'Grady* (1987) the Court dismissed an appeal that the blows causing the death of the victim had been struck by *D* under a drunken and unreasonable mistake that a deadly attack was being made on him.

The principles are the same whether the intoxication is by alcohol or drugs.

> *Lipman* (1970). *D* took LSD and during hallucination killed his girl-friend not knowing what he was doing. *D*'s conviction of manslaughter was upheld.

There is very little authority on involuntary drunkenness but it is open for the courts in a *Lipman* situation, but where *D*'s intoxication was not self-induced and where he was not at fault in any way, to hold that *D* was in a state of automatism and so not liable for murder *or manslaughter*.

Prevention of Crime: Arrest

S. 3(1) of the Criminal Law Act, 1967, provides that a person may use such force as is reasonable in the circumstances in the prevention of crime or in effecting or assisting in the lawful arrest of offenders.

As Williams points out, this 'gives no clear guidance on what we are allowed to do', especially on what offences are so serious that extreme force is justified to prevent them.

Private Defence

This will excuse crimes against the person or property, provided the force used is necessary to avoid the attack and is reasonable. If *D* is mistaken in his belief that there is need for defence, he will be excused only if his belief is reasonable (*Rose*, 1847).

At common law there were rules as to the duty to retreat if possible before acting in defence. It is not clear whether those rules remain or have been replaced by s. 3(1) of the Criminal Law Act, 1967; but according to Williams they have not; also queried in *Bird* (1985).

The occupier of premises may use force against a trespasser provided it is necessary and reasonable. In *Hussey* (1924) it was assumed by the Court of Criminal Appeal that it was still good law that a man may defend his dwelling against unlawful eviction even to the extent of taking life. However, it is doubtful whether the courts would take that view today.

Under s. 6 of the Criminal Law Act, 1977, a displaced residential occupier may use necessary and reasonable force to re-enter. Similar force may be used to prevent dispossession of chattels.

Necessity

Is it a defence for *D* to break the law in order to prevent greater harm? In the American case of 'The William Gray' it was held that the captain of a ship was justified in entering port against the regulations where he did so in a storm in order to save the ship, lives and cargo.

Opinions differ as to whether necessity is a general defence at common law or whether it is confined to the definitions of particular offences. Some statutes contain a defence in respect of acts done in an emergency, e.g. Control of Pollution Act, 1974; in other offences a justification may be implied, e.g. careless driving. At common law there is a number of cases in which necessity has been held to be a defence, e.g. prisoners leaving prison which was on fire, pulling down a house to prevent a fire spreading, jettisoning cargo in a storm at sea for the safety of passengers, force-feeding prisoners on hunger-strike in gaol. But it is not clear how far the defence extends beyond such cases. Williams has argued that there must be a general defence otherwise the doctor who operates on an unconscious victim of a road accident would have no defence to assault.

In the English case of *Dudley & Stephens* (1884) it was held not to be a defence to murder where some of the shipwrecked crew killed and ate the cabin boy to save their own lives. Nevertheless, there are no doubt circumstances where necessity would be a defence to murder.

Duress

If *D* commits any crime, other than murder, as a principal in the first degree (*Abbott*, 1977) and some forms of treason (*Oldcastle*, 1419), under the threat of immediate (*Gill*, 1963) death or serious personal violence (*A.-G.* v. *Whelan*, 1934) he may have the defence of duress. In *Howe* (1987) the House of Lords held that duress was not available as a defence in murder to either a principal or secondary party. Duress was also held to involve an objective as well as a subjective test.

A threat to property is not sufficient.

Coercion

By s. 47 of the Criminal Justice Act, 1925, on a charge against a wife for any offence other than treason or murder, it shall be a good defence to prove that the offence was committed in the presence of, and under the coercion of, the husband.

Whereas duress amounts to physical compulsion, coercion is concerned with 'moral or spiritual' influence. But it is seldom put forward as a defence; the only reported case seems to be *Pierce* (1941).

Superior Orders

There is little authority on this but although they are not usually a defence to a criminal charge it has been held in the South African case of *Smith* (1900) that a soldier would have a defence if he honestly believes he is doing his duty in obeying the commands of his superior and the orders are not so manifestly illegal that he ought to have known them to be unlawful.

8. Inchoate Offences

There are three such offences:

(*a*) **Incitement.** It is incitement to counsel, procure, advise, encourage or persuade a person to commit a crime, even though that crime is not committed. If the crime is committed, the inciter becomes an accessory to the crime.

(*b*) **Conspiracy.** By the Criminal Law Act, 1977, it is a statutory conspiracy for two or more persons to agree to commit a crime, even though the offence is not committed. The Act in abolishing common-law conspiracy nevertheless preserved three conspiracies at common law: conspiracy to defraud, to corrupt public morals and to outrage public decency.

> *Scott* v. *Metropolitan Police Commissioner* (1975). The House of Lords held that *D* was rightly convicted of conspiracy to defraud where he had agreed with employees of cinema owners to pay them for lending him without the owners' consent films which he could copy in breach of copyright and sell for profit. An agreement dishonestly to deprive a person of something which is his or to which he might be entitled, or to injure some proprietary right of his suffices for the offence.

This offence is therefore wider than agreements to commit offences under the Theft Act.

> *Nock* (1978). The House of Lords held that an agreement to do what was in fact impossible was not a common law conspiracy; and quashed the conviction for conspiracy to produce a controlled cocaine-based drug from powder which in fact contained no cocaine.

It seems likely that the courts will treat Nock as applying also to statutory conspiracies.

(*c*) **Attempt.** It is an offence at common law to attempt to commit any indictable offence or an offence triable either way.

The *mens rea* for an attempt is nothing less than intention to commit the crime aimed at; recklessness is not sufficient (*Mohan*, 1976). Attempted murder requires the intent to kill (*Whybrow*, 1951).

The act must be 'proximate' to the crime attempted. The courts have said that to be proximate it must go beyond mere preparation.

> *Robinson* (1915). A jeweller was held not guilty of attempted obtaining by false pretences where he had staged a fake robbery of his jewellery, insured against theft, and allowed himself to be found by the police, bound and

gagged. He had not gone beyond preparation since he had not claimed from the insurance company.

Today Robinson could be charged under s. 5(2) of the Criminal Law Act, 1967, of causing the wasteful employment of the police.

The courts have not had much success in laying down more precise rules as to what constitutes a proximate act; and prosecutions often fail on this score. Another difficulty of attempt is the question of impossibility. Until recently a long line of authorities as far back as 1870 had held that factual impossibility was not a defence to attempt, and thus *D* could be convicted of attempting to steal from a pocket which was in fact empty (*Ring*, 1892) or attempting to obtain by false pretences where the person approached was not deceived (*Hensler*, 1870). But in *Haughton* v. *Smith* (1975) the House of Lords restated the rules with regard to this aspect in holding that *D* could not be guilty of attempting to handle goods which had in fact ceased to be stolen. The aim of the Criminal Attempts Act, 1981, was to clarify the law relating to attempts generally and, in particular, to reverse these decisions. S. 1(2) of the Act provides that a person may be guilty of attempting to commit an offence, even though the facts were such that the commission of the offence would have been impossible.

In *Shivpuri* (1986), the House of Lords held that since the Act, impossibility was no bar to a conviction for attempt. This decision overruled their previous decision in *Anderton* v. *Ryan* (1985), which tried to exclude some situations of impossibility from the effect of s. 1 of the Act.

9. Burden of Proof

In criminal cases the burden is throughout on the prosecution to establish the case against the accused beyond reasonable doubt. If the jury or magistrates have such doubt then they should acquit (*Woolmington*, 1935).

At the close of the prosecution case, counsel for the defence may submit that there is no case to answer; if the judge agrees he will direct the jury to acquit.

Normally, if the accused puts forward a defence he does not have to prove it but must adduce sufficient evidence to go to the jury (the evidential burden) and if it creates a reasonable doubt in the minds of the jury they should acquit. In some cases, however, he must prove a defence on balance of probabilities, i.e. the civil burden of proof, e.g. insanity, diminished responsibility and under the Prevention of Corruption Act, 1916 (s. 2), where a gift shall be deemed to have been given or received corruptly unless *D* proves the contrary.

In the Crown Court the judge directs the jury on the relevant law and the jury apply the law to the facts of the case in returning a verdict of guilty or not guilty.

10. Offences Against the Person

Homicide, the killing of a man, may be lawful if it is done for self-defence or prevention of violence or if it is accidental, i.e. without *mens rea* or negligence.

The forms of unlawful homicide are murder, manslaughter, infanticide and causing death by reckless driving.

Murder

Coke C.J. defined murder as 'when a man of sound memory and of the age of discretion unlawfully killeth any reasonable creature *in rerum natura* under the King's peace, with malice aforethought, either expressed by the party or implied by law, so as the party wounded, etc., die of the wound or hurt, etc., within a year and a day after the same'.

'A man of sound memory, etc.' means a man who is responsible according to the general principles of criminal law. 'Under the King's peace' excludes only an enemy in time of war. A killing by a citizen of the U.K. and Colonies may be murder or manslaughter even if committed outside the U.K. Killings on a British ship or aircraft by anyone are triable in the U.K. 'A reasonable creature, etc.' means any human being; but a foetus does not become a person until it has an existence independent of the mother; and a person becomes a corpse when his brain is dead.

If death occurs more than a year and a day after the injury, it is not unlawful homicide (*Dyson*, 1908).

In homicide, problems of causation can arise. *D* will be liable only if his act was a substantial cause of the death; if, for example, the victim received medical treatment after the injury the court will have to determine whether the injury or the treatment was the cause.

> *Jordan* (1956). *D* stabbed *P* who was admitted to hospital, was given an antibiotic after intolerance had been shown and died a few days later. The Court of Criminal Appeal quashed *D*'s conviction holding that the cause of death was the 'palpably wrong' (negligent?) treatment, not the wound which had almost healed.

> *Smith* (1959). *D* stabbed *P*, another soldier, in a fight. *P*'s comrade dropped him twice in carrying him to the medical centre. The medical officer considered the wound to be superficial, whereas in fact it had pierced a lung, and consequently gave the wrong treatment. *D*'s conviction of murder was upheld on the ground that at the time of death the original wound was still an operating and substantial cause.

The common law rule that neglect of the injury by *P* does not exempt *D* (*Holland*, 1841) has been applied in the recent case of *Blaue* (1975), where *D* stabbed *P*, a young girl, and pierced her lung. As a Jehovah's witness she refused a blood transfusion which she was told was necessary to save her life. She died from loss of blood; and her refusal to have a transfusion was held not to have broken the chain of causation, and *D*'s conviction of manslaughter was upheld.

Killing means accelerating death; even if *P* is in any case expected to die within a short time (*Adams*, 1957).

The malice aforethought for murder has traditionally been regarded as follows:

(i) Intention to kill (*Salisbury*, 1553).

(ii) Intention to cause grievous bodily harm (*Vickers*, 1957—approved by the House of Lords in *D.P.P.* v. *Smith* (1961) and followed by the Court of Appeal in Ellerton, 1978).

(iii) Recklessness as to death (*Desmond*, 1868, and *Serne*, 1887) or grievous bodily harm (*Barnes and Richards*, 1940, *Buckett*, 1964).

In spite of the authorities, in (iii) recklessness has been an uncertain *mens rea* and such cases have usually been treated as manslaughter.

Today the leading case on malice aforethought is *Moloney* (1985), where *D* and his stepfather were very drunk, following a family party. As a result of a challenge by the stepfather, *D* blew the stepfather's head off with a shotgun. He admitted manslaughter but maintained that he had no foresight whatsoever of the possibility of death or injury to his victim. The House of Lords held that *D* should be acquitted of murder if, in his drunken state, he might have failed to foresee death or injury at all. That only intent to kill or cause serious harm would suffice for malice aforethought. This decision has been followed in both *Hancock* (1986) and *Nedrick* (1986). The emphasis is on distinguishing intent from foresight.

Defences to murder. *D* is entitled to be acquitted of murder if he killed in execution or advancement of justice, in self-defence or prevention of violence, or if the death was accidental.

Manslaughter

The two types of manslaughter are:

(*a*) **Voluntary Manslaughter.** *D* may have the malice aforethought for murder but if one of the following mitigating circumstances is present the jury may convict of manslaughter instead of murder.

(i) *Provocation.* A classic definition of the common law rule, approved by the Court of Criminal Appeal, was stated by Devlin J. in *Duffy* (1949): 'Provocation is some act, or series of acts, done by the dead man to the accused, which would cause in any reasonable person and actually causes in the accused, a sudden and temporary loss of self-control rendering the accused so subject to passion as to make him for the moment not master of his mind.'

This rule has been modified by s. 3 of the Homicide Act, 1957, which provides: 'Where on a charge of murder there is evidence on which the jury can find that the person charged was provoked (whether by things done or by things said or by both together) to lose his self-control, the question whether the provocation was enough to make a reasonable man do as he did shall be left to be determined by the jury; and in determining that question the jury shall take into account everything both done and said according to the effect which, in their opinion, it would have on a reasonable man.'

In *Brown* (1972) it was laid down that the judge should ask the jury two questions and in this order:

(1) Did *D* as a result of the provocation lose self-control? If so

(2) Was the provocation enough to make a reasonable man do as *D* did?

Even if the judge thinks the evidence is slight, he should leave it to the jury to decide whether *D* did lose control (*Bullard*, 1957). One matter which will be important is whether there has been time for the blood to cool (*Hayward*, 1833).

S. 3 prevents the judge from withdrawing the defence from the jury on the ground that there is no evidence on which a jury can find that no reasonable man would have been provoked; or that the mode of retaliation was not reasonably related to the provocation. It also presumably prevents the judge from telling the jury to disregard physical or mental peculiarities of *D*. In *Camplin* (1977) the House of Lords held that the jury could consider what effect the provocation would have on a reasonable boy of 15, the age of *D*. But in *Wardrope* (1960) Edmund Davies J. directed the jury that 'the reasonable man is not a violent-tempered man, not a drunken man'. *McCarthy* (1954) seems therefore still to be good law; in that case the jury were directed that they were not entitled to consider the fact that *D* was drunk and therefore more likely to lose self-control.

In *Davies* (1975) it was held that under s. 3 the provocation could come from a third party.

(ii) *Diminished responsibility*. S. 2 of the Homicide Act, 1957, provides: 'Where a person kills or is a party to the killing of another, he shall not be convicted of murder if he was suffering from such abnormality of mind (whether arising from a condition of arrested or retarded development of mind or any inherent causes or induced by disease or injury) as substantially impaired his mental responsibility for his acts and omissions in doing or being a party to the killing.' A jury can convict of manslaughter instead. S. 2(2) puts the burden of proof on

D, and in *Dunbar* (1958) it was held that the standard of proof was on balance of probabilities.

By s. 6 of the Criminal Procedure (Insanity) Act, 1964 on a plea of diminished responsibility the Crown may adduce evidence of insanity.

In *Byrne* (1960) the Court of Criminal Appeal indicated the scope of 'abnormality of mind': 'It appears to us to be wide enough to cover the mind's activities in all its aspects ... also the ability to exercise will-power to control physical acts in accordance with that rational judgment.' Thus irresistible impulse, which had never been recognized under the *M'Naghten* rules, is admitted under the new defence.

It should be noted that the courts have power under s. 60 of the Mental Health Act, 1959, to make hospital orders committing persons who have committed imprisonable offences to a mental hospital or to guardianship of a health authority.

(iii) *Killing in the course of a suicide pact*. S. 4 of the Homicide Act, 1957, provides that 'it shall be manslaughter ... not murder, for a person acting in pursuance of a suicide pact between him and another to kill the other or be a party to the other being killed by a third person'. The burden of proof of the pact is on the defence.

By the Suicide Act, 1961, suicide is no longer a crime; but it is an offence to aid, abet, counsel or procure the suicide of another or an attempt by another to commit suicide (*Att. Gen.* v. *Able*, 1983). Whether *D* is guilty of manslaughter or of the offence under the 1961 Act will depend on who does the act which kills.

(iv) *Excessive self-defence*. There is some old authority for the rule that if *D* in defending himself kills by using more force than he is allowed to he is entitled to a verdict of manslaughter not murder. But in *Palmer* (1971) the Privy Council and in *McInnes* (1971) the Court of Appeal did not accept this rule. It seems therefore that in such cases *D* should rely on the defence of provocation not self-defence.

Involuntary Manslaughter

There appear to be three types:

(*a*) **Killing by gross negligence.** The classic definition of this is by Lord Hewart in *Bateman* (1925): '... whatever epithet be used and whether an epithet be used or not, in order to establish criminal liability the facts must be such that, in the opinion of the jury, the negligence of the accused went beyond a mere matter of compensation between subjects and showed such disregard for life and safety of others as to amount to a crime against the State and deserving of punishment'. This definition was approved by Lord Atkin in *Andrews* v. *D.P.P.* (1937) and has been followed by many judges. The test envisaged by it is clearly an objective one. But in some later cases judges have directed in terms of recklessness (*Cato*, 1976, *Lowe*, 1973) or equated recklessness with criminal negligence (*Lamb*, 1967). Even Lord Atkin in *Andrews* used 'reckless' obscurely. This is unfortunate since the legal meaning of recklessness differs from its everyday meaning.

(*b*) **Killing by intentionally doing an unlawful and dangerous act (Constructive manslaughter).** It is not sufficient that the act is unlawful; it must also be dangerous (*Franklin*, 1883).

In *Church* (1966) the Court of Criminal Appeal stated that 'the unlawful act must be such as all sober and reasonable people would inevitably recognize must subject the other person to at least the risk of some harm resulting therefrom, albeit not serious harm'. This was approved and applied by the House of Lords in *D.P.P.* v. *Newbury* (1976), which also held that the test of dangerousness is objective, i.e. *D* need not have known of the risk. In this case two 15-year-old boys threw part of a paving stone from a railway bridge on to an oncoming train, they said in order to hit the train. It went through a window and killed the guard. Since the unlawful act here is criminal damage, and an offence against property has hitherto been regarded as not sufficient for manslaughter, the House of Lords in upholding the conviction of manslaughter appears to be overruling *Franklin*, which however was not referred to in the speeches.

Of this type of manslaughter Williams says: 'The present position is that (it) is committed only by a killing in the course of certain kinds of unlawful acts and then only when the defendant is negligent as to causing bodily injury ... apart from the special case of abortion, constructive manslaughter now requires a criminal act of actual or constructive aggression, whether by force or by poisoning.'

(*c*) **Killing by an intentional act, being reckless whether bodily harm less than grievous bodily harm results.** If recklessness as to grievous bodily harm is sufficient for murder, it is logical that recklessness as to a lesser degree of harm should suffice for manslaughter; but the authority is slight.

> *Pike* (1961). *D* caused his consenting mistress to inhale the vapour of a cleaning chemical as an aphrodisiac. He had done this to other women over several years with no ill-effects except temporary loss of consciousness. On this occasion the woman died. The jury were directed that *D* was guilty of manslaughter if he knew that inhaling would expose *P* to physical harm and yet recklessly caused her to inhale. The Court of Criminal Appeal approved this direction.

Today the charge might perhaps be gross negligence.

Infanticide

S. 1(i) of the Infanticide Act, 1938, provides that where a woman causes the death of her child under the age of twelve months but at the time the balance of her mind was disturbed by reason of not having fully recovered from the effect of giving birth to the child she shall be guilty of infanticide, not murder, and dealt with as for manslaughter.

Causing Death by Reckless Driving

Since juries have always been reluctant to convict fellow-motorists of manslaughter, and the police therefore do not prosecute for it, Parliament provided the offence of causing death by dangerous driving, with an objective test for danger. The Criminal Law Act, 1977, changed this offence to causing death by reckless driving. Common law recklessness is subjective, i.e. it involves foresight. The Court of Appeal quashed a conviction of causing death by reckless driving and substituted a conviction for driving without due care and attention. There was evidence that the defendant ought at least to have been convicted of the lesser offence, an alternative which the trial judge had refused to put to the jury (*Fairbanks*, 1986).

In *Lawrence* (1981) the House of Lords upheld the quashing of a conviction of causing death by reckless driving on the direction that a driver is guilty of driving recklessly if he deliberately disregards the obligation to drive with due care and attention, or is indifferent as to whether or not he does so, and thereby creates a risk of an accident which a driver driving with due care and attention would not create.

Child Destruction and Abortion

It is not murder to kill a child in the womb or while being born. But it may be one of the following offences:

(i) By the Infant Life (Preservation) Act, 1929, it is child destruction for any person who with intent to destroy the life of a child capable of being born alive by any wilful act causes a child to die before it has an existence independent of its mother, provided that the act was not done in good faith for the purpose only of protecting the life of the mother. Evidence that at the material time the woman had been pregnant for 28 weeks or more shall be *prima facie* proof that she was pregnant of a child capable of being born alive.

(ii) As regards an earlier stage of pregnancy, s. 58 of the Offences against the Person Act, 1861, makes it an offence for a pregnant woman with intent to procure her miscarriage, unlawfully to administer to herself any poison or other noxious thing or use any instrument or other means whatsoever; or for another person to do such act with intent to procure the miscarriage of a woman, whether or not she is pregnant. This is the offence of illegal abortion.

(iii) By the Abortion Act, 1967, medical termination of pregnancy is protected if two medical practitioners are of the opinion that continuance of the pregnancy would involve risk to the mother's life or injury to her physical or mental health, account being taken of environmental factors; or that there was a substantial risk that if the child were born it would suffer from such physical or mental abnormalities as to be seriously handicapped. The operation must be carried out in a N.H.S. hospital or other approved place. One medical practitioner may perform the operation in an emergency. Abortions performed otherwise than within the terms of this Act are unlawful; and thus even a doctor may be prosecuted under s. 58 of the Offences against the Person Act (*Smith*, 1974).

Assault and Battery

At common law these are two distinct offences: assault is any act by which *D* intentionally or recklessly (*Venna*, 1975) causes *P* to apprehend immediate and unlawful personal violence; battery is the intentional or reckless infliction of unlawful personal violence on *P*. The courts, however, often use 'assault' to cover both.

If *P* does not observe *D*'s act it is not an assault; nor if it is obvious that *D* cannot carry out his threat. Words may 'unmake' an assault, as in *Tuberville* v. *Savage* (1669), where *D*, laying his hand on his sword, said 'If it were not assize time I would not take such language.' But it is questionable whether words alone will constitute an assault, although there is a dictum of Lord Goddard that they may (*Wilson*, 1955). It seems neither offence can be committed by omission, e.g. in *Fagan* (1968) where *D* in parking his car accidentally ran a wheel on to a policeman's foot and took his time in removing it, it was held that it was battery by a continuing act, not by an omission.

Consent, either express or implied, may be a defence to both offences. It is implied, for example, in taking part in sports or in everyday contact in buses, trains or streets. But it will not be a defence where the victim is too young to understand the nature of the act, where it is obtained by duress or fraud, or in sexual offences against children. *P* cannot consent to serious bodily harm, except in surgical operations for medical purposes. He can consent to some degree of likely bodily harm in lawful sport; but he does not consent to deliberate injury outside the rules of the game (*Billinghurst*, 1978). Also, on grounds of public policy the courts may refuse the defence even when there is only a slight degree of harm, e.g. *Donovan* (1934) apparently because of the element of indecency.

Two other defences are: lawful physical chastisement (i.e. moderate and reasonable) by parents of their children, or by school teachers in respect of children at school or on the way to or from school; and self-defence.

Assault occasioning Actual Bodily Harm

This offence is provided by s. 47 of the Offences against the Person Act, 1861. The harm need not be serious but presumably there must be some harm, e.g. a bruise. If the harm was reasonably foreseeable, the prosecution need not prove that *D* foresaw it; the *mens rea* for the assault is sufficient (*Roberts*, 1971).

Malicious Wounding

By s. 20 of the Offences against the Person Act, 1861, it is an offence unlawfully and maliciously to wound or inflict any grievous bodily harm upon any other person. 'Grievous' means 'really serious' (*D.P.P.* v. *Smith*, 1961). 'Maliciously' means 'intentionally or recklessly' (*Cunningham*, 1957). In *Mowatt* (1968) it was held that 'it is enough that (*D*) should have foreseen that some physical harm to some person, albeit of a minor character, might result'. This seems wrong in principle. 'Inflict' has been held to connote an assault (*Clarence*, 1888).

Wounding with Intent

By s. 18 of the same Act it is an offence unlawfully and maliciously to wound or cause any grievous bodily harm to any person with intent to do some grievous bodily harm to any person, or with intent to resist or prevent the lawful apprehension of any person. The maximum penalty is life imprisonment. 'Wounding' means to break the two layers of skin, so that an internal injury cannot constitute a wound, as there must be a break in the skin (*C* (*a minor*) v. *Eisenhower*, 1983). 'Causes' is wider than 'inflicts' in s. 20. S. 18 requires intention; recklessness is not sufficient (*Belfon*, 1976). If *D* intentionally strikes at *P* but hits *X* the intention can be transferred to *X* (transferred malice).

Administering Poison

Sections 23 and 24 of the same Act provide two offences of administering poison or other noxious thing to another person.

Assault on, Resistance to, or Obstruction of a Police Constable in the Execution of his Duty

These offences are in s. 51 of the Police Act, 1964. Such an assault is considered more serious than common assault; but by the Criminal Law Act, 1977, it becomes a summary offence only. There is much case law on 'execution of his duty' (*Collins* v. *Wilcock*, 1984).

Firearms and Offensive Weapons

In an endeavour to prevent serious offences against the person, the Firearms Act, 1968, regulates the manufacture, sale, use and possession of firearms (as explained in *Hall* v. *Cotton* (1986)), and the Prevention of Crime Act, 1953, prohibits the carrying of offensive weapons in public places without lawful authority or reasonable excuse. In the latter Act, the wide definition includes three categories of articles: (i) those made for causing injury; (ii) those adapted for such use; and (iii) those carried for causing injury (*Simpson*, 1983 and *Court*, 1986).

The courts have construed 'reasonable excuse' narrowly and have held that even if *D* carries a weapon only for self-defence, to have an excuse he must show that there was 'an imminent particular threat.' (*Evans* v. *Hughes*, 1979).

Sexual Offences

The main Act is the Sexual Offences Act, 1956. The offences include:

(*a*) **Rape.** By s. 1 of the Act and s. 1 of the Sexual Offences (Amendment) Act, 1976, a man commits rape if he has unlawful sexual intercourse with a woman who at the time does not consent, and at that time he knows that she does not consent or he is reckless as to whether she consents or not.

The least degree of penetration *per vaginam* is sufficient, and it is not necessary to prove that the hymen is ruptured (*Lines*, 1844).

If the woman's consent is obtained without the use of threats, force or fraud *D* will not be guilty of rape.

A husband cannot rape his wife unless the parties are separated or the court has by injunction forbidden him to interfere with his wife or he has given an undertaking to the court not to interfere with her.

A boy under 14 cannot be guilty of rape; but he can be convicted of indecent assault.

(*b*) **Intercourse with girls under 16.** By s. 5 intercourse with a girl under 13 is punishable with life imprisonment. Consent is no defence; nor is reasonable belief that the girl is over 13 (*Prince*, 1875).

By s. 6 intercourse with a girl under 16 carries a penalty of two years' imprisonment. *D* will have a defence if he is under 24 and has not previously been charged with a like offence and he reasonably believes that the girl is over 16.

(*c*) **Incest.** By s. 10 of the Act it is an offence for a man to have sexual intercourse with a woman he knows to be his grand-daughter, daughter, sister or mother.

By s. 11 there is a corresponding offence for a woman in respect of her grandfather, father, brother or son.

Consent is no defence. Where the female is a girl under 13 the maximum penalty is life imprisonment.

(*d*) **Indecent assault.** By s. 14 indecent assault by any person on a woman is punishable with two years' imprisonment (five years if against a girl under 13); and by s. 15 indecent assault by any person on a man has a maximum penalty of 10 years' imprisonment. The offence consists of a physical or psychic assault accompanied by circumstances of indecency (*Rolfe*, 1952). Children under 16 cannot consent.

(*e*) **Indecency with children.** The Indecency with Children Act, 1960, provides that any person who commits an act of gross indecency with or towards a child under the age of 14, or who incites a child under that age to such an act with him or another shall be guilty of an offence. This offence is thus wider than indecent assault in not necessarily requiring an assault.

11. Offences against Property

Offences under Theft Act, 1968

Theft

S. 1 defines theft as dishonestly appropriating property belonging to another with the intention of permanently depriving the other of it. S. 1(2) provides that 'it is immaterial whether the appropriation is made with a view to gain, or is made for the thief's own benefit'.

The *actus reus* is appropriating property belonging to another. S. 3(1) provides that 'any assumption by a person of the rights of an owner amounts to an appropriation, and this includes where he has come by the property (innocently or not) without stealing it, any later assumption of a right to it by keeping or dealing with it as owner'. The term obviously covers a taking, and such cases as:

> *Rogers* v. *Arnott* (1960). The bailee of a tape-recorder offered to sell it to another person. It was held that his offer, even though it was not taken up, amounted to conversion as a bailee.

The Court of Appeal has interpreted the term widely in *Monaghan* (1979), where a shop assistant was held to have appropriated money when she put cash in the shop till without registering it; and in *Anderton* v. *Wish* (1980) where a customer swapped labels on tins in a supermarket to pay a lower price. The House of Lords upheld these Court of Appeal decisions in:

> *Morris* (1983), where D, who had taken a number of articles from shelves of a supermarket store, swapped labels and therefore paid a lower price at the checkout. *Held:* D had appropriated the articles by assuming some (not necessarily all) of the rights of the owner.

It is arguable that in each case *D* did no more than a preparatory act.

If a shop assistant sells his employer's goods at less than the correct price, he appropriates since he goes outside his authority. In *Pilgram* v. *Rice-Smith* (1977) *D*'s conviction for theft was upheld when in a supermarket she had charged a customer friend less than the price of the goods. Whether there is an appropriation will depend on the intention with which an act is done. In a supermarket the contract is made at the cash-desk (*Pharmaceutical Society* v. *Boots*), so that in *Eddy* v. *Niman* (1981), *D*, who had placed goods in a receptacle with the intention of stealing them, and had then changed his mind and left the store without them, was held not to have appropriated the goods. However, in *Macpherson* (1973) it was held that a customer appropriates when he takes goods from a shelf if he is clearly dishonest, e.g. puts them in his pocket intending not to pay for them.

S. 3(2) excepts a *bonda fide* purchaser for value from s. 3(1).

S. 4 defines 'property' widely to include 'money and all other property real or personal, including things in action and other intangible property', e.g. debts, patents. But land can only be stolen by

(i) A trustee who appropriates the land for his own purposes.
(ii) A person not in possession who appropriates by severing the land, e.g. cuts down a tree or takes away the top soil.
(iii) A tenant who appropriates fixtures or structures let to be used with the land, e.g. he sells a greenhouse.

Things growing wild cannot be stolen unless the whole plant is taken or the flowers, etc., are picked for a commercial purpose.

Wild creatures cannot be stolen unless the creature is tamed or ordinarily kept in captivity or it has been reduced into possession of another person and possession has not since been lost or abandoned.

To be stolen, property must belong to another; thus abandoned property cannot be stolen, nor can it be if *D* believes it to be abandoned. But there are some situations where the property in the goods is by s. 5 notionally put in another person for the purposes of the Act. By s. 5(1) 'property shall be regarded as belonging to any person having possession or control of it, or having in it any proprietary right or interest'. Therefore the owner can steal from someone with a lesser but prior interest, e.g. a bailee. In *Rose* v. *Matt* (1951) *D* pawned his clock and then retrieved it when the broker was not looking, and was convicted of what would now be theft.

By s. 5(2) a trustee, who has the legal ownership of the trust property, is regarded as stealing from the person having the right to enforce the trust.

S. 5(3) provides that 'where a person receives property from or on account of another, and is under an obligation to the other to retain or deal with it in a particular way, the property or its proceeds shall be regarded as belonging to the other'.

By s. 5(4), 'where a person gets property by another's mistake, and is under an obligation to make restoration (in whole or in part) of the property or its proceeds or the value thereof, then ... the property ... shall be regarded ... as belonging to the person entitled to restoration and an intention not to make restoration shall be regarded accordingly as an intention to deprive that person of the property or proceeds'. In *Ghosh* (1982) the Court of Appeal stated that it had to be shown that *D* acted dishonestly by the standards of ordinary people and, if so, he must have realized that his acts were dishonest by those standards. It has been held (in *Attorney-General's Ref.* (*No. 1 of 1983*), that the same situation would apply where an employer mistakenly instructs his bank to credit an employee's bank account with a sum in excess of the employee's proper entitlement.

To be theft the appropriation must be made dishonestly and there must be the intention permanently to deprive the other person of the property.

S. 2 does not define dishonesty but it provides that a person is not dishonest if he appropriates:

(i) 'in the belief that he has in law the right to deprive the other of it' (claim of right);
(ii) 'in the belief that he would have the other's consent if the other knew of the appropriation and the circumstances of it'; or
(iii) 'in the belief that the person to whom the property belongs cannot be discovered by taking reasonable steps', e.g. where he finds lost property.

If none of these provisions applies, the accused may still be found not dishonest, the matter being left to the jury (*Feeley*, 1972), e.g. where the manager of a shop against the rules takes money from the till knowing that he can repay it within a few days.

S. 6 provides that 'a person shall be regarded as having the intention of permanently depriving if his intention is to treat the thing as his own to dispose of regardless of the other's rights, even without meaning the other permanently to lose the thing itself; and a borrowing or lending of it may amount to so treating it if . . . the borrowing or lending is for a period and in such circumstances making it equivalent to an outright taking or disposal'.

Robbery

By s. 8 robbery is 'stealing and immediately before or at the time of doing so, and in order to do so, using force on any person or putting or seeking to put any person in fear of being then and there subjected to force'. The penalty is life imprisonment. If there is no theft there is no robbery.

> *Skivington* (1968). *D* went to his sister's firm to collect wages due to her. When the cashier refused to pay him on that day he obtained the money by threatening the cashier with a knife. *Held:* not robbery because not theft since *D* had a claim of right.

It must be force to the person and used in order to obtain the property. Force against a third person is sufficient, e.g. a passerby who intervenes.

The Court of Appeal in *Hale* (1979) held that appropriation is a continuing act and it is for the jury to decide when it is over. In consequence, they upheld a conviction of robbery where the force was used some minutes after the theft.

By s. 8(2) an assault with intent to rob carries the same penalty as robbery.

Burglary

By s. 9 burglary is either:

(*a*) Entering a building or part of a building or an inhabited vehicle or vessel as a trespasser with intent therein to steal, to inflict grievous bodily harm, to rape or to do unlawful damage, or,

(*b*) Having entered as a trespasser to steal or attempt to steal therein or inflict or attempt to inflict grievous bodily harm.

'Entering' is not defined, thus the common law rules no doubt apply. According to these, insertion of any part of the body was sufficient entry. In *Davis* (1823) *D* pushed in a pane and his finger was seen to be inside. In *Machent* v. *Quinn* (1970) *D* broke a shop window and stole from the window-display; he was convicted of burglary. In *Collins* (1972) the Court of Appeal spoke of 'substantial entry' but did not elaborate. If an instrument is inserted, it will amount to an entry if inserted for the purpose of committing the ulterior offence, even though no part of the body enters, e.g. barrel of a gun inserted to shoot a person inside. But not if it is inserted only to gain entry.

The trespass must be intentional or reckless; and it will not be trespass if the entry is negligent or involuntary. In *Jenkins and Jenkins* (1983) it was held that assault is not an essential requirement of inflicting grievous bodily harm within s. 9. Entry obtained by a false pretence is probably trespass, since fraud usually negatives consent.

By s. 10 it is aggravated burglary if a person commits burglary 'and at the time has with him any firearm or imitation firearm, any weapon of offence or any explosive'.

Removal of Articles from Places open to the Public

Borrowing does not amount to theft, subject to the provisions of s. 6; but the borrowing of exhibits in museums and of vehicles had become a nuisance which needed controlling. S. 11 provides that it is an offence without lawful authority to remove from a building or its grounds articles displayed or kept for display where the public have access to the building in order to view the building or a collection housed in it. 'A collection made or exhibited for the purpose of effecting sales or other commercial dealings' is not within the section.

Taking a Motor Vehicle or other Conveyance without Authority

This is the other borrowing offence. By s. 12 it is an offence if a person 'without having the consent of the owner or other lawful authority, takes any conveyance for his own or another's use or, knowing that (it) has been taken without such authority, drives it or allows himself to be carried in or on it'.

It is not an offence if the act is 'done in the belief that he has the lawful authority to do it or that he would have the owner's consent if the owner knew of his doing it and the circumstances of it'.

If *D* has authority to use a vehicle for one purpose but uses it for another, he may commit the offence (*McKnight* v. *Davies*, 1974).

In *Bogacki* (1973) the Court of Appeal held that 'taking' involved some element of movement, however small, and therefore where *D* boarded a bus and tried to start the engine but the bus did not move he did not commit the offence.

'Conveyance' means one 'constructed or adapted for the carriage of a person or persons whether by land, water or air . . .'. A conveyance for the carriage of goods is not included unless it has a place for a driver, e.g. a lorry but not a goods trailer.

By s. 12(5) the taking of pedal cycles is a summary offence.

Abstracting of Electricity

Electricity cannot be stolen and therefore cannot be the subject of burglary. But by s. 13 it is an offence dishonestly to use without due authority, or dishonestly cause to be wasted or diverted, any electricity. The penalty is up to five years' imprisonment. If there is no dishonesty there is no offence. In *Boggeln* v. *Williams* (1978) *D*'s supply had been cut off; he re-connected it to the meter and informed the electricity board; he was held not to have been dishonest.

Obtaining Property by Deception

The difference between this offence and theft is that here the owner has voluntarily handed over the property in consequence of the fraud of *D*. By s. 15(1) the offence is committed by 'a person who by any deception dishonestly obtains property belonging to another, with the intention of permanently depriving the other of it'.

'Obtain' includes obtaining for another or enabling another to obtain or retain. *D* obtains property under s. 15 if he obtains ownership, possession or control of it; thus if he obtains possession by a trick, that is theft by a trick, but it is also obtaining by deception and it would be better to charge *D* under s. 15.

The obtaining must be induced by the deception, therefore it is not the offence if *P* is not deceived, but it is an attempt (*Hensler*, 1870, approved by the House of Lords in *Haughton* v. *Smith*); and the obtaining must not be too remote, as in *Clucas* (1949) where *D*, by a false pretence, induced bookmakers to accept credit bets, his practice being not to pay if his horse did not win, but to collect his winnings if the horse did win; on this occasion it won and the court held that the effective cause of obtaining the money was not the deception but backing the winner.

The deception may be by 'words or conduct and as to fact or as to law, including a deception as to the present intentions of the person using the deception or any other person'. Active concealment of defects would amount to 'conduct'; as would going into an Oxford tailors' wearing an undergraduate gown if the person is not a member of a college (*Barnard*, 1837).

A promise made not intending to fulfil it is sufficient; and so is an implied promise, as where a person orders a meal in a restaurant (*Jones*, 1878).

S. 15 says nothing about statements of opinion, but on principle it should count as deception where the opinion is not honestly held.

The deception may be 'deliberate or reckless'. With regard to statements, the House of Lords in *Derry* v. *Peek* (1889), a case on the tort of deceit, held that the defendants could not be liable if they honestly believed what they had said (see p. 155).

'Property' is wider than in theft: the s. 4 limitations do not apply.

Apart from being 'deliberate or reckless' the deception must be dishonest. If the same view as in *Feely* (1973), a theft case, is taken then the matter of dishonesty should be left to the jury.

Obtaining a Pecuniary Advantage by Deception

Since s. 16(2)(a) has been repealed, this offence is committed by a person who by deception dishonestly obtains for himself or another one of the following advantages: 'He is allowed to borrow by way of overdraft, or to take out any policy of assurance or annuity contract, or obtains an improvement of the terms on which he is allowed to do so; or he is given the opportunity to earn remuneration or greater remuneration in an office or employment, or to win money by betting'. *Clucas* (1949) would now come within this section.

'Deception' has the same meaning as in s. 15 and must be made deliberately or recklessly and dishonestly.

False Accounting

This offence, wider than the last offence and forgery, is by s. 17 'where a person dishonestly, with a view to gain for himself or another or with intent to cause loss to another

(*a*) destroys, defaces, conceals or falsifies any account or any record or document made or required for any accounting purpose; or

(*b*) in furnishing information for any purpose produces or makes use of any account or any such record or document as aforesaid, which to his knowledge is or may be misleading, false or deceptive in a material particular.'

'A person who makes or concurs in making in an account or other document an entry which is or may be misleading, false or deceptive in a material particular, or who omits or concurs in omitting a material particular from an account or other document, is to be treated as falsifying the account or document.'

The records or documents are restricted to those made or required for any accounting purpose, e.g. ledgers, cash-books, meters, cash-tills.

The section is useful particularly as it covers omissions as well as acts. In *Monaghan* (1979) a charge under this section might have been better than for theft.

Liability of Company Officers for Offences by the Company

By s. 18 if an offence by a corporation under sections 15, 16 or 17 is proved to have been committed with the consent or connivance of a director, manager, secretary, etc., he shall also be guilty of the offence. This offence is wider than aiding and abetting.

False Statements by Company Directors, etc.

By s. 19 it is an offence for an officer of a corporation, with intent to deceive members or creditors of the corporation about its affairs, to publish or concur in publishing a written statement or account which to his knowledge is or may be misleading, etc.

A false statement in a prospectus is also covered by s. 70 of the Companies Act, 1985.

Suppression of Documents

Under s. 20 a person who dishonestly, with a view to gain for himself or another or with intent to cause loss to another, destroys, defaces or conceals any valuable security, any will, etc. (the conduct of Squeers in *Nicholas Nickleby*), or by deception procures the execution of a valuable security, shall be guilty of an offence (*Beck* (Brian), 1985).

Blackmail

By s. 21 it is blackmail if, with a view to gain for himself or another or with intent to cause loss to another, a person makes any unwarranted demand with menaces; and it is unwarranted unless he makes it in the belief

(*a*) that he has reasonable grounds for making the demand, and

(*b*) that the use of the menaces is a proper means of enforcing the demand.

'Menaces' was used in the previous Act and no doubt Lord Wright's definition in *Thorne* v. *Motor Trade Association* (1937) is likely to be followed: 'I think the word "menace" is to be liberally construed and not as limited to threats of violence but as including threats of any action detrimental to or unpleasant to the person addressed. It may also include a warning that in certain events such action is intended.'

The test for whether the demand is warranted is clearly subjective.

No doubt *Skivington* (1968) could have been charged under this section; and *Bernhard* (1938) would probably be acquitted on a claim of right as under the old law; she believed she had a legal right to enforce a promise of payment of a sum of money made by her ex-lover and threatened that unless he paid she would tell his wife of their association.

Handling Stolen Goods

This offence carries a penalty of 14 years, which is higher than the penalty for theft.

By s. 22 'a person handles stolen goods if (otherwise than in the course of the stealing) knowing or believing them to be stolen goods he dishonestly receives the goods, or dishonestly undertakes or assists in their retention, removal, disposal or realization by or for the benefit of another person, or if he arranges to do so'.

Goods are 'stolen' for the purposes of this section if obtained by an offence under sections 1, 15 or 21, or if obtained in a foreign country the act would have been a crime in that country and would have been an offence under sections 1, 15 or 21 if done in England or Wales (s. 24(1) and (4)).

D must know or believe the goods to be stolen; and they must actually be stolen at the time of the offence. If they have ceased to be stolen by being taken into the possession of the owner or the police, *D* cannot be convicted of the offence or an attempt (*Haughton* v. *Smith*, 1975).

The forms of the offence are:

(i) receiving;
(ii) arranging to receive;
(iii) undertaking or assisting in their retention, etc.;
(iv) arranging to undertake or assist.

Where *D* is charged with receiving, to be guilty he must have the *mens rea* at the time. Nor will he be guilty of theft if he was a *bona fide* purchaser for value and only later knew that the goods were stolen (s. 3(2)).

To be guilty of undertaking, etc., *D* must be acting for the benefit of another person.

> *Pitchley* (1973). *D*'s son stole £150 and gave it to *D* to look after. *D* paid it into his bank account and only later learned that it was stolen; he did nothing about it. *Held:* he was guilty of assisting in retaining.

This decision is open to the objection that *D* alone retained, therefore he could hardly be said to assist. A better charge would have been theft, since *D* would not come within s. 3(2).

The *mens rea* of the offence is knowledge or belief. The test is subjective and therefore negligence is not sufficient; nor is mere suspicion or wilful blindness, since knowledge and belief are something positive (*Ismail*, 1977; *Stagg*, 1978).

Dishonesty is an essential ingredient. Therefore if *D* knows the goods are stolen but intends to return them to the owner (*Matthews*, 1950), he will not be guilty.

Proof of *mens rea* in handling cases is assisted by s. 27(3) which enables evidence of previous handling or of previous convictions of theft or handling to be given, and by the common law rules which enable a jury to infer guilty knowledge where *D* is in possession of recently stolen property and he gives no satisfactory explanation.

Offences under the Theft Act, 1978

This Act was passed to remedy certain defects of the 1968 Act, and provides for three offences:

Obtaining Services by Deception

By s. 1 it is an offence dishonestly to obtain services from another by deception, i.e. 'where the other is induced to confer a benefit by doing some act, or causing or permitting some act to be done, on the understanding that the benefit has been or will be paid for'.

The liability need not, it seems, be legally enforceable.

Evasion of Liability by Deception

S. 2 covers three situations:

(*a*) 'Where a person by any deception

(i) dishonestly secures the remission of the whole or part of any *existing liability* to make a payment, whether his own liability or another's; or

(ii) with intent to make permanent default in whole or in part on any *existing liability* to make a payment, or with intent to let another do so, dishonestly induces the creditor or any person claiming payment on behalf of the creditor to wait for payment (whether or not the due date for payment is deferred) or to forgo payment; or

(iii) dishonestly obtains any exemption from or abatement of liability to make a payment.'

In this section 'liability' means legally enforceable liability (s. 2(2)).

S. 2(3) provides that a person who takes in payment a cheque etc. 'by way of conditional satisfaction of a pre-existing liability is to be treated not as being paid but as being induced to wait for payment.'

Making off Without Payment

Unlike the other two offences this does not require any deception and was designed to cover the 'bilking' cases.

By s. 3(1) it is an offence if 'a person who, knowing that payment on the spot for any goods supplied or service done is required or expected of him, dishonestly makes off without having paid as required or expected and with intent to avoid payment of the amount due'. 'Payment at the time of collecting goods on which work has been done or in respect of which service has been provided' is included (s. 3(2)). *D* can only be guilty of this offence if he intends to avoid payment permanently (*Allen* (Christopher), 1985).

The section does not apply where the supply of goods or the service is contrary to law or where payment is not legally enforceable.

The section is intended to catch such cases as

> *Edwards* v. *Ddin* (1976). *D* asked an attendant to fill his car tank with petrol. When this had been done he decided he could not wait, and drove off without paying. *Held*: that he had not stolen the petrol because the property in it passed to him when it was put in the tank, therefore it was not property belonging to another.

The offence is expressly made an arrestable one (s. 3(4)).

Criminal Damage

The Criminal Damage Act, 1971, contains one basic offence, one aggravated offence and two subsidiary offences.

The basic offence by s. 1(1) is without lawful excuse destroying or damaging any property *belonging to another* intentionally or recklessly. For the interpretation of the meaning of 'recklessly' see *Caldwell* (1981) and *Miller* (1983) on page 316. 'Destroy' means to break up, demolish, etc. 'Damage' may be slight but there must be some perceptible physical harm.

> *'A'* (*a juvenile*) (1978). *D*, a football supporter, spat on a constable's raincoat. The prosecution argued that it must have been damaged because it needed dry-cleaning. *Held:* a raincoat is not damaged in this way though, for example, a satin wedding dress might have been.

'Property' is widely defined by s. 10(1) as of a tangible nature, whether real or personal, including money and wild creatures reduced into possession, but excluding mushrooms, flowers, fruit or foliage of a plant growing wild on any land. It belongs to another by s. 5 if another has custody or control of it, or any proprietary interest in it or a charge on it.

By s. 5 *D* will have a lawful excuse where:

(i) he believes *P* had consented or would have consented had he known of the damage and the circumstances (as in *Denton*, 1981); or

(ii) he is protecting property or a right or interest in the property and at the time he believes

(*a*) the property was in immediate need of protection and

(*b*) the means adopted were reasonable in the circumstances.

Here it is a question of honest belief not reasonable belief.

Also, existing defences in law are preserved by s. 5(2) e.g. infancy, necessity.

D also has a defence if he believes wrongly that he owns the property or has a claim of right.

Smith (1974). *D* wrongly believed that wiring which he had installed in his flat belonged to him and removed it when he left. In law it had become a landlord's fixture. *Held:* honest belief that the property was his own was a defence.

The aggravated offence by s. 1(2) is without lawful excuse to destroy or damage any property, *whether belonging to D or another*

(*a*) intending to destroy or damage it or being reckless as to that and
(*b*) intending by the destruction or damage to endanger the life of another or being reckless as to that (*Sangha*, 1988).

The House of Lords in *Steer* (1987) explained that in the case of aggravated criminal damage, the element of the *mens rea* relating to the endangering of life must refer to the endangering resulting from the damage, as opposed to the means used to cause the damage.

This offence does not require intent to kill and is therefore wider than attempted murder; it is also wider because a preparatory act may suffice which is not sufficient for attempt.

S. 5 does not apply to this offence; but since the definition itself includes the words 'without lawful excuse' there must be circumstances which would excuse. Smith and Hogan suggest that such a case would be where the police damage property to prevent a serious offence against a person even though they know it might endanger *D*'s life.

If the offence under s. 1(1) or s. 1(2) is committed by fire, it must be charged as arson (s. 1(3)) and the penalty is life imprisonment, the same as for s. 1(2).

The two subsidiary offences are based on threats and possession.

By s. 2 it is an offence without lawful excuse 'to make to another a threat, intending that he would fear it would be carried out

(*a*) to destroy or damage any property belonging to that other or a third person, or

(*b*) to destroy or damage his own property in a way which he knows is likely to endanger the life of that other or a third person.'

By s. 3 it is an offence for a person to have '*anything* in his custody or under his control intending without lawful excuse to use it or cause or permit another to use it

(*a*) to destroy or damage any property belonging to some other person, or

(*b*) to destroy or damage his own or the user's property in a way which he knows is likely to endanger the life of some other person.'

The maximum penalty under s. 1(1), s. 2 and s. 3 is 10 years' imprisonment.

S. 8, which is now superseded by s. 1 of the Criminal Justice Act, 1972, empowered all courts, on application or otherwise, on conviction of a person to order him to pay compensation for the destruction or damage to the person to whom the property belonged.

It should be noted that sections 35, 36, 47, 58 and 72 of the Malicious Damage Act, 1961, dealing with railways and shipping, were not repealed by the 1971 Act. The charge against the protestors who in July 1980 halted a train carrying nuclear waste in Gloucestershire was under s. 35, which makes it an offence 'to place wood, etc., on railway lines with intent to obstruct ... an engine'.

Forgery

S. 1 of the Forgery and Counterfeiting Act, 1981, provides that a person is guilty of forgery if he makes a false instrument in order that it may be used as genuine: s. 8 defines instrument as either any formal or informal document or any form of sound recording such as a disc, tape or sound track. In accordance with s. 2 it is now a separate offence to make a photostat copy of a forged document.

At common law 'document' usually means a writing. A painting with a false signature has been held not to be a document (*Closs*, 1858); and so has a printed wrapper on a baking powder (*Smith*, 1858).

At common law the rule was that 'a document must not only tell a lie, it must tell a lie about itself'.

> *Re Windsor* (1865). A teller in a bank fraudulently entered in his journal a greater sum than the actual asset. *Held:* not a forgery since the journal did not tell a lie about itself.

However, in the later case of *Hopkins and Collins* (1957) the Court of Criminal Appeal did not follow this rule and held on similar facts, but where a figure had been altered, that the document was a forgery. Even under the Forgery and Counterfeiting Act, 1981, it is not clear what the present position is. However, in *Donnelly* (*Ian*) (1984) the Court of Appeal held that the Act is a reforming statute and that an instrument which would not be a forgery under the old law could fall within the definition provided by the new Act.

The House of Lords has held that the log-on procedure for assessing computer databases such as Prestel does not constitute forgery.

> *Gold and Schifreen* (1987). Illicit access to a database obtained by using someone else's identity number. *Held:* not forgery.

Buckley J. in *re London and Globe Finance Corporation Ltd.* (1903) defined defraud and deceive as 'to deceive is by falsehood to induce a state of mind; to defraud is by deceit to induce a course of action'. The House of Lords in *Welham* v. *D.P.P.* (1961) held that defrauding is not confined to an economic loss; and *D* was held to have intended to defraud where his intention was to cover up a breach of credit regulations to avoid a prosecution.

Bassey (1931). *D* was held to have an intent to defraud where he forged documents in order to gain admission as a student to the Inner Temple.

S. 13 has now abolished the offence of forgery at common law.

Trespass

In recent years, squatting has caused problems; and in order to give some, though limited, legal protection against it, five offences are enacted in the Criminal Law Act, 1977:

(i) S. 6 provides that it is an offence for any person without lawful authority, to use or threaten violence for the purpose of securing entry into any premises for himself or another, provided that

(*a*) there is someone present on those premises at the time who is opposed to the entry, and

(*b*) the person using or threatening the violence knows that that is the case.

The violence may be against person or property. The right to occupy the premises will not excuse a violent entry: but a displaced residential occupier has a defence provided the force used is reasonable.

(ii) By s. 7 any person on the premises as a trespasser having entered as such is guilty of an offence if he fails to leave on being required to do so by or on behalf of

(*a*) a displaced residential occupier of the premises requiring the premises for occupation as a residence, or

(*b*) an individual who is a protected intending occupier of the premises, i.e. a person who has purchased a freehold interest, or a leasehold interest with not less than 21 years to run, or a person authorized to occupy by, for example, a local authority or a housing association.

In both cases the person must be excluded by a trespasser and must hold a written statement or a certificate as to occupation as a residence.

(iii) S. 8(1) makes it an offence for a trespasser on any premises having entered as such to have with him, without lawful authority or reasonable excuse, on the premises any weapon of offence.

(iv) By s. 9(1) a person who enters or is on foreign diplomatic or consular premises as a trespasser is guilty of an offence.

(v) S. 10(1) provides that it is an offence to resist or obstruct an officer of the court engaged in executing process issued by the court for the purpose of enforcing any judgment or order for the recovery of any premises or for the delivery of possession of premises.

Unlawful Eviction and Harassment of a Residential Occupier

This is made an offence by s. 1 of the Protection from Eviction Act, 1977.

12. Other Offences

Bigamy

S. 57 of the Offences against the Person Act, 1861, provides that 'whosoever, being married, shall marry any other person during the life of the former husband or wife, whether the marriage shall have taken place in England or Ireland or elsewhere', commits the offence.

But it will not be bigamy if at the time of the second ceremony the first marriage had been dissolved or annulled by a court of competent jurisdiction; or if the second ceremony took place abroad and the defendant is not a citizen of the United Kingdom and Colonies; or if the spouse shall have been continually absent from the other spouse for the past seven years and not known by that spouse to be living within that time.

It has also been held that *D*'s reasonable belief that the spouse was dead shall be a defence, even though there has not been seven years' absence (*Tolson*, 1889).

In *King* (1964) the court accepted that *D* would have a defence where he believed on reasonable grounds that the alleged first marriage was void. Similarly, in *Gould* (1968) *D*'s reasonable belief that he was divorced was held to be a defence.

The elements which must be proved for the offence are: the first marriage, that it was still subsisting at the time of the second ceremony, and a second ceremony known to and recognized by law. It is immaterial that the second ceremony is invalid for other reasons, e.g. non-compliance with residential requirements.

Problems have arisen in recent years with regard to polygamous marriages. Is such a marriage a basis for bigamy? The position seems to be that the first marriage must be a monogamous marriage; but marriages potentially polygamous when contracted may become monogamous through change of domicile or by legislation, in which case *D* may commit bigamy.

> *Sagoo* (1975). *D* married in Kenya where he was domiciled. The Kenyan government later converted the marriage into a monogamous one. He came to England and married another woman. *Held:* bigamy.

No one domiciled in England can contract a polygamous marriage. If a person acquires a domicile in England, a marriage contracted where he was earlier domiciled will be converted into a monogamous marriage.

Road Traffic Offences

Offences under the Road Traffic Acts are construed strictly unless *mens rea* is expressed or implied or the offence is one of negligence.

Some of the offences are:

Careless driving. By s. 3 of the 1972 Act it is an offence to drive 'a motor vehicle on a road without due care and attention'. The standard is objective and is the same for learner drivers as for experienced ones (*McCrone* v. *Riding*, 1938); i.e. it is an offence of negligence. In *Simpson* v. *Peat* (1952) Lord Goddard stated the test as: 'Was the accused exercising that degree of care and attention that a reasonable and prudent driver would exercise in the circumstances?'

The same facts may amount to some other offences as well as careless driving; in which case *D* should not be convicted of both.

Inconsiderate driving. It is also an offence by s. 3 to drive 'a motor vehicle on a road without reasonable consideration for other persons using the road'. For this offence other persons must be using the road. Instances are: *D* drives slowly and holds back following traffic; *D* drives through an avoidable puddle near the kerb and splashes pedestrians.

Reckless driving. By s. 2 of the 1972 Act, as amended by s. 50(1) of the Criminal Law Act, 1977, a person who drives a motor vehicle on a road recklessly shall be guilty of an offence. The section previously included dangerous driving which, like careless driving, was based on negligence. The offence has now been abolished.

The test for recklessness at common law is subjective, the deliberate taking of an unjustifiable risk (see p. 316). The House of Lords in *Lawrence* (1980) stated that *mens rea* was a constituent in reckless driving, and that for there to be a conviction the vehicle should be driven in such a way as to create an obvious and serious risk and that it must be proved that the accused had given no thought to the possibility of risk or had proceeded despite the risk.

Causing death by reckless driving has already been discussed (see p. 332).

Driving under the influence of drink or drugs. By s. 5 of the 1972 Act a person who, when driving or attempting to drive or when in charge of a motor vehicle on a road or other public place, is unfit to drive through drink or drugs shall be guilty of an offence.

In view of the indulgent attitude of juries to fellow-motorists, this offence has been found difficult to prove; therefore most prosecutions for drinking and driving are brought under s. 6, in spite of its procedural difficulties, because it has an objective test; but s. 5 must be used when drugs are concerned.

Driving with a blood-alcohol concentration above the prescribed limit. By s. 6 it is an offence if a person drives or attempts to drive or is in charge of 'a motor vehicle on a road or other public place, having consumed alcohol in such a quantity that the proportion thereof in his blood, as ascertained from a laboratory test for which he subsequently provides a specimen under s. 9 of the Act, exceeds the prescribed limit at the time he supplies the specimen'. There is much case law on this section including the breathalyser cases (Transport Act, 1981).

The Criminal Law Act, 1977, has reduced the offences under sections 5 and 6 to summary offences, with a penalty of six months' imprisonment and/or a fine of £1,000.

Conviction under s. 5 or s. 6 of driving or attempting to drive also carries a mandatory disqualification from driving for at least twelve months, unless there are special reasons for the court to do otherwise; and for at least three years if the defendant has previously been convicted within a period of ten years.

Disqualification is not obligatory for conviction of being in charge.

Assisting Arrestable Offenders

By s. 4(1) of the Criminal Law Act, 1967, where a person has committed an arrestable offence, any other person who, knowing or believing him to be guilty of such an offence, does without lawful authority or reasonable excuse any act with intent to impede his apprehension or prosecution, is guilty of an offence.

It was necessary to enact this offence to replace that of being an accessory after the fact to felony.

Concealing an Arrestable Offence

By s. 5(1) of the same Act, where a person has committed an arrestable offence, any other person who, knowing or believing that such an offence has been committed, and that he has information which might be of material assistance in securing the prosecution of an offender for it, shall be guilty of an offence if he accepts or agrees to accept for not disclosing that information any consideration other than the making good of loss or injury caused by the offence, or the making of reasonable compensation for the loss or injury.

Causing Wasteful Employment of the Police

By s. 5(2) of the same Act it is an offence to cause 'any wasteful employment of the police by knowingly making to any person a false report tending to show that an offence has been committed, or to give rise to apprehension for the safety of any persons or property, or tending to show that he has information material to any police inquiry'.

13. Criminal Injuries Compensation Board

This Board, established in 1964, consists of a chairman of wide legal experience and 7 other legally qualified members appointed by the Home Secretary and Secretary of State for Scotland after consultation with the Lord Chancellor. Its function is to entertain applications for *ex gratia* payments of compensation, in certain circumstances, to victims of crimes of violence in Great Britain or on a British vessel or aircraft, including since 1979 victims within the family.

It must be shown that the injury is one for which compensation of at least £150 would be awarded by the courts. The circumstances of the injury must have been reported to the police without delay, or have been the subject of criminal proceedings in the courts. An applicant must have given the Board all reasonable assistance to substantiate his claim. Compensation, which is assessed on the basis of common law damages, amounts to several million pounds per annum. About 12,500 applications are made yearly to the Board. Monthly reports are issued by the Board giving details of the amount of compensation paid and some of the more important cases.

The scheme does not apply to Northern Ireland where there is statutory provision in certain circumstances for compensation from public funds for criminal injuries and also for malicious damage to property.

14. Exercises

1. What are 'arrestable offences' and 'other offences' under the Criminal Law Act, 1967?
2. *Actus non facit reum nisi mens sit rea.* Explain. Are there any exceptions to this principle?
3. Describe what is meant by an 'attempt to commit crime'.
4. Describe the defence of 'diminished responsibility'.
5. 'Mistake is no defence to a prosecution for crime.' Do you agree? How far is duress a defence?
6. How far may drunkenness be a defence to a criminal charge?
7. Can a Corporation be indicted for crime? Give example, if any.
8. Define 'murder'. What is meant by 'malice aforethought' and 'under the Queen's peace'?
9. Define 'bigamy'. What are the facts of *R.* v. *Tolson* (1889)?
10. Define 'theft'. What is meant by 'appropriation' and 'property' under the Theft Act, 1968?
11. Explain three offences under the Criminal Damage Act, 1972.
12. Discuss the offences under s. 3 of the Road Traffic Act, 1972.
13. What is the Criminal Injuries Compensation Board and what are its functions?

13

PROCEDURE

The following is an outline of the procedure applicable to civil and criminal cases.

1. Civil Procedure

General. Where a person considers he has a civil claim against another he will normally consult his solicitor. If he is unable to afford this he may first visit a Citizens' Advice Bureau and take advantage of the facilities available under the Legal Aid and Advice Acts (see p. 75). There is no obligation to consult a solicitor, but legal procedure is technical and detailed and it is a matter of common sense to take advice from those who are experienced and qualified to give it.

The first step of the solicitor is to ascertain whether a cause of action is disclosed or whether the matter agitating the mind of a citizen may be overcome by a straightforward letter to, for example, a debtor asking for payment. This may be all that is required but, if legal action is needed, the next step is to see whether the action will be taken in the county court or the High Court (the jurisdiction of each is dealt with in Chapter 4). No court can entertain an action unless it is legally empowered to do so.

2. County Court Procedure

Proceedings in the county court are divided into two classes: (*a*) **matters** and (*b*) **actions**.

(*a*) Where a person brings a proceeding, such as an adoption order, or a declaration of legitimacy, his initial proceeding is by **originating application**. Where a person seeks to bring an action for divorce or judicial separation, bankruptcy, or winding up a company, his application is begun by a **petition**. Originating applications and petitions are collectively called 'matters', as opposed to 'actions', described below.

(*b*) An action is a legal proceeding which is begun by a **plaint**. Broadly, all proceedings are begun by means of a plaint where one person, a plaintiff, brings an action against another, a defendant; as in claims for damages for breach of contract, a tort or when a plaintiff claims an equitable remedy.

Actions are of two kinds: **ordinary actions** and **default actions**, each with its own technical rules and steps.

Steps in an Ordinary Action

The general rules are that the plaintiff obtains from the county court office a request for the summons and completes it. The document sets out full particulars of (*a*) the parties, (*b*) the nature of the claim, and (*c*) the amount of damages the plaintiff claims. The plaintiff files the completed request in the county court office together with particulars of claim.

The particulars of claim lay down the basis of the plaintiff's case. Thus, in a road accident case, in which the plaintiff sustained a fracture of his left leg, was severely cut on the face and suffered shock, the claim will detail any allegations of negligence, such as driving a motor-car carelessly, or at an excessive speed and details of the injury and damage to property, together with the cost and details of any other losses, such as wages during the plaintiff's incapacity.

The registrar of the court then prepares a summons for service on the defendant. Affixed to the summons are (*a*) particulars of claim; (*b*) the form of admission (should the defendant admit the allegations and/or particulars) and (*c*) the form of defence and counterclaim.

The documents so prepared must be served upon the defendant (or each of the defendants if there are more than one). There must be 21 days between the date of service and the date for the hearing of the action.

Once the summons has been served the defendant will have to decide what he, himself, will do. Normally he will consult a solicitor, if he has not already done so.

The defendant may within 14 days admit liability for all or part of the claim. He can make payment of the sum claimed, with costs, into court or he may pay a lesser sum which the plaintiff may decide to accept in full settlement. The defendant may, if he cannot pay all the sum due at once, offer to pay at a later date or by instalments, e.g. £5 a month. If the plaintiff accepts the offer the court will enter judgment accordingly but, if he does not, the action proceeds.

Where the defendant disputes the claim and wishes to contest the action he must 'file a defence'. He may also make a counterclaim, if he has one, and this should be served on the plaintiff, normally within 14 days.

At this stage there is (*a*) the claim of the plaintiff with his allegations, and (*b*) the defence of the defendant with his side of the case. The defence may be a denial of the allegations made by the plaintiff that, for example, the defendant drove too fast, with any counterclaim the defendant may make against the plaintiff.

Pre-trial Review. This is a preliminary consideration of the action by the registrar at which he will give directions to ensure a speedy and just disposal of the action. In effect he will try to narrow down the issue in dispute, see whether admissions may be made by one or both sides, whether witnesses need be called, what documents may be admitted in evidence without proof, etc.

If the defendant does not appear at this proceeding judgment may be entered, by the registrar, for the plaintiff. If the defendant appears, the registrar fixes the day for the trial of the action after considering the two sides of the case. He gives notice to every party so that all can be present.

The trial date being fixed the action proceeds on the date named and in the court named. Normally civil actions are brought to the court in the district where the defendant usually resides or carries on his business. But there are exceptions to this rule, as where the ownership of land is in dispute the proceedings are brought in the district where the land is situated.

Many things may cause hitches, e.g. the illness of the plaintiff, defendant, or an important witness and similar matters, so that adjournments may have to be made.

If, after all the documents have been served, the defendant does not appear at the action on the date named the trial may proceed in his absence and judgment may be entered for the plaintiff, usually with costs. If, however, the plaintiff does not appear at the court and gives no explanation for his absence the action will generally be struck out for want of prosecution. The action may be reinstated for sufficient cause on the plaintiff's application.

Let us assume that both parties are present with their witnesses and their respective solicitors or counsel. The steps to be followed in the contest will take the following form.

At the trial before the judge (or registrar in certain county court cases) the usual procedure is as follows:

(*a*) Plaintiff's lawyer makes an opening speech, describing the issue to be resolved and explaining how he proposes to prove the points at issue.

(*b*) Plaintiff's lawyer calls his witnesses and examines them. They are then cross-examined by the defendant's lawyer, in order to test the truth of what each witness says on oath.

(*c*) Defendant's lawyer calls his witnesses, who testify what they know of the matter. Defendant's lawyer examines the witnesses, and they are cross-examined by plaintiff's lawyer.

(*d*) Defendant's lawyer makes his speech to the judge, comments on the points relevant to the issue and, if a point of law is concerned, he brings to the notice of the judge the relevant statute or cases. He asks for judgment in his favour.

(*e*) Plaintiff's lawyer makes his speech in reply, giving his side of the story, commenting on the relevant factors, arguing points of law and asking for judgment in his favour.

(*f*) The judge thereupon makes his decision. If the judge sits alone he will give his judgment which is entered on the court records. If a jury is present he will address the jury on the facts and the law, and ask them to retire and consider their verdict. Juries are very rare in county courts.

Steps in a Default Action

Where the plaintiff is claiming a debt or a liquidated (i.e. ascertained) demand, he must proceed by default action, not by an ordinary action. He may then enter judgment in default without the case going to trial if the defendant fails to take the appropriate steps, i.e. file a defence, counterclaim or admission or pay into court the sum claimed with costs. Even where the claim is for a debt or liquidated demand, there are some exceptions to the above rule and an ordinary action must be brought, e.g. against a person under disability or to recover a sum secured by mortgage.

The same initial steps must be taken by the plaintiff's solicitor as those taken in ordinary actions described above. However, after the defendant has been served with the summons and the particulars of claim he may take one of several courses:

(*a*) If the defendant after receiving the summons does nothing within 14 days (i.e. the defendant defaults) the plaintiff may enter judgment.

(*b*) If after receiving the summons the defendant pays into court either the whole amount claimed or an amount which the plaintiff is prepared to accept in settlement, the action will in most cases be stayed.

(*c*) If the defendant admits the whole, or part, of the debt claimed and, at the same time offers to pay the sum claimed at a specified rate (say £10 per month) and the plaintiff accepts (i) the amount admitted and (ii) agrees to accept the mode of payment, judgment will be entered for the plaintiff.

(*d*) If the defendant admits the *whole* of the claim, but the plaintiff does not agree to accept the mode of payment (say £10 per month) a date will be set by the registrar for the decision of the question of the mode of payment. Much depends on the means of the defendant about which inquiries will be made.

(*e*) If the defendant admits only a *part* of the claim, and the plaintiff does not wish to accept the amount admitted by the defendant and the form of payment which the defendant proposes, the registrar will fix a pre-trial review and then a date for hearing.

(*f*) If the defendant does not admit the claim at all the registrar will fix a pre-trial review at which the action may be disposed of or a date fixed for the hearing.

The Enforcement of County Court Judgments

There are, of course, rights of appeal against the judgments given in a county court. Generally, however, once judgment is given in the county court that is the end of the matter. The sum adjudged to be paid to the plaintiff is sent to the court; or to the plaintiff by the defendant; or, if the dispute is over the possession of land, the possessor either stays on in occupation or removes in favour of the plaintiff.

Where the judgment is ignored, however, we have to consider how the judgment is enforced by the court. There are two general kinds of enforcement: (*a*) those where a judgment is given for a sum of money, and (*b*) other judgments (e.g. for possession of land or a chattel).

(*a*) **Enforcing Judgments for a Sum of Money.** The following methods of enforcement are available:

(i) *Warrant of Execution.* The warrant is issued under the authority of the court directing the bailiffs to seize sufficient of the property of the debtor, including money, negotiable instruments and his goods, and to sell the same if need be to satisfy the amount of the judgment plus costs. The clothing and bedding of the debtor and his family and the tools of his trade to the value of £50 may not be seized.

(ii) *Attachment of Earnings Order.* Under the Attachment of Earnings Act, 1971, a county court is empowered to issue this order, which directs the employer of the judgment debtor to make periodical payments from the debtor's earnings and to pay the amounts so deducted to the collecting officer of the court at certain specified intervals. The sums so paid over by the employer are allocated to the judgment creditor in satisfaction of his judgment.

(iii) *Bankruptcy Proceedings.* Where the judgment is for £200 or more the judgment creditor may serve a bankruptcy notice on the debtor. If the latter does not pay the sum claimed this omission will constitute an 'act of bankruptcy' and proceedings will ensue in the normal way.

(iv) *Garnishee Proceedings.* This form of enforcement is available where a third party owes a sum of money to the judgment debtor. Thus where *A*, the judgment creditor, is owed £100 by *B*, the judgment debtor, and *X* (a third party) owes £100 to *B*, garnishee proceedings may be issued against *X*, the garnishee, to pay the sum of £100 to *A*, the judgment creditor, instead of to *B*. The debt is thereby extinguished and the judgment is satisfied.

(v) *Appointment of a Receiver.* Where a judgment debtor refuses to pay the judgment debt and the debtor has lands or houses which yield rents and profits, the court may on the application of the judgment creditor appoint a receiver, who is thereupon an officer of the court to collect the rents and profits. These are applied in reducing the debt due. When the whole of the judgment debt (plus costs) is paid the appointment of the receiver ends.

(vi) *Charging Order.* Where the judgment debtor owns land and certain other forms of property, the judgment creditor may apply to the court for a charging order the effect of which is that the property owned by the debtor is charged with the payment of the sum due on the judgment (plus costs). The property subject to the charge may be sold in settlement of the judgment debt, any surplus being handed over to the judgment debtor.

(vii) *Judgment summons* in a few cases.

(viii) *Administration order* providing for the administration of an insolvent judgment debtor's estate by the court.

(*b*) **Enforcing Other Judgments.** Sometimes a county court is called upon to decide ownership of land or goods which the defendant refuses to give up in favour of the rightful owner or possessor. The following authorize enforcement in such cases.

(i) *Warrants of Delivery or Possession.* A warrant may be issued by the court to authorize the bailiff to take by force if need be the goods to be delivered to the person adjudged to have rightful ownership. Similarly where a judgment for the recovery of land has been obtained, and the defendant will not give up the land, a warrant may be issued by the court to the bailiff to enter on the land and place the rightful owner in possession. Any interference with the bailiff is a punishable offence.

(ii) *Warrant of Attachment.* A warrant may be issued by the court to attach the defendant for contempt. The warrant authorizes the bailiff to arrest the defendant and convey him to the prison named. This form of enforcement is available where a defendant wilfully fails to comply with an order of the court.

Costs

The general rule regarding the costs involved in taking and defending actions, which include barristers' fees and solicitors' charges, together with court fees and other disbursements, are in the discretion of the court. Usually the court orders the costs to be paid by the party losing the action.

3. Civil Proceedings in the Queen's Bench Division

The first step in an action, e.g. in tort or a breach of contract, is begun by a writ issued in the Central Office of the Supreme Court (or in a District Registry). The writ is a document requiring the defendant to enter an appearance (see below) within 14 days, or risk the plaintiff proceeding to judgment in the absence of the defendant.

The writ is dated with the day of issue and it specifies the division to which it is intended that the action should be assigned.

Every writ is indorsed with short particulars of the plaintiff's claim, and in certain cases with a 'special indorsement' (see below). The address of the plaintiff and the name and address of the solicitor issuing the writ are also indorsed, with the address for service. Normally leave is not required to issue a writ.

The writ so obtained must be served. This may be done by handing it to the defendant (personal service), serving it by post or, in certain cases, by advertisement.

Leave of the court is required both for the issue and service of a writ outside the jurisdiction.

The writ is indorsed with short particulars of the plaintiff's claim. The object of this is to show the defendant immediately the nature of the demand made against him.

There are three kinds of indorsement:

(*a*) **General.** This need not set out details of the claim, but is simply a general description of the nature of the claim. Where libel is alleged the indorsement must identify the publication(s) containing the alleged libel.

(*b*) **For an Account.** This is used where the defendant has received money on behalf of the plaintiff who does not know the exact amount. The plaintiff can call for an account to be taken.

(*c*) **Special.** This is a statement of claim and is used where the plaintiff seeks to recover a liquidated sum or to recover land or articles and in certain other cases. The special indorsement is a full statement of the cause of action and the plaintiff cannot serve another statement of claim except to amend the indorsement.

The advantage of a special indorsement is that as soon as the defendant gives notice of his intention to defend, the plaintiff may apply for summary judgment under Order 14.

'Enter an Appearance' formerly meant what it said: the defendant had to appear at the court and, if need be, ask for an adjournment to arrange his defence. Today a defendant 'Enters an Appearance' by his solicitor completing a form, in duplicate, and filing the document (or 'entering' it) at the Central Office in London (or District Registry) within 8 days from service of the writ. A memorandum of the appearance sealed with the official seal is sent to the plaintiff. This notifies the plaintiff and his solicitor of the defendant's intention to defend.

If the defendant does not enter an appearance the plaintiff is entitled to judgment in default of appearance (unless the defendant is a minor, or of unsound mind). If the writ is specially indorsed for a liquidated sum the plaintiff can enter final judgment for the sum, plus interest, and costs. If the claim is for damages (not a liquidated demand) the damages must be assessed, and the plaintiff may have interlocutory judgment followed by final judgment when the damages are assessed.

If the defendant appears and the writ is specially indorsed under Order III (R.S.C.) the plaintiff may, on affidavit—verifying the cause of action and the amount claimed and stating that in his belief there is no defence—take out a summons under Order XIV before a master for leave to sign final judgment for the amount indorsed on the writ (or for the recovery of the land, if that is the issue) and costs. The master may, however, on reviewing the claim and the facts, give leave to defend (subject to any conditions he may lay down) or give the plaintiff leave to sign judgment.

Where leave to defend is given by the master the latter has considerable powers (similar to those of the registrar in the county court already described) to give directions as to how the matter is to proceed; to admit affidavit evidence, for example, with a view to narrowing the issue and to ensure a speedy and efficient disposal of the action so avoiding extra costs to which the parties might otherwise be put.

Pleadings in a legal action consist of statements in writing by both the plaintiff and the defendant. They exist to show the court (and the jury if there is one) the questions at issue between the parties and the facts on which each party relies. Pleadings must be as brief as the nature of the claim or defence allows; they must state concisely the material facts upon which a party relies, but not the evidence by which those facts are to be proved. The pleadings must be divided into numbered paragraphs. When the pleadings are closed two completed copies are lodged with the court.

The first pleading is the statement of claim. This must be clear and detailed; it must not be ambiguous. In tort the right which has been violated need not be set out, unless the right is peculiar to the plaintiff. In breach of contract the contract must be proved and then the breach.

The statement of claim must be delivered either with the writ, or within 14 days.

The next pleading is the defence which must be delivered within 14 days of the delivery of the statement of claim. The defence must contain every material fact which is to be relied on at the trial and the denials made by the defendant must be specific.

If the defendant has a claim against the plaintiff he may set this up by way of set-off or counterclaim.

The next pleading following the delivery of the defence is the reply of the plaintiff. Where there is no counterclaim by the defendant the reply would normally contain simply a joinder of issue, e.g. a **traverse** which means that the plaintiff denies the facts alleged by the defendant.

No pleading after reply is allowed as a general rule. At this stage we know the claim of the plaintiff and the defence of the defendant, together with the reply of the plaintiff. The parties join issue. At this stage a summons for directions must be taken out by the plaintiff. The directions are determined by the master and indicate the future course of the action and are aimed to secure the just, expeditious and economical disposal of the case.

The duties of the master are mainly (*a*) to limit the issues, and (*b*) to make orders which will reduce the costs of the evidence (by limiting the number of witnesses, particularly expert ones, who may be expensive, and by ensuring that evidence may, where possible, be allowed by affidavit). The master may make orders as to discovery, when each party must swear on affidavit as to the documents which are or have been in his possession, or power, relating to the matters in question in the action. The master may make an order allowing the discovery of facts by means of **interrogatories**, which are questions addressed to the other party to the action to which reply must be made. The answers must be given on oath.

Following the summons for directions the next step is to give notice of trial which may be on the application of plaintiff, or, if he does not do so, of the defendant.

The form of the trial whether before a judge alone or before a judge and jury is decided by the master. In cases of fraud, defamation, malicious prosecution or false imprisonment, for example, there is a right to trial by jury unless prolonged examination of documents or accounts is involved which cannot well be made with a jury.

The procedure at the trial is that described elsewhere (see p. 355) except that where the issue is exceptional in terms of the amount claimed, or there are considerable legal complexities, there will be two counsel—a Q.C. and a junior—on each side.

After the witnesses produced by both sides have been examined, cross-examined, and re-examined, and after the speeches by the counsel on both sides, the judge sums up and explains to the jury (if there is one) the point upon which their verdict is required. The judge also directs the jury as to the proper measure of damages if the verdict should be given to the plaintiff. The jury then retire to consider their verdict which is later announced in court by the foreman chosen by the jurymen from among their number. If there is no jury the judge delivers his judgment and finding, which are entered on the records of the court. At the same time the judge makes his order as to costs.

Enforcement of Judgments in the High Court

Once a judgment is made by the judge it follows that the judgment will have to be obeyed. If the party, against whom judgment is given, pays the damages and costs awarded against him that is the end of the matter. Sometimes the judgment is not obeyed and the party to whom the money is due or, if land is in dispute, the party entitled to possession, will have to take steps to enforce the judgment. There are two classes: judgments for payment of money, and judgments for other matters such as possession of land or goods. Writs of execution are issued by the court, as follows:

(*a*) *Fieri facias*. This is a writ which is directed to the sheriff commanding him that out of the goods and chattels of the debtor he do cause to be made the sum endorsed on the writ with interest and costs. The sheriff who acts through bailiffs thereby becomes entitled to take possession of the goods of the debtor, except the wearing apparel and bedding and tools of trade to a total value of £50, and to sell the goods in satisfaction of the writ. The sheriff can enter the lands of the debtor to do this.

(*b*) *Garnishee order*. This is similar to that described on p. 357.

(*c*) *Charging order* (see p. 358).

(*d*) *Appointment of a receiver* (see p. 357).

(*e*) *Sequestration*. The writ of sequestration authorizes commissioners (up to 4) to enter the debtor's lands, to take possession and collect the rent and profits from the debtor's real and personal estate and to hold the land and personal estate until the debtor has paid the amount due. This writ is available where the debtor is in contempt of court by refusing or neglecting to obey the order of the court to pay the specified amount.

(*f*) *Attachment of Earnings*. This is available to the plaintiff only where the defendant neglects or refuses to obey a maintenance order made by the High Court.

(*g*) *Committal to Prison*. A rare method, but available where the defendant neglects or refuses to obey an order of the court.

(*h*) For possession of land or delivery of goods.

4. Criminal Procedure

This section deals briefly with the procedure followed in the prosecution of a case in (*a*) a magistrates' court, and (*b*) the Crown Court.

All criminal prosecutions are in theory taken in the name of the Crown and are cited: *Rex* (*or Regina*) v. *Smith* (defendant). That form is followed in Crown Court proceedings. In summary trials the Crown Prosecution Service will institute proceedings as prosecutor against a defendant (see p. 84).

But a private citizen may institute criminal proceedings.

5. Proceedings in Magistrates' Courts

Process by Summons

Refer to p. 314 and note the distinction between summary offences and indictable offences. This section deals with the procedure followed in the prosecution of a summary offence. These are by far the most numerous and include road traffic offences of all sorts.

Let us assume a simple case. *X* a college student rides his bicycle away from the college after dark without a front light. *X* is stopped on the highway by a P.C. The constable notes down any explanation *X* may give for his omission to have a light on his bicycle. The constable then informs *X* that he will be reported for summons.

What happens now? The P.C. submits his report and from this an **information** is prepared, the first legal process. An information is merely a statement which may be oral, but is usually written, setting out the details of the alleged offence.

From the information the clerk to the justices prepares a summons which is signed by a J.P.

The summons is then served on the defendant. Service may be effected simply by handing *X* a copy personally, or more usually by sending him a copy by post. The summons informs *X* of the date, time and place of the alleged offence and the statute (or common law rule) infringed. The summons commands the attendance of *X* at a court on a date named in the summons.

In most cases the defendant *X* must appear at court. Indeed if *X* does not attend the court the magistrates may issue a warrant for his arrest. Note they *may* do so. In minor offences, however, the Magistrates' Courts Act, 1952, provides a procedure by which a defendant may avoid attendance at court by sending a form through the post to the clerk of the court pleading guilty. He may make any written explanation he desires, which will be considered by the court. This saves much time and the case is quickly disposed of, usually by a fine.

If our defendant *X* pleads 'Not Guilty' he should attend the court on the day named. He may consult a solicitor to assist him in his defence. On the facts, however, there is not likely to be a defence. If the lamp was stolen by a fellow student on the day, *X* may consider this a defence. However, it is not a defence, though it may be a mitigating circumstance which the court may take into consideration when fixing the sentence if it finds the defendant guilty.

If *X* feels he must contest the case he will attend the court on the day named. When the magistrates are ready to hear the case, *X*'s name will be called out. *X* will be directed to a position in the court (see diagram on p. 58). The alleged offence is read out to him and he is asked to plead. *X* pleads 'Not Guilty'. First the solicitor will give a short outline of the facts, and then ask the P.C. to enter the witness box. He will be sworn and will give his evidence. *X* (or his solicitor) will be invited to ask any questions on the evidence of the P.C. The solicitor for the prosecution may re-examine the P.C. to clear up any doubts raised by *X* (or his solicitor). Any other prosecution witnesses will then be called to give their evidence and may be cross-examined by *X* or his solicitor. The prosecution is then at an end. *X* will now be invited to do one of two things: (*a*) to go into the witness box and be sworn on oath to give his evidence of what happened; or (*b*) he may make a statement from outside the witness box giving his side of the story. If *X* adopts course (*a*) he will be liable to be cross-examined by the prosecuting solicitor to test the truth of what *X* says. He, *X*, may then be re-examined by his own solicitor, if he has one. Otherwise after both sides i.e. the police (the prosecution) and *X* (the defendant) have given their versions the justices announce their verdict of Guilty or Not Guilty.

As to course (*b*) it will be apparent that if *X* decides not to go into the witness box his statement will not be as convincing as that which he is prepared to testify to in the witness box. But note—this decision is *X*'s alone, and he is not forced to take either course. He may say nothing at all.

In the example given the magistrates will decide on a penalty. It may be a fine, but this is a matter for the court, and if *X* was riding home to tend to his sick mother the court may give him an absolute discharge.

To sum up this is the simplest example of a case often before a magistrates' court, but in many cases in these courts there are more serious matters such as driving a car to the danger of the public, when there may be several witnesses for the defence and several for the prosecution. The burden of proving the guilt of the accused beyond reasonable doubt rests on the prosecution throughout the trial. The accused person is presumed innocent until the contrary is proved.

Process by Warrant

A warrant is another means of starting a prosecution. Let us assume that *X* has stolen £100 from *Y* and that *X* has absconded. *Y* reports the matter to the police and gives a description of the offence and the offender. Theft is an 'arrestable offence'. After the police investigation the police may apply to the magistrates for a warrant. First an information in writing and on oath must be laid by the police before a magistrate, who may then issue a warrant for the arrest of *X*.

The warrant authorizes the police to whom it is directed to arrest *X*. The warrant may direct that *X* on arrest be granted bail. This is entirely in the discretion of the magistrate. If *X* is arrested in some other part of the U.K. he will be handed over by the police of that area to the police of the area where the offence occurred. *X* will then be brought before the court whence the warrant was issued to answer the charge of theft. The powers of a police officer regarding stop and search; entry search and seizure; arrest; detention and questioning, are now contained in the Police and Criminal Evidence Act, 1984.

On being brought before the court the magistrates will give *X* a choice of being tried either by (*a*) the magistrates' court or (*b*) the Crown Court, since theft is an offence triable either way. (Sections 21, 22 and 23 of the Criminal Law Act, 1977, provide that in the case of offences triable either way, even if the magistrates consider that the offence is more suitable for summary trial, they must commit to the Crown Court unless the accused consents to summary trial; that if they consider the offence more suitable for trial on indictment they must commit to the Crown Court; and that certain offences, e.g. criminal damage, where the value involved does not exceed £200 must be tried summarily.) Let us assume that the defendant opts for (*a*). The charge will be read out to him, and he will be asked to plead Guilty or Not Guilty. If he does not plead one or the other or says anything which casts doubt on his plea of Guilty, a plea of Not Guilty will be entered for him.

Note: *X* will be given facilities to consult a solicitor who will advise him what course of action to take and how the defence should be conducted, i.e. obtaining evidence and witnesses for the defence. If he is unable to afford a solicitor he may be granted by the court the services of a solicitor (see Legal Aid and Advice, p. 75). *X* may apply for bail or for an adjournment to enable him and his solicitor to arrange his defence. These matters are decided by the court.

When the case is ready for trial the case proceeds in the normal way: Prosecuting solicitor outlines the main facts of the case. He then calls witnesses, who are examined, and may then be cross-examined. Prosecution solicitor addresses the court. The defence solicitor addresses the court, calls his witnesses who give evidence. They are examined, cross-examined and may be re-examined to clear up any points raised by the prosecution. The prosecution solicitor addresses the court, followed by the defence solicitor. At the conclusion of the case the magistrates may retire to consider their verdict.

The magistrates will, if they find the defendant guilty, then hear the antecedents (i.e. the history) of the accused. The magistrates then decide the appropriate penalty. If the magistrates find the case not proved they will return a verdict of Not Guilty and the defendant will go free from the court.

A warrant of arrest may not be issued against a person 17 or over unless the offence is (i) indictable, or (ii) is punishable by imprisonment, or (iii) the address of the defendant is not sufficiently established for a summons (to be served on him) (Criminal Justice Act, 1967, s. 24(2)).

6. Proceedings in the Crown Court

Cases committed to the Crown Court by the magistrates are triable by judge and jury.

Indictment

This is a written or printed accusation of the crime for which a person is to be tried by the Crown Court. More than one person may be charged in an indictment, as where two or more persons are charged jointly or where the crime necessarily involves more than one person, e.g. conspiracy. Moreover, several crimes may be charged in an indictment. Each offence will be described in a separate paragraph called a 'count'.

A 'bill of indictment' must be given to the clerk of the court. When the judge (or recorder) is satisfied that the requirements of the law are complied with he may direct the clerk to sign the Bill and, when he does so, the document becomes an 'Indictment'.

Any person may prefer a bill of indictment before the Crown Court and, if it is properly drawn up and signed, a trial may take place. Where the Court of Appeal orders a new trial it will direct a fresh indictment to be preferred; a bill may be preferred by a judge of the High Court; and where a person commits perjury (Perjury Act, 1911) in the Crown Court a bill of indictment may then and there be drawn up and the person may be charged, tried and convicted. The usual channel however is by means of preliminary investigation at the magistrates' court, followed by a committal for trial to the Crown Court.

What follows is a general description of a trial when, e.g. a defendant, *X*, is charged with theft under the Theft Act, 1968. Complicated trials (some have lasted 100 days) involve complex rules. Only the broad general procedure can be noted here.

Arraignment

The defendant, *X*, is 'arraigned' when the clerk of the court calls the defendant by name to the bar (i.e. the bar of the dock, see p. 56) and asks: 'How say you, are you guilty or not guilty?'

The actual pleading to this question, i.e. guilty or not guilty, must be by the defendant himself, not his counsel.

Guilty Pleas. Where the defendant pleads guilty, the prosecuting counsel outlines the broad facts of the case to the court, and the antecedents of the defendant are read out to the court by the police officer in charge of the case. Defendant's counsel may then make a speech in mitigation, pointing out any circumstances, e.g. upbringing, mental depressions, personal accidents, etc. which should be borne in mind by the court in fixing the sentence to be passed on the defendant. The judge, who may retire to consider the sentence, delivers his decision of the penalty in open court.

Not Guilty Pleas. In these cases the procedure is as follows. A jury is empanelled from those jurymen called to attend the court. They take the oath and are sworn to 'well and truly try the case according to the evidence'.

After this prosecuting counsel outlines the facts of the case, shows how he proposes to prove the case, the number of the witnesses he proposes to call and the exhibits at his disposal.

Prosecuting counsel calls his witnesses. Each is examined; and then cross-examined by defence counsel. Each may be re-examined by prosecuting counsel to clear up doubtful points.

Defence counsel then outlines his defence. He may, however, state that no case has been disclosed and that the defendant should go free. If that submission is accepted the court makes its finding and may then free the prisoner. Usually there is a *prima facie* case, and the defence counsel, if he is calling witnesses to fact other than the defendant, may make an opening speech to the jury, after which he will call his witnesses. Each witness is examined, cross-examined by prosecuting counsel, and re-examined by defence counsel.

The defendant, *X*, may if he so elects, go into the witness box and give evidence on oath. If he does so and wishes to protest his innocence he will be examined by his own counsel, but will also be exposed to cross-examination by prosecuting counsel. This is usually a vital moment in every trial since both what he says and how he says it will be under close scrutiny by the jury and all those present in court. If he negotiates this stage he will be re-examined by his own counsel.

If the defendant elects not to go into the witness box he may make any statement he wishes from the bar or other appointed place. Naturally any statement not on oath will not be as convincing as that which is subject to cross-examination under oath.

Prosecuting counsel now makes his closing speech asking that the accused be found guilty. The last speech, however, will be that of defence counsel who will make his final plea to the jury.

The judge (or recorder) then directs the jury on the law, sums up and explains that the burden lying on the prosecution is to prove that the accused committed the offence beyond reasonable doubt. He will also direct them as regards majority verdicts. The jury then retires and deliberates in secret without any interference from anyone. The verdict is theirs and theirs alone.

If the jury disagree (e.g. where 8 consider the defendant guilty, whilst 4 consider him not guilty) the judge will order a retrial when a different jury will be empanelled.

If the defendant is found guilty by the jury, defence counsel will make a plea in mitigation bringing out those facts which ought to be borne in mind by the court before the sentence of the court is awarded by the judge.

If the defendant is sentenced to prison a committal warrant is prepared and the defendant is taken to the prison where his sentence is to be served.

In accordance with s. 43 of the Powers of the Criminal Courts Act, 1973, forfeiture may be ordered of any property which has been used for the purpose of committing or facilitating the commission of an offence (or which it was intended to be used for that purpose) by the person convicted of the offence.

Proceedings against Children and Young Persons

All offences committed by children and young persons must be dealt with summarily by juvenile courts. These are special courts (see p. 61) set up for each petty sessional area, and are presided over by specially experienced J.P.s.

The following offences committed by either a child or a young person may not be dealt with summarily:

(i) homicide.

(ii) where the child or young person is charged jointly with a person over 17 years and the court considers it necessary in the interests of justice that the defendants be committed for trial.

In these classes of cases the court of trial will be the Crown Court.

Arrest and Habeas Corpus

The police have wide powers of arrest both at common law and under statute. Private citizens also have powers of arrest but in practice they are not frequently used.

If a person is detained in custody (e.g. in police cells or a prison or elsewhere) he, or someone acting on his behalf, may apply for a writ of *habeas corpus* against the person, e.g. a police superintendent or prison governor, who detains him. The detaining person will be required to appear in court on a day named to justify the detention of the prisoner.

An application for such a writ is made to the Divisional Court of the Queen's Bench Division. If the court is not sitting then application may be made to a single judge who will inquire into the matter.

Where the imprisonment is lawful the prisoner will be returned to custody. Otherwise the court will order release. Under the civil law where a person has been imprisoned wrongfully damages may be claimed against the person responsible. However we should note that where a police officer has reasonable suspicion that an arrestable offence has been committed he may arrest that person even though it turns out that no offence has been committed. In *Mohammed-Holgate* v. *Duke* (1983) where *P* had been arrested for questioning and then released without being charged, the House of Lords held that such an arrest was not unlawful.

7. Standard Works

The standard books used by lawyers are:

(1) *County Court Practice* for County Court proceedings (commonly called the Green Book).

(2) *Annual Practice* containing the rules of the Supreme Court (R.S.C. for short) for High Court proceedings (commonly called the White Book).

(3) *Stone's Justices' Manual* for the law and procedure of magistrates' courts.

(4) *Archbold Criminal Pleading, Evidence and Practice.*

8. Exercises

1. Outline the procedure in bringing an ordinary action in a County Court.
2. What are the three kinds of indorsement of a High Court writ? What is meant by the phrase 'Entering an Appearance'?
3. Explain the meaning of: (*a*) Interrogatories, (*b*) an Order of Discovery, and (*c*) Statement of Defence.
4. Describe the methods available for the enforcement of judgments in the High Court.
5. Explain the terms: (*a*) Indictment; (*b*) Arraignment; (*c*) *Habeas Corpus.*
6. Describe in broad outline the procedure to be followed in a Crown Court where the defendant pleads Not Guilty.

Appendix 1

GLOSSARY OF TERMS

ab initio	from the beginning
actio personalis moritur cum persona	a personal action dies with the person
ad litem	with respect to a suit at law
administrator cum testamento annexo	administrator with the will annexed (which the court appoints him to administer)
administrator durante minore aetate	administrator during infancy (of the true appointee)
administrator pendente lite	administrator during the litigation (of a disputed will)
animus manendi	the intention to remain in that place or country
animus revocandi	the intention to revoke
audi alteram partem	hear the other side
bona fide	in good faith
bona vacantia	ownerless property
caveat emptor	let the buyer beware
certiorari	to be informed (an order of *certiorari* is explained on p. 71)
cestui que trust	the person for whose benefit a trust is created; a beneficiary
chattels personal	personal goods
chattels real	a lease, forming part of personalty
chose in action	a thing in action; a personal right of property which can only be claimed or enforced by an action at law and not by taking physical possession
chose in possession	a thing that is the subject of physical possession (contrast with chose in action)
consensus ad idem	mutual agreement on the same point
cujus est solum ejus est usque ad caelum	the owner of land owns all the land below the surface and all the space above the land
cum testamento annexo	with the will attached
Curia Regis	The King's Court
Cy-près	so near; as nearly as possible
damnum sine injuria	damage without legal injury (or wrong)
delegatus non potest delegare	one to whom power has been delegated cannot delegate that power to another

de minimis non curat lex	the law takes no notice of trifles
de novo	anew
distress damage feasant	the right of an occupier of land to seize animals doing damage thereon
donatio mortis causa	a gift in anticipation of death
durante minore aetate	during infancy
ejusdem generis	of the same kind, or nature
equitas sequitur legem	equity follows the law
escrow	a sealed writing delivered conditionally, which condition being performed it operates immediately as a deed
estoppel	a rule of evidence whereby a party is precluded by some previous act to which he was party or privy from asserting or denying a fact. For example, a party cannot aver that a state of things is different from what he has led the other party to believe if the other party has acted upon such belief and changed his position
ex gratia	as a matter of favour
ex nudo pacto non oritur actio	a bare promise (without consideration) does not give rise to any action
ex officio	arising from an official position, by virtue of his office
ex parte	on the application of. (An *ex parte* hearing is one at which only one side is represented)
ex post facto	after the event
expressio unius est exclusio alterius	the express mention of one thing implies the exclusion of another
ex turpi causa non oritur actio	no action arises out of a base cause
ibid. = ibidem	in the same place
ignorantia juris haud excusat *ignorantia juris neminem excusat* *ignorantia juris non excusat*	ignorance of the law excuses no one
in consimili casu	in similar case to
in extremis	in imminent peril of death
in personam	against a person
in pari delicto potior est conditio possidentis	where two parties are equally in the wrong, the condition of the possessor is the stronger
in pari delicto potior est conditio defendentis	of two wrong-doers it is better to be the defendant
in re	in the matter of
in rem	against a thing; a right *in rem* is a right in property such as land which is good against the whole world
in terrorem	as a threat, to cause fear

indenture	a deed to which there are two or more parties
injuria sine damno	legal injury without damage
inter alia	among other matters
inter se	among themselves
inter vivos	during life
jus accrescendi	right of survivorship
jus tertii	the right of a third party
laches	delay, e.g. in pursuing a remedy at law
lex loci contractus	the law of the place where the agreement was made
mandamus	we command (an order of *mandamus* is explained on p. 70)
Magnum Concilium	the Great Council
mens rea	guilty mind
mesne	intermediate
nec per vim, nec clam, nec precario	peaceably, openly and as of right
nemo dat quod non habet	no one can give what he does not have
non est factum	not my deed
noscitur a sociis	the meaning of a word can be gathered from its context
obiter dicta	sayings by the way
overt	open
pendente lite	during the litigation
per se	by itself, by *or* through himself
per subsequens matrimonium	by subsequent marriage
per capita	by the number of individuals
prima facie	at a first view
puisne	lesser in importance
pur autre vie	for another's life
quantum meruit	as much as he has deserved
quasi	as if, as it were
quid pro quo	a mutual consideration; tit for tat
qui facit per alium facit per se	he who does a thing through another does it himself
ratio decidendi	the reason for the decision
res	thing
res ipsa loquitur	the thing speaks for itself
restitutio in integrum	restoration to the original position
sans recours	without recourse
sciens	knowing
scienti non fit injuria	one who knows cannot be harmed
seisin	effective possession of land by a freeholder (see p. 267)

sic utere tuo ut alienum non laedas	so use your own property as not to injure your neighbour's
sine die	without fixing a day
stare decisis	to stand by past decisions
status quo	the state in which a thing exists
sue	to take proceedings in a civil action
sui juris	of full legal capacity
surrogate	deputy
tortfeasor	a person liable on a tort
trover	an early form of conversion in which a finding (*trover*) of the goods was alleged
uberrimae fidei	of the utmost good faith
ubi remedium ibi jus	where there is a remedy there is a right
ultra vires	beyond the powers of
viva voce	by word of mouth
volens	willing
volenti non fit injuria	no wrong can be done to one who consents to what is done

Appendix 2

EXAMINATION TECHNIQUE

At the end of each chapter you will find questions to enable you to test your knowledge. Use these questions constantly throughout your course, for revision is a vital requirement in all studies and particularly in law. However able your tutor may be, in the final result the examination will test *your* knowledge and *your* learning. Constant revision is vital for those of us with average powers. The secret of success is adequate preparation.

Law Questions

These are usually of two types: (*a*) a textbook type of question, and (*b*) a problem question. The approach to each is slightly different.

(*a*) **Textbook Questions.** These seek to test your knowledge of a particular portion of the law. A question may call for a description of a development in legal history, or a court: for example 'How was the common law of England formed?' 'What is the composition and jurisdiction of a county court?' A thorough knowledge of the textbook will enable you to answer all such questions normally asked. Deal with historical questions in chronological order as a general rule; and if you are tackling a question on the courts deal with it in the order asked, i.e. (i) composition, and (ii) jurisdiction.

(*b*) **Problem Questions.** These usually set down facts, based on one or more decided cases. The question may ask you to discuss the problem, or to consider the liability of persons named in the case. These questions test your knowledge of the law and, secondly, your application of the law to the facts. The general approach here is first to set down quite clearly the general rule of law, which may be statutory or a decided case. Then lead on to the exception to the general rule, which may be the result of another case decided in the courts and, therefore, law. In all your statements on the law quote authorities, i.e. statute law or case law. At this stage apply the law to the facts in the question, noting any distinctions you may observe, and come to a conclusion.

The following simple rules will guide you in answering all law-examination questions:

(i) Read the question *carefully*.
(ii) Read it again, underlining the *key word or words*.
(iii) Make *rough* notes of your answer.
(iv) Arrange your points in *order*.
(v) Write your answer from your *plan*.

English Style. Examiners want clear and concise answers. Remember the 'ABCD Rule':

A = Accurate
B = Brief
C = Clear
D = Direct (i.e. be relevant).

Legal text-writers, judges, and examiners prefer simple, clear, and direct statements. Avoid showy, extravagant, and facetious language or comments. This wastes time, earns no marks, and may be penalized. Aptness and suitability should be the aim.

Spelling, Grammar, and Handwriting. Whatever views we may personally hold on these matters, the fact remains that a grammatically correct, well-paragraphed, and well-written paper will commend itself to any examiner. Untidy, blotched, and scribbled efforts ask for the red pencil and will not justify good marks.

Citing Authorities. Examiners seek to test your knowledge of English law. Include your authorities for your statements, e.g. 's. 136 of the Law of Property Act, 1925', or (if your authority is a decided case) '*Nash* v. *Inman* (1908)', '*Roscorla* v. *Thomas* (1842)', and so on. It is customary practice in law examinations to underline the titles of cases. This helps to draw the attention of the examiner to the important references you make. If you do not know the name of the case, or if it escapes your memory, give the facts and the principles of law which it demonstrates.

Example 1

Question: What do you understand by equity? What reasons led to the creation and growth of the Court of Chancery?

Rough Notes: Definition of equity: supplementary to common law. Creation of Court of Chancery: petitions to King; reference to Council, then Chancellor; Court set up by end of fifteenth century.

Growth: Earl of Oxford's case 1616; principles established, case law developed; finally, delays and abuses till Judicature Act, 1873–5; now Chancery Division.

Model Answer: Equity in a general sense corresponds to natural justice or fairness in the adjustment of conflicting interests or controversies. As administered in the courts, however, equity means that portion of natural justice which eventually formed itself into technical rules operating according to certain clear-cut principles. Before the Judicature Acts, 1873–5, equity comprised those rules administered and enforced by the Court of Chancery in cases where the courts of common law gave no remedy or gave an inadequate remedy to a plaintiff notwithstanding that there was a right, based on conscience, to relief. In this sense, therefore, equity may be looked upon as a gloss (or appendix) to the common law, filling in the gaps and making the English legal system more complete.

The germ of the idea of equity lies in the notion of the King as 'fountain of justice' to whom a subject could present a petition for relief in any cause and for any reason. Where no relief was obtainable in the common law courts or under the common law, a subject sent his petition to the King. The petitions became numerous and were sometimes examined by the King and his Council, relief being granted, as a matter of grace, or refused. Owing to pressure of business in the Council the petitions were sent to the Chancellor who, as Chief Secretary of State and Keeper of the King's Conscience, eventually dealt with them alone.

By the end of the fifteenth century the Chancellor had established his own court, the Court of Chancery, and assumed a jurisdiction in disputes, applying his own procedures (e.g. *subpoena* and interrogatories) and granting relief by decree (e.g. specific performance of contracts and injunction). In due course of time the Chancellor's jurisdiction grew because of its popularity. Eventually his jurisdiction competed with and conflicted with the common law itself, and resulted in open dispute in the celebrated *Earl of Oxford's* case (1616) in which the King personally interposed his will. Thereafter, where the rules of common law and equity conflicted, equity prevailed.

Despite its initial popularity, equity as administered in the Chancery Court came under criticism. Jurisdiction grew, particularly in the administration of trusts and mortgages, but abuses occurred and there were frequent delays in dealing with cases, so that in course of time the Court became the exact opposite of its original intention and purpose.

Finally the Judicature Acts, 1873–5, were passed which brought into being a new system of courts and a fusion of the *administration* of law and equity. The Court of Chancery was abolished, but was re-created as one of the divisions of the High Court and named the Chancery Division. It retained most of its original jurisdiction, but may now grant in any case coming before it not only its traditional equitable remedies (referred to above) but also common law remedies.

Example 2

Question: (*a*) Discuss the meaning of trespass to the person and distinguish between the different forms that it may take. (*b*) State with reasons whether *F* and *G* are guilty of the tort of assault in the following cases:

(i) *F*, a farmer, after a quarrel with his neighbour *H*, points his gun at him. In fact, unknown to *H*, the gun is not loaded.

(ii) *G*, who with his wife has been playing cards with Mr. and Mrs. *K*, has an argument with *K*, who has accused him of cheating. *G* says to *K*: 'If there were no ladies present I should give you the biggest hiding you ever got.' (*A.E.B.*)

Rough Notes: (*a*) Three forms of trespass: assault, battery, and false imprisonment. Cases: *R.* v. *St. George*, *Bird* v. *Jones.*

(*b*) (i) Assault even if gun unloaded, *R.* v. *St. George*. (ii) No assault here, *Tuberville* v. *Savage*.

Model Answer: (*a*) Trespass to the person comprises three kinds: (i) assault, (ii) battery, and (iii) false imprisonment.

(i) An assault is an act which causes another to apprehend immediate and unlawful personal violence. An assault may be committed by striking at another person with a stick or a fist, or by throwing water or a stone at another; it is immaterial that the person who aims the blow misses his aim. It has been held that words alone do not constitute an assault; there must be some force used by the defendant.

(ii) Battery consists in *applying* force to the person of another hostilely or against his will. It is a battery even though the amount of force applied is slight. Common examples include giving a man a 'black eye', throwing water over another which splashes him, and holding a man by the arm (as where a police officer arrests a prisoner). Merely touching a person to draw his attention to some matter does not constitute an assault; similarly it is no assault where a pedestrian collides with another on the footpath accidentally. It appears that it is essential in this type of case to prove that the defendant acted intentionally or negligently: *Fowler* v. *Lanning* (1959).

(iii) False imprisonment consists in the infliction of bodily restraint on another without lawful justification. There need be no imprisonment such as detention in police cells. The mere holding of the arm of another is sufficient provided that the detention is complete. Thus, to restrain a person from going in three ways while leaving a fourth way open to him is not false imprisonment: *Bird* v. *Jones* (1845). Similarly, it was held that there was no imprisonment where employers refused to allow miners employed at the coal face to come to the surface to discuss a dispute, where the miners were working on a shift which had not been completed: *Herd* v. *Weardale Steel etc. Co.* (1915).

(*b*) (i) Applying the rules stated at (*a*) (i) above, the test is: Did the neighbour, *H*, fear violence from *F*? Pointing a gun is a threat to apply unlawful force to the person of another. Therefore an assault has been committed if *H* is put in fear, as would be the case with any reasonable person in his position. It is material whether *H* knew the gun was loaded or unloaded: *R.* v. *St. George* (1840). In the circumstances *H* may sue *F* for assault.

(ii) Words alone do not constitute an assault, it is said, but may 'unmake' it. In the present case *G* qualifies his statement by the words 'If there were no ladies present . . .'. There is no decided case where these particular words have been uttered in the circumstances shown, but it was held in *Tuberville* v. *Savage* (1669) that where a defendant uttered 'If it were not assize time, I would not take such language from you' and at the same time put his hand on his sword (a threat), there was no assault. Arguing by analogy from this early case, we may state that *G* has committed no assault.

Appendix 3

TEST PAPERS

The following questions are taken mainly from examination papers set by the Associated Examining Board for the General Certificate of Education at Advanced Level, and by the Royal Society of Arts for the Ordinary National Certificate in Business Studies (Joint Examination Scheme of the R.S.A. and the L.C.C.). The author acknowledges gratefully the kindness of both examining authorities for permission to reproduce the questions here.

Chapters 1–6: English Legal System

Answer six questions. Time allowed three hours.

1. What is meant by the 'sources of law'? Distinguish clearly between the different meanings attached to this term. (*A.E.B.*)

2. Describe briefly the origins and nature of the common law. Mention the defects which appeared in the common law system and state the effects of the Judicature Acts, 1873–5. (*R.S.A.*)

3. What is meant by 'delegated legislation'? What are its advantages and disadvantages? (*A.E.B.*)

4. What is meant by equity? Give a brief account of the ways in which equity sought to remedy the defects of the common law. (*R.S.A.*)

5. What influence, if any, have the following had on the development of English law: (i) the Church; (ii) mercantile practice; (iii) Roman law? (*A.E.B.*)

6. Describe the jurisdiction and composition of each of the following courts: (i) the Court of Appeal (Civil and Criminal Divisions); (ii) the county court; (iii) the quarter sessions. (*R.S.A.*)

7. Give an account of the part played by laymen in the administration of justice in England today. How does the English legal system benefit from this use of laymen? (*R.S.A.*)

8. (*a*) What are administrative tribunals? What kinds of work do they do and what advantages are they said to enjoy over the ordinary courts?

(*b*) By what means may the activities of administrative tribunals be controlled? (*R.S.A.*)

9. Distinguish carefully between the following:

(*a*) domicile and nationality;
(*b*) corporations sole and corporations aggregate;
(*c*) adoption and legitimation. (*A.E.B.*)

10. (*a*) In what ways do the functions of a barrister differ from those of a solicitor?

(*b*) Explain what the following do: (i) Queen's Counsel; (ii) The Law Society; (iii) The Council of Legal Education. (*A.E.B.*)

11. (*a*) Explain each of the following rules of statutory interpretation:

(i) the literal rule; (ii) the golden rule; (iii) the mischief rule.

(*b*) The Betting Act, 1853, prohibited the keeping of 'a house, office, room or other place' for betting purposes. *P* is charged with a contravention of the Act by keeping an uncovered area of a race-course for betting purposes. Discuss the application of the Act to these facts. (*R.S.A.*)

12. Trace the history of law reporting in England and consider to what extent law reporting has influenced the growth and development of the common law. (*A.E.B.*)

13. What do you consider to be the advantages and disadvantages of the English system of judicial precedent? (*A.E.B.*)

14. Explain in outline the main provisions of the Crown Proceedings Act, 1947.

15. Explain and comment on the scheme for legal aid and advice.

Chapter 7: Law of Contract

Answer six questions. Time allowed three hours.

1. (*a*) State the rules of the law of contract governing the acceptance of an offer.

(*b*) *A* lost his gold watch and offered £10 reward for its return. *B* found the watch and returned it to *A* at a time when he did not know of the reward. *B* subsequently heard that the reward had been offered and claimed it from *A*, who refused to pay. Discuss. (*R.S.A.*)

2. (*a*) What are the rules regarding the revocation of an offer? In what circumstances will an offer be irrevocable?

(*b*) Jones has offered to sell his grand piano to Brown for £50. What will be the legal position if:

(i) Jones dies before the offer has been accepted.
(ii) Brown dies before he has accepted the offer.
(iii) Brown dies after accepting the offer? (*A.E.B.*)

3. (*a*) Define consideration and summarize the rules which govern this element of a valid contract.

(*b*) *A* and *B* agree that *A* shall transfer his business to *B* in consideration of *B*'s paying *A* an annuity of £500 per annum during *A*'s lifetime, and after *A*'s death to *A*'s widow, *C*, for life. The business is transferred to *B* and he pays *A*'s annuity until *A*'s death, whereupon *B* refuses to pay the annuity to *C*. *C* is *A*'s sole surviving relative. Advise her. (*R.S.A.*)

4. (*a*) In what circumstances, if at all, can a debt be legally discharged by the payment of a smaller sum of money?

(*b*) *X*, an electrician, has agreed to rewire *Y*'s house for £150. The work having been completed, *Y* delays payment although he is pressed for it by *X*. Eventually, *Y* offers to discharge the debt by a payment of £120 and he tells *X* that if he were to refuse to accept this sum in full settlement he (*X*) could 'whistle for' his money. *X*, who is short of ready cash, then accepts a cheque for £120 and signs a receipt stating that he has accepted this sum in full settlement. He now asks your advice as to whether he can still claim the balance of £30. Explain the legal position to *X*. (*A.E.B.*)

5. (*a*) Certain contracts made by infants are treated as 'void', while others are said to be 'voidable'. Name the contracts falling into the two categories and explain the meaning of 'void' and 'voidable' in this context.

(*b*) *M*, an infant, bought an electric guitar for £40, paying £10 at the time of purchase and promising to pay the balance in six monthly instalments of £5 each. What would be the legal position if:

(i) *M* fails to pay any of the instalments and refuses to return the guitar:

(ii) *M*, who has failed to pay any of the instalments, sells the guitar to his friend Bingo (who is over 21) and delivers the guitar to him;

(iii) *M* finds that he cannot play the guitar and wants to return it and reclaim the £10 that he has already paid? (*A.E.B.*)

6. (*a*) What is meant by innocent and by fraudulent misrepresentation? What are the legal remedies available to the party misled (i) at common law, and (ii) under the Misrepresentation Act, 1967?

(*b*) *E* wishes to buy a caravan trailer to use on a touring holiday. *F*, a dealer, tells him that model '*X*' would be most suitable for his needs and could easily be pulled by *E*'s existing car. *E* buys the trailer but discovers after a week's trial run that the trailer is too heavy for his car and would damage it if used for any length of time. What redress, if any, will *E* have against *F*? What difference would it make to your answer if the contract specifically excluded liability for misrepresentation? Give reasons. (*A.E.B.*)

7. Simpson wrote a letter to Brown in which he said 'I offer to buy for the sum of £2,500 that painting by Constable which you keep in your study.' Brown knew that the painting referred to was not by Constable but by an unknown artist. Nevertheless, Brown sent a telegram to Simpson accepting this offer and the next day Simpson paid Brown £2,500 and took the painting away. Five years later an art dealer informed Simpson of his mistake, and that the painting was worth only £100. Advise Simpson. (*R.S.A.*)

8. (*a*) Which contracts are illegal at common law? What are the effects of this illegality?

(*b*) State with reasons which, if any, of the following contracts would be illegal:

(i) Mr. and Mrs. *X* agree to live apart and for Mr. *X* to pay his wife a monthly allowance of £100.

(ii) Mr. and Mrs. *X* agree to part in five years' time when their children will have grown up. The financial arrangements are as under (i).

(iii) Utopia imposes for political reasons a surcharge on import duty on goods which have originated in Ruritania. A British exporter handling products originating in Ruritania agrees with an importer in Utopia that the goods should be invoiced as British products in order to avoid payment of the surcharge. (*A.E.B.*)

9. (*a*) Discuss the extent to which a party to a contract may assign: (i) his rights and (ii) his liabilities under that contract. In what forms may such assignments be made?

(*b*) *X* owes *Y* £100. *Y* owes *Z* £75. Can *Y* transfer to *Z* £75 of the £100 which *X* owes him? If so, how? (*R.S.A.*)

10. (*a*) Distinguish between liquidated damages and unliquidated damages as remedies for breach of contract. Upon what principles do the courts assess the measure of damages to be awarded for a breach of contract?

(*b*) R. Co. Ltd., agreed to employ Smith as Company Secretary for two years certain at a salary of £6,000 a year. After he had been employed for four months Smith was wrongfully dismissed by R. Co. Ltd. Before his dismissal Smith had begun negotiations to buy Green's house for £15,000 and he had paid Green a deposit of £1,500 for the house. Because of his lack of employment Smith was unable to proceed with the purchase of the house and he forfeited his £1,500 deposit. Advise Smith as to his claim against R. Co. Ltd.

(*R.S.A.*)

11. (*a*) How far is writing an essential requirement for the validity and enforceability of a contract?

(*b*) George Smith orally agreed to sell his house to William Robertson for £18,000. Smith subsequently sent a letter through the post to Robertson which read as follows:

> Dear Sir, 1 March 1978
>
> I confirm that we have agreed today on the sale of my house Greenacre to you at a price of £18,000. Completion of the contract and payment of the purchase price are due to take place on 1 November 1978.
>
> Yours faithfully,
> George Smith.

Smith subsequently refused to complete the contract. Consider carefully the circumstances in which Robertson may be able to enforce it against him.

(*A.E.B.*)

12. (*a*) In what circumstances will the court award an order of specific performance or an injunction for breach of contract?

(*b*) *W* is the works manager of C. Co. Ltd., and he is employed under a five-year contract which provides that he should devote his entire working time to his employers. After two years, when the contract has still three years to run, *W* decides to leave since he has received a better offer from one of his employers' competitors. Will C. Co. Ltd., be likely to secure:

(i) an order for specific performance to compel *W* to serve out the full term of his contract;

(ii) an order for an injunction to stop him from working for C. Co.'s competitors;

(iii) damages for breach of contract?

Give reasons for your answers. (*A.E.B.*)

13. (*a*) Explain what is meant in the law of contract by (i) accord and satisfaction, (ii) frustration.

(*b*) *A* orders machinery to be made by *B* at a price of £15,000, and *B* agrees to make it. *A* later realizes that he does not really need the machinery and wants to cancel his order. Advise him of the legal position. How, if at all, would your answer differ if *A* had been buying a house from *B* instead of machinery? (*R.S.A.*)

14. (*a*) Explain the difference between 'duress' and 'undue influence'. How far do they respectively affect the validity of a contract?

(*b*) *M* has agreed to sell his house to *N* for less than its market value. Will this contract be binding on *M* if he was induced to sell his house by:

(i) *N*'s threat to start bankruptcy proceedings against *M* for some unpaid judgment debts;

(ii) *N*'s threat to refuse to allow his daughter to marry *M*'s son;

(iii) *N*'s threat to prosecute *M*'s son, whom he had employed and who had embezzled some funds belonging to *N*? Give reasons for your answers. (*A.E.B.*)

15. (*a*) What is meant by a contract of guarantee? How does it differ from a contract of indemnity? Why is it important to distinguish between these two contracts?

(*b*) A local tennis club was considering the replacement of the wire-netting round its courts. *C*, the chairman of the club, asked *T*, a contractor, to do the work and told him that he (*C*) would see to it personally that *T* was paid. When the work was completed the club refused to pay on the ground that *C* had acted without authority. *T* then sued *C* for payment. Discuss whether *T* is likely to succeed. (*A.E.B.*)

Chapter 8: Law of Torts

Answer six questions. Time allowed three hours.

1. (*a*) Define and distinguish between a tort and a crime.

(*b*) Describe any *two* general defences to an action for tort. Give illustrations. (*R.S.A.*)

2. (*a*) In what circumstances will a person be vicariously liable for the tort of another?

(*b*) Mr. Smith has given his twelve-year-old son, John, an air-gun as a Christmas present. The Smith family live on a farm and John has been forbidden by his father to use the gun outside the farm grounds. One day, John and his friend Paul go into the woods and John takes the gun with him to show off to his friend. On his way to the wood, John trips over a stone and accidentally presses the trigger. Paul, who is walking in front, is injured. Discuss whether Paul has a right of action against Smith senior. (*A.E.B.*)

3. (*a*) What do you understand by the tort of trespass, and what forms may trespass take?

(*b*) A group of children whose ages range from 8 to 11 years go on to a building site at the entrance to which there is a notice: 'Dangerous—Trespassers will be prosecuted.' Jack, aged 9 years, falls down a hole on the site and suffers injuries. Consider his chances of success in an action for damages which has been started against the occupiers of the site. (*R.S.A.*)

4. (*a*) How far is malice an essential ingredient of tortious liability?

(*b*) *Y*, a bed-ridden invalid, lives in a terraced house. He finds it impossible to sleep in the afternoons because his neighbour *X* is giving piano lessons at that time. *Y* has asked *X* to rearrange his lessons for some other time, but *X* has refused to do so. By way of retaliation, *Y* starts hammering on the wall as soon as the lessons commence. Explain (i) whether *Y* has any legal remedy against *X*, and (ii) whether *X* has any legal remedy against *Y*. (*A.E.B.*)

5. (*a*) Define and distinguish between public nuisance and private nuisance.

(*b*) What remedies are available to a person who claims he has sustained loss by reason of a nuisance committed by his neighbour? (*R.S.A.*)

6. (*a*) What defences are open to the defendant in an action for negligence?

(*b*) Jones, a visitor in a botanical garden, eats a berry taken from a bush. There is a large notice exhibited in the garden warning visitors against touching any of the plants, as some are poisonous. If Jones falls ill as a result of eating the berry would he have any redress against the proprietors of the garden? Would it make any difference to your answer if Jones was a child? (*A.E.B.*)

7. (*a*) Discuss the rule in *Rylands* v. *Fletcher*.

(*b*) *X* is the tenant of office premises situated on the second floor of an office building. One evening the washbasin in the men's cloakroom in *X*'s offices overflows with the result that the premises of *Y* on the first floor are flooded. Consider whether *X* will be liable in damages to *Y* if the flooding occurred because:

(i) the tap was left running by an employee of *X*;

(ii) the tap was left running by a burglar who had a wash after opening *X*'s safe;

(iii) a pipe had burst after frost. (*A.E.B.*)

8. (*a*) What is meant by contributory negligence in the law of tort? What are its legal consequences?

(*b*) *H* is driving his wife, *W*, to visit her mother in the country. The car is involved in a crash caused by the joint negligence of *H* who drove too fast and of *T*, the driver of another car, who backed his car into the main highway. *W*, who is injured in the crash, brings an action for damages against *T*. Advise *T*.

9. (*a*) Consider the circumstances in which the principle of *res ipsa loquitur* will apply in an action for negligence.
(*b*) Discuss the reasons whether this principle can be applied in the following cases:

(i) *X*'s stationary car is run into by *Y*'s car which has skidded on a greasy road;
(ii) *W*, while walking on the pavement, is knocked out by a flower pot falling from an upstairs window;
(iii) *Z*, a child, falls out of the door of a moving corridor train half an hour after the train has left the station. (*A.E.B.*)

10. Write notes on *two* of the following cases, bringing out in each instance the *ratio decidendi* of the case:

(*a*) *Donoghue* v. *Stevenson* (snail in the bottle);
(*b*) *Haynes* v. *Harwood* (runaway horse);
(*c*) *Overseas Tankships* (*U.K.*) *Ltd.* v. *Morts Dock and Engineering Co. Ltd.* (the *Wagon Mound* case: liability for damages);
(*d*) *Tulk* v. *Moxhay* (restrictive covenants). (*A.E.B.*)

Chapters 9–11: Trusts, Property, and Succession

Answer six questions. Time allowed three hours.

1. What is meant by an estate of freehold? Distinguish carefully between the main types of estate of freehold. (*A.E.B.*)

2. (*a*) What is meant by a fee simple absolute in possession? How does this estate differ from a leasehold estate?
(*b*) Describe the nature and the extent of the rights of the owner of an estate in fee simple absolute in possession. Mention any limitations upon the right of the owner of this kind of estate to deal with his property as freely as he wishes. (*R.S.A.*)

3. (*a*) Describe briefly the ways in which the owner of a freehold interest in land might mortgage his land as security for a loan.
(*b*) Palmer borrowed £20,000 from an oil company to build a petrol filling station. The terms of the loan were: (i) Palmer would pay the oil company 6 per cent per annum interest on the loan until he repaid it; (ii) Palmer would not buy petrol from any other company for a period of twenty years. After five years Palmer repaid the loan in full and then wished to buy petrol from another company. Advise the oil company which made him the loan. (*R.S.A.*)

4. What legal estates exist in English law at the present time? Give a short account of the nature of each of these estates. (*R.S.A.*)

5. (*a*) Can an infant ever make a valid will? State the relevant law.

(*b*) Thompson, a widower with two children, made a will in 1963 leaving his whole estate to be divided equally on his death between his two children. In 1965, at the suggestion of his rascally solicitor under whose influence he had fallen, Thompson made a codicil to his will leaving £5,000 to the solicitor. In 1967 Thompson married Miss Barton. In July 1968 Thompson died. Advise his children who are now aged 25 and 22 years, respectively, on the law arising out of this matter. (*R.S.A.*)

6. Define and distinguish between: (i) ownership and possession; (ii) real property and personal property. Give examples to illustrate your answer. (*R.S.A.*)

7. (*a*) Explain fully, with the help of examples, the difference between legal estates and equitable interests in land.

(*b*) Which of the following can exist as legal estates: (i) a life interest in a house; (ii) the fee simple of a farm; (iii) a twenty years' lease of a field? (*A.E.B.*)

8. Define a trust. Discuss its essential features and explain the purposes for which trusts are created today.

9. Distinguish between (i) a trust for sale, and (ii) a strict settlement.

10. (*a*) Explain in relation to trusts what is meant by the 'three certainties' rule.

(*b*) Distinguish (i) between an executory trust and an executed trust; and (ii) between an incompletely constituted trust and a completely constituted trust.

11. How and by whom may trustees be appointed? It is said that a trustee must not delegate his duties and must not make a profit from his trust. How far is this true?

12. Explain, with examples, the following: (*a*) a general legacy; (*b*) a specific legacy; (*c*) a demonstrative legacy.

13. Explain how a will may be revoked. What do you understand by the doctrine of 'dependent relative revocation'?

14. Write notes on:

(*a*) a *profit à prendre*;
(*b*) an easement;
(*c*) a resulting trust; and
(*d*) an administrator *cum testamento annexo*.

Chapters 12–13: Criminal Law and Procedure

1. *Actus non facit reum nisi mens sit rea*. Explain this maxim. Are there any exceptions to the doctrine of *mens rea*? What is *mens rea*?

2. What are the M'Naghten Rules? What is diminished responsibility?

3. What is automatism and when is it a defence?

4. Distinguish between murder and manslaughter.

5. Distinguish between (*a*) burglary, and (*b*) robbery. What is meant by 'aggravated burglary'?

6. In what circumstances will the finder of lost goods be guilty of theft if he keeps them?

7. How does obtaining by deception differ from theft?

8. What is blackmail?

9. What offences are created by the Criminal Law Act, 1977?

10. Explain what is meant by: (i) Order for Discovery; (ii) Interrogatories; (iii) Sequestration; (iv) Garnishee order.

Appendix 4

LIST OF ABBREVIATIONS: LAW REPORTS

[1891] A.C.	The Law Reports, Appeals to the House of Lords and the Judicial Committee of the Privy Council and Peerage cases, from 1891 onwards.
Ad. & El..	Adolphus and Ellis's Reports, Queen's Bench. 12 volumes. 1834–40.
[1936] All E.R... ..	All England Law Reports from 1936 onwards.
[1923] All E.R. Rep. ..	All England Reports Reprint.
App. Cas..	The Law Reports, Appeals to the House of Lords and the Judicial Committee of the Privy Council. 15 volumes. 1875–90.
B. & Ad.	Barnewall and Adolphus's Reports, King's Bench. 5 volumes. 1830–4.
B. & Ald..	Barnewall and Alderson's Reports, King's Bench. 5 volumes. 1817–22.
B. & S.	Best and Smith's Reports, Queen's Bench. 10 volumes. 1861–70.
Beav.	Beavan's Reports, Rolls Court. 36 volumes. 1838–66.
Bing.	Bingham's Reports, Common Pleas. 10 volumes. 1822–34.
Bing. N.C.	Bingham's New Cases, Common Pleas. 6 volumes. 1834–1840.
Bro. Parl. Cas... ..	Brown's Parliamentary Cases. 8 volumes. 1702–1800.
C.B.	Common Bench Reports. 18 volumes. 1845–56.
C.B. (N.S.)	Common Bench Reports, New Series. 20 volumes. 1856–1865.
C. & P.	Carrington and Payne's Reports, Nisi Prius. 9 volumes. 1823–41.
C.P.D.	The Law Reports, Common Pleas Division. 5 volumes. 1875–80.
[1891] Ch.	The Law Reports, Chancery Division, from 1891 onwards.
1 Ch.D.	The Law Reports, Chancery Division. 45 volumes. 1875–1890.
Cha. Ca...	Choyce Cases in Chancery. 1557–1606.
Cl. & F...	Clark and Finelly's Reports, House of Lords. 12 volumes. 1831–46.
Co. Rep...	Coke's Reports. 13 parts. 1572–1616.
Cox C. C.	Cox's Criminal Law Cases. 1843–1945.
Cro. Car..	Croke's King's Bench Reports during the time of King Charles I. 1 volume. 1625–41.
Curt.	Curteis's Ecclesiastical Reports. 3 volumes. 1834–44.
De G. M. & G.. ..	De Gex, Magnachten and Gordon's Reports, Chancery. 8 volumes. 1851–7.
Dowl.	Dowling's Practice Reports. 9 volumes. 1830–41.
E. & B.	Ellis and Blackburn's Queen's Bench Reports. 8 volumes. 1852–8.

Eq. Case. Abr.	Abridgement of Cases in Equity. 2 volumes. 1667–1744.
Exch.	Exchequer Reports (Welsby, Hurlstone and Gordon). 11 volumes. 1847–56.
Ex.D.	The Law Reports, Exchequer Division. 5 volumes. 1875–1880.
Foster.	Foster's Crown Cases. 1 volume. 1708–60.
Gal. & Dav.	Gale and Davison's Queen's Bench Reports. 3 volumes. 1841–3.
H. & C.	Hurlstone and Coltman's Exchequer Reports. 4 volumes. 1862–6.
H. & N.	Hurlstone and Norman's Exchequer Reports. 7 volumes. 1856–62.
H. & T.	Halls and Twells's Chancery Reports. 2 volumes. 1846–50.
H.L.C.	Clark's House of Lords Cases. 11 volumes. 1847–66.
Jur..	Jurist Reports. 18 volumes. 1837–54.
[1901] K.B.	The Law Reports, King's Bench, from 1901 onwards.
Keb.	Keble's King's Bench Reports. 3 volumes. 1661–79.
Kel.	Sir John Kelying's Reports, Crown Cases. 1 volume. 1662–1707.
L.J.Ch.	Law Journal Reports, Chancery. 118 volumes. 1831–1949.
Lev.	Levinz's King's Bench Reports. 3 volumes. 1660–97.
[1951] Lloyd's Rep. ..	Lloyd's List Law Reports, cited by date from 1951 onwards.
L.J.C.P.	Law Journal Reports, Common Pleas. 1831–75.
L.J.Ex.	Law Journal Reports, Exchequer. 1831–75.
L.J.(o.s.)C.P.	Law Journal, Old Series. 1822–31.
L.J.P.	Law Journal Reports, Probate, Divorce and Admiralty. 1875–1946.
L.J.P.C.	Law Journal Reports, Privy Council. 1865–1946.
[1947] L.J.R.	Law Journal Reports. 1947–9.
L.R.App.Cas.	The Law Reports, Appeals to the House of Lords and the Judicial Committee of the Privy Council. 15 volumes. 1875–90.
L.R.C.C.R.	The Law Reports of Crown Cases Reserved. 2 volumes. 1865–75.
L.R.C.P...	The Law Reports, Common Pleas. 10 volumes. 1865–75.
L.R.Ex.	The Law Reports, Exchequer. 10 volumes. 1865–75.
(1875)7 H.L.1	The Law Reports, English and Irish Appeals to the House of Lords. 7 volumes. 1865–75.
L.R.P. & D.	The Law Reports, Probate and Divorce. 3 volumes. 1865–1875.
L.R.Q.B.	The Law Reports, Queen's Bench. 10 volumes. 1865–75.
L.T.	Law Times Reports. 1859–1947.
L.T.(o.s.)	Law Times, Old Series. 34 volumes. 1843–60.
Leach	Leach's Crown Cases. 2 volumes. 1730–1815.
M. & W.	Meeson and Welsby's Exchequer Reports. 16 volumes. 1836–47.
Mer.	Merivale's Chancery Reports. 3 volumes. 1815–17.
Mod. Rep.	Modern Reports. 12 volumes. 1669–1755.
Moo. & S.	Moore and Scott's Reports, Common Pleas. 4 volumes. 1831–4.
Moore K.B.	Sir F. Moore's Reports, King's Bench, Folio. 1 volume. 1485–1620.

New Rep..	New Reports. 6 volumes. 1862–5.
[1891] P...	The Law Reports, Probate, Divorce and Admiralty Division, from 1891 onwards.
P.D.	The Law Reports, Probate Division. 15 volumes. 1876–90.
Ph..	Phillips's Reports, Chancery. 2 volumes. 1841–9.
Q.B.	Queen's Bench Reports (Adolphus and Ellis, New Series). 18 volumes. 1841–52.
[1891] Q.B.	The Law Reports, Queen's Bench Division, from 1891 onwards.
Q.B.D.	The Law Reports, Queen's Bench Division. 25 volumes. 1875–90.
Rep. Ch...	Reports in Chancery. 3 volumes. 1615–1710.
Rob. Eccl.	Robertson's Ecclesiastical Reports. 2 volumes. 1844–53.
Smith L. C.	Smith's Leading Cases. 2 volumes.
Sol. Jo.	Solicitor's Journal, from 1856 onwards.
S.T.	State Trials. 34 volumes. 1163–1820.
State Tr. (N.S.)	State Trials, New Series. 8 volumes. 1820–58.
Str..	Strange's King's Bench Reports. 2 volumes. 1716–47.
Starkie	Starkie's Reports, Nisi Prius. 3 volumes. 1814–23.
T.L.R.	*The Times* Law Reports. 1885–1952.
Term. Rep.	Term Reports (Durnford and East). 8 volumes. 1785–1800.
Toth.	Tothill's Transactions in Chancery. 1 volume. 1559–1646.
Ves.	Vesey Junior's Chancery Reports. 19 volumes. 1789–1817.
W. & T.L.C.	White and Tudor's Leading Cases in Equity. 2 volumes.
W. Bl.	Sir William Blackstone's King's Bench Reports. 1746–80.
[1953] W.L.R.	Weekly Law Reports, from 1953 onwards.
W.R.	Weekly Reporter. 54 volumes. 1852–1906.
W.N.	Weekly Notes. 1866–1952.

Appendix 5

SPECIMEN LEGISLATIVE DOCUMENTS

A

B I L L

TO

Abolish the power of local authorities to levy rates on domestic householders.

A.D. 1981

BE IT ENACTED by the Queen's most Excellent Majesty, by and with the advice and consent of the Lords Spiritual and Temporal, and Commons, in this present Parliament assembled, and by the authority of the same, as follows:—

Abolition of domestic rates.

1. The power of local authorities to levy rates on domestic householders is hereby abolished.

Repeal of enactments.

2. All enactments under which powers are given to local authorities to levy rates on domestic householders are hereby repealed to the extent that they confer such powers.

Short title and commencement.

3.—(1) This Act may be cited as the Domestic Rating (Abolition) Act 1981.

(2) This Act shall come into force on the beginning of the financial year 1983–84.

Domestic Rating (Abolition)

A

BILL

To abolish the power of local authorities to levy rates on domestic householders.

Presented by Mr. Christopher Murphy

supported by

Mr. Richard Alexander, Mr. David Bevan, Mr. Tim Brinton, Mr. John Carlisle, Mr. Den Dover, Mr. Bob Dunn, Mr. Peter Griffiths, Mr. Warren Hawksley, Mr. Iain Mills, Mr. James Pawsey and Mr. Richard Shepherd

Ordered, by The House of Commons, *to be Printed, 3 February* 1981

LONDON

Printed and published by
Her Majesty's Stationery Office
Printed in England at St Stephen's
Parliamentary Press

30p net

[Bill 57] (51684) 48/2

ELIZABETH II

Criminal Evidence Act 1979

1979 CHAPTER 16

An Act to amend paragraph (*f*)(iii) of the proviso to section 1 of the Criminal Evidence Act 1898 and corresponding enactments extending to Scotland and Northern Ireland. [22nd March 1979]

BE IT ENACTED by the Queen's most Excellent Majesty, by and with the advice and consent of the Lords Spiritual and Temporal, and Commons, in this present Parliament assembled, and by the authority of the same, as follows:—

Amendment of section 1 of Criminal Evidence Act 1898, etc., and transitional provision.

1.—(1) In paragraph (*f*)(iii) of the proviso to each of the following enactments, that is to say, section 1 of the Criminal Evidence Act 1898, sections 141 and 346 of the Criminal Procedure (Scotland) Act 1975 and section 1 of the Criminal Evidence Act (Northern Ireland) 1923 (under which an accused person who has given evidence against another person charged with the same offence may be cross-examined about his previous convictions and his bad character), for the words " with the same offence " there shall be substituted the words " in the same proceedings ".

(2) Notwithstanding subsection (1) above, a person charged with any offence who, before the coming into force of this Act, has given evidence against any other person charged in the same proceedings shall not by reason of that fact be asked or required to answer any question which he could not have been asked and required to answer but for that subsection.

Short title and commencement.

2.—(1) This Act may be cited as the Criminal Evidence Act 1979.

(2) This Act shall come into force at the end of the period of one month beginning with the date on which it is passed.

PRINTED IN ENGLAND BY BERNARD M. THIMONT
Controller of Her Majesty's Stationery Office and Queen's Printer of Acts of Parliament

STATUTORY INSTRUMENTS

1980 No. 1978

COAL INDUSTRY

The Opencast Coal (Rate of Interest on Compensation) (No. 3) Order 1980

Made - - - -	16*th December* 1980
Laid before Parliament	18*th December* 1980
Coming into Operation	8*th January* 1981

The Treasury, in exercise of the powers conferred upon them by sections 35(8) and 49(4) of the Opencast Coal Act 1958(**a**) and of all other powers enabling them in that behalf, hereby make the following Order:—

1. This Order may be cited as the Opencast Coal (Rate of Interest on Compensation) (No. 3) Order 1980, and shall come into operation on 8th January 1981.

2. The rate of interest for the purposes of section 35 of the Opencast Coal Act 1958 shall be 14½ per cent. per annum.

3. The Opencast Coal (Rate of Interest on Compensation)(No. 2) Order 1980(**b**) is hereby revoked.

John MacGregor,
David Waddington,
Two of the Lords Commissioners
of Her Majesty's Treasury.

16th December 1980.

EXPLANATORY NOTE

(*This Note is not part of the Order.*)

Section 35 of the Opencast Coal Act 1958 provides that interest shall be payable in addition to compensation in certain circumstances. This Order decreases the rate of interest from 16½ per cent. to 14½ per cent. per annum and revokes the Opencast Coal (Rate of Interest on Compensation) (No. 2) Order 1980.

(**a**) 1958 c.69. (**b**) S.I. 1980/1365.

Appendix 6

SPECIMEN FORMS

(*a*) Information

In the County of Somerset, Petty Sessional Division of Oxbridge Borough.

THE INFORMATION of Watson Holmes, Chief Inspector of Police, who upon oath states that Richard Roe, of 5 Fore Street, Blacktown, on the 30th day of June, 1980, at Oxbridge in the County aforesaid, did drive a motor-vehicle on a certain restricted road called South Road at a speed exceeding thirty miles per hour, contrary to sections 71 and 78A of the Road Traffic Regulation Act, 1967. TAKEN AND SWORN before me this 10th day of July, 1980.

R. W. Emerson (signed)
Justice of the Peace for the County first above mentioned.

(*b*) Summons

In the County of Somerset, Petty Sessional Division of Oxbridge Borough.

To: Richard Roe, of 5 Fore Street, Blacktown, Somerset.

INFORMATION has this day been laid before me, the undersigned Justice of the Peace, by Watson Holmes, Chief Inspector of Police, of Oxbridge, Somerset, that you on the 30th day of June, 1980, at South Road, Oxbridge, in the County aforesaid, did drive a motor-vehicle at a speed exceeding thirty miles per hour, contrary to sections 71 and 78A of the Road Traffic Regulation Act, 1967.

YOU ARE THEREFORE HEREBY SUMMONED to appear on Friday, the 12th day of August, 1980, at the hour of 10.30 in the forenoon, before the MAGISTRATES' COURT sitting at the Shire Hall, Oxbridge, to answer to the said information.

R. W. Emerson (signed)
Justice of the Peace for the County first above mentioned.

(*c*) Recognizance

IN The County of Somerset, Petty Sessional Division of Oxbridge.

THE UNDERMENTIONED PERSONS each acknowledges that he owes to Our Sovereign Lady the Queen the following sums, namely William Sykes of 1 High Street, Oxbridge, as Principal, the sum of Twenty Pounds; John

Doone, of 12 Blackmore Vale, Oxbridge, as Surety, the sum of Ten Pounds; and William Smith, of 21 South Street, Oxbridge, as Surety, the sum of Ten Pounds, payment thereof to be enforced severally against them by due process of law if he (the Principal) fails to comply with the condition endorsed hereon.

(signed) William Sykes,	Principal
(signed) John Doone, (signed) William Smith,	Sureties

TAKEN before me on 20th day of August, 1980.

Ralph W. Emerson (signed)
Justice of the Peace for the County first above mentioned.

THE CONDITION of this recognizance is:

That the said Principal keep the peace and be of good behaviour towards Her Majesty and all Her liege people, and especially towards Josephine Faithless for the term of one year from the date of this recognizance.

(*d*) **Warrant of Arrest**

In the County of Somerset, Petty Sessional Division of Oxbridge.

TO each and all of the constables in the Borough of Oxbridge.

INFORMATION on oath has this day been laid before me, the undersigned Justice of the Peace, by Watson Holmes, Chief Inspector of Police, that William Sykes (hereinafter called the defendant) on the 5th day of July, 1980, at Blacktown in the County aforesaid did steal one gold watch, one silver chain and one fountain-pen the property of John Jones, of 1 High Street, Oxbridge, contrary to section 1(1) of the Theft Act, 1968.

YOU ARE HEREBY COMMANDED to bring the defendant before the Magistrates' Court sitting at Oxbridge forthwith to answer to the said information.

DATED the 12th day of August, 1980.

R. W. Emerson (signed)
Justice of the Peace for the County first above mentioned.

(*e*) **Indictment**

The Queen v. William Meurtrier

The Crown Court sitting at Bristol

William Meurtrier is charged with the following offence:

Statement of Offence
Murder

Particulars of Offence
William Meurtrier on the 29th day of August, 1980, in the County of Somerset murdered William Jones.

Appendix 7

FINANCIAL PROVISION ON DIVORCE, ETC.

When a court grants a decree of divorce, nullity or judicial separation it may in addition order financial provision under the Matrimonial Causes Act, 1973 (ss. 21–25), as amended by s. 3 of the Matrimonial and Family Proceedings Act, 1984. In assessing the most suitable type of provision and the amount, the court *must* take into account a list of factors set out in the newly amended s. 25. The most important of these are:

(*a*) The present and future income and earning capacity of the parties, including, in the opinion of the court, that which it would be reasonable to expect a party in respect of earning capacity to take steps to acquire.
(*b*) The present and future financial needs and obligations of the parties.
(*c*) The parties' standard of living before the marriage broke down.
(*d*) The age of the parties and the length of the marriage.
(*e*) Any disabilities of the parties.
(*f*) Their contributions to the welfare of the family during the marriage, e.g. the fact that the wife devoted herself to caring full-time for the children.
(*g*) The parties' conduct, but only if it is such that it would be inequitable to disregard it.
(*h*) The loss of benefits, e.g. a pension, arising from dissolution.

S. 25 also sets out the matters to which the court must have regard when making orders in relation to a child of the family in respect of financial provision, property adjustment or sale of property. This includes his financial needs, income, earning capacity (if any), property and other financial resources, disabilities, education and training.

The new s. 25A imposes additional obligations on the court to consider the appropriateness of a 'clean break' when exercising its powers to order financial provision, property adjustment or sale of property in favour of a party to the marriage. In this connection it may limit the term of any periodical payments order (a deferred 'clean break') or dismiss an application for periodical payments (without agreement) and direct that no further application be made for such an order.

TABLE OF CASES

Adams v. Lindsell (1818) 1 B. & Ald. 681 120
Adams v. Ursell [1913] 1 Ch. 269 221
Adams v. War Office [1955] 3 All E.R. 245; [1955] 1 W.L.R. 1116 111
Addis v. Crocker [1960] 2 All E.R. 629; [1960] 3 W.L.R. 339; [1961] 1 Q.B. 11 .. 242
Ailsa Craig Fishing Co. Ltd. v. Malvern Fishing Co. Ltd. [1983] 1 W.L.R. 964; [1983] 1 All E.R. 101 145
Ainsbury v. Millington [1987] 1 W.L.R. 379; [1987] 1 All E.R. 929 7
Alexander v. Railway Executive [1951] 2 K.B. 882; [1951] 2 All E.R. 442; [1951] 2 T.L.R. 69 144
Al-Kandari v. J. R. Brown & Co. [1987] 2 W.L.R. 469; [1987] 2 All E.R. 302 .. 85
Allen v. Whitehead [1930] 1 K.B. 211, 29 Cox C.C. 8, 99 L.J.K.B. 146 318
Alpenstow Ltd. and Another v. Regalian Properties PLC [1985] 1 W.L.R. 721; [1985] 2 All E.R. 545 292
Anderton v. Ryan [1985] 2 W.L.R. 981; [1985] 2 All E.R. 355 326
Anderton v. Wish [1980] Cr. L.R. 319, 657 336
Andrews v. D.P.P. [1937] A.C. 576, [1937] 2 All E.R. 552, 26 Cr. App. Rep. 34 . 330
Anns v. L.B. of Merton [1977] 2 All E.R. 492 [1977] 2 W.L.R. 1024 224
Appleson v. Littlewood (H) Ltd. [1939] 1 All E.R. 464 122
Armory v. Delamirie (1721) 1 Str. 505 217
Ashbury Railway Carriage & Iron Co. v. Riche (1875) L.R. 7 H.L. 653; 44 L.J. Ex. 185; 33 L.T. 450; 24 W.R. 794 .... 104, 138
Ashford v. Thornton (1819) B. & Ald. 405 33
Attia v. British Gas PLC [1987] 3 W.L.R. 1101; [1987] 3 All E.R. 455 225
Attorney-General v. Able [1983] 3 W.L.R. 845 [1984] 1 W.L.R. 277 330
Attorney-General v. P.Y.A. Quarries Ltd. [1957] 2 Q.B. 169 218
Attorney-General's Ref (No. 1 of 1983) [1984] 3 W.L.R. 686; [1984] 3 All E.R. 369 337
Attwood v. Lamont [1920] 3 K.B. 571; 90 L.J.K.B. 121; 124 L.T. 108; 36 T.L.R. 895 165
Avery v. Bowden (1856) 6 E. & B. 953; 26 L.J.Q.B. 3 171
Attorney-General v. Whelan [1934] I.R. 518 324

Baily v. De Crespigny (1869) L.R. 4 Q.B. 180; 19 L.T. 681 171
Bainbridge v. Firmstone (1838) 8 Ad. & El. 743 124
Baker v. T. E. Hopkins & Sons Ltd. [1959] 3 All E.R. 225; [1959] 1 W.L.R. 966 196
Ballet v. Mingay [1943] K.B. 281; [1943] 1 All E.R. 143 .... 135, 201
Banque Keyser Ullmann SA v. Skandia (UK) Ins. Co. Ltd. and Others [1987] 2 W.L.R. 1300; [1987] 2 All E.R. 923 159
Barnes v. Richards [1940] 2 All E.R. 229, 56 T.L.R. 379 328
Baroness Wenlock v. River Dee Co. (*see* Wenlock (Baroness) v. River Dee Co.) 138
Bartlett v. Barclays Bank Trust Co. Ltd. [1980] 2 W.L.R. 430, [1980] 1 All E.R. 139 256
Basely v. Clarkson (1682) Lev. 37 150
Beard v. London General Omnibus Co. [1900] 2 Q.B. 530 206
Bebee v. Sales (1916) 32 T.L.R. 413 201
Becke v. Smith (1836) 2 M. & W. 191 39
Bell v. Lever Brothers Ltd. [1932] A.C. 161; [1931] All E.R. Rep. 1; 101 L.J.K.B. 129; 146 L.T. 258; 48 T.L.R. 133 .... 149, 152
Benjamin v. Storr (1874) L.R. 9 C.P. 400 217
Beresford v. Royal Insurance Co. Ltd. [1938] A.C. 586; [1938] 2 All E.R. 602; 107 L.J.K.B. 464; 158 L.T. 459; 54 T.L.R. 789 162
Berg v. Sadler & Moore [1937] 2 K.B. 158; [1937] 1 All E.R. 637 167
Beswick v. Beswick [1968] A.C. 58; [1967] 2 All E.R. 1197 .... 182, 185

Bigos v. Bousted [1951] All E.R. 92 167
Bird v. Holbrook (1828) 4 Bing. 628; 6 L.J. (o.s.) C.P. 146 232
Bird v. Jones (1845) 7 Ad. & El. 742 .... 210, 376, 377
Bliss v. Hall (1838) 4 Bing. N.C. 183; 6 Dowl. 442 .... 220, 222
Boggeln v. Williams [1978] 2 All E.R. 1061, [1978] Crim. L.R. 242 340
Bolton v. Stone [1951] A.C. 850; [1951] 1 All E.R. 1078 .... 149, 222
Boulton v. Jones (1857) 2 H. & N. 564; 27 L.J.Ex. 117 .... 115, 153
Bowater v. Rowley Regis Corporation [1944] K.B. 476; [1944] 1 All E.R. 465 196
Brace v. Calder [1895] 2 Q.B. 253; 64 L.J.Q.B. 582; 72 L.T. 829 178
Bradford Building Society v. Borders [1941] 2 All E.R. 205 244
Branca v. Cobarro [1947] K.B. 854; [1947] 2 All E.R. 101 119
Brandt's (William) Sons & Co. v. Dunlop Rubber Company [1905] A.C. 454; 74 L.J.K.B. 898 188
Bratty v. A-G for Northern Ireland [1963] A.C. 386, [1961] 3 All E.R. 523, [1961] 3 W.L.R. 965 322
Brice v. Brown [1984] 1 All E.R. 997 225
Bridle v. Ruby and Another [1988] 3 W.L.R. 191; [1988] 3 All E.R. 64 285
Brinkibon Ltd. v. Stahag Stahl [1982] 2 W.L.R. 264; [1982] 1 All E.R. 293 120
B.R. Board v. Herrington [1972] T.L.R. 16.2.72 233
British Reinforced Concrete Engineering Co. Ltd. v. Schelff [1921] 2 Ch. 563; [1921] All E.R. Rep. 202; 91 L.J. Ch. 114; 126 L.T. 230 164
Brown v. Lewis (1896) 12 T.L.R. 455 106
Burnard v. Haggis (1863) 14 C.B.N.S. 45; 2 New Rep. 126; 32 L.J.C.P. 189; 8 L.T. 320; 11 W.R. 644 201
Burns v. Bidder [1967] 2 Q.B. 227, [1966] 3 All E.R. 29, [1966] 3 W.L.R. 99 320
Burrows v. Rhodes [1899] 1 Q.B. 816; 68 L.J.Q.B. 545; 80 L.T. 591 245
Butler (*or* Black) v. Fife Coal Co. Ltd. [1912] A.C. 149; 106 L.T. 161 223
Byrne v. Boadle (1863) 2 H. & C. 722; 3 New Rep. 161 227
Byrne v. Van Tienhoven (1880) 5 C.P.D. 344; 49 L.J.Q.B. 316 .... 117, 120

C (a minor) v. Eisenhower [1983] 3 W.L.R. 537 [1983] 3 All E.R. 230 334
Cadell v. Palmer (1833) 1 Cl. & F. 372 254
Callaghan, *re* [1984] 3 W.L.R. 1076 [1984], 3 All E.R. 790 146
Callisher v. Bischoffsheim (1870) L.R. 5 Q.B. 449 125
Candler v. Crane, Christmas & Co. [1951] 2 K.B. 164; [1951] 1 All E.R. 426 226
Carlill v. Carbolic Smoke Ball Co. [1892] 2 Q.B. 484; 61 L.J.Q.B. 696; affirmed (1893) 1 Q.B. 256; 62 L.J.Q.B. 257 .... 115, 118, 119
Carmarthenshire C. C. v. Lewis [1955] A.C. 549; [1955], 1 All E.R. 565 224
Carritt v. Bradley [1903] A.C. 253; 51 W.R. 636; 88 L.T. 633 291
Carter v. Mace [1949] 2 All E.R. 714 320
Cassell & Co. Ltd v. Broome [1972] 2 W.L.R. 645 178
Cassidy v. Daily Mirror Newspapers Ltd. [1929] 2 K.B. 331 .... 238, 243
Cassidy v. Ministry of Health [1951] 2 K.B. 343, [1951] 1 All E.R. 574 227
Castle v. St. Augustine's Links (1922) 38 T.L.R. 615 222
Cellulose Acetate Silk Co. Ltd. v. Widnes Foundry (1925) Ltd. [1933] A.C. 20; (1932) All E.R. Rep. 567 179
Central London Property Trust Ltd. v. High Trees House Ltd. [1947] K.B. 130; (1956) 1 All E.R. 256 n 128
Century Insurance Co. v. Northern Ireland Road Transport Board [1942] A.C. 509; [1942] 1 All E.R. 491 206
Chandler v. Webster [1904] 1 K.B. 493; 73 L.J.K.B. 401 173
Chapelton v. Barry U.D.C. [1940] 1 K.B. 532; [1940] 1 All E.R. 356; 109 L.J.K.B. 213 .... 143, 144
Chatterton v. Secretary of State for India in Council [1895] 2 Q.B. 189; [1895–9] All E.R.Rep 1035 .... 241, 242
Cheese v. Lovejoy (1877) 2 P.D. 251 301
Chillingworth v. Esche [1924] 1 Ch. 97; [1923] All E.R.Rep. 97; 93 L.J.Ch. 129; 129 L.T. 808; 40 T.L.R. 23 119
Christie v. Davey [1893] 1 Ch. 316; 62 L.J.Ch. 439 .... 195, 221
Clay v. A. J. Crump and Sons Ltd. [1964] 1 Q.B. 533; [1963] 3 All E.R. 687 226

Clifford Davis Management Ltd *v.* WEA Records Ltd [1975] 1 W.L.R. 61, [1975] 1 All E.R. 237 161
Colchester Estates *v.* Carlton Industries [1984] 3 W.L.R. 693; [1984] 2 All E.R. 601 24
Collins *v.* Wilcock [1984] 1 W.L.R. 1172; [1984] 3 All E.R. 374 334
Combe *v.* Combe [1951] 2 K.B. 215; [1951] 1 All E.R. 767 129
Condon *v.* Basi [1985] 1 W.L.R. 860; [1985] 2 All E.R. 453 225
Condor *v.* Barron Knights Ltd. [1966] 1 W.L.R. 87 172
Conry *v.* Simpson [1983] 3 All E.R. 369 246
Constantine (Joseph) Steamship Line *v.* Imperial Smelting Corporation [1942] A.C. 154; [1941] 2 All E.R. 165; 165 L.T. 27 173
Cooke *v.* Midland Great Western Railway of Ireland [1909] A.C. 229; [1808–10] All E.R.Rep. 16 233
Cooper *v.* Phibbs (1867) L.R. 2 H.L. 149; 16 L.T. 678 148
Cope *v.* Sharpe [1912] 1 K.B. 496; 81 L.J.K.B. 346 198
Coppen *v.* Moore (No. 2) [1898] 2 Q.B. 306, 67 L.J.Q.B. 689, 19 Cox C.C. 45 .. 318
Cornish *v.* Midland Bank PLC (Humes, Third Party) [1985] 3 All E.R. 513 . . 226
Couchman *v.* Hill [1947] K.B. 554; [1947] 1 All E.R. 103; 176 L.T. 278; 63 T.L.R. 81 141
Coutts & Co. *v.* Browne-Lecky [1947] K.B. 104; [1946] 2 All E.R. 207 135
Couturier *v.* Hastie (1852) 8 Exch. 40; 22 L.J. Ex. 97; reversed *sub nom* Hastie *v.* Couturier (1853) 9 Exch. 102; [1843–60] All E.R.Rep. 280 affirmed (1856) 5. H.L.C. 673; 25 L.J. Ex. 253 148
Cowern *v.* Nield [1912] 2 K.B. 419; [1911–13] All E.R.Rep. 425; 81 L.J.K.B. 865 136
Craddock Brothers *v.* Hunt [1923] 2 Ch. 136; [1923] All E.R.Rep. 394 152
Craven-Ellis *v.* Canons Ltd. [1936] 2 K.B. 403; [1936] 3 All E.R. 1066; 105 L.J.K.B. 767 180
Cresswell *v.* Sirl [1948] 1 K.B. 241; [1947] 2 All E.R. 730 199
Crowhurst *v.* Amersham Burial Board (1879) 4 Ex. D. 5; 39 L.T. 355 .... 234, 236
Cumming *v.* Ince (1847) 11 Q.B. 112; 17 L.J.Q.B. 105 160
Cundy *v.* Lindsay (1878) 3 App. Cas. 459; 38 L.T. 573 .... 148, 150
Currie *v.* Misa (1875) L.R. 10 Ex. 153; 44 L.J. Ex. 94; affirmed *sub nom* Misa *v.* Currie (1876) 1 App. Cas. 554; [1874–80] All E.R.Rep. 686 121
Curtis *v.* Chemical Cleaning & Dyeing Co. [1951] 1 K.B. 805; [1951] 1 All E.R. 631; [1951] 1 T.L.R. 452 .... 143, 144
Cutler *v.* United Dairies London Ltd. [1933] 2 K.B. 297; [1933] All E.R.Rep. 594 197
Cutter *v.* Powell (1795) 6 Term Rep. 320; [1775–1802] All E.R.Rep. 159; 2 Smith L.C. 1, n 181

D. & C. Builders Ltd. *v.* Rees (1966] 2. Q.B. 617; (1965) 3 All E.R. 837; (1966) 2 W.L.R. 288 .... 125, 129
Dann *v.* Hamilton [1939] 1 K.B. 509; [1939] 1 All E.R. 59 197
Dashwood *v.* Magniac [1891] 3 Ch. 306; 60 L.J.Ch. 210 46
Davies *v.* DPP [1954] A.C. 378, [1954] 1 All E.R. 507, [1954] 2 W.L.R. 343 319
Davis Contractors Ltd *v.* Fareham U.D.C. [1956] A.C. 696; [1956] 2 All E.R. 145 173
Derry *v.* Peek (1889) 14 App.Cas. 337; 58 L.J.Ch. 864; [1886–90] All E.R.Rep. 1; 61 L.T. 265 .... 155, 226, 244, 341
Dickinson *v.* Dodds (1876) 2 Ch. D. 463; 45 L.J.Ch. 777; 34 L.T. 607 117
Dimes *v.* Grand Junction Canal (Proprietors) (1852) 3 H.L. Cas. 794; 8 State Tr. N.S. 85 69
Donaldson *v.* McNiven (1952) 2 All E.R. 691; 96 Sol. Jo. 747 202
Donoghue *v.* Stevenson. *See* McAlister (*or* Donoghue) *v.* Stevenson (1932) A.C. 562; (1932) All E.R.Rep. 1 .... 223, 284
Dorset Yacht Co. *v.* Home Office [1969] 2 Q.B. 158; [1969] 2 W.L.R. 673; [1969] 2 All E.R. 119 225
Doughty *v.* Turner Manufacturing Co. Ltd. [1964] 1 Q.B. 518; [1964] 1 All E.R. 98 204
Dove *v.* Banhams Locks Ltd. [1983] 2 All E.R. 833 246
Doyle *v.* White City Stadium Ltd. [1935] 1 K.B. 110; [1934] All E.R.Rep. 252; 104 L.J.K.B. 140; 152 L.T. 32 136
D.P.P. *v.* Beard [1920] A.C. 479, 89 L.J.K.B. 437, 14 Cr. App. Rep. 159 322

D.P.P. *v.* Newbury [1967] A.C. 500, [1976] 2 All E.R. 365, [1976] 2 W.L.R. 918 331
D.P.P. *v.* Smith [1961] A.C. 290, [1960] 3 All E.R. 161, [1960] 3 W.L.R. 546.... 334
Dudley and Stephens (1884) 14 Q.B.D. 273, 54 L.J.M.C. 32 15 Cox C.C. 624 .. 324
Dunlop Pneumatic Tyre Co. Ltd. *v.* New Garage and Motor Co. Ltd. [1915] A.C. 79: [1914–15] All E.R.Rep. 739; 83 L.J.K.B. 1574; 111 L.T. 862; 30 T.L.R. 625.......... 179
Dunlop Pneumatic Tyre Co. Ltd. *v.* Selfridge and Co. Ltd. [1915] A.C. 847: [1914-15] All E.R.Rep. 333: 84 L.J.K.B. 1680: 113 L.T. 386: 31 T.L.R. 399 183

Eccles *v.* Bryant & Pollock [1948] Ch. 93: [1947] 2 All E.R. 865: [1948] L.J.R. 418.......... 119
Edington *v.* Fitzmaurice (1885) 29 Ch. D. 459, 476: 55 L.J. Ch. 650: [1881-5] All E.R.Rep. 856.......... 154
Edwards *v.* Odin [1976] 3 All E.R. 705, [1976] 1 W.L.R. 942.......... 345
Ellis *v.* Sheffield Gas Consumers Co. (1853) 2 E. & B. 767: 23 L.J.Q.B. 42..... 207
Entores Ltd. *v.* Miles Far Eastern Corporation [1955] 2 Q.B. 327: [1955] 2 All E.R. 493.......... 129
Evans *v.* Cross [1938] 1 K.B. 694: [1938] 1 All E.R. 751.......... 40
Evans *v.* Hughes [1972] 3 All E.R. 412, [1972] 1 W.L.R. 1452 56 Cr. App. Rep. 813.......... 335

Felthouse *v.* Bindley (1863) 1 New Rep. 401: 7 L.T. 835.......... 118
Firth *v.* Bowling Iron Co. (1878) 3 C.P.D. 254.......... 234
Fisher *v.* Bell [1961] 1 Q.B. 394: [1960] 3 All E.R. 731.......... 116
Fitch *v.* Dewes [1921] 2 A.C. 158: [1921] All E.R.Rep. 13: 90 L.J.Ch. 436: 125 L.T. 744: 37 T.L.R. 784.......... 164
Foley *v.* Classique Coaches Ltd. [1934] 2 K.B. 1: [1934] All E.R.Rep. 88: 103 L.J.K.B. 550.......... 234 142
Foster *v.* Driscoll [1929] 1 K.B. 470: [1928] All E.R.Rep. 130: 98 L.J.K.B. 282: 140 L.T. 479.......... 126, 162
Foster *v.* MacKinnon (1869) L.R. 4 C.P. 704: 38 L.J.C.P. 310.......... 137
Fouldes *v.* Willoughby (1841) 8 M. & W. 540.......... 216
Four Maids Ltd. *v.* Dudley Marshall (Properties) Ltd. [1957] Ch. 317, [1957] 2 W.L.R. 931, [1957] 2 All E.R. 35.......... 2191
Fowler *v.* Lanning [1959] 1 Q.B. 426: [1959] 1 All E.R. 290....... 209, 211, 215, 377
Froom and others *v.* Butcher [1976] Q.B. 286.......... 228

George, Mitchell (Chesterhall) Ltd. *v.* Finney Lock Seeds Ltd. [1982] 3 W.L.R. 1036; [1983] 1 All E.R. 108 (C.A.).......... 146
Giles *v.* Walker (1890) 24 Q.B.D. 656.......... 236
Gill *v.* Gill [1909] P. 157.......... 301
Glasgow Corporation *v.* Taylor [1922] 1. A.C. 44.......... 233
Glassbrook Brothers Ltd. *v.* Glamorgan County Council [1925] A.C. 270: [1924] All E.R.Rep. 579: 94 L.J.K.B. 272: 132 L.T. 611.......... 124
Goddard *v.* O'Brien (1882) 9 Q.B.D. 37: 46 L.T. 306.......... 125
Goldsworthy *v.* Bricknell and Another [1987] 2 W.L.R. 133; [1987] 1 All E.R. 853.......... 161
Goodwin *v.* Robarts (1875) L.R. 10 Exch. 337: 44 L.J.Ex. 157: affirmed (1876) 1 App.Cas. 476: 45 L.J.Q.B. 748.......... 19
Gordon *v.* Gordon (1821) 3 Swan 400.......... 159
Grant *v.* Australian Knitting Mills [1936] A.C. 85: [1935] All E.R.Rep. 209.... 227
Grant *v.* Maddox (1846) 15 M. & W. 737: 16 L.J.Ex. 227.......... 46
Great Northern Railway *v.* Witham (1873) L.R. 9 C.P. 16: 43 L.J.C.P. 1: 29 L.T. 471 W.R. 48.......... 121
Green *v.* Burnett [1955] 1 Q.B. 78, [1954] 3 All E.R. 273, [1954] 3 W.L.R. 631 .. 318
Green *v.* Chelsea Waterworks Co. (1894) 70 L.T. 547.......... 235, 236
Greenstreet, *In the estate of* (1930) 74 S.J. 188.......... 305
Grist *v.* Bailey [1967] Ch. 532 [1966] 2 All E.R. 875: [1966] 3 W.L.R. 618...... 149

Hadley *v.* Baxendale (1854) 9 Exch. 341: 23 L.J.Ex. 179: 23 L.T. (o.s.) 69: 2 W.R. 302.......... 177

Haigh *v.* Brooks (1839) 10 Ad. & El. 309; 9 L.J.Q.B. 99, 194; affirmed *sub nom* Brooks *v.* Haigh (1840) 10 Ad. & El. 323 124
Hall *v.* Brooklands Auto-Racing Club [1933] 1 K.B. 205 195
Hall *v.* Cotton [1986] 3 W.L.R. 681; [1986] 3 All E.R. 332 334
Hannah *v.* Peel [1945] K.B. 509; [1945] 2 All E.R. 288 262
Harding *v.* Price [1948] 1 K.B. 695; [1948] L.J.R. 1624; 64 T.L.R. 111; [1948] 1 All E.R. 283 40
Harris *v.* James (1876) 45 L.J.Q.B. 545 220
Harris *v.* Nickerson (1873) L.R. 8 Q.B. 286; 42 L.J.Q.B. 171 116
Harrison *v.* Michelin Tyre Co. Ltd. [1985] 1 All E.R. 918 206
Harvey *v.* Facey [1893] A.C. 552; 62 L.J.P.C. 127 116
Haughton *v.* Smith [1975] A.C. 476, [1973] 3 All E.R. 1109, [1974] 2 W.L.R. 1 .... 326, 340, 343
Haynes *v.* Harwood [1935] 1 K.B. 146; [1934] All E.R.Rep. 103 .... 196, 384
Hedley Byrne & Co. Ltd. *v.* Heller and Partners Ltd. [1964] A.C. 465; [1963] 2 All E.R. 575 [1963] 226
Hemmings *v.* Stoke Poges Golf Club [1920] 1 K.B. 720; [1918 19] All E.R.Rep. 798 214
Herd *v.* Weardale Steel Coal & Coke Co. [1915] A.C. 67; 84 L.J K.B. 121 .. 210, 377
Henshall (John) (Quarries) Ltd. *v.* Harvey [1965] 2 Q.B. 233, [1965] 1 All E.R. 725 [1965] 2 W.L.R. 758 318
Herne Bay Steam Boat Co. *v.* Hutton [1903] 2 K.B. 683; [1900–3] All E.R.Rep. 627; 72 L.J.K.B. 879; 89 L.T. 422 172
Hill *v.* Baxter [1958] 1 Q.B. 277, [1958] 1 All E.R. 193, [1958] 2 W.L.R. 76 320
Hill *v.* Chief Constable of West Yorkshire [1988] 2 W.L.R. 1049; [1988] 2 All E.R. 238 224
Hivac Ltd. *v.* Park Royal Scientific Instruments Ltd. [1946] Ch. 169; [1946] 1 All E.R. 350 165
Hochster *v.* De La Tour (1853) 2 E. & B. 678; 22 L.J.Q.B. 455; [1843–60] All E.R.Rep. 12 170
Hoenig *v.* Isaacs [1952] 2 All E.R. 176; [1952] 1 T.L.R. 1360 181
Hollins *v.* Fowler (1875) L.R. 7 H.L. 757 217
Hollywood Silver Fox Farm Ltd. *v.* Emmett [1936] 2 K.B. 468; [1936] 1 All E.R. 825 221
Holmes *v.* Mather (1875) L.R. 10 Ex. 261; 44 L.J.Ex. 176 197
Home Brewery Co. Ltd. *v.* William Davis & Co. (Leicester) Ltd. [1987] 2 W.L.R. 117; [1987] 1 All E.R. 637 236
Honeywill & Stein Ltd. *v.* Larkin Brothers [1934] 1 K.B. 191 208
Hopkins *v.* Collins (1957) 41 Cr. App. Rep. 231 347
Household Fire and Carriage Accident Insurance Co. Ltd. *v.* Grant (1879) 4 Ex. D. 216; 48 L.J.Q.B. 577; 41 L.T. 298 120
Howatson *v.* Webb [1907] 1 Ch. 537; 76 L.J.Ch. 346; affirmed [1908] 1 Ch. 1; 77 L.J.Ch. 32; 97 L.T. 730 151
Hughes *v.* Lord Advocate [1963] A.C. 837; [1963] 2 W.L.R. 799; [1963] 1 All E.R. 705 204
Hulton & Co. *v.* Jones [1910] A.C. 20 238
Huth *v.* Huth [1915] 3 K.B. 32 239
Hyde *v.* Hyde (1866) L.R. 1 P. & D. 130, 133; 14 L.T. 188 92
Hyde *v.* Wrench (1840) 3 Beav. 334; 4 Jur. 1106 117

Income Tax Special Commissioners *v.* Pemsel [1891] A.C. 531; 61 L.J.Q.B. 265 . 252
Inland Revenue Commissioners *v.* McMullen [1980] 2 W.L.R. 416, [1980] 1 All E.R. 884 252
International Drilling Fluids Ltd. *v.* Louisville Investments (Uxbridge) Ltd. [1986] 2 W.L.R. 581 (C.A.) 282
Investors in Industry Commercial Properties Ltd. *v.* South Bedfordshire District Council (Ellison and Partners (A Firm) and Others, Third Parties) [1986] 2 W.L.R. 937; [1986] 1 All E.R. 787 224

Jackson *v.* Hopperton (1864) 16 C.B. (N.S.) 829 242

Jennings *v.* Rundall (1799) 8 Term Rep. 335 201
John Michael Design PLC *v.* Cooke and Another [1987] 2 All E.R. 332 164
Jones *v.* Boyce (1816) 1 Starkie 493 228
Jones *v.* Llanrwst Urban District Council [1911] 1 Ch. 393 234
Jones *v.* Vernon's Pools Ltd. [1938] 2 All E.R. 626 122
Jordan *v.* Norton (1838) 4 M. & W. 155; 7 L.J.Ex. 281 118
Joyce *v.* Director of Public Prosecutions [1946] A.C. 347, 368; 115 L.J K.B. 146; 174 L.T. 206; [1946] 1 All E.R. 186 33

Karsales (Harrow) Ltd. *v.* Wallis (1956) 2 All E.R. 866; [1956] 1 W.L.R. 936 144
Kealey *v.* Heard [1983] 1 W.L.R. 573; [1983] 1 All E.R. 973 227
Keech *v.* Sandford (1726) 2 Eg.Cas.Abr. 741 .... 251, 256
Kier (J.L.) & Co. Ltd. *v.* Whitehead Iron & Steel Co. Ltd. [1938] 1 All E.R. 591; 158 L.T. 228 121
King *v.* Phillips [1953] 1 Q.B. 429 225
Knight *v.* Knight (1840) 3 Beav. 148; 9 L.J.Ch. 354 249
Knightsbridge Estates Trust Ltd. *v.* Byrne [1939] Ch. 441; 55 T.L.R. 196; 160 L.T. 68; affirmed [1940] A.C. 613; 109 L.Ch. 200; [1940] 2 All E.R. 401 292
Knuller *v.* D.P.P. [1973] A.C. 435, [1972] 2 All E.R. 898, [1972] 3 W.L.R. 143 313
Koeppler's Will Trusts *v.* Slack, *re* [1985] *The Times* 21 May 252
Kreglinger *v.* New Patagonia Meat and Cold Storage Co. Ltd. [1914] A.C. 25; 83 L.J.Ch. 79; 109 L.T. 802 292
Krell *v.* Henry [1903] 2 K.B. 740; [1900–3] All E.R.Rep. 20; 72 L.J.K.B. 794; 89 L.T. 328 172
Kruse *v.* Johnson [1898] 2 Q.B. 91; 67 L.J.Q.B. 782; 78 L.T. 647; 14 T.L.R. 416 37

Lampleigh *v.* Braithwait (1615) Moore (K.B.) 866; 1 Smith L.C. (13th ed.) 151 127
Lancashire Loans Ltd. *v.* Black [1934] 1 K.B. 380; [1933] All E.R.Rep. 201 161
Langridge *v.* Levy (1837) 2 M. & W. 519, 531 245
Latimer *v.* A.E.C. Ltd [1952] 2 Q.B. 701; [1952] 1 All E.R. 1302; affirmed [1953] A.C. 643; [1953] 2 All E.R. 449 225
Law *v.* Llewellyn [1906] 1 K.B. 487 200
Leach (Deceased), Re; Leach *v.* Lindeman and Others [1985] 3 W.L.R. 413; [1985] 2 All E.R. 754 306
Leaf *v.* International Galleries [1950] 2 K.B. 86; [1950] 1 All E.R. 693 158
Leakey *v.* National Trust [1980] 2 W.L.R. 65, [1980] 1 All E.R. 17 236
Leigh *v.* Gladstone (1909) 26 T.L.R. 139 198
Le Lievere *v.* Goulf [1893] 1 Q.B. 491 222
Lemmon *v.* Webb [1851] A.C. 1; [1894] 3 Ch. 1 220
Leslie (R) Ltd. *v.* Sheill [1914] 3 K.B. 607; [1914–15] All E.R.Rep. 511; 83 L.J.K.B. 1145 .... 135, 201
L'Estrange *v.* Graucob Ltd. [1934] 2 K.B. 394; [1934] All E.R.Rep. 16; 103 L.J.K.B. 730 .... 143, 144, 151
Lever Brothers Ltd. *v.* Bell, *see* Bell *v.* Lever Brothers Ltd.
Lewis *v.* Averay [1972] 1 QB 198, [1971] 3 All E.R. 907 .... 150, 154
Liesbosch Dredger *v.* Edison Steamship [1933] A.C. 449; [1933] All E.R.Rep. 144 203
Limpus *v.* London General Omnibus Co. (1862) 1 H. & C. 526; 32 L.J.Ex. 34 206
Lister *v.* Romford Ice & Cold Storage Co. Ltd. [1957] A.C. 555; [1957] 1 All E.R. 125; [1957] 2 W.L.R. 158 207
Lloyd *v.* Grace, Smith & Co. [1912] A.C. 716; [1911–13] All E.R.Rep. 51 206
Lloyds Bank Ltd *v.* Bundy [1975] Q.B. 326, [1974] 3 W.L.R. 501, [1974] 3 All E.R. 757 161
Loftus *v.* Roberts (1902) 18 T.L.R. 532 141
London & Globe Finance Corpn Ltd., *re* [1903] 1 Ch. 728, 88 L.T. 194 19 T.L.R. 314 347
Lumley *v.* Wagner (1852) 1 De G.M. & G. 604; [1843–60] All E.R.Rep. 368; 21 L.J.Ch. 898 182
Lyons, Sons & Co. *v.* Gulliver [1914] 1 Ch. 631 218

M. & S. Drapers (A firm) *v.* Reynolds [1956] 3 All E.R. 814: [1957] 1 W.L.R. 9. 165
McCrone *v.* Riding [1938] 1 All E.R. 157, 54 T.L.R. 328, 30 Cox CC 670 349
McGowan *v.* Stott (1923) 143 L.T. 217: 99 L.J.K.B. 357 n 227
McKnight *v.* Davies [1974] R.T.R. 4 339
Machent *v.* Quinn [1970] 2 All E.R. 255 339
Maddison *v.* Alderson (1883) 8 App.Cas. 467: [1881–5] All E.R.Rep. 742: 52 L.J.Q.B. 737 133
Mahon *v.* Osborne [1939] 2 K.B. 14: [1939] 1 All E.R. 535 227
Malone *v.* Laskey [1907] 2 K.B. 141 219
Mathew *v.* Bobbins (1980) *The Times* 20 June 163
Meering *v.* Graham White Aviation Co. (1919) 122 L.T. 44 210
Mercantile Union Guarantee Corporation Ltd. *v.* Ball [1937] 2 K.B. 498: [1937] All E.R. 1: 106 L.J.K.B. 621 136
Mercer *v.* Denne [1905] 2 Ch. 538: [1904–7] All E.R.Rep. 71: 74 L.J.Ch. 723: 93 L.T. 412 44
Metropolitan District Asylum Board *v.* Hill (1881) 6 App.Cas. 193 199
Metropolitan Police Commission *v.* Caldwell [1981] 2 W.L.R. 509 [1981] 1 All E.R. 961 ...... 316, 345
Metropolitan Water Board *v.* Dick, Kerr & Co. [1918] A.C. 119: [1916–17] All E.R.Rep. 122: 87 L.J.K.B. 370 172
Mighel *v.* Sultan of Johore [1894] 1 Q.B. 149: 61 L.J.Q.B. 593 140
Miller *v.* Jackson [1977] Q.B. 966, [1977] 3 W.L.R. 20, [1977] 3 All E.R. 338 ... 218
Mint *v.* Good [1951] 1 K.B. 517: [1950] 2 All E.R. 1159 221
Mogul Steamship Co. *v.* McGregor Gow & Co. [1892] A.C. 25: [1891–4] All E.R.Rep. 263: 61 L.J.Q.B. 295: 66 L.T. 1 193
Morris (Herbert) Ltd. *v.* Saxelby [1916] A A.C. 688: [1916–17] All E.R.Rep. 305: 85 L.J.Ch. 210: 114 L.T. 618 164
Morriss *v.* Marsden [1952] 1 All E.R. 925: (1952) 1 T.L.R. 947 202
Moynes *v.* Cooper [1956] 1 Q.B. 439, [1956] 1 All E.R. 450, [1956] 2 W.L.R. 562 337
Murray *v.* Ministry of Defence [1988] 1 W.L.R. 692; [1988] 2 All E.R. 521 210

Napier *v.* National Business Agency Ltd. [1951] 2 All E.R. 264: 95 Sol.Jo 528 .. 167
Nash *v.* Inmann [1908] 2 K.B. 1: [1908–10] All E.R.Rep. 317: 77 L.J.K.B. 626 136, 375
National Coal Board *v.* Evans [1951] 2 K.B. 816: [1951] 2 All E.R. 310 . 198, 211, 215
National Telephone Co. *v.* Baker [1893] 2 Ch. 186 334
National Westminster Bank PLC *v.* Morgan [1985] 2 W.L.R. 588: [1985] 2 All E.R. 821 161
Neale *v.* Merrett (1930) W.N. 189 119
Newstead *v.* London Express Newspaper Ltd. [1940] 1 K.B. 377: [1939] 4 All E.R. 319 ...... 238, 243
Newton *v.* Smith [1962] 2 W.L.R. 19 220
Nichols *v.* Marsland (1876) 2 Ex.D.1: 46 L.J.Q.B. 174 235
Noakes & Co. Ltd. *v.* Rice [1902] A.C. 24, 31, 34: 71 L.J.Ch. 139: 86 L.T. 62: 50 W.R. 305: 18 T.L.R. 196 291
Nordenfeldt Case. *See* Maxim Nordenfeldt Guns and Ammunition Co. *v.* Nordenfeldt 164

O'Connell *v.* Jackson (1971) 3. W.L.R. 463 228
O'Connor *v.* Swan & Edgar Ltd. (1963) 107 Sol.Jo. 215 232
Oldcastle's Case (1419) 1 Hale P.C. 50, 1 East P.C. 364 324
Olley *v.* Marlborough Court Ltd. [1949] 1 K.B. 532: [1949] 1 All E.R. 127: 65 T.L.R. 95 143
Osborn *v.* Boulter [1930] 2 K.B. 226 242
Oppenheim *v.* Tobacco Securities Trust Co. Ltd. [1951] A.C. 297, [1951] 1 All E.R. 3, [1951] 1 T.L.R. 118 253
Owens *v.* Brimmell [1977] Q.B. 859, 2 W.L.R. 943 [1976] 3 All E.R. 765 197
Owgo *v.* Taylor [1987] 3 W.L.R. 1145; [1987] 3 All E.R. 961 196

Parker *v.* Alder [1899] 1 Q.B. 20, 68 L.J.Q.B. 7, 19 Cox C.C. 191 317
Parker *v.* Clark [1960] 1 All E.R. 93: [1960] 1 W.L.R. 286 122

Pirelli General Cable Works Ltd. *v*. Oscar Faber & Partners [1983] 2 W.L.R. 6 [1983] 1 All E.R. 65 246
Planché *v*. Colburn (1831) 8 Bing 14; 1 Moo & S. 51 .... 180, 190
Poulton *v*. London and South Western Railway (1867) L.R. 2 Q.B. 534 207

Quelch *v*. Collett [1948] 1 K.B. 478 317

R. *v*. 'A' (a juvenile) [1978] CR. L.R. 689 345
R. *v*. Abbott [1977] A.C. 755, [1976] 3 All E.R. 140, [1976] 3 W.L.R. 462 324
R. *v*. Allen (1872) L.R. 1 C.C.R. 367; 26 L.T. 644; 20 W.R. 756 40
R. *v*. Allen (Christopher) [1985] 1 W.L.R. 50; [1985] 1 All E.R. 148 345
R. *v*. Barnard (1837) 7 C. & P. 784 340
R. *v*. Bassey (1931) 47 T.L.R. 222, 22 CR.App.Rep. 160 347
R. *v*. Bateman (1925) 94 L.J.K.B. 791, 28 Cox CC 33, 19 CR.App.Rep. 8 330
R. *v*. Beck (Brian) [1985] 1 W.L.R. 22; [1985] 1 All E.R. 571 342
R. *v*. Belfon [1976] 1 W.L.R. 741, [1976] 3 All E.R. 46, Cr.App.Rep. 46 334
R. *v*. Benn & Church (1795) 6 Term. Rep. 198 69
R. *v*. Billinghurst [1978] Cr. L.R. 553 333
R. *v*. Bird [1985] 1 W.L.R. 816; [1985] 2 All E.R. 513 323
R. *v*. Blaue [1975] 1 W.L.R. 1411, [1975] 3 All E.R. 446, 61 Cr.App.Rep. 271 327
R. *v*. Bogacki [1973] QB 832, [1973] 2 All E.R. 864, 57 Cr.App.Rep. 593 340
R. *v*. Boshears (1961) *The Times* 8 February 320
R. *v*. Briggs [1977] 1 W.L.R. 605, [1977] 1 All E.R. 475, [1976] Cr. L.R. 438 316
R. *v*. Brown [1972] 2 Q.B. 229, [1972] 2 All E.R. 1328, [1971] 3 All E.R. 11 329
R. *v*. Buck [1960] Cr. L.R. 730, 33 Cr.App.Rep. 213 320
R. *v*. Buckett (1964) 7 W.L.R. 271 328
R. *v*. Byrne [1960] 2 Q.B. 396, [1960] 3 All E.R. 1, [1960] 3 W.L.R. 440 330
R. *v*. Cato [1976] 1 W.L.R. 110, [1976] 1 All E.R. 260, 62 Cr.App.Rep. 41 331
R. *v*. Church [1966] 1 Q.B. 59, [1965] 2 All E.R. 72, [1965] 2 W.L.R. 1220 331
R. *v*. Clarence (1888) 22 Q.B.D. 23, L.J.M.C. 10, 16 Cox C.C. 511 334
R. *v*. Closs (1858) Dears & Bell 460, 27 L.J.M.C. 54, 7 Cox C.C. 494 347
R. *v*. Clucas [1949] 2 Q.B. 226, [1949] 2 All E.R. 40, 33 Cr.App.Rep. 136 .... 340, 341
R. *v*. Collins [1973] Q.B. 100, [1972] 2 All E.R. 1105, (1972] 3 W.L.R. 243 339
R. *v*. Cunningham [1957] 2 Q.B. 396, [1957] 2 All E.R. 412, [1957] 3 W.L.R. 76 .... 316, 334
R. *v*. Davies [1975] Q.B. 691, [1975] 1 All E.R. 890, [1975] 2 W.L.R. 586 329
R. *v*. Davis (1823) R. and R. 499 339
R. *v*. Denton [1981] 1 W.L.R. 1446 [1982] 1 All E.R. 65 345
R. *v*. Desmond (1868) *The Times* 28 April 328
R. *v*. Donovan [1934] 2 K.B. 498, 103 L.J.K.B. 683, 25 Cr.App.Rep. 1 333
R. *v*. Duffy [1949] 1 All E.R. 932 n 328
R. *v*. Dyson [1908] 2 K.B. 454, 77 L.J.K.B. 813, 1 Cr.App.Rep. 13 327
R. *v*. Electricity Commissioners. *Ex. parte* London Electricity Joint Committee Co. (1920) Ltd. & Others [1924] 1 K.B. 171 71
R. *v*. Ellerton [1978] Cr. L.R. 166, 67 Cr.App.Rep. 63 328
R. *v*. Feely [1973] Q.B. 530, [1973] 1 All E.R. 341, [1973] 2 W.L.R. 201 .... 338, 341
R. *v*. Franklin (1883) 15 Cox C.C. 163 331
R. *v*. Gill (1963) 1 W.L.R. 841, [1963] 2 All E.R. 688, 47 Cr.App.Rep. 166. 324
R. *v*. Gould [1968] 2 Q.B. 65, [1968] 1 All E.R. 849, [1968] 3 W.L.R. 643 349
R. *v*. Ghosh [1981] 1 W.L.R. 110; [1982] 2 All E.R. 689 336
R. *v*. Hale [1979] Cr. L.R. 596 338
R. *v*. Hancock [1986] 1 All E.R. 641 328
R. *v*. Hayward (1833) C. C. & P. 157 329
R. *v*. Hensler (1870) 22 L.T. 691, 11 Cox C.C. 570 .... 326, 340
R. *v*. Holland (1841) 2 Mood & R. 351 327
R. *v*. Hussey (1924) 89 J.P. 28, 41 T.L.R. 205, 18 Cr.App.Rep. 160 323
R. *v*. Ismail [1977] Cr. L.R. 557 343
R. *v*. Jenkins and Jenkins [1983] 1 All E.R. 1000 339
R. *v*. Jordan (1956) 40 Cr.App.Rep. 152 327

R. *v*. Duffy [1949] 1 All E.R. 932 n 328
R. *v*. Dyson [1908] 2 K.B. 454, 77 L.J.K.B. 813, 1 Cr.App.Rep. 13 327
R. *v*. Electricity Commissioners. *Ex. parte* London Electricity Joint Committee Co. (1920) Ltd. & Others [1924] 1 K.B. 171 71
R. *v*. Ellerton [1978] Cr. L.R. 166, 67 Cr.App.Rep. 63 328
R. *v*. Fairbanks [1986] 1 W.L.R. 1202 332
R. *v*. Feely [1973] Q.B. 530, [1973] 1 All E.R. 341, [1973] 2 W.L.R. 201 .... 338, 341
R. *v*. Franklin (1883) 15 Cox C.C. 163 331
R. *v*. Gill (1963) 1 W.L.R. 841, [1963] 2 All E.R. 688, 47 Cr.App.Rep. 166. 324
R. *v*. Gould [1968] 2 Q.B. 65, [1968] 1 All E.R. 849, [1968] 3 W.L.R. 643 349
R. *v*. Ghosh [1981] 1 W.L.R. 110; [1982] 2 All E.R. 689 336
R. *v*. Gold; R. *v*. Schifreen [1987] 3 W.L.R. 803; [1987] 3 All E.R. 618 347
R. *v*. Hale [1979] Cr. L.R. 596 338
R. *v*. Hancock [1986] 1 All E.R. 641 328
R. *v*. Hayward (1833) C. C. & P. 157 329
R. *v*. Hensler (1870) 22 L.T. 691, 11 Cox C.C. 570 .... 326, 340
R. *v*. Holland (1841) 2 Mood & R. 351 327
R. *v*. Howe [1987] 2 W.L.R. 568; [1987] 1 All E.R. 771 324
R. *v*. Hussey (1924) 89 J.P. 28, 41 T.L.R. 205, 18 Cr.App.Rep. 160 323
R. *v*. Ismail [1977] Cr. L.R. 557 343
R. *v*. Jenkins and Jenkins [1983] 1 All E.R. 1000 339
R. *v*. Jordan (1956) 40 Cr.App.Rep. 152 327
R. *v*. Kemp [1957] 1 Q.B. 399, [1956] 3 All E.R. 249, [1956] 3 W.L.R. 724 .... 320, 322
R. *v*. King [1964] 1 Q.B. 285, [1963] 3 All E.R. 561, [1963] 3 W.L.R. 892 349
R. *v*. Lamb [1967] 2 Q.B. 981, [1967] 2 All E.R. 1282, [1967] 3 W.L.R. 888 331
R. *v*. Lawrence [1980] Cr. L.R. 574 .... 332, 356
R. *v*. Lines (1844) 1 Car. & Kir. 393 335
R. *v*. Lipman [1970] 1 Q.B., 152, [1969] 3 All E.R. 410, [1969] 3 W.L.R. 819 323
R. *v*. Lowe [1973] Q.B. 702, [1973] 1 All E.R. 805, [1973] 2 W.L.R. 481 331
R. *v*. McCarthy [1954] 2 Q.B. 105, [1954] 2 All E.R. 262, [1954] 2 W.L.R. 1044 . 329
R. *v*. McInnes [1971] 1 W.L.R. 1600, [1971] 3 All E.R. 295 330
R. *v*. MacPherson [1973] R.T.R. 157, [1973] Cr. L.R. 457 336
R. *v*. Males [1962] 2 Q.B. 500, [1961] 3 All E.R. 705, [1961] 3 W.L.R. 1297 326
R. *v*. Matthews [1950] 1 All E.R. 137, 34 Cr.App.Rep. 55 344
R. *v*. Miller [1983] 2 W.L.R. 539 [1983] 1 All E.R. 978 .... 316, 345
R. *v*. Mitchell [1983] 2 W.L.R. 983; [1983] 2 All E.R. 427 331
R. *v*. Moloney [1985] 2 W.L.R. 648; [1985] 1 All E.R. 1025 328
R. *v*. Monaghan [1979] Cr. L.R. 673 .... 336, 342
R. *v*. Morris [1983] 2 W.L.R. 768; [1983] 2 All E.R. 448 336
R. *v*. Mowatt [1968] 1 Q.B. 421, [1967] 3 All E.R. 47, [1967] 3 W.L.R. 1192 334
R. *v*. Nedrick [1986] 1 W.L.R. 1025; [1986] 3 All E.R. 1 328
R. *v*. O'Grady [1987] 3 W.L.R. 321 323
R. *v*. Palmer [1971] A.C. 814, [1971] 1 All E.R. 1077, [1971] 2 W.L.R. 831 330
R. *v*. Pierce (1941) 5 J. Cr. L. 124 324
R. *v*. Pike [1961] Cr. L.R. 547 331
R. *v*. Pitchley (1973) 57 Cr.App.Rep., 30 [1972] Cr. L.R. 705 343
R. *v*. Prince (1875) L.R. 2 C.C.R. 154, 44 L.J.M.C. 122, 13 Cox C.C. 138 .... 317, 335
R. *v*. Quick [1973] Q.B. 910, [1973] 3 All E.R. 347, [1973] 3 W.L.R. 26 320
R. *v*. Rand (1866) L.R. 1 Q.B. 230 69
R. *v*. Ring (1892) 61 L.J.M.C. 116, 66 L.T. 300, 17 Cox C.C. 491 326
R. *v*. Roberts (1971) 56 Cr.App.Rep. 95, [1972] Cr. L.R. 27 334
R. *v*. Robinson [1915] 2 K.B. 342, 31 T.L.R. 313, 11 Cr.App.Rep. 124 325
R. *v*. Rolfe (1952) 36 Cr.App.Rep. 4 335
R. *v*. Rose (1884) 15 Cox 540 321
R. *v*. Sagoo [1975] Q.B. 885, [1975] 2 All E.R. 926, [1975] 3 W.L.R. 267 349
R. *v*. St. George (1840) 9 C. & P. 483 .... 376, 377
R. *v*. Salisbury (1553) 1 Plow d 100 328
R. *v*. Sangha [1988] 1 W.L.R. 519; [1988] 2 All E.R. 385 346
R. *v*. Serne and Goldfinch (1887) 16 Cox C.C. 311 328
R. *v*. Shivpuri [1986] 2 W.L.R. 988; [1986] 2 All E.R. 334 326

R. *v*. Simpson [1983] 1 W.L.R. 1494; [1983] 3 All E.R. 789 334
R. *v*. Skivington [1968] 1 Q.B. 166, [1967] 1 All E.R. 483, [1967] 2 W.L.R. 665 . 338
R. *v*. Smith (1858) Dears & B.566, 27 L.J.M.C. 225, 8 Cox C.C. 32 347
R. *v*. Smith [1959] 2 Q.B. 35, [1959] 2 All E.R. 193, [1959] 2 W.L.R. 623 327
R. *v*. Smith [1974] Q.B. 354, [1974] 1 All E.R. 632, [1974] 2 W.L.R. 20 . 321, 333, 346
R. *v*. Stagg [1978] Cr. L.R. 227 343
R. *v*. Steer [1987] 3 W.L.R. 205; [1987] 2 All E.R. 833 (HL) 346
R. *v*. Sussex Justices, *Ex parte* McCarthy [1924] 1 K.B. 256 69
R. *v*. Tolson (1889) 23 Q.B.D. 168, 58 L.J.M.C. 97, 16 Cox C.C. 321, 349
R. *v*. Venna [1976] Q.B. 421, [1975] 3 All E.R. 788, [1975] 3 W.L.R. 737 333
R. *v*. Vickers [1957] 2 Q.B. 664, [1957] 2 All E.R. 741, [1957] 3 W.L.R. 326 328
R. *v*. Wardrope [1960] Cr. L.R. 770 329
R. *v*. Wilson [1955] 1 W.L.R. 493, [1955] 1 All E.R. 744, 39 Cr.App.Rep. 12 ... 333
Raffles *v*. Winchelhaus (1864) 2 H. & C. 906; 33 L.J.Ex. 160 .... 148, 152
Rainham Chemical Works *v*. Belvedere Fish Guano Co. [1921] 2 A.C. 465 234
Ramsgate Victoria Hotel Co. *v*. Montefiore (1866) L.R. 1 Ex. 109; 4 H. & Co. 164; 35 L.J.Ex. 90 117
Rann *v*. Hughes (1778) 7 Term.Rep. 350 n.; Bro. Parl. Cas. 27 122
Rapley's Estate, *re* [1983] W.L.R. 1069 [1983] 3 All E.R. 248 300
Ratcliffe *v*. Evans [1892] 2 Q.B. 524 246
Rawlinson *v*. Ames [1925] Ch. 96; 94 L.J.Ch. 113; 132 L.T. 370 133
Read *v*. Lyons & Co. Ltd. [1946] A.C. 156; [1946] 2 All E.R. 471; 175 L.T. 413; 62 T.L.R. 646 236
Rickards *v*. Lothian [1913] A.C. 263; 108 L.T. 225; [1911–13] All E.R.Rep. 71; 29 T.L.R. 281 235
Rickards (Charles) Ltd. *v*. Oppenheim [1950] 1 K.B. 616; [1950] 1 All E.R. 420 . 168
Ridge *v*. Baldwin [1964] A.C. 40; [1963] 2 All E.R. 66 70
Roberts *v*. Gray [1913] 1 K.B. 520; [1911–13] All E.R.Rep. 870; 82 L.J.K.B. 362; 108 L.T. 232; 29 T.L.R. 149 136
Robinson *v*. Davison (1871) L.R. 6 Ex. 269; [1861–73] All E.R.Rep. 699; 40 L.J.Ex. 172 172
Robinson *v*. Kilvert (1889) 41 Ch. D. 88; 58 L.J.Ch. 392 221
Robson and Sharpe *v*. Drummond (1831) 2 B. & Ad. 303; [1824–34] All E.R.Rep. 158 186
Rogers *v*. Arnott [1960] 2 Q.B. 244, [1960] 2 All E.R. 417, [1960] 3 W.L.R. 73 .. 336
Rondel *v*. Worsley [1969] 1 A.C. 191; [1967] 3 All E.R, 993 226
Rookes *v*. Barnard [1964] A.C. 1129; [1964] 1 All E.R. 367 [1964] 1 Lloyd's Rep. 28 184
Roscorla *v*. Thomas (1842) 3 Q.B. 234; 2 Gal. & Dav. 508; 11 L.J.Q.B. 214 127
Rose and Frank Co. *v*. J. R. Crompton & Brothers Ltd. [1925] A.C. 445; 94 L.J.K.B. 120; 132 L.T. 641 122
Ross *v*. Caunters [1980] Ch. 297 85
Ross *v*. Matt [1951] 1 K.B. 810, [1951] 1 All E.R. 361, 35 Cr.App.Rep. 1 337
Rylands *v*. Fletcher (1868) L.R. 3 H.L. 330; 37 L.J.Ex. 161; 19 L.T. 220 .... 208, 236, 383

St. Helen's Smelting Co. *v*. Tipping (1865) 11 H.L.Cas. 642; 35 L.J.Q.B. 66; 12 L.T. 776 221
Saunders *v*. Anglia Bldg. Society [1970] 3 W.L.R. 1078 151
Sayers *v*. Harlow Urban District Council [1958] 2 All E.R. 342; [1958] 1 W.L.R. 623 228
Scammell (G) and Nephew Ltd. *v*. Ouston [1941] A.C. 251; [1941] 1 All E.R. 14; 100 L.J.K.B. 197; 164 L.T. 379; 57 T.L.R. 280 141
Scott *v*. London and St. Katherine's Docks Co. (1865) 3 H. & C. 596; 34 L.J. Ex. 220; 13 L.T. 148 227
Scott *v*. Metropolitan Police Commissioner [1975] A.C. 819, [1974] 3 All E.R. 1032 [1974] 3 W.L.R. 741 325
Scott *v*. Shepherd (1773) 2 W. Bl. 892 .... 209, 228
Scriven Brothers & Co. *v*. Hindley & Co. [1913] 3 K.B. 564; 83 L.J.K.B. 40; 109 L.T. 526 148

Scruttons Ltd. *v.* Midland Silicones Ltd. [1962] A.C. 446: [1962] 1 All E.R. 1: [1961] 2 Lloyd's Rep. 365 184
Sedleigh Denfield *v.* O'Callagan [1940] A.C. 880: [1940] 3 All E.R. 349: 109 L.J.K.B. 893: 164 L.T. 72: 56 T.L.R. 887 218
Shadwell *v.* Shadwell (1860) 9 C.B. (N.S.) 159: 30 L.J.C.P. 145: 3 L.T. 628: 9 W.R. 163 124
Shaw *v.* D.P.P. [1962] A.C. 220, [1961] 2 All E.R. 446, [1961] 2 W.L.R. 897 313
Simpkins *v.* Pays [1955] 3 All E.R. 10: [1955] 1 W.L.R. 975 121
Simpson *v.* Peat [1952] 2 Q.B. 24, [1952] 1 All E.R. 447, 1 T.L.R. 469 349
Skinner *v.* London, Brighton and South Coast Railway Co. (1850) 5 Exch. 787 . 227
Smith *v.* Chadwick (1882) 20 Ch.D. 27: 51 L.J.Ch. 597: 46 L.T. 702 affirmed (1884) 9 App.Cas. 187: [1881–5] All E.R.Rep 242 155
Smith *v.* Leech Brain & Co. Ltd. [1962] 2 Q.B. 405: [1961] 3 All E.R. 115: 204
Smith *v.* Wilson (1832) B. & Ad. 782: 1 L.J.K.B. 194 46
Smith and Others *v.* Littlewoods Organisation Ltd. [1987] 2 W.L.R. 480; [1987] 1 All E.R. 710 225
Solle *v.* Butcher [1950] 1 K.B. 671: [1949] 2 All E.R. 1107 .... 149, 152
South Place Ethical Society *In re* (1980) *The Times* 18 June 252
Spurling (J) Ltd. *v.* Bradshaw [1956] 2 All E.R. 121: [1956] 1 W.L.R. 461 144
Stanley *v.* Powell [1891] 1 Q.B. 86: 60 L.J.Q.B. 52 .... 198, 211
Steinberg *v.* Scala (Leeds) Ltd. [1923] 2 Ch. 452: [1923] All E.R.Rep. 239: 92 L.J.K.B. 944: 129 L.T. 624: 39 T.L.R. 542 137
Storey *v.* Ashton (1869) L.R. 4 Q.B. 476 206
Sturges *v.* Bridgman (1879) 11 Ch.D 852: 48 L.J. Ch. 785: 41 L.T. 219 220
Sugden *v.* Lord St. Leonards (1876) 1 P.D. 154 301
Sumpter *v.* Hedges [1898] 1 Q.B. 673: 67 L.J.Q.B. 545: 78 L.T. 378: 46 W.R. 454 181
Sybron *v.* Rochem [1983] 3 W.L.R. 713; [1983] 2 All E.R. 707 149

Tarry *v.* Ashton (1876) 1 Q.B.D. 314: 45 L.J.Q.B. 260: 34 L.T. 97 208
Taylor *v.* Caldwell (1863) 3 B. & S. 826: 2 New Rep. 198: 32 L.J.Q.B. 164: 8 L.T. 356 172
Taylor *v.* Laird (1856) 1 H. & N. 266: 25 L.J.Ex. 239 116
Thorne *v.* Motor Trade Association [1937] A.C. 797, [1937] 3 All E.R. 157, 24 Cr.App.Rep. 51 342
Thornton *v.* Mitchell [1940] 1 All E.R. 339 320
Thornton *v.* Shoe Lane Parking Ltd. [1971] 2 W.L.R. 585; [1971] 1 All E.R. 686 143
Tolley *v.* J. S. Fry & Sons Ltd. [1931] A.C. 333: [1931] All E.R.Rep. 131: 100 L.J.K.B. 328: 145 L.T. 1: 47 T.L.R. 351 238
Tool Metal Manufacturing Co. Ltd. *v.* Tungsten Electric Co. Ltd. [1955] 2 All E.R. 657: [1955] 1 W.L.R. 671 129
Tsakiroglu & Co. Ltd. *v.* Noblee Thorl G.m.b.H. [1962] A.C. 93: [1961] 2 All E.R. 179 173
Tuberville *v.* Savage (1669) 2 Keb. 545: 1 Mod.Rep. 3 .... 209, 333
Tulk *v.* Moxhay (1848) 1 H. & T. 105: 18 L.J.Ch. 83: 2 Ph. 774 286
Tweddle *v.* Atkinson (1861) 1 B. & S. 393: 30 L.J.Q.B. 265: [1861–73] All E.R.Rep. 369: 4 L.T. 468 .... 126, 184, 185

Valentini *v.* Canali (1889) 24 Q.B.D. 166: 59 L.J.Q.B. 74: 61 L.T. 731: G.T.L.R. 75: 38 W.R. 331 137
Vaughan *v.* Taff Vale Railway Co. (1860) 5 H. & N. 679 199
Victoria Laundry (Windsor) Ltd. *v.* Newman Industries Ltd. [1949] 2 K.B. 528: [1949] 1 All E.R. 997: 65 T.L.R. 274 177
Vizetelly *v.* Mudie's Select Library [1900] 2 Q.B. 170 240

Wachtel *v.* Wachtel (1973) Fam. 72, p. 95 305
Wade *v.* Simeon (1846) 2 C.B. 548: 15 L.J.C.P. 114 125
Wakeham *v.* Mackenzie (1968) 2 All E.R. 783: 1 W.L.R. 1175 132
Walton Harvey Ltd. *v.* Walker and Homfrays Ltd. [1931] 1 Ch. 274 171
Ward *v.* Byham [1956] 2 All E.R. 318: [1956] 1 W.L.R. 496: 100 Sol.Jo. 341 124
Warner Brothers Pictures Incorporated *v.* Nelson [1937] 1 K.B. 209: 106 L.J.K.B. 97: 155 L.T. 538: 53 T.L.R. 14 182

Webster *v.* Cecil (1861) 30 Beav. 62 152
Webley *v.* Buxton [1977] Q.B. 481, [1977] 2 All E.R. 595 326
Welham *v.* D.P.P. [1961] A.C. 103, [1960] 1 All E.R. 805, [1960] 2 W.L.R. 669 . 347
Westminster City Council *v.* Croyalgrange Ltd. [1986] 1 W.L.R. 674; [1986] 2 All E.R. 353 161
White *v.* Bluett (1853) 23 L.J. Ex. 36; 2 W.R. 75 123
Whitwood Chemical Co. *v.* Hardman [1891] 2 Ch. 416; 60 L.J.Ch. 428; 64 L.T. 716; 7 T.L.R. 325; 39 W.R. 433 183
Wilkinson *v.* Downton [1897] 2 Q.B. 57 194
William Gray, The 29 Fed. Cas. 1300 324
Williams (Deceased), Re, Wiles and Another *v.* Madgin and Others [1985] 1 W.L.R. 905; [1985] 1 All E.R. 964 295
Wilson *v.* Pringle [1986] 3 W.L.R. 1; [1986] 2 All E.R. 440 209
Windsor, *Re* (1865) 6 B. & S. 552, 34 L.J.M.C. 163, 10 Cox C.C. 118 347
Wings Ltd. *v.* Ellis [1984] 3 W.L.R. 965; [1984] 3 All E.R. 577 158
With *v.* O'Flanagan [1936] Ch. 575; [1936] 1 All E.R. 727; 105 L.J.Ch. 247 154 L.T. 634; 80 Sol.Jo. 285 155
Wren *v.* Weild (1869) L.R. 4 Q.B. 730; 38 L.J.Q.B. 327 245

Yachuk *v.* Olivier Blais Co. Ltd. [1949] A.C. 386 225
Youssoupoff *v.* Metro-Goldwyn-Mayer Pictures Ltd. (1934) 50 T.L.R. 581 237

TABLE OF STATUTES

Abortion Act 1967 332
Act of Settlement 1701 7
Act of Union with Scotland. *See* Union with Scotland Act
Administration of Estates Act 1925 .. .. 269, 277, 308, 309, 311
Administration of Justice Act 1960 54
Administration of Justice Act 1964 54
Administration of Justice Act 1969 47
Administration of Justice Act 1970 and 1973 .. .. 50, 51, 290
Administration of Justice Act 1982 .. .. .. 63, 68, 229, 230, 298, 299, 301
Administration of Justice Act 1985 .. .. 86, 247
Administration of Justice (Miscellaneous Provisions) Act 1933 74
Adoption Act 1958 and 1976 .. .. 96, 97
Agricultural Holdings Act, 1948 280
Animals Act, 1971 .. .. 199, 214
Arbitration Acts 1950, 1975 and 1979 73
Betting and Loans (Infants) Act 1892 134
Bill of Rights 1689 241
Bills of Exchange Act 1882 .. .. 127, 130, 134, 188
British Nationality Act 1948, 1981 89

Chancery Amendment Act 1858 22
Chancery Procedure Act 1852 21
Charities Act 1960 253
Children Act 1975 96
Civil Aviation Act 1949 212
Civil Jurisdiction and Judgments Act 1982 5
Civil Liability (Contribution) Act 1978 .. .. 208, 257
Coal Industry Nationalization Act 1946 102
Common Law Procedure Act 1854 21
Companies Act 1985 .. .. 101, 102, 103, 130, 139, 155, 158, 159, 188
Congenital Disabilities (Civil Liability) Act 1976 201
Consolidation Act 1978 62
Consolidation of Enactments (Procedure) Act 1949 33
Consumer Protection Act 1987 .. .. 158, 317
Contracts of Employment Act 1972 131
Control of Pollution Act 1974 324
Conveyancing Act 1881 272
Copyright Act 1956 130
Coroners Acts 1887 to 1980 63
Corporate Bodies' Contracts Act 1960 139
County Courts Act 1846 51
County Courts Act 1959 51
County Courts Act 1984 51
Court of Probate Act 1857 .. .. 21, 297
Courts Act 1971 .. .. 54, 59, 82
Criminal Appeal Act 1968 54
Criminal Attempts Act 1981 326
Criminal Damage Act 1971 .. .. 217, 345
Criminal Justice Act 1925 324
Criminal Justice Act 1967 .. .. 42, 61, 74, 346, 365
Criminal Justice Act 1972 74

Criminal Law Act 1967 .. .. .. 33, 43, 213, 214, 314, 319, 323, 325, 326, 332, 334, 347, 350, 365
Criminal Law Act 1977 .. .. 60, 63, 314, 370
Criminal Procedure (Insanity) Act 1964 330
Crown Proceedings Act 1947 199
Crown Proceedings (Armed Forces) Act 1987 111

Dangerous Drugs Act 1965 83
Defamation Act 1952 .. .. 44, 237, 243
Defective Premises Act, 1972 232
Diplomatic Privileges Act 1964 140
Divorce Reform Act 1969 99
Domestic Proceedings and Magistrates Courts Act 1978 427
Domicile and Matrimonial Proceedings Act 1973 91

Education Act 1944 34
Emergency Powers (Defence) Act 1939 36
Employers' Liability (Compulsory Insurance) Act 1969 223
Employers' Liability (Defective Equipment) Act 1969 224
Employment Acts 1980 and 1982 108
Employment Protection Act 1975 66
Employment Protection (Consolidation) Act 1978 .. .. .. 62, 66
Equal Pay Act 1970 63
European Communities Act 1972 .. .. 42, 104

Factories Act 1961 .. .. 33, 229, 230
Fair Trading Act 1973 .. .. 62, 165
Family Law Reform Act 1969 .. .. 98, 99, 133, 310
Fatal Accidents Act 1976 .. .. 229, 246
Firearms Act, 1968 334
Forfeiture Acts 1870 and 1982 292
Forgery Act 1913 84
Frauds, *See* Statute of Frauds

Gaming Act 1845 161
Guardianship of Minors Act 1971 97
Guardianship Act 1973 102

Health and Safety at Work Act 1974 .. .. 229, 316
Hire Purchase Act 1965 130
Homicide Act 1957 .. .. 313, 314, 329, 330
Housing Act 1957 281

Import Duties Act 1932 36
Incitement to Disaffection Act 1934 84
Industrial Relations Act, 1971 108
Industrial Training Act, 1964 66
Infant Life (Preservation) Act, 1929 332
Infanticide Act 1938 331
Infants Relief Act 1874 .. .. 133, 135, 137, 201
Inheritance (Family Provision) Act 1938 .. .. 44, 304
Inheritance (Provision for Family and Dependants) Act 1975 305
Insolvency Act 1986 309
Interpretation Act 1978 38
Intestates' Estates Act 1952 309

Juries Act 1974 .. .. 33, 75
Jurisdiction Act 1876 22
Justices of the Peace Act 1949 59

Land Charges Act 1925, 1972 .. .. 269, 286, 294
Land Registration Act 1925 .. .. 269, 295
Landlord and Tenant Act 1927, 1954 .. .. 280, 282
Latent Damage Act 1986 247
Law Commission Act 1965 .. .. 6, 43
Law of Property Act 1925 .. .. .. 100, 106, 130, 131, 184, 185, 186, 187, 269, 270, 271, 272, 277, 278, 279, 286, 287, 288, 289, 292, 301
Law Officers Act 1944 83
Law Reform (Contributory Negligence) Act 1945 .. .. 43, 227
Law Reform (Enforcement of Contracts) Act 1954. 131
Law Reform (Frustrated Contracts) Act 1943 174
Law Reform (Husband and Wife) Act 1962 .. .. 43, 202
Law Reform (Limitations of Actions, etc.) Act 1954 .. .. .. 175, 229
Law Reform (Married Women and Tortfeasors) Act 1935 .. .. 139, 202, 298
Law Reform (Miscellaneous Provisions) Act 1934 .. .. .. 180, 229
Leasehold Reform Act 1967 280
Legal Aid and Advice Acts 1949 to 1982. .. .. 75, 76, 77
Legitimacy Act 1926, 1959, 1976 96
Libel Act 1843 242
Libel Act 1845 242
Limitation Acts 1939 to 1980 .. .. 43, 113, 127, 130, 174, 246, 258, 262
Limited Partnerships Act 1907 108
Local Government Act 1888 102
Local Government Act 1972 31

Magistrates' Courts Act 1952 .. .. 33, 96, 363
Magistrates' Courts Act 1978 96
Malicious Damage Act 1961 346
Marine Insurance Act 1906 184
Marriage Act 1949 92
Marriage Act 1983 92
Marriage (Enabling) Act 1960 92
Married Women's Property Act 1882 .. .. 184, 202, 298
Matrimonial Causes Act 1857 .. .. 21, 94
Matrimonial Causes Act 1937 .. .. 32, 44
Matrimonial Causes Act 1967 52
Matrimonial Causes Act 1973 .. .. 98, 396
Matrimonial and Family Proceedings Act 1984 396
Medical Act 1956 68
Mental Health Act 1959 .. .. 61, 94, 330
Mercantile Shipping Act 1894 140
Mines and Quarries Act, 1954 229
Minors' Contracts Act 1987 137
Misrepresentation Act 1967 .. .. 157, 158
Moneylenders Act 1927 .. .. 130, 162
Municipal Corporation Act 1882 70
Murder (Abolition of Death Penalty) Act 1965 32

National Insurance Act 1946 36
National Insurance Act 1965 66
National Insurance (Industrial Injuries) Act 1965 .. .. 64, 66
National Service Act, 1948 40

Observance Act, 1677 33
Occupiers' Liability Act 1957 .. .. 43, 230, 231
Occupiers' Liability Act 1984 .. .. 230, 231
Offences against the Person Act 1861, 1974 .. 5, 39, 316, 332, 333, 334, 348
Official Secrets Acts 1911 to 1939 .. .. 83, 84

Parliament Act 1911 32
Parliament Act 1949 32

Parliamentary Papers Act 1940 241
Partnership Act 1890 .. .. 34, 106
People Act 1969 100
Perjury Act 1911 1
Perpetuities and Accumulations Act 1964 254
Pharmacy and Poisons Act 1933 318
Police Act 1964 .. .. 34, 200, 334
Police and Criminal Evidence Act 1984 365
Policies of Assurance Act 1867 188
Post Office Act 1953, 1969 .. .. 41, 110
Powers of the Criminal Courts Act 1973 368
Prescription Act 1832 285
Prevention of Corruption Act, 1916 326
Prevention of Crime Act, 1953 334
Profane Oaths Act 1745 33
Property. *See* Law of Property Act
Prosecution of Offences Act 1985 84
Provisions of Oxford 1258 13
Public Order Act 1936 83
Punishment of Incest Act 1908 84

Race Relations Act 1965 and 1976 63
Race Relations Act 1968 41
Recreational Charities Act 1958 252
Redundancy Payments Act 1965 66
Reform Act 1832 17
Rent Act 1968, 1974, 1977 280
Resale Prices Act, 1976 183
Reservoirs Act, 1975 235
Restrictive Practices Court Act 1976 .. .. 62, 166
Restrictive Trade Practices Acts 1956, 1968, 1976, 1977 .. .. 62, 163, 165, 184
Rights of Light Act 1959 285
Road Traffic Act 1972 .. .. 33, 34, 184
Royal Assent Act 1967 32

Sale of Goods Act 1893, 1979 .. .. 34, 135, 139, 142, 146, 174
Settled Land Act 1882 275
Settled Land Act 1925 .. .. 269, 275, 276
Sex Discrimination Acts 1975 and 1986 .. .. 63, 164
Sexual Offences Act 1967 335
Solicitors Acts 1957 to 1974 .. .. 33, 68, 84
Stamps Act 1891 130
Statute of Appeals 1532 19
Statute of Forcible Entry 1381 214
Statute of Frauds 1677 131
Statute of Military Tenures 1660 297
Statute of Treason 1351 39
Statute of Westminster II 1285 13
Statutory Instruments Act 1946 36
Suicide Act 1961 330
Supply of Goods (Implied Terms) Act 1973 146
Supply of Goods and Services Act 1982 146
Supreme Court of Judicature Acts 1873 and 1875 .. .. 12, 14, 15, 19, 182, 186

Television Act 1954 102
Tenures Abolition Act. *See* Statute of Military Tenures
Theft Act 1968 and 1978 .. .. .. 38, 41, 43, 134, 155, 257, 314, 336, 344
Torts (Interference with Goods) Act 1977 215
Town and Country Planning Act 1971 260
Trade Descriptions Act 1968 .. .. 158, 317
Trade Disputes Act 1965 184

Trading with the Enemy Act 1939 163
Trade Union Act 1984 .. .. 108, 200
Trade Union and Labour Relations Act 1974 .. .. ..65, 67, 108, 109, 183
Transport Acts 1962 and 1981 350
Treason Act 1351 .. .. 6, 33, 69
Tribunals and Inquiries Act 1958 .. .. 43, 71
Tribunals and Inquiries Act 1971 .. .. 37, 71, 79
Truck Act 1831 .. .. 1, 162
Trustee Act 1925 .. ..255, 257, 258
Trustee Investments Act 1961 256

Unfair Contract Terms Act 1977 .. .. 145, 226
Union with Scotland Act 1707 5

Wages Act 1986 162
Wills Act 1837.. .. .. 298, 299, 300, 301, 303
Wills Act 1968.. 299
Wills Act Amendment Act 1852 298
Wills (Soldiers and Sailors) Act 1918 300

Index

Abatement,
  legacy of, 303
Abortion,
  illegal, 332
  lawful, 332
Acceptance,
  contract in, 115
  mental, 118
  post by, 120
  subject to contract, 119
  unqualified, 119
Actus reus, 315
Administrative tribunals, 64
Administrator (intestacy), 306
Admiralty,
  Court of, 20, 79
  lay assessors and, 79
Adoption, 96
  child of, 96
  jurisdiction in, 97
Agency,
  privity and, 184
Agreement,
  commercial and business, 122
  contract discharged by, 167
Aliens, 90
  contracts by, 140
  status of, 140
  torts and, 202
Appeal,
  County Court, from, 52
  criminal cases, in, 54
  Crown Court, from, 57
  High Court, from, 24
  House of Lords, to, 24, 37
  Justices, from, 62
Arbitration, 72
Arches, Court of, 19
Arrest, 368
Arrestable offences, 314
Assault, 333
  aggravated, 334
  battery and, 209, 210, 333
  common, 333
  crime and, 192
  intent to rob with, 338
  occasioning Actual Bodily Harm, 333
  PC, on, 334
  sexual, 335
  tort as, 209
Assignment, 185
  chose in action, of, 187
  contractual rights, of, 186
  equitable, 187
  legal, 186
  liabilities, of, 186
  notice of, 187
  novation, and, 186
  operation of law, by, 188
Assisting arrestable offender, 350
Assize,
  Commission of, 10
Attempt, 325
  to commit crime, 350
Attorney General, 83
Audi alterem partem, 69
Automatism, 320

Bankruptcy,
  contracts and, 175
Barrister, 85
  duties of, 86
  Inns of Court, disciplinary powers of, 85
Battery, 333
Bias,
  rule against, 69
Bigamy, 348
  defences, 349
Bill of Exchange,
  consideration and, 127
Binding precedent, 24
Blackmail, 342
Blackstone, Sir William,
  commentaries of, 44
Bona vacantia, 319
Borough-English, 9
Bracton,
  De legibus, etc., 44
Breach of contract,
  anticipatory, 170
  discharge by, 170
  remedies for, 176
  repudiation and, 170–1
  subsequent impossibility, by, 171

Bribery, 163
Burglary, 338
By-laws, 34

Canterbury,
  Court of Arches, 19
Capacity,
  contract, of parties to, 133
  criminal law, under, 99
  infants, of, 99, 133
  tort, parties to actions in, 199
Care,
  duty of, 222
  standard of, 224
Case,
  citation of, 29
  law, 25
  stated, appeal by way of, 57
  Caveat emptor, 149
Causing death by reckless driving, 332
Causing wasteful employment of police, 351
Certiorari, 71
Champerty, 163
Chancery,
  Amendment Act (1858), 22
  Court of, 14
  York, 19
  High Court of, 50
    composition, 50
    creation of, 50
    jurisdiction of, 50
  Procedure Act (1852), 21
Chartered companies, 102
Chattels,
  meaning of, 263, 265
  personal, intestacy under, 309
  real, 263, 264, 265
Child,
  adoption of, 96
  destruction, 332
  illegitimate, intestacy and, 310
  legitimation of, 96
Children, and criminal intent, 319
Chose in Action,
  assignment of, 187
  classes of, 265
Church courts, 18
Circuits, 11
Civil law, 3
Classifications, 314
Codification,
  English law, of, 6, 33
Coercion, 324
Coke, Chief Justice, 44, 101
Commission,
  Assize, of, 10
  gaol delivery, of, 10
  oyer and terminer, of, 10
Committal,
  trial, for, 61
Committee stage,
  statute, of, 31
Common Law Procedure Act (1854), 21
Common Pleas,
  Court of, 12
Communication,
  offer, of, 115
  revocation, of, 117
Company,
  articles of association, 102
  directors etc., 342
  form of contracts of, 138
  limitations of liability, 103
  memorandum of association, 102
  objects clause of, 102
  private, 103
  public, 103
  share capital of, 104
  termination of, 105
  ultra vires rule, and, 104
  unlimited, 103
  winding-up, 105
Compensation,
  for injuries, 351
  victims of crimes of violence, 351
Concealing arrestable offence, 351
Condition
  contract, as terms of, 146
Conflict,
  common law and equity, between, 14
  laws, of, 5
  statute and common law, between, 32
Consensus ad idem, 112
Consent,
  contract, in, 112, 160
  crime as defence to, 333
  tort, as defence in, 210
Consideration, 122
  adequacy of, 124
  contract, for, 122
  definition of, 123
  executed, 123
  executory, 123
  legality of, 126
  must move from promisee, 126
  must not be past, 127
  real nature of, 123
  rules of, 123

Consolidation,
statutes, of, 33
Conspiracy, 325
Constitution,
law, of, 4
Consumer protection,
Trade Descriptions Act, 1968, 158
Contract,
acceptance of, 115, 118
aliens, and, 140
assignment,
liabilities of, 186
rights of, 186
bankruptcy and, 175
breach of,
claim on *quantum meruit*, 180
damages for, 176
remedies for, 176
capacity to make, 133
classes of, 113
condition as term of, 146
consensus ad idem, 112
consent to, 112, 160
consideration, 122
corporation, by, 138
damages for breach of, 176
death and, 117, 172, 176
deed, by, 130
definition of, 112
discharge, 167
agreement, by, 167
operation of law, by, 174
breach, by, 170
disclosure in, 158
drunkenness, effect of, 139
duress, induced by, 159
escrow, 114
essential elements of, 112
executed, 114
executory, 114
exemption clauses, 143
express, 114
form of, 129, 140
fraud and, 153
fraudulent misrepresentation in, 155
frustration, by, 171
performance, by, 173
guarantee, 131
illegality of, 147, 161, 166
implied terms in, 142
impossibility of performance, 171
indemnity, 146
indenture, 114
inducing breach of, 184
infants, by, 133
injunction against breach of, 182
innocent misrepresentation in, 153
insanity, effect of, 139
intention of parties to create legal relations, 121
interpretation of, 188
invitation to treat distinguished from, 116
judgments, and, 113
law of, 112
legality of objects, 147, 161
limitations, of action in, 174
material alteration of, 175
merger, 175
misrepresentation, effect of, 153
mistake, effect of, 147
offer and, 115
parol evidence in interpretation of, 188–9
part performance, 132
performance, 168
possibility of performance, 171
privity of, 183
quantum meruit, claim on, 180
quasi-contract, nature of, 189
recognizances and, 113
record, of, 113
rectification of, 152
refusal to perform, 170
rescission, 157
severance and, 167
simple, 114
specialty, 113
specific performance and, 181
Statute of Frauds, and, 131
termination of offer, 117
terms of, 140
tort, and, 134, 201
ubberimae fidei, 158
undue influence and, 159
unenforceable, 113
void, 113, 133, 147
voidable, 113, 147
warranty as term of, 146
women and, 139
writing, and, 130
Conversion, 215
destruction, by, 216
detention, by, 216
doctrine of, in trusts for sale, 276
nature of, in tort, 215
taking, by, 216
wrongful delivery, by, 216
Conveyance,
mortgage and, 287

Coroner,
  Court of, 63
Corporation,
  aggregate, meaning of, 101
  capacity in tort, 200
  chartered, 102, 138
  Companies Act and, 102
  contracts of, 104, 138, 139
  criminal liability, 318
  definition, 100
  legal person, as, 100
  liability, 318
  registered, 102
  sole, meaning of, 101
  statutory, 102, 138
  tort, liability in, 200
  ultra vires, doctrine of, 104
Corruption, 162
County Courts,
  jurisdiction of, 51
Course of employment,
  vicarious liability in, meaning, 206
Court,
  Admiralty, of, 20, 50
  Appeal, of, 24, 48, 54
  Arches, of, 19
  Church, 18
  Common Pleas, of, 12
  Coroners', 63
  County, 51
  Crown, 54
  Crown cases reserved, 22
  Curia Regis, 11
  Divisional, 57
  Ecclesiastical, 18
  Equity (Chancery), 14
  Exchequer, of, 12
  Franchise, 8
  High, 24, 49
  House of Lords, 22, 24, 54
  Hundred, 8
  Juvenile, 61
  Local, 20
  King's Bench, of, 12
  Magistrates', 58
  Merchant, 20
  Moot, 9
  nineteenth century, 21
  nisi prius, 10
  Piepowder, 20
  Probate, of, 21
  quarter sessions, 55
  Restrictive Practices, 62
  Shire, 8
Court of Appeal,
  Civil Division, 48
  Criminal Division, 54
  judges of, 48, 54
  jurisdiction of, 48
Courts-Martial
  Appeal Court, 62
Crime,
  defences to, 320
  defined, 313
  diminished responsibility, 329
  documents, suppression of, 342
  duress, 324
  electricity, abstracting of, 340
  evasion of liability by deception, 344
  eviction and harassment, 348
  exemptions from liability, 319
  false accounting, 341
  firearms, 334
  forgery, 347
  handling stolen goods, 343
  incitement, 325
  infanticide, 331
  insanity, 321
  intention, 316
  intoxication from drink or drugs, 322
  liability for, 315
  making off without payment, 344
  malicious wounding, 336
  manslaughter, 328
  mens rea, 315
  mistake, 321
  murder, 327
  necessity, 324
  negligence, 316
  obtaining property by deception, 340
  obtaining a pecuniary advantage by deception, 341
  obtaining services by deception, 344
  offensive weapons, 334
  parties to, 319
  poisoning offences, 336
  prevention of, 323
  private offence, 323
  provocation, 328
  recklessness, 316
  removal of articles from places open to public, 339
  road traffic offences, 349
  robbery, 338
  sexual offences, 335
  sources of law, 313
  squatting offences, 347
  strict liability, 317
  superior orders, 324

Crime—*continued*
taking a conveyance without authority, 339
theft, 336
trespass on premises, 347
vicarious liability, 317
wounding with intent, 336
Criminal,
damage, 345
Law Revision Committee, 43
Criminal damage, 345
Criminal law, 3, 313
burden of proof, in, 326
duress, as a defence in, 324
intent, in, 316
recklessness, in, 316
Criminal procedure, 362
Crown,
contracts and, 109
employer, as, 109
proceedings against, 109
servants, 111
tort and, 109, 199
Crown Court, 54
proceedings in, 366
Crown Proceedings Act, 109
Curia Regis, 11
Custom,
local, 21
source of law, as, 21
trade, of, 142
Cy-près,
doctrine of, 253

Damages,
classification of, 176
contemptuous, 178
contract, breach of, 176
damnum sine injuria, 193
exemplary, 178
general, 178
interest and, 180
liquidated, 178
measure of, 176
minimization of, 177
nominal, 178
penalty, distinguished from, 179
remoteness of, in contract, 176–7
in tort, 203
special, 178
unliquidated, 178
Danelaw, 8
Deceit, 244
intent, 244
nature of, 244
statement of fact, 244
Deception,
obtaining property by, 340
Declaratory theory, 29
Deed, 113
Defamation, 195, 236
apology and amends, 242, 243
defences, 240
definition of, 236
dissemination, 239
fair comment, 240
innuendo, 237
justification, 240
libel and, 236
proof of, 237
privilege and, 241
publication and, 239
remedies, 243
repetition and, 239
slander and, 237
Default Actions, steps in, 356
Defences, to criminal liability, 320
Delegated legislation, 34
by-laws, 34
consultation and control of, 36
court, control by, 37
criticisms of, 35
growth of, 35
Orders in Council, 34
Parliament, control by, 37
publication of, 38
Select Committee on, 37
statutory instruments, 34
sub-delegation, 36
Devise,
meaning of, 302
Diminished responsibility, 329
Director of Public Prosecutions, 84
Discharge,
agreement, by, 167
operation of law, by, 174
performance, by, 168
substituted agreement, by, 168
Dispossession, 214, 264
Divisional Court, 57
Divorce, 94, 396
domicile, and, 91
ecclesiastical courts, jurisdiction of, 18
High Court, jurisdiction of, 52
presumption of death, 95
Domestic proceedings,
Magistrates courts and, 95
Domicile, 91
animus manendi and, 91
choice, of, 91

Domicile—*continued*
dependent persons, of, 91
divorce and, 91
legitimation and, 92
marriage validity and, 92
origin, of, 91
proof of, 92
wills and, 92
Drunkenness,
contract, effect on, 139
defence in crime, 322
Duress,
contract induced by, 159
crime, defence to, 324

Earl of Oxford's case, 14
Easement,
acquisition of, 284
creation of, 284
nature of, 283
Ecclesiastical Courts, 18
Ejectment, action of, 213
Ejusdem generis, 40
Electricity, abstracting of, 340
Employers' Associations, 108
Employment,
Appeal Tribunal, 62
course of, wrongs committed in, 206
Equitable estoppel, 128
Equity, 13
Court of (Chancery), 14
Judicature Acts and, 14, 23
nature of, 14–16
Escrow, 114
Estate,
administration of, 306
fee simple, in, 268
land, in, 268
legal, kinds now subsisting, 268, 270
life, for, 268
meaning of, 268
pur autre vie, 268
term of years, 270
Estoppel, equitable, 128
Evidence,
burden of proof, of, 326
Exchequer, Court of, 12
Division, 22
Ex turpi causa non oritur actio, 161
Executed contract, 114
Executors, 306
Executory contract, 114
Exemption clauses,
in contract, 143
misrepresentation and, 143
Express contract, 116
Expressio unius est exclusio alterius, 40
Eyre, general, 10

False accounting, 424
False imprisonment, 209, 368
Family arrangements, 159
Family law, 4
fiat, 109
Firearms, 324
First Reading, of statute, 31
Forgery, 347
Franchise Court, 8
Frank-pledge, 9
Frauds,
contract, in, 153
Fraudulent misrepresentation,
contract, in, 155
remedies for, 155
Frustration of contract, 171
Fusion of common law and equity administration, 15, 16

Gaol delivery, commission of, 10
Garnishee proceedings, 357
gavelkind, 9
General Eyre, 10
Gift,
donatio mortis causa, 312
inter vivos, 311
lapse of, 303
Golden Rule, 39
Grant, lost modern, 285
Guardian, 97
ad litem, 100
appointed of, for infant, 97

Habeas Corpus, 368
Handling stolen goods, 343
High Court, 49
creation of, 22
divisions of, 49
judges of, 49
Homicide,
justifiable, 328
misadventure, 328
self-defence, rules of, 210, 323
Hotchpot, 311
House of Lords,
appeal to, 22, 54
composition of, 47, 54
jurisdiction of, 37, 47
Hundred Court, 8
Husband and wife,
coercion, doctrine of, 324

Illegality,
  bribery, 163
  champerty, 163
  consideration of, 126
  contracts, in, 147, 161, 166
  corruption, 162
  effects of, 161
  honours, purchase of, 163
  maintenance, 163
  restraint of trade, 163
  sexual immorality, 162
  statutory, 161
  trading with enemy, 163
Illegitimacy, 98
  custody and maintenance in, 98
  property rights in, 98
Immunity,
  diplomatic, 200
  judicial, 7, 200
Implied contract, 114
Implied terms, 142
Imprisonment,
  false, 209
Incitement, 325
Indemnity, guarantee and, 146
Indentures, 114
Independent contractor,
  torts of, liability for, 207
Indictment,
  offences, triable on, 60
  procedure in Crown Court, 366
Industrial Tribunals, 66
Industrial injuries, 66
Inevitable Accident, 198
Infant (*see* Minor)
Infanticide, 331
Injunction,
  contract, against breach of, 182
  tort, in action in, 213
Innocent misrepresentation,
  contract, in, 153
  remedies for, 156
Insanity,
  as a defence, 321
  effect in contract, 139
Insurance, contract of, 158
Intention in crime, 316
Intention to create legal relations, 121
Interpretation, 38
  Act (1978), 38
  common-law rules, 39
    Ejusdem generis, 40
    expressio unius est exclusio alterius, 40
    Golden Rule, 39
    literal rule, 39
    mischief rule, 39
    nosciter a sociis, 40
  contracts of, parol evidence in, 188–9
  presumptions and, 40
  statutes, of, 38–9
  statutory definitions and, 38–9
Intestacy, 309
  Crown rights under, 312
  family provision in, 305
  succession under, 309
    illegitimate child, 310
    parents, 310
    spouse, 309
Invitation to treat, 116
Itinerant justices, 11

Joint tortfeasors, 208
Judgment, enforcement of, 357, 361
Judges,
  circuit, 82
  county court, 82
  Court of Appeal, 54
  Crown Court, 54
  High Court, 82
  House of Lords, 54
  Recorders, 82
Judicature,
  Acts (1873–5), 22, 23
  Commission (1867), 22
Judicial Committee of Privy Council, 46
  jurisdiction, 48
  procedure, 48
Judicial immunity, 7, 200
Judicial precedent, 24
  Table of Courts, 24
Judicial separation, 95
Judiciary,
  independence of, 7
Jury,
  civil, 74
  criminal, 74
  functions of, 74
  qualifications for, 74
Justices,
  clerk to, 59
  itinerant, 11
  Peace, of, 78
    appointment, 59
    numbers, 59
Justification,
  in defamation, 240
Juvenile Court, 61

King's Bench, Court of, 12

Land,
  certificate of registration, 295
  charges, 294
  contract for sale of, 131, 159, 293
  conveyances, 293
  co-ownership, 277
  copyhold tenure of, 267
  estate in, 268
  fee-simple absolute in possession, 270
  freehold, meaning of, 265, 267
  future estates in, 273
  joint ownership, 277
  leasehold, 264, 265, 279
  quia emptores statute, 267
  re-entry on, 214
  registration of, 293, 294
  sale of, 292
  Settled Land Act, 275
  settlements, 273
  tenure of, 266
  trespass to, 211, 213
  trusts for sale, 273, 276
  uberrima fidei, contracts and, 158
Land charge,
  estate contracts, 294
  general equitable, 294
  limited owners' charge, 294
  puisne mortgages, 294
  registration of, 293
Lapse of offer, 117
Law,
  administrative, 4
  canon, 18
  case, 7
  civil, 3
  classification of, 3
  common, nature of, 8
  compulsion and, 1, 2
  Constitutional, 4
  content of, 3
  contract, of, 3, 112
  criminal, 3, 313
  custom, morality and, 1
  enforcement of, 2
  family, 4
  interpretation of, 38
  judicial character of, 6
  justice and, 3
  laymen and, 78
  mercantile, 19
  merchant, 19
  Mercian, 8
  nature of, 1
  order in, 1
  private international, 5
  procedural, 5
  property, of, 4, 262
  public international, 5
  reform, 42
  reports, 27
  sources, 8
    custom, local, 21, 44
    judicial precedent, 24
    legislation, 18
    obiter dicta, 26
    textbooks, 44
  substantive, 4
  succession, of, 4, 297
  tort, of, 4, 191
  Wessex, 8
Law Commission, 43
Law reform, 42
  Committee of, 42
Law Reports, 27
Law revision, 42
Lawyers,
  independence of, 7
Lay courts, 10
Laymen,
  law and, 78
Lease,
  covenants in, 282
  form of, 281
Leasehold,
  periodic tenancies, 279
  tenancies, 279
    at sufferance, 279, 280
    at will, 279, 280
  terms of years absolute, 269, 279
Legacy, 302
  abatement of, 303
  ademption of, 303
  demonstrative, 302
  general, 302
  specific, 302
Legal aid, 75
  civil proceedings, 76
  contributions, 77
  criminal proceedings, 77
  disposable capital, 77
  disposable income, 77
  legal advice, 78
  procedure, 79
Legal personality, 88
Legal profession, 84
Legislation, 16, 17
  delegated, 34
  source of law, 18
  stages in, 31
Legality, object of, 113

Legitimacy, 96
Legitimation, 96, 98
Letters of administration, grant of, 307
Liabilities,
  assignment of, 186
  strict, 234
Libel, 236
Licensed conveyancers, 86
Limitation of actions, 246
Literal Rule, 39
Local,
  courts, 20
  customs, 21, 44
  by-laws, 34
Lord Chancellor, 81
Lord Chief Justice, 81
Lords,
  of Appeal in Ordinary, 82
  Justices of Appeal, 82

Magistrates,
  jurisdiction, 59
  proceedings before, 60, 363
  stipendiary, 59
Magnum Concilium, 10
Malicious falsehood, 195, 245
  slander of goods, 245
  slander of title, 245
Malicious prosecution, 194
Mandamus, 70
Manslaughter, 328
  categories of, 328, 330
Maritime Courts, 19
Marriage, 92
  capacity and, 92
  contract of, 93
  divorce and, 94
  formalities required, 93
  void, 94
  voidable, 94
Married women,
  contract and, 139
  legal capacity of, 202
Masters of the High Court, 83, 84
Mens rea, 315
Mental disorder,
  criminal charge, defence to, 321
Mercantile Law, 19
Mesne profits, 214
Minor, 99
  adoption of, 96
  capacity to own property, 100
  capacity in tort, 99
  contracts by, 133, 135
  criminal liability of, 99
  definition of, 99
  guardianship of, 97
  illegitimate, 98
  intestacy, entitled under, 309
  liability in tort, 99, 201
  litigation rights, 100
  necessaries and, 134
  property rights and, 100
  void contracts and, 133
  voidable contracts and, 136
  voting rights, 100
  will made by, 100
Mischief Rule, 39
Misfeasance, 212
Misrepresentation,
  effect on contract, 153
  fraudulent, 153, 156
  innocent, 156
  reliance upon, 154
  remedies for, 155
Misrepresentation Act (1967), 156
Mistake,
  contract void on grounds of, 147
  defence to crime, as a, 321
  equity, in, 152
  existence of subject-matter, as to, 148
  fact, of, 147
  identity of subject-matter, as to, 148
  identity of person, as to, 149
  in tort, 197
  law of, 147
  nature of document, as to, 151
  operative, 147
  quality, as to, 148
Monarchy, constitutional position, 17
Moot, 8
Mortgages, 287
  charge by way of, 288
  demise, by, 288
  equitable, 289
  foreclosure under, 290
  legal, 288
  mortgagee rights of, 289
  mortgagor rights of, 290
  possession, right to, 289
  receiver, appointment of, 290
  remedies, 289
  sale, right of, 290
Murder, 327
  diminished responsibility, as a defence to, 329
  provocation as defence to, 328

Nationality, 88
  British, 89

Nationality—*continued*
deprivation of, 90
incorporation of territory and, 90
marriage and, 90
protected persons and, 90
renunciation of, 90
Naturalization, 90
Necessaries,
contract for, 134
Necessity,
as defence in crime, 324
as defence in tort, 198
Negligence, 222, 316
by bailee, 224
by carriers, 224
contributory, 227
death and, 229
duty of care, 222
highway, 199, 223
misstatement, 225
professional persons, 224
res lipsa loquitur, 226
survival of actions in, 229
Negotiable instrument, privity and, 184
Nisi prius, 10
Non est factum, 151
Non-feasance, 212
Norman Conquest, 9
Novation, contract of, 186
Nuisance, 217
abatement of, 220
defences to, 220
lawful use of land and, 218, 220
malice and, 219
occupier and, 219
prescription, 219
private, 218
public, 217
remedies, 220
sensitivity and, 219
trespass and, 221
triviality and, 220
utility of, 219

Obsolete statutes, 32
Occupier's liability, 230
children and, 232
dangerous premises, 231
defences to, 232
invitee, 230
licensee, 230
trespassers and, 232
visitors, and, 231
Offences,
against property, 336
against the person, 327
arrestable, 314
indictable and summary, 314
Offensive weapons, 334
Offer,
contract, in, 115
counter-offer, and, 118
lapse of, 117
option, and, 119
rejection of, 118
statement of price, and, 116
termination of, 117
Operative mistake, 147
Options, 119
Orders in Council, 34
Ownership, distinguished from possession, 262
Oxford, Provisions of, 13
Oyer and terminer, commission of, 10

Parental authority, 211
Parliament,
rise of, 17
sovereignty of, 30
Partnership, 106
contractual authority and, 107
dissolution of, 107
general, 108
liability, 107
limited, 108
management, 107
numbers of partners in, 107
personality and, 107
Uberrima fidei, contracts in, 158
Payment,
appropriation of, 169
composition, 126
early, 125
mode altered, 125
sufficiency of consideration, and, 124
Performance, 168
contract discharged by, 168
possibility of, in contract, 113
tender of, 169
time and, 168
Persons of unsound mind,
contracts by, 139
tort and, 203
Personal representatives, 306
abatement, 303
ademption, 303
appointment, 308
classes of, 306
duties of, 308
insolvent estate, 309

Personal representatives—*continued*
  liabilities of, 308
  powers of, 308
Personalty, 264
Piepowder Courts, 20
Possession, 26
  animus possidendi, 261
  bailee, 261
  corpus possessionis, 261
Post Office, 110
Precedent,
  binding, 26
  judicial, 24
  persuasive, 26
Prerogative orders, 70–1
Prescription,
  easement acquired by, 284
  profits à prendre, 284
Price maintenance, privity and, 183
Prima facie, 60
Primogeniture, 9
Private Bills, 32
Private international law, 5
Private law, 4
Private Member's Bill, 32, 44
Privilege,
  absolute, 241
  defamation, defence to action in, 241
  qualified, 241
Privity of contract, 183
Privy Council,
  Judicial Committee of, 47
    jurisdiction, 48
    origins of, 47
    procedure, 48
Probate, 307
  Court of, 22
  grant of, 307
  High Court, jurisdiction of, 50
Procedural Law, influence of, 5
Procedure,
  County courts, in, 353
  Crown Court, in, 366
  magistrates' courts, in, 363
  Queen's Bench Division, in, 359
Profits à prendre, 284
Prohibition, 71
Property, 262
  bankruptcy, subject, 175
  chattels,
    personal, 263, 265
    real, 263, 264, 265
  choses,
    in action, 265
    in possession, 265
  criminal damage to, 345
  deception, obtaining by, 340
  defence of, 210
  law of, 260
  offences against, 336
  ownership, 260
  possession, 261
  real, meaning of, 268
Prospectuses, of companies, 155
Provisions of Oxford (1258), 13
Public international law, 5
Public law, 4

Quantum meruit,
  claim on, 180
Queen's Counsel, 86
Queen's Bench Division, 34
  procedure in, 358

Rape, 335
Realty, 264
Recklessness in crime, 316
Recognizances, 113
Rectification of contract, 152
Redundancy payments, tribunals, 66
Registration,
  of companies, 102
  nationality and, 89
Remedies,
  equitable, 16, 182
  injunction, 16, 182, 213
  specific performance, 16, 181
Rent tribunals, 67
Report stage of statute, 31
Reports, Law, 27
Representation, definition of, 153
Res ipsa loquitur, 226
Rescission of,
  contract, 157
Restraint of trade,
  contract, in, 163
  employees, 164
  sale of business, 163
Restrictive covenants, 285
  constructive notice of, 285
  negative nature of, 286
Restrictive Practices, 62
Reversing decisions, 25
Revocation,
  of offer, 117
  of will, 300
Robbery, 338
Roman Law, 7
Royal Assent to,
  statute, 32
Royal judges, 10

Rylands v. *Fletcher*, rule in, 233
defences to, 235

Second reading of statute, 31
Self-defence, 199, 210, 323
Servant,
course of employment, 206
definition of, 205
tort, liability in, 206, 207
Servitudes, 282
lost modern grant, 285
Prescription Act, and, 285
Settlement, 273
trust for sale, 276
Severance,
in contracts, 167
words of, 278
Sexual offences, 335
Shire Court, 8
Simon de Montfort's Parliament, 17
Solicitors, 84
duties of, 85
history of, 84
tribunals and, 68
Solicitor-General, 82
Sources of English Law, historical, 8
Specialty contracts, 113
Specific performance,
contracts, on breach of, 181
Squatting offences, 347
Stare decisis, 11
Statute of Westminster, 13
Statutes
codification of, 33
consolidation of, 33
definition, 30
full title, 41
interpretation of, 38
making of, 30
obsolescence, 32
official reference to, 41
short title, 41
Statutory companies, 102
Statutory instruments, 34
reference to, 41
Select Committee on, 37
Statutory trusts, 310
Stipendiary magistrate, 59
Strict liability, 234, 317
Strict settlements, 273
Substantive law, 4
Succession,
law of, 297
wills and, 297
Suicide,
aiding and abetting, 330
pact, 330
Summary offences,
definition of, 60
procedure at trial, 40, 363
Superior orders in crime, 324
Supreme Court of Judicature, 22
Suretyship, *uberrima fidei* contracts in, 159
Survivorship, right of, 278

Taxing Masters, 84
Tenant,
covenants by, in lease, 282
duties of, 281
in common, 277
joint, 277
Tender,
legal, 169
payment of, 169
Tenders, 121
Tenement,
dominant, 283
servient, 283
Terms,
certainty, of, 141
contract, of, 140
express, 140
implied, 142
Textbooks, 44
Blackstone, 44
Bracton, 44
Cheshire, 44
Coke, 44
Dicey, 44
Foster, 44
Glanvil, 44
Hale, 44
Littleton, 44
Salmond, 44
Smith and Hogan, 44
Williams, 44
Winfield, 44
Theft, 336
Third Reading of statute, 31
Time,
lapse of offer, 117
performance and, 168
Tort,
actionable *per se*, 214
assault, 209
battery, 209
breach of statutory duty, 229
capacity of parties, 199
consent, as defence to action in, 210

Tort—*continued*
contract, distinguished from, 192
conversion, 215
corporation, liability of, 200
crime, distinguished from, 192
damage, 193
proof of, 194
remoteness of, 203
death: survival of actions, 229
deceit, nature of, 244
defamation, 195, 236
defences to, 195, 235
defined, 191, 192
detinue, 215
dispossession, 214
duty of care, 222
imprisonment, 209
infant, liability of, 201
injuria sine damno, 193
law of, 193
malice and, 194
malicious,
falsehood, 195, 245
prosecution, 194
mistake, 196
negligence, 222
nuisance, 217
persons of unsound mind, 202
reasonable foresight, 203
Rylands v. *Fletcher*, rule in, 233
slander,
goods, 245
title, 245
trade unions and, 200
trespass, 209
against the person, 209
to land, 211, 213
to chattels, 217
vicarious liability, 204
volenti non fit injuria, as defence to, 195
Trade Unions, 108
requirements, 108
Trading with the enemy, 163
Treason, 314
Trespass, 209, 347
ab initio, 212
criminal, 347
goods, to, 214
land, to, 211, 213
person, against the, 209
Trial by jury, 74
Tribunals,
administrative, 64
and *audi alterem partem*, 69
bias, 69
council on, 71
dentists and, 68
doctors and, 68
domestic, 67
industrial injuries, 66
judicial control of, 68, 70
National Insurance Acts and, 66
redundancy payments and, 66
rent, 67
solicitors and, 68
trade unions and, 67
Trinity House, Admiralty Court and, 79
Trusts, 248
beneficiary, action by, 257
breach of, 257
charitable, 252
completely constituted, 250
constructive, 251
corporation, 255
certainty,
intentions, of, 249
objects, of, 250, 255
subject-matter, of, 250
cy près, 253
deed, 275
definition of, 249
express, 249
implied, 251
perpetuity rules in, 253, 254
private, 249
public, 252
resulting, 251
variation of, 257
Trustees, 255
appointment of, 255
duties and powers of, 256
liability for breaches of trust, 257
remuneration, 257
termination of trusteeship, 256
Trusts for sale, 273, 276

Uberrimae fidei contracts,
company prospectuses, 159
family arrangements, 159
insurance, 158
land, 159
partnership, and suretyship, 158, 159
Undue influence, 159
Unenforceable contracts, 113
Unincorporated associations, 105
committees, 106
contract in, 106
ownership of land and, 106
representative action and, 106

Vesting deed, 275
Vicarious liability, 204
  crime, in, 317
  tort, in, 204
Void contracts, infants and, 133
Voidable contracts, infants and, 136
Volenti non fit injuria, 195

Warrants, kinds of, 364
Warranty, contracts in, 146
Wills, 297, 303
  additions and alterations, 299
  attestation of, 298
  dispositions and, 302
  family provision, 304
  formalities, 298
  legacies and devises in, 302
  nature of, 297
  revocation of, 300
  revival of revoked, 301
  soldiers', etc., 299
  testamentary capacity, 298
Wounding with intent, 336
Writ,
  debt, 13
  detinue, 13
  habeas corpus, of, 373
  original, 12
  prerogative, 70–1
  trespass, 13, 191

York, Chancery Court of, 19